50TH INTERNATIONAL EUCH/

PROCEEDINGS OF THE INTERNATIONAL SYMPOSIUM OF THEOLOGY

The Ecclesiology of Communion
Fifty Years after the Opening of Vatican II

Published 2013 by
Veritas Publications
7–8 Lower Abbey Street
Dublin 1
Ireland
publications@veritas.ie
www.veritas.ie

ISBN 978 1 84730 423 0

10 9 8 7 6 5 4 3 2 1

A catalogue record for this book is available from the British Library.

Cover design by Martin Barlow, 2b: creative
Typesetting by Suzanne Moncelet, izus design
Printed in the Republic of Ireland by Hudson Killeen Limited, Dublin

Veritas books are printed on paper made from the wood pulp of managed forests. For every tree felled, at least one tree is planted, thereby renewing natural resources.

50TH INTERNATIONAL EUCHARISTIC CONGRESS 2012

PROCEEDINGS OF THE INTERNATIONAL SYMPOSIUM OF THEOLOGY

The Ecclesiology of Communion
Fifty Years after the Opening of Vatican II

St Patrick's College, Maynooth, County Kildare, Ireland
6th–9th June, 2012

CONTENTS

PROCEEDINGS OF THE INTERNATIONAL SYMPOSIUM OF THEOLOGY

Introduction from **Monsignor Hugh G. Connolly** 16
President, St Patrick's College, Maynooth

Foreword by **Prof. Brendan Leahy** 18
Chariman of the Symposium Organising Comittee, St Patrick's College, Maynooth

KEYNOTE SPEAKERS

AT THE INTERNATIONAL SYMPOSIUM OF THEOLOGY
50TH INTERNATIONAL EUCHARISTIC CONGRESS 2012

WEDNESDAY 6TH JUNE 2012

FORMAL OPENING AND KEYNOTE ADDRESS

CHAIR: Most Rev. Diarmuid Martin
(Archbishop of Dublin and Primate of Ireland)

SPEAKER: **His Eminence Marc Cardinal Ouellet PPS**
Prefect of the Congregation for Bishops
The Ecclesiology of Communion, Fifty Years after the Opening of Vatican II 30

THE EUCHARIST, COMMUNION AND PEOPLE IN IRISH CHRISTIANITY

CHAIR: Rev. Dr Thomas O'Connor
(National University of Ireland, Maynooth)

SPEAKER: **Dr Jennifer O'Reilly**
School of History, University College Cork; Royal Irish Academy
The Body of Christ in the Book of Kells 52

SPEAKER: **Prof. Salvador Ryan**
St Patrick's College, Maynooth
Merita Missae: The Eucharist and the Lived Reality of Irish Christians in the Late Medieval and Early Modern Periods 63

SPEAKER: **Rev. Fr Brendan McConvery CSsR**
St Patrick's College, Maynooth
Eucharistic Faith and Practice of the People as seen by some Irish Artists 74

THURSDAY 7TH JUNE 2012

EXPLORING SOURCES AND WAYS OF COMMUNION

CHAIR: Ms Gillian Kingston (*Lay Leader of the Methodist Church in Ireland and Co-chair of the Theology Forum of the Irish Inter-Church Meeting) and* His Eminence Cardinal Seán Brady DD *(Archbishop of Armagh and Primate of All Ireland)*

SPEAKER: **Sr Prof. Teresa Okure SHCJ**
Catholic Institute of West Africa, Nigeria
The Eucharist: A Way of Life for Jesus and the Christian According to the Scriptures **90**

SPEAKER: **Rev. Prof. Martin Stuflesser**
Julius-Maxmillians University, Würzburg, Germany
Drawn Day by Day: Eucharistic Ecclesiology from the Perspective of a Liturgical Theologian **134**

CHAIR: Most Rev. Gérald Cyprien Lacroix DD *(Archbishop of Québec)*

SPEAKER: **Rev. Prof. Piero Coda**
Sophia University Institute, Loppiano, Florence
Il 'Corpo donato per voi': origine e forma della chiesa comunione (The 'Body Given Up for You' as Origin and Form of Communion) **165**

SPEAKER: **Rev. Prof. Brian Johnstone CSsR**
Catholic University of America, Washington DC
The Resurrection and the Eucharist **178**

CHAIR: Rev. Prof. Liam Tracey OSM *(St Patrick's College, Maynooth)*

SPEAKER: **Rev. Prof. Finbarr Clancy SJ**
Milltown Institute, Dublin
Some Patristic Insights into the Eucharist Understood as Communion **192**

CHAIR: Sr Bríd Liston FCJ *(St Patrick's College, Maynooth)*

SPEAKER: **Dr Clare Watkins**
Westminster Seminary, London
'The Domestic Sanctuary of the Church' (*Apostolicam Actuositatem*, 11): Living Eucharist in the Family Today **223**

CHAIR: Rt Rev. Mons. James Cassin
(Council for Education, Irish Bishops' Conference)

SPEAKER: **Rev. Fr Michael Drumm**
Executive Chairperson of the Catholic Schools Partnership, Maynooth
Being Educated in Communion **238**

CHAIR: Prof. Dan Bradley *(Trinity College, Dublin)*

SPEAKER: **Rev. Dr Brendan Purcell**
Notre Dame University, Sydney
Beyond the Big Bang: The Eucharist at the Heart of Cosmic, Evolutionary and Human History **250**

CHAIR: Rev. Dr Declan Marmion SM *(St Patrick's College, Maynooth)*

SPEAKER: **Prof. Gill Goulding CJ**
University of Toronto
The Irreducible Particularity of Christ: Beauty, Eucharist and Communion **266**

CHAIR: Rev. Dr Michael Shortall *(St Patrick's College, Maynooth)*

SPEAKER: **Rev. Prof. Paul O'Callaghan**
Pontifical University of the Holy Cross, Rome
The Anthropological Roots of Communion **287**

CHAIR: Rev. Dr Kevin O'Gorman SMA *(St Patrick's College, Maynooth)*

SPEAKER: **Rev. Prof. Slawomir Nowosad**
Catholic University of Lublin, Poland
Responding to the Great Challenges Facing the Church Today: Blessed John Paul II and the Ecclesiology of Communion **302**

CHAIR: Rev. Prof. Michael Conway *(St Patrick's College, Maynooth)*

SPEAKER: **Prof. Robert D. Enright**
University of Wisconsin-Madison
Becoming Eucharist for One Another through Forgiving **326**

SPEAKER: **Dr Geraldine Smyth OP**
Irish School of Ecumenics, Dublin
Forgiveness: Between Created Wisdom and Reconciling Grace **334**

CHAIR: Most Rev. Phillip Boyce OCD, DD *(Bishop of Raphoe)*

SPEAKER: **Rev. Prof. Thomas Norris**
International Theological Commission
The Church's Marian Profile and the Reception
of Vatican II's Ecclesiology **362**

CHAIR: Rev. Fr Laurence Murphy SJ *(St Patrick's College, Maynooth)*

SPEAKER: **Rev. Prof. Eamonn Conway**
Mary Immaculate College, University of Limerick
'With Reverence and Love': Being a Priest in a Detraditionalised
Cultural Context **382**

CHAIR: Rev. Fr Paul Crosbie *(Diocese of Meath)*

SPEAKER: **Rev. Dr Dermot A. Lane**
Mater Dei Institute of Education, Dublin City University
Eucharist as Sacrament of the Eschaton: A Failure of the
Imagination? **399**

CHAIR: Dr Lorna Gold (*Trócaire: The Overseas and Development Agency of the Catholic Church in Ireland)*

SPEAKER: **Prof. Stefano Zamagni**
Department of Economics, University of Bologna
Civilizzare L'Economia: Comunione e Gratuità Nell'agire Economico
Alla Luce Della Dottrina Sociale Della Chiesa **415**

CHAIR: Dr Vera Donnelly OP

SPEAKER: **Rev. Dr Oliver Treanor**
St Patrick's College, Maynooth
The Eucharist: Apostolicity of Communion **446**

CHAIR: Rev. Dr Patrick Mullins O Carm *(Milltown Institute, Dublin)*

SPEAKER: **Rev. Prof. Michael Mullaney**
St Patrick's College, Maynooth
Laity and Ministry in the Church as Communion:
Canonical Perspectives **464**

SPEAKER: **Most Rev. Piero Marini**
President, Pontifical Committee for International and Eucharistic Congresses
Homily **484**

FRIDAY 8TH JUNE 2012
LEARNING FROM ECUMENISM

CHAIR: Most Rev. Thomas Dabre DD *(Bishop of Pune, India)*

SPEAKER: **His Eminence Kurt Cardinal Koch**
President, Pontifical Council for Promoting Christian Unity
The Relation between the Eucharist and Ecclesial Communion: An Ecumenical View **488**

CHAIR: Most Rev. Richard Clarke
(Church of Ireland, Bishop of Meath and Kildare)

SPEAKER: **Rev. Prof. Nicholas Sagovsky**
Member of ARCIC III
Ut Unum Simus: What I Learnt from Jean-Marie Tillard **502**

SPEAKER: **Dr Julie Canlis** *University of Aberdeen*
Reforming Ascent: Calvin's Communion Motif **517**

CHAIR: Most Rev. Anthony Farquhar DD *(Chairman of the Council for Ecumenism of the Irish Catholic Bishops' Conference)* and Sr Elizabeth Cotter IBVM *(Vicar for Religious, Archdiocese of Dublin)*

SPEAKER: **Rev. Prof. Geoffrey Wainwright** *Duke University Divinity School, Durham, North Carolina*
From *Communio Imperfecta* through *Communio in Via* to 'Full Communion in Faith, Mission and Sacramental Life'? **530**

SPEAKER: **His Eminence Metropolitan Emmanuel Adamakis of France**
President of the Conference of European Churches
Dialogue and Communion: An Orthodox Perspective **559**

SATURDAY 9TH JUNE 2012
LOOKING TO THE FUTURE:
THE INTERACTION OF COMMUNION AND MISSION

CHAIR: Most Rev. Kieran O'Reilly SMA DD *(Bishop of Killaloe)* and Sr Conchita McDonnell MSHR *(President of the Conference of Religious of Ireland (CORI))*

SPEAKER: **Rev. Prof. Michael McCabe SMA**
Head of the Mission Studies Department, Tangaza College, Nairobi
Mission: Climax and Consummation of the Eucharist **574**

SPEAKER: **His Eminence Oscar Andrés Cardinal Rodríguez Maradiaga SDB**
Archbishop of Tegucigalpa, Honduras
La Eucaristia es el Punto Culminante de la Misión **583**

CHAIR: Rev. Prof. Hugh Connolly *(President of St Patrick's College, Maynooth)* *and* Rev. Fr John Guiney SJ *(President of the Irish Missionary Union)*

SPEAKER: **Rev. Dr Theodore Mascarenhas SFX**
Member of the Pontifical Council for Culture
Communion with Christ: Mission and Evangelisation in Asia **614**

SPEAKER: **Prof. Dr Joris Geldhof**
Catholic University, Leuven
The End of the Mass for the Masses? Reflections on the Source and Summit of the Christian Life of Faith in Secular Cultures **624**

CONTENTS

EMERGING SCHOLARS
AT THE INTERNATIONAL SYMPOSIUM OF THEOLOGY
50TH INTERNATIONAL EUCHARISTIC CONGRESS 2012

WEDNESDAY 6TH JUNE 2012

THE ECCLESIOLOGY OF COMMUNION IN JOSEPH RATZINGER/ POPE BENEDICT XVI
CHAIR: Rev. Dr Tom Dalzell SM *(All Hallows College, Dublin)*

SPEAKER: **Rev. Seán Corkery**
St Patrick's College, Maynooth
Christological Hermeneutic: Sacrament and Scripture in the Work of Joseph Ratzinger 648

SPEAKER: **Mr Anthony Valle**
Pontifical University of the Holy Cross, Rome
Retrieving the Christological Core of Joseph Ratzinger's Communio Ecclesiology 664

SPEAKER: **Dr Mary McCaughey DD**
St Patrick's College, Maynooth
Joseph Ratzinger's Contextual Understanding of the Church as Communion: Embodied, Existential, Ecstatic Praxis 682

EVANGELISATION TODAY
CHAIR: Dr Ann Codd PBVM *(Council for Pastoral Renewal and Adult Faith Development, Irish Bishops' Conference)*

SPEAKER: **Mr Matthew Halbach**
Catholic University of America, Washington DC
The Incarnational Dimension of Catechesis and the Work of the New Evangelisation 700

SPEAKER: **Rev. Fr Norlan Julia SJ**
Heythrop College, University of London
Beyond Basic Ecclesial Communities (BECs): Challenges to the Reception of Communio Ecclesiology in Asia 711

SPEAKER: **Ms Christina Strafaci**
Diocese of Phoenix, USA
'Food Indeed': Consequences of the Americanisation of the Family Table for an Ecclesiology of Communion 722

THE MARIAN PROFILE OF THE CHURCH
CHAIR: Rev. Prof. Thomas Norris *(International Theological Commission)*

SPEAKER: **Mr Paudie Holly**
Mary Immaculate College, Limerick
The All-Embracing Maternal Church: The Communion Ecclesiology of Henri de Lubac 739

SPEAKER: **Sr Chau Nguyen OP**
Catholic University of America, Washington DC
Mariological Dimensions of an Ecclesiology of Communion: Reading *Lumen Gentium* Anew 748

SPEAKER: **Dr Paul O'Hara**
Catholic Theological Union, Chicago
A Lonerganian Analysis of the Marian Profile of the Church in the Theology of Hans Urs Von Balthasar 759

LITURGY
CHAIR: Rev. Patrick Jones *(National Liturgy Centre, Maynooth)*

SPEAKER: **Dr James A. Wickman**
Georgetown University, Washington DC
Toward a Renewed Understanding of Internal Participation in the Eucharist 787

SPEAKER: **Rev. Fr Sojan Karottu**
Catholic University, Leuven
The Communitarian and Social Dimensions of the Liturgy Introduced in the Enarxis of the Eucharistic Liturgy of the Syro-Malabar Church 797

THE ECCLESIOLOGY OF COMMUNION: SACRAMENTAL AND HIERARCHICAL PERSPECTIVES
CHAIR: Rev. Dr Oliver Treanor *(St Patrick's College, Maynooth)*

SPEAKER: **Rev. Fr John Anthony Berry**
University of Malta
Communion and Co-responsibility in the Church 811

SPEAKER: **Rev. Fr Thabang Nkadimeng OMI**
Catholic University of America, Washington DC
The Sacramental Ecclesiology of Communion and the Hierarchical Ecclesiology of Communion, with Insights from Antonio Acerbi's '*Due Ecclesiologie*' **821**

SPEAKER: **Mr Edward Trendowski**
Catholic University of America, Washington DC
The Bishop as Servant to Communion: Vatican II Revisited **831**

MUSICOLOGY AND COMMUNION
CHAIR: Dr John O'Keeffe and Ms Giovanna Feeley
(St Patrick's College, Maynooth)

SPEAKER: **Ms Anne Mary Keeley**
University College, Dublin
The Ecclesiology of Communion: A Musicological Perspective **842**

SPEAKER: **Dr Maeve Louise Heaney VDMF**
Santa Clara University
Music as *Locus Theologicus*: An Expression of Harmonic Grace **854**

THURSDAY 7TH JUNE 2012

CHAIR: Dr Catherine O'Leary *(National University of Ireland, Maynooth)*

SPEAKER: **Mr Aurelio Cerviño**
The Alphonsian Academy, Rome
El eslabón perdido de la comunión: el mandamiento nuevo **868**

CHAIR: Rev. Dr David Kelly OSA *(Milltown Institute, Dublin)*

SPEAKER: **Ms Nollaig M. Ní Mhaoileoin**
St Patrick's College, Maynooth
Gairdín an Anama mar Iomhá: Samplaí as na Leabhair Urnaithe ón Naoú Aoise Déag sa Leabharlann Ruiséal, Coláiste Naoimh Phádraig, Má Nuad, le nascanna agus macallaí ón dtraidisiúin Eireannach chomh maith leis an Mhór Roinn **880**

CHAIR: Dr Tony Hanna *(Director of Pastoral Renewal and Family Ministry, Archdiocese of Armagh)*

SPEAKER: **Ms Patricia Kelly**
Centre for Catholic Studies, Durham University, UK
'The Workbench is your Altar': Jozef Cardijn's Understanding of the Role of the Eucharist in the Life of the Worker **891**

CHAIR: Sr Eleanor Campion OCSO *(Cistercian Generalate, Rome)*

SPEAKER: **Mr José Pedro Lopes Angélico**
Catholic University of Portugal
'The Eucharist as the Eager Longing of Creation': The Relational Wholeness of Reality and the Mystery of Communion **902**

CHAIR: Rev. Dr Gearóid Dullea
(Secretary to the Irish Catholic Bishops' Conference)

SPEAKER: **Rev. Dr Alessandro Clemenzia**
Sophia University Institute, Loppiano, Italy
The Ecclesial 'We' and the Eucharist: In Dialogue with the 'Theo-logic' of Heribert Mühlen **910**

CHAIR: Dr Dáire Keogh *(St Patrick's College, Drumcondra)*

SPEAKER: **Rt Rev. Antonio Luiz Catelan Ferreira**
Catholic University of Paraná, Brazil
L'ecclesiologia di comunione di Jerome Hamer **920**

FRIDAY 8TH JUNE 2012

CHAIR: Very Rev. Kieran McDermott
(Episcopal Vicar for Evangelisation and Ecumenism, Archdiocese of Dublin)

SPEAKER: **Mr Eimhin Walsh**
Trinity College, Dublin
Communion, Church and Crisis: Communion Ecclesiology in an Anglican Context **944**

CHAIR: Dr Suzanne Mulligan *(St Patrick's College, Maynooth)*

SPEAKER: **Rev. Dr Tomás Surlis DD**
Gregorian University, Rome
The Second Vatican Council and the Ecclesiology of Communion with Special Reference to Matthew 18:20 **955**

CHAIR: Sr Mary T. O'Brien PBVM *(St Patrick's College, Thurles)*

SPEAKER: **Rev. Dr Izunna Okonkwo**
Archdiocese of Glasgow, Scotland
The Eucharist as Community Builder: Eucharistic Communion and Social Transformation **967**

CHAIR: Sr Consilio Rock RSM
(Member of the Theology Forum of the Irish Inter-Church Meeting)

SPEAKER: **Ms Anastasia Wooden**
Catholic University of America, Washington DC
The Eucharistic Ecclesiology of Nicholas Afanasiev and Catholic Ecclesiology: History of Interaction and Future Perspectives **981**

CHAIR: Rev. Paul Prior
(St Patrick's College, Maynooth)

SPEAKER: **Rev. Dr Billy Swan**
Gregorian University, Rome
The Eucharist, Communion and Formation **993**

CHAIR: Mr Brendan O'Reilly
(National Director for Catechetics, Irish Bishops' Conference)

SPEAKER: **Ms Siobhan Leahy**
All Hallows College, Dublin
Nurturing Children's Spirituality in the Presence of the Eucharist **1003**

CHAIR: Rev. Dr Michael Shortall (St Patrick's College, Maynooth)

SPEAKER: **Rev. Dr Antonio José de Almeida**
Pontifical Catholic University of Paraná, Brazil
Comunità e Eucaristia nella V Conferenza Generale dell' Episcopato dell' America Latina **1015**

INTRODUCTION

MONSIGNOR HUGH G. CONNOLLY
President, St Patrick's College, Maynooth

For three days in June 2012, St Patrick's College, Maynooth, an institution synonymous with more than two centuries of priestly and theological training, played host to a veritable kaleidoscope of colour, culture, scholarship and fellowship as up to 400 delegates from every corner of the world visited our beautiful campus for the International Symposium of Theology. These days of friendship, fellowship and generous sharing of scholarship and spirituality were a truly wonderful precursor to the magnificent gathering that is the International Eucharistic Congress.

Despite unseasonably cold and damp weather, the warmth of the encounter was remarked upon by all the delegates. Here was an extraordinary cross-section of the people of God, the body of Christ, coming together to explore our understanding of the Eucharist and in particular the theme: 'Communion with Christ and with One Another.' Delegates from Quebec, the previous Congress hosts, chatted excitedly in the cloisters with prelates from Rome; emerging Irish scholars exchanged contact details with their peers from overseas; priests and parishioners from the four corners of our country made new friendships with their counterparts from Asia, Africa and the all the Americas. Challenges of language, culture and custom seemed to dissolve as if by magic as an all-pervading spirit of communion and solidarity took hold.

The symposium was very significant because it allowed people of faith and of various faith traditions at home and abroad to share their insight, wisdom and spirituality as a living reality with their brothers and sisters, and to do so in a manner which linked in a very practical and real way with the Eucharistic Congress. It was noteworthy in this regard that the 50th International Eucharistic Congress coincided with the 50th anniversary of the opening of the Second Vatican Council, a gathering of the Church that had so strongly underlined the ecclesiology of communion. The symposium of theology thus set itself the task of examining the *status questionis* fifty years on.

One entire morning was dedicated to biblical, systematic and moral explorations; later there were smaller, focussed seminars such as Communion and the Word; Communion and Social Justice, Communion and Art/Architecture/Music, Mission/Evangelisation, Communion and Ecology and the theme of Communion in the Irish tradition. Additionally, an entire day was dedicated to ecumenism. Major figures from across the Christian traditions availed of the opportunity to engage in frank and serious dialogue. Finally, missionary and pastoral themes concluded the symposium and served to reinvigorate the delegates with a sense of new resolve and mission so as to face ever more enthusiastically the challenges of the New Evangelisation.

As well as a myriad of workshops, lectures and parallel seminars in a host of languages, there was also ample opportunity for some *collegialitas affectiva*. For instance, all the participants were treated to an organised tour of a college exhibition entitled Gifts and Blessing: The Eucharist, the Irish Church and its People Through the Ages, which highlighted several treasures from the early books and manuscripts of St Patrick's College. Others travelled to some of the ancient monastic and pilgrimage sites which still bear such vivid witness to St Patrick, St Brigid, St Kevin and so many other great saints of the Irish Tradition. There were moments aplenty too to truly share, to dialogue, to savour and especially to pray and to celebrate the Eucharist together in the magnificent College Chapel, which has itself seen throughout the course of its history more than 11,000 young men ordained to the priesthood.

The Symposium and the Eucharist Congress were thus wonderful opportunities for all of us to rediscover the very bedrock of our faith, as well as to encounter our brothers and sisters in Christ from all across the globe. This was really a blessed time where we shared a little portion of our journey of faith and where *our eyes were opened and our hearts stirred.*

I trust that in perusing these pages those who were not fortunate enough to share these days of communion, fellowship and joy with us will nevertheless experience something of the camaraderie, the scholarly rigour and the fraternal ambiance of an event which truly allowed us to experience the very theme which we sought to explore, namely: 'Communion with Christ and with One Another.'

FOREWORD BY

PROF. BRENDAN LEAHY
Chairman of the Symposium Organising Committee
St Patrick's College, Maynooth

In his apostolic letter *Porta Fidei*, announcing the Year of Faith,[1] Pope Benedict XVI expresses his conviction that the Council, interpreted in terms of 'reform in continuity' will be increasingly important for the ever necessary renewal of the Church. What emerged from the Council was an ecclesiology of communion as a compass to guide the Catholic Church into the third millennium.

The ecclesiology of communion is a 'task', as Cardinal Kasper has put it, laid on us by the last council, and 'we are by no means at the end of the task. We are only at the beginning. With the council, Pope John XXIII wanted to take a leap forward ... A great deal still has to be done ... if we are to arrive at a renewal from the depths and from the sources, which will be at the same time a response to the signs of the time.'[2]

Fifty years after the opening of the Council is an opportune moment to reflect on how things are going in our understanding and implementation of the ecclesiology of communion. Accordingly, when Archbishop Diarmuid Martin of Dublin asked St Patrick's College, Maynooth, to host the International Symposium of Theology leading up to the International Eucharistic Congress, the choice of topic almost suggested itself, for the Eucharistic Congress had as its theme 'The Eucharist: Communion with Christ and with One Another'. The Symposium of Theology, from 6th–9th June 2012, would focus on The Ecclesiology of Communion Fifty Years after Vatican II.

It is sometimes debated as to whether the Council was theological or pastoral. While no new previously undefined doctrines were 'defined' at the Council, the event of the Spirit and its documents were a pressing invitation to conversion in our view of the Church in terms both of inner ecclesial renewal and outreach in dialogue. In that sense, it was indeed highly theological. The conversion it proposed finds its source in a renewed focus on the link between theology and anthropology that is found in Jesus Christ, the fullness of the triune God's revelation as communion. It is our participation in this communion that is to be lived 'on earth as it is in heaven'.

To use an image, the Council was like viewing a familiar object or landscape. Move even a few centimetres and you have a new perspective on that object or landscape. It isn't that the object you are looking at changes, but that you see it in a new way. Likewise, the Second Vatican Council invites us still today to take a new look at the Church, understand it from a particular angle, in this case communion, and act accordingly. Taking up the Council's vision, Blessed John Paul II reminded us as we entered the third millennium that 'to make the Church the home and the school of communion' is 'the great challenge facing us' at this time.[3]

It is significant that the opening paragraph of *Lumen Gentium* notes that in presenting the Church's nature and mission, the conciliar assembly wanted to do so 'following faithfully the teaching of previous councils'. Building on the clarifications and teachings of previous councils to do with Jesus Christ and the Trinity, grace, ministry and the sacraments, the Second Vatican Council offered a new beginning, linking God-Trinity and humanity/history/sociality. This is what lies at the root of the Council's emphasis on the ecclesiology of communion.

In his opening address during the Symposium of Theology, His Eminence, Marc Cardinal Ouellet observed that 'fifty years after the opening of the Second Vatican Council, the Church can better gauge the scope of this event and the import of its texts, which profoundly marked her life and her relation to the world'. He noted that the 'ecclesiology is ... richer and more promising than certain debates make it appear'. It is still an ecclesiology in development, enriched not least by ecumenical dialogue and directed towards the evangelising mission of the Church:

> Let us rejoice at this fruitfulness of the Council, which is far greater than the phenomena of regression or ideological reception. Among the consequences of the Council, we note the Church's renewed commitment to peace and justice in the world, her promotion of interreligious dialogue, and an extension of solidarity to a global scale, in the spirit of the encyclical *Caritas in Veritate*. However, the ecclesiology of communion still requires deeper theological

reflection and pastoral implementation. At the end of these fifty years, this ecclesiology appears more and more to be the concrete realisation of the Church, the Sacrament of salvation.

Among the topics that Cardinal Ouellet suggested for further exploration are: the relationship between the universal and the particular churches; the theology of Christian initiation; the ecclesiology of communion and eucharistic piety; the nuptial perspective of ecclesiology; the Church's Marian profile; the emergence of charisms; and the family as the domestic church.

The Symposium of Theology held in Maynooth from 6th–9th June 2012, saw thirty-four major scholars and twenty-eight emerging scholars from Ireland and around the world address many themes linked directly or indirectly to the ecclesiology of communion. The first sessions on Wednesday 6th June, which were those of the emerging scholars, set the tone for lively discussion and engagement with the topic both inside and outside the lecture halls over the next few days.

The main programme of the symposium began with an introductory session on 'The Eucharist, Communion and People in Irish Christianity', presenting the Irish setting of this international gathering of almost 400 participants from over thirty different countries and five continents. That evening, following Cardinal Ouellet's wide-ranging overview of the ecclesiology of communion, mentioned above, participants attended a reception that was marked by a warm atmosphere that continued and grew throughout the course of the symposium – despite inclement weather on two of the days of our gathering in Maynooth.

It would be impossible in this short introduction to attempt a summary of the many excellent papers delivered. Perhaps an overview of the structure of the symposium will assist the readers of this volume to navigate their way through the wealth of texts contained in it.

The first full day of the symposium, Thursday 7th June, was entitled 'Exploring Sources and Ways of Communion'. The morning was dedicated to scriptural and systematic, moral and liturgical foundations of the theme. The afternoon, on the other hand, provided an array of lectures on special topics to aid participants in considering particular dimensions of the theme of communion and its resonance in various fields – from patristic theology to the domestic church; from education to economics; from evolutionary history to the theme of beauty; from anthropology to reconciliation; from the Church's Marian profile to priesthood, eschatology, laity and ministry; from analysis of Mark's Gospel to the apostolicity of communion. Not least among the papers was the lecture by Prof. Slawomir Nowosad of Lublin on Blessed John Paul II and the ecclesiology of communion.

It is well known that one of the main concerns and objectives of the Second Vatican Council was Christian unity. For a symposium held in Ireland, this topic was bound to have a high profile. No surprise, therefore, that Friday 8th June was devoted entirely to 'learning from ecumenism'. We were honoured to have had his Eminence Kurt Cardinal Koch (president of the Pontifical Council for Promoting Christian Unity) deliver a paper entitled 'The Relation between the Eucharist and Ecclesial Communion: An Ecumenical View'.

This was followed by the Anglican scholar, Canon Nicholas Sagovsky's account of what he learnt (and did not learn) from the leading ecumenist, the late Jean-Marie Tillard OP. Doctor Julie Canlis, Presbyterian of the University of Aberdeen, shared the fruits of her recent research on the communion motif in the reformer, John Calvin. A key player of the ecumenical movement in the twentieth century, the Methodist ecumenist Rev. Prof. Geoffrey Wainwright delivered a carefully prepared text entitled 'From *Communio Imperfecta* through *Communio in Via* to Full Communion in Faith, Mission and Sacramental Life?' His Eminence, Metropolitan Emmanuel Adamakis of France (President of the Conference of European Churches) crowned the day's study with a deep reflection on the Orthodox perspective on dialogue and communion.

With the day's theological exploration done, the symposium participants all joined in a moving ecumenical evening prayer in the beautiful college chapel, the location of splendid liturgy and music each day of the symposium. The Gala Dinner that evening in Pugin Hall was followed by a prayerful concert of music by Irish composer Mr Ronan McDonagh, performed by *Fuaimlaoi*.

Reflection on the missionary, evangelising goal of communion is another theme very much at home in Ireland, a country that has a rich missionary history. The final day of the symposium, Saturday, 9th June, was entitled 'Looking to the Future: The Interaction of Communion and Mission'. Following missiologist Prof. Michael McCabe's very fine overview, the passion of His Eminence Oscar Cardinal Rodríguez Maradiaga's talk on the Eucharist and Mission warmed the hearts and minds of the participants. Our exploration of the theme was further developed by Rev. Dr Theodore Mascarenhas of the Pontifical Council for Culture's paper on mission and evangelisation in Asia and Prof. Joris Geldhof of the Catholic University of Leuven's stimulating paper entitled 'The End of the Mass for the Masses? Reflections on the Source and Summit of the Christian Life of Faith in Secular Cultures'.

As participants began to leave Maynooth on the concluding day of the symposium (the sun was finally shining!), there was gratitude expressed to one another for the positive and encouraging event that had been experienced together. New contacts made, addresses exchanged, papers requested. We had experienced something of the joy and spirit of communion of which the first letter of John speaks (1 Jn 1:1-4). In that light we saw light. And now, many of the pilgrim participants were moving on to take part in the International Eucharistic Congress due to start the day afterwards in the RDS, Dublin.

As I conclude this short introduction to the proceedings published in this volume, I need to express a big 'thank you' to all who, in any way, contributed to the success of the symposium, especially to the very fine speakers for their careful preparation of papers and attendance, as well as to the many eager participants who made the symposium a lively and Spirit-filled event. We are very grateful to those participants who chaired sessions, led us in prayer and presided over liturgies.

The International Theology Symposium wasn't just made up of speakers or the scholarly participants. Many contributed in other ways – the ever welcoming volunteers, the enthusiastic teams that prepared the liturgies (the staff and seminarians of St Patrick's College as well as the National Liturgy Centre) and the wonderful choirs: the Maynooth Symposium Choir, the Choir of Trinity College Chapel, Dublin, the Maynooth Parish Choir and the NUI Maynooth Chamber Choir.

Particular thanks is due to Monsignor Hugh Connolly, president of St Patrick's College, for his keen interest in and support of the symposium from the beginning. Likewise, thanks to members of the Faculty for the many ways they helped in its preparation. The symposium wouldn't have happened without the faithful commitment of my fellow members of the St Patrick's College organising committee (Prof. Michael Mullaney; Prof. Salvador Ryan; Dr Michael Shortall; Ms Fidelma Madden and Dr Bill Tinley). Warm thanks are due to the liturgy committee (Prof. Liam Tracey OSM; Dr John O'Keefe; Rev. Patrick Jones; and Sr Moira Bergin RSM), the Office of the President (especially Ms Cora Hennelly), the Development Office (Mr Dominic McNamara and Ms Louise Hennessy), the Accounts Office and the Theology Office (especially Ms Sheila Browne, Ms Colette Scully and, Admissions Officer, Ms Sandra Norgrove).

Gratitude is due also to the Catholic Communications office (especially Mr Martin Long and Ms Brenda Drumm), the staff of *Intercom* (especially Mr Francis Cousins) and *The Furrow* (especially Prof. Ronan Drury), the staff of the Russell Library, the Maynooth Campus Conference and Accommodation Centre (especially Mr Bill Tinley and Ms Daire Dillon), Campus Services, Security and the Domestic Supervisors, the Catering team (especially Ms Dearbhaile Finn, Mr David Kealy and Ms Michelle Bergin), Mr Andrew Moloney in AV Support, the translators, Mr Paulo Colonetti and Ms Ilaria Bonavita.

In a very special way, thanks are due to His Grace Archbishop Diarmuid Martin, president of the 50th International Eucharistic Congress, for inviting St Patrick's College to host the symposium and spreading the word about it. For their encouragement, support and promotion of the symposium, thanks is due also to His Eminence Seán Cardinal Brady and the Irish Bishops' Conference, as well as the Eucharistic Congress Office in Rome (especially Archbishop Piero Marini, Fr Vittore Boccardi and Sr Sara Galati).

Throughout the period of preparation, we in Maynooth were in constant contact with the International Eucharistic Congress Office in Dublin (especially Fr Kevin Doran, Ms Anne Griffin, Mr Dara McNally, Ms Mary Anne Stokes, Ms Teresa Menendez) and we are grateful to them for all their help, patience and hard work. In her capacity as theology intern for the symposium, a deep debt of gratitude is due to Dr Mary

50TH INTERNATIONAL EUCHARISTIC CONGRESS 2012

KEYNOTE SPEAKERS

at the International Symposium of Theology

St Patrick's College, Maynooth, County Kildare, Ireland
6th–9th June, 2012

Wednesday 6th June 2012

THE EUCHARIST, COMMUNION AND PEOPLE IN IRISH CHRISTIANITY

KEYNOTE SPEAKERS

at the International Symposium of Theology 50TH INTERNATIONAL EUCHARISTIC CONGRESS

• • 1 • •

FORMAL OPENING AND KEYNOTE ADDRESS

CHAIR: **MOST REV. DIARMUID MARTIN**
(Archbishop of Dublin and Primate of Ireland)

SPEAKER: **HIS EMINENCE MARC CARDINAL OUELLET PPS**
Prefect of the Congregation for Bishops
The Ecclesiology of Communion Fifty Years after the Opening of Vatican II

• • 2 • •

CHAIR: **REV. DR THOMAS O'CONNOR**
(National University of Ireland, Maynooth)

SPEAKER: **DR JENNIFER O'REILLY**
School of History, University College Cork; Royal Irish Academy
The Body of Christ in the Book of Kells

SPEAKER: **PROF. SALVADOR RYAN**
St Patrick's College, Maynooth
Merita Missae: *The Eucharist and the Lived Reality of Irish Christians in the Late Medieval and Early Modern Periods*

SPEAKER: **REV. FR BRENDAN McCONVERY CSsR**
St Patrick's College, Maynooth
Eucharistic Faith and Practice of the People as seen by some Irish Artists

THE ECCELESIOLOGY OF COMMUNION, FIFTY YEARS AFTER THE OPENING OF VATICAN II

HIS EMINENCE MARC CARDINAL OUELLET PPS
Prefect of the Congregation for Bishops
Papal Legate to the 50th International Eucharistic Congress

Fifty years after the opening of the Second Vatican Council, the Church can better gauge the scope of this event and the import of its texts, which profoundly marked her life and her relation to the world at the turn of the third millennium.

Blessed John XXIII set two main goals for the Council: to bring the presentation of the Church's doctrine up to date and to promote the unity of Christians.[1] These two objectives were intended to renew the Church's relation with the modern world and thus to revive her universal mission.

In order to attain these objectives, the Council Fathers undertook a fundamental reflection on ecclesiology, in the hopes of better defining the Church's profound nature, her essential structure, and the meaning of her mission in a world increasingly emancipated from her influence and tradition.

The ecclesiology of communion is the fruit of this reflection, which ripened through the gradual reception of the conciliar texts – with notable divergences, according to which theological or pastoral interpretation privileged reform within continuity or rupture with the Tradition. Thus, after the 'explication' and 'reception' of the Council had been promoted, orientation for its interpretation became necessary. The 1985 Synod of Bishops provided this by declaring, 'The ecclesiology of communion is the central and fundamental idea of the Council's documents.'[2]

Pope Benedict XVI contributed greatly to this reflection, noting the need for it: 'Why has the implementation of the Council, in large parts of the Church, thus far been so difficult? Well, it all depends on the correct interpretation of the Council or – as we would say today – on its proper hermeneutics, the correct key to its interpretation and application.'[3] It is enough to mention liturgical reform, episcopal collegiality, synodality and ecumenism, to touch on the well-known key points of the ecclesiology of communion and its interpretation.

This ecclesiology is, however, richer and more promising than certain debates make it appear. Within the framework of this International Eucharistic Congress, I propose to offer a brief retrospective of the ecclesiology of communion since the Council, followed by a few indications for further development, with a view to concluding with the global significance of this ecclesiology for the Church's mission in the third millennium.

I. A BRIEF RETROSPECTIVE OF THE ECCLESIOLOGY OF COMMUNION SINCE VATICAN COUNCIL II

A. The emergence of an ecclesiology of communion

A fifty-year anniversary is a propitious moment for assessing the path trod by ecclesiology since Vatican Council II. Already in 1982, Cardinal Ratzinger wrote, 'To mention only the more important theological results: the Council reinserted into the Church as a whole a doctrine of primacy that was dangerously isolated; it integrated into the one mysterium of the body of Christ a too-isolated conception of the hierarchy; it restored to the ordered unity of the faith an isolated Mariology; it gave the biblical word its full due; it made the liturgy once more accessible; and, in addition, it made a courageous step forward toward the unity of all Christians.'[4]

All these extremely important but not exhaustive results illustrate the emergence of an 'ecclesiology of communion' before the term itself arises. In 1985, the extraordinary Synod confirmed this as the fundamental orientation of the Council.

1) People of God

At first glance, this ecclesiology of communion makes us think of the Church's sociological dimension, with its structures of participation based on the common priesthood of the faithful and on the charisms the Holy Spirit stirs up so that the Church can accomplish her universal mission. Chapter two of *Lumen Gentium* refers to this dimension of the Church with the term 'people of God'.

We think of pastoral councils at the level of parish communities; presbyteral and pastoral councils at the diocesan level; and finally episcopal conferences as permanent structures that are represented at the Synod of Bishops. The multiple structures of participation in the new people of God make manifest a basic principle of Christianity: 'it is only in the community of all the brothers and sisters of Jesus Christ that one is a Christian, not otherwise'.[5]

We encounter the ecclesiology of communion concretely in these new structures, which implement the orientation of the Council. But this visible, functional and participatory dimension of the Church is not all or even the essential of the ecclesiology of communion. The starting point of this ecclesiology can be found in the first paragraph of the Constitution, *Lumen Gentium*: 'The Church is in Christ like a sacrament or as a sign and instrument both of a very closely knit union with God and of the unity of the whole human race' (LG, 1). This sacramental point of departure will mark the entire development of the ecclesiology of communion. Let us not forget that, in order to define the Church's nature and mission, the first chapter of the Dogmatic Constitution on the Church, *Lumen Gentium*, speaks first and above all of the 'mystery' of the Church and hence of her divine dimension, which proceeds from the Trinitarian missions of the Son and the Spirit in history: 'The Spirit dwells in the Church and in the hearts of the faithful, as in a temple (cf. 1 Cor 3:16; 6:19) ... He both equips and directs with hierarchical and charismatic gifts and adorns with his fruits (cf. Eph 4:11-12; 1 Cor 12:4; Gal 5:22) ... Thus, the Church has been seen as "a people made one with the unity of the Father, the Son and the Holy Spirit"' (LG, 4).

This Trinitarian vision of the mystery of the Church is not new. It belongs to the great tradition, but was obscured in modern times by a predominantly juridical approach to ecclesiology, that of the *societas perfecta*. It was taken up again at the Council on the basis of the expanded notion of 'sacrament,' applied to the Church as such.[6] This bold intuition invites us to see the visible realities of the Church immersed in the invisible reality of Trinitarian communion. We will come back to this later on.

2) Sacramental foundation

In a few paragraphs that take their inspiration from sacred scripture, the Council brings to light the sacramental foundation of the ecclesiology of communion: baptism and the Eucharist, which incorporate us into Christ. Through baptism we are formed in the likeness of Christ: 'For in one Spirit we were all baptised into one body' (1 Cor 12:13). Really partaking of the body of the Lord in the breaking of the eucharistic bread, we are taken up into communion with him and with one another. 'Because the bread is one, we though many, are one body, all of us who partake of the one bread' (1 Cor 10:17). In this way all of us are made members of his body, 'but severally members one of another' (Rm 12:5) (LG, 7).

Contemporary exegesis of 1 Corinthians 10:16-17 has once again brought to the foreground the ecclesial sense of eucharistic communion.[7] According to St Paul, communion in the eucharistic body of Christ builds up the Church as his Body. The eucharistic celebration actualises the mystery of the covenant, that is, the total gift that Christ makes of his body to the Church his bride, to sanctify and nourish her (Eph 5:27) and to associate her to his own fruitfulness, for the salvation of the world (cf. LG, 7). This ecclesial sense of the Eucharist was very strong at the origins. Unfortunately, this sense took an individualist turn during the second millennium, under the influence of a more dialectical theology that had lost the profound sense of symbolism of the Church Fathers.

Henri de Lubac traced the history of the semantic shift that marked the evolution of eucharistic theology and its relation to the Church. At its origin, *corpus mysticum* referred to the eucharistic body of Christ in closest relation with the ecclesial body associated with him. In the Middle Ages, Bérenger's heresy prompted a reaffirmation of the real presence of Christ in the sacrament; the expression *corpus verum* was substituted for *corpus mysticum*, and the latter was relegated to the level of spiritual presence. It then referred to the ecclesial body in a purely spiritual sense, which lost its basis in the realist and concrete notion of sacrament.

This was followed by a weakening of the bond between the Eucharist and the Church. A more individualistic eucharistic piety developed that was centred on the real presence, despite the fact that St

Thomas Aquinas still clearly maintained *à propos* of the Eucharist that 'the reality (res) of the sacrament is the unity of the mystical body'.[8]

3) Eucharistic ecclesiology

It is important to stress here that the ecclesiology of communion promoted by the Council takes its inspiration from the Eucharistic ecclesiology of the Orthodox, especially Afanassief, who is cited in the texts. The Council's ecclesiology is thus of great ecumenical import. The intervention of John Zizioulas, the Metropolitan of Pergamon, at the 2005 Roman Synod of Bishops on the Eucharist, testifies to this: 'The ecclesiology of communion promoted by Vatican II and deepened further by eminent Roman Catholic theologians can make sense only if it derives from the eucharistic life of the Church. The Eucharist belongs not simply to the *bene esse* but to the *esse* of the Church. The whole life, word and structure of the Church is eucharistic in its very essence.'[9] Walter Kasper agrees whole-heartedly and holds that 'eucharistic ecclesiology has become one of the most important foundations of the ecumenical dialogue between the Catholic Church and the Orthodox Churches.'[10]

B. Stages of development of the ecclesiology of communion

1) *Ecclesia domestica*

Alongside the foundations laid by the Council in terms of a eucharistic ecclesiology, we can add the discreet mention of the *ecclesia domestica*, which refers to the family founded on the sacrament of marriage. The family has the 'mission to be the first and vital cell of society ... It will fulfil this mission if it appears as the domestic sanctuary of the Church by reason of the mutual affection of its members and the prayer that they offer to God in common, if the whole family makes itself a part of the liturgical worship of the Church' (*Apostolicam Actuositatem* 11; cf. also LG, 11). The *ecclesia domestica* rests on the 'conjugal covenant' in Christ, through marriage, which establishes 'the intimate partnership of married life and love' that forms the couple (*Gaudium et Spes,* 48§1).

This notion of the *ecclesia domestica* was taken up again systematically in the post-synodal exhortation *Familiaris Consortio,* which has given rise to an abundant literature under the impulse of John Paul II, the Pope of the family.[11] If it is indisputable that baptism and the Eucharist constitute the Church, the body of Christ, the sacrament of marriage confers an ecclesial status upon the conjugal bond between a man and a woman. This status is recognised by the application of the term *ecclesia domestica* to the Christian family. At a time when we are witnessing an unprecedented anthropological crisis, characterised by the loss of a sense of marriage and the family, the Church can and must count on the resource of the family founded on sacramental marriage in order to confront the challenges of secularised societies. The evangelising potential of such a sacramental reality still remains to be discovered and promoted, so that the Church's endeavour for the new evangelisation can become a reality.[12]

2) *Ecclesia de Eucharistia*

The publication of the encyclical *Ecclesia de Eucharistia* in 2003 was an important step in the development of the ecclesiology of communion. John Paul II's encyclical filled a lacuna left by the Council, which had exalted the preeminence of the Eucharist in the Church's life but had not systematically defined its relation to the Church.[13] This relation is now defined in the sense of a reciprocal dependence, in which the Church receives the Eucharist as the 'gift par excellence' (EE, 11), a gift that presupposes incorporation into Christ through baptism but also 'reinforces' this incorporation, because it is the 'unifying power of the body of Christ' (EE, 24). The *leitmotif* of this encyclical is that the Church lives from the Eucharist. If we must add that the Church 'makes' the Eucharist, she does so on the basis of the more profound causality of the Eucharist, which 'makes' the Church.[14] Reviving the biblical and patristic perspective mentioned above, the encyclical deepens the apostolic dimension of the Eucharist and draws out the riches of its nuptial symbolism. It does so in the context of a Trinitarian and Marian ecclesiology that opens the way to a new equilibrium of ecclesial consciousness and practice.

Ecclesia de Eucharistia promotes spiritual and practical attitudes that allow us to live the Church's blessed dependence on the Eucharist more profoundly and intensely: 'The Eucharist ... appears as both the source and the summit of all evangelisation, since its goal is the communion of mankind with Christ and in him with the Father and the Holy Spirit' (EE, 22).[15] In fact, ecclesial communion, nourished by the sacrament of the Eucharist, includes in its invisible dimension 'communion with God the Father by identification with his only-begotten Son through the working of the Holy Spirit' (EE, 34). In the visible dimension, it also implies 'communion in the teaching of the Apostles, in the sacraments and in the Church's hierarchical order' (EE, 35). This magisterial intervention significantly confirms the ecclesiology of communion and revives the Council's commitment to the cause of ecumenism by highlighting the witness of Catholics in this area.

The 2005 Synod of Bishops on the Eucharist draws out the pastoral and ecumenical consequences of the fundamental relationship between the Eucharist and the Church. The title itself of the post-synodal document, *Sacramentum Caritatis,* contains an entire programme intended to realise the Church's identity as Christ's body and bride, as well as the universal scope of her mission as *sacramentum unitatis*. In this light, the apostolic exhortation makes an important clarification with regard to the relation between the universal Church and the particular Churches:

> The unity of ecclesial communion is concretely manifested in the Christian communities and is renewed at the celebration of the Eucharist, which unites them and differentiates them in the particular Churches, *'in quibuset ex quibusuna et unica Ecclesia catholica exsistit'*. The fact that the one Eucharist is celebrated in each diocese around its own bishop helps us to see how those particular Churches subsist in and *ex Ecclesia*. (SC, 15)

In fact, the oneness of the eucharistic Body of the Lord implies the oneness of his mystical body, which is the one and indivisible Church. This principle of unity leads to the openness of each community and of every particular Church to all the others that celebrate the Eucharist in the Lord. *Sacramentum Caritatis* adds, 'Consequently, in the celebration of the Eucharist, the individual members of the faithful find themselves in their Church, that is, in the Church of Christ' (SC, 15). This position has great ecumenical significance, because it recognises both the proximity of the Orthodox Churches and a basis for dialogue with the ecclesial communities that have their origins in the Reformation.

This rapid overview of the ecclesiology of communion through the past fifty years remains fragmentary. Nevertheless, it leaves an impression of fruitfulness with respect to the fundamental orientation of the Second Vatican Council. With Pope Benedict XVI, we can clearly affirm that Vatican Council II and its ecclesiological development were a providential work of the Holy Spirit in our age. If it is true that we can criticise a number of post-conciliar developments that left a negative mark on the liturgy, the family, vocations and consecrated life, we must acknowledge that the emergence of the ecclesiology of communion has borne abundant fruit in the areas of episcopal collegiality, synodality, the apostolate of the laity, charismatic and ecclesial movements, ecumenism, and the Church's dialogue with the modern world.

Obviously, theological discussion must continue in order further to clarify the ecclesiology of communion. I will evoke three themes which, in my opinion, merit particular attention: the relation between the universal Church and the particular Churches, the theology of Christian initiation, and the integration of modern forms of eucharistic piety in an ecclesiology of communion.

C. Theological discussions to be pursued

1) Universal and particular Church

An issue of great importance for both ecumenism and the *mission ad gentes* is the way we conceive of the relation between the universal Church and the particular Churches. This question occupied an important place in Vatican Council II. It was occasioned by the discussion of the sacramentality of the episcopate, in which the relation between the primacy of Peter and episcopal collegiality was clarified. In this context, the Council clearly affirmed that 'in virtue of his office, that is as Vicar of Christ and pastor of the whole Church, the Roman Pontiff has full, supreme and universal power over the Church. And he is always free to exercise this power' (LG, 22). According to some, the power of the college of bishops seems to be expressed in a more restricted fashion, which leaves little initiative to the particular Churches, episcopal conferences, and synods.

The rapid development of the ecclesiology of communion revived this debate, which has to do with the Church's profound nature, her unity in diversity, the presence of the universal Church in the particular

Churches, and the concrete meaning of episcopal collegiality. To counter the relativist interpretations of the ecclesiology of communion, the Congregation for the Doctrine of the Faith published a *Letter to the Bishops of the Catholic Church on Some Aspects of the Church Understood as Communion* (28th May 1992). This letter prompted a number of criticisms, such as that of Walter Kasper, who worried about a vision of the Church that 'becomes completely problematic if the one, universal Church is tacitly identified with the Roman Church, de facto with the Pope and the Curia'. According to Kasper, this would be, not 'an aid for the clarification of the ecclesiology of communion', but rather 'its abandonment, and a kind of attempt to restore Roman centralisation'.[16]

This strong criticism prompted a reaction from Cardinal Joseph Ratzinger, who defended the ontological primacy of the universal Church over the particular Churches against Kasper's empirical interpretation, which affirmed their interdependence. Once the misunderstandings had been dispelled, the divergences between the two authors remained relatively minimal. However, the debate served to balance Orthodox-inspired eucharistic ecclesiology with a reminder of the baptismal ecclesiology that is more fundamental for Protestants. The debate also helped us the better to understand the profound nature of the Church as a unique subject who 'subsists' (LG, 8) in the Catholic Church. Concretely, she subsists in each local community presided over by a bishop in communion with the college of the successors of the apostles and its head, the successor of Peter. This subsistence of the Church cannot be affirmed of the other Churches and ecclesial communities, but permits the recognition of elements of ecclesiality in them.

The unique, universal Church is in fact always at the same time a local reality, incarnated in concrete persons – if only, before every local community, in the Virgin Mary, the Mother of the Saviour, who is given a share by God in the birth and the growth of the one, holy, Catholic, and apostolic Church.

On the level of ecumenism, Pope John Paul II invited the other Churches and ecclesial communities to tell him in what way he might exercise his Petrine ministry to respond better to the expectations of other Christians (cf. *Ut Unum Sint*, 95–6). This invitation to dialogue carries great weight, for it presupposes an availability to adapt the exercise of the primacy and of collegiality to the new conditions of ecclesial communion *ad intra* and *ad extra*.

A great deal of flexibility is possible for ecclesiastical discipline in the areas of the liturgy, the clergy, synodality, the nomination and the governance of bishops, etc., but unity of teaching in matters of faith and morals nonetheless requires a doctrinal authority that decides in the final instance, according to the role traditionally attributed to the Sovereign Pontiff.

Between the universal Church and the particular Church, there is thus no opposition, but rather a mutual immanence that has its source in Christ's primacy over the Church. There is no particular Church that is not first and always the universal Church welcoming God's children, whom Christ gives her through faith and the sacraments celebrated in a given place.

The particular Church is rightly valued if we consider it as a 'portion' of the universal Church, and not only as a part or a geographical region. 'Portion' means the universal Church is present in this portion and is the foundation for its communion with all the other portions. Together, they form a single Church. This presence of the unique Church in each portion implies a relation of communion between the bishops. For each bishop, this means full episcopal authority over the portion he has been given to shepherd, and whose communion with the universal Church he must ensure. The Pope bears 'anxiety for all the churches' (2 Cor 11:28) as the Pastor of the universal Church, but he accomplishes this service as the guarantor of unity. That is to say, he does not substitute the authority of the local bishop, but confirms it from within. As the bishop of Rome, who presides over the college of bishops, of which he is the head, he has universal authority over the pastors and the faithful. His role is to keep watch over the unity of the whole Church, first of all by caring for the communion of the bishops with him and among themselves. The bishops, for their part, are not vicars of the Pope. They, too, are vicars of Christ, but in dependence on the head of the college in everything that touches on the doctrinal and disciplinary unity of the universal Church.

In brief, the relation between the universal Church and the particular Churches presupposes a eucharistic ecclesiology based

comprehensive vision of eucharistic and ecclesial communion. The adoration of the Blessed Sacrament, for example, is a form of spiritual communion, which prolongs sacramental communion or replaces it when an obstacle hinders the reception of the sacrament. We must always try to show the ecclesial meaning of other manifestations of eucharistic piety by reattaching them to the eucharistic celebration. The Church's eucharistic tradition is so rich that it cannot be reduced to the celebration of the Eucharist alone. We need all the Church's eucharistic culture in order to keep all of its aspects in balance. The dialogue between theologians, pastors and the faithful must thus be carried out in a climate of openness and respect for spiritual traditions.

II. PERSPECTIVES FOR THE FUTURE

A. For an ecclesiology of communion in a nuptial perspective

Earlier we evoked the relation between baptism and the Eucharist, which configures the ecclesiology of communion. Baptism highlights the belonging to the universal Church, since it incorporates the believer into Christ, who is unique and universal. The Eucharist highlights the belonging to the particular Church, since it is always celebrated in a concrete community, which thus becomes more the Body of Christ. This difference does not justify an opposition between two ecclesiologies, because the two sacraments of the new covenant are ordered to one another.

The Catechism of the Catholic Church offers us the right perspective for the ecclesiology of communion when it proposes nuptial symbolism to describe the articulation of the sacraments:

> The entire Christian life bears the mark of the spousal love of Christ and the Church. Already baptism, the entry into the people of God, is a nuptial mystery; it is so to speak the nuptial bath (cf. Eph 5:26-27), which precedes the wedding feast, the Eucharist. Christian marriage in its turn becomes an efficacious sign, the sacrament of the covenant of Christ and the Church. Since it signifies and communicates grace, marriage between baptised persons is a true sacrament of the new covenant.[18]

Even if we cannot demonstrate it here, this nuptial perspective on the Christian life in general and on the Eucharist in particular is rooted in the biblical notion of *mysterion*.[19] This term has multiple semantic connotations, but its sacramental significance gradually unfolds in the direction of the 'great mystery' St Paul expresses in Ephesians 5:32, which refers to Christ's 'nuptial love for the Church'. The (Trinitarian) mystery hidden in God from all ages unveils its interiority through the mystery of the incarnation of the Word – a mystery that culminates in the nuptial relationship of Christ and the Church.[20] When God gradually reveals his mystery in salvation history, he privileges nuptial symbolism, particularly in Genesis, the prophets, the Song of Songs, the gospels, the Pauline letters and the Book of Revelation. This biblical notion of *mysterion* is taken up again by the Fathers, who understood it rather broadly as the foundation of the sacramental economy and the keystone of the relation between the Eucharist and the Church. Cardinal Henri de Lubac draws our attention once again to this relation in the Fathers, with its profoundly nuptial harmonies, by re-circulating the famous patristic expression that structures John Paul II's encyclical 'The Eucharist makes the Church.'[21]

This systematic articulation is more important than it appears, for it gives us a new model to think of the synergy between Christ and the Church in the economy of sacramental grace. The sacraments are efficacious signs of the new covenant; they are acts of Christ and the Church performed in an intimate synergy, in the one Spirit.

On the theological level, *Sacramentum Caritatis* further clarifies the relation between the Church and the other sacraments when it affirms, 'The Church receives and at the same time expresses what she herself is in the seven sacraments' (SC, 16). This clarification is important, since the Church is both active and passive in her relationship to Christ through faith and the sacraments. She is not an autonomous subject who appropriates and manages Christ's foundational gestures as she sees fit. She remains always the body that depends on the head, and the bride attentive to the will of the bridegroom.

One might object that this nuptial perspective has above all an aesthetic value, and that it does not sufficiently involve communion on the level of the dramas and conflicts of human life. The response to this objection depends on a further development of the ecclesiology of communion under the sign of Mary.

B. Mary, the Eucharist and the Church

The intimate relationship between the Eucharist and the Church, such as it appears in the First Letter to the Corinthians and in a strong liturgical tradition of the first millennium, invites us to reaffirm in sacramental practice the unity of the body of Christ, who rises with his eucharistic and his ecclesial body. This strict but differentiated unity implies the participation of different actors at the level of the rite, but also at the level of the mystery, of which the sacrament is the memorial. *Ecclesia de Eucharistia* reaffirmed the apostolicity of the Eucharist, against the widespread tendency to relativise the role of the ordained minister in order to affirm the conscious and active participation of the assembly in Christ's sacrificial offering.

This tension on the liturgical level invites us to ask, on the theological level, about the Church's participation in the sacrifice of the Redeemer. 'Is the Mass a sacrifice of the Church?' asked Hans Urs von Balthasar shortly after the Council. The Catholic conception of the Eucharist presupposes this participation but does not always make its foundation explicit. The ecclesiology of communion would benefit by listening here to the theologian from Basel, who takes up the question once again within the framework of his theo-drama: 'So the question is, is the Church already the body of Christ in offering her sacrifice, or is it only by her action that she becomes such?'[22]

Balthasar adds, 'The community's celebration of the Eucharist led to the more and more conscious insight that faith in his sacrifice, which already includes us, "passively", by way of anticipation, also demands our active collaboration.'[23] This apparently sibylline question is extremely important for ecumenism, since Protestants reproach Catholics for diminishing the work of Christ by claiming to add something to his redemptive sacrifice, from which flows all the grace of our salvation. Balthasar is very aware of this objection; he attempts to receive it and to respond to it fully.

In his account of the drama of the Eucharist, he shows the place and the archetypical role of Mary's 'yes', which, in the grace of the Spirit, precedes and encompasses every other 'yes' in the Church of sinners to the sacrifice of Christ: 'In so far as Mary's Yes is one of the presuppositions of the Son's incarnation, it can be, beneath the Cross, a constituent part of his sacrifice.'[24]

Balthasar further deepens our understanding of this question in relation to the mediation of the ministers of the Eucharist. He affirms that 'Christ is entrusted to the hands of Mary at birth and at his death: this is more central than his being given into the hands of the Church in her official, public aspect. The former is the precondition for the latter.'[25] This profound vision helps us correctly to integrate the essential role of the ordained minister in the sacramental offering of the eucharistic sacrifice, but without isolating it from the community. His role remains essentially dependent on the Marian faith in which and from which he can exercise his liturgical function. There is a function that represents Christ in the Church because the Church is already constituted by Mary's faith, which is communicated to us at baptism.

The Church is confirmed and strengthened in her identity as the body and bride of Christ through the Eucharist. She participates as the bride of the lamb in the offering entrusted to the hands of her ordained ministers; but this offering was first placed by the Spirit of the Redeemer in the heart and the hands of Mary at the foot of the cross.

Such a vision allows us to understand the primacy of the baptismal priesthood, which culminates in Mary's act of faith, offering Jesus to the Father and offering herself with him. Consequently, we can say that, thanks to her, it is the entire community of the baptised that participates in offering the eucharistic sacrifice, even if the community's role is to receive, like Mary at the foot of the cross, the sacramental gift that the minister accomplishes in Christ's name.

Lastly, Balthasar demonstrates the hidden presupposition that makes possible this participation of Mary in the redemptive sacrifice: her Immaculate Conception, which permits her to be in perfect solidarity with her Son in the sacrificial offering. She does not add a surplus, as a 'work' that would be proper to her, but consents to let God's will be accomplished in the unique redemptive sacrifice. This humble and painful consent remains the permanent foundation of the Church's participation in Christ's eucharistic offering.

Balthasar notes the paradox: it is through the mediation of the mystery of Mary, in whom everything is grace, that we can overcome the Protestant objection, which reproaches Catholics for adding their own works and merits to the unique sacrifice of Christ.

C. The ecclesiology of communion and charisms

Vatican Council II certainly was a breath of Pentecost that freed the Church from her isolation from the modern world and her ecclesiological limits. The Council did not only reestablish the balance between the primacy of Peter and episcopal collegiality, or simply articulate the royal priesthood of the baptised in relation to the hierarchical ministry. It also provided a broad opening to the charisms the Spirit distributes for the renewal or the expansion of the Church: 'To each is given the manifestation of the Spirit for the common good' (1 Cor 12:7). In the words of *Lumen Gentium*, 'These charisms, whether they be the more outstanding or the more simple and widely diffused, are to be received with thanksgiving and consolation for they are perfectly suited to and useful for the needs of the Church' (LG, 12).

I remain profoundly convinced that the Council greatly contributed to the appearance of a multitude of charisms, which now have full rights of citizenship in the Church. Old and new communities of consecrated life, ecclesial movements, the lay apostolate, and everything St Paul describes in his non-exhaustive list of charisms – all of this belongs to the Church of Christ, which the Holy Spirit abundantly enriches to make of her a beautiful and resplendent bride, according to the divine will. All this dynamism forces theology to rethink the ecclesiology of communion, systematically integrating these new realities along with the old. Both belong to this order of realities destined to build up the Church.

Taking up again the expression of Zizioulas cited earlier, I would say that the charisms are generally seen as useful to the Church's *bene esse*, but not as necessary to her *esse* as such. We would have to say more in order to support the new evangelisation, and we can thanks to an ecclesiology of communion that integrates all the gifts of the Spirit, both hierarchical and charismatic (LG, 4), in a comprehensive vision of the Church as the sacrament of salvation.[26]

CONCLUSION

Fifty years after the opening of the Second Vatican Council, we have seen that its chief inspiration was the ecclesiology of communion, which a right interpretation of the Council gradually identified and emphasised. The ecclesiology of communion is still in the process of development. It is enriched by ecumenical dialogue with the Orthodox and their eucharistic ecclesiology, as well as by dialogue with the ecclesial communities that have their source in the Reformation and maintain the primacy of a baptismal ecclesiology.

Within the Catholic Church, the ecclesiology of communion gives value to the episcopal ministry, the episcopal conferences, and the Synod of Bishops, while giving renewed impetus to reflection on the primacy of Peter; it promotes the search for a new equilibrium between primacy and collegiality in the relation between the universal Church and the particular Churches. At the level of the particular Churches, the sacramental dimension of the ecclesiology of communion extends the Church's consciousness into the family, the *ecclesia domestica*. It demands a renewed pastoral practice of Christian initiation, as well as the harmonious integration of charisms for an efficacious new evangelisation.

The ecclesiology of communion has thus revitalised the Church *ad intra* and multiplied her ecumenical and missionary openings *ad extra*. Let us rejoice at this fruitfulness of the Council, which is far greater than the phenomena of regression or ideological reception. Among the consequences of the Council, we note the Church's renewed commitment to peace and justice in the world, her promotion of interreligious dialogue and an extension of solidarity to a global scale, in the spirit of the encyclical *Caritas in Veritate*.

However, the ecclesiology of communion still requires deeper theological reflection and pastoral implementation. At the end of these fifty years, this ecclesiology appears more and more to be the concrete realisation of the Church, the sacrament of salvation. The notion of sacrament applied to the Church is to be understood not only as the efficacy of the seven sacraments, but as the participation of ecclesial communion in the communion of the Trinity, given to the world in Jesus Christ. 'God is love, and whoever abides in love abides in God, and God abides in him' (1 Jn 4:16).

The sacramentality of the Church therefore means ecclesial communion as a force of attraction and evangelisation. Let us not forget that the evangelising power of the first Christians emanated from their witness of reciprocal love, which attracted and converted the pagans: 'See how they love one another!'[27] The Church thus becomes a sacrament, or 'a sign and instrument both of a very closely knit union with God and of the unity of the whole human race' (LG 1), in accordance with the general definition of sacrament. As 'sign', she is the bearer of a mysterious divine reality that no image or analogy of this world will adequately express. As 'instrument', she works efficaciously for the salvation of the world through her union with Christ, who associates her to his unique priesthood as his body and bride. The Church's mission thus coincides with the sacramental form of the love that reveals God at work in the world, in an intimate synergy with the witnesses of the new covenant.

The future of the Church's mission passes through her witness of unity and her dialogue with all of humanity in the name of the Trinitarian communion. This communion is destined for everyone, and she is its sacrament. Her sacramental mission means more than a reference to the Holy Trinity as an ideal or a model; it means a communion that is an authentic participation in the witness of the Trinity in history. 'There are three witnesses, the Spirit, the water and the blood, and these three agree in one. If we receive the testimony of men, the testimony of God is greater ... And this is the testimony, that God gave us eternal life, and this life is in his Son. He who has the Son has life; he who has not the Son of God has not life' (1 Jn 5:7-9, 11-12).

NOTES

1 John XXIII, Address on the occasion of the solemn opening of the Most Holy Council, 11th October 1962.

2 The Final Report of the Extraordinary Synod of Bishops, The Church, in the Word of God, Celebrates the Mysteries of Christ for the Salvation of the World, 1985, II, C., 1. Cf. also on this subject: Rino Fisichella, ed., *Il Concilio Vaticano II: Recezione e attualità alla luce del Giubileo,* Milan: San Paolo, 2000; René Latourelle, ed., *Vatican II: Bilanet perspectives, vingt-cinqans après* (1962–1987), Montréal/Paris: Bellarmin/Cerf, 1988, (*Vatican II: Assessment and Perspectives 25 Years Later,* New York: Paulist Press, 1988–9).

3 Benedict XVI, Address to the Roman Curia offering them his Christmas greetings, 22nd December 2005.

4 Joseph Ratzinger, 'Review of the Postconciliar Era: Failures, Tasks, Hopes', *Principles of Catholic Theology: Building Stones for a Fundamental Theology,* San Francisco: Ignatius Press, 1987, p. 370.

5 Ibid., p. 75.

6 Semmelroth, O., *Die Kirche als Ursakrament,* Knecht, Frankfurt a.M., 1955, 1963; *Die Kirche als Sakrament des Heils,* in *Mysterium Salutis. Grundriß heilsgeschichtlicher Dogmatik.*, 4/1, pp. 309–56.

7 Cf. Xavier Léon-Dufour, 'Corps du Christ et Eucharistieselon Saint Paul', *Le corps et le corps du Christ dans la première Épître aux Corinthiens* (Congrès de l'ACFEB, Tarbes,1981), Paris: Cerf, 1983, pp. 225–55; Hervé Legrand, 'Communion eucharistique et communion ecclésiale. Une relecture de la première lettre aux Corinthiens', *Centro Pro Unione Bulletin* 67 (spring 2005), pp. 21–32.

8 *Summa Theologica,* III, 73, 3.

9 John Zizioulas, intervention at Vatican Synod of Bishops, 11th October 2005, cited in Walter Kasper, 'Ecclésiologie Eucharistique: de Vatican II à l'exhortation *Sacramentum Caritatis*', *L'Eucharistie, don de Dieu pour la vie du monde. Actes du Symposium international de théologie,* Ottawa: CECC, 2009, p. 196.

10 Walter Kasper, ibid., p. 198.

11 John Paul II, apostolic exhortation *Familiaris Consortio: The Role of the Christian Family in the Modern World* (1981); apostolic letter *Mulieris Dignitatem: On the Dignity and Vocation of Women* (1988); *Letter to Families* (1994). On *Familiaris Consortio,* see, for example, *L'Esortazione sulla famiglia, Familiaris consortio. Introduzione alla lettura, testo, sussidi per incontri pastorali, indice analitico per argomenti* (Milan: Ed. Massimo, 1982); 'La famiglia cristiana 'velut Ecclesia domestica' nell'Esortazione Familiaris Consortio', *La Scuola Cattolica,* 111 (1983), pp. 107–52.

12 Cf. Marc Ouellet, *Mistero e Sacramento dell'amore. Teologia del matrimonio e della Famiglia per la nuova evangelizzazione,* Siena, Cantagalli, 2007.

13 Cf. Giuseppe Colombo, *Teologia sacramentaria,* Milan: Glossa, 1997, pp. 320–38.

14 A complementary clarification is offered by *Sacramentum Caritatis*: 'in the striking interplay between the Eucharist which builds up the Church, and the Church herself which "makes" the Eucharist, the primary causality is expressed in the first formula: the Church is able to celebrate and adore the mystery of Christ present in the Eucharist precisely because Christ first gave himself to her in the sacrifice of the Cross. The Church's ability to "make" the Eucharist is completely rooted in Christ's self-gift to her' (*Sacramentum Caritatis* 14; cf. John Paul II, *Redemptor Hominis* 20; *Dominicae Cenae* 4).

15 Cf. Marc Ouellet, *Ecclesia de Eucharistia*, Conference at the International Eucharistic Congress of Guadalajara, 6th October 2004, p. 13. www.eglisecatholiquedequebec.org/documents/pdf/congres_euch.pdf.

16 Walter Kasper, 'Zur Theologie und Praxis des bischöflichen Amtes', *Auf neue Art Kirche Sein. Wirklichkeiten – Herausforderungen – Wandlungen,* Munich: Bernward bei Don Bosco, 1999, p. 44. For the essential texts of the dialogue initiated by this text of Kasper's, see:

a) Joseph Ratziner, 'L'ecclésiologie de la Constitution conciliare *Lumen Gentium*', *La Documentation Catholique*, 2223 (2nd April 2000), pp. 303–12;

b) Walter Kasper, 'On the Church. A Friendly Reply to Cardinal Ratzinger,' *America* 184 (23rd–30th April 2001), 8–14 (original: 'Das Verhältnis con Universalkirche und Ortskirche: Freundschaftliche Auseinandersetzung mit der Kritik von Joseph Kardinal Ratzinger,' Stimmen der Zeit 218 (2000), pp. 795–804;

c) Joseph Ratzinger, 'A Response to Walter Kasper: The Local Church and the Universal Church', *America* 185 (19th November 2001), pp. 7–11.

17 Cf. L'adoration eucharistique: 'Ponenza dell'Em.mo Card. Marc Ouellet, Arcivescovo di Québec', *Notitiae* 46, 3–4, 2009, pp. 130–49.

18 *Catechism of the Catholic Church* 1617. Cf. Code of Canon Law, canon 1055, §2; DS 1800 (Session 24 of the Council of Trent): 'Whereas therefore matrimony, in the evangelical law, excels in grace, through Christ, the ancient marriages; with reason have our Holy Fathers, the Councils, and the tradition of the universal Church, always taught, that it is to be numbered amongst the sacraments of the new law.'

19 Cf. G. Bornkam, 'Mysterion', *Grande Lessico del Nuovo Testamento,* vol. VII, 645–716; C. Rocchetta, *Sacramentaria Fondamentale,* Bologna: EDB, 1989, pp. 191–242.

20 See Pope John Paul II's historical footnote regarding the term *mysterion* in his catecheses on human love, *Uomo e Donna lo creò,* Città Nuova – Libreria Ed. Vaticana, 1995, p. 363. John Paul II, *Man and Woman He Created Them:*

A Theology of the Body, Michael Waldstein, trans., Boston: Pauline Books & Media, 2006, pp. 489–90.

21 Henri de Lubac, *Corpus Mysticum: L'Eucharistie et l'Eglise au Moyen Âge,* Paris: Aubier, 1939 (Corpus Mysticum: The Eucharist and the Church in the Middle Ages, Gemma Simmonds trans., (Notre Dame, IN: University of Notre Dame Press, 2007); cf. Paul McPartlan, *The Eucharist Makes the Church: Henri de Lubac and John Zizioulas in Dialogue,* Edinburgh: T&T Clark, 1993.

22 Hans Urs von Balthasar, *Theo-Drama: Theological Dramatic Theory IV: The Action,* Graham Harrison trans., San Francisco: Ignatius, 1994, p. 394.

23 Ibid., 395.

24 Ibid.

25 Ibid., 397.

26 Cf. Marc Ouellet, *L'apport des mouvements ecclésiaux. Unité et diversité dans l'Esprit,* Bruyères-le-Châtel: Nouvelle Cité, 2011.

27 Tertullian, *Apology* 39, 7.

or calf, which had Old Testament associations as a priestly sacrificial victim, to St Luke as his evangelist symbol. Hiberno-Latin writers were thoroughly familiar with these traditions, and also with the New Testament and patristic interpretation of Christ as the new high priest, 'after the order of Melchisedech', who offered himself as a unique and perfect sacrifice, superseding the Old Testament priesthood of Aaron and its repeated propitiatory offerings of blood sacrifices (Heb 5:6; 7:11; 9:11-12).[5]

In the Book of Kells these ideas are not illustrated in a literal or didactic manner, as for the uninformed. The images presuppose familiarity with a *living* tradition of the spiritual interpretation of Scripture, sanctified in the New Testament and used in the liturgy, the monastic office and *lectio divina*, in patristic and insular biblical commentaries and many other genres, including homilies, hymns and hagiography. Using the visual equivalent of the rhetorical techniques employed by exegetes to engage the reader who seeks the underlying spiritual significance of the literal text of scripture, much of the prodigious illumination in the Book of Kells entices the meditative viewer – by means of allusions, paradox, variety, surprise and delight – to puzzle out and recognise known truths with a deeper insight.

FOLIOS 200R–202R
THE PRIESTLY GENEALOGY OF CHRIST AND HIS PEOPLE

The sacramental theme begun with the ornamentation of Zachariah's name is continued in the illumination of Luke's account of Christ's human genealogy. In Luke's Gospel the list of Christ's human ancestors is a priestly as well as a royal genealogy and, significantly, it is positioned immediately after Christ's baptism, where his identity as the Son of God is affirmed by the Father (Lk 3:22). In the Book of Kells the ancestral names in the genealogy (Lk 3:23-38) are decoratively set out over five pages, with a line for each entry (ff. 200r–202r). Some of the names are visually glossed, revealing that it is also the genealogy of the Church, the whole people of God.[6]

FOLIO 201V

On folio 201v the listing of the names of 'Jacob, who was the son of Isaac, who was the son of Abraham', is accompanied by a small figure who is seated above the name of Abraham.[7] He is reclining with his legs drawn up, as at table, and raises a cup or chalice, to drink from it. The three patriarchs, who repeatedly represent God's original chosen people in the Old Testament, were distinguished by God's promise to Abraham: 'And in your seed all the tribes of the earth will be blessed' (Gn 12:3; cf. 17:5; 22:18), a promise literally fulfilled in the birth of Abraham's son Isaac and grandson Jacob, the father of the eponymous ancestors of the twelve tribes of Israel. But the promise was interpreted by St Paul (Gal 3:16) as having been spiritually fulfilled in the birth of Christ and in the formation of the Church, not just from the literal descendants of Abraham, from whom Christ took his human flesh, but from all the tribes of the earth: 'for by one Spirit were we all baptised into one body, whether Jews or gentiles, whether bond or free: and in one Spirit we have all been made to drink' (1 Cor 12:13).[8]

Patristic commentators on the genealogy quote Christ's prophecy: 'Many shall come from the east and the west and shall sit down (*recumbent*) with Abraham and Isaac and Jacob in the kingdom of heaven' (Mt 8:11). This text was directly associated in exegesis and liturgy with the heavenly banquet and with Christ's promise to drink the fruit of the vine with his disciples in his Father's kingdom (Mt 26:29).[9] These biblical images of the formation of the ecclesial body of the new chosen people of God through baptism were applied by insular writers to their own society. The text about sitting down with the patriarchs had been quoted centuries before the Book of Kells by St Patrick in each of his epistles. He refers to those coming from east and west to join Abraham and Isaac and Jacob and 'banquet with Christ' in the heavenly kingdom and identifies them with recent converts in Ireland, anointed with chrism, 'a people newly coming to belief whom the Lord took from the uttermost parts of the earth as long ago he promised through his prophets'. Patrick shows the prophecy of Hosea 1:10 has been fulfilled through their baptism and the outpouring of the Holy Spirit on them: 'Those who were not my people I will call "my people" ... they will be called "sons of the living God". Consequently, then, in Ireland, they who had never had knowledge of God ... have lately been made a people of the Lord and called the children of God.'[10]

FOLIOS 201V–202R

In the Book of Kells the page bearing the names of Abraham, Isaac and Jacob faces the final page of the Lucan priestly genealogy of Christ, which is also the spiritual genealogy of the whole Church. At the bottom of the page, f.201v, is a winged calf, priestly sacrificial victim and Luke's evangelist symbol; it directs attention to the ornamented panel which forms the end-piece of the genealogy on the facing page, f.202r.[11] In the context of discussing the Lucan priestly genealogy and the revelation of Christ as a priest 'after the order of Melchisedech', St Ambrose's influential commentary had noted that the calf always points to this sacerdotal mystery.[12] The ornamented panel to which the calf points in the Book of Kells is not simply a decorative space-filler, but alludes to the priestly sacrifice of Christ. It depicts a pair of peacocks next to vine-scrolls stemming from a chalice. The Mediterranean motif, wonderfully translated into an abstract, two-dimensional insular idiom of highly stylised interlacing forms, signifies the sacramental body of Christ and the hope of eternal life which will sustain all the people of God.[13]

Commenting on Luke's account of Christ's baptism and anointing with the Holy Spirit, which prefigures the descent of the Holy Spirit on the whole Church at pentecost, Ambrose pictured the growth, composition and calling of the Church. He did so by means of the biblical and patristic tradition of expounding the abiding spiritual significance of the historical temple built by Solomon in the earthly Jerusalem, a tradition familiar to insular commentators. Expounded in its many contexts in the literal text of scripture the temple may variously and simultaneously apply figuratively to Christ himself (Jn 2:19-21), 'who became the temple of God by assuming human nature', to his ecclesial body, the universal Church, each of whose individual members becomes a temple of the Holy Spirit at baptism (1 Cor 3:16; 6:16; Rm 8:11), and to the heavenly life of all.[14] Ambrose cited the key texts from 1 Peter 2 and Ephesians 2 to describe not only priests and bishops, but all the members of the body of Christ, 'as living stones built up, a spiritual house, a holy priesthood, to offer up spiritual sacrifices'(1 Pt 2:5); drawn from all peoples, Jew and gentile, it is 'built upon the foundation of the apostles and prophets, Jesus Christ himself being the chief cornerstone, in whom all the building, being framed together, grows into a holy temple in the Lord. In whom you also are built together into a habitation of God in the Spirit' (Eph 2:20-22).[15]

FOLIOS 202V–203R. THE SPIRITUAL TEMPLE

In the Book of Kells an extraordinary image on the verso of the last page of the genealogy presents the body of Christ through this metaphor of the living temple. The distinctive shape of the temple in Jerusalem in the picture is probably derived from that of an early Irish church or house-shaped shrine, but it evokes an invisible spiritual building, encompassing past, present and future and still in the course of being built up. The temple is pictured surmounted by the bust-length figure of Christ, who is its head and cornerstone, and the individual 'living stones' below, built into its fabric, are formed by rows of small figures who are members of Christ's body on earth. The image faces a page bearing the words *Iesus autem plenus spiritus sancto*, 'Jesus full of the Holy Spirit', which begin the verse that immediately follows the genealogy in Luke's Gospel. The verse goes on to describe how 'Jesus, full of the Holy Spirit', returned from his baptism in the Jordan and was led by the Spirit into the desert (Lk 4:1), where he was to withstand the temptations of the devil, the last being the challenge to cast himself off from a pinnacle of the temple in Jerusalem (Lk 4:2-14).

The opening words alone are isolated and enlarged to fill the whole page, which is framed and heavily ornamented, so that the brief text acts as a *titulus* for the facing picture of the temple as the body of Christ, filled with the Holy Spirit.[16] It is a living temple, partly on earth and partly in heaven, where it will eventually receive its completion. Meanwhile, its members on earth, associated with the divine nature, are called to be a fit dwelling for the Holy Spirit, perfecting the gifts of the Spirit to remain vigilant under Christ against the continuing attacks of the devil expelled at their baptism.[17]

FOLIO 114R. THE MYSTERY OF THE BODY OF CHRIST

Like the image of the unity of Christ and his Church, depicted as the spiritual temple on f. 202v in Luke's Gospel, the image of Christ flanked and touched by two human figures on f.114r in Matthew's Gospel is a very rare example among early medieval Latin gospel books of a figural image positioned within the gospel text.

It has often been described as an illustration of the arrest of Christ, but several features question this identification.[18] The picture is placed, for example, five pages before Matthew's account of the arrest begins 'Then they came up and laid hands on Jesus and held him' (Mt 26:50), a passage which is not visually highlighted in any way. The few words on the verso of the picture, however, are enlarged to fill the whole page and are ornamented and framed. They signal the beginning of his passion, for they are the opening words spoken by Christ *before* going with his disciples to Gethsemane, announcing the imminent fulfilment of prophecy in the desertion of the disciples that night: *Tunc dicit illis Ihs [Iesus] omnes vos scan[dalum]* (Mt 26:31).[19]

Secondly, it seems unlikely that the picture simply depicts the arrest because its whole character is not that of a narrative illustration of an event in time, but of a timeless hieratic image. The two men who symmetrically flank the monumental figure of Christ are shown unarmed and robed, not in the short tunics of soldiers at the arrest; their legs are seen in profile, moving inwards, as though they are being drawn to Christ. They are not identical but shown to be in close harmony. The composition radically renews early Christian iconographic conventions in which the exalted Christ, usually represented by the abstract sign of the cross or the *chi-rho*, is manifested beneath an honorific arch or is symmetrically flanked and sometimes touched by attendant figures or creatures shown in profile. Some early Christian and insular representations of the crucifixion show Christ standing with arms outstretched in cruciform or *orans* posture, but without the cross itself being shown. In the Book of Kells image Christ is set in frontal, orant pose between the two crosses which prominently form the capitals of the arch, evoking the crucifixion. The X-shaped letter *chi*, the Greek initial of his sacred title Christ, 'the anointed one', which is a recurring symbol throughout the manuscript, sometimes hidden, sometimes overt, is concealed in the diagonal cross formed by his splayed arms and legs, highlighted in blue.[20]

The inscription overhead but within the picture provides a further aid to its interpretation: 'And a hymn being said, they went out to the Mount of Olives' (Mt 26:30). The words conclude Matthew's account of the Last Supper.

The preceding text has been carefully arranged so that the page which faces the picture on f.114r consists entirely of Christ's institution of the Eucharist and his allusion to the risen life of which it is the foretaste (Mt 26:26-29): 'I shall no more drink of the fruit of the vine until I drink it new with you in my Father's kingdom.'

The Book of Kells has the 'mixed Irish text' of the gospel, incorporating Old Latin or pre-Vulgate readings, but there is an insertion in Mt 26:26 on this page, f.113v, which is not paralleled in other insular gospel books and probably represents a liturgical reminiscence. It occurs in the words of Christ, when he took bread, blessed and broke it and gave it to his disciples: 'Take and eat this all of you. This is my body *which is broken for the life of the world* (*quod confringitur pro saeculi vita*)'. The verb *confringere* is not found in the Roman Canon of the Mass but appears in other early liturgical contexts in the western rite. St Ambrose's treatise on the sacraments, for example, quotes the commemoration of the institution of the sacrament in the Mass prayers as *hoc est enim corpus meum, quod pro multis confringetur.*[21] The eclectic Irish Stowe Missal has the Roman Canon, but one of the prayers or confessions of faith at the breaking of the bread speaks of the breaking of Christ's body: *Credimus in hac confractione corporis et effusione sanguinis nos esse redemptos.*[22] In the Kells text Christ's blood is 'poured out for you and for many for the remission of sins'.[23]

The Stowe Missal has a fixed lection beginning, 'As often as you eat this bread and drink this cup, you show forth the Lord's death till he come' (1 Cor 11:26). The belief, developed by the fathers and expressed in the liturgy, that the passion and resurrection are made present at the eucharistic altar, and that through the breaking of bread the faithful partake of the body of Christ and become one body with him (1 Cor 10:16-17), came to be expressed through detailed allegorical parallelism in which bringing the offering of the paten and chalice to the altar calls to mind Christ being brought to his passion. In the Irish commentary on the Mass appended to the Stowe Missal, c. 800, the breaking of the host is seen as a figure of the seizing of Christ; the host on the paten is his flesh on the cross; the fraction on the paten is the breaking of the body of Christ broken with nails and spear.[24]

Such 'signs of our salvation' had been pictured much earlier by the fathers. Theodore of Mopsuestia, for example, had most vividly contrasted those who seized Christ with the deacons who represent the angels of the heavenly liturgy, invisibly present at every Mass:

> We must think of Christ at one time being led to his passion, and at another time stretched out on the altar to be sacrificed for us. And when the offering which is to be placed [on the altar] is brought out in the sacred vessels of the paten and the chalice [by the deacons] we must think that Christ our Lord is being led and brought to his passion, not, however, by the Jews ... but by the invisible hosts of ministry ... who were present when the Passion of our Salvation was being accomplished.[25]

The gesture of the two attendant robed figures in the Kells image, who lay their hands on Christ's outstretched arms, may carry a reminiscence of the liturgical ceremony of *sustentatio*, which is described in the earliest Roman *ordines*. Two deacons support the outstretched arms of the celebrant, who bears the priestly role of Christ, as he enters the sanctuary, at the offertory and at the Communion.[26]

In the Book of Kells the two columns which flank the two figures are ornamented with vines rising from chalices. As already seen, this was an early Christian motif representing the eucharistic and eschatological incorporation of the faithful into Christ. Christ, vested in human flesh, is robed in red; with his priestly gesture of oblation he both evokes his passion and articulates the text on the facing page: 'Take, eat ... This is my body which is broken for the life of the world.' The image and the facing text form a diptych, though the image is not a literal illustration of the Last Supper. Rather, it shows the sacramental means by which, since the resurrection, Christ's life-giving offering continues to be received and it prompts further meditation on the mystery of the body of Christ, made present at every celebration of the Eucharist. His iconic gaze invites the faithful to draw near into union with him and with each other.

NOTES

1 The Book of Kells, Dublin, Trinity College Library, A.I.6 (58). The exact date and place of origin remain uncertain. Peter Fox, *The Book of Kells*, 2 vols. (Verlag: Lucerne 1990), facsimile and commentary; for reproductions and commentary see Françoise Henry, *The Book of Kells*, London: Thames and Hudson, 1974; Bernard Meehan, *The Book of Kells*, London: Thames and Hudson, 1994. For discussion of the manuscript in its insular contexts, see George Henderson, *From Durrow to Kells. The Insular Gospel*, books 650–800, London: Thames and Hudson, 1987, pp. 130–98.

2 Reproduced in Henry, *Book of Kells*, pl.26; Meehan, *Book of Kells*, fig. 63; J.J.G.Alexander, *insular Manuscripts, 6th to the 9th Century*, London: Harvey Miller, 1978, catalogue no. 52, fig. 243. Carol Farr, 'Cosmological and eschatological images in the *Book of Kells*: folios 32v and 114r', *Listen, Isles O, Unto Me: Studies in Medieval Word and Image*, Elizabeth Mullins and Diarmuid Scully, eds, Cork: Cork University Press, 2011, pp. 291–301, pl.34.

3 In the present pagination of the manuscript, f.32v precedes the richly ornamented cross-carpet and *chi-rho* pages, which announce the Incarnation at Mt 1:18.

4 Henry, *Book of Kells*, pl.14, 103; Meehan, *Book of Kells*, figs. 10, 69.

5 Gen 14:18; Ps 109 (110):4; Heb 4:14-16 and chapters 5; 7-9.

6 Henry, pl. 63–7. Jennifer O'Reilly, 'Exegesis and the Book of Kells: The Lucan genealogy', *The Book of Kells*, Felicity O'Mahony, ed., Aldershot: Scolar Press, 1994, pp. 344–97, pl. 37–43.

7 Henry, pl.66, Meehan, fig. 50.

8 For early exegeis on the theme see, for example, G.W. Barkley, trans., *Origen: Homilies on Leviticus*, Washington DC: Catholic University of America, 1990, Homily 7.2, p. 137.

9 The names of the three patriarchs, in allusion to Mt 8:11 and the heavenly banquet, are cited, for example, in a Mass for the dead in the Irish Stowe Missal, c. 800: F. E.Warren, *The Ritual and Liturgy of the Celtic Church*, Oxford, 1881, 248.

10 *Confessio*, 39, 40; *Epistola ad milites Corotici*, 18: Daniel Conneely, *The Letters of St Patrick*, Maynooth: An Sagart, 1993, 42–3, 71–2; 56, 80, Latin text and translation.

11 Henry, pl. 66–7, 109; Meehan, fig. 70.

12 Ambrose, *Expositio evangelii secundum Lucam*, CCSL, 14, 83.

13 Henry, pl.67, 109; Meehan, fig. 70.

14 See, for example, Bede's magisterial commentary *De templo*, CCSL 119A, 147–8, Seán Connolly, trans., *Bede: On the Temple*, Liverpool: Liverpool University Press, 1999, pp. 5–6; Introduction, xvii–xxxiii.

15 For Christ as the cornerstone see also Ps 117:22; Is 28:16; Mt 21:42; Lk 20:17; Acts 4:11; Rm 9:33.

16 Henry, pl. 68–9; Meehan, fig. 6.

17 For further discussion of f.202v and the temple, see George Henderson, *From Durrow to Kells*, pp. 168–74; O'Reilly, 'Exegesis and the Book of Kells: The Lucan genealogy', pp. 358–97; Carol Farr, *The Book of Kells: Its Function and Audience*, London: British Library, 1997, pp. 51–103.

18 This final section, like the brief entry on the Book of Kells, f.114r, in *The Treasures of Irish Christianity*, Salvador Ryan and Brendan Leahy, eds, Dublin: Veritas, 2012, draws in part on research more fully discussed and documented in Jennifer O'Reilly, 'The *Book of Kells*, folio 114 : A Mystery Revealed yet Concealed', *The Age of Migrating Ideas: Early Medieval Art in Britain and Ireland*, John Higgitt and R. M. Spearman, eds, Stroud: Alan Sutton and National Museums of Scotland, 1993, pp. 106–14.

19 Folios 114r–114v reproduced in Henry, *Book of Kells*, pl.45, 46; Meehan, *Book of Kells*, figs. 54, 57. See Carol Farr, *The Book of Kells: Its Function and Audience*, pp. 104–39, and 'Cosmological and Eschatological images in the Book of Kells: folios 32v and 114r', pp. 297–301.

20 Suzanne Lewis, 'Sacred Calligraphy: The *Chi-rho* Page in the Book of Kells', *Traditio* 36 (1980) pp. 139–59.

21 *De sacramentis* IV, 5. 21; J. A. Jungman, *The Mass of the Roman Rite: Its Origin and Development*, New York: Benziger, 1951, p. 52. The Kells text reads *Accipite edite ex hoc omnes. Hoc est enim corpus meum quod confringitur pro saeculi vita.*

22 F. L. Warren, *The Liturgy and Ritual of the Celtic Church*, Oxford, 1881, p. 241.

23 *Hic est enim sanguis meus novi testamenti qui effundetur pro vobis et pro multis in remissionem peccatorum.*

24 George F. Warner, ed., *The Stowe Missal*, vol. II, Henry Bradshaw Society 31, 1915, p. 41.

25 A. Mingana, trans., *Commentary of Theodore of Mopsuestia on the Lord's Prayer and on the Sacraments of Baptism and the Eucharist*, Woodbrook Studies VI, Cambridge: W. Heffer & Sons, 1933, pp. 85–6.

26 O'Reilly, 'The Book of Kells, folio 114: A Mystery Revealed yet Concealed', pp. 112–14; Éamonn Ó Carragáin, '*Traditio evangeliorum* and *sustentatio*: The Relevance of Liturgical Ceremonies to the Book of Kells', *The Book of Kells*, Felicity O'Mahony, ed., pp. 399–436; pp. 417–22.

MERITA MISSAE: THE EUCHARIST AND THE LIVED REALITY OF IRISH CHRISTIANS IN THE LATE MEDIEVAL AND EARLY MODERN PERIODS

PROF. SALVADOR RYAN
St Patrick's College, Maynooth

In the year 1215, the Fourth Lateran Council's decree *Omnis utriusque sexus* enjoined upon Christians to receive the Eucharist at least once a year – and, by extension, the sacrament of penance beforehand. This development, coupled with the consolidation of the recently formulated doctrine of transubstantiation, would have a far-reaching effect on the lives of medieval Christians in general. For many Christians, the injunction to receive once a year would be followed to the letter to the extent that they would only receive once annually and no more.

Part of the reason for the reluctance of the laity to receive communion frequently was surely a consciousness of the awesome nature of the sacrament and the necessity of approaching it with a pure heart in order to avoid, as St Paul warned in 1 Corinthians 11:29, 'eating and drinking God's judgement'. The fifteenth-century Irish bardic poet Tuathal Ó hUiginn (d. 1450), in a poetic treatment of the Eucharist, makes the point several times: 'The Lord's body avails not if I receive it in spite of my sin; before its reception sin's root must be plucked out' and again 'to receive it with sin in my heart is death; it is fruitless for him who receives it lightly, though its reception is (meant to be) a presage of salvation.'[1] One account found in a thirteenth-century collection of preacher's tales known as the *Liber Exemplorum*, compiled by an English Franciscan who spent much of his life in Ireland, tells how a man from near York received the Eucharist unworthily at Easter without first having availed himself of the sacrament of penance. The story relates how 'after dinner that day he brought up all that he had eaten' and not only that day but for the succeeding days too; in fact, 'he did not stop vomiting until he died'.[2] As the Irish bardic poet Fearghal Óg Mac an Bhaird warned in a poem composed in the early seventeenth century, receiving the Lord's Body without love was akin to consuming poison.

The Eucharist could, indeed, be a dangerous thing if not approached properly – in the proper presence of mind or indeed the proper state of soul. This danger, of course, was not confined to the laity. The priests too were expected to celebrate the liturgy with the utmost care and attention and to ensure that proper care was accorded the consecrated host during the course of the liturgy and also afterwards if being carried to the sick. In a version of the ninth-century Stowe Missal Old Irish Mass tract which appears in the fifteenth-century *Leabhar Breac* manuscript, we get a clear insight into the heightened importance given to the recitation of the words of consecration when it is warned that the priest is not to be disturbed during the words of consecration in order that his mind not separate from God even for one syllable; it is for this reason, it continues, that this is known as the *periculosa oratio* – the perilous or dangerous prayer.[3]

The most dangerous prayer. Yes, it could be dangerous if not performed properly. Again, such a concern would have a long history. Many older priests and indeed older lay people will recall how in the pre-Vatican II liturgy there was something called (unofficially, of course) the 'holy cough'. For those few moments when the words of consecration would be recited by the priest congregations were expected to hold their breath (and more importantly their coughs, snorts or any other potentially disturbing utterances!) until the elements were consecrated. Then, when the bell would ring signalling that this had been done, previously suspended outbursts of coughing could be given free rein throughout the church! It was not unknown for priests to take it upon themselves to recite the words of consecration a second time if they were distracted in some way. These were, indeed, crucial moments for both priest and people. Indeed in the early Irish Church the rather strict Penitential of Cummean (d. 662) states explicitly that 'If the minister stammers over the Sunday prayer which is called the "perilous" [*periculosa*], if once, he shall be cleansed with fifty strokes; if a second time, with one hundred; if a third time, he shall keep a special fast.'[4] It is no accident that similar words are found in the much earlier Penitential of Gildas which uses the Welsh word *periglawr* to describe the priest saying Mass: literally, the 'danger man', he who ran the risk of pronouncing these sacred words without stumbling.[5]

Belief in the power of the consecrated host in the later Middle Ages instilled in most a deep sense of reverence and awe before the sacrament. An indication of how seriously this reverence was taken is found in the common practice of swearing oaths *super sacramentum* or 'over the sacrament'. Oath taking was a serious business and the penalties for perjury were severe. It was generally accepted, therefore, that those who swore on the sacrament would have the appropriate awe and reverence to resist profaning it by perjury, which was believed to provoke divine retribution. When a consecrated host could not be procured, parties were often content to swear on Mass books which contained the sacred words of the Holy Sacrifice. We know, for instance, that in 1597 Hugh O' Neill, earl of Tyrone, upon meeting one Captain Warren in Dundalk, 'called for a Mass book and swore in the presence of Captain Warren ... that he looked for no aid from Spain'.[6]

In the late-medieval period, the respect that was to be accorded the eucharistic host by both clergy and laity was perhaps most effectively transmitted through the use of didactic stories called *exempla* in popular preaching. It was especially the mendicant orders that specialised in this form of preaching, and a large number of these cautionary tales survive in medieval and early modern manuscripts. One of the most notable of these is found in the *Liber Flavus Fergusiorum*, a fifteenth-century Roscommon manuscript now held at the Royal Irish Academy. The story recounts how a priest travelling to visit a sick man came upon a swarm of bees on his way. Leaving down the host, he proceeded to capture the swarm. When he later returned to fetch the eucharistic host, it had disappeared. After spending a year in penance, an angel appeared to him to tell him where to locate the missing host. The swarm of bees had recovered the host and brought it to their hive where they had built 'a fair chapel of wax and an altar, and a mass-chalice and a pair of priests, fashioning them fairly of wax, to stand over the Host'. The angel instructed the priest to bring people with him so that they, too, could attest the miracle. A similar tale in the thirteenth-century *Liber Exemplorum* relates how even more industrious German bees rescued a host that had been buried in a man's garden and built it a church complete with bell tower, bells, altar, chalice, corporal and paten.[7]

A variation on this tale told how bees had venerated a host that had been placed in a hive by its owner in order to increase the yield of honey and a friar Duncan absolved an Irishwoman in the thirteenth century for procuring the host to increase the price of her wine.[8] This reflects an attitude to the Eucharist that was common in the late-medieval world and one in which the eucharistic species was considered powerful in helping to attain all manner of worldly gains. Religion in this period, as in many others, was often not just about safely securing an afterlife worth living: it was also about improving one's lot in the here and now. Medieval Irish Christians expected to reap some reward as a result of their religious fervour well in advance of Judgement Day. It was not uncommon, therefore, for religious devotional texts to offer this-worldly favours as sweeteners to encourage devotees to remain loyal for the long haul. Thus, the well-known list of benefits for attending Mass, known as the *merita missae,* which appeared in many fifteenth-century Irish manuscripts, offered something both for this world and the next: among the benefits to be received were the following: one would gain all one's needs that day (the implication is that this included both spiritual and practical needs); one wouldn't lose the sight of one's eyes after viewing the host; one wouldn't suffer sudden death that day (always helpful if one was not properly prepared); one would not suffer from indigestion; one's time in purgatory would be shortened; and, perhaps the most novel of all, for the length of time one spent at Mass, one would not age; also, one's venial (or less serious) sins would be forgiven each time one attended Mass.[9] In the case of the latter, there is some evidence that this boon was taken to its extremes if the report of an English government official on the rebelliousness of the Irish, written in 1582, is to be believed: 'And hearing Mass on Sunday or Holyday, they think all the week after they may do what heinous offence soever, and it is dispensed withal.'[10] Here, then, the aptness of the familiar rhyme holds true: 'Paddy Murphy went to Mass; never missed a Sunday; Paddy Murphy went to hell for what he did on Monday'!

For many Christians, the *merita missae* were specifically linked to viewing the eucharistic host at the elevation and thus benefits such as these often led to many people zealously exhibiting a kind of merit mania in rushing from church to church to catch as many eucharistic consecrations as possible. One interesting feature of these lists, as found in Irish manuscripts such as the fifteenth-century *Liber Flavus Fergusiorum* and an early sixteenth-century book of devotion compiled for a Donegal noblewoman,[11] is a *proviso* contained within the title of each of the versions of the text. The merits are said to be available to all who attend Mass *ó tosach go deiredh* (from beginning to end), thus depriving those who wished to accumulate a quick spiritual fortune by running from church to church to 'catch' as many elevations as they possibly could.[12]

At a time when regular reception of the host was not very common, the question of a person's worthiness or unworthiness moved from their consumption of the host to the very act of viewing the consecrated species. Indeed William of Auxerre (d. 1232) and others in the thirteenth century had raised the question of whether a person in mortal sin, and thus unworthy to receive the Eucharist, committed further sin by merely looking at the sacred host when it was elevated at Mass.[13] This concern that the very act of 'seeing' the Eucharist should be only carried out by those free from mortal sin was also extended to the act of viewing the wooden pax-board, an image of Christ passed around the congregation to be kissed, which replaced the custom of exchanging an actual kiss. In a fifteenth-century poem recounting the experience of Mary the mother of Jesus at Christ's crucifixion, one Irish bardic poet points to the Virgin Mary as the perfect Mass-goer when he states that 'Mary fled not from his murderers but gazed on his body ... '[14] The added inference here, of course, is that as Mary was considered to be completely free from sin she was deemed to be the most worthy of adorers.

Given the benefits accorded those who viewed the eucharistic host at Mass (both secular and spiritual), little wonder then that it was so often stolen in medieval Europe by laity who wished to harness the power of Christ's presence for their own varied needs. Stories relating to the theft of the host for all manner of uses are well-known: it is known to have been stolen and ground to powder and then sprinkled over crops as an insecticide; as noted above, we have a thirteenth-century example of an

Irishwoman stealing the host in order that it might increase the price of her wine; it was also used as a love potion whereby those who wished to woo the object of their affection kept the host in their mouth as they went in for a kiss. Here, then, we have examples of what might be called 'DIY' religion – the appropriation of the sacrament and use of same in an extra-liturgical and clearly illicit fashion.

It could be argued that extra-liturgical use of the consecrated host for worldly objectives does not necessarily imply a lack of respect or reverence for the sacrament. Those who engaged in such activity obviously believed strongly in its efficacy, a belief grounded in the doctrine that this was not ordinary bread but the body, blood, soul and divinity of Jesus Christ. Viewed from this perspective it is little wonder that some people were prepared to employ the real presence of Christ in the blessing of their crops, the healing of their ailments and the sanctification of their romantic relationships. The fact that such actions constituted a thoroughly inappropriate use of the sacrament might indeed have been lost on a great many people. Many undoubtedly surmised that if the consecrated host was powerful during Mass then why not outside of it? To expect miraculous results from an extra-liturgical use of the host for a particular good undeniably marked a deep, if misplaced, faith in its power, which was understood simply as Christ working in his world.

To abuse the host out of contempt, scorn or, indeed, refusal to accept the reality of Christ's presence, however, was a different matter indeed. This kind of abuse was associated with heretics, unbelievers and, most commonly, medieval Jews – and this constitutes one of the more painful and regrettable legacies of medieval eucharistic piety. The latter group was perhaps the most vilified in this regard. Stories which recounted supposed abuse of the eucharistic host by medieval Jews abounded in medieval literature and are attested even in Gaelic Irish sources from the period.[15] In a bardic poem composed for the feast of Corpus Christi, we find the story of a Jew who enters a Christian Church and out of scorn stabs the eucharistic host declaring that 'never was there body without blood in it', whereupon the host begins to spurt blood and this flow of blood quickly turns into a flood which flows right out of the church and into the streets.[16] This torrent of blood then proceeds to drown the principal Jewish protagonist and much of the Jewish community, while at the same time buoying up the Christian population and sweeping them to safety. Here we have an example of how the eucharistic blood of Christ was understood to discern between believers and unbelievers and to save or condemn these accordingly. It also demonstrates how, in the past, we have sometimes understood the Eucharist's 'Christ-for-*us*' also as 'Christ-against-*them*', the 'them' being variously interpreted as unbelievers, heretics, Jews, etc. 'Communion with Christ and with one another' have not always sat as happy bedfellows.

Although for the greater part of the later medieval period the chalice had been withdrawn from the laity, popular devotion nevertheless became consumed with ever more graphic representations in both art and literature of Christ's Passion and, in particular, the number and extent of his wounds. At the Last Day it was expected that the crucified Christ would appear in the sky lying upon his cross with his wounds bleeding afresh. For those who looked upon the wounds of Christ and begged for mercy, this would be available. However, for those who rejected the saving blood of Christ, condemnation was assured. The distinction between salvation and condemnation was thus literally in the eye of beholder. The medieval tale of the dying knight to whom Christ appears showing his wounds and asking him to trust in them was popular in Ireland as elsewhere. Upon rejecting Christ's offer, the Christ figure was shown to cast his blood in the knight's face after which he was quickly and unceremoniously then dragged off to hell by a troop of demons. The blood of Christ, therefore, was a double-edged sword, working for the weal of those who placed their trust in it, and to the detriment of those who did not. Thus the story of the Jew stabbing the eucharistic host which then spurted blood captures something of this popular understanding.[17]

The most striking Irish image of devotion to Christ's blood is, in fact, a Marian one. The famous *pietà* scene in which the dead Christ lies in Mary's lap was recalled in many popular medieval lives of Christ and Mary which circulated around Europe. When one of these, the *Liber de Passione Christi*, was translated from Latin into Irish in the fifteenth century, however, an additional feature crept into the account. The Virgin Mary was portrayed as bending her head down to kiss and then drink the blood from Christ's wounds, and protesting vehemently when the body was taken away as she had not had her fill. Here the mother of Christ performs an act which resembles part of the Gaelic Irish keening ritual, for which there are many references in Irish literature and, indeed, some claims that the action was witnessed historically. Typically, when a male died violently, the principal female mourner (most often, wife or female companion) would drink the blood from the wounds of the dead body, not allowing any of his blood to seep into the ground. This is most famously exemplified in Eibhlín Dubh Ní Chonaill's late-eighteenth-century lament *Caoineadh Airt Uí Laoghaire* ('The Lament for Art O'Leary'). However, in the case of the Virgin Mary, her drinking of Christ's blood almost certainly contains other layers of meaning. This might include a deep respect for Christ's blood and the concomitant fear, seen in a normal eucharistic setting, that it would ever spill to the ground – part of the reason, surely, for the withdrawal of the chalice from the laity in the first instance. Furthermore, Mary's craving to be allowed to drink her fill of Christ's blood is reminiscent of medieval mystical literature, as exemplified in the fourteenth-century Middle English text, *A Talking of the Love of God*. This speaks of Mary drinking the blood from Christ's feet and although she drinks her fill she is left wanting more. In this image, then, the figure of Mary is an amalgam of *Mater Dolorosa*, Gaelic Irish keening woman and medieval mystic in her devotion to Christ's blood.[18]

Bleeding hosts were not the only means by which God could, by miraculous intervention, inspire faith in Christ's presence in the Eucharist. There are many tales that relate how doubters who gazed on the host were sometimes shown a child in its stead. A seventeenth-century Irish collection of exempla found in the Bibliothèque Royale in Brussels contains the story of a priest who doubted the reality of Christ in the sacrament. Having consecrated the bread at Mass without thinking of what he was doing, the host was suddenly lifted out of his two hands and disappeared. Calling upon the Virgin Mary for help, she then appeared to him with the baby Jesus at her breast saying, 'Behold the one whom you blessed on the dish a while ago … behold the one who will be eaten in his blood and in his body, in his divinity and in his humanity …' Upon leaving the infant on the altar the priest stretched out his hands towards him and suddenly the vision was transformed back into the shape of a host.[19] The idea that one received the Child Jesus in Holy Communion would live on in the popular imagination. The early seventeenth century Irish poet Aonghus Fionn O Dálaigh, in a poem dedicated to the Eucharist, welcomes the king of angels and takes delight in the paradox of addressing the host as 'O young child yet ever old'.[20] A woman in County Mayo in the 1690s, who was asked on leaving church what happened at Mass and who replied that she received the Virgin Mary with the Child Jesus in her arms, may have been influenced by pious stories such as that concerning the doubting priest.[21] Even as late as the twentieth century, it was not uncommon to find communion hosts embossed with the image of the Christ-Child.

From the above brief survey it would seem that late-medieval devotion to the Eucharist was fixated upon its vertical aspect – with an almost exclusive concern with ones relationship with Christ – to the neglect of its horizontal implications: striving to be at one with members of the wider community. Yet this is too simplistic a judgement and there are many counter-examples one could cite. For instance, Colmán Ó Clabaigh has recently recalled a tale of reconciliation between two communities living at opposite sides of the river Boyne in Drogheda in 1412, brought about by a sermon preached by a Dominican friar on the feast of Corpus Christi which resulted in reconciliation between the rival factions and their petitioning the king for the establishment of a single united borough.[22] Examples such as this aside, it might nevertheless be argued that we have recovered more fully in recent times the notion of 'Communion with one another'. In fact, a beautiful example of this aspect of Eucharist is found in an Irish folk-tale collected in the twentieth century.[23] The story recounts how a young priest departing from home told his mother to place a pebble in a box for every morning that she attended Mass until he returned again. Having been faithfully present at Mass every day for a considerable time, one morning the priest's mother arrived late at the church on account of her turning back to drive cattle out of a neighbour's potato field. When her son returned and enquired as to how many Masses she had attended since he was last there, she showed him the box, expecting it to be full, and, with regret, saw only one pebble. She explained to her son that one morning she had 'missed' Mass by arriving late. Looking at the lone pebble in the box, her son proceeded to tell her that this very Mass that she had turned up late for (owing to her good deed) was the only one she had truly properly heard. In this tale, 'Communion with Christ and with One Another' appears as a seamless whole.

EUCHARISTIC FAITH AND PRACTICE OF THE PEOPLE AS SEEN BY SOME IRISH ARTISTS

REV. FR BRENDAN McCONVERY CSsR
St Patrick's College, Maynooth

Some three years before the celebration of the first Eucharistic Congress in Dublin in 1932, another celebration was held in Dublin that in several respects might be seen as a dress-rehearsal for the Congress. It attracted more than a quarter of a million people to its final High Mass in Phoenix Park, Dublin, which was followed by a procession of the Blessed Sacrament and pontifical benediction on Watling Street Bridge. Although it attracted fewer visitors from overseas, this celebration of the centenary of Catholic emancipation marked a watershed the history of Irish Catholicism. It is worth recalling that, when Dublin celebrated its first Eucharistic Congress, Catholics had only enjoyed the right to the open and public practise of their faith in the land in which they were the majority for little over one hundred years. One of the early signs of the thaw of the winter of the penal days was the passing by the Irish Parliament in 1795 of an act establishing a college in Maynooth 'for the better education of persons professing the Popish or Roman Catholic religion' – it is that college that is the host of our symposium.

FROM THE MASS ROCK TO THE STATION MASS

The centuries from the Reformation to Catholic emancipation are often known in Ireland as the 'penal years'. They left a mark on the faith, and especially on the practise, of the Irish Church. Although some medieval churches, often those of the mendicant orders, continued in a more or less unbroken chain the discreet and clandestine celebration of the Mass, little of the ceremonial and ritual of the Church survived in public. By the middle of the eighteenth century, there were some signs of a Catholic liturgical revival, especially in the towns. In many parts of Ireland, one will still find today 'Mass rocks', which tradition associates with the celebration of the Mass during this period and which remain places of pilgrimage for the local community. A familiar picture in many Irish Catholic homes in the early twentieth century depicted just such a scene. It is called *A Christmas Mass in the Penal Days – The Alarm.*[1] It is a chromolithograph by John Dooley Reigh, originally distributed free with Christmas number (1884) of the *United Ireland* journal but often reproduced. Reigh (*floruit* 1875–c. 1914) was a cartoonist who contributed to Irish national journals at the end of the ninteenth century. He was also an accomplished artist who exhibited paintings in 1880 at the Royal Hibernian Academy of Arts.

Reigh's melodramatic illustration takes the viewer to a snowy morning, presumably on Christmas Day, to witness devout men, women and children crowded around the Mass rock. As the priest raises the host during the consecration, armed lookouts posted on the hillside cry out. A column of soldiers is approaching their secret place of worship. The captain has spotted them and uses his sabre to direct the troops to attack. Most of the people are lost in prayer; others at the edge hear the call. But will the tiny flock have time to scatter? Will their priest make a safe getaway? Will the Catholic worshippers use their guns in self-defence?[2]

As the journal title might suggest, Reigh's popular picture developed the association between the penal laws and the growing political and cultural movement for Irish nationalism. Its continuing influence can be seen in a modern rendering on a street corner mural from a Republican (Catholic) area in Belfast.

The Mass rock scene appears relatively frequently in stained glass and other artistic forms in Irish Church art. A somewhat more artistic rendering of a similar scene in *opus sectile* was incorporated in the typaneum of the Franciscan church in Athlone, built in 1931. It is the work of Catherine O'Brien (1881–1963), a member of *An Tur Gloine,* that grew out of the revival of Irish arts and crafts in the early twentieth century.

THE STATION MASS

Emmet Larkin has described the station Mass as 'the most interesting and important religious practice to emerge in pre-famine Ireland'.[3]

According to Larkin, the term 'Mass stations' designated places where Mass was celebrated on Sundays and holy days of obligation, in church or chapel, or under a shed or on a Mass rock. Mass had been celebrated, confessions heard and communion received in private houses in Ireland for at least a hundred years or more before the 1750s, but from that time onwards the term 'station Mass' began to assume a particular meaning. The harsher implementation of the anti-Catholic penal laws in the years following the Williamite wars in Ireland led to a fall in the total number of clergy, but from the early years of the eighteenth century there was something of a resurgence of vocations.[4] In a community with few churches, private houses were the most convenient place in which to celebrate Mass, and there seems to have been a consolidation of this system in the years between 1770 and 1850. The reforming Synod of Thurles in 1850, under Paul Cardinal Cullen, attempted to put an end to this system which, with the growing number of churches, was seen to be an abuse. It was so strongly embedded in popular feeling, however, that it survived and continues to survive especially in rural areas to this day. Indeed, it may be said to have touched a cord in the reform of the liturgy in the years following the Second Vatican Council. Stations were held several times a year in a designated house to which the families of the station area were invited. A recent popular writer, Alice Taylor, who has recorded life in rural Ireland during the twentieth century, describes the station Mass:

> On the day of the station, the pastor and his curate arrived early in the morning and while one priest said Mass in the kitchen (living room) the other heard confessions by the fire in the parlour. There was a warm feeling about this Mass and communion, with all the neighbours gathered around the kitchen table. We had worked and played together, and now we were sharing in something much greater which formed a different bond between us. It was like the Last Supper.[5]

ALOYSIUS O'KELLY: *MASS IN A CONNEMARA CABIN*

The best artistic representation of a station Mass is probably *Mass in a Connemara Cabin* by Aloysius O'Kelly (1853–1941). O'Kelly received his early art training in Paris and exhibited this picture in the Paris Salon in

1884 and four years later in London.[6] It attracted favourable comment for its style, particularly for what critics regarded as its artistic realism and attention to detail. The Irish newspaper *The Freeman's Journal* (2nd June 1888) described it as most notable for drawing, both as to beauty of facial form and drapery and for the infinitude of detail sedulously followed. The shawl on the back of one of the women nearest the priest is a marvel in this latter respect in itself. As a composition it certainly must take exceptionally high rank.

Despite this high critical praise, the painting disappeared from view for more than one hundred years and was presumed lost until it was rediscovered hanging on the wall of the presbytery of the Catholic Church of St Patrick in Edinburgh, then the home of a Redemptorist Community. It is now on long-term loan from the Archdiocese of Edinburgh to the collection of the National Gallery of Ireland and is currently on display in the Museum of Country Life near Castlebar, County Mayo.

The painting represents a typical station Mass. The congregation, numbering some twenty people of varying ages, is gathered around the young priest celebrating the Mass on an ordinary kitchen table spread with a white cloth. He appears to be speaking to the people, perhaps delivering the homily at the Mass. His top hat and overcoat lie on a wooden chair beside the altar. Striking are the various representations of the people's devotion. An elderly woman in red in the second row of the worshippers raises her hands in the ancient *orante* position of prayer, known from figures in the art of the catacombs; another prostrates herself, her face towards the ground in adoration, while the rest kneel devoutly with bowed heads. The clothing is typical of Irish country people of the period, with heavy patterned shawls or scarves for the women and girls. The man kneeling on one knee at the front wears typical work clothes with heavy boots. The house is clean, but simply furnished. The dresser against the wall on the right-hand side probably contains the family's best collection of coloured dishes. Against it rests a churn for making butter and a small tin bath-tub hangs from a hook at the end of the dresser. On the rear wall, there is a simple unframed picture of the Sacred Heart, the standard religious image in an Irish home. The ceiling of the room is formed by wooden beamed rafters, through which can be seen the remainder of the annual supply of hay or straw, while a simple lamp hanging from the ceiling provides the only source of light apart from the windows.

O'Kelly, the artist, was known as something of a political radical. The Land League had been founded to fight for a more equitable distribution of land and treatment of tenants in Castlebar in 1879, not long before this picture was painted. Critics have speculated that O'Kelly might not have intended his picture to mirror the close egalitarian relationship between priest and people that was a key to any profound social change in nineteenth-century Ireland. If this is in fact the case, the setting of the station Mass allows him to do this in a strikingly vivid manner. The priest is on the same level as the people, not raised above them on an altar in the sanctuary of a church or in a pulpit. The setting for the celebration of the Eucharist is the every day world of work and family life, indeed even of rural poverty. While this may be interpreted as a political statement, it is also one that has a profound theological truth: priest and people form a community through celebrating the Mass together and sharing in the Body of Christ: 'because there is one bread, we who are many are one body, for we all partake of the one bread' (1 Cor 10:17).

MATTHEW LAWLESS: *THE SICK CALL*

One of the historical factors that lead to the foundation the Irish Land League had been the suffering, death and social upheaval caused by the great Irish Famine of 1845–52. It is impossible to say how many people died directly from starvation or disease as a result of the famine. One of the long-term results of the famine was a dramatic decline in population. Immediately before the famine, Ireland had a population of more than 8 million: by the census of 1901, it was 4.4 million, much of it attributable to emigration. The daily round of pastoral work for priests in the famine-stricken areas was truly horrendous. One priest, Fr Hugh Quigley, who ministered in the diocese of Killaloe has left an account of it:

> We arise at four o'clock ... when not obliged to attend a night call ... and proceed on horse-back a distance of four to seven miles to hold stations of confession for the convenience of the poor country people, who flock in thousands to prepare themselves for the death they look upon as inevitable. At these stations we have to

> remain up to five o'clock pm administering both consolation and instruction to the famished thousands. The confessions are often interrupted by calls to the dying, and generally on our way home, we have to minister the last rites to one or more fever patients.[7]

The Sick Call by Matthew Lawless is in the collection of the National Gallery in Dublin and takes as its theme the administration of the sacraments of the sick to the dying. It is the work of an Irish artist, Matthew James Lawless (1837–64) and was painted barely a decade after the end of the famine (1860). It depicts a priest being brought by boat to attend a sick person. He wears a black cloak over his white surplice and sits with eyes cast down, solemnly intent on the task that lies before him. He is accompanied by three acolytes, wearing white albs, with one carrying a liturgical lantern. Another boy sits near the priest, with another lantern beside him and a sickle. A strong able-bodied man rows the boat and the final person in the composition is a woman weeping with her face in her hands, probably a relative of the person to whom the sacraments are to be brought. The setting of the picture is not Ireland. The walled town and canal might suggest Belgium as a more likely locale, where Holy Communion was brought to the sick with a certain amount of ceremony. Such public ceremony was unknown in Ireland due to the reticence imposed by several centuries of penal legislation. Nevertheless, the priest novelist, Canon Sheehan, describes his first sick call at night in his new parish:

> I had quite an escort of cavalry, two horsemen who rode side by side with me the whole way to the mountain, and then when we had to dismount and climb through the boulders ... I had two link-men or torch-bearers, leaping on the crest of the ditch on either side and lighting me up to the door of the cabin.[8]

The older and wiser canon remarks that it is likely that such reverence for the Blessed Sacrament is a survival among the people of older ways that have not been totally forgotten. The painting was so highly regarded for its technical merits that it was exhibited in the Royal Academy in London in 1860.[9] The artist was already in the advanced stages of consumption when he painted the picture. Matthew Lawless was just twenty three years of age and it is truly a remarkable work for such a young man. He was known by his contemporaries as a devout young Catholic man, and it is not unlikely that the painting expresses a personal faith in the meaning of the last sacraments and his hope to receive them before his own death. It has been suggested that some of the figures in the painting are based on people he knew, for example, that the face of the priest is modelled on that of the doctor who treated him in his final illness. The artist may have chosen to set this scene outside of Ireland, as it enabled him to call on some of the ceremonies associated with bringing Holy Communion to the sick in traditionally Catholic countries. Much of the imagery in the picture suggests that death is close at hand. The colour of the sky suggests that evening is coming. A boat is a common symbol of death – with Chairon the ferryman who rows the souls of the departed across the river of death. The reaping hook on the stern of the boat suggests that the harvest of life is at hand. The lantern beside it does not contain a candle, another suggestion perhaps that life has run its course. Despite the sadness of the subject, the mood the painting conveys is one of grave serenity and trust that in the final journey into death, the believer will be strengthened for the journey by the bread of life.

RAY CARROLL: *THE SUPPER AT EMMAUS*

If *Mass in a Connemara Cabin* is a picture that has been recovered from oblivion, our final one is, sadly, one that has been destroyed beyond recovery. It was commissioned for the Blessed Sacrament Chapel of Longford Cathedral in 1982 by Cardinal Cathal Daly (1917–2009), when he was Bishop of Ardagh and Clonmacnoise. It hung there until the cathedral was tragically destroyed by fire on Christmas Day 2009 and this picture, among many other treasures was destroyed beyond recovery. The Emmaus scene has long been a favourite subject of artists. This one is by the Irish artist, Ray Carroll, who contributed much to the renewing of Church art and architecture in the decades after Vatican II.[10] It is very striking in several respects. First of all, it is a simple picture with little detail but it demands attention by its simplicity and elegance of line and its vibrant colour. It has been noticed that the loaf of bread being brought to the table is very like the traditional Irish soda bread, baked in the form of a cake with a cross incised into it. By choosing this scene for a Blessed Sacrament Chapel, Carroll is clearly alert to the biblical renewal of Vatican II that has recognised and appropriated the profoundly eucharistic and ecclesial dimension of the Emmaus story.

Secondly, when you look closely at this painting, what is most striking about it is the presence of women.[11] One woman is serving, the other, the seated lady in the red dress and blouse, is clearly one of the travellers who has come with Jesus. The artist may be striking imaginatively here on a detail that is often forgotten. The text of Luke tells us that Jesus met two travellers on the road to Emmaus but names only one of them. It is often assumed, by Lucan commentators as well as by artists, that both are male. The named companion is Cleophas. It is the only time he is mentioned by name in the gospels – or is it? There is a woman mentioned in St John's account of the death of Jesus, Mary (wife? daughter?) of Clopas, Μαρία ἡ τοῦ Κλωπα (Jn 19:25). The difference between the spellings (Κλεοπας/Κλωπα) is so slight that many translations, including the Vulgate,[12] take them to be variant forms of the same name; a view shared by some commentators, who then proceed to argue that, if the two persons are identical, then Cleophas's companion is more likely to have been his wife than anyone else.[13] Other scholars (for example, Joseph Fitzmeyer) are less persuaded that they are.[14]

If that way to solving the identity of the unnamed disciple at Emmaus is blocked, then it might be helpful to remember that in his gospel, Luke assigns roles of importance to women. He alone, for example, gives a list of women disciples who accompanied Jesus and provided for him out of their own resources (Lk 8:2-3), he alone matches the term 'Son of Abraham' with 'daughter of Abraham' (Lk 13:16), or encloses a parable involving a woman seeking for a lost coin between two parables of men searching for lost sheep and a lost son (Lk 15: 3-32). That perhaps is the beauty of art as biblical commentary. It can take a fresh view of things, and in setting women at table with the Risen Jesus at Emmaus, Ray Carroll reminds us that their place in the eucharistic community is one to be valued and treasured.

NOTES

1 So titled in the Print Collection of the National Library of Ireland, Dublin.

2 Lawrence W. McBride, 'Historical Imagery in Irish Political Illustrations, 1880–1910', *New Hibernia Review/Iris Éireannach Nua*, Vol. 2, no. 1 (spring, 1998), pp. 9–25, p. 17.

3 Emmet Larkin, *The Pastoral Role of the Roman Catholic Church in Pre-Famine Ireland*, Dublin: Four Courts Press, 2006, chapter IV 'The Rise of the Stations in Ireland', pp. 189–258, p. 189.

4 Larkin, *Pastoral Role*, p. 191.

5 Alice Taylor, *To School through the Fields: An Irish Country Childhood*, Dingle: Brandon Books, 1988, pp. 10–11. There are many references to station Masses in Irish popular literature, for example, William Carlton, 'The Station' in *Works of William Carlton*, Vol 3, 1881 (a negative assessment by a northern Catholic who had abandoned the Church); Patrick Augustine Sheehan, *My New Curate,* 1902 (Sheehan was a parish priest and writes with evident sympathy of the station Mass and its significance in the life of the community); Dermot Healy, *Long Time No See* (2011), a recent novel which describes a station Mass and its impact on the young protagonists of the novel.

6 Niamh O'Sullivan, 'The Priest and the People: Mass in a Connemara Cabin', *From the Edge: Art and Design in Twentieth Century Ireland,* Circa Supplement, National College of Art and Design, Summer, 2000.

7 Cited in Donal Kerr, *The Catholic Church and the Famine*, Dublin: Columba Press, p. 19.

8 P. A. Sheehan, *My New Curate*, p. 18.

9 Christopher Baily, 'James Matthew Lawless', *Irish Arts Review*, Vol. 4, No. 2 (Summer, 1987), pp. 20–4.

10 On Ray Carroll as an artist, see Wilfred Cantwell, 'Ray Carroll: A Memorial to an Artist and a Prophet', *New Liturgy*, autumn–winter (1994), no. 83–84, pp. 25–8. Carroll has also left a personal statement of how he perceived the relationship between theology and art, see, 'The Image of Christ: And an Apologia for the Artist', *The Furrow*, Vol. 32, No. 8 (Aug 1981), pp. 496–503.

11 Even in Caravaggio's famous *Supper at Emmaus*, all the characters are male. The sole exception might be Diego Velázquez, *Kitchen Maid at the Supper at Emmaus* (c. 1618), now in the National Gallery of Ireland, Dublin.

12 See for example the variants in J. Wordsworth and H.J. White, *Novum Testamentum*, Oxford: Clarendon Press, p. 634.

13 Howard Marshall, *Gospel of Luke* (New International Greek Testament Commentary), Exeter: Paternoster Press, 1975. Bruce Metzger includes in his *Textual Commentary on the Greek New Testament* (London: United Bible

Societies, 1975), a selection of early manuscript marginalia that attempted to identify the unnamed disciple (p. 185).

14 He holds that Cleophas is a shortened form of the Greek name Cleopatros (male form of Cleopatra) and that Clopas is a form of a Semitic name *qlwp* or similar, *Gospel According to St Luke* vol 2 (Anchor Bible 28 A), New York: Doubleday, 1985, p. 1563.

Thursday 7th June 2012

EXPLORING SOURCES AND WAYS OF COMMUNION

KEYNOTE SPEAKERS

at the International Symposium of Theology
50TH INTERNATIONAL EUCHARISTIC CONGRESS

• • 1 • •

CHAIR: **MS GILLIAN KINGSTON** (Lay Leader of the Methodist Church in Ireland and Co-chair of the Theology Forum of the Irish Inter-Church Meeting) and **HIS EMINENCE CARDINAL SEÁN BRADY DD** (Archbishop of Armagh and Primate of All Ireland)

SPEAKER: **SR PROF. TERESA OKURE SHCJ**
Catholic Institute of West Africa, Nigeria
The Eucharist: A Way of Life for Jesus and the Christian According to the Scriptures

SPEAKER: **REV. PROF. MARTIN STUFLESSER**
Julius-Maxmillians University, Würzburg, Germany
Drawn Day by Day: Eucharistic Ecclesiology from the Perspective of a Liturgical Theologian

• • 2 • •

CHAIR: **MOST REV. GÉRALD CYPRIEN LACROIX DD**
(Archbishop of Québec)

SPEAKER: **REV. PROF. PIERO CODA**
Sophia University Institute, Loppiano, Florence
Il 'Corpo donato per voi': origine e forma della chiesa comunione
(The 'Body Given Up for You' as Origin and Form of Communion)

SPEAKER: **REV. PROF. BRIAN JOHNSTONE CSsR**
Catholic University of America, Washington DC
The Resurrection and the Eucharist

• • 3 • •

CHAIR: **REV. PROF. LIAM TRACEY OSM** (St Patrick's College, Maynooth)

SPEAKER: **REV. PROF. FINBARR CLANCY SJ**
Milltown Institute, Dublin
Some Patristic Insights into the Eucharist Understood as Communion

• • 4 • •

CHAIR: **SR BRÍD LISTON FCJ** (St Patrick's College, Maynooth)

SPEAKER: **DR CLARE WATKINS**
Westminster Seminary, London
'The Domestic Sanctuary of the Church' (Apostolicam Actuositatem, 11):
Living Eucharist in the Family Today

• • 5 • •

CHAIR: **RT REV. MONS. JAMES CASSIN**
(Council for Education, Irish Bishops' Conference)

SPEAKER: **REV. FR MICHAEL DRUMM**
Executive Chairperson of the Catholic Schools Partnership, Maynooth
Being Educated in Communion

• • 6 • •

CHAIR: **PROF. DAN BRADLEY** (Trinity College, Dublin)

SPEAKER: **REV. DR BRENDAN PURCELL**
Notre Dame University, Sydney
Beyond the Big Bang: The Eucharist at the Heart of Cosmic,
Evolutionary and Human History

• • 7 • •

CHAIR: **REV. DR DECLAN MARMION SM** (St Patrick's College, Maynooth)

SPEAKER: **PROF. GILL GOULDING CJ**
University of Toronto
The Irreducible Particularity of Christ: Beauty, Eucharist and Communion

• • 8 • •

CHAIR: **REV. DR MICHAEL SHORTALL** (St Patrick's College, Maynooth)

SPEAKER: **REV. PROF. PAUL O'CALLAGHAN**
Pontifical University of the Holy Cross, Rome
The Anthropological Roots of Communion

• • 9 • •

CHAIR: **REV. DR KEVIN O'GORMAN SMA** (St Patrick's College, Maynooth)

SPEAKER: **REV. PROF. SLAWOMIR NOWOSAD**
Catholic University of Lublin, Poland
Responding to the Great Challenges Facing the Church Today: Blessed John Paul II and the Ecclesiology of Communion

• • 10 • •

CHAIR: **REV. PROF. MICHAEL CONWAY** (St Patrick's College, Maynooth)

SPEAKER: **PROF. ROBERT D. ENRIGHT**
University of Wisconsin-Madison
Becoming Eucharist for One Another through Forgiving

SPEAKER: **DR GERALDINE SMYTH OP**
Irish School of Ecumenics, Dublin
Forgiveness: Between Created Wisdom and Reconciling Grace

• • 11 • •

CHAIR: **MOST REV. PHILLIP BOYCE OCD, DD** (Bishop of Raphoe)

SPEAKER: **REV. PROF. THOMAS NORRIS**
International Theological Commission
The Church's Marian Profile and the Reception of Vatican II's Ecclesiology

• • 12 • •

CHAIR: **REV. FR LAURENCE MURPHY SJ** (St Patrick's College, Maynooth)

SPEAKER: **REV. PROF. EAMONN CONWAY**
Mary Immaculate College, University of Limerick
'With Reverence and Love': Being a Priest in a Detraditionalised Cultural Context

• • 13 • •

CHAIR: **REV. FR PAUL CROSBIE** (Diocese of Meath)

SPEAKER: **REV. DR DERMOT A. LANE**
Mater Dei Institute of Education, Dublin City University
Eucharist as Sacrament of the Eschaton: A Failure of the Imagination?

• • 14 • •

CHAIR: **DR LORNA GOLD** (Trócaire: The Overseas and Development Agency of the Catholic Church in Ireland)

SPEAKER: **PROF. STEFANO ZAMAGNI**
Department of Economics, University of Bologna
Civilizzare L'Economia: Comunione e Gratuità Nell'agire Economico Alla Luce Della Dottrina Sociale Della Chiesa

• • 15 • •

CHAIR: **DR VERA DONNELLY OP**

SPEAKER: **REV. DR OLIVER TREANOR**
St Patrick's College, Maynooth
The Eucharist: Apostolicity of Communion

• • 16 • •

CHAIR: **REV. DR PATRICK MULLINS O CARM**
(Milltown Institute, Dublin)

SPEAKER: **REV. PROF. MICHAEL MULLANEY**
St Patrick's College, Maynooth
Laity and Ministry in the Church as Communion: Canonical Perspectives

SPEAKER: **MOST REV. PIERO MARINI**
President, Pontifical Committee for International and Eucharistic Congresses
Homily

THE EUCHARIST: A WAY OF LIFE FOR JESUS AND THE CHRISTIAN ACCORDING TO THE SCRIPTURES

SR PROF. TERESA OKURE SHCJ
Catholic Institute of West Africa, Nigeria

INTRODUCTION

Set within the context of the 50th International Eucharistic Congress, this symposium marks the 50th anniversary of the opening of the Second Vatican Ecumenical Council. The symposium therefore celebrates a double fiftieth jubilee: that of the Eucharistic Congress and of the opening of the Second Vatican Council. This double jubilee context invites us to address in our discussions the concept of jubilee itself and its crucial importance for understanding the Eucharist as life and a way of life for Christ and Christians; people called to communion with him, with one another, and with all God's people.

A leitmotif of the Second Vatican Council, which John XXIII declared open in 1962, was *aggiornamento,* the renewal of the Church. Popularly the Council was viewed as an opening of windows of the Church to let in fresh air. Jokingly some remarked that when the windows were opened, plenty of things in the life of the Church flew out of them. This could be a grace or something regrettable, depending on what flew out. As a grace, it would be comparable to Jeremiah's mission, to go, uproot and knock down in order to build and to plant (Jer 1:10). Jeremiah's mission was God's agenda of renewing the covenanted people, welcome or unwelcome (Jer 1:19). The Vatican Council carried out the Church's renewal by revisiting most of the Church's teachings and practices (starting with the liturgy).[1] It restructured the order of ecclesiastical disciplines,[2] emphasised that all ecclesiastical disciplines (including Canon Law) must be based on scripture;[3] most importantly for our context, it reviewed the whole understanding of Church (*Lumen Gentium*) and the Church's attitude towards the modern world (*Gaudium et Spes*).

In particular, the Council advised religious congregations to return to the charism of their founders, that is, to their roots, as sure way to achieve authentic renewal. As the congregations did this, many things and even religious themselves flew out of the window, to the joy or regret of the viewer depending on one's stance. Nonetheless, it has been remarked that while mother Church advised congregations to do this, the Church leadership did not return in appreciable and systematic way to the charism of its own founder Jesus of Nazareth. Though the Council reiterated the traditional belief in apostolic succession, raised the office of bishops to the status of ordination/consecration, and introduced the notion of collegiality, it did not make a similar appreciable effort to return to Jesus' model of leadership; to the apostolic leadership traditions of the New Testament and their ecclesial communities; or assess systematically the theology that shaped these apostolic communities as a way of promoting a renewed gospel-based 'ecclesiology of communion'.

This notwithstanding, the advice to religious congregations bore and continues to bear rich fruit especially in promoting mature and responsible men and women who undertake personal and communal responsibility for living the charism of their founders and participating in the mission of their respective religious congregations. Of interest for our topic is the fact that the Council did call for a return to roots as the way forward in genuine renewal. In March this year, Pope Benedict XVI in a message to the Catholic Church in Ireland commended them on their improvement on various fronts and urged them to return to the 'foundations' of the faith, namely, scripture and the traditions of the Church, as resources for sustaining that improvement.[4] It is appropriate therefore, that in reflecting on the Eucharist as life and way of life for Christ and the Christian, we take a solid scriptural approach, since 'the study of the sacred page should be, as it were, the very soul of theology',[5] and of the life of the Church. In this presentation we treat first the jubilee motif in relation to the Eucharist, then the Eucharist as life and way of life for Christ and the Christian. The approach is essentially a reflection on the scriptural traditions on the Eucharist and the communion life of the Church based on the Eucharist.

BIBLICAL JUBILEE MOTIF IN RELATION TO THE EUCHARIST

The call to return to the roots is the core of biblical jubilee, made up of seven weeks of years (forty-nine plus one) as found in Leviticus (25:8-55). Briefly, God requires of the Israelites to return to their ancestral land (and faith); to recapture and live the spirit of their free and gratuitous election by God; to renew their call to be God's people; and to exist in communion with one another and with the strangers living in their land. Through celebrating the jubilee, Israel was to remind itself that everything it is and has comes from God. It is Israel's faith that the land, indeed the earth and all it holds, belong to God (Deut 10:14; Ps 24:1-2). As God's covenanted people, they were to live this gift in the jubilee year by setting free slaves, giving rest to the animals that ploughed the land and to the land itself by refraining from sowing, planting or harvesting (into barns) during the jubilee year.

By these measures they were to exercise dependence on God's ability to provide for their needs for three years running. In the jubilee year, they were to depend solely on what the land produced of its own accord; and in the year following the jubilee year, by trusting that what the land had produced the year before the jubilee year would sustain them till the harvest of that year was ready: 'I shall order my blessing to be on you ... which will yield you enough produce for three years' (Lev 25:21-22).[6] The jubilee year was thus a God-given agenda to Israel for grace-based social justice, respect for humans (all humans, irrespective of their racial and social standing in the community) and recognition of the rights of the land. While scholars debate whether this year, occurring every fifty years, was ever kept, the fact remains that scripture enjoined it as a divine imperative for God's chosen people: people who accepted to be in communion covenant with God and in virtue of that covenant, to be in communion with one another and with others outside the covenanted community. In that community all were provided for such that there was to 'be no poor among them'; they were equally to care for the poor strangers who would always be among them (Deut 15:1-11).

In the New Testament, Jesus' inaugural discourse in his home town in Nazareth, 'where he had been brought up', that is, where he had his roots (Lk 4:18-19), makes this jubilee injunction his missionary agenda, the purpose of his having been anointed, 'christened' (*echrisen*), made the Messiah, commissioned and sent by God. The divine jubilee year rules out vengeance on the wicked, a motif present in the Isaiah passage cited by Jesus (Is 61:1-2). God's general amnesty excludes nobody and no age. Its Johannine corollary is John 10:10: 'Others come to steal and to plunder. I have come so that they may have life in ever increasing abundance.' The declaration of God's general amnesty to Israel and the entire creation constitutes the core of Jesus' liberating and life-giving mission. He declares this year of God's favour by the totality of his life, ministry, passion, death and resurrection.

Jesus' conception, practice, method and fulfilment of his mission are firmly rooted in the biblical jubilee. Throughout his life and mission, Jesus returned to the roots of God's promise to save humanity from their illegal allegiance with Satan (Gn 3:1-7) and restore them to God (Gn 3:15). In his person ('the Word became flesh'; Jn 1:14), God in person established the enmity between humanity and Satan in a way that can never ever again be broken: 'It is accomplished, done' (Jn 19:30). The good news to be proclaimed to all nations (Mt 28:19-20; Lk 24:47; Acts 1:8) was God's fulfilment of the promise of restoration in Christ. Peter sees Pentecost, the outpouring of God's 'Spirit upon all flesh' (such that even menservants and maidservants, the young and the old, daughters and sons all prophecy, as the fulfilment of God's general amnesty to humanity and creation (Acts 2:14-21).[7]

The jubilee motif is linked to the Eucharist because in the Eucharist God provides for humanity food for eternal life, one that unites them with God and with one another in and through Christ. As the land provided free food for the people at creation and during the jubilee year, so in this divine jubilee year this food is given free of charge. As the covenant people were required to have faith in God and God's ability to provide for them during the jubilee year, so does the reception of this food in God's year of favour depend on faith. The evangelist John sees *believing* as the *one and only 'work'* God requires of recipients (Jn 6:39). At a deeper level, God's year of favour marks God's own return to the divine roots: the restoration of God's first creation (vitiated by the sin of our first parents). This is the most fundamental return to the roots that makes all other returns possible and indispensable. The Eucharist is the food God provides for those who in Christ have become a new creation (2 Cor 5:17). It is the food which constitutes the Church, all God's people (LG 2), as and into ecclesial communion.

THE CHURCH'S JUBILEE CELEBRATIONS IN RELATION TO THE EUCHARIST

John Paul II captured the spirit underlying biblical jubilee in his reflection on the great jubilee of our Lord (2000). Inspired by this spirit (the call to return to land and roots), he called on the universal Church, all and sundry, to return to our gospel roots as the way forward in the march towards becoming authentically Church, the *ekklesia* of God, in the twenty-first century. This return to our roots is the leitmotif of his apostolic letter *Novo Millennio Ineunte* (NMI, *At the Beginning of the New Millennium*).[8] Reflecting on the life and mission of the Church during the past two thousand years, the Pope observed that over that entire period, we as Church, like the disciples in the fishing episode (Lk 5:1-11), 'have laboured all night and caught nothing'. At the dawn of this new millennium, we are to see and listen to Jesus standing on the shore, asking us to recognise the emptiness of our two thousand years of fruitless labour (in all aspects of life, what it means to be Church and in theologising and missionary undertaking); then follow his instructions as he directs us to launch into the deep: 'pair down your nets for a catch.' Only by so doing will we catch the abundant fish of fruitful life and mission in this dawning millennium. The Pope emphasised that the letter is his personal insights gained from reflecting on the events that marked the celebrations of the great jubilee. He urged all Christians to join him in doing their personal reflection as a way of engaging in authentic renewal. A memorable event in the great jubilee celebration mentioned in the letter was the Eucharistic Congress of that year.[9]

The organisers of this symposium have rightly observed that 'John Paul II underlined the spirituality of communion' in his *Novo Millennio Ineunte*. Spirituality is essentially about how we live our life in the Spirit (cf. Gal 5:13-26), at the personal and communal levels. The Eucharist is the spirituality of communion par excellence, 'the centre of spiritual life in the kingdom founded by Jesus'.[10] Jesus declares that the one who eats his flesh and drinks his blood lives in him and he in the person (Jn 6:56). It is the Spirit who causes to live (Jn 6:63). The same

Spirit that anointed Jesus and sent him to declare God's jubilee year by the sumtotal of his life and mission, is also given to the Christian, one 'configured to Christ' by baptism 'with an indelible character and made a member of the Church' (Canon 849), to continue to declare this divine jubilee year in the same way as Jesus did.

Jesus carried out his call and mission to be God's good news, to proclaim God's jubilee year for humanity and creation in the totality of his life. This mission climaxed in the giving of that life as Eucharist, food and drink, for all humanity through death and resurrection. The Christian, who is another Christ in the world today, is equally called and commissioned to continue this same life-giving mission, as individuals and as community of believers, *ecclesia de eucharistia*. To do this is to be truly a Church in communion with God in, with and through Christ and resultantly in communion with one another and with the entire creation. The task before us now is to explore how the Eucharist, according to the scriptures, uniquely constitutes this life and way of life of communion for the Christian as it did for Christ.

THE EUCHARIST, LIFE AND WAY OF LIFE FOR CHRIST

In the thinking of the Church, the Eucharist is the source and summit of all Christian life. Not surprisingly, the Eucharist, bread of life, food for the world, is arguably one of the most, if not the most written about aspects of our Christian faith. The literature right from Christian origins takes a plethora of forms: creeds and reflections in the New Testament, teachings of the Fathers of the Church, papal encyclicals and decrees, apostolic letters and exhortations, theological treatises and exposés, hymns,[11] prayers, and so forth. The interests cover a variety of topics, positive and negative.[12] To borrow from John Evangelist, we may say that if all the books/works written on the Eucharist were to be reviewed in this our current context, the entire time of the symposium and the subsequent Eucharist Congress would be quite insufficient to review them.[13]

Sadly though, despite this overwhelming interest, the Eucharist which Jesus intended to unite all Christians in him, and through them all humanity (Jn 17:21), remains the single most important point of division among Christians. The Catholic Church is not exempt from this, especially in terms of who is qualified or not by sex to be an ordained minister of the Eucharist, and the issue of the clergy/laity divide. The fault is not in the Eucharist itself, but in extraneous causes rooted in history and in culture-based interpretations of our Jesus traditions, some embedded in the sacred texts themselves. They include issues of, apostolic succession: belief or lack of it in the Eucharist as truly not symbolically the body and blood of Christ; debates on whether the Eucharist is a true enactment of what Jesus did at the Last Supper or a mere ritual remembrance of it; whether, after consecration, the bread and wine become truly Christ's Body and Blood.[14] Other concomitant issues revolve around authority, power and control.

Our concern here is not with these vexing though important questions. Rather it is with the Eucharist as life and a way of life for Jesus and the Christian. The reason is simple. We eat physical food to live or sustain life; the proof that we are alive is that we act. Eucharist is life for Jesus and the Christian in a symbiotic type of relationship. Since Christ and the Christian relate to one another as the body and its members (1 Cor 12:12-27) or the vine and its branches (Jn 15:1-17), what applies to one applies equally to the other. Jesus' relationship with God was one of exact correspondence: whatever the Father does, the Son/Child does too, for 'the Son can do nothing except what he sees the Father doing'; [15] honour given to the Son is given to the Father; rejection of the Son is rejection of the Father (Jn 5:19-23). Still more, the Father lives, acts, and speaks in the Son (Jn 14:10-11). Christ extends the same correspondence to the relationship between him and the Christian. One who believes in him will do the same works as he does and even greater works because he goes to the Father (Jn 14:12). Whatever is done to any of the believers is done to him; rejection of the believer is rejection of him; persecution of the believer (as Paul did) is persecution of him: 'I am Jesus and you are persecuting me' (Acts 9:5).

In view of this, we seek to discover what the Eucharist signified for Jesus, the Messiah (*ho christos*) as a way to discovering what it should signify for the Christian, one *christened*, or configured to him in baptism. The focus of this presentation on the Eucharist as food and way of life for Christ and the Christian is based on how Jesus himself perceived and lived the Eucharist and proposed it to us in the scriptures. He saw himself comprehensively as 'the life' (Jn 14:6), 'the bread of life' (Jn 6:35, 48), 'the living bread which has come down from heaven' (Jn 6:51); to give eternal life to all who eat of this bread, which concretely is his 'flesh and blood' (Jn 6:48-58). He posited the eating of his flesh and drinking of his blood as indispensable condition for having endless life, a life like his, a life that is God's own life in the receiver/believer. He anchored in the Eucharist his identity as 'the life' and mission to give life. How was Eucharist life for Christ (not just mission) and a way of life for him?

THE EUCHARIST AS FOOD AND LIFE FOR CHRIST

Food and life in all its forms go together. We are accustomed to see the Eucharist as food and life for the believer. Jesus declared it to be essentially so, 'my flesh is real food and my blood is real drink' given for the life of world; one must eat it if one is to have endless life (Jn 6:51-58). As God-Word become flesh (Jn 1:1-2, 14, 18), Jesus, the Messiah/Christ, was the life from whom all created life derived. He came so that all might have life in its fullness (Jn 10:10). He came not to be served but to serve and to give his life as a ransom for many (Mt 20:28). The Father commissioned him to give life to all those he chooses to give life (Jn 5:21) and this excludes no one. Yet as a human being, Jesus also needed food in the spiritual as in the physical order, a food which sustained his life and mission and formed his way of life: 'My food is to do the will of the one who sent me and to complete his work' (Jn 4:34). The completion of this work was rooted inextricably in the Eucharist, the giving of his life as food and drink in death and resurrection for the life of the world. As Jesus drew life from the Father, even so does the one who eats him draw life from him (Jn 6:52). Over the centuries the Church teaches that the Eucharist is the foundation of the Church. 'Without the Eucharist there is no Church and without the Church there is no Eucharist.' In this reflection we are saying that without the Eucharist there is no Christ and without Christ there is no Eucharist. How can the Eucharist be food and life for one who is the very bread of life? To help clarify this better we first consider the relationship between food and life in general.

FOOD AND LIFE

Food and life go together. We need food to live and sustain life. People who choose to die a gradual death out of protest for a given cause go on hunger strike, hoping that before death strikes, the cause for which they went on the hunger strike would have been satisfactorily addressed. Not surprisingly, the biggest human industry in the world is that of food, seconded by that of clothing. By industry here I do not mean the big and multinational corporations or supermarkets, but whatever human beings, from the highest to the grassroots do to provide food for themselves and their own, or sell to earn a living. The food industry is open to all and can be accessed by all. One requires no special skills to engage in it; petty traders along the roads sell fruits, biscuits and all sorts of drinks; others have the sign 'Food is ready' dotted in small shops almost everywhere where human beings work and so need food. Men and especially women engage in selling what in Nigeria is popularly called 'Mama put' (roadside cooked food). Canteens, cafés and restaurants are the most frequented and crowded places at airports, train and bus stations and other public places. Regular and frequent suppliers, buyers and caterers of all kinds of foodstuffs feature in educational institutions, at functions, weddings, gatherings. All human beings need food to live, and this need unites humanity across the globe.

The first thing God did after creating man and woman, male and female in the divine image and likeness was to provide food for them and for all living creatures: 'I give you all the seed bearing plants for food' (Gn 1:29-29). We are not told that the man and woman gave thanks for the food God provided for them. What we know is that they desired and eventually ate of the tree of good and evil of which God had said, 'On the day you eat of it you will die' (Gn 2:16-17; 3:3). The result was death (Gn 3:19). But the God who is life and the giver of life cannot see God's own work defeated by death caused 'by the devil's envy' (Wis 2:24). God came to their rescue: to overcome death by the promise a new life in a new creation. At first, God created the man and woman in the divine image and likeness (Gn 1:26-27; 5:1-2) and destined them for immortality (Wis 2:23). Now in the new creation (2 Cor 5:17), God ensures that the man and woman have the divine life inside them, substantially, by regenerating them as God's sons and daughters in the Son (Rm 8:14-17; Gal 4:4-6). This time God also provides the food which must be received or eaten in faith (Jn 6:29) to sustain this new life eternally: the Eucharist.

EUCHARIST: JESUS' IDENTITY AND MISSION AS FOOD AND DRINK

The Eucharist is essentially about food (and giving thanks for it): he gave thanks and said: 'Take, eat this is my body.' 'Take, drink, this is my blood.' He was very aware that he himself was food: 'I am the bread of life'; 'I am the living bread come down from heaven.' This indicates that he knew that his identity and way of life was to be food, life vitals for others. Scholars debate endlessly whether the Lord's Supper was the celebration of the Paschal meal or something outside it, unique to Jesus: his Supper. Interesting as this question may be, it cannot distract from the essentially food nature of this celebration. Jesus' identity as food and giver of food goes back to his ancestry and the circumstances of his birth. By his human origin and birth, Jesus was destined to be food for the world.

JESUS AS FOOD IN HIS ANCESTRY

Jesus was popularly called 'Son of David' by his people, especially the poor and needy who saw him as providing their diverse life needs as did David his ancestor.[16] David descended from Ruth and Boaz through the union of an Israelite and a Moabitess, in circumstances marked by famine in the land (therefore connected with food). This famine drove Noami, her husband and their two sons to the land of Moab. Her eventual return with a daughter-in-law in place of a husband and two sons was because 'God had visited his people and given them food' (Ruth 1:6-7). Scripture associates David the king,[17] descendant of Boaz and Ruth through Jesse, with food. As a boy, he was a shepherd, which meant his profession was to care and provide food for sheep. Not surprisingly, when Jesus was born in Bethlehem, shepherds were the first to whom God's angel revealed his birth as the Messiah. They were to go to Bethlehem, the city of David, to discover the Messiah by 'the sign' of 'a baby in swaddling clothes and lying in the manger' (Lk 2:11-12). We will return to this shortly.

As king, David distributed food to everybody in his kingdom the day the ark was carried to its rest, singing, dancing and giving thanks to God before the ark, offering abundant sacrifices and feasting all the people one by one (2 Sm 6:12-19). When pursued by his son Absalom, stricken by hunger, David assumed the freedom to enter the sanctuary, eat the loaves of sacrifice and give the same to his followers, though only the priests were entitled to eat such loaves (1 Sm 21:2-7). For him life was primary. In his footsteps, Jesus would give his disciples freedom to pluck, rub and eat ears of corn on the Sabbath despite the laws prohibiting such action, citing in justification this action of his ancestor David (Mk 2:23-28).

Beth-le-hem, house of food, house of bread, where Jesus was born, was the 'city of David' (Lk 2:1-28). His legal father, Joseph, husband of his mother, hailed from this city and served as the bridge in his genealogy as 'son of David', son of Abraham (Mt 1:16-25).[18] He was not just born in this 'house of food' or 'house of bread', but in a particular place in it: the manger. Among its possible meanings, a manger is essentially where animals are fed. Place of birth is a required entry in one's passport, because where one first lands in life as human being is significant for one's life. In America and Ireland, for instance, birth in the country automatically makes one a citizen, and in the US qualifies one to become president, something naturalisation does not confer. Among my people, the Ibibio, people often traditionally received names from the places where they were born, for example *Usungurua* (market road), if a child was born when the mother was on the way to the market; *Inwan* (farm), if the boy was born on the farm. Similarly, Jesus' birthplace in Bethlehem, *House of Food*, was not neutral to his life identity. His mother laid him in a manger in preparation for the food he was to become for humanity. This insight gives a new perspective, a eucharistic perspective, to the crib which we visit and sing around at Christmas. From birth and by descent from David, Jesus was destined to become food for humanity.

As Jesus grew up, and was popularly called Son of David, he would naturally have studied and tried to connect with his ancestor so as to place himself in David's track, to give, and more so, to be bread to the hungry. Jesus did not lose touch with his human roots; he habitually studied scripture to discover what was said there about him (Lk 1:18-20; 24:25-27; Jn 5:39). His mother would have helped him to this. The popular hymn 'The Baker Woman' says it all: 'Bake us the bread Mary, Mary … Bake us the bread we need to be fed.' This hymn extends Jesus' food character right to the womb, where Mary, the baker woman, baked him to life as bread for us, her woman human substance. Gabriel emphasised at the annunciation that she would conceive *in her womb* (that is, not spiritually or symbolically, but physically, and bear a child. The body that Jesus later gave as bread – 'Take eat, this is my body', he took 100 per cent from Mary's woman body – by God's deliberate and deliberative will and act. His mother also had a key role to play in his alpha sign at Cana in Galilee where he turned water into wine (Jn 2:1-11), an action that looked to his omega sign in the events surrounding his last supper, passion and death and resurrection; Calvary being the first real altar of sacrifice where she also featured as concelebrant with other named women (Jn 19:25-27).

LIFE AND FOOD IN JESUS' MINISTRY

Jesus' life and ministry were characterised by being/giving food. He frequently tied food and life together. When he raised the daughter of Jarius from death, the first thing he asked was that she be given something to eat (Lk 8:54-55). No mention is made of eating immediately after the raising of Lazarus (four days dead; Jn 11:39), but later a party was given to honour Jesus ('the resurrection and the life') and Lazarus was one of the guests (Jn 12:1-11). Jesus worked his first or omega sign at the wedding in Cana of Galilee, where eating and drinking was plentiful and free of charge according to the traditions of the time (as in African cultures). Wedding signifies the beginning of new life, for the couples as for the children who would be born of the wedlock. Food and eating featured prominently in Jesus' parables, in his contacts with the self-righteous (Simon the Pharisee; Lk 7:36-50); with social outcasts, tax collectors and sinners (Levi, Mk 2:13-17; Zacchaeus, Lk 19:1-10); and with friends, Martha and Mary (Lk 10:38-42). As mentioned earlier, he gave freedom to his disciples to break ears of corn and eat on the Sabbath to sustain life, citing as precedence what David did. He personally ate and drank with tax collectors and sinners, contrary to societal laws of decency. Table fellowship with sinners did not defile him. Rather it raised and empowered those sinners to become authentic members of the community that God destined them to be by virtue of their descent from Abraham in whose covenant and promises they shared: 'Today is salvation come to this house for he too is a son of Abraham' (Lk 19:9-10).

Equally Jesus made his disciples aware that it was their duty to give food to the crowd. When they complained that they did not have enough to feed the crowd, he worked a miracle to supply their lack. Jesus describes Peter's leadership mission of the flock in terms of feeding and tending his (Jesus') little sheep, after Jesus' own example of feeding and empowering him and his companions (Jn 21:1-19). When they asked him to teach them how to pray, prayer for daily bread formed part of this prayer (The Lord's Prayer).

The point is made. Food and life go together at the natural and spiritual levels. For one who came that human beings may have life to the full (natural life and spiritual life), food could not but be integral aspect of his mission. These examples are not exhaustive. Jesus simply had a passion for food. He desired with desire to eat his Passover with his disciples (Lk 22:15) where he would give them his Body and Blood as living food for endless life.

THE EUCHARIST AS SACRIFICE IN RELATION TO JESUS AS FOOD

A firm belief of the Church rooted in scripture is that the Eucharist is both food/meal and sacrifice. What, if any, is the intrinsic connection between the two? While not denying the sacrificial nature of what Jesus did the night before he suffered, according to the usual understanding of sacrifice (and we will return to this shortly),[19] I prefer first to view Jesus' sacrifice in relation to his being food/meal for us. In normal life, raw food needs to be cut, cooked, boiled and eaten. Even food that does not need to be cooked (vegetables for salad and fruits), is normally chewed (that is, destroyed in its original form) before it is swallowed. Perhaps if we saw Jesus' passion, death and resurrection in this light, as food that is thoroughly and richly cooked for us, in the crucible of suffering unto death and resurrection, we would appreciate more the love that undergirds his having loved us to the utmost limit: giving himself to us as food and drink through death and resurrection (transformation of the flesh/humanity). His love 'to the end' (*eis telos*) is love that reaches a limit beyond which it was utterly impossible to go; this makes more sense than does the traditional view of it as sacrificial expiation for sin to appease the anger of a vengeful God.[20]

Jesus expatiates on this in his farewell or Last Supper discourse (Jn 15:13): 'Greater love has no human being than to lay down his or her life for those he/she loves.' Centuries later he tells Julian of Norwich in *Revelations of Divine Love* that if there was anything else he could possibly have done to prove how much he loved us he would have done it. Dying for us was the limit beyond which it was utterly impossible for any human being to go; the sign of utmost, unsurpassable love. If we saw his passion, death and resurrection in this light, as utmost love beyond comprehension, a love which only God can give to God's creatures, we would come to appreciate Jesus' gift of self as food and drink more profoundly than we do by seeing his death as supposedly satisfying God's anger against us or treating the Eucharist as a mere symbol or vague remembrance; we would also appreciate better the challenge of this sacrificial love for us Christians.

The Johannine Jesus himself declares that his death is the utmost proof of love (Jn 15:13). His love for us is itself a corollary of God's own incredible love for the world (Jn 3:16). 'God loved the world so much that he gave' the best, the most precious thing God could possibly give, the *monogenes theos*, 'only begotten-God' (Jn 1:18), the *yahid*, his own life entrails; so as to draw us closest to the divine self, no longer as slaves or even friends but finally and definitively as siblings of Jesus, God's own beloved children, 'heirs of God and co-heirs with Christ' (Rm 8:14-18; Gal 4:4-6).[21] Patristic scholars using the modes of cultural expression of their time, and before them the New Testament authors, interpreted Jesus' death in terms of Jewish atonement theology and their own cultural mindsets: the satisfaction of God's wrath. This led to the belief that Jesus' death was satisfactory vengeance exacted by God to meet the enormity of the offence to God (as Anselm thought). Yet Hebrews makes it clear that the sacrifice of Jesus is different from what we understand by 'sacrifice'. In the sacrifice of Jesus, God personally offers the divine self for humanity to bring humanity closest to the divine self, for good ('once for all').[22] This indeed is a great mystery which we need to re-discover in this third millennium to help us launch into the deep (*duc in altum*) and truly appreciate God's incomprehensible and overwhelming love for us, shown concretely in and through Christ.[23]

When Jesus said to his audience, 'Unless you eat the flesh of the son of man [that is, this human being][24] and drink his blood, you shall not have life in you, for my flesh is real food and my blood is real drink, whoever eats my flesh and drinks my blood abides in me and I will raise the person up on the last day', he would have had no illusion that for him personally, this would entail *death*. He would have known

The pain of betrayal (Judas; Mt 26:20-25), denial (Peter), being abandoned by all his disciples (Mk 14:50-52; Mt 26:56) and rejected by his leaders in preference for Barabbas, a brigand and a murderer (Mk 15: 6-15; Jn 18:40); his rejection as king by his people in preference for Caesar (Jn 19:15). All these pains added to the great pangs of childbirth (Jn 12:24) for one who was to become the mother and ground of being of the new humanity (Eph 4:13; Rm 5:12-21; Cor 15:22). He gave birth and life to this humanity on the cross as the Fathers of the Church held long ago.[25] His death on the cross was the necessary action by which he drew all humanity to himself (Jn 12:32). His Father loved him precisely because of his own free will, he laid down his life for his sheep so that they might have life, real life, abundantly and ever increasingly (*perisson*; Jn 10:10, 17-18) and unendingly.

These examples could go on. In this century we need to 'launch into the deep': reposition our thinking about the reasons for Jesus' death. The core reason is unsurpassable love; love which levels all ranks and brings all into one communion. This is crucial in a world where selfish love is rampant; a world where people live on others rather than for others; a world where religion itself has become the biggest and most lucrative and labour and cost-free business in what is popularly tagged 'the religion industry', with no national or international laws attached to it. Or where it has become one of the greatest reasons for fanatically, recklessly destroying the life of others as is evident in many parts of the world. These negative actions go against the nature of Eucharist as life-giving and thanksgiving.

EUCHARIST AS A THANKSGIVING WAY OF LIFE FOR JESUS

Etymologically, the noun 'Eucharist' (*eucharistia*) derives from the Greek verb *eucharistein* (to give thanks). Eucharist signifies 'thanksgiving'. We give thanks for what we receive as gift from others. Jesus gave his body and blood to us as food and drink. Did he then need to give thanks? Why did he give thanks? Was his action a mere ritual thanksgiving or blessing before meals or was there a deeper significance in what he did which has subsequently given the most poplar name to his Last Supper?[26] Can we say that thanksgiving was a way of life for him? It would seem so. Jesus gave thanks to God throughout his life because he realised that he himself was God's pure grace and gift to humanity. The law, what one does and receives credit for, was given through Moses. 'Grace and truth', the real ('the substance', as Paul would put it), 'came through Jesus Christ' (Jn 1:16-17). God-Word though he was, as Word become flesh, everything Jesus was, was God's pure grace. The human race could do nothing to merit that God should become substantially one of this race; anymore than could human beings merit becoming God's real children (1 Jn 3:1-3). Jesus was first blessed in the womb by Elizabeth (Lk 1:42) and this beatitude accompanied him through life. He knew and declared that his life, his words, his works and even his disciples came from God (Jn 14:6; 17:6-7); therefore they were a blessing and a matter for gratitude.

Not surprisingly, Jesus' entire life was marked, defined and characterised by thanksgiving. Instances abound in the gospels where he gave thanks to God. In many of these instances, the thanksgiving is connected with food: the loaves and fish which he miraculously increased using gestures evocative of what he did at the Eucharist, even after the resurrection.[27] He admired, praised God's wise ways and thanked God for revealing the mysteries of the kingdom to mere children, the simplest of humans (Mt 11:25-26). He thanked God for hearing his prayer on the occasion of raising Lazarus, a prayer said out loud for the sake of his audience, but which defined his inner relationship with God 'I know you always hear me' (Jn 11:41-42). He thanked God for giving the disciples to him, though they belonged to God (Jn 17:6). He admired and thanked God for the gifts and beauty of nature: the lilies of the field which not even Solomon in all his glory could rival, and the birds of the air which neither sow nor gather, but whom the heavenly Father feeds (Mt 6:26-29). Admiring God's work in nature, marveling at the beauty of God's creation, is integral part of the liturgy of life of thanksgiving.

Thanksgiving defines the attitude, mindset and worldview of one who is and sees self as a steward or servant; who knows and accepts that what one is, has and does in a gift from God. Who is aware that all these gifts, including personal talent and ministry, come from God. Thanksgiving defines sound stewardship which translates into open accountability. Its opposite is to convert stewardship to ownership as exemplified by the wicked tenants of the vineyard:[28] my church, my diocese, parish, office, congregation, and so forth. Jesus' prayer in John 17, in my view, is his public prayer of accountability to God for the work God entrusted to him to 'do and complete' (Jn 4:34; 17:4); it is said publicly before his disciples who were eye-witnesses to his stewardship and who therefore can vouch for its veracity.[29] The story is told of John XXIII, who was excruciatingly struggling and worrying because things were flying out of the Church's windows. Then he took himself to the chapel, knelt down and prayed; 'Lord the Church is yours, and I am going to bed.' He probably slept very well that night. To appropriate what is given to us in trust is a form of self abuse. No matter how vehemently we claim it, it will never and can never be ours.

Thanksgiving defined Jesus' entire life and way of life as a true servant and steward of God's mysteries who knows that all is grace. He lived to the full the spirit of gratitude that Paul enjoins on the Corinthians: 'What have you that you did not first receive? And if you have received it why boast as if you had not received it?' (1 Cor 4:7). Jesus himself was God's grace, gift to humanity (Jn 1:17). His life of thanksgiving was not limited to prayer of thanksgiving. It oiled, seasoned and greased all his activities and his entire attitude and outlook in life, a life lived for others. Peter sums up his life for Cornelius thus: 'He went about doing good' (Acts 10:38). He was sensitive to people's need for physical food; even when they came for physical healing, or to listen to his teaching, he fed them at the cost of his own rest and that of his disciples (Mk 6:30-44). All these activities were only pointers to the food proper, the Eucharist, the food of foods, where he would give his own body and blood for endless life (Jn 16:21). His passion, death and resurrection were the crowning point of his life of thanksgiving through self-giving. It was enacted in the institution of the Eucharist itself. 'This is my body given for you; this is my blood of the covenant poured out for you and for many.' By giving thanks, Jesus accepted wholeheartedly his death as God's supreme gift of love for humanity. What a mystery.

Thanksgiving by nature enlarges the thanks-giver even as it glorifies God to whom the thanks are given. Without thanksgiving, we remain like the wheat grain that refuses to fall to the ground and die; but if it dies it bears much fruit (Jn 12:24). The miracle of the multiplication of the loaves happens in the sharing: blessing, thanking and giving. Had the little boy with five loaves and two fish eaten his lunch all by himself, it would have ended there (Jn 6:8-9). But because he surrendered it to be blessed, prayed over and shared, it multiplied to feed five thousand men and leave twelve baskets full, first for the apostles, then symbolically for the nation Israel (with its Twelve Tribes), and more profoundly still, for humanity (with its innumerable tribes, nations and tongues). If Jesus had not given himself for our food and drink in death and resurrection, he would have remained alone, 'a single grain' (Jn 12:24), just Jesus of Nazareth. But because he surrendered his life for us in death and resurrection, he became the 'the new humanity', 'the cosmic Christ' as scholars call him. The designation originates from Jesus himself who declared: 'When I am lifted up from the earth, I will draw all peoples to myself '(Jn 12:32). 'All' (*pantas*) here stands for all humans (male and female, animate and inanimate things taken together); he is the one from whom, through whom and to whom all things came to be; for whom they were made (Jn 1:3; Rm 11:36); 'in whom all things hold together' (Col 1:17) and through whom God reconciles to the divine self 'all things' both in heaven an on earth (Col 1:17, 20). Those drawn to him are by that very deed drawn also into living his eucharistic life.

EUCHARIST: FOOD AND WAY OF LIFE FOR THE CHRISTIAN

As one configured to Christ by baptism, the Christian is called into permanent ecclesial communion in the eucharistic Church (*ecclesia de eucharistia)*, a Church that as the body of Christ stands or falls on the Eucharist.[30] The Christian is essentially a disciple of Christ. Discipleship has four basic components: *akolouthein* (to follow) *manthanein* (to learn step by step), *diakonein* (to serve) and *koinonein* (to have and enjoy communion, be at one with). Service is the content of what the disciple learns from Jesus (Jn 13:12-17); it is precisely here that communion or being-at-one-ness takes place. In view of this, all that is said above about Christ as Eucharist – a life that is defined by total self-giving as food in continued thanksgiving to God – applies equally to the Christian. Like Christ, the Christian needs to cultivate and sustain a *eucharistic mindset* and way of life. In this section we reflect first on how the Eucharist is food that sustains life for the Christian, then on how as food and as thanksgiving it should define the life of the Christian and the ecclesial community as it defined that of Christ.

EUCHARIST AS LIFE-GIVING FOOD FOR THE CHRISTIAN

We say it again: food and life go together for the spiritual as for the physical life. At the first creation, God provided food for humans and all living creatures. In the new creation ('When anyone is in Christ, that person is a new creation, the old has passed away' [2 Cor 5:17]), brought into existence by the totality of Christ's eucharistic life, God the giver of this new life also provides the food that goes with it. That food is inseparable from the person of Jesus. 'In all truth I tell you, unless you eat of the flesh of the son of man and drink his blood, you have no life in you ... My flesh is real food and my blood is real drink. Whoever eats my flesh and drinks my blood lives in me and I live in the person. As the living Father sent me and I draw life from the Father, whoever eats me draws life from me' (Jn 6:53-57). This 'bread of life' is both 'living' (it has life in itself) and 'life-giving' (Jn 6:48, 51); it differs from what the ancestors ate and are dead. Whoever eats this one 'lives forever'. Even if the person dies, 'I shall raise that person up on the last day' (Jn 6:54). The phrase 'draw life from me' evokes the action of a foetus who draws life from the mother through the placenta, and as a baby sucks the mother's breast for the complete food it needs, at times up to the first three years of its existence (cf. 2 Mac 7:27).

The synoptic gospels speak of the Eucharist, this food and drink, as Jesus' 'body and blood'; John's Gospel, rated to be the most rooted in Jewish traditions, speaks of it as 'flesh and blood'. Though the synoptic terminology may have originated from Hellenistic rather than Palestinian context, arguably the simplest explanation is that Hebrew had no word for body. 'Flesh and blood' designated the human reality,[31] just as 'bone of bones and flesh of flesh' designated close kinship (Gn 2:23-24; 2 Sm 5:1). Still the Johannine usage draws closest attention to the fact that it is in the person of Jesus, concretely in his humanity (flesh and blood) that this life is found; in him it must be rooted and sustained. One must 'remain' or be at one with him in all aspects of life as prove that one lives in or 'draws life' from him; just as his deeds in the body, as a human being, were proof that he lived in and drew life from God (Jn 14:9-12), in whose bosom he permanently was (Jn 1:18).

As Christians we were constituted into being, given birth at the Last Supper, which reached its climax and completion on the cross. We saw earlier that Jesus' birth place and the history surrounding it were not neutral to his identity of being bread and life for the world. Like him, the Christian must appropriate the significance of his/her birth stool, the Eucharist, at the Paschal event from Holy Thursday to Easter Sunday. He or she cannot simply be satisfied with eating the body and drinking the blood of Jesus without doing everything possible to become in turn food and drink for others, breaking the bread of his or her life so that others may eat and drink and have life in all its fullness. When Jesus said, 'Do this in memory of me', he was not thinking merely of a ritual celebration such as we have developed around the Eucharist over the past 2,000 years. The increasing practice of making a living out of the Eucharist: seeking for titles, honours, money, power and control (all values in the world which have penetrated, infiltrated into the Church),[32] is anti-eucharistic. These practices are opposed to the eucharistic form of life where 'the whole of life should be a spiritual worship offered to God' (Rm 12:1).[33] Eucharist is essentially about giving one's life for others (not making a living out of it): a life lived in and nourished by Jesus in a relationship of the vine and its branches or the body and its members.

Celebrating the Eucharist 'in memory of Jesus' is intimately linked with the new commandment, the greatest, indeed the one and only commandment Jesus gives to people of the new covenant: 'A new commandment I give you, that you love one another as I have loved you. By this will all know that you are my disciples, by the love you have for one another' (Jn 13:34-35). At the Last Supper, Jesus symbolically illustrates this love by washing the disciples' feet (Jn 13:1-17) as the sign of a unsurpassable love (*eis telos*); he actualised it in his passion, death and resurrection: 'Greater love than this has no one than to lay down one's life for his friends' (Jn 15:13). Unfortunately we have reduced the symbolic foot washing to a mere ritual celebration once a year on Holy Thursday at the celebration of the Lord's Supper. Yet Jesus intended it to be an example of humble, mutual service to be exercised in real life by *all* his disciples; not a mere ritual celebration confined to the chief celebrant at the Last Supper Mass, with selected feet to be washed and to the exclusion of women, though some courageous church communities have started to include women in the exercise both ways.

What Jesus did was not a mere ritual, but something he did with the totality of his life. The foot washing was a way of giving them a part with him, as he explains to protesting Peter. It also served as a concrete and timely reminder that he had lived among his disciples as one who serves, their Lord and Master though he was (Jn 13:13-15). Even after his resurrection, he prepared breakfast for them on a charcoal fire with his sacred, risen hands (Jn 21:9-14). On the basis of this concrete example, he gave the mandate to Peter to feed his little sheep and look after his sheerings (Jn 21:15-19) as proof of his love 'above all others' and continued discipleship ('Follow me', Jn 21:19). Jesus thus established and anchored the Petrine ministry in his eucharistic ministry, the summit of his own love for Peter and all of us. From this incident, too, it was essential to this ministry that Peter empowers all the sheep to respond to the vocation to love Jesus above all other things ('Whoever loves father or mother, or wife or children or own life more than me is not worthy of me'). Even as Jesus empowered Peter himself to live up to his pre-resurrection boast that he loved him more than all the other disciples and would not deny him even if others did.[34]

Jesus' criteria at the last judgement will not be the number of times we 'received' the Holy Communion, or whether we were regular communicants, daily Mass attendants (even without receiving Communion) or organised conferences and wrote beautiful exposés on the Eucharist. Rather it will be a love like his which translates into concrete actions to sustain, nourish and ennoble the life of others (Mt 25:30-46). Paul castigates the rich Corinthians who ate without 'discerning the body'. Traditionally we take this to mean receiving Holy Communion 'unworthily'; or not in 'a state of grace'.[35] The literary and social contexts of the letter (in a house church) where the rich displayed their wealth and drank their fill to the humiliation of the poor, leads to the conclusion that Paul was talking about failure to recognise 'the physical (not sacramental) body of Christ', namely, the community of believers gathered in worship who form *one* body in Christ in the *one* loaf and *one* cup (1 Cor 10:16-17). He develops this concept further in chapter 12 of his letter (the body and its members). Throughout his letters, Paul consistently emphasises the intimate relationship between Christ and all believers. The birth-gift of this awareness was his initial encounter with Jesus on the way to Damascus: 'Who are you sir?' 'I am Jesus whom you are persecuting' (Acts 9:5). Thus Jesus claimed as himself the men, women and children (the body of believers) whom

Paul was persecuting: 'Whatsoever you did to the least of these my brothers and sisters you did it to me' (Mt 25:40, 45).

Interpreting the 'eating and drinking without discerning the body' in this light, challenges many things we do as normal in our ecclesial and liturgical, specifically in eucharistic, celebrations. How can a divided Christ be in communion with himself? How can members divided along class and oftentimes ethnic, sex and racial lines be in communion with one another? 'A kingdom divided against itself cannot stand' (Mk 3:22-30). Paul asks the Corinthians whether Christ has been divided up by their factions based on preference for the ministers, boasting about charisms (pure gifts) received from the Holy Spirit, social class conflicts between the rich and the poor and theological issues of who is strong or weak in faith.[36] He advocates Christ-like love above all things, as the most desired gift (1 Cor 13); citing himself and his own Christological principles as example (1 Cor 9); and challenging them to imitate him as he imitates Christ (1 Cor 11:1).

EUCHARIST AS THANKSGIVING WAY OF LIFE FOR THE CHRISTIAN

For the Christian as for Christ, the Eucharist is comprehensively *the liturgy of life,* a life of thanksgiving and breaking the bread of one's life so that others may eat, live and have life ever increasingly. Jesus' food and drink (what sustained his life), was to do and complete God's work (Jn 4:31; 17:4). He glorified God by so doing (Jn 17:5). God in turn glorified him (Jn 12:28). People glorified, praised and thanked God for the great works they saw Jesus do. It should be the same for the Christian.

Paul tells the Corinthians, 'Whatever you eat, whatever you drink, whatever you do at all [that is, whatever you do to sustain your life and show that you are alive], do it for the glory of God' (1 Cor 10:31). 'Whatever you do [in word and deed], do it in the name of the Lord Jesus giving thanks to God the Father through him' (Col 3:17). Let God be glorified in the totality of your life. Paul himself was constantly giving thanks to God for his life and for the faith of his brother and sister converts.[37] The spirit of thanksgiving and prayer characterised his stewardship as apostle of the gentiles. Concretely for him and his converts (1 Cor 10:33-11:1) this meant that they do nothing offensive to Jew or gentile (we may add Christian, Muslim, traditional religionist, or any other religious adherent); that they let not their own needs and concerns be the driving force of their life; instead they should break away from the sin of lack of communion and enjoy and promote God's general amnesty for all creation; spend and be spent for others, making others the number one in all they do.

A eucharistic ecclesiology of communion urges us to imitate the first Christian communities where the breaking of the bread of the word and the Eucharist resulted in breaking away from selfishness and sharing of everything they had in common, such that none of their members was ever in want (Acts 2:42-47; 4:32-37). It urges us to flee the modern tendency to worship and serve the false 'trinity' of me, myself and I (with its corresponding branches of me, my family, my community; me, my community, my nation, and so forth). It makes us aware that 'if there is hunger anywhere in the world, the celebration of the Eucharist is somehow incomplete everywhere in the world'.[38] In sum, it invites us to take Christ as our model, since by baptism we are configured to him – prophet, priest and king – with an indelible character and made permanent members of his ecclesial community.

These are some practical ways of being Eucharist, breaking the bread of one's life with a heart full of thanksgiving and love for others to eat and have life to the full. By these actions one lives as a true Christian, another Christ in the world. By them Christ's Eucharist is continually commemorated everywhere in the world. Yet it is impossible to do this without *believing* that God has made us God's beloved sons and daughters. This faith is rooted in God who is love (1 Jn 4:16), a love which not even death can destroy.[39] The victory over death based on this love is not limited to Jesus. Whoever accepts, believes and lives by it, eats his body and drinks his blood, has endless life; even if the person dies, Jesus the resurrection and the life will raise him or her up on the last day. At baptism we are baptised into Christ's death, so that by rising with him we may lead a new life (Rm 6:3-7). Through the food of the Eucharist, Christ lives and acts in every believer, just as the blood circulates and acts in each organ of the body and empowers it to perform its function, like the sap of the vine in the branches. Cut up from him by words and deeds, the believer can do nothing; he or she is dead. These truths have consequences not only for the individual but also for the Church and the world as a whole.

CONSEQUENCES FOR THE CHURCH OF THE EUCHARISTIC WAY OF LIFE

This symposium seeks to promote a eucharistic ecclesiology of communion fifty years after the opening of the Second Vatican Council. In view of this, it is imperative that we revisit as of first importance our self-understanding as Church and the structures by which we govern ourselves as ecclesial community that is the one body of Christ (1 Cor 12:12; Rm 12:4-5). We relate this undertaking to the jubilee call to return to our roots in Christ and that of John Paul II in *Novo Millennio Ineunte,* to change our rules of fishing and learn to fish in daylight under the direction of Christ, the light and life of the world, as a sure way to true, in depth ecclesial communion in this century (*duc in altum*).

Here we are going to face very challenging and fearful issues. Yet our life in Christ and the Church's repeated injunctions about the importance of communion ecclesiology encourages us to boldly revisit and ask Christological questions about our self-understanding as Church and the operative structures thereof. Key areas are the clergy–laity structure, the place of women in the Church, the dichotomy between our rich theologies of oneness in Christ and our operating policies which contradict that oneness. To this we add the subversive nature of language itself (rooted in culture) which plays a key socialising and conditioning role in all this. For practical purposes we will address briefly only the clergy–laity issue. We have taken this for granted as part and parcel of our being a eucharistic Church; but in many respects the structure poses serious obstacles to our being a eucharistic people, truly 'one' (Gal 3:28) in 'the one body of Christ'.

About the women issue, it is perhaps better to say nothing here than to say too little. Yet it is an area we must address in light of Christological truth, the core of our Christian faith: the truth that Jesus took his human body and blood (which he gave as food and drink) 100 per cent from woman; that woman like man is configured to him at baptism through water and the Holy Spirit and becomes 'one' person with him (Gal 3:25-29); Jesus himself claims women along with men as integral part of himself, to cite but a few core truths. A major obstacle to overcome in discussing this issue with Christological freedom is the fear of breaking with tradition. Jesus, and after him Paul, allowed the Spirit to lead them into the complete truth (*duc in altum*) which empowered them to place the gospel and its imperatives above all human traditions, however ancient.

In the last analysis, the issue of women in the Church is not about women or men, much less a case of women versus men and vice versa. It is fundamentally about Jesus himself and the mystery of his incarnation. Did he truly and fully assume humanity, created male and female by God? Or was there something lacking, a deficiency in his assumption of humanity: the female element? Yet he took this humanity 100 per cent from woman by God's deliberate and deliberative will and design. If there was a deficiency, is he in truth the new humanity in whom women and men find their new identity as 'a new creation' (2 Cor 5:17)? If it is true that by his incarnation Christ assumed and united inseparably in himself humanity (male and female), have we the right and authority to separate under any pretext whatsoever what God has consubstantially united to the divine self in Christ? Or was there a part of his humanity which was not involved in his total self-giving in the Eucharist and on the cross? When the discourse on the inclusion of women with particular reference to the Eucharist is put in these terms, a completely new light emerges. We need Peter's humility to listen to Jesus and follow him as he directs us to launch into the deep; plumb the depths of the mystery of his incarnation, his full humanity with reference to men and women. But as said, we leave aside this matter in our ensuing reflection.

THE CLERGY–LAITY ISSUE

To adequately and objectively address the contentious clergy–laity issue we need to return to our New Testament roots. Key questions are these: does the current clergy–laity structure and the sustained theologies on the ministerial priesthood, inseparably connected with being a eucharistic Church, visibly promote our communion in the one body of Christ? Do the current roles assigned to the laity (with the tag, 'at their own level') promote their full dignity and status rooted and centred in Christ and participation as Christ's body in the eucharistic celebration? Fifty years after the opening of the Second Vatican Council, many would agree that 'The ecclesiology which governs our thinking is that the Church is a hierarchy and a clergy to whom the laity serve as clients.'[40] Similarly, how does the abiding tendency to draw permanent lines between the teaching Church (*ecclesia docens,* the clergy) and the learning Church (*ecclesia discens,* the laity) promote the Christian maturity of both parties and ultimately the growth of the entire body into the 'full maturity of Christ' (Eph 4:13)?[41]

On the level of Church as communion, do these divisions promote and mirror forth the truth that the Church is the one body of Christ and that the one Christ lives and acts in all his members without distinction of ranks? Related to this issue is the division between the sacred sphere assigned to sacred ministers and the secular sphere, assigned to the lay faithful whose responsibility is to evangelise. Yet Christ is one. To what extent is it true that the lay faithful live in the secular sphere or have the secular sphere as their mission domain while the clergy and consecrated persons live in the sacred sphere when in reality the entire Church is 'in the world', even if not 'of the world' and the Church as a whole is 'sent to the world' as Jesus 'was sent to the world' (Jn 17:6, 11, 14-15, 18)?[42] The desire to live fully a eucharistic way of life and make the Eucharist a liturgy of life calls us to revisit this clergy–laity issue with Spirit-filled openness so that the Spirit may lead us to the complete truth; so that we may be 'consecrated in the truth' of our call to oneness in Christ; so that we may visibly live that oneness today in answer to Jesus' prayer 'that they may be one as we are one' (Jn 17:22).

The ecclesiology that sees the Church as 'a hierarchy to whom the laity serve as clients' is held by clergy and laity alike. All are socialised into and conditioned by it. The lay faithful for the most part tend to see themselves mainly as people who *attend* Mass, *book* Mass, *offer* Mass intentions, *receive* Holy Communion, *go to* confession, *contribute financially* to Church (indeed the sole financial contributors, by paying tithes [in my part of the Church], Annual Missionary Collection [AMC], and other levies), but who, despite the Second Vatican Council's dogmatic position that the Church is the people of God (LG, chapter 2), do not see themselves, nor are they seen in practice, as being fully integral members of the Church as are members of a family. Our language too betrays us. When we speak, for example, of what the Church says, teaches or desires, we instinctively equate this Church with the Magisterium. Is there a corresponding instance in our thinking where 'Church' applies exclusively or predominantly to the laity? This divide is most prominent in the liturgical and eucharistic life of the Church, the source and summit of Christian life and worship. Yet this is the area where we should concretely manifest, inside and outside the liturgical context, what we say we are in theological discourse. How visibly is the liturgical celebration centred in Christ in all his members? How visible does the one Christ (who lives and acts in all his members) exercise his one priestly ministry in these members?

The demotion of the 'ordinary' Christians from active agents to clients, and their confinement to the status of permanent learners (the term 'laity' connotes apprentice) is not inimical only to the laity. It impoverishes Jesus himself, in so far as he is prevented from coming fully into his own in these so-called laity. The rich talents the Spirit gives to each for the building up of Christ's body, the Church, till it reaches its perfect maturity in Christ (cf. 1 Eph 4:1-16), are suppressed, stifled and prevented from growing, at times deliberately by the person 'in charge' who feels threatened by these talents, instead of welcoming them as free gifts of the Spirit. Such actions are anti-eucharistic and anti-Christ. They impoverish the Church and consolidate the perpetrator in selfishness.

The Constitution on the Sacred Liturgy, the first conciliar document produced by the Council, speaks of the Christocentric nature of the liturgy. The Dogmatic Constitution of the Church (*Lumen Gentium*) is replete with rich theologies of the unity and equality of all the baptised in Christ, specifically through the Eucharist. Subsequent popes have also hammered on this truth.[43] One thing about a circle is that all points from the circumference are equidistant from the centre, though each point is unique. To use the terms of our conference, they are equidistant in communion with Christ, the centre. If Christ is the centre and all baptised are configured to him on equal terms with equal dignity (each given 'the dignity of the firstborn' [Heb 12:22-23] because each is incorporated on equal terms into Christ the first born) and if this configuration is pure grace, then nobody is or should be seen, feel or be made to feel as being 'less' or 'lesser' or 'inferior' in dignity, rank and status to another, as is frequently assumed in our theological and ecclesiological discourse.

Equally, no function in the Church should be seen as being inferior to the other; the body has many parts and each part plays a different but unique God-given function that is essential and indispensable to the body and can therefore not be treated as inferior or expendable. No human being thinks of any of his or her body parts in terms of inferior or superior or as sacred and secular. Our natural body is one; so too the body of Christ, the entire body of the baptised, made sacred, consecrated by God in Christ at baptism. We need to work concertedly to deconstruct our language about us as Church; for language is not neutral to meaning; it forms and informs attitudes and consolidate in internalised perception of self and others.

Perhaps the most disturbing aspect of our current provision for the Eucharistic celebration is that it leaves millions of Catholics worldwide without the Eucharist, in some cases for months. The shortage of priests is something that calls for urgent action, not to wait till we have enough priests, but to pay attention to the needs and right of every Christian to be and to celebrate the Eucharist with the Lord in our midst. The current shortage of priests worldwide may be a blessing in disguise: to lead us to return to our New Testament roots and draw the liberating grace on how to meet this shortage.

The people in the rural areas are not alone deprived. In some urban places priests are available but may choose not to celebrate; or they may celebrate for themselves at their own convenience, since the law tells them that even if they celebrate privately, it is the Church that celebrates. In some cases the people wake up very early in the morning, trek long distances or sweat through heavy morning traffic to go to Mass. When they arrive, the priests may debate whose turn or right it is to say the Mass. Or being only 'resident' or 'visiting' priests, they may feel or be made to feel it not their duty to celebrate for the people. So the people wait in vain for hours then go home 'empty'. Communities of Sisters often wait for a designated chaplain to come and celebrate Mass for them at an agreed time. After over an hour of waiting, they may resort to 'closing' with prayers; or if they have enough consecrated hosts, may conduct Communion service. These and similar situations, by no means rare, should be a matter of grave concern for a eucharistic Church; they call for urgent redress. They amount to injustice to the eucharistic people who come to celebrate the Lord's Supper but cannot, because the one ordained to do so 'for them' decides to be absent.

On the other hand, some committed priests say as many as four Masses a day, especially on Sundays, in some cases travelling distances to do so in the 'out stations', at times with confessions before each Mass in order to meet the needs of the people. Physically and mentally they are exhausted. Even when consecrated persons or committed lay faithful are present, they are deemed unfit to 'assist' in giving Communion (though not to receive it). Who benefits from this whole situation and what does it say about Christ in the Christian?

The jubilee call to return to our roots maps a sure way forward in addressing these matters. The New Testament Churches converted by Paul and the unnamed Christians of Antioch (the 'mother Church' in outreach to gentiles), one that provided inclusive theological and missionary formation for Paul and Barnabas (Acts 11:19-26), would have celebrated the Lord's Supper, though all the apostles stayed put in Jerusalem (Acts 8:1, 4). They would have done so through their faith in the Lord Jesus, who said that where two or three are gathered in his name, he is there in their midst. The real celebrant in the Eucharist is the Lord, whose sacrificial body and blood we celebrate and share. John Paul II holds that at consecration the priest '*puts his voice at the disposal of the one who spoke these words in the Upper Room* and who desires that they be repeated in every generation by all those who in the Church ministerially share in his priesthood'.[44] The theology and perimeters of our current 'ministerial priesthood' are set by Church leadership; not by Christ. A renewed eucharistic ecclesiology invites us as Church to return to revisit how a eucharistic community in whose midst is the living Lord, can lend its voice to the Lord in diverse situations so that the majority of Christians, body of Christ, may not be deprived for days, even months, on end from partaking in the Eucharist.

The Corinthian Christians evangelised by Paul also celebrated the Lord's Supper without him (1 Cor 11:17-34).[45] The same applied to the many other 'Churches of God' mentioned in the letter to the Corinthians and other letters. We need to place our current understanding and exercise of ministerial priesthood alongside the daily needs and Christological right of the people to celebrate the Eucharist, receive the body and blood of Christ. Let us allow the Lord and the New Testament Christians, our ancestors in the faith, to lead us forward to a christocentric (as opposed to a priest-centric) approach to the celebration of the Eucharist. If we listen in faith and humility with disciples' ears (as Peter did in Lk 11:1-5), the Lord will show us the right way forward so that the Eucharist and the sacraments can be readily accessible to many 'ordinary' people who are otherwise deprived through no fault of their own. The New Testament Churches had a diversity of ministries. Interestingly, priesthood is not one of them. This does not mean that it is irrelevant. The priesthood is central to the Eucharist because it is the one priesthood of Christ. The issue at stake is how we, equal members of this one Christ, administer and participate in his priesthood, with specific reference to the Eucharist.

THE WAY FORWARD FOR A EUCHARISTIC CHURCH IN SEARCH OF COMMUNION ECCLESIOLOGY

Jesus, 'the way, the truth, and the life', is the only way forward in this matter. The laity/clergy like the man/woman issue in the Church calls us to boldly and courageously launch into the deep (*duc in altum*) at Jesus' instructions for an abundant catch. This requires that we courageously desist from elaborating and holding unto theologies that defend and sustain inherited empire-based Church structures and traditions. If it is true that Christ is one; that all the baptised are incorporated into him on equal terms and that 'one should not believe that Christ is in the head but not in the body; rather he is complete in the head and the body',[46] then we need to revisit from a Christological standpoint such terms as '*in persona Christi*' (applied exclusively to the ordained priest) and the belief that our union in Christ is both 'hierarchical' and 'fraternal', as if Christ was 'divided up' (1 Cor 1:10-13). These terms are rooted in unevangelised cultures that originated mainly from the donation of Constantine, not from Christ.[47] They divide up Christ and his priesthood, as does the belief that priests only share in the fullness of the bishop's priesthood, rather than in that of Christ.

The evident confusion between faith and practice in these matters needs to be humbly acknowledged and addressed dispassionately in the light of the Christ of the gospels. Jesus had a clear place for leadership in his Church, so leadership is not irrelevant. No group can exist and function well without a leader. Jesus' 'hierarchical' leadership was a reversed pyramid, where the leaders are actually, not theoretically, at the bottom, as servants of the people. The washing of the feet, set in the context of the Last Supper and the Eucharist, concretises this. Paul understood and imbibed this spirit when he described his ministry and that of Apollo among the Corinthians as 'servants through whom' the Corinthians believed (1 Cor 3:5). In his reversed pyramid, they (Paul, Apollos and Cephas) are at the bottom, with everything including themselves 'for' the people, the people for Christ and Christ for God (1 Cor 22-23). Furthermore, though all things have been subjected to Christ, ultimately Christ will subject even himself to God 'so that God may be all in all' (1 Cor 15:24-28). Needless to say, in the reversed pyramid, the servants, 'stewards entrusted with God's mysteries', are at the bottom; they need and receive the most abundant grace to enable them to render effective, trustworthy service to God's people (1 Cor 4:1-13), the body of Christ.

Revisiting the inherited empire structures will help us to promote a deeper and more *visible* celebration of the Eucharist as Christ alive and active in his brothers and sisters in the liturgy and in real life. Actively making Christ the centre and focus in all aspects of our life as Christians, especially in the liturgy, will minimise and eventually eliminate the tendency to reduce the Eucharist to mere ritual celebration, which often does not flow into the life of participants (priests and people) and the tendency by some to make it a matter of boasting ('I am a Catholic priest, without me you can do nothing in the sacraments and the parish'). Christ gave his life for us in the Eucharist, yet many priests tend to make a living and a status symbol out of it. Revisiting the structures and values inherited from the empire will also shed light on many ecumenical questions where our history-based criteria impede the unity for which Christ died; for which he prayed and which he left us in his dying will.

It can also lead to discovering unexpected priestly figures in the New Testament, such as the Syrophoenician woman (Mk 7:24-30),[48] the boy with five loaves and two fish and the widow who put in all she had to live on in the treasury. By surrendering the totality of her life into the treasury (Mk 12:21-44), she exemplifies on the one hand the foolishness of love that stops at nothing, not even the saving of one's life, and on the other, the critique of a religion that would condition a destitute widow to do this. She is, in all respects, a Christ figure, who surrendered his entire life to God 'for us and for our salvation'. Soon after noticing and praising the woman's action in the Marcan schema, Jesus would experience his own total rejection by a religious leadership that had converted stewardship of the Torah into ownership (Mk 12–16). He would put not merely his livelihood or 'all he had to live on', but his entire life into God's hands (Lk 22:46) in death and resurrection, so that all humanity may have life in its fullness.

As we launch into the deep, we draw inspiration from the New Testament Churches which had a diversity of ministries,[49] rather than centring every ministry in the priest, consequently overburdening him and in the process curtailing the effectiveness of the ministry, reducing a powerful workforce – by far the largest body of ministers of the Lord, the so-called laity – to largely passive onlookers in what they tag *Uka Fada* (Igbo, 'Father's Church').[50] The need to diversify ministries is necessary, not merely because there is a sharp decline in priestly vocations (especially in the west); but essentially because our faithfulness to being a eucharistic Church in the one body of Christ requires it. It is a matter of allowing Christ to come fully and in practice into his own in all his members.

ON THE GLOBAL LEVEL

The eucharistic way of life (self-giving, sharing and thanksgiving), is rooted in the recognition that everything we have and are as individuals, Church and human family, comes from God as grace: pure unmerited gift (1 Cor 4:7). We gave ourselves nothing: race, colour, sex, nationality, abilities, intelligence, prowess, astuteness, life itself. Creation and the earth's ability to produce food are God's gift (Gn 1:11-12). Even our technological discoveries are possible because God put in creation the conditions which make them possible. Besides, our generation today builds on the cumulative knowledge and discoveries of past generations going back to the most ancient times, especially ancient Egypt and Africa as a whole.[51]

Embracing the Eucharist as a way of life launches us on the path of authentic communion, in line with the will of our creator God. Because it is essentially a life of self-giving and sharing, it holds the key to sustainable solutions to our human problems at all levels; solutions to domestic, ethnic, political, economic, gender-based and religious violence; all forms of exploitation in the home, in society and in the Church. It holds the key for how to tackle the multifaceted problems of international relations and the raging and reigning issues of ecology, environmental degradation and global warming, the manufacture and proliferation of arms and the 'grabbing' of land in developing countries by rich foreigners.

Concerning the arms race, embracing the Eucharist as a way of life moves us to review the tacit approval of the arms industry as a normal way to make a living, when in reality it is and should be viewed as the greatest of crimes against humanity. If arms were not manufactured and sold, we would have no wars, destruction of innocent lives (especially women, children and the aged), child soldiers, militarism and related crimes that ravage our world. We live in fear of the threat of nuclear war. Yet this threat is not from forces inimical to humanity. It is human beings themselves who manufacture these nuclear and other weapons of mass destruction that risk exterminating all of us. Is it muted that powerful nations have nuclear projects as backup to protect themselves from other human beings in case of necessity. How honest are we with ourselves that we want a nuclear-free world? Is it really impossible to beat our swords (weapons of mass destruction), now carried out by robots and drones, into ploughshares (means of life-sustenance) to feed the increasing masses of hungry, homeless and jobless people worldwide? It is sober to remember that we are all in one big airboat, our planet earth. If it explodes, we all get blown up together, regardless of our sophisticated measures of self protection. The earth, all its peoples and all it holds belong to God (Ps 24:1; 89:11). Natural disasters, such as tsunami, are a warning that it is not in our power to control, command and dominate nature. Let the wise learn from these disasters.

Embracing the Eucharist as a way of life gives us the inexhaustible energy to promote in a sustained and committed way the fundamental human rights adopted by the United Nations in 1948 (over fifty years ago): that nobody shall be discriminated against on the basis of race, sex, nationality, colour, religion or any reason whatsoever; and to meet the UN millennium development goals, especially with regard to the eradication of poverty. Since everything is unmerited grace from God, no body or group or nation has the right to deprive, intimidate, control, exploit another or nature in whatever manner. Rather all are called to recognise, celebrate, promote, share and give thanks to God for creation, to serve and reverence the gift which is the other in *the liturgy of life*. This *liturgy of life,* rooted in selfless service, not only promotes the other, it also ennobles and enables the one who practises it to move freely, respectfully and with joy in the world, knowing that at creation God gave the earth with all it holds to humanity as heritage and trust (Gn 1:28-29) to tend and cultivate; a joy that increases from knowing that through the mystery of the incarnation, God personally entered our world more wonderfully to recreate it anew and become one of us.

At the last judgement, Jesus, 'the son of man' ('the human being'), will take his seat on the judgement throne and all humanity (not just Christians) will assemble before him. Some will go to eternal life because they served him in the needs of other human beings.[52] Others will go to eternal punishment, because they did not serve him in other human beings. The service in question is about sustaining life in its most basic necessities: 'I was hungry and you gave me food, thirsty and you gave me drink. I was a stranger and you made me welcome. Lacking clothes and you clothed me, sick and you visited me, in prison and you came to see me' (Mt 25:34-35). As Jesus' disciples it is our duty to feed the people, not to send them away to fend for themselves (Mk 6:35-37) or, worse still, like bad shepherds (Jn 10:1-13; Ez 34), to feed on them under cover of being ministers of the Lord. When we obey his instructions, Jesus will empower us to feed the millions of hungry people and have a surplus, though we may initially complain that we do not have enough and that the earth's resources are diminishing. The miracle happens in the sharing.

The *Eucharist way of life* by nature reaches out to those in need, in the jubilee spirit. It calls for thanksgiving and sharing rooted in the recognition that we have no right or authority whatsoever to appropriate, usurp and accumulate for ourselves, our families, nations or geo-political zones or economic blocks, the fruits of the earth and the cumulative and progressive technological knowledge of all humanity to the increasing impoverishment of others tagged 'outsiders', weak, poor (better 'impoverished') or developing. The parables of the rich fool (Lk 12:16-21) and of the rich man and Lazarus (Lk 16:19-31) challenge all of us individually and collectively to awareness of the futility of hoarding up this world's goods (whatever their nature) for ourselves and those we regard as 'ours', thus dehumanising ourselves and impoverishing others in the process.

TOWARDS A CONCLUSION

The celebration of 'the Eucharist as ecclesiology of communion' in this fiftieth jubilee year of its International Congress is an invitation to embrace more consciously the *Eucharist as a way of life* and *the liturgy of life*. This jubilee, strictly speaking, is the first real jubilee in the biblical sense of the word. As recalled at the beginning, the jubilee was to be celebrated every fifty years; for most people that is once in a lifetime. Its core message is a return to the roots for renewed vision, energy and impetus to live the covenanted life. For us Christians the covenanted life is rooted in the Eucharist with its new commandment to love as Jesus loves us (Jn 13:34-35; 15:13); it is a life of thanksgiving and of setting free captives (ourselves and others) from anti-eucharistic practices. This love alone marks us out as authentic followers of Christ, whatever our walk in life. May this current celebration propel us to return to our roots in Christ, the living bread of life, who has been with us throughout this session. In him, with him and through him we will arrive at that ecclesiology of communion which is not only for Christians, let alone Catholics, but which John Paul II calls '*a project of solidarity* for all of humanity'.[53]

May we together cultivate that *eucharistic mindset* which will make us a living and visible ecclesial community anchored in Jesus who indivisibly united in himself the whole of humanity to divinity,[54] and who invites us to do the same. May Jesus help us to embrace the Eucharist as our God-given identity in him. When we do this, our celebration of the 50th International Eucharistic Congress will be a true proclamation, in our communities and today's world, of God's general amnesty to the entire human family and creation. Our celebration will be a true communion of love, nourished and sustained by Christ who is the bread of life for the world and who invites us to be the same. We pray for the grace to listen to him with hearts full of love and launch into the deep for a Christ centred ecclesial communion that is rooted in the Trinity, into whose life and communion all

Christians are baptised and continually drawn. The Trinity has one mind and heart, holds all things in common and acts in unison for the good of the entire creation; so may it be with us who through Jesus' eucharistic way of life are privileged to be Eucharist with him as substantial members of his body, his brothers and sisters, 'heirs of God and co-heirs with Christ'. May God give us all the grace together to courageously and fearlessly launch into the deep as Jesus directs us.

Amen.

NOTES

1 Many regarded it a special blessing that the decree on the Sacred Liturgy, *Sacrosanctum Concilium*, was the first treated by the Council, because the Liturgy deals with the worship life of the Church, with the Eucharist forming the 'source and summit of all Christian life'; see also Peter Schineller SJ and Justin Ukpong, eds, *Eucharist: Source and Summit of Christian Life: Reflections on the Eucharist in Relation to Christian Life*, Port Harcourt: CIWA Publications, 1982.

2 Before the Council, dogmatic or systematic theology ranked before scripture, while scripture was seen largely as the handmaid of dogma, with the mission to find proof texts for the Church's dogmatic declarations in a process tagged 'dogmatic exegesis'. The Council reversed this order by putting scripture in the first rank and recognising that 'sacred theology' relies on scripture as its 'permanent foundation' (DV, 24)

3 This recognition has a long history as the following references in chronologically descending order show: Benedict XVI, *Verbum Domini* (VD, 31; citing the Second Vatican Ecumenical Council on the Dogmatic Constitution on Divine Revelation *Dei Verbum* (DV, 24; also Leo XIII, Encyclical Letter *Providentissimus Deus, ASS* 26 (1893–94), 269–92; and Benedict XV, Encyclical Letter *Spiritus Paraclitus, ASS* 12 (1920), 385–422.

4 This message was reported on EWTN news on 23 March 2012. Naturally if in the exercise one notices a clash between the traditions of the Church and the teaching of scripture, scripture will take corrective precedence over the traditional practice.

5 Second Vatican Council, DV, 24, also cited by Benedict XVI, VD, 31.

6 What is said here is essentially of the Sabbath, but it applies equally in the jubilee year which comes after a Sabbath of seven weeks of years.

7 This is Peter's interpretation of the Pentecost event. The event was not merely God's 'sending of the Holy Spirit on the apostles' as we have it in the third glorious mystery and in paintings of the Pentecost event featuring only the Twelve and our Lady in their midst; she could not be conveniently left out as were the other men and several women disciples, numbering 'about a hundred and twenty' (Acts 1:15). On Peter's interpretation of Pentecost, see also, Teresa Okure, ed., *To Cast Fire upon the Earth: Bible and Mission Collaborating in Today's Muticultural Global Context,* Pietermaritzburg: Cluster Publications, 2000, pp. 5–6.

8 Pope John Paul II, trans., At the Beginning of the New Millennium: Apostolic Letter, *Novo Millennio Ineunte* Nairobi: Paulines Publications Africa, 2001. See in particular, section 'III: Starting Afresh with Christ', nos. 29–41; with no. 35 on 'The Sunday Eucharist'. Earlier the Pope had decried what he called 'our deviations from the gospel'.

9 See NMI, 11.

10 The New Jerusalem Bible, note 'e' on Luke 22:15. See in particular, Benedict XVI, Post-Synodal Apostolic Exhortation *Sacramentum Caritatis, The Sacrament of Charity*, Vatican City: Libreria Editrice Vaticana, 2007; Nairobi: Paulines Publications, 2007, 'Spirituality and Eucharistic Culture', no. 77.

11 One thinks of 'O Bread of Heaven beneath this veil' or the most celebrated hymn composed for a previous International Eucharistic Congress, 'You satisfy the hungry heart, with gifts of bread and wine'.

12 Joseph Cardinal Ratzinger, Benedict XVI, *Jesus of Nazareth, Part Two: Holy Week: From the Entrance into Jerusalem to the Resurrection*, Vatican City: Libreria Editrice Vaticana; India: ACT Publications, 2011, gives a good survey of the relatively recent literature on this issue; see esp., 'The Last Supper', pp. 103–44.

13 A quick way to access the abundant literature is to do a Google search on 'the Eucharist'. On recent Church documents we may cite *Ecclesia de Eucharistia* of John Paul II (Vatican City: Libreria Editrice Vaticana, 2003), with rich references to previous Church documents and theological works; the Post-Synodal Apostolic Exhortations of Benedict XVI: *Sacramentum Caritatis* (on the Eucharist); *Verbum Domini*, no. 54 (this extends into the section on the 'Sacramentality of the Word', no. 56, and passim); *Africae Munus: Africa's Commitment to Christ* (on the Second African Synod; Vatican City: Libreria Editrice Vaticana, 2011), esp., 'Spirituality of communion' (nos. 34–5, 'the gift of Christ: the Eucharist and the word of God', 39–41, and 'the Eucharist', nos. 152–4). The very fact that this is the 50th International Eucharistic Congress since the Second Vatican Ecumenical Council speaks for itself of the abiding interest in the Eucharist.

14 To note in passing, if the natural food that sustains our natural life is real not symbolic, why should the food we eat to sustain our spiritual life be symbolic, not naturally spiritual? As real physical life requires real physical food, so does real spiritual life require real spiritual food. 'It is the Spirit that causes to live' (Jn 6:63); that is why the only condition for receiving this food is to believe in Jesus, God's bread from heaven as he propounds its meaning to us. Both the physical and the spiritual food are provided by one and the same God who gives and has the right to provide sustenance for each type of life. Human beings have no authority or right whatsoever to veto or negotiate what God offers for enduring life-sustenance us as pure grace.

15 The primary reference of the terms Son and Father in this discussion as in John's Gospel and other New Testament works is not 'maleness'. Their primary reference is origin and exact correspondence (like Father/Parent, like Son/Child). Jesus declares that all that is done to the Son is done to the Father; all that the Father does the Son does, since the Father and Son are one (Jn 5:19, 21, 26). Revelation 12:5, which speaks of 'a male son' (*hyion arsen*), is clear indication that the primary reference to 'son' (*hyios*) is not maleness since it would make little sense to speak of 'a male male son'. African languages have no problem in this matter; most if not all of them,

have separate words for child (male or female; *eyen* in my language, Ibibio) and son and daughter (*eyen eden* or *awuden* and *eyen anwan* or *awuan* in Efik/Ibibio, respectively). It is perhaps because Father signified source or ground of our being that Jesus forbade us to call anyone on earth 'father since we all have only one Father and he is in heaven'. Secondly, the earthly practice by which a child is called after the father to the exclusion of the mother may be an added reason. Jesus had an earthly biological mother but no biological father. Joseph was his legal father. Perhaps too he spoke of his heavenly Father to distinguish this from his earthly legal father, which Joseph became through faith, even as Mary became his biological mother through faith. That was all God's work. See further my '"Joseph Husband of Mary"' (Mt 1:18-25): A Gospel Recipe for Conflict Resolution and Reconciliation for the Church in Africa', a paper given at the XIVth Congress of the Panafrican Association of Catholic Exegetes (PACE), on Conflicts and Reconciliation in the Bible, St Gall Major Seminary, Ouidah, République de Bénin, 2nd–9th September 2009.

16 See for instance Bartimaeus, the blind man at Jericho (Mk 10:46-52ss.); the Scribes (Mk 12:35-37ss.); and comprehensively by the crowds at his triumphant entry in Jerusalem (Mt 21:1-11ss), where Jesus' entry into Jerusalem is interpreted as 'the coming kingdom of David our father' (Mk 11:10).

17 Remarkably the title 'King' was always affixed to David right to the genealogy of Jesus though other kings lacked such designation. As a person and ruler, he was 'a man after my [God's] own heart'.

18 For my extensive analysis of this linkage, see my '"Joseph Husband of Mary"', note 15 above; forthcoming.

19 In brief, sacrifice from the African traditional and other contexts is something by which the one who offers it seeks to appease the gods of the land, ask a favour, seek the cause and solution for problem in the land, and so forth. It is essentially something that the lesser offers to the greater to obtain something. I have developed this in my 'Hebrews: Sacrifice in an African Perspective', *Global Bible Commentary*, Daniel Patte, J. Severino Coratto, Archie Lee, Teresa Okure, and Nicole Duran, eds., Nashville: Abingdon, 2004, pp. 535–8.

20 The traditional hymn, 'Help Lord the Souls which thou has made' captures well this theology.

21 Friends in the New Testament era was not just a 'pal' type of relationship but a political title or honour whereby the one so honoured received a special social post from the one who gave that friendship. The rank in the social order was family, friends, and then close associates. The story of the seven Maccabees, where Antiochus promises to give the last son the title of 'Friend of the King' (2 Mac 7:24) illustrates this.

22 See Teresa Okure, note 16 above.

23 See in particular Rm 5:6-11; 8:31-39; 2 Cor 5:14-15.

24 Scholars have written volumes on the meaning of 'son of man' in the New Testament, especially in John's Gospel. My simple understanding is that when we listen closely to the contexts in which Jesus refers to himself as 'the son of man' (Aramaic: *bar enash or enosh*), the core referent is his humanity. What Bultmann would call 'the scandal of the flesh' (*sarx*). In Ibibio/Efik/Annang the translation would be '*eyen owo*', which means 'child of a human being', irrespective of whether the child is male or female.

25 A classic example here is John Chrysostom, 'As a woman nourishes her child with her own blood and milk, so does Christ unceasingly nourish with his own blood those to whom he himself as given life', *Catechesis* 3, 13–19; *Sources Chrétiennes* 50, 174–7; see also Second Reading of the Office of Readings for Good Friday.

26 The Eucharist has other names: The Lord's Supper, the Last Supper, the Supper of the Lamb (in the recent rite of the Church, picking up from Revelations) and 'the mysteries' in the works of the Fathers of the Church.

27 See the feeding of 'four thousand men' (Mk 6:44); 'four thousand people' (Mk 8:10), and 'five thousand men' (Jn 6:10) with their parallels in Matthew and Luke. For after the resurrection see Lk 24:30-31 and Jn 21:13.

28 Mk 12:1-12; Mt 21:33-46; Lk 20:9-19.

29 Teresa Okure, *The Johannine Approach to Mission: A Contextual Study of John 4:1–42*, WUNT 2.31 (Tübingen: JCB Mohr [Paul Siebeck], 1988), p. 217; ibid. 'John', in *International Bible Commentary: A Catholic and Ecumenical Commentary for the Twenty-First Century,* William R. Farmer et al., eds, Collegeville: Liturgical Press, 1998, pp. 1438–1505.

30 John Paul II observes that '*A causal influence of the Eucharist* is present at the Church's very origins', *Ecclesia de Eucharistia,* no. 21; he develops this further in nos. 21–5, 'the Eucharist builds the Church'.

31 See also, Raymond E. Brown, *The Churches the Apostles Left Behind,* New York/Ramsey: Paulist Press, 1984, 89, n. 130.

32 We may cite here, Brown, who says, 'Money and power are two principal values in this world; and it would be a sociological miracle if church institutions, inescapably patterned on surrounding institutions, would not be tempted to take over such institutions' (*The Churches the Apostles Left Behind,* p. 55).

33 Benedict XVI speaks this of at length in *Sacramentum Caritatis,* Part III, nos. 70–93: 'The Eucharist: A Mystery to be Lived.'

34 See further, Teresa Okure, 'John', p. 1501.

35 Actually, from Jesus' declaration of God's general amnesty to all creation, every human being is in sate of or under the dominion of grace ('not of sin'), God's grace open to all; for grace and truth, not law and merit or personal holiness and achievement, came with Jesus Christ (Jn 1:17).

36 For more on this see, Teresa Okure, 'The Ministry of Reconciliation' (2 Cor 5:14-21): Paul's Key to the Problem of 'the Other' in Corinth', *Mission Studies* 23.1 (2006), pp. 105–21.

37 Every one of his letters (except Galatians) begins with greetings, an address, thanksgiving and prayer (e.g. 1 Th 1:2-10; Rm 1:8-9; Cor 1:4-9; 2 Cor 1:1-11; Phil 1:3-11, etc.). Then there are the more extended thanksgiving and prayers in the Pauline letters: Eph 1:3-14; 3:14-21; Col 1: 3-14, etc.

38 From an address of Fr Pedro Arrupe SJ, at the International Eucharistic Congress in 1976, some thirty-six years ago. Cited in Augustine Nebechukwu, 'The Eucharist and Hunger for Food', *Eucharist Source and Summit of Christian Life*, Peter Schineller and Justin Ukpong, eds, p. 61.

39 Jn 15:13; 1 Cor 13: 1-13; Songs 8:6.

40 A. de Sousa, 'Wanted: A Seminary for a New Way of Being Church', *Vidjayoti* 65 (2001), pp. 60–5, p. 61. The author here decries the current operative system which makes the priest believe that merely by becoming a priest he has the expertise for everything, from Church matters to economics, architecture and so forth, such that he can say 'without me you can do nothing', without him there is no sacraments and even Church.

41 Raymond E. Brown, *The Church the Apostles Left Behind,* New York/Ramsey: Paulist, 1984, pp. 43–5, outlines the dangers and mutual impoverishment which this dichotomy between the teaching church and the learning Church causes to both the teachers and the taught. Ultimately it is the body of Christ that suffers.

42 See also Teresa Okure, 'The Church in the World: A Dialogue in Ecclesiology', *Theology and Conversation: Towards a Relational Theology*, J. Haers & P. De Mey, eds., BETL CLXXII; Leuven: Leuven University Press Peeters, 2003, pp. 393–437, esp. pp. 400–4.

43 See for instance, John Paul II, *Ecclesia de Eucharistia,* pp. 22–3 (where he remarks that 'the Eucharist reinforces the incorporation into Christ which took place at baptism through the gift of the Spirit'), and cites 1 Cor 10:16-17 on '*the unifying power*' of the Eucharist; ibid., *Mane Nobiscum* 21 (where he speaks of the Eucharist as '*the epiphany of communion*' [italics in original]); Benedict XVI, *Sacramentum Caritatis* 36 (quoting Augustine [*Treatise on John's Gospel*, 28,1; *Pl* 35, 1622]) says 'one should not believe that Christ is in the head but not in the body; rather he is complete in the head and the body'.

44 John Paul II, *Ecclesia de Eucharistia* 5, Nairobi: Paulines Publications Africa, 2003, 2009; italics in original.

45 One gets the impression from what Paul says that theirs was truly a communal or ecclesial celebration. The problem was not that they celebrated without him but that they celebrated without recognising Christ's presence in each one of them, especially among the poor. Respect of ranks in the community, according to James is a contradiction in terms for Christ's people a breaking of the law of love (2:1-9). Respect of persons

is not the same as respect for persons. None should be deprived of respect in the house and family of God.

46 Benedict XVI, *Sacramentum Caritatis* 36 (see note 43 above).

47 The clergy–laity divide as we have it today is a donation of Constantine, who, to stabilise his empire, stopped the persecution of Christians, raised bishops to the rank of senators and the clergy to the next rank; thus giving them 'exalted positions' after the manner of the kings of the gentiles. In the process we progressively developed theologies to sustain this donation and other legacies from the empire, at the expense of the gospel; they are with us till today.

48 See further Teresa Okure, 'A Syrophoenician Woman's Share in Jesus' Priestly Ministry', *Healing Priesthood*. Women's Commission of the UK Bishop's Conference, London: Darton, Longman and Todd, 2003, pp. 115–18.

49 I have explored this issue at some length in 'The Church in the World: A Dialogue in Ecclesiology', pp. 417–21.

50 Though Vatican Council II opened the windows for the laity to look through them to see what was happening inside the Church, as some lay faithful describe their status; these lay faithful want to come right inside not only to see but also to be full participants in what is happening inside the Church. It is their baptismal right to do so as members of God's family.

51 The foundational role of Africa in promoting civilisation is becoming increasingly acknowledged. Africa taught humanity to walk, talk; taught science, organised religion, monotheism, the idea of life after death and so forth. The Museum of Origins in Johannesburg and increasing research by African scholars at home and the diaspora testify to this see www.origins.co.za; email: info@originscentre.co.za.

52 This is the point why Jesus designates himself here as a son of man, a human being. Whatever is done to a *human being* is done to him. Greek says *adelpoi mou* 'my siblings', since the term embraced all classes of kindred alive, male and female. The New Revised Standard Version of the Bible translates it as 'members of my family' using inclusive language. The point is that all human beings are brothers and sisters of Jesus, the new humanity. So what is done to any of human being is done to him. This too is worth a thought.

53 John Paul II, Apostolic Letter for the Year of the Eucharist 2005, *Mane Nobiscum*, Nairobi: Paulines Publications Africa, 2004, 2005, no. 27; (italics in original); here the Pope further cites Vatican Council II which sees the Church as 'sign and instrument' not only of intimate union with God but of the unity of the whole human race' (LG, 1).

54 See, for instance, John Paul II, *Redemptor Hominis* 13; *Redemptoris Missio* 10, 2; *Novo Millennio Ineunte* 49, where he also cites previous Church documents on the matter.

DRAWN DAY BY DAY
EUCHARISTIC ECCLESIOLOGY FROM THE PERSPECTIVE OF A LITURGICAL THEOLOGIAN

PROF. DR MARTIN STUFLESSER
Julius-Maxmillians University, Würzburg, Germany

1. INTRODUCTORY REMARKS: CONSIDERATIONS ON THE OCCASION OF TWO ANNIVERSARIES

Next week, from 10th–17th June, 2012, when the International Eucharistic Congress gathers in Dublin, the meeting marks a double anniversary. On the one hand, the 50th International Eucharistic Congress is being celebrated. On the other, the Congress is taking place fifty years after the opening of the Second Vatican Council by Blessed John XXIII. In my paper, I will seek to link both anniversaries. I wish to link reflection on this year's Congress, 'The Eucharist: Communion with Christ and with One Another'[1] with a re-reading of what the Second Vatican Council has now, fifty years on, given us regarding what we as Roman Catholics celebrate when we celebrate the Eucharist. The Pontifical Committee for the International Eucharistic Congress recalls that 'The Second Vatican Council could be described as a Pentecostal event that remains a sure compass by which the Church today too takes its bearings.'[2]

My remarks will be bound by this compass. As a liturgical theologian I will base my comments above all on the text of the Liturgy Constitution, *Sacrosanctum Concilium* (SC). Next year, 4th December 2013, is the fiftieth anniversary of its promulgation as the first document of the Second Vatican Council. In view of this anniversary of almost fifty years of what, in my opinion, has been a thoroughly successful reform of the liturgy in our Church, the following considerations seek to provide a deeper understanding of the fundamental liturgical affirmations and paradigms of the Liturgy Constitution. The title of my talk comes from this document, where it says:

> The Church, therefore, earnestly desires that Christ's faithful, when present at this mystery of faith, should not be there as strangers or silent spectators; on the contrary, through a good understanding of the rites and prayers they should take part in the sacred action conscious of what they are doing, with devotion and full collaboration. They should be instructed by God's Word and be nourished at the table of the Lord's body; they should give thanks to God; by offering the Immaculate Victim, not only through the hands of the priest, but also with him, they should learn also to offer themselves; through Christ the Mediator, they should be drawn day by day into ever more perfect union with God and with each other, so that finally God may be all in all.[3]

This article from SC guides what follows in outlining the contours of a eucharistic ecclesiology.[4] I will reflect on the theme of the Eucharistic Congress, 'The Eucharist: Communion with Christ and with One Another', under the theme of participation (1 Cor 10:16-17)[5] in the (Paschal) mystery, which is celebrated in the Eucharist because 'in the Eucharist we discover the genetic code of communion that is at the heart of the Church's identity'.[6]

Building on this foundation, I shall develop the paper as follows: in asking what are the possibilities for celebrating communion with Christ and with one another in the Eucharist, we must first understand what we celebrate when we celebrate the eucharistic liturgy. SC 48 speaks of 'this mystery'. We need to understand this. So firstly, what is the meaning of the celebration of the Eucharist? Then, how is this meaning expressed appropriately in the form (shape) of the celebration? In other words, how do we celebrate the (eucharistic) liturgy in an appropriate manner? Once again, SC 48 offers a model when it states that we should 'take part in the sacred action conscious of what (we) are doing, with devotion and full collaboration'. What is meant precisely by this? Finally, I want to summarise what has been said up to this point and then conclude with a theology of sacrifice.

2. ASCERTAINING WHAT WE CELEBRATE WHEN WE CELEBRATE THE (EUCHARISTIC) LITURGY?

As already noted, in reference to the Eucharist, SC 48 speaks of a 'sacred action' that the celebration of the 'mystery of faith' represents. This 'mystery' is something that the faithful, as the desire of the council puts it, should come to understand. So it seems useful at this point to verify what the council means when it speaks in the constitution on the liturgy of 'mystery,' or more precisely, of the 'Paschal mystery'.

2.1. Entrance: A Prayer with Important Contents

> Gedenke ... (Good Friday prayer text)[7]
> Remember your mercies, O Lord
> and with your eternal protection sanctify your servants,
> for whom Christ your Son,
> by the shedding of his blood
> established the Paschal mystery,
> who lives and reigns for ever and ever. Amen.

Thus begins the Good Friday liturgy of the suffering and death of our Lord. Our God is asked to think about the great deeds of salvation which he worked in the past for his people. The petition in this prayer makes it clear that the greatest deed is the Easter redemptive act, the Paschal mystery that his Son, our Lord Jesus Christ, consecrated in his suffering, death and resurrection. Indeed the question asked at the start of this paper – what do we celebrate when we celebrate the eucharistic liturgy? – is answered only with the help of this prayer. Two major key concepts stand out in this prayer. The liturgy is described as a memorial and the content of this memorial-celebration is described as the 'Paschal mystery'. We will look now at both these concepts and seek to clarify them in order to show what they have to do with the memorial of the Paschal mystery in the liturgy.

2.2. The Core of Liturgical Theology: Memorial of the Paschal Mystery

2.2.1. 'Remember, Lord ... ' What does Anamnesis/Memory mean?

To answer this question we must look once more at what is happening in the so-called Anamnesis, that is, in the first section of the Good Friday prayer.[8] The liturgist Hans Bernhard Meyer explains the Anamnesis in liturgical prayer as follows:

> Anamnesis is the mediated contemporaneity of the celebrants, through the liturgical celebration, with past history, but also with

> the situation of the future-promised redemption, in which they have obtained a share, as well as an encounter with its foundation, the Triune God and Sovereign Lord ... [9]

Anamnesis, the celebration of memorial, is not about what we subjectively remember, but rather through the Anamnesis, the redemptive act of God becomes present in the liturgical celebration, so continues Meyer, just as we are present to the event. By way of example of how Anamnesis of God's redemptive act means more than simply a 'devout remembering', think of the Jewish Passover celebration. Today still in 2012, when a Jewish family celebrates the Passover, the youngest participant asks the father of the house: why is this night so different to all the other nights? And the father of the house answers: once we were slaves, now we are free!

The freeing of Israel from slavery in Egypt is recounted as a present event. The Anamnesis of the salvific event is not reporting something in the past. No, God's saving action appears here and now, even though the flight of the Israelites from Pharoah, goes back hundreds and indeed thousands of years. Hans Bernhard Mayer would say that the Jewish family gathered for the Passover meal is contemporary with the event, and they obtain a share in this freedom which has been given through God's saving action.

On the basis of this understanding of Anamnesis, it becomes possible for the prayer over the gifts of the second Sunday in the year, which is also the prayer over the gifts for Holy Thursday, to describe the presence of Christ's offering in the following words:

> Grant us, O Lord, we pray,
> that we may participate worthily in these mysteries,
> for whenever the memorial of this sacrifice is celebrated
> the work of our redemption is accomplished.
> Through Christ our Lord.

Going by the Latin text[10] which also lies behind the Liturgy Constitution *Sacrosanctum Concilium* 2, the verb of the original version *exseritur* ('come out, be revealed, be audible, visible, tangible') was weakened to *exercetur*.[11] If you take the original version of *exseritur* literally, it means that in the liturgical celebration of the memorial, the saving deeds of the past are happening here and now.

This liturgical Anamnesis is directed firstly to God the Father. 'celebration of the memorial' means confronting God with his own saving action. Not because God might be forgetful, but rather because in terms of the inner logic of prayer, we can do no other than confront God with his own saving action: The one who is praying is firstly in the presence of God; praising God 'here and now'. He remembers the former saving action of God, thanks God for his saving action in the past and then finally – trusting that God is faithful and will fulfill his promises – he utters a prayer to God that draws him towards the future. The very first opening prayer of the Good Friday celebration of the suffering and death of Christ expresses this in a very concentrated form: 'Remember your mercies, O Lord, and with your eternal protection sanctify your servants.'

2.2.2. 'Easter Mystery': What does the Paschal Mystery Mean?
When we try to clarify what the notion of 'Easter mystery' ('Paschal mystery') means, in German we come up against an issue of translation. 'Mystery', according to a dictionary means 'something that is unknowable and cannot be clarified'.[12] So, in contemporary German, 'mystery' reminds us of a gothic novel, *Harry Potter* or fantasy tales. Reiner Kaczynski comments: 'the word "mystery/mysteries" often just expresses what is undefined and puzzling, unknowable, not to be clarified, the unimaginable, indeed scary'.[13]

The Greek word, mustηrion, however, means something else. It has to do with what (in faith) can be (theologically) clarified. This is how Paul states it at the end of the Letter to the Romans, 16:25-27:[14]

> Now to God who is able to strengthen you according to my gospel and the proclamation of Jesus Christ, according to the revelation of the mystery that was kept secret for long ages but is now disclosed, and through the prophetic writings is made known to all the gentiles, according to the command of the eternal God, to bring about the obedience of faith.

In Paul, mystery does not mean what remains hidden but rather what is disclosed, it refers to the plan of God both as a whole and each of the single phases of the fulfillment of that plan of which Jesus Christ is the centre.[15] Klemens Richter maintains 'that the translation of this concept with the German (word) "mystery" is not able to reproduce the contents of the concept of *mysterium*.'[16]

In the celebration of the liturgy we share in this mystery, in this saving action of God. That sounds a mystery that is paradoxical – it both is and is not a mystery. On the one hand, it is and remains a mystery of faith that God became man in Jesus Christ and that Jesus Christ preached the kingdom of God, suffered and died and on the third day rose again. And yet, as Paul says so clearly, it is precisely this mystery that has been revealed in Christ, that is preached and so also to be celebrated in the liturgy.

To the central question: what do we celebrate in the liturgy of the Church? The Second Vatican Council responded that the celebration of the liturgy is always a celebration of the Paschal mystery of Jesus Christ. The Council clarified the meaning of 'Paschal mystery' in the Constitution on the Liturgy where it says:

> The wonderful works of God among the people of the Old Testament were but a prelude to the work of Christ the Lord in redeeming mankind and giving perfect glory to God. He achieved his task principally by the Paschal mystery of his blessed passion and resurrection from the dead, and his glorious ascension ... (SC 5)

In the Second Vatican Council, the Paschal mystery is the Easter saving action of God on and in his Son, Jesus Christ.[17] The Council takes up once more the dimensions of salvation history[18] contained in the New Testament notion of mustηrion. And the Council insists that we celebrate this saving action of God in each of the various forms of liturgical celebration. But this means that what we celebrate in the liturgy is not marginal but the core of our faith. In his post-Synodal Apostolic Exhoration, *Sacramentum Caritatis*, Pope Benedict XVI underlines this when he emphasises: 'Our faith and the eucharistic liturgy both have their source in the same event: Christ's gift of himself in the Paschal mystery' (no. 34).[19]

So we can affirm, with regard to the celebration of the Eucharist, that it is also a celebration of the suffering, death and resurrection of Christ; it is always the memorial of the self-giving of Jesus on the cross; it is always the entrance of the community into this self-giving of Jesus. It is also the praise and thanksgiving offering of the Church of Jesus Christ; it is always a sharing in Jesus' destiny and so a share in his Body and Blood. It is not by chance that as a community gathered for the liturgy we confess at a central point this 'mystery of our faith': 'We proclaim your death, O Lord and profess your resurrection until you come again.'

Commenting on the first draft of the Liturgy Constitution, *Schema I*, the French liturgist A.G. Martimort insisted that the liturgy should rightly be referred to as *mysterium* because it holds true that *res visibilis* (est/M.St.) *in qua Deus invisibiliter agit.*[20] Klemens Richter writes: 'In Christ the mystery of God has become visible for us; It continues in the community that is itself thereby *mysterium* and this *mysterium* is to be celebrated in symbolic actions, in Word and Sacrament' (cf. SC 7).[21]

Finally, what is the relationship between the liturgical celebration and the concrete saving action of God in history as witnessed by scripture?

We celebrate the liturgical Anamnesis of God's saving actions in his son Jesus Christ. What Pope Leo the Great wrote applies when he said that all that 'was visible in our redeemer (Jesus Christ/M.S.) passed over into the mysteries (of the liturgy/M.S.)'.[22] Liturgy is therefore the continuation of the priestly work of Christ whereby this priestly office is shared with all who through baptism become members of Christ's body. The result of this is that all are bearers of the liturgy.[23]

If all are bearers of the liturgy then the question of how we take part appropriately in celebrating the liturgy of the Paschal mystery becomes even more significant. During the Council debates, Archbishop Wronka (Gnesen) referred expressly to this: *Mysterium significat actum redemptivum Christi, in quo fidelis aliquomodo participare potest.*[24] *Mysterium* is therefore an action of Christ, with the redemption of humankind as its goal, and in which we share. Therefore in the very notion of *mysterium* we find the basis of the idea of people's participation in the salvific work of God which is mediated and celebrated ritually in the liturgy.

The Latin notion of *participatio* corresponds to the notion of participation and with this we come to a further key notion of the liturgical theology of the Constitution on the Liturgy, namely, *participatio actuosa*. So what is the appropriate form of taking part and participation in the (eucharistic) liturgy?

3. A STEP FURTHER: HOW DO WE CELEBRATE THE (EUCHARISTIC) LITURGY?

'Active participation' is a key concept when we turn to the question, *how* can we celebrate the (eucharistic) liturgy appropriately.[25] To understand this key phrase of the Council, we must refer back to article 48 of the Liturgy Constitution which shows precisely how critical the Council Fathers were at the end of the 1950s when they looked at the actual celebration of the liturgy. The Council Fathers emphasised that the faithful should not participate merely passively in the Mass as 'strangers and silent spectators' and this is what they wanted to change through the reform of the liturgy. How had it come to such a juncture?

It is true that the official liturgical texts as well as official Church publications had always maintained that the celebration of liturgy under the direction of the bishop or the priest was a matter for the whole assembled people of God. However, an ever-increasing emphasis over the centuries on the difference between clergy and lay people had led inexorably to the conclusion that the clergy, to some extent specialists, celebrated the liturgy while the people were forced into the position of spectators. While the priest 'read the Mass', the people prayed their pious devotions or the rosary. There is no objection either to pious devotions or to the rosary. It was a cause for concern, however, that the faithful did not follow the sacred action, because at times they were unable to follow the Latin liturgical language and therefore prayed in their own way in order to fill up a vacuum.

It was already a matter of concern for Saint Pope Pius X, who wished that the faithful should not pray 'in the liturgy', that is, where possible parallel and in any way they chose, but rather: 'pray the liturgy'! Thus we should not be surprised that it was the same Pope who already in 1903, sixty years before the Constitution on the Liturgy, in a papal document expressed the wish for an 'active participation' (*partecipatione attiva*) of all the baptised in the liturgy.

First therefore it must be stated: on the eve of the Second Vatican Council there was need for action. Although some groups today in the Church are again trying to persuade us otherwise,[26] the liturgical times before the Council were not golden times, in the sense of 'previously everything was better'. The Council Fathers at least saw this in a quite different way;[27] otherwise they would not have passed the Constitution on the liturgy on the 4th December 1963 with 2,147 votes in favour and only four votes against.

With this in mind, there is no need for an explanation of the preconciliar situation. The assembled bishops of Vatican II saw a greater need for reform in the preconciliar format of the liturgy with a view to the participation of all the baptised in the Paschal mystery.

In the Liturgy Constitution *Sacrosanctum Concilium* (SC) of 4th December 1963, the concept of active participation in the liturgy takes a central place and indeed becomes a leitmotif which runs through all the statements of the Constitution on the liturgy. Altogether the concept of participation in the Latin form participatio/participare occurs twenty-eight times in the Constitution on the Liturgy.[28] Central to this is, as Vatican II fills out the concept of participation, not only article 48, but also article 14 of the Liturgy Constitution which states:

> Mother Church earnestly desires that all the faithful be led to that full, conscious, and active participation in liturgical celebrations which is demanded by the very nature of the liturgy. Such participation by the Christian people as 'a chosen race, a royal priesthood, a holy nation, a purchased people' (1 Pt 2:9; cf. 2:4-5), is their right and duty by reason of their baptism. (SC, 14)

In the restoration and promotion of the sacred liturgy, this full and active participation by all the people is the aim to be considered before all else; for it is the primary and indispensable source from which the faithful are to derive the true Christian spirit.

All believers have a share in the priesthood of Jesus Christ as the royal priesthood of the new covenant, which,'by power of baptism, has a right to and is obliged to this liturgy'.[29] Appealing to 1 Peter 2:9, the Council grounds *actuosa participatio* in the liturgy as a consequence that flows from baptism. The presupposition for the active participation of the baptised in the liturgy is, according to Reiner Kacynski in his commentary on the Liturgy Constitution, their taking part in the threefold office of Christ ... their participation in which flows from their participation in Jesus Christ. Thus *Participatio* means primarily a participation on the basis of what they have received from, and is the condition of and obligation to full participation.[30] Liturgy is thus an exercise of the priestly office of Christ (cf.

SC, 7) in which the baptised are given a part by virtue of baptism. If all the baptised have been baptised precisely for participation in the mystery of the Eucharist, then a criterion for the correctness of the liturgy is full, conscious and active participation of the laity. Liturgy is not a private action (cf. SC, 26)[31] but rather the fundamental action of the Church and therefore can never be merely a clerical liturgy (cf. LG, 11).

The celebration of the liturgy may not exclude the baptised and so the Church ensures, as is expressed in SC, 48, that Christians do not experience this mystery of faith as strangers and silent spectators. By means of rites and prayers they should rather learn to understand this mystery and so actively celebrate the sacred event in a conscious, pious and active manner.[32] The Council grounds *actuosa participation* (active participation) in the essence of the liturgy.[33] Active participation is the leitmotif of SC and is considered in SC, 79 to belong to the *norma primaria*.[34]

With the Constitution on the Liturgy, the Council considered the desires for reform which had been expressed in the Church over many decades and from them chose what was valid for the whole Church, and finally provided a binding trajectory for the whole Church. The then Cardinal Joseph Ratzinger expressed this clearly in his lecture in 2003 to mark the forthieth anniversary of the Liturgy Constitution:

> It is not the task of the Councils to bring forth what was hitherto unknown but rather from the currents of the time it should filter out what is valid and that has grown out of the faith of the Church. In this way it should create togetherness and set the direction for the road ahead.[35]

However, the Council Fathers, the bishops assembled in Rome, did not begin their deliberations from zero. Already since the beginning of the twentieth century especially coming from the youth movement and in conversation with contemporary theology (especially in France and Germany) the biblical and liturgical movements had developed as the twin lungs which brought the liturgical movement to birth: the rediscovery of Holy Scripture as the foundational document of our faith and the rediscovery of the liturgy as a community celebration. Just as Cardinal Ratzinger had written, what was valid was filtered out of 'the currents of the time' and brought fresh into consciousness.

What was really new in the Constitution on the liturgy was 'the explicit magisterial declaration of the full, conscious and active participation of all Christians in the liturgical celebration'.[36] From this official Church codification came the reform of the liturgy which served the purpose of promoting the full, active and common participation as article 21 the *Magna Charta* of the liturgical reform emphasises.[37] So it may be added fifty years later, progress must constantly be checked to see how far the liturgical reform has reached this goal. In this sense the postconciliar renewed liturgy remains a *liturgia semper reformanda*.[38]

The participation of the faithful is described and specified more fully in the Constitution on the liturgy by means of adjectives. A participation which is: *debita, communitatis propria, interna and externa, vera, genuina, congrua, sciens and conscia, perfecta, efficax and fructuosa, actuosa, viva, plena and pia*.[39] These additional adjectives indicate precisely how the Council understands *participatio* (participation).[40] Even if the Council provides no comprehensive theology of 'active participation', nevertheless the accompanying adjectives give a direction and contain a precise image of how the participation expressly wished for by the Council might be implemented and conceived.

The qualifying additional adjectives indicate starting points for the postconciliar liturgical theological reflection that critically accompanied the pastoral-liturgical experiences of the postconciliar period and, in content, frequently guided it forward. It is the responsibility of scientific liturgical reflection to consider further this 'heart-word'[41] of Vatican II, to evaluate it theologically, and to protect it from all one-sided misinterpretations and any ideological abuses.[42]

In the foundational article 14 of the Liturgical Constitution, only the adjectives 'full', 'conscious' and 'active' are used in the first part. To elucidate more fully the liturgical-theological programme presented by Vatican II, in the next section I wish to turn our attention to the three most frequently used concepts in the Liturgy Constitution: *participatio plena, participation conscia* and finally *participatio actuosa*.

3.1 *Participatio Plena* – Full Participation: the Council Sets a Goal

When the Council speaks of *participatio plena*[43] this 'full' participation is, first of all, taken to mean the opposite of 'partial' or 'incomplete' participation.[44] The Council is setting out an ambitious goal here, as it is of course very aware that this vision of the full participation in the liturgy of all those baptised, as Winfried Haunerland critically puts it, 'has not been a guiding force over the centuries and the liturgical books generally only had the actions of the clergy in mind …'[45] The Council, on the other hand, emphasises that by virtue of baptism every believer has a right and a duty in this respect.[46] Two conclusions can be drawn from this.

First, the Council Fathers clearly considered the liturgical practice of their time to be inadequate.[47] While the participation of the baptised had never been completely absent from the history of the Church, it was however, sporadically at least, not 'full' but rather 'partial' and 'incomplete'. Second, it was the stated goal of the liturgical reform of the Second Vatican Council that 'after reform has been carried out, participation henceforth be a *full* participation'.[48] The Council Fathers were certainly not so naïve as to presume that this goal would be simple or easy, or that it could, so to speak, be achieved overnight[49] – nevertheless, the theological objective is clearly and unequivocally formulated: 'It should not be the fault of the reform of the liturgy if *actuosa participatio* falls short of the ideal.'[50]

So has the reform of the liturgy succeeded in its goal of bringing about *a participatio plena*? This question can, of course, be answered in different ways. Firstly, we need to grasp that the term 'full participation' implies that *in*complete forms of participation have, could and always will exist as well.

Appropriate as it undoubtedly is to assume an ideal target group in the case of such a goal, as is the case here, with the concept of *participatio plena*, we find every possible degree of participation in our congregations. Only twenty-five years after the promulgation of the Constitution of the Liturgy, the Tübingen dogmatician Bernd Jochen Hilberath proposed differentiating considerations on this.[51] He distinguishes between believers who are truly *plene incorporati* as defined by the Council, others who do indeed participate in the liturgy but not in a strictly *plene et actuose* manner, right down to those who rarely go to church anymore but still somehow consider themselves to be practising 'Christians'.[52] Hilberath's differentiating analysis would certainly require further specification today, almost twenty-five years later, and would possibly turn out even more complex. Many intermediary stages are possible between peripheral (that is to say, incomplete) participation and full participation, and not all are necessarily *plene incorporati* (see LG, 14). This has concrete consequences on the celebration of the liturgy, the tangible forms of which, in my opinion, we must much more forcefully consider.[53]

Thus the question of how to achieve the full participation of all in the liturgy of the Church remains, even almost fifty years after the *Sacrosanctum Concilium*, a pressing task. This is because – if you'll pardon the pun – as seen from the outside at least, our Church services since Vatican II are most definitely not getting any 'fuller'. Having been in decline for decades, Mass attendance figures are now settling down at a low level. So has the liturgical reform of the Second Vatican Council led to empty churches rather than to full participation?

Reiner Kaczynski takes on these concerns in his commentary on *Sacrosanctum Concilium*, seeing steadily emptying churches as a logical consequence of the principle of *actuosa participatio*: 'the constant charge since the very beginnings of the liturgical reform that it served to *de*crease rather than to increase attendance figures at Sunday services came as absolutely no surprise to those responsible for the liturgical renewal. Right from the start they were in fact very clear about the fact that a liturgy that was to be "actively co-celebrated" by all rather than "attended" as a matter of duty would necessarily lead to smaller congregations, all the more so if the "full and active", that is to say, engaged participation was not supported by intensive instruction.'[54]

Ultimately: need I not first of all understand what it is that I am celebrating in order to act actively at all, or, as Reiner Kaczynski puts it, so as to be able to celebrate in an 'engaged' way? This, indeed, raises the question of liturgical education – a broad field.

3.2 *Participatio Conscia* – Conscious Participation: Consciousness of One's Baptism as the Basis of all Liturgical Formation

When the Council speaks about *participatio conscia*,[55] this again expresses a contrast to the 'strangers or silent spectators' (SC, 48). But conscious participation means, first of all, not a superficially rational intelligibility, but rather 'the effect on the deepest layers of the psyche, of the heart, an effect that expresses itself, out of an inner necessity, through taking part in prayer and song'.[56] As Josef Pascher critically noted as early as 1966, the Council did not intend *participatio conscia* to mean that intelligibility 'might sink to remedial school level', but rather 'that there must also be further explanations'.[57]

It must be said, however, that liturgy, even if not instantly clear in every detail, must at the very least be comprehensible.[58] In this respect the *participatio conscia* points also to the question of the vernacular and the intelligibility of the rites.[59] This very question of the vernacular liturgy is a good example of the development of the principle of *participatio (conscia)* in the post-Council reform period.

The Council itself is initially very cautious in its comments on the question of the vernacular: in principle Latin is to be retained as the language of the liturgy (SC, 36), those parts that can also be translated into the vernacular, and to which, as the Council puts it, should be 'allotted a suitable place', are listed in detail. The use of the vernacular in 'the readings' and 'the common prayer', but also, as local conditions may warrant, to those parts which pertain to the people', is expressly mentioned (SC, 54).

In the immediate aftermath of the Council, however, it emerged, as Winfried Haunerland explains, that '... in the Church's new understanding of the liturgy, there are no longer any important parts that *do not* pertain to the people. Thus it transpired that within the space of less than four years virtually the entire liturgy of the Mass could be celebrated in the vernacular.'[60]

It is very much the Council's intention then, that the vernacular be granted greater scope in the post-Conciliar reform of the liturgy, and that the rites be, as hoped by the Council, 'distinguished by a noble simplicity; they should be short, clear and unencumbered by useless repetitions' (SC, 34). In order to allow for *participatio conscia*, the liturgical rites should be sufficiently followable and comprehensible so as to 'not require much explanation' (SC, 34), which does not, of course, rule out the catechetical and mystagogical interpretation[61] of rites and symbols or efforts towards ensuring comprehensive liturgical formation.[62]

It follows, then, that as debates currently rage in the English-speaking world over a suitable translation of the *Missale Romanum* from Latin into English, we need to remember that the primary goal of such a translation, from the Council's point of view, cannot be the creation of new possible sacral languages (in the vernacular), but rather the promotion of the conscious participation of all those baptised in the liturgy of the Church.[63] Any new translation of the Missal that might once again turn the celebrating congregation into 'strangers or silent spectators', would draw the criticism of the Constitution of the Liturgy.

The deeper dimensions of the *participatio conscia* mentioned at the outset needs to be recalled here. *Sacrosanctum Concilium* 11, quotes almost directly from the *Regula Benedicti* to exhort how necessary it is for the faithful to come to the liturgy, 'with proper dispositions, that their minds should be attuned to their voices' in order that the liturgy may be the source and summit of all ecclesial activity (SC 10) another goal, *Participatio conscia* (conscious participation) in the liturgy,[64] then, is more than following and understanding individual texts, prayers, rites and songs. Conscious participation focuses on the deeper spiritual dimensions of the liturgy, it involves a 'conscious, active and spiritually fruitful participation in the liturgy'.[65]

When the subsequent article 12 of the Liturgical Constitution states, drawing on Romans 6: 3-8, that 'we must always carry around in our bodies the dying of Jesus', it is clear that this liturgical spirituality is to be grounded in baptism; the consciousness of one's own baptism is taken up into the Paschal mystery: 'The sacrament of baptism, by which we were conformed to Christ, incorporated in the Church and made children of God, is the portal to all the sacraments. It makes us part of the one body of Christ (cf. 1 Cor 12:13, a priestly people)' (*Sacramentum Caritatis*, 17).[66]

In order to achieve a consciousness of one's own baptism catechetical and mystagogical instruction is necessary. In recent times, there have been repeated complaints about the virtually non-existent awareness of a baptismal consciousness in our communities and warnings about the overall negative effect this has on the formation of Christian identity. If an awareness of baptism is lacking, this cannot but have negative consequences for implementing an understanding of the liturgy, that as we have seen, regards precisely this baptism – based on scripture and tradition – as the very foundation basis for all liturgical activity. How can someone who is unaware of the fundamental meaning of baptism for his or her own Christian existence be in a position to discover in the actual performance of the liturgy, the common priesthood of the baptised, to practise it actively (that is to say, to participate fully and actively), and to make it spiritually fruitful for him- or herself?

3.3 *Participatio Actuosa* – Active Participation: A Taut Balance between Internal and External Participation

When the Council speaks of *participatio actuosa,* internal and external participation must be seen here as a tautly balanced entity. This is also suggested by SC, where it states: 'With zeal and patience, pastors of souls must promote the liturgical instruction of the faithful, and also their active participation in the liturgy *both internally and externally,* taking into account their age and condition, their way of life, and standard of religious culture' (SC, 19).

No other word can illustrate this tension quite as clearly as the adjective *actuosus* itself. As with all Latin words ending in *-osus, actuosus* means the state of being internally filled with something, in this case, with activity. This state of being 'filled with activity' is expressed in German with the successful translation of *tätige Teilnahme,* or in English 'active participation', as translated by the liturgical movement.[67]

'Active' participation does not mean that every participant in the liturgy must constantly undertake something extraordinary or engage in some external actions. Doing things for the sake of it is not what the Council has in mind here. Interpreting the pronouncements of the Liturgical Constitution to that effect would certainly lead to major misunderstanding; on the contrary, the Council explicitly emphasises that 'in liturgical celebrations each person, minister or layman, who has an office to perform, should do all of, but only, those parts which pertain to his office by the nature of the rite and the principles of liturgy' (SC, 28). A 'movement of externalisation' whose criterion is 'everybody should have something to do',[68] cannot base itself on the spirit or letters of the Council. Accordingly, we must once again clarify 'that the word "participation" does not refer to mere external activity during the celebration'[69] mindless activism is not the same as spiritual and fruitful participation.[70]

On the other hand, the Council clearly expects that this active participation will not be limited to purely abstract inwardness, but rather that it also reveal itself outwardly. *Sacrosanctum Concilium,* 30 reads 'to promote active participation, the people should be encouraged to take part by means of acclamations, responses, psalmody, antiphons and songs, as well as by actions, gestures and bodily attitudes. And at the proper times all should observe a reverent silence'. The *actuosa participatio* of all the faithful expresses itself, therefore, 'in shared attitudes, but also in shared speaking and singing, in acclamations and in other songs that are so much a matter for the whole congregation that only rarely can they be assigned to a choir'.[71]

In terms of the actual celebration of the liturgy, then, it is imperative that the tension between internal and external participation be preserved.[72] Active participation implies neither meaningless action for action's sake nor pure inwardness.[73] When the Council defines the *actuosa participatio* as internal and external, it in so doing resists 'a spiritualisation and dematerialising ... alien to the nature of the Liturgy. It is, in fact, its very distinguishing feature that the internal and the external are so inextricably bound, and that liturgy not only implies internal prayer, but rather that it also takes human corporality seriously.'[74]

This internally and externally executed active participation is the right and the duty of the faithful by virtue of their baptism.[75] But in the totality of the community of the baptised, there are always a variety of different charisms, functions and ministries. Aidan Kavanagh, doyen of American liturgics, describes the essential distinction between the ministerial priesthood[76] and the common priesthood of all the baptised in this way: 'The Church ... baptises to priesthood: it ordains only to executive exercise of the priesthood in the major orders of ministry ... Nor does sacerdotality come upon us for the first time ... at one's ordination. In constant genesis in the font, the Church is born there as a sacerdotal assembly by the Spirit of the Anointed One himself.'[77]

When the Council considers the common priesthood of all the baptised as the theological foundation for *particiatio actuosa* in the Mass, this also implies that not only the ministry of presiding, but also the liturgical lay ministries as exercised by 'virtue of baptism' are true liturgical ministries.[78] Thus, readers and altar servers are not derived ministries filling in for a cleric.[79] If these ministries are performed by virtue of baptism, this also means the reverse in consequence, namely that any clericalisation of the laity is to be avoided.[80] These concrete and genuine liturgical lay ministries help the active participation of all. The ministerial character of these liturgical lay ministries also means that parishioners will be chosen for this purpose 'who are in each case suitable and who are to be instructed and prepared accordingly'.[81]

4. OUTLOOK: *COMMUNIO* – PARTICIPATION THROUGH CONTRIBUTION

4.1 Active Participation: Your Right, Your Duty?[82]

We must not forget the historical context in which the Fathers of the Second Vatican Council formulated their thoughts on active participation in the celebration of the Paschal mystery. Historical research into Vatican II and the post-Vatican liturgical reform is a relatively new field of scholarship, and all the more exciting for it. The Constitution of the liturgy was adopted barely two years after a Catholic stood on the steps of Capitol Hill in Washington DC on 20th January 1961 and addressed his countrymen and the world at large:

> And so, my fellow Americans: ask not what your country can do for you – ask what you can do for your country. My fellow citizens of the world: ask not what America will do for you, but what together we can do for the freedom of man.

The high degree of personal responsibility invoked here with a certain pathos by the American president John F. Kennedy in his inauguration speech corresponds to the spirit of the times. Would it, then, really be so wrong to read and interpret the *participatio actuosa* in this light? Applied to the liturgy, it would go: 'And so, my dear baptised: ask not what the liturgy can do for you – ask what you can do for the liturgy. My dear people of good will: ask not what the Church can do for you, but what you can do for the Church for the salvation of humankind.'

This does, I admit, sound somewhat odd at first, but I wish now to briefly substantiate and open out this thesis theologically. Recall again the theological grounding of active participation: the common priesthood of all the baptised. The community of the baptised, as the Council says, is one of the principal ways of the presence of Jesus Christ in his Church: 'He is present, lastly, when the Church prays and sings, for he promised: 'Where two or three are gathered in my name, I am there among them' (Mt 18:20). In article 7 of *Sacrosanctum Concilium*, the Council teaches that the foundational sign of the presence of Christ in the liturgy is the liturgical assembly itself. This is a huge claim, as the assembled congregation is hereby the clearest sign of the Church; it is its effective sign. It becomes the basic sacrament for the presence of Jesus Christ because it is the body of Christ, because Christ, ultimately in it and acting through the Church, is present in the Church as the *Ursakrament*.[83] The American liturgist Judith Kubicki notes:

> our impulse to gather for worship is itself a response to an invitation that God gestures to humankind through the life, death and resurrection of Jesus Christ. Baptism enables us to respond to God's invitation by plunging us into the Paschal mystery ... Baptism authorises us to do Eucharist since it is through baptism that we receive Christ's mandate to 'do this in remembrance of me'.[84]

If we understand active participation in the liturgy of the Church in accordance with the pronouncements of the Second Vatican Council, as a right and a duty resulting from baptism, then it is necessary to look closely at how the faith celebrated in the liturgy and everyday faith relate to one another. Active participation extending only to the liturgy but having no relevance to the drudge of everyday life would be purely superficial.[85]

4.2 Communion with Christ and with One Another: Sharing in the Sacrifice of the Lord

It is telling that criticism of a purely external understanding of the participation of the faithful in the liturgy often goes hand in hand with complaints about the ideological instrumentalisation of the liturgy (in the sense of one-way indoctrination) and with concerns over the oft-encountered trivialisation of our worship services.[86] The American theologian Richard Niebuhr (c. 1962) summed up these trivialising tendencies as follows: 'A God without wrath brought men without sin into a kingdom without judgement through the ministrations of a Christ without a cross.'[87]

When the content of our worship services is banal and arbitrary it should hardly come as any surprise that participation in them is declining. If, however, we wish at this point to formulate the demands active participation in the liturgy makes of us as baptised Christians, then it is not enough – to take up Joseph Pascher's well-known *dictum* – that we merely follow the rubrics, the external ceremonial prescriptions and the directions of the liturgical books. Much more important are the things in black, the inner claim of the liturgical texts printed in black.[88] But do we even know what mystery it is that we are celebrating here? And if so, does this have any kind of relevance for our lives?[89]

It is interesting to note the kind of contexts in which the oft-cited terms 'strangers' and 'silent spectators' are applied in article 48. The Council probably had catechetical instruction in mind at first ('through a good understanding of the rites and prayers', resulting in conscious, devout and active participation). The celebration of the faith in the liturgy presupposes knowledge of the faith.

The context in which the Council refers to active participation here is, of course, the celebration of the Eucharist, or more precisely, the celebration of the Eucharistic sacrifice, the memorial celebration of the sacrifice of Jesus, its offering through the Church or the sacrifice of the Church in the celebration of the Eucharist.[90]

This brings us then to the fulcrum of Christian faith: if the liturgy is the celebration of the Paschal mystery of Jesus Christ, and if we, through our baptism, have been received into this Paschal feast of Jesus Christ, then with every Eucharist we celebrate his self-giving, out of love, ultimately to death (Eph 5:2), and we celebrate that we have been taken up into Jesus' self-giving to the Father and, with him, offer ourselves. It is no more and no less than precisely this. Active participation in the liturgy also means participation in that which we are celebrating in the liturgy: an active participation in the suffering, death and resurrection of Jesus Christ, because 'that which cost Christ His life cannot be ours, cannot become our life without becoming our death'. *Sing To The Lord,*[91] a document issued by the American bishops in 2007, expresses this connection between the celebration of the Eucharist as the sacrifice of Jesus Christ and the Church, and active participation, tersely and concisely:

In the celebration of Mass the faithful form a holy people, a people whom God has made his own, a royal priesthood, so that they may give thanks to God and offer the spotless victim not only through the hands of the priest but also together with him, and so that they may learn to offer themselves' (GIRM 95). This is the basis for the 'full, conscious, and active participation' of the faithful demanded by the very nature of the Liturgy.[92]

Drawing on article 95 of the *General Instruction of the Roman Missal*, the bishops insist that the sacrifice of Christ and our entering into Jesus' self-giving of himself to the Father are the very foundation of our active participation.[93] According to Hermann Volk: 'The Mass engrosses us, and the more powerful the Mass the more powerfully we are engrossed. The more we let ourselves be engrossed, the closer we correspond to the Mass in which Christ's total giving of himself to the heavenly Father is made present.'[94] Further developing the meaning of the Paschal mystery, he continues: 'If we can boast then with all certainty that the sacrifice of the cross is made present in the Mass as a celebration of the Paschal mystery, then what the desire and authority for conscious, active and spiritually profitable participation in this actually means is that we don't try to somehow spare ourselves, in the sense that while we may indeed do *something*, we in so doing try to protect *our own inner selves*. Rather, in the Christian liturgy we should deliver ourselves unconditionally up to Christ, he who first unconditionally sacrificed himself for us.'[95]

To take up Emil Joseph Lengeling's famous dialogue model:[96] if the liturgy is a dialogue between God and humans, and if God addresses us through his Word, through the incarnate logos Jesus Christ who gave himself up for us on the cross, then the celebration of the liturgy is a means of responding to God. If, then, we participate consciously and actively in this way, it is clear that this is more than just a question of outward action. It is, rather, a question of our own selves, of our inner willingness to walk along with Jesus, through suffering and the cross towards the glory of the resurrection – and it is, in fact, this inner willingness that must also be made concrete through action.

In fact, this concretisation must happen, not only in the activities taking place within the liturgy, but also – if we are to take seriously that it involves our own deeper selves – in actions that permeate every aspect of our daily lives. As Paul the apostle writes to the community in Rome, 'I appeal to you therefore, brothers and sisters, by the mercies of God, to present your bodies as a living sacrifice, holy and acceptable to God, which is your spiritual worship' (Rm 12:1). This also means, that as we include ourselves in the love of Jesus Christ for God and humanity, we ourselves become a 'living sacrifice' (Rm 12:1), a sacrifice that takes place, not just during the Sunday Mass, but rather in the mundane toil of the everyday.[97]

Active participation in the sense of the absolute giving of the self, which, as such, cannot be merely external but must, rather, embrace every aspect of our lives, permeates liturgy and *diakonia*, the praise of God and everyday living, *lex orandi* and *lex credendi*.[98] Participation in Jesus Christ's 'love unto the uttermost'[99] is not something that ends as soon as the liturgy is over.[100] The decision to engage with and then to follow the path of Jesus should, in fact, lead to greater decisiveness in every aspect of our lives. *Ahme nach, was Du vollziehst* – literally, 'Imitate that which you carry out' – the wording in German of the task entrusted to ordinands with the presentation of the chalice and the paten, is thus equally applicable to all the baptised.[101] This is made even clearer in the official English version of these words of administration: 'Imitate the mystery you celebrate!'[102]

The celebration of the liturgy (*lex orandi*) keeps the memory of the Paschal mystery of Christ alive in every Eucharist. In this celebration, the Church places itself before the true God, reminds him of his saving action in history, and bases on that their – expressed in petitions – believing confidence (*lex credendi*) that God will treat them in the same way. The celebration of the Paschal mystery thus brings the eucharistic meal back to the events on the cross; the objects of bread and wine become symbols of the self-giving life of Jesus, symbols of his radical sacrifice on the cross.

The Church lets itself be drawn into this free giving of his life. Its full, conscious and active participation manifests itself in its devotion to God and neighbour (*lex agendi*). And so the Church proclaims the suffering, death and resurrection of the Lord and awaits his second coming: 'We proclaim your death, O Lord, and profess your Resurrection until you come again.'

NOTES

1 *The Eucharist: Communion with Christ and with One Another.* Theological and Pastoral Reflections in Preparation for the 50th International Eucharistic Congress, Dublin, Ireland, 10th–17th June 2012. Dublin 2011.

2 *The Eucharist: Communion with Christ and with One Another,* no. 2.

3 Second Vatican Council, *Sacrosanctum Concilium* (Hereinafter referred to as SC), Rome: Libreria Editrice Vaticana, 1963, 48.

4 Cf. Richter, Klemens, 'Das Verhältnis von Kirche und Liturgie. Zur Rezeption des Zweiten Vatikanischen Konzils', *Heiliger Dienst* 54 (2000), 171–180.

5 Cf. *The Eucharist: Communion with Christ and with One Another,* no. 10.

6 Ibid.

7 Cf. Wohlmuth, Joseph, *Jesu Weg – unser Weg, Kleine mystagogische Christologie,* Würzburg 1992, 136.

8 Cf. Pahl, Irmgard, 'Das Paschamysterium in seiner zentralen Bedeutung für die Gestalt christlicher Liturgie', *Liturgisches Jahrbuch* 46 (1996), 71–93.

9 Meyer, Hans-Bernhard. art. 'Anamnese, V. Liturgisch', *Lexikon für Theologie und Kirche,* W. Kasper et al., eds, Vol. 1. Freiburg ³1993, pp. 592–3, here: 592.

10 *'Concede nobis, quaesumus, Domine, haec digne frequentare mysteria, qui, quoties huius hostiae commemoratio celebratur, opus nostrae redemptionis exercetur'* (Super oblata; Dominica II per Annum).

11 Cf. Meyer, Hans-Bernhard, *Eucharistie* (Gottesdienst der Kirche. Handbuch der Liturgiewissenschaft 4), Regensburg 1989, 448, Footnote 1.

12 Wahrig, *Deutsches Wörterbuch,* Gütersloh 1968, 1428.

13 Kaczynski, Reiner, 'Was heißt "Geheimnisse feiern"?', *Münchener Theologische Zeitschrift* 38 (1987), 241–55, here p. 255.

14 Regarding the concluding doxology in the Letter to the Romans cf. Wilckens, Ulrich, *Der Brief an die Römer* (Röm 12–16, Vol. 3. (EKK VI, 3), Zürich ²1989, here: 147f.

15 Richter, Klemens, *Was die sakramentalen Zeichen bedeuten. Zu Fragen aus der Gemeinde von heute,* Freiburg, 1988, 14f.

16 Ibid., 15.

17 Cf. on this understanding see the general outline in Pahl, *Das Paschamysterium in seiner zentralen Bedeutung für die Gestalt christlicher Liturgie,* 71–93.

18 Regarding the theological reduction which occurred in translating the Greek μυστηριον into the Latin 'sacramentum', cf. the fundamental discussion in Kaczynski, *Was heißt 'Geheimnisse feiern'?,* esp. 243; also: Richter, *Was die sakramentalen Zeichen bedeuten,* 15.

19 Post-Synodal Apostolic Exhortation *Sacramentum Caritatis* of the Holy Father Benedict XVI to the Bishops, Clergy, consecrated Persons and the Lay Faithful on the Eucharist is the Source and Summit of the Church's Life and Mission. February 20, 2007 (http://www.vatican.va/holy_father/benedict_xvi/apost_exhortations/documents/hf_ben-xvi_exh_20070222_sacramentum-caritatis_en.html); here no. 34.

20 Martimort, A. G., Observationes of September 13, 1961, p. 4.

21 Richter, Klemens, 'Die Signalfunktion der Liturgiekonstitution', *Münchener Theologische Zeitschrift 54* (2003) 98–113, here 100.

22 *Sermo* 74,2 (PL 54, 398)

23 Richter, ibid., 100.

24 AS I/II, 321. Wronka spoke during the debate on chapter III on November 6 and 7, 1962 in general congregations 13 and 14. Wronka continued by emphasising the Council's intentions: *'Et ad talem activam participationem haec Sacrosancta Synodus vult fidelibus sternere.'*

25 Cf. *Eucharist: Communion with Christ and One Another*, no. 22.

26 Motu proprio 'Tra le sollecitudini' by Pope Pius X on November 22, 1903. In: ASS 36 (1903–4, here 331: 'Essendo infatti Nostro vivissimo desiderio che il vero spirito cristiano rifiorisca per ogni modo e si mantenga nei fedeli tutti, è necessario provvedere prima di ogni altra cosa alla santità e dignità del tempio, *dove appunto i fedeli si radunano per atingere tale spirito dalla sua prima ed indispensabile fonte, che è la partecipazione attiva ai sacrosanti misteri e alla preghiera pubblica e solenne della Chiesa.* Ed è vano sperare che a tal fine su noi discenda copiosa la benedizione del Cielo, quando il nostro ossequio all'Altissimo, anzichè ascendere in odore di soavità, rimette invece nella mano del Signore i flagelli, onde altra volta il Divin Redentore cacciò dal tempio gli indegni profanatori.'

27 Cf. on this analysis of a 'Liturgy in Need of Reform', Ferrone, Rita, *Liturgy. Sacrosanctum Concilium* (Rediscovering Vatican II. Vol. 4), New York, 2007, 1–5.

28 Cf. Schmidt, Herman. *Die Konstitution über die heilige Liturgie.* Text – Vorgeschichte – *Kommentar.* Freiburg 1965, here 201ff.

29 Richter, Klemens. Liturgiereform als Mitte einer Erneuerung der Kirche, In: Idem, ed., Das Konzil war erst der Anfang. Die Bedeutung des II. *Vatikanums für Theologie und Kirche.* Mainz 1991, 53–74, here 66.

30 Kaczynski, Reiner. Theologischer Kommentar zur Konstitution über die Heilige Liturgie Sacrosanctum Concilium. B. Kommentierung. In: Hünermann, P./Hilberath, B. J., eds,. Herders Theologischer Kommentar zum Zweiten Vatikanischen Konzil.Vol. 2: *Sacrosanctum Concilium. Inter mirifica. Lumen Gentium.* Freiburg 2004, here 80. Cf. also the fundamental work of: Jungmann, Josef Andreas, *'Kommentar zur Liturgiekonstitution: Sacrosanctum Concilium,* Höfer, J./Rahner, K. et al., eds, *Lexikon für Theologie*

und Kirche 12. Das Zweite Vatikanische Konzil. Vol. I. Freiburg[2] 1966, 10–109, here 28. Also: Lengeling, Emil Joseph. *Die Konstitution des Zweiten Vatikanischen Konzils über die heilige Liturgie.* Lateinisch-deutscher Text mit einem Kommentar (Lebendiger Gottesdienst 5/6), Münster[2] 1965, here 40f.

31 Kunzler, Michael, Liturge sein, *Entwurf einer Ars celebrandi*, Paderborn, 2007, here 167.

32 This fundamental statement of the Constitution seems to some extent to have fallen victim to a quite selective hermeneutic and reception of Vatican II. At least this highly important argument for the post-conciliar liturgical reform does not occur frequently in the current discussion about the reintroduction of the so-called 'Tridentine' Mass (for example, the extraordinary form of the Roman Rite) by the Motu Proprio *Summorum Pontificum* on July 7th, 2007. The statement of the US Bishops' Conference about SC, 14 on active participation being still valid in the extraordinary rite according to the *Missale Romanum* 1962, seems rather questionable: http://www.usccb.org/liturgy/bclnewsletterjune07.pdf (Newsletter from June 2007, no. 3, p. 27.)

33 Cf. also: SC, 26–31.

34 Haunerland, Winfried, Vom 'Gottesdienst' zur 'Gemeindefeier'? Prinzipien und Herausforderungen nachkonziliarer Liturgiereform, *Theologisch-praktische Quartalschrift* 153 (2005), 67–81, here 73.

35 Joseph Ratzinger, 40 Jahre Konstitution über die heilige Liturgie. Rückblick und Vorblick, *Liturgisches Jahrbuch* 53 (2003) pp. 209–21, here 209.

36 Kunzler, *Liturge sein*, 167f.

37 SC, 21: 'In order that the Christian people may more certainly derive an abundance of graces from the sacred liturgy, holy Mother Church desires to undertake with great care a general restoration of the liturgy itself ... In this restoration, both texts and rites should be drawn up so that they express more clearly the holy things which they signify; the Christian people, so far as possible, should be enabled to understand them with ease and to take part in them fully, actively, and as befits a community. Wherefore the sacred Council establishes the following general norms: ... ' Cf. on this: Schrott, Simon, 'The Need for Discontinuity: Considerations on a Hermeneutic of Liturgical Reform according to *Sacrosanctum Concilium*', *Studia Liturgica* 41 (2011), pp. 56–67.

38 SC, 21 states accordingly: 'For the liturgy is made up of immutable elements divinely instituted, and of elements subject to change. These not only may but ought to be changed with the passage of time if they have suffered from the intrusion of anything out of harmony with the inner nature of the liturgy or have become unsuited to it. 'In the same way SC, 50: 'The rite of the Mass is to be revised in such a way that the intrinsic nature and purpose of its several parts, as also the connection between them, may be more clearly manifested, and that devout and active participation by

the faithful may be more easily achieved. For this purpose the rites are to be simplified, due care being taken to preserve their substance; elements which, with the passage of time, came to be duplicated, or were added with but little advantage, are now to be discarded; other elements which have suffered injury through accidents of history are now to be restored to the vigor which they had in the days of the holy Fathers, as may seem useful or necessary.' It is quite remarkable how in the current discussion about the recent liturgical reform this rather critical assessment of the contemporary liturgical reality of the Council Fathers is largely ignored. (Cf. the survey of such critical opinions: Baldovin, *Reforming the Liturgy*, pp. 134–57, esp. 134ff.) This might lead to the (historically wrong) impression that the pre-conciliar liturgy was not in need of any reform at all. The vast majority of the Council Fathers clearly held a different opinion on that.

39 Cf. Kaczynski, *Kommentar*, 80.

40 Winfried Haunerland notes critically that this clarification of the meaning of participation carried more far-ranging consequences that most of the Council Fathers might have been aware of: '... mehr Konsequenzen, als den meisten Konzilsvätern schon bei der Verabschiebung der Konstitution bewusst gewesen sein dürfte', Haunerland, *Vom 'Gottesdienst' zur 'Gemeindefeier'*?, 74.

41 Häußling, Angelus. 'Pascha-Mysterium'. Kritisches zu einem Beitrag in der dritten Auflage des Lexikon für Theologie und Kirche, *Archiv für Liturgiewissenschaft* 41 (1999), 157–65.

42 Cf. Haunerland, Winfried, 'Erneuerung der Liturgie als bleibende Aufgabe. Zur aktuellen Herausforderung durch die Konstitution Sacrosanctum Concilium, *Studia Westprimiensia* 2006/I–II, 109–23, here 118ff.

43 SC, 14, 21, 41.

44 Vgl. Kohlschein, *Bewusste, tätige und fruchtbringende Teilnahme*, 43.

45 Haunerland, Vom 'Gottesdienst' zur 'Gemeindefeier'?, 73.

46 See the literal translation of the Latin original of SC, 14: '... vi Baptismatis ius habet et officium.'

47 Cf. also: SC, 50.

48 Pascher, Josef, 'Das Wesen der tätigen Teilnahme. Ein Beitrag zur Theologie der Konstitution über die Hl. Liturgie', *Miscellanea Liturgica* (Festschrift G. Lercaro), Vol. I. Rom 1966, pp. 211–29, here p. 227.

49 Cf. the self-critical reflections and words of warning given by the former Council Father and Bishop of Mainz, Hermann Volk in: Volk, Hermann. *Theologische Grundlagen der Liturgie. Erwägungen nach der Constitutio de Sacra Liturgia*, Mainz 1964, esp. 60f.

50 Pascher, Das Wesen der tätigen Teilnahme, 227. Against this background

should be read the practical instructions of SC, 30: 'To promote active participation, the people should be encouraged to take part by means of acclamations, responses, psalmody, antiphons, and songs, as well as by actions, gestures, and bodily attitudes. And at the proper times all should observe a reverent silence.'

51 Hilberath, Bernd Jochen. 'Participatio actuosa'. Zum ekklesiologischen Kontext eines pastoralliturgischen Programms, Becker, H., ed., Gottesdienst – Kirche – *Gesellschaft. Interdisziplinäre und ökumenische Standortbestimmungen nach 25 Jahren Liturgiereform,* (Pietas Liturgica 5). St Ottilien 1991, 319–38

52 Hilberath, 'Actuosa participatio', 337.

53 Also cf. on this, the bright pre-conciliar analysis of Bishop and Cardinal Hermann Volk, that to a great extent sounds like a description of today's situation, with the same pastoral concerns and problems, Volk, Hermann. Sonntäglicher Gottesdienst, *Ders. Gesammelte Schriften* (Vol. 3), Mainz 1978, pp. 98–132, esp. 106f.

54 Kaczynski, *Kommentar*, 80.

55 SC,11, 48 and 79.

56 Schmidt, Die Konstitution über die heilige Liturgie, 203.

57 Pascher, Das Wesen der tätigen Teilnahme, 226. Cf. Ratzinger, 40 *Jahre Konstitution über die heilige Liturgie*, 216.

58 Cf. the distinctinon between 'instantly clear in every detail' and being at least comprehensible': Stuflesser, Martin. *Liturgisches Gedächtnis der einen Taufe. Überlegungen im ökumenischen Kontext.* Freiburg 2004, 318–320.

59 Cf. Schmidt, *Die Konstitution über die heilige Liturgie*, 203.

60 Haunerland, Vom 'Gottesdienst' zur 'Gemeindefeier'?, 74. Cf. by the same author, regarding the use of the vernacular in post-conciliar liturgy: *Lingua vernacula. Zur Sprache der Liturgie nach dem II. Vatikanum.* In: *Liturgisches Jahrbuch* 42 (1992), pp. 219–238.

61 Cf. see my further thoughts in: Stuflesser, Martin. 'Das Geheimnis lasst uns künden, das uns Gott im Zeichen bot...' *Überlegungen zur mystagogischen Erschließung liturgischer Feiern.* In: *Liturgisches Jahrbuch* 56 (2006), 83–97.

62 Cf. SC, 14.

63 Cf. on this see the highly critical, yet accurate remarks about the meaning of active participation in the Council's documents: Trautman, Donald W., 'The Language of the New Missal in Light of the Constitution on the Sacred Liturgy', *The Jurist* 70 (2010), pp. 455–72, esp. p. 471f. And: Stuflesser, Martin. 'How to pray the vernacular. Überlegungen zu Fragen der Liturgiesprache am Beispiel des neuen Roman Missal in den USA', Anzeiger für die *Seelsorge* 121 (2012), pp. 18–22.

64 SC, 11. Cf. the quotation from the Regula Benedicti: 'mens concordet voci'; Reg. Ben. 19. Cf. Lengeling, *Kommentar*, 34.

65 Kazcynski, *Kommentar*, 75.

66 *Sacramentum Caritatis*, no. 17.

67 This example illustrates that a translation always includes a certain amount of interpretation by the translator, too. The official English translation of 'actuosa participatio' with 'active participation' is much less ambiguous and interprets the lexeme by solving its intrinsic tension in favour of a specific aspect of its originally broader meaning (compared for example to the German translation *tätige Teilnahme* which is a much more literal translation of the Latin).

68 Ratzinger, Joseph, '40 Jahre Konstitution über die Heilige Liturgie. Rückblick und Vorblick', *Liturgisches Jahrbuch* 53 (2003), pp. 209–221, here p. 219.

69 *Sacramentum Caritatis*, no. 52.

70 Haunerland, Vom 'Gottesdienst' zur 'Gemeindefeier'?, 74f.

71 Haunerland, Vom 'Gottesdienst' zur 'Gemeindefeier'?, 75.

72 This tension is also detectable in the instruction *Redemptionis Sacramentum*: Congregation for Divine Worship and the Discipline of the Sacraments. Instruction *Redemptionis Sacramentum* on certain matters to be observed or to be avoided regarding the Most Holy Eucharist (http://www.vatican.va/roman_curia/congregations/ccdds/documents/rc_con_ccdds_doc_20040423_redemptionis-sacramentum_en.html); March 25, 2004; here n. 39f.

73 Cf. the statement in *Sacramentum Caritatis*, no. 52, where the corresponding conciliar teaching (especially SC, 48), under the caption 'authentic participation', is ascertained to have 'lost none of its force'.

74 Haunerland, Vom 'Gottesdienst' zur 'Gemeindefeier'?, 75.

75 SC, 14.

76 LG, 10: 'Though they differ from one another in essence and not only in degree, the common priesthood of the faithful and the ministerial or hierarchical priesthood are nonetheless interrelated: each of them in its own special way is a participation in the one priesthood of Christ.'

77 Kavanagh, Aidan, 'Unfinished and Unbegun Revisited: The Rite of Christian Initiation of Adults', *Worship* 53 (1979), 338. Nathan D. Mitchell comments on this: 'Laypeople who minister have neither the desire nor the intention of taking over the ordained priest's function. They instinctively understand the difference between what they do and what he does. Most lay Catholics who minister at Sunday Eucharist do so with dignity and gratitude. They are grateful to stand in God's presence and serve, grateful for God's gracious initiative that calls them to faith and ministry; grateful for Jesus' lively

presence in Word, prayer, and song, in gathered people, in bread and wine; grateful to all who minister (clergy included; see SC, no. 7). They understand in their bones that what binds us together is more imporant than what separates or divides.' Mitchell, Nathan D. Meeting *Mystery: Liturgy, Worship Sacraments,* New York/USA: Orbis Books, 2006, here 243.

78 The Constitution on the Sacred Liturgy says in art. 29: 'Servers, lectors commentators, and members of the choir also exercise a genuine liturgical function.'

79 This is an actual innovation compared to the CIC/1917 and also the instruction of the Congregation of the Rites on September 3, 1985. Until then laypeople needed an official assignment (*deputatio ecclesiae*) to act 'liturgically' in the liturgy, that is, to carry out a 'genuine liturgical function' (SC, no. 29). Since Vatican II this delegation of liturgical functions that were originally reserved for the clergy no longer exists, these are now viewed as performed in virtue of Baptism. Cf. Schmidt, *Die Konstitution über die heilige Liturgie,* 201f.

80 Cf. *Redemptionis Sacramentum*, 45: 'To be avoided is the danger of obscuring the complementary relationship between the action of clerics and that of laypersons, in such a way that the ministry of laypersons undergoes what might be called a certain "clericalizatio", while the sacred ministers inappropriately assume those things that are proper to the life and activity of the lay faithful.'

81 Haunerland, Vom 'Gottesdienst' zur 'Gemeindefeier'?, 75.

82 The heading is borrowed from a pastoral letter by the former Archbishop of Los Angeles/USA, Roger Card. Mahony: 'Gather Faithfully Together. Guide for Sunday Mass.' Los Angeles 1997, esp. pp. 28–35. In the chapter 'Your Right, Your Duty' (pp. 28–35) this letter offers plenty of valuable practical and spiritual suggestions for the liturgy.

83 Richter, Klemens. Klemens, 'Die Konstitution über die heilige Liturgie Sacrosanctum Concilium', Bischof, Franz Xaver, ed., *Vierzig Jahre II.* Vatikanum. Zur Wirkungsgeschichte der Konzilstexte. Würzburg 2004, 29–49, here esp. 31f.

84 Kubicki, Judith M, *The Presence of Christ in the Gathered Assembly,* New York: Continuum, 2006, here 36.

85 Cf. Die Eucharistie: *Communio mit Christus und untereinander,* no. 47.

86 Cf. Ratzinger, 40 Jahre Konstitution über die heilige Liturgie, 218ff.

87 'A God without wrath brought men without sin into a kingdom without judgment through the ministrations of a Christ without a cross', Niebuhr, Richard, *The Kingdom of God in America,* New York, 1959, here 193.

88 Cf. Ratzinger, '40 Jahre Konstitution über die heilige Liturgie', 219.

89 Cf. Regarding the current situation of the Catholic Church in Ireland after the sexual abuse scandals, see the highly self-critical considerations in the document *The Eucharist: Communion with Christ and with One Another*, nos. 5, 31 and 46. No. 31 says: 'It cannot be denied that some find it difficult even to enter the doors of a church after what they have experienced through the actions of priests and religious or the inaction of their superiors ... It is to be hoped, however, that those who, for whatever reason, feel alienated from the Church, might consider revisiting it and taking a new look at its message in the context of the Congress. It is to be hoped that they will discover a community that in recent years has recognised more clearly its faults and failings, seeking now in a spirit of repentance and reconciliation to heal memories and begin anew in the commitment to *be* and *speak* of Jesus' life-giving message.'

90 Cf. *Die Eucharistie: Communio mit Christus und untereinander*, no. 109.

91 Volk, *Theologische Grundlagen der Liturgie*, 63.

92 United States Conference of Catholic Bishops, *Sing to the Lord*, issued November 14, 2007, here no. 24. (Published as a PDF document via www.usccb.org).

93 Cf. *Sacr. Caritatis*, no. 64: 'The Church's great liturgical tradition teaches us that fruitful participation in the liturgy requires that one be personally conformed to the mystery being celebrated, offering one's life to God in unity with the sacrifice of Christ for the salvation of the whole world. For this reason, the Synod of Bishops asked that the faithful be helped to make their interior dispositions correspond to their gestures and words. Otherwise, however carefully planned and executed our liturgies may be, they would risk falling into a certain ritualism. Hence the need to provide an education in eucharistic faith capable of enabling the faithful to live personally what they celebrate.'

94 Volk, *Theologische Grundlagen der Liturgie*, 62.

95 Ibid., 63.

96 Cf. Lengeling, Emil Joseph, *Liturgie – Dialog zwischen Gott und Mensch*, Klemens Richter, ed., Altenberge[2] 1991.

97 Ökumenischer Arbeitskreis evangelischer und katholischer Theologen. Das Opfer Jesu Christi und seine Gegenwart in der Kirche. Klärungen zum Opfercharakter des Herrenmahles.(Dialog der Kirchen Vol.3), K. Lehmann and E. Schlink.Freiburg, eds, 1983, here 238.

98 Cf. Seasoltz, R. Kevin, *God's Gift Giving: In Christ and Through the Spirit*. New York: Continuum, 2007, 33ff.

99 Ratzinger, '40 Jahre Konstitution über die heilige Liturgie', 214. Cf. *Sacr. Caritatis*, no. 64.

100 Regarding the Eucharist Karl Lehmann substantiates this in, Lehmann,Karl Gemeinde, *Christlicher Glaube in moderner Gesellschaft*. Fasc. 29, Freiburg 1982, 31–3.

101 Cf. Stuflesser, Martin/Winter, Stephan, eds, 'Ahme nach, was du vollziehst ... ' *Positionsbestimmungen zum Verhältnis von Liturgie und Ethik*. Regensburg 2008.

102 Cf. *The Eucharist: Communion with Christ and with One Another*, no. 110.

IL 'CORPO DONATO PER VOI' ORIGINE E FORMA DELLA CHIESA COMUNIONE

REV. PROF. PIERO CODA
President of the Sophia University Institute, Loppiano, Florence

1. La contemporaneità di Gesù – sottolineava Sören Kierkegaard – non è un'idea. E neppure un'aspirazione. È un evento tangibile: qualcosa, meglio qualcuno, che – nella sua sconvolgente e invitante alterità – si vede, si tocca, si mangia. L'Eucaristia.

Discorrere intorno alla contemporaneità di Gesù, e intorno al significato e alla provocazione che ne vengono per la Chiesa oggi, non raggiunge il 'dunque' sin quando non ci s'impatta con Gesù nell'Eucaristia. È così, infatti, nell'Eucaristia, che Gesù autoattesta e rende attiva ed efficace la sua contemporaneità. Non solo attraverso l'eco vivente della sua Parola, ma nella sostanzialità del Pane e del Vino. '*Questo* è il mio corpo ... *questo* è il mio sangue'. Stanno in ciò la grazia e il 'nocciolo duro' dell'esperienza cristiana.

Nel libro VII delle *Confessioni*, riandando con la memoria al suo primo incontro con Dio (*'cum primum te cognovi'*, quando ti ho conosciuto per la prima volta – egli scrive, vibrante ancora di stupore e gratitudine), Sant'Agostino testimonia d'aver ascoltato da Dio, con la voce dell'anima, la promessa viva della straordinaria ed eccedente contemporaneità di Gesù alla storia, nella Chiesa, attraverso l'Eucaristia:

> riverberasti l'infermità del mio sguardo – ricorda – raggiando verso di me con veemenza, e tremai tutto di amore e di tremore, e scoprii che ero lontano da te nella regione della dissomiglianza, come se ascoltassi la tua voce dall'alto: 'Io sono il nutrimento degli adulti: cresci e ti nutrirai di me. E tu non trasformerai me in te come cibo della tua carne, ma tu sarai trasformato in me.[1]

Il compito teologico di cui ci è chiesta l'esecuzione è quello di risalire da *questa* Presenza, di cui la *koinonía* nella e della Chiesa si alimenta, e in cui la *koinonía* nella e della Chiesa proletticamente si consuma, all'istituzione che ne ha predisposto Gesù e all'intenzione che vi ha annesso e che attraverso i secoli li incastonava nell'eterno presente di Dio. In modo da cogliere e accogliere, con intelligenza d'amore sempre più piena e rigeneratrice, *nel 'corpo dato per voi' l'origine e la forma della Chiesa,* che il Concilio Vaticano II ha inteso descrivere e promuovere, appunto, come *koinonia.*

> nella frazione del Pane eucaristico – insegna la *Lumen Gentium* – partecipando noi realmente del Corpo del Signore, siamo elevati alla comunione con Lui e tra noi: 'Perché c'è un solo pane, un solo corpo noi siamo, quantunque molti, partecipando noi tutti di uno stesso pane' (1 Cor 10:17). Così noi tutti diventiamo membra di quel Corpo (cfr. 1 Cor 12:27), e singolarmente siamo membra gli uni degli altri (Rm 12:5) (no. 7).

Questa realtà – sottolinea Giovanni Paolo II nella *Novo millennio ineunte* – 'incarna e manifesta l'essenza stessa del mistero della Chiesa' (no. 42). La Chiesa che è in Cristo *koinonia* rinvia per sé alla Pasqua e alla cena del Signore – non l'una senza l'altra. La presenza di Gesù alla Chiesa che la plasma *koinonia* è appesa a questi due *gesti fondatori,* l'uno dall'altro indissolubile. Due gesti, in cui il primo anticipa e offre 'una volta per sempre' la verità salvifica del secondo; mentre il secondo nel memoriale del primo si perpetua.

Ovviamente, quando per pasqua s'intenda l'integralità di ciò che essa è: morte e risurrezione, sacrificio e convivialità. Essendo la pasqua, così intesa, il dispiegarsi abbreviato e puntuale dell'evento intero di Gesù – esistenza e missione – è chiaro che nella cena, suo anticipo e significato, si compendia tutto il bene della Chiesa: Cristo Gesù intero – anima, corpo, sangue e divinità, come ama dire la *Traditio vivens* che fa la Chiesa, anzi: la *Traditio vivens* dell'evento di Gesù Cristo che la Chiesa stessa è.

In effetti, a guardar le cose dritti negli occhi, la pasqua di Gesù senza la cena sarebbe svuotata del senso sostanziale che la rende contemporanea *oggi, qui, per noi.* Quel senso che si dispiega tra la cena di Gesù con gli apostoli nel cenacolo, prima della sua pasqua, e, dopo di essa, la cena dei discepoli a Emmaus – paradigmatica d'ogni altra Eucaristia.

La pasqua riceve senso dalla prima e dà senso – sostanziale – alla seconda. E quando dico 'sostanziale' intendo rimarcare la sua irriducibile, perché densa di mistero procedente dal cuore stesso di Dio Trinità, corposità e incisività storica. Quella, per intenderci, assumendo la quale i discepoli di Gesù sono investiti nel loro essere e agire dalla contemporaneità di Gesù e, a loro volta, se ne fanno attori irradianti nella storia come corpo di Cristo, 'sacramento, in Lui, e cioè segno e strumento dell'intima unione con Dio e dell'unità di tutto il genere umano'(LG, 1).

Che cosa, dunque, avviene nella pasqua, che è anticipato nel significato permanente che essa irradia dalla cena di Gesù e che perciò, nel memoriale di essa, ci è donato in ogni cena eucaristica?[2]

2. Cominciamo dal racconto della cena. Lo considero qui nella convergenza dei dati storici e teologici che ci offrono le due grandi linee di tradizione che l'esegesi ha riconosciuto nell'attestazione neotestamentaria: quella paolino-lucana e quella marciano-mattaica, cui si congiunge, nella sua ricca originalità, la tradizione del quarto vangelo.

Ora, il primo e fondamentale dato teologico che ci viene offerto, e che c'introduce al cuore dell'intenzione istitutrice di Gesù, è che la cena – e quanto essa anticipa e dischiude della pasqua – è racchiusa e avvolta dallo sguardo sconfinato e perseverante d'amore, per l'uomo, di quel Dio che Gesù ha vissuto e testimoniato al mondo come l'*Abbà*. L'*incipit* della cena e, di conseguenza, lo spazio che in essa si apre, son segnati, infatti, dalla *eucharistia* (Paolo e Luca) ovvero dalla *euloghía* (Marco e Matteo): due termini che rinviano alla *berakhá*, la grande preghiera di ringraziamento e di lode in cui si condensa l'ispirazione della preghiera ebraica.[3]

È Dio, dunque, l'*Abbà* il protagonista di ciò che sta per accadere. Come lo è stato, sin dall'inizio, *en arché* – per dirla col vangelo di Marco – quando Gesù ha preso ad annunciare l'*euanghélion*: '*il tempo è compiuto e il Regno di Dio sta venendo; convertitevi e credete nel Vangelo*' (Mc 1:15). La morte di croce, verso cui Gesù sta andando, non è un incidente di percorso, un fuori d'opera imprevisto, la fine e il fallimento di tutto.

Nella paradossalità tragica e oscura che la investe, l'enigmatica e sconcertante morte di Gesù è in tutto e per tutto avvolta e penetrata dall'amore misterioso ed efficace del Padre. Essa, anzi, è veramente e in modo definitivo il luogo e l'ora dell'accadimento del Regno che viene a noi, attraverso il Figlio, dall'*Abbà*, nella forza dello Spirito. Il contesto di preghiera – lo mostrerà, subito appresso, l'episodio di Getsemani – esprime l'adesione piena del Figlio, con sofferta e angosciata consapevolezza, alla volontà del Padre (cfr. Mc 14: 32-36 e par.). E offre la prima e fondamentale coordinata che permette di decifrare e far nostro il senso della pasqua che la cena proletticamente esibisce.

Tutto è sotto lo sguardo di misericordia dell'*Abbà*, dunque, tutto è disposto dal e nel suo disegno di salvezza che si dispiega nel Figlio. Niente sfugge alla forza redentrice e trasformatrice del suo amore. Ma il disegno di Dio si fa storia dell'uomo, appunto, grazie all'adesione del Figlio che si dispone a vivere il sacrificio di sé, sino alla morte, entro la trama insensata e peccaminosa di ciò che gli è ingiustamente e insensatamente inflitto: '*non ciò che voglio io, ma ciò che vuoi tu*' (cfr. Mc 14:36). La cena è radicalmente *eucaristia*, ringraziamento e lode, *eucaristia* cristica e universale, panumana e cosmica rivolta dal Figlio e nel Figlio all'*Abbà*: perché il Figlio, sulla croce, adempie infine e definitivamente la buona e bella notizia del disegno di salvezza del Padre.

La coscienza cristiana delle origini, e l'ininterrotta tradizione della Chiesa, fissando questo nome – *eucaristia* – tra i molti disponibili, per designare il memoriale della cena celebrato dai discepoli in memoria del Maestro e Signore, con l'infallibile senso soprannaturale della fede, ne coglie ed esprime l'intima e ultima verità.

3. Di qui, senza soluzione di continuità, un secondo dato, altrettanto radicale e decisivo. Se l'*Abbà* è l'indiscusso, nascosto regista del dramma di salvezza che sta per consumarsi – regista quant'altri mai presente e piegato con tutto se stesso a seguirlo passo passo – il Figlio, Gesù, ne è il protagonista.

E ciò significa, innanzi tutto, che egli è l'attore libero, consapevole e responsabile, di ciò che sta accadendo. La libertà di Gesù, nell'aderire, meglio ancora, nel *far accadere* la volontà d'amore dell'*Abbà* come storia, è il cuore pulsante della cena. E dunque della pasqua. Senza di essa nulla avrebbe senso. La libertà di Gesù, di fronte al Padre, meglio sotto lo sguardo d'amore del Padre, nell'intima unione d'amore e di reciproca intesa con lui, se, da un lato, disambigua per sempre il volto e il cuore di Dio – in lui non c'è tenebra, né doppiezza, né rivendicazione, né giustizia vendicativa – dall'altro, penetra con la luce dell'amore, che è libertà, e della libertà che è amore, la tenebra anche più fitta e impenetrabile del cuore umano.

Il lessico di cui – con qualche variante che, alla fine, arricchisce l'intelligenza della cosa – fanno uso i racconti della cena, nella sua quotidiana e limpida semplicità, è del tutto eloquente. Ecco il racconto di Marco: il più scarno ed essenziale. *'Prese, spezzò, diede...'* (cfr. Mc 14:22-23). L'intenzione di Gesù ha come oggetto il destino della sua esistenza e missione. Che egli, in tutto, riceve dall'*Abbà*. E che assume e fa proprio nel suo senso risolutivo, con gesto sovrano, sereno e solenne, di libertà e consapevolezza (*prese*), per condividerne il frutto (*spezzò*) e per donarlo (*diede*): e cioè per parteciparlo, a tutti, in libera convivialità.

In questi gesti di Gesù, egli, il Figlio dell'uomo che è il Figlio di Dio, espone se stesso, si espone – come Dio, l'*Abbà*, si è esposto e si espone al mondo in lui. Se lo 'spezzare' allude, da un lato, al realismo – cruento – della dedizione di sé, che non è un fatto idealistico e velleitario, ma ha la concretezza del corpo innalzato sulla croce e del sangue da essa versato, e, dall'altro, alla dinamica distributiva implicita in questo gesto, per cui ciascuno è oggetto e termine inteso e voluto di tale gesto; il 'dare' esibisce la logica profonda e intenzionale dell'esistenza di Gesù. Egli *si dà*. E cioè, non solo, liberamente – aderendo all'amore del Padre – offre il suo corpo, se stesso, rivelando così, all'estremo, quanto già ha donato con la parola, lo sguardo, i gesti. Ma, con ciò stesso, si comunica, anzi si trasferisce in chi l'accoglie.

Per questo, il *diede loro* si esprime e si traduce nel *prendete*. La dedizione si realizza e compie quand'è assunta e nella misura in cui è assunta. Con questa parola – *prendete* – i discepoli sono costituiti tali, discepoli: perché coinvolti e abilitati nel far vivere in sé il Figlio dell'uomo che è il Figlio di Dio.

Diventa evidente, nella logica di una dedizione così intesa, dedizione che da sé suscita l'accoglienza che la assume e la rivive, la coscienza che in Gesù dimora, luminosa e lucida – nella sua relazione all'*Abbà* – del senso di ciò che sta per accadere. Egli – dirà il quarto vangelo – '*offre la sua vita e così la prende di nuovo*' (cfr. Gv 10, 17). La ri-prende non solo nel senso che è donando la sua vita che la riceve nuova in sé: ecco la risurrezione; ma nel senso che, donandola, la riceve nuova anche in chi l'accoglie e la fa sua: ecco Gesù '*primogenito tra molti fratelli*' (Rm 8, 29).

La dedizione, in tal modo, suscita la convivialità e la fraternità, e cioè la Chiesa nella sua essenza, vocazione e missione di comunione. La Chiesa tale è e diviene, se sempre di nuovo riscopre e rivive la sua radice e la sua forma nella dedizione di sé: '*egli ha dato la sua vita per noi, quindi anche noi dobbiamo dare la vita per i fratelli*' (1 Gv 3:16). È questo che Gesù '*ha imparato dal Padre*' (cfr. Gv 6:45): '*Come infatti il Padre ha la vita in se stesso, così ha dato anche al Figlio di avere la vita in se stesso*' (Gv 5:26). La cena – e la pasqua – sono la comunicazione di quella dedizione di sé che ha sua sorgente nel Padre, attraverso il Figlio – che dal Padre anch'egli ha in sé la vita – a chi lo accoglie riconoscendolo e accogliendolo per chi egli è: *il* Figlio.

Ma ciò non basta, anche se permette d' intuire il 'filo d'oro' che lega la cena – e in prospettiva il ministero e l'evento tutto di Gesù – alla pasqua. Nei racconti della cena, e nella ripresa che ne fa la tradizione apostolica nelle sue molteplici declinazioni, ricorre una preposizione: *hypér*, '*per*' che, nella sua esiguità, dischiude un abisso – l'abisso più profondo della dedizione di Gesù e della comunione nuova e fraterna che essa suscita e plasma. Tanto che Benedetto XVI è giunto a dire che questo 'per' può considerarsi la 'parola-chiave non solo dei racconti dell'ultima cena, ma della figura stessa di Gesù'.[4]

È lo stesso 'per' che, riecheggiando e sviscerando il significato preannunciato, nel Primo Testamento, dai carmi del Servo sofferente di Jhwh, è al cuore del *lóghion* cristologico più essenziale e concentrato della tradizione pre-pasquale: *il Figlio dell'uomo non è venuto per farsi servire, ma per servire e per dare la propria vita in riscatto per molti* (Mc 10, 45). In questo *lóghion*, il *servire* è esplicitato nel *dare la vita in riscatto* (*lútron*). La stessa dinamica e finalità che sono espresse nel 'per' pronunciato da Gesù nell'ultima cena. Esso racchiude così, densamente, nel loro reciproco implicarsi, il significato di *espiazione* e quello di *riconciliazione* – per usare il lessico neotestamentario – della croce e della cena.

Si tratta di prendere sul serio, e sino in fondo, la potenza del male come peccato di opposizione a Dio e al suo disegno di amore, e la fatticità della tragica realtà che ne è l'effetto – nella vita personale e nella storia del mondo. Se non si fa ciò, se si rimuove cioè o si fa finta di non veder il male e la sequela tragica delle sue strutture e dei suoi effetti, la dedizione di Gesù e la grazia di riconciliazione e di comunione che 'a caro prezzo' (per Gesù e per noi, al seguito di lui) ne scaturisce, si svuotano di senso, di serietà e sincerità, d'incisività ed efficacia spirituale e storica.

Il dar-si di Gesù – prolungamento ed espressione trinitaria del dar-si dell'*Abbà* – implica, proprio perché è vero e risolutivo, lo scendere nell'abisso di morte in cui il peccato ha imprigionato l'uomo. Solo così, solo prendendo su di sé la conseguenza della contraddizione tragica dell'amore dell'*Abbà* che è il peccato dell'uomo, Gesù può attestare che *'più forte della morte è l'amore'* (cfr. Ct 8:6), l'amore dell'*Abbà*. I due linguaggi, quello della cena e quello del sacrificio, quello dell'espiazione vicaria e quello della convivialità fraterna, non sono antagonisti, né vanno assorbiti l'unto nell'altro: vanno piuttosto coniugati in profondità alla luce dell'amore dell'*Abbà* che tutto illumina di sé, nel Figlio crocifisso e risorto.

Prendere sul serio la 'potenza immane del negativo' – come arditamente lo chiama il pensiero moderno – decifrare, cioè, con lucidità e coraggio, ovunque essi si annidino, i tratti e le trame della strategia d'inganno e malvagità disegnati dal 'principe di questo mondo', significa, in definitiva, prendere sul serio la sapienza e la potenza dell'amore di Dio: Cristo crocifisso. '*Perché* – insegna l'apostolo Paolo – *ciò che è stoltezza di Dio è più sapiente degli uomini, e ciò che è debolezza di Dio è più forte degli uomini*' (1 Cor 1:25).

La speranza cristiana è tale solo se è inchiodata alla croce. E da essa più non si schioda.

4. È per questo, per il suo essere inchiodata alla croce di Gesù, che la speranza – attesta l'apostolo Paolo – *non delude: perché l'amore di Dio è stato riversato nei nostri cuori per mezzo dello Spirito Santo che ci è stato dato* (Rm 5:5). La dedizione del Figlio, espressione della dedizione dell'*Abbà*, è accolta nei cuori e li accende alla fede, alla speranza e all'amore – *per mezzo dello Spirito Santo*.

È lo Spirito Santo il terzo co-agonista, tutto divino – eppure così intimamente vicino al nostro cuore da esservi dentro versato! – del dramma della cena e della croce.

Certo, a un primo sguardo, dello Spirito Santo non si dice parola, nell'uno e nell'altro caso. Ma egli, in verità, è il soffio di vita in cui accadono il dono del Padre e il dono del Figlio. È, anzi, il dono stesso che, dal Padre, il Figlio versa nei nostri cuori.

Versare. Il verbo è lo stesso (*ekchéo*): nel lessico di Paolo che parla dello Spirito *versato nei nostri cuori*, e in quello del vangelo di Marco, che mette questa parola sulle labbra di Gesù nell'offrire ai discepoli *il sangue dell'alleanza versato per molti*. Del resto, l'alleanza, di cui qui si tratta, quella che prende origine e vigore dal e nel sangue versato di Gesù, è la 'nuova e definitiva alleanza' che Dio ha promesso d'instaurare col suo popolo. Quella di cui dicono Geremia:

> Ecco, verranno giorni – oracolo del Signore – nei quali con la casa d'Israele e con la casa di Giuda concluderò un'alleanza nuova ... porrò la mia legge dentro di loro, la scriverò sul loro cuore. Allora io sarò il loro Dio ed essi saranno il mio popolo. Non dovranno più istruirsi l'un l'altro, dicendo: 'Conoscete il Signore, perché tutti mi conosceranno, dal più piccolo al più grande – oracolo del Signore – poiché io perdonerò la loro iniquità e non ricorderò più il loro peccato (Ger 31:31, 33-34);

ed Ezechiele: 'Vi darò un cuore nuovo, metterò dentro di voi uno spirito nuovo, toglierò da voi il cuore di pietra e vi darò un cuore di carne. Porrò il mio spirito dentro di voi e vi farò vivere secondo le mie leggi e vi farò osservare e mettere in pratica le mie norme' (Ez 36: 26-27).

Il sangue *versato* da Gesù sulla croce, che egli offre col calice ai discepoli nella cena, se, da un lato, evoca senz'altro, nella sua separazione dal *corpo dato*, il realismo estremo e cruento della morte; dall'altro, esprime il dono di sé *sino alla fine* (cfr. Gv 13:1): sino, appunto, all'effusione del sangue. E si propone come il segno vero e tangibile e il veicolo concreto ed efficace della comunicazione che Gesù – sulla croce e nella cena – fa di sé, della vita di Dio in sé – lo Spirito Santo – agli uomini. Scrive Santa Caterina da Siena, Dottore della Chiesa: 'l sangue [del Cristo crocifisso] è intriso con la calcina della deità e con la fortezza e il fuoco della carità', che è lo Spirito Santo.[5]

Il *sangue versato* dal Crocifisso è – possiamo ben dire – il 'sangue di Dio', la sua stessa vita: lo Spirito Santo. Il quarto vangelo, narrando la scena della croce, lo richiama, in forma densamente simbolica, quando pone il sigillo sulla morte di Gesù dicendo che egli, *reclinato il capo, consegnò lo Spirito* (19:30), per poi certificare l'avvenuta effusione della vita come consegna dello Spirito nell'attestazione del riversarsi, dal costato di Gesù squarciato dalla lancia, di *sangue ed acqua* (Gv 19:34).

In essi, nel sangue e nell'acqua, i Padri della Chiesa riconosceranno i segni, vivificati dallo Spirito del Risorto, dell'Eucaristia e del Battesimo. Lo ribadisce la Costituzione *Sacrosanctum Concilium* del Vaticano II, sintetizzando densamente la grande lezione della Tradizione: *De latere Christi in cruce dormientis ortum est totius Ecclesiae mirabile sacramentum* (no. 5).

È dunque il sangue di Cristo, espressione tangibile e irrevocabile dell'effusione escatologica e 'senza misura' (cfr. Gv 3:34) dello Spirito, che, versato nei nostri cuori, fa scorrere in essi la vita di Dio, lo stesso suo sangue. La nuova alleanza abbraccia cielo e terra: perché, ormai, un'unica vita, quella dell'amore 'sino alla fine', quella che sgorga dal Padre e pulsa nella missione del Figlio, viene da lui versata col dono di sé sino al sangue, mediante lo Spirito Santo, nel cuore dei credenti.

Questo accade nella pasqua. Questo dice e compie la cena.

5. Ci resta da fare un ultimo passo. Sinora abbiamo cercato di leggere la pasqua alla luce della cena, e viceversa. Ci resta di fissare l'attenzione, brevemente, sulla *cena dei discepoli* quale *culmen et fons* della vita e missione della Chiesa (cfr. *Sacrosanctum Concilium,* 10), in quanto in essa, a memoriale della cena di Gesù, si fa contemporanea a noi la pasqua del Signore, sorgente e forma della Chiesa comunione. Come preannunciato, guardiamo al ben noto, ma sempre nuovo e provocante, racconto dei discepoli di Emmaus (Lc 24:13-35).

Di esso, in questa sede, mi pare suggestivo richiamare un aspetto soltanto, in ordine al compito che c'impegna. Si tratta di questo. Come sappiamo, i due discepoli scendono da Gerusalemme verso Emmaus sconsolati e spenti, nella mente e nel cuore. Non hanno afferrato il senso e la grazia – misteriosa – di quant'è accaduto, avendo per protagonista Gesù Nazareno. Fin quando un viandante, che è Gesù stesso, il Risorto, si accosta a loro e interpreta in tutte le Scritture ciò che lo riguarda. Al punto che, seduto infine a tavola con loro, ripete i gesti della cena: *Prese il pane, disse la benedizione, lo spezzò e lo diede loro* (24:30). È nel rivivere *questo* atto, l'evento della cena, che *si aprirono loro gli occhi e lo riconobbero* (24:31). In quel 'riconoscimento' trova conferma e sigillo l'ardore che bruciava nel loro petto *mentre* – si dicono l'un l'altro – *conversava con noi lungo il cammino, quando ci spiegava le Scritture* (24:32).

Qual è il significato di questo riconoscimento (*epígnosis*)? È il fatto che essi, rivivendo con Gesù la cena, alla luce della Scrittura da lui interpretata, ora, con lui vivo in mezzo a loro, mediante quei gesti, entrano vitalmente e *insieme* in una conoscenza nuova e vera e definitiva di lui. Essi, cioè, non solo riconoscono in colui che ha camminato con loro quel Gesù che nella cena – senza che ancora lo si potesse appieno comprendere – aveva anticipato il senso e la verità della croce: quel senso e quella verità che sono lui stesso, il Vivente e il Risorto. Ma comprendono e accolgono anche il tenore di quel '*prendete* e mangiate, *questo* è il mio corpo... *prendete* e bevete, *questo* è il mio sangue'. Accade che – come spiega in modo bellissimo Benedetto XVI – 'mediante quelle parole, il nostro momento attuale viene tirato dentro il momento di Gesù. Si verifica ciò che Gesù ha annunciato in *Giovanni* 12, 32: dalla croce egli attira tutti a sé, dentro di sé'.[6] E nella *Deus caritas est* il Papa spiega:

> la 'mistica' del Sacramento ha un carattere sociale, perché nella comunione sacramentale io vengo unito al Signore come tutti gli altri comunicanti: 'Poiché c'è un solo pane, noi, pur essendo molti, siamo un corpo solo: tutti infatti partecipiamo dell'unico pane', dice san Paolo (1 Cor 10:17). L'unione con Cristo è allo stesso tempo unione con tutti gli altri ai quali Egli si dona. Io non posso avere Cristo solo per me; posso appartenergli soltanto in unione con tutti quelli che sono diventati o diventeranno suoi. La comunione mi tira fuori di me stesso verso di Lui, e così anche verso l'unità con tutti i cristiani. Diventiamo 'un solo corpo', fusi insieme in un'unica esistenza. Amore per Dio e amore per il prossimo sono ora veramente uniti: il Dio incarnato ci attrae tutti a sé (no. 14).

È quel che nel racconto lucano dei discepoli di Emmaus, paradossalmente, si attualizza in ciò: che l'evento del riconoscimento del viandante coincide col *diventare egli non (più) veduto da loro* (24, 31). Egli, infatti, vive ora, e come tale ha da vivere, *in loro*: in ciascuno di loro e in mezzo a loro, nel loro diventare *koinonia* in Lui. È questa l'intenzionalità del *prendete. Io in loro e Tu in me* – chiede Gesù nella preghiera all'*Abbà*, nell'ultima cena.

Il Padre in Gesù, Gesù nei discepoli. È quanto Gesù realizza nella pasqua e comunica nell'Eucaristia.

6. Nel memoriale della cena si attualizza, dunque, da Cristo Gesù, tutto il bene della Chiesa per la salvezza del mondo. Senza Eucaristia non vi è Chiesa e non vi è dispensazione della salvezza, che è la vita di Dio – cioè il suo sangue, lo Spirito Santo – in noi, a favore di tutti.

I Padri della Chiesa, con formula pregnante, insegnano che il Figlio di Dio s'è fatto Figlio dell'uomo, perché noi, figli e figlie dell'uomo, possiamo diventare in Lui figli di Dio. Con preciso e suggestivo linguaggio filosofico, il beato Antonio Rosmini scrive che Gesù Cristo, nell'incarnazione e sulla croce, di cui l'Eucaristia offre il frutto sostanziale, si è 'inoggettivato' in noi: ha cioè 'trasportato' se stesso in noi al punto da 'in-esistere' in noi (e cioè da esistere-dentro-di-noi). Ma ciò si realizza – nella logica del *diede* e del *prendete* – solo attraverso la nostra reale 'inoggettivazione' di risposta in lui. È 'questa 'inoggettivazione' morale in Gesù Cristo – spiega Rosmini – la formula più breve della cristiana perfezione, di qui viene l'espressione solenne: *in Cristo*. L'uomo cristiano deve sentire, pensare, fare, e patire, avere, essere ogni cosa, *in Cristo*'.[7] Insieme, gli uni come membra degli altri (cfr. Rm 12, 5; Ef 4, 25).

Occorre dunque, in virtù dell'Eucaristia, seguire Cristo nel suo movimento di dedizione e identificazione riconciliatrice che lo porta a scendere negli abissi – sino agl'inferi – del cuore, della mente, della vita dell'uomo, di ogni uomo, in ogni tempo e in ogni situazione. A tutti i livelli e in tutte le dimensioni del suo essere e della sua esperienza: fisica, psichica, spirituale e culturale. Solo così Cristo, in noi, nei 'poveri vasi d'argilla' (cfr. 2 Cor 4:7) che accolgono la sua grazia, *diventa contemporaneo*. Là e quando – scrive Teresa di Lisieux, il Dottore della Chiesa che Dio ci ha donato nel nostro tempo – ciascuno di noi e il popolo della nuova alleanza, in tutte le forme del suo esistere ed agire, 'accetta di mangiare quanto a lungo voi vorrete, Gesù, il pane del dolore', e 'non vorrà alzarsi dalla tavola piena di tristezza e pena, dove mangiano i poveri peccatori ... sino a quando a voi, Gesù, così piacerà'.[8]

Questa la contemporaneità che Gesù chiede alla sua Chiesa come 'sacramento, e cioè segno e strumento, in Lui, dell'unione con Dio e dell'unità di tutto il genere umano' (LG 1). Di qui si irradiano la verità e l'efficacia nella *comunione* della sua missione: religiosa e civile. 'Finché egli venga' (1 Cor 11:26).

NOTES

1 Agostino, *Confessioni*, VII, 10.16

2 La cornice teologica di quanto qui verrò esponendo è disegnata nel mio *Dalla Trinità. L'avvento di Dio tra storia e profezia*, Città Nuova, Roma 2012^2, in particolare, parte III: 'L'evento. L'*Abbà* del Figlio fatto uomo nello Spirito', pp. 205–326.

3 Cfr. J. Ratzinger (Benedetto XVI), *Gesù di Nazaret*, II. *Dall'ingresso in Gerusalemme fino alla risurrezione*, Libreria Editrice Vaticana, Città del Vaticano 2011, pp. 145–6.

4 J. Ratzinger (Benedetto XVI), *Gesù di Nazaret*, II, cit., p. 152.

5 Caterina da Siena, *Il dialogo della divina provvidenza* ovvero *Libro della divina dottrina*, a cura di G. Cavallini, Edizioni Cateriniane, Roma, 1968, XXVII, 60.

6 J. Ratzinger (Benedetto XVI), *Gesù di Nazaret*, II, cit., p. 158.

7 A. Rosmini, *Teosofia*, parte I: *Ontologia*, Libro III *L'essere trino*, Sez. III, Cap. I, Art. IV, n. 899; *Opere*, vol. 13, a cura di M. Adelaide Raschini e P.P. Ottonello, Istituto di Studi Filosofici – Centro Internazionale di Studi Rosminiani – Città Nuova, Roma 1998 , p. 209.

8 Thérèse de l'Enfant Jésus, *Manuscrit 'C'*, Folio 6 r., *Manuscrits autobiographiques*, Carmel de Lisieux, Lisieux 1957, p. 251 (trad. nostra).

THE RESURRECTION AND THE EUCHARIST

REV. PROF. BRIAN JOHNSTONE CSsR
Professor of Moral Theology/Ethics,
Catholic University of America, Washington DC

In the opening presentation of the symposium Dr Jennifer O'Reilly led us to contemplate the Book of Kells. One of the representations to which she drew our attention was that of the risen Christ. Christ is shown seated beneath an arch and immediately above his head is a small cross. At either side of Christ we see the figure of the pelican. The pelican was believed to feed its young with its own blood, and was adopted as a symbol of Christ who fed believers spiritually with his flesh and blood in the Eucharist. These three images, the risen Christ, the cross and the Eucharist are the main themes of my presentation. In particular I want to draw attention to the close connection between the risen Christ and the Eucharist.

In this presentation I will propose that the Eucharist is an active, saving memorial, not only of the sacrificial death of Jesus but also of the resurrection. When we participate in the Eucharist we are liberated from sin by the redeeming death of Christ and we are positively transformed by the power of his resurrection. The same divine power that raised Christ now transforms us so that we rise to a new and richer spiritual life. The pastoral significance of this is that by linking the Eucharist to Christ's resurrection we can develop a richer understanding of the Eucharist; at the same time by connecting the resurrection to our participation in the Eucharist we can relate the resurrection closely to our religious experience. Each time we receive the Eucharist we rise again and the energy of that rising again empowers our daily lives. In our present circumstances we are very aware of our need to rise again to new life and new hope: it is in participating in the Eucharist that we are given the power to do so.

To support these suggestions I will review some of the major liturgical texts that express the meaning of the celebration of the Eucharist.

I will focus on the Eucharistic prayers themselves, in particular on the *anaphoras,* the memorial prayers that follow the words of consecration. These texts, as I will show, consistently include not only the memory of the passion and death of Christ but also of the resurrection. The purpose of this presentation is not to provide a detailed analysis of the theology of the texts, but to show that, although there is significant variation, all the texts include a reference to Christ's resurrection. However, while the texts consistently attribute a saving role to the passion and death of Jesus, it is not clear whether they always give a similar salvific role to his resurrection. Catholics could generally agree that the Eucharist is an active memorial of the passion and death of Jesus and that participating in the Eucharist is therefore a saving event for us. But they may not perhaps also appreciate that the Eucharist is an active memorial of Christ's resurrection and that when we participate in the Eucharist we share in the saving power of the resurrection. They may think of the resurrection as a personal victory for Christ but not also a saving event for them. What I will suggest in this presentation is that is that if we were to appreciate the connection between the Eucharist and the resurrection we could come to a deeper appreciation of the meaning of the Eucharist and, at the same time, become more aware that our spiritual lives are a sharing in the resurrection of Christ.

To show the connection between the Eucharist and the resurrection I will study some Eucharistic prayers both from the early Church and from the present. I will begin with some of the most ancient texts.[1]

THE LITURGY OF ST BASIL

The Liturgy of St Basil or, more formally, the Divine Liturgy of St Basil the Great, is a term for several Eastern Christian texts that have been attributed to St Basil the Great, who was Bishop of Cæsarea in Cappadocia from 370 to 379. The following is the text of one of the anaphoras from this liturgy.

> He gave himself as ransom to death in which we were held captive, sold under sin. Descending into Hades through the cross, that he might fill all things with himself, he loosed the bonds of death. He rose on the third day, having opened a path for all flesh to the resurrection from the dead, since it was not possible that the author of life would be dominated by corruption. So he became the first

> fruits of those who have fallen asleep, the first born of the dead, that he might be himself the first in all things. Ascending into heaven, he sat at the right hand of your majesty on high and he will come to render to each according to his works. As memorials of his saving passion, he has left us these gifts which we have set forth before you according to his commands. Do this in remembrance of me. For as often as you eat this Bread and drink this Cup, you proclaim my death, and you confess my resurrection. Therefore, Master, we also, remembering his saving passion and life-giving cross, his three-day burial and resurrection from the dead, his ascension into heaven, and enthronement at your right hand, God and Father, and his glorious and awesome second coming.[2]

I will not attempt to enter into a detailed theological analysis of this or the following texts, a task which would be beyond my competence. For the purposes of this presentation chapter it is sufficient to have shown that the resurrection was included in these ancient prayers. However, there are two points which deserve mention. The first is the 'descent into hell'. This would, it seems, refer to the ancient tradition according to which Christ descended into hell to liberate the souls who were retained there; Christ descended into 'hell' to liberate the souls who were in hell as a consequence of 'disobedience' (1 Pt 3:18-19). According to David Power, the influence of Paschal homilies may have led to '... the use of Paschal imagery that portrays the descent into hell by voluntary death as the conquest of the powers of the underworld, death and sin. While the death anticipates the resurrection, the image of voluntary descent gives primacy to the significance of Christ's death in the work of redemption.'[3] I will not attempt to discuss the various interpretations of this difficult passage. In his commentary, Donald P. Senior notes the traditional notion of a descent by Christ into hell or Hades in the time between his death and resurrection.[4] This would convey a recognition of the full reality of Christ's death and an anticipation of his saving victory over death. However, according to Senior, the text of the Epistle 'offers scant ground for this interpretation'. There are reasons for interpreting the text as referring to a journey of Christ after the resurrection. Indeed, the text may not be not a message of liberation offered to just souls constrained in Hades, but '... triumphant announcement of victory over the forces of death and evil hurled at hostile spirits'.[5] If the visit of Christ is presented as happening after the resurrection and if the text does refer to an announcement of victory over evil spirits, then we could say that it indicates a saving action on the part of Christ. It is not clear how the liturgical texts themselves understand this action on the part of Christ, but at least we can say that contemporary interpretations on the part of scripture scholars would support the view that this action of Christ is a saving one.

A further question is whether the resurrection itself was recognised as having such a saving role. Power recognises that the early theologies as reflected in the liturgies, while they proclaimed the resurrection of Christ together with his death, saw the Eucharist as a memorial of the passion.[6] By this I understand him to imply that these texts present the Eucharist as a memorial of the passion rather than also of the resurrection. This is the issue that I will discuss in this presentation; I will suggest that a reading of some of the texts supports the interpretation that the Eucharist is a memorial of the passion together with the resurrection.

THE LITURGY OF HIPPOLYTUS

This was included in a document entitled 'The Apostolic Tradition'. This anaphora was at one time associated with Hippolytus of Rome and dated to the mid-third century. However, according to some recent studies, the anaphora probably attained its final form around the middle of the fourth century AD and it is not to be related to Rome but to West Syria or even to Egypt.[7] According to Jungmann, this text '... certainly does not adequately represent the whole tradition'.[8]

When he was about to hand himself over to voluntary suffering, in order to destroy death and break the chains of the devil, to crush hell beneath his feet, to give light to the just, to establish the rule [of faith?], and to show forth the resurrection, he took bread, gave you thanks, saying, 'Take, eat, this is my body which is broken for you.' Likewise the cup, while saying, 'This is my blood which is poured out for you. When you do this, you do it in memory of me.' Recalling his death and his resurrection, we offer you this bread and this cup. We give thanks to you for having judged us worthy to stand before you and serve you.[9]

Another translation has:

> Now, therefore, making the anamnesis of his death and resurrection, we offer to thee the bread and the cup, giving thee thanks because thou hast made us worthy to stand before thee and minister as priests to thee. Humbly we pray thee and implore thee, O Holy of Holies, by the favour of thy goodness, that the fullness of thy Holy Spirit may descend upon us and upon these gifts and bless them and sanctify them.[10]

THE LITURGY OF ST JAMES

The Liturgy of St James is the oldest complete form of the Eastern varieties of the divine liturgy still in use among certain Christian Churches. It is based on the traditions of the ancient rite of the Early Christian Church of Jerusalem, as the *Mystagogic Catecheses* of St Cyril of Jerusalem imply. Forming the historical basis of the Liturgy of Antioch, it is still the principal liturgy of the Syriac Orthodox Church. It is also occasionally used in the Eastern Orthodox Church and Melkite Catholic Church.

> Therefore, we sinners too, remembering his life-giving sufferings and the saving cross, his death and burial, and resurrection from the dead on the third day, his ascension into heaven and sitting at your right hand, his God and Father, and his second, glorious and fearsome coming, when he comes in glory to judge the living and the dead, when he will render to each according to their works – Spare us, O Lord![11]

I now move on to a study of later anaphoras. We can begin with the meaning of the words 'remembering' or 'memorial' that are included in all the texts. According to Kevin Irwin, what is involved is an 'act of memory', an 'enactment of the word of God here and now, which action and event become operative for us in a unique way in and through the liturgy'. He continues, 'Words are proclaimed at liturgy so that God can do something among us for our sakes and our salvation.' The notion of memory as enactment will be the key to the interpretation that will be offered in this book. Irwin comments that the phrase 'for our salvation' shows clearly that the liturgical prayers do not merely 'describe' Christ's Paschal mystery, but 'draw us into experiencing it in all its fullness through the action of the Eucharist'.[12]

However, while this text clearly indicates the saving role of the passion, it does not explicitly attribute a saving role to the resurrection.

I would further suggest that the tendency to interpret the 'memorial' as a purely mental event, rather than as a 'real' transformation may be an indication of an underlying problem that contributed to the strange forgetfulness of the resurrection. By this I refer to the separation of subject and object, which has been a feature of Western thinking for centuries. In the framework of this separation it could happen that the resurrection is thought of as a purely interior or subjective transformation or, on the other hand, as an 'objective' fact, apart from any engagement of the part of the subject. But, in the liturgy we do not merely remember the Paschal mystery, we enact it and we experience the effective power of the resurrection in the real actions that constitute the liturgy, 'transformation, memorial, offering and supplication', or more succinctly, 'take, bless, break, give'.[13] Transformation, in the preceding citation no doubt refers to the transformation of the bread and wine into the Body and Blood of the Lord, but I suggest that it would have to include also the transformation of the those who participate in the liturgy, a transformation that St Thomas called the 'resurrection of the soul' or what we could call the 'spiritual resurrection'.[14] The spiritual transformation engenders a bodily transformation; those who are spiritually transformed express the spiritual transformation in the actions of celebration, receiving the Body and Blood of the Lord, giving the sign of peace and then, beyond the formal liturgy, in healing the sick and feeding the hungry. These bodily acts could, I suggest, be called a 'bodily resurrection'; they are an anticipation of the complete transformation of soul and body in the final resurrection. It is in this way that the notion of remembering or 'making memory' may be interpreted. We can now examine the texts in detail.

THE MASS OF PIUS V

The Mass of Pope St Pius V was promulgated on 14th July 1570, by the apostolic constitution *Quo Primum*.[15] It was replaced by the Mass of Pope Paul VI in 1969.

> *Unde et memores, Domine, nos servi tui, sed et plebs tua sancta, ejusdem Christi Filii tui Domini nostri tam beatae Passionis, necnon et ab inferis Resurrectionis, sed et in coelos gloriosae Ascensionis. Offerimus*

> *praeclarae majertati tuae de tuis donis ac datis hostiam puram, hostiam sanctam, hostiam immaculatam, Panem sanctum vitae aeternae, et calicem salutis perpetuae.*

It is of interest that this text included *ab inferis Resurrectionis,* which would be translated literally as 'resurrection from hell' or the underworld. We can note that the reference is to resurrection from hell but not the descent into hell.[16] Is this resurrection process considered as salvific? One would have to concede that a definite answer to this question is not possible. Centuries before, St Thomas had treated the theme of the descent into hell (*ad infernum*) and quite explicitly affirmed that this descent was a salvific act.[17] The same Latin text is reproduced in the First Eucharistic Prayer of the new order of the Mass, known as the Mass of Paul VI (1969).[18] Thus, I will reserve any further comment on it to the following section. There are approved translations of the Latin text and I will refer to these in the discussion that follows.

THE NEW ORDER

This has four Eucharistic Prayers.

THE FIRST EUCHARISTIC PRAYER

As has been noted the Latin text is the same as that of the Mass of Pius V cited above.

The first approved English translation had:[19]

> Father, we celebrate the memory of Christ, your Son. We, your people and your ministers, recall his passion, his descent among the dead, his resurrection from the dead, and his ascension into glory; and from the many gifts you have given us we offer to you, God of glory and majesty, this holy and perfect sacrifice: the bread of life and the cup of eternal salvation.

The passion of Christ, his descent into hell and his resurrection from the dead are all included but they are not qualified as 'saving'. The sacrificial element is, however, clearly expressed. Furthermore, the saving role of the sacrifice is affirmed by the final phrase, 'eternal salvation'. The 'bread of life' would seem to refer to the new (risen) life given through the sacramental reality of the Eucharist. It seems clear that the translators did not know what to do with the descent into the 'inferis' that is 'hell'. Thus they used a double formula, which is not in the Latin: 'his descent among the dead, his resurrection from the dead.' But this fails to bring out the saving purpose of this descent; Christ descended into 'hell' to liberate the souls who were in hell as a consequence of 'disobedience' (1 Pt 3:18-19). Those in 'hell' were not merely dead, they were, in some sense, sinners, and by Christ's descent into hell and resurrection they were liberated not only from death, but from sin.

The new translation has:[20]

> Therefore, O Lord, as we celebrate the memorial of the blessed passion, the resurrection from the dead, and the glorious ascension into heaven of Christ, your Son our Lord, we, your servants and your holy people, offer to your glorious majesty from the gifts that you have given us, this pure victim, this holy victim, this spotless victim, the holy bread of eternal life and the chalice of everlasting salvation.

Again, the passion, the resurrection and the ascension are all elements of the memorial. This translation has omitted his 'descent among the dead', but has kept the phrase 'the resurrection from the dead', and thus again has missed the reference to the *inferis*. Thus, again, the saving role of the resurrection is less clear.

THE SECOND EUCHARISTIC PRAYER

> *Memores igitur mortis et Resurrectionis eius, tibi, Domine, panem vitae et calicem salutis offerimus, gratias agentes quia nos dignos habuisti astare coram te et tibi ministrare.*

The first English translation had:

> In memory of his death and resurrection, we offer you, Father, this life-giving bread, this saving cup. We thank you for counting us worthy to stand in your presence and serve you.

'In memory' does not express the 'making-memory' sense of *memores*. The death is mentioned as is the resurrection but there is no explicit indication of their saving role. The saving element, however, is expressed, as already noted in the words, 'life-giving bread ... saving cup'.

The new English translation has:

Therefore, as we celebrate the memorial of his death and resurrection, we offer you, Lord, the bread of life and the chalice of salvation, giving thanks that you have held us worthy to be in your presence and minister to you.

Here the phrase, 'celebrate the memorial' occurs again; the difficulties which this creates have already been mentioned. There is no saving role explicitly attributed to either the death or the resurrection.

THE THIRD EUCHARISTIC PRAYER

This presents the Paschal mystery more fully:

Memores igitur, Domine, eiusdem Filii tui salutiferae passionis necnon mirabilis Resurrectionis et ascensionis in caelum, sed et praestolantes alterum eius adventum, offerimus tibi, gratias referentes, hoc sacrificium vivum et sanctum.

The text attributes a saving role to the passion, but not explicitly to the resurrection, which is designated simply as *mirabilis*. The eschatological fulfilment in the second coming is included. Again the sacrificial aspect is clearly indicated.

The first English official translation rendered the text as:

Father, calling to mind the death your Son endured for our salvation, his glorious resurrection and ascension into heaven, and ready to greet him when he comes again.

The translation, like the Latin text, attributes 'salvation' to the death of 'your son' but not to the resurrection.

The new translation has:

Therefore, O Lord, we celebrate the memorial of the saving passion of your Son, his wondrous resurrection and Ascension into heaven, and as we look forward to his second coming, we offer you in thanksgiving this holy and living sacrifice.

Here again, the passion is 'saving'; but the resurrection is only 'wonderous'.

THE FOURTH EUCHARISTIC PRAYER[21]

The text has, before the consecration:

'To accomplish your plan, he gave himself up to death, and rising from the dead, he destroyed death and restored life.'

This is the clearest expression of the saving power of the resurrection in the official texts: the rising Christ destroyed death and restored life.

The same prayer also has, after the consecration:

> *Unde et nos, Domine, redemtionis [*sic*] nostrae memoriale nunc celebrantes, mortem Christi eiusque descensum ad inferos recolimus, eius Resurrectionem et ascensionem ad tuam dexteram profitemur, et, exspectantes ipsius adventum in gloria, offerimus tibi eius Corpus et Sanguinem, sacrificium tibi acceptabile et toti mundo salutare.*

This is the most complete of all the prayers; it includes the death of Christ, the descent into hell and the resurrection, the Ascension and also the eschatological fulfilment. The sacrificial element is also clearly affirmed, as is the eschatological fulfilment.

The first English translation had:

> Father, we now celebrate this memorial of our redemption. We recall Christ's death, his descent among the dead, his resurrection, and his ascension to your right hand; and, looking forward to his coming in glory, we offer you his body and blood, the acceptable sacrifice which brings salvation to the whole world.

It is noteworthy that what we 'recall' according to the English is the death of Christ, his descent among the dead, his resurrection and his ascension. In the Latin, however, what is 'recalled' is his descent into 'hell', the underworld. Perhaps the translators wanted to avoid the harsh word 'hell' but this translation 'among the dead' obscures the saving role of the descent and the resurrection. By his descent into 'hell', Christ not only liberates from death but from sin.

The new English translation has:

> Therefore, O Lord, as we now celebrate the memorial of our redemption, we remember Christ's death and his descent to the realm of the dead, we proclaim his resurrection and his ascension to your right hand, and, as we await his coming in glory, we offer you his Body and Blood, the sacrifice acceptable to you which brings salvation to the whole world.

The translation recognises the 'descent into the realm of the dead', as well as the resurrection itself. However, again I would suggest that the 'realm of the dead' does not convey the full meaning of 'hell'; as I have noted Christ's descent to the underworld was for the purpose of saving the souls in sinful condition.

In this text the Latin has the phrase, *redemptionis nostrae memoriale celebrantes* occurs, which could be translated, 'we now celebrate this memorial' but the memorial is the memorial of 'our redemption'. This focus of attention is firstly not on the death and resurrection of Christ but on what we might call the 'effects' of his death and resurrection, namely our redemption. After this reference to our redemption the text then moves, as we would expect, to the events that bring about our redemption, that is, we could say to the 'causes' of our redemption: the death, resurrection and ascension. The fourth Eucharistic Prayer was composed under the influence of the Liturgy of St Basil of the Greek Orthodox Church. The theological richness of these texts clearly surpasses what is provided in the texts that have been cited previously, with the exception, of course, of the fourth Eucharistic Prayer.

Having documented and analysed the relationship between the resurrection and the Eucharist in the liturgical prayers, I now pass to a consideration of how this relationship is presented in the *Catechism*.

THE CATECHISM OF THE CATHOLIC CHURCH

The section on the Eucharist mentions the resurrection a number of times:

1330 'The *memorial* of the Lord's passion and resurrection.'

1337 '... he instituted the Eucharist as the memorial of his death and resurrection, and commanded his apostles to celebrate it until his return; 'thereby he constituted them priests of the new testament'.

1343 It was above all on 'the first day of the week', Sunday, the day of Jesus' resurrection that the Christians met 'to break bread'.

1359 The Eucharist, the sacrament of our salvation accomplished by Christ on the cross, is also a sacrifice of praise in thanksgiving for the work of creation. In the eucharistic sacrifice the whole of creation loved by God is presented to the Father through the death and the resurrection of Christ.

The mention of the resurrection in these texts would seem to be rather *pro forma*.

What shall we conclude? It would be safe to say that, compared with the liturgies of St James, St Basil and the fourth Eucharistic Prayer, the other liturgical texts reflect a less comprehensive theology of the Eucharist and the resurrection. In particular, the Western texts do not explicitly indicate the saving role of the resurrection or the risen Christ. This, however, is clearer in the Eastern texts. I suggest that, on this point, Western theology and spirituality might learn much from the East. The Eucharist is active memory of the passion and death of Jesus and thus for participants it is a saving event; the grace of the Eucharist is the divine power that liberates from sin. But surely it is not only this. The Eucharist is at the same time an active memory of the resurrection of Christ such that the faithful who participate in the Eucharist share in the power that raised Jesus and is now raising them to new and richer life.

Perhaps the best solution would be to adopt the term 'the Paschal mystery', understanding it to include all the events that have been discussed: the redeeming passion and death of Jesus, his resurrection, his victory of the evil spirits and his ascension. Questions about the saving function of particular events would then become less important and even irrelevant. However, it would still be important to insist that within the whole saving process, the resurrection itself is not an appendage but a saving action on the part of the Risen Christ. The resurrection does something for us or better, the Risen Christ saves us.

We might end by returning to the representation of the Risen Christ in the Book of Kells with which my presentation began. The figure of the Risen Christ is clearly central and dominant; the cross is present, but adorns the risen Christ, the eucharistic reference is clear, but the figures of the pelicans are set around the central figure of the risen Christ. This image presents what I wanted to say more clearly than all the words that I have written here.

NOTES

1 Since this is not intended as an historical study, I will not enter into discussions of precise dating.

2 http://www.goarch.org/chapel/liturgical_texts/basil (accessed, 1st March 2012).

3 Anscar Chupungco, *Handbook for Liturgical Studies*, III, Collegeville, Minnesota: The Liturgical Press, SA Pueblo Book, 1999, Chapter 15, 'Theology of Eucharistic Celebration' by David Power. In this chapter at p. 343, Power states that the theme of the descent into hell appears in the *Apostolic Tradition*. However, I have not found it in this text.

4 Donald P. Senior, C.P., *I Peter, Sacra Pagina*, Daniel J. Harrington SJ, ed., Collegeville: The Liturgical Press, 2003, p. 108.

5 Senior, *1 Peter,* 109.

6 Chupungco, *Handbook for Liturgical Studies*, III, p. 346.

7 Lawrence J. Johnson, *Worship in the Early Church: An Anthology of Historical Sources. Vol 1.*, Collegeville: Liturgical Press, 2009, p. 194.

8 Josef A. Jungmann SJ, *The Mass of the Roman Rite: Its Origins and Development*, vol. 2, Francis A. Brunner CSsR, trans., New York: Benziger, 1955, p. 157.

9 Lawrence J. Johnson, *Worship in the Early Church: An Anthology of Historical Sources,* CD-ROM, www.litpress.org, vol. 2, p. 259–60, 1758.

10 http://roman-orthodox.tripod.com/liturgy.html (accessed 3rd March 2012).

11 www.anastasis.org.uk (accessed 3rd March 2012).

12 Kevin Irwin, *Models of the Eucharist*, New York, Mahwah: Paulist Press, 2005,135.

13 'Joseph S. O'Leary Homepage: Another Messy Translation: The Third Eucharistic Prayer', 133.

14 St Thomas Aquinas, S. Th., III, 56, 2.

15 Josef A. Jungmann, *The Mass, An Historical, Theological, and Pastoral Survey,* Julian Fernandes SJ, trans., Mary Ellen Evans, ed., Collegeville: The Liturgical Press, 1976.

16 Joseph A. Jungmann, *The Mass of the Roman Rite,* vol.2, 218–26 analyses the memorial prayer, 'Unde et memores', but does not provide any comment on this phrase.

17 St Thomas Aquinas, S. Th., III, 52, 1.

18 'The Mass of Paul VI' means the Mass promulgated by Pope Paul VI in 1969. It is commonly called the *Novus Ordo* to distinguish it from the Traditional

Latin Mass. On 7 July 2007, in *Summorum Pontificum,* Pope Benedict XVI declared that the Mass of Paul VI is the ordinary form of the Roman Rite, while the Traditional Latin Mass is the extraordinary form.

19 The approved English translations are those published in the *Roman Missal,* revised by the Decree of the Second Vatican Council and published by Authority of Pope Paul VI, The Sacramentary, approved for use in the dioceses of the United States of America by the National Conference of Catholic Bishops and Confirmed by the Apostolic See. English translation prepared by the International Commission on English in the Liturgy, New York: Catholic Book Publishing Co., 1985.

20 The New Translations are from the *Roman Missal,* renewed by Decree of the Most Holy Second Ecumenical Council of the Vatican, promulgated by authority of Pope John Paul II, English translation according to the Third Typical Edition, for use in the dioceses of the United States of America, approved by the United States Conference of Catholic Bishops and Confirmed by the Apostolic See, New Jersey: Catholic Book Publishing Corp., 2011.

21 Jungmann, *The Mass of the Roman Rite,* p. 200.

SOME PATRISTIC INSIGHTS INTO THE EUCHARIST UNDERSTOOD AS COMMUNION

REV. PROF. FINBARR G. CLANCY SJ
Milltown Institute, Dublin

INTRODUCTION

Patristic insights into the Eucharist are enormously rich. They help us to glimpse something of the vibrant faith of the early Church as it gathered to celebrate the divine mysteries in her varied liturgical traditions. Even a cursory glance at three papal encyclicals on the Eucharist, Leo XIII's *Mirae caritatis* (1902), Paul VI's *Mysterium fidei* (1965) and John Paul II's *Ecclesia de Eucharistia* (2003) leave us in no doubt as to the continued importance and helpfulness of some of these pivotal Patristic insights on the Eucharist in formulating the Church's doctrine about this great mystery.

The Fathers commented on the Eucharist in a great variety of literary texts and genres. From earliest times the Patristic writers liked to identify prefigurements or types of the Eucharist in the Old Testament. The Lenten and Easter periods of the liturgical year were privileged times of catechesis for catechumens and neophytes, respectively, concerning the sacraments. The legacy of catechetical and mystagogical treatises or instructions on the sacraments in general, and on the Eucharist in particular, is truly impressive, especially in the fourth and fifth centuries. Explanations of various texts from scripture also provided a valuable locus for commentary and exposition on the Eucharist. Homiletic material often addressed the mystery of the Eucharist in very concise manner, encouraging the faithful to active and frequent participation in the liturgy, while also seeking to foster sentiments of reverence as they approached the awesome rites. Episcopal letters occasionally dealt with liturgical matters and addressed specific issues or aberrant practices concerning the celebration of the Church's liturgy. Liturgical texts themselves, and commentaries on them by the Fathers, also furnish us with valuable insights into the Eucharist. The specific petition of the *Pater noster* dealing with 'daily bread' often drew a pluriform interpretation in Patristic commentaries on the Lord's Prayer. The 'daily bread' was variously linked with material needs, the daily celebration of the Eucharist, and the very words of scripture itself. The poet-theologian Ephrem the Syrian often addressed the topic of the Eucharist in his various hymn cycles, texts destined for both catechetical and liturgical usage.

The 50th International Eucharistic Congress focuses on the theme of 'The Eucharist: Communion with Christ and with One Another'. The present paper seeks to look at some Patristic insights relevant to this theme, focusing in particular on how the Eucharist was understood in terms of communion. I do not intend to give an exhaustive analysis of the theme, but rather to chart some of the major insights from some of the better known Fathers as they reflect on the Eucharist. I propose to examine the topic under a number of headings. These will include: (1) the unitive significance of the eucharistic elements; (2) the significance of mixing water and wine in the chalice; (3) communion with Christ; (4) communion with one another; (5) the communal offering of the eucharistic sacrifice; and (6) the use of nuptial symbolism by the Fathers in reflecting on the sacraments and the Church flowing from Christ's wounded side on the cross (cf. Jn 19:34).

THE UNITIVE SIGNIFICANCE OF THE EUCHARISTIC ELEMENTS

In writing to the Corinthians, Paul stressed the unity of the ecclesial community, despite the diversity of its members. He argues that the diversity of members formed an organic unity because 'The fact that there is only one loaf means that, though there are many of us, we form a single body, because we all have a share in this one loaf' (1 Cor 10:17). This theme enjoyed great popularity in Patristic literature from the earliest times, Paul's insight being applied not only to the one loaf but also to the contents of the chalice.

One of our earliest liturgical documents, the *Didache*, stipulates that the following prayer was to be offered over the particles of bread: 'As this broken bread, once dispersed over the hills, was brought together and became one loaf, so may the Church be brought together from the ends of the earth into your kingdom.'[1] This brief text, which displays a strong eschatological flavour, eloquently captures the vision of the ears of wheat growing on the hillside fields being gathered and formed into the one loaf of bread for use in the Eucharist. The seeds of a Eucharistic ecclesiology are also evident here, as the symbolism of the gathered wheat spills over into the gathering of the community of the Church into God's kingdom. This same theme is re-echoed in the neighbouring paragraph of the *Didache*: 'Be mindful of your Church, O Lord; deliver it from all evil, perfect it in your love, sanctify it, and gather it from the four winds into the kingdom you have prepared for it.'[2]

Two letters from Cyprian of Carthage employ a similar type of symbolism, in one case incorporating reference to the chalice as well as the bread. The first example comes from Cyprian's *Letter* 69 to a fellow bishop Magnus. Here he states:

> Even the very sacrifices of the Lord show Christian unanimity knit together by firm and inseparable charity. For when the Lord calls bread, which is made up of the union of many grains, his body, he indicates our people whom he bore united together; and when he calls wine, which is pressed from many bunches and clusters and drawn into one, his blood, he likewise signifies our flock joined together by the mingling of a united multitude.[3]

In his famous letter to Caecilius of Biltha, dealing with the problem of the *Aquarii*, who insisted on only using water in the chalice, Cyprian used a similar line of argument:

> Thus the cup of the Lord is not water alone, or wine alone, but both are mixed together, just as flour alone or water alone cannot be the Body of the Lord, unless both have been united and joined and made solid in the structure of a single bread. By this very sacrament our people is shown to be united. Just as the many grains, collected and milled and mixed, make one bread, so let us know that in Christ, who is the heavenly bread, there is one body, to which our number has been joined and united.[4]

We meet some typical Cyprianic vocabulary in these two quotations, with his characteristic emphasis on unity, unanimity and being 'joined together by the mingling of a united multitude'.

Augustine of Hippo clearly follows Cyprian's insight, ecclesial concerns and emphasis in two famous Easter day sermons addressed to the *Infantes* on the Eucharist. He further embellishes the imagery by linking the different stages of the formation of the catechumens with the sequence involved in baking bread. In *Sermo* 227, Augustine, having cited Paul's text (1 Cor 10:17), continued as follows:

> By means of this bread he impresses on you how you must love unity. For was this bread made from one grain? Were there not many grains of wheat? Yet before they became bread, they were separate. They were joined together through water, and that after some grinding, for unless wheat is milled and moistened with water, it never reaches that form which is called bread.

He next makes the link with the stages of formation of catechumens:

> So you too, in a certain sense, were first milled by the humiliation of fasting and the sacred rites of exorcism. Next came baptism and water. You were moistened, as it were, to come to the form of bread. But there is yet no bread without fire. What, then, does fire signify? The chrismation of oil. For what feeds our fire is the sacrament of the Holy Spirit ... The Spirit manifests itself in fiery tongues, for he breathes into us the charity whereby we blaze towards God and disdain the world, and our straw is burnt away, and the heart is purified like gold. The Holy Spirit comes, then, as fire after water, and you are made bread which is the body of Christ. And for that reason, unity is signified in a particular way.[5]

Similar imagery occurs in Augustine's *Sermo* 272, coupled with many famous and memorable phrases from Augustine about the Eucharist. The relevant section of this very succinct sermon is introduced with the exclamation 'Unity! Verity! Piety! Charity! One bread'. Augustine explains:

> Remember that bread is not made from one grain, but from many. When you were exorcised you were, after a fashion, milled. When you were baptised you were moistened. When you received the fire of the Holy Spirit you were baked. Be what you see and receive what you are (*Estote quod videtis; et accipite quod estis*).

Next Augustine introduces, like Cyprian, the symbolism of the cup, furthermore linking it with the exemplary *koinonia* of the early Church:

> This is what the Apostle said about the bread, and he has already indicated quite well what we are to understand of the cup, even though he did not say it. For just as in the preparation of the bread which you see, many grains were moistened into a unity, as if there were taking place what holy scripture says about he faithful: 'They had one mind, one heart towards God' (Acts 4:32), so also in the case of the wine. Brothers, recall whence wine comes. Many grapes hang in the cluster, but the juice of the grapes is mixed in unity. So also did Christ the Lord portray us. He willed that we belong to Him. He consecrated the mystery of our peace and unity upon his table.[6]

Augustine concludes here by speaking of 'the mystery of unity' and warns that those who do not preserve 'the bond of peace' receive the Eucharist unworthily and as 'a testimony against himself'.[7]

Commenting on the bread of life discourse in John's Gospel, Augustine refers to the Eucharist as 'the bread of concord' (*panis concordiae*). He explains that those who eat this bread do not strive against each other, but seek to preserve harmony and a united household.[8] In this same sermon he uses a famous trilogy of phrases to refer to the Eucharist: 'O mystery of piety! O sign of unity! O bond of charity!'[9] The familiar appeal to the unitive significance of the eucharistic elements appears once more: 'Our Lord Jesus Christ has pointed our minds to his body and blood in those things, which from being many are reduced to some one thing. For a unity is formed by many grains forming together; and another unity is effected by the clustering together of many berries.'[10]

Gaudentius of Brescia was a direct contemporary of St Ambrose and a prominent member of the Italian episcopate. The second of his surviving *Tractates* is a mystagogical address to the newly baptised about the Eucharist. Towards the end of this comprehensive *Tractate* we witness Gaudentius employ familiar imagery based on the unitive significance of the eucharistic elements. Once again he refers to the various stages of the formation of bread from wheat, linking them this time not with the stages of formation of catechumens prior to Easter, but with significant stages in Christ's own life:

> ... It is necessary that bread be made from many grains of wheat reduced to flour, and that it be compounded with water and

> completed by means of fire, it is reasonable that the figure of the body of Christ be accepted in it. We know that he has been made one body from the multitude of the entire human race, completed through the fire of the Holy Spirit. For he was born of the Holy Spirit, and because it thus suited him to fulfil all justice (see Mt 3:15). He enters the waters of baptism so that he might consecrate them. Then filled with the Holy Spirit who had descended on him in the form of a dove, he returns from the Jordan, as the evangelist bears witness: 'Now Jesus, full of the Holy Spirit, returned from the Jordan' (Lk 4:1).

Gaudentius continues here by associating the production of wine from many grapes with the winepress of Christ's cross:

> Similarly also, the wine of his blood, gathered from the many grapes of the vine planted by him, is pressed out in the winepress of the cross, and of its own power it begins to ferment in the capacious vessels of those who receive it with faithful heart.[11]

We see in Gaudentius' *Tractate* on the Eucharist a deeply Christocentric approach to the theme of unity. The unitive significance of the eucharistic elements is closely linked with details of Christ's conception, his baptism in the Jordan and the salvific event of the cross. There is also an ecclesial message in terms of the familiar Pauline insight on the many different members forming the one body of Christ.

One of the Church's earliest martyrs, St Ignatius of Antioch, is also hailed as the father of eucharistic ecclesiology because of his repeated emphasis on the centrality of the Eucharist at the heart of the Church's life. In his famous letters, written while en route to his martyrdom in Rome, he issues clear clarion calls to the Ephesians (Eph 5,13, 20, the Philadelphians (Phil 4) and the Smyrnaeans (Smyr 7–8) to foster unity in the community through regular attendance at the Eucharist in union with their bishop. In his *Letter to the Romans* he outlines his understanding of his forthcoming martyrdom. Interestingly he identifies his martyrdom mystically with the Eucharist itself. He expresses his passionate desire 'to become purest bread for Christ by being ground by the lions' teeth' in the arena.[12] He continues by stating that he is 'fain for the bread of God and craves that blood which is love imperishable'.[13] He clearly saw his approaching martyrdom as the way of perfecting his discipleship and imitating the passion of his Saviour. He pleads earnestly with the Roman faithful not to deter him from his chosen path of discipleship. He had reminded the Ephesians that the Eucharist was 'the medicine of immortality, the sovereign remedy by which we escape death and live in Jesus Christ for ever more'.[14] Cyprian, too, had argued that the Lord's disciple would be fit for the 'chalice of martyrdom' if they had been fortified 'by the Lord's chalice'.[15]

ON THE SIGNIFICANCE OF MIXING WATER AND WINE IN THE CHALICE

Various apocryphal texts (*Acts of Peter; Acts of Thomas*) and a number of Fathers (Filaster of Brescia, Irenaeus of Lyons, Clement of Alexandria, Epiphanius of Salamis, John Chrysostom, Theodoret and Leo the Great) refer to a sect in the early Church known as the *Aquarii*.[16] These refused to use wine in the celebration of the Eucharist and consequently only used bread and water. Irenaeus attributed this wrongful practice to a faulty Christology based on a refusal to believe in the union of the two natures in Christ and a deficient understanding of salvation.[17] Cyprian of Carthage also condemned this aberrant practice in his famous *Letter* 63, one of our earliest pre-Nicene treatises on the Eucharist, without identifying who the *Aquarii* were in the immediate context.

Cyprian's long *Letter* 63 is addressed to Caecilius of Biltha, condemning the practice of the *Aquarii*. It is a deeply scriptural letter and in typical style, Cyprian marshals the scriptural evidence from both Old and New Testaments concerning the admixture of wine and water in several instances. His grasp of the relevant texts is truly impressive. In addition to scriptural evidence he makes repeated appeals in this letter to Dominical precedent in terms of Christ having used a mixed cup of wine and water at the Last Supper. Cyprian argues in his letter that in order to be faithful to established tradition, the Church must imitate exactly what our Lord did at the Last Supper.

In the course of his letter to Caecilius, Cyprian explains the reason for the Dominical practice and the established liturgical tradition of the Church: 'But when water is mixed with wine in the cup the people are signified in the water, but in the wine the blood of Christ is shown. But when water is mixed with wine in the cup, the people are united to it and the multitude of believers is linked and joined to him in whom they believed.'

He continues:

> This association and mingling of water and wine are so mixed in the cup of the Lord that the mixed elements cannot be separated from one another. Wherefore nothing can separate the Church, that is the multitude established faithfully and firmly in the Church, persevering in him in whom it has believed, from Christ; nothing can keep it from clinging and abiding in undivided love. But thus, in consecrating the cup of the Lord, water alone cannot be offered, just as wine alone cannot. For, if anyone offers wine alone, the blood of Christ is without us; but if the water is alone, the people are without Christ. But when both are mixed and joined to each other in the indiscriminate union, then the spiritual and heavenly sacrament is completed.[18]

Familiar Cyprianic concerns are clearly evident in the passages quoted here. It is no surprise that he next introduced his example of the bread being made from several grains of wheat in completing his argument, a section of the letter which we have earlier examined.

The mixed cup, containing water and wine, symbolised the inseparable union of Christ and the faithful. This was the key to both the nature of the sacrifice offered and the fruit of that sacrifice, ecclesial unity and the unity of all the faithful with Christ. We can recognise the Eucharistic Congress theme here. Cyprian's writings always display a passionate concern for ecclesial unity with typical emphasis being placed on words like 'unanimity', 'harmony', 'concord', 'unity', etc. His *Commentary on the Lord's Prayer* specifies the type of sacrifice that is most pleasing to God: 'That we be a people drawn into the unity of the Father, the Son and the Holy Spirit.'[19] This is the ultimate fruit of the Eucharist, being drawn into the life of the Trinity itself.

COMMUNION WITH CHRIST

Many of the texts that we have so far examined already put before us, in various ways, the theme of the Eucharist bringing about our communion with Christ. The Fathers use a colourful array of terminology and imagery to describe how this union with Christ is effected. The very fact that the Eucharist is received in the form of food and drink clearly puts the theme of nourishment and growth before us. Tertullian displays a wonderful appreciation of the two levels at which sacraments are perceived and work. In his work *De resurrectione carnis* he comments on the rites of Christian initiation. Having treated of baptism, chrismation, and being signed with the sign of the cross, he proceeds to describe the reception of the Eucharist as follows: 'The flesh feeds on the body and blood of Christ that the soul likewise may fatten on God – *ut et anima de deo saginetur.*'[20] Elsewhere, commenting on the return home of the prodigal son and the banquet that celebrated his home-coming, Tertullian speaks analogously of the communicant: 'feeding on the abundance of Christ's body' in the Eucharist.[21] The 'daily bread' which we petition in saying the Lord's Prayer is a petition 'asking to live forever in Christ and never to be separated from his body'.[22]

Ambrose of Milan can speak of Christ feeding his Church on the sacraments 'by which the substance of the soul is made strong'.[23] The bread of eternal life received in the Eucharist 'supports the substance of our soul'.[24] Addressing the *neophytes* on the sacraments Ambrose states: 'Receiving the flesh of Christ, you share in the food of his divine nature.'[25] Ambrose's various psalm commentaries are a fertile source for some of his teaching on the sacraments. Commenting on Psalm 1 he repeatedly urges his congregation to 'drink Christ' both in the scriptures and in the Eucharist.[26] The faithful feast daily on the Lord's passion in the sacrament of the Eucharist.[27] The nourishment we receive in the sacraments does not make the body fat, but it strengthens the heart.[28] The faithful are invited to heed Ambrose's repeated call – *Accedite ad eum!* Otherwise, by adopting a policy of keeping their distance, they run the risk of perishing, as Psalm 72:27 warns.[29] The eucharistic chalice is a *poculum inebrians*, which brings forgiveness of sins, a strengthening of the footsteps of the soul, and courage in face of martyrdom, while watering the seed of eternal life within the human soul.[30]

Augustine, like many other Fathers, uses food imagery in speaking of our union with Christ through the Eucharist. Not surprisingly he often moves to a deeper level in so doing. In one of his popular sermons he notes that in the Eucharist: 'We receive a tiny portion, and in our minds we take our fill. So it is not what is seen but what is believed that feeds us – *modicum accipimus et in corde saginamur. Non ergo quod videtur sed quod creditur pascit.*'[31] We are fed by Christ from what we receive from the cross, for we receive his very Body and Blood.[32] We encounter one of Augustine's most famous and profound statements on the Eucharist in his *Confessions:*

> Your light shone upon me in its brilliance, and I thrilled with love and dread alike. I realised that I was far away from you. It was as though I were in a land where all is different from your own and I heard a voice calling from on high saying: 'I am the food of full-grown men. Grow and you shall feed on me. But you shall not change me into your own substance, as you do with the food of your body. Instead you shall be changed into me.'[33]

As we digest the normal food we eat it becomes part of us. As we feed upon Christ in the Eucharist we are assimilated ever more deeply into his mysterious reality. It is no wonder that Augustine addressed the *neophytes* on Easter morning, encouraging and challenging them simultaneously, as he said: '*Estote quod videtis, et accipite quod estis* – Be what you see, receive what you are.'[34] It is their mystery that is placed upon the table. They must be members of the body of Christ, so that their *Amen* may be true and not a shallow or routine response.

Cyril of Jerusalem in his *Mystagogical Catecheses* on the Eucharist reminds his *neophytes* that 'by partaking of the body and blood of Christ you may become one body and one blood with him'. He uses the lovely image that when the sacred elements are imparted to our bodies 'we become χριστοφόροι – Christ-bearers'.[35] Significantly, Cyril supports his point here by citing 2 Peter 1:4 about us becoming 'partakers of the divine nature'. He continues by noting that the mystical table gives us communion with God.[36] Like many of the other Fathers already mentioned, Cyril too speaks of the Eucharist as spiritual food which strengthens the heart.[37] In keeping with a phrase already found in the *Didache*, he stresses: 'So things and persons correspond: both are holy.'[38]

Ephrem the Syrian, the poet theologian and hymn writer, speaks movingly of Christ's union with the faithful through receiving Holy Communion. Once again using imagery taken from making bread, he states: 'His body is kneaded into our bodies, his blood is poured into our arteries. All of him is kneaded into all of us.'[39] Referring to the liturgical rite of consignation, where drops of blood from the chalice were placed on the consecrated host, Ephrem says: 'Behold your image is portrayed with the blood of the grape upon the bread and portrayed on the heart by the finger of love, with pigments of faith.'[40] We are privileged to receive unlimited nourishment in the Eucharist. This leads Ephrem to exclaim: 'We have eaten you, Lord, we have drunk you; not to exhaust you, but to live by you.'[41] This same hymn famously speaks of the fire that lies hidden in the eucharistic elements, a fire that cleanses and transforms its recipients.

The awesome rites of the celebration of the Eucharist invite us 'to gaze with the inner eye at the blood flowing from Christ's side'.[42] Ephrem delights in expressing the paradox of the Christian mysteries. For us 'the Shepherd has become the food for his sheep' and 'the Planter of the garden (of Eden) has become food for our souls'.[43] In one of his homilies Ephrem speaks of the sacraments giving us, in increasing measure, the 'treasures of divine life', encouraging us simultaneously to see them like a mirror in which we glimpse the mystery of the resurrection.[44] Very like Ignatius of Antioch's reference to the Eucharist as 'medicine of immortality', Ephrem loves to refer to the Eucharist as 'medicine of life' or 'living medicine'. The Eucharist is compared to an eagle bringing us heavenward.[45] As an antidote to death and its conqueror, the Eucharist causes death to vomit forth all it has greedily consumed.[46]

John Chrysostom is hailed as the great *doctor eucharistiae* because of his rich contribution to our understanding of the multi-faceted importance of the Eucharist in our lives and in the life of the Church. In one of his homilies on Matthew's Gospel he states:

> He also commingles himself with us and makes us his body, not by faith only, but in very fact ... By him we are fed, with him we are commingled, and we are made one body and one flesh of Christ ... What shepherd feeds his sheep with his limbs? ... He himself feeds us with his own blood, and in every way entwines us with himself ... He mingles himself with each one of the faithful through the mysteries.[47]

Commenting on a key Pauline text on the Eucharist and unity (1 Cor 10:16-17), Chrysostom states:

> When we receive communion, we do not only participate and receive but we are also united. For just as that body was united

> to Christ, so also are we united to him through this bread ... He submits to be broken that he may fill all partaking of the one body ... We become the body of Christ who partake of it.[48]

He next continues here with the familiar appeal to the unitive symbolism of the eucharistic elements. By receiving the Eucharist we are conjoined with Christ and with one another. He makes appeal to the idyllic *koinonia* of the early Church (Acts 4:32) and contrasts it with the incidence of disharmony which we often encounter, a counter-sign to the Eucharist.

Chrysostom, like St Ephrem, also refers to the Eucharist making us like eagles, capable of soaring heavenwards, gazing at the Sun of Righteousness.[49] This same homily speaks of the great privilege of holding and eating the Eucharist. It is an experience belonging to 'intense love, whereby Christ draws us to an even greater love'. Not to partake of this mystical supper is tantamount to spiritual famine and death. Using a rich cascade of terms, Chrysostom exclaims: 'For this table is the sinews of our soul, the bond of our mind, the foundation of our confidence, our hope, our salvation, our light, our life.'[50] The eucharistic mystery causes heaven to be realised already here on earth.

In his commentary on the bread of life discourse in John's Gospel, Chrysostom once again appeals to the theme of being commingled with Christ:

> Let us become commingled with that flesh. This, in truth, takes place by means of the food which he has given us as a gift, because he desired to prove the love which he has for us. It is for this reason that he joined himself to us, and has brought his body down to our level, namely, that we might be one, just as a body is joined with the head. For this indeed is characteristic of those who love greatly.

Chrysostom continues by noting that it is not sufficient to see and to touch, we must go further and eat of this mystic reality and savour deeply the intense love the Head has for his members:

> This blood makes the image of our King bloom in us, it produces an inconceivable beauty; it does not permit the nobility of soul to fade, since it waters and nourishes it without ceasing ... this blood at once waters the soul and creates a certain power in it.

> This blood, when worthily received, drives away demons and puts them far from us, and summons to us the angels and the Lord of the angels. Where they see the blood of the Lord demons flee, but angels gather. This blood, poured out, has cleansed the whole world.[51]

The Eucharist cleanses, beautifies and enflames the soul, making heaven accessible to it.

COMMUNION WITH ONE ANOTHER

Closely allied with the theme of communion with Christ, by means of the Eucharist, is the twin theme of communion with each other. This should be clear already from our previous reflection on the unitive significance of the eucharistic elements. Union with Christ the Head necessarily involves union with his members. This theme finds abundant expression in Patristic sources and involves several interrelated aspects. The Eucharist is always understood as a communal celebration, with emphasis put on the gathering of the assembly for the awesome rites and the joy of the assembly in welcoming the newly baptised into their midst.

Another important aspect hinges on Jesus' teaching in the Sermon on the Mount about the need for reconciliation in the community prior to offering sacrifice to God (cf. Mt 5:23-24). This is closely connected to the significance of the 'kiss of peace' in the eucharistic liturgy and the need for unison between heart and lips, if the exchange of a sign of peace is to be a meaningful gesture. The petition for forgiveness in reciting the *Pater noster,* immediately before receiving communion, was also important in this regard. From earliest times the eucharistic assembly saw itself as a caring and compassionate assembly. This expressed itself in prayer for penitents, the sick, the dead and the different categories of those in need. Similarly collections were made for the needy. Communion was brought to the sick and housebound. The Eucharist was seen to send people to care for the needy and mediate the Good Shepherd's love and care to them. We will explore these themes with some representative Patristic texts.

In the description of the Sunday assembly for the breaking of bread in the *Didache,* the author(s) firstly remind the congregation of the need 'to make confession of your faults so that your sacrifice may be a pure one'. With a clear reference to the Sermon on the Mount, the text also refers to the need for reconciliation with anyone with whom one holds a difference, once again in order to avoid profanation of the sacrifice to be offered.[52] We find similar appeals to Jesus' teaching on reconciliation prior to receiving the Eucharist in both Cyril of Jerusalem and John Chrysostom. Commenting on the exchange of the kiss of peace, in *Mystagogical Catechesis* 5, Cyril speaks of it 'effecting a commingling of souls, pledging complete forgiveness'. It is a sign of true union of hearts and the banishing of any grudges among the brethren.[53]

In his *Sermon on the Betrayal by Judas*, Chrysostom states eloquently: 'This sacrifice was instituted for the sake of peace with your brother.' The time of the awesome mysteries reminds us of no other commandment but that of reconciliation. He encourages his congregation to believe that they receive healing from 'the table of peace'. Consequently, feelings of wrath against one's brother, holding grudges and harbouring resentment must be banished. The faithful must cultivate reverence for the goal of the sacrificial offering. Chrysostom states that the time of the 'holy kiss and awe-inspiring embrace' must not be perfunctory actions: 'Let us blend into one body, not mingling bodies, but joining our souls to one another with the bond of love. For thus will we be able to enjoy the table set before us.'[54]

Ephrem frequently associates the Eucharist with healing and forgiveness. The Eucharist is described as a 'fountain of healing'.[55] The altar is often referred to as the 'table of reconciliation'.[56] Freedom is linked with the reception of Christ's bread, just as the erasure of debts is associated with receiving from the chalice.[57] Ephrem states that if the dead receive benefit from God at the sacred moment of the fraction of the host, how much more do those still living receive the gift of forgiveness at this same moment.[58]

Justin Martyr's *First Apology* preserves a precious account for us of one of the earliest know celebrations of the Sunday Eucharist in the Early Church and the special celebration of First Holy Communion for the newly baptised. He describes how the newly baptised were escorted into the main assembly and received the kiss of peace as new members. He also describes the distribution of communion by the deacons to those present and to those who were absent.[59] He displays a keen awareness that the Eucharist is not ordinary food and that it nourishes our flesh and blood by assimilation.[60] The opening lines of his description of the Sunday Eucharist describe how the members visit each other, showing special solicitude for all who are in want.

Justin gives a moving description of people gathering from the town and countryside for the celebration of the Sunday Eucharist. All the details of the liturgy he describes are recognisable to us. Once again he describes the deacons distributing communion and bringing it to those who were absent. The members of the congregation were invited to contribute to the collection being taken up, according to their means. He sketches for us the different categories of people for whom the collection was intended, and how the collection was left with the president for distribution to the needy, as he thought best.[61] The rich tradition of *diaconia* in the Early Church, often entrusted to the deacons or monastic centres, owes its inspiration to the institutionalisation of this caring attitude of the Christian community towards the needy, which found concrete expression when the community assembled to celebrate the Eucharist.[62]

The writings of many of the Fathers remind us that they were not only skilled exegetes, preachers and theologians. They also possessed a keen social consciousness and an ability to stand up as prophetic champions of the poor, often offering a scathing critique of the extravagance of societal lifestyle and the accompanying chronic neglect of the poor. One great champion of the poor was St John Chrysostom.[63] The manner in which he connected the Eucharist with care for the poor is noteworthy. In his twenty-seventh homily on 1 Corinthians, Chrysostom notes that Jesus considered everyone worthy of the same eucharistic table, a table that is awesome and surpasses the dignity of all.[64] This insight carries with it an ethical imperative for those who receive the Eucharist:

> If, therefore, you come to the Eucharist, do not do anything unworthy of the Eucharist. Do not shame your brother or neglect him in his hunger. Do not be intoxicated, do not insult the Church. You come giving thanks for what you have enjoyed, so give back something in exchange and do not cut yourself off from your neighbour. For Christ gave equally to all, when he said: 'Take,

> Eat.' He gave his body equally, but you do not even share ordinary bread equally.[65]

Chrysostom continues here by noting that we cannot make a remembrance of Christ at the Eucharist and then continue by despising the poor. One partakes unworthily of the Eucharist if one neglects the poor.

In this same homily, Chrysostom challenges his congregation to learn to recognise, love and serve the poor by frequenting the awesome table at which the Master feeds everyone without distinction, by giving of himself generously to all. Sharing in the spiritual food of the Eucharist must lead us to share our material food with the needy. Chrysostom here weaves in the parable about the unforgiving debtor (cf. Mt 18:23-35) to good effect. He states:

> You have partaken of a table so wonderful, and when you should be gentler than anyone, and like the angels, you become more cruel than any. You have tasted the blood of the Lord and not even thus do you acknowledge your brother. What pardon can you deserve? Indeed if you did not know him before this, you should have come to know him from the table. But now you dishonour the very table, for he was counted worthy to partake of it, but you do not count him worthy of your food. Have you not heard how much the one who demanded the one hundred *denarii* suffered, how he made void the gift bestowed on him?[66]

Chrysostom notes that the behaviour which Paul reprimanded among the Corinthians is still afflicting society. People are happy to approach the table of the Eucharist with the poor, but on going out from Church they do not notice the poor and 'hurry past the hungry'. They are culpable of a gross neglect of the poor, being caught up in a cocoon of materialism and the pursuit of luxury. He warns that the 'evils of luxury' are fatal 'after the communion of the mysteries'. Making reference to the parable of the last judgement (cf. Mt 25:31-46), Chrysostom advises his congregation: 'Let us feed Christ, let us give him to drink, let us clothe him. These things are worthy of that table.'[67]

Similar themes to these recur in John Chrysostom's famous fiftieth *Homily on Matthew.* Here his 'golden mouth' is truly in evidence as he challenges his congregation once more to tend Christ in the poor, rather than spending their money in decorating the sanctuary of the Church in lavish manner. God needs 'golden hearts', not 'golden vessels'. Chrysostom once again refers to the last judgement scene in developing his thought:

> Would you honour the body of Christ? Do not despise his nakedness; do not honour him here in Church clothed in silk vestments and then pass him by unclothed and frozen outside. Remember that he who said: 'This is my body' (Mt 26:26), and made good his words, also said: 'You saw me hungry and gave me no food', and, 'in so far as you did it not to one of these, you did it not to me' (Mt 25:42, 45). In the first sense the body of Christ does not need clothing but worship from a pure heart. In the second sense it does need clothing and all the care we can give it.[68]

Christ needs to be honoured in an appropriate way. Chrysostom is not against the kindness of benefactors decorating and ennobling Churches, but he calls for a judicious discernment and balance in these matters:

> What is the use of loading Christ's table with gold cups while he himself is starving? Feed the hungry and then if you have any money left over, spend it on the altar table. Will you make a cup of gold and withhold a cup of water? What use is it to adorn the altar with cloth of gold hanging and deny Christ a coat for his back! What would that profit you? Tell me: if you saw someone starving and refused to give him any food but instead spent your money on adorning the altar with gold, would he thank you? Would he rather not be outraged? Or if you saw someone in rags and stiff with the cold and then did not give him clothing but set up golden column in his honour, would he not say he was being made a fool of and insulted?[69]

John Chrysostom invites us to consider that Christ comes in the guise of the tramp seeking a night's lodging. Just as with the fabric of the Church, Chrysostom is not against people having homes that are nice and comfortable. However, they must not neglect the poor in their need: 'Adorn your house if you will, but do not forget your brother in distress. He is a temple of infinitely greater value.' In his homilies on Lazarus and Dives (cf. Lk 16:19-31), Chrysostom movingly refers to the destitute Lazarus being like a pearl stuck in the mud or a gold coin by the side of the road, a pearl and gold coin which the rich man failed to notice and tend.[70] As Chrysostom had stated in an earlier *Homily on Matthew*, the Lord has devised many means of bringing us together in unity. Chief among these in the eucharistic cup: 'For our Father, wishing to bring us to familial affection, has devised this also, that we should drink from one cup.'[71] This is a reality that belongs to 'intense love'.

THE COMMUNAL OFFERING OF THE EUCHARISTIC SACRIFICE

Various Patristic texts, going back to some of our earliest witnesses, refer to the Eucharist using sacrificial categories. The Fathers liked to see the Eucharist as a sacrifice fulfilling its Old Testament prefigurements. A particularly close association was always seen between the Jewish Passover sacrifice and the Christian celebration of the Eucharist. Parallel developments tended to take place whereby the theology of the cross and that of the Eucharist both came to be understood in terms of sacrifice. Notable, too, is the early and repeated interpretation of a text from the prophet Malachi (Mal 1:11, 14) with reference to the Eucharist. The Eucharist was seen to be the pure sacrifice that is offered universally to God by all the nations, in fulfilment of Malachi's prophecy.

The description of the celebration of the Jewish Passover in the Book of Exodus puts great emphasis on the communal nature of the festive celebration. It was a celebration of the whole community (cf. Ex 12:3, 6). Smaller households were to join with a larger group (cf. Ex 12:4). As if anticipating the later technical liturgical term *anamnesis*, the Passover celebration is described as being 'a day of remembrance for you' (Ex 12:14). It has a certain timeless quality about it and it was to be observed for all generations as a day of festival. We can easily see how many of these ideas colour the Christian approach to the offering of the eucharistic sacrifice. Thus Cyprian can state: 'The passion of the Lord is, indeed, the sacrifice which we offer.'[72]

Among all of the Fathers it is Augustine who gives us the most systematic exposition about the nature of Christian sacrifice, specifically with reference to the Eucharist. Book ten of his *Confessions* concludes with a deeply personal comment on how important he considered the Eucharist to be in his own life and ministry as a bishop.[73] This section was preceded by one describing Christ as both 'priest and sacrifice, and priest because sacrifice' (Conf. 10.43.69). Augustine describes Jesus Christ as the *verissimus sacerdos* who offers the *verissimum sacrificium*.[74] In a very succinct statement Augustine links the stages of prefigurement, fulfilment and sacramental celebration with reference to the Eucharist as follows:

> Before the coming of Christ, the flesh and blood of this sacrifice were *foreshadowed* in the animals slain; in the passion of Christ the types were *fulfilled* by the true sacrifice; after the ascension of Christ, this sacrifice is *commemorated* in the sacrament.[75]

Both the manna and the Passover of the Old Testament are merely a shadow (*umbra*) of the truth (*veritas*) revealed in Christ. It is in book ten of the *City of God* that Augustine gives his most thorough exposition on the nature and purpose of Christian sacrifice. It is clear from his definitions that the twin goals of 'cleaving to God' and 'seeking our neighbour's good' lie at the core of his understanding of the concept of sacrifice. We can see the theme of the Eucharistic Congress shining forth here. Augustine states: Thus the true sacrifice is offered in every act which is designed to unite us to God in a holy fellowship, every act, that is, which is directed to that final Good which makes possible our true felicity.[76]

A little later in the same section Augustine relates this specifically to the Eucharist, building on the Pauline notion of the union of head and members constituting the one body of Christ, the Church:

> This is the sacrifice of Christians, who are 'many, making up the body of Christ' (Rm 12:5). This is the sacrifice which the Church continually celebrates in the sacrament of the altar, a sacrament well-known to the faithful, where it is shown to the Church that she herself is offered in the offering which she presents to God.[77]

A final stone in the mosaic of his thought here is his description of the Church being organically united with Christ's offering of himself to the Father:

> Thus, he is both the priest, himself making the offering, and the oblation. This is the reality, and he intended the daily sacrifice of

> the Church to be the sacramental symbol of this; for the Church being the body of which he is the head, learns to offer herself through him.[78]

Thus, for Augustine the concept of sacrifice involves our cleaving to God, with the pleasing dispositions of a contrite heart and mercy, and seeking to build a 'holy fellowship' with one another. This is only possible with Christ's pivotal role as our mediator. It is through, with, and in Christ, the head and members forming the *Christus totus*, that we learn to offer ourselves with him in our regular celebrations of the Eucharist. It is no wonder that Augustine could identify himself as bishop with 'the poor who long to be filled' with this saving mystery (see Conf. 10.43.70).

Many of the Fathers liked to draw a close association between martyrdom and the Eucharist. Indeed Ignatius of Antioch's description of his desire to become 'pure bread for Christ', having been pulverised into flour by the mouths of the lions, suggests such a relationship. The account of the martyrdom of Polycarp also shows close links with the details of the gospel passion narratives and with the Eucharist. Here we find Polycarp being described like 'a loaf of bread being baked in an oven', emitting a pleasing aroma.[79] Cyprian was at pains to see that those in prison, during periods of persecution under Decius and Valerian, were fortified by receiving the Eucharist as they approached the possibility of their own martyrdom. Indeed, he states that one is fit for the chalice of martyrdom if fortified by the Lord's chalice.[80] Augustine likewise can hail St Laurence, deacon and martyr, as one who 'ate and drank well' in the Eucharist, observing carefully what was on the altar at which he served, and imitating these same mysteries in his own self-offering as a martyr.[81]

THE CROSS, THE CHURCH AND THE SACRAMENTS

The fruits of Christ's Paschal mystery are celebrated in the sacraments by the Church. It was common for the Fathers to articulate the vital links between the cross and the Church's sacramental celebrations. In doing so, they often have recourse to nuptial imagery to describe Christ's close relationship with his spouse the Church. A favourite text here is John 19:34 describing the wound inflicted in Christ's side by the soldier's lance after the crucifixion. The streams of blood and water flowing from Christ's wounded side were seen to be symbolic of the sacramental life of the Church, the blood being commonly linked with the Eucharist and the water with baptism.

All three strands of the Patristic tradition, Greek, Latin and Syriac, exhibit a certain predilection for linking John 19:34 with the description of Eve being formed from Adam's side in Genesis 2:21-22. Just as Adam was led into a deep sleep, so too, Christ, as second Adam, endured the sleep of death on the cross. From Adam's side a rib was extracted and built up into Eve. From Christ's wounded side, blood and water flowed forth, the fountains of sacramental life of the Church by which she, as second Eve, is formed. Just as Eve's name was interpreted as 'mother of the living' (Gn 3:20), so too, the Church becomes a 'mother of the living', giving birth to new members in baptism and nourishing her members with the Eucharist. As Eve became Adam's spouse and helpmate, the Church likewise fulfils these role in regard to Christ her spouse. The two are united in a close and loving union, as Paul had stressed in Ephesians 5:31-32.

This pattern of typology is extremely common in the Fathers.[82] We shall just examine a few texts by way of illustration of the deep bonds of communion between Christ, the Church and the sacrament of the Eucharist. Commenting on the wounding of Christ's side in John's passion narrative, Chrysostom states:

> Moreover, in addition to this, an ineffable mystery was also accomplished, for 'there came out blood and water'. It was not accidentally or by chance that these streams came forth, but because the Church has been established from both of these. Her members know this, since they have come to birth by water and are nourished by flesh and blood. The mysteries have their source from there, so that when you approach the awesome chalice you may come as if you were about to drink from his very side.[83]

In one of his *Baptismal Catecheses,* Chrysostom speaks to the *neophytes* about the wound in Christ's side as a breach in the wall of the temple, whence he received the treasure and the gift of salvation emanating from the sacrifice on the Cross. The Church, the New Eve, was fashioned from this same wound in Christ's side.[84]

Ambrose likes to describe the wound in Christ's side as being a source of reconciliation and healing. It is no foul and festering wound, as wounds often are, but rather one exhaling the 'perfume of grace', like a fountain of life, bringing healing wherever it flows.[85] In one place he compares Jesus' wounded side to a balsam tree in the vineyards of Engedi:

> In the vineyard of Engedi, grows a tree which, if gashed, yields a fragrant balm. If you do not cut the tree, the balm refuses to flow. Once its bark has been cut by the hand of the master, the tears begin to flow. Just as the tears of Christ, crucified on the tree of temptation, were shed to wipe away the sins of the people, a balm poured from a merciful heart. All the while he cried: 'Father, forgive them, for they do not know what they are doing' (Lk 23:34). So Jesus pierced upon the tree by a lance, poured out blood and water, sweeter than any perfume.[86]

Ambrose also compares Christ to a scented apple hanging on the tree, the sweetest of the orchard's fruits. This apple is wounded, but is sweet to the taste, and 'Christ is good to eat'.[87]

Augustine, too, writes eloquently using this typology. He liked to link the wound in Christ's side with the door on the side of Noah's ark (cf. Gn 6:16). The wound is described as an *ostium vitae*, or doorway to life. In one place he stresses that the soldier 'opened' Christ's side, as if opening a door, rather than piercing or puncturing Christ's side. The wounded side of Christ becomes a doorway to salvation, just as the door in Noah's ark was the way to safety for Noah, his family and the animals, as they were rescued at the time of the flood.[88] Augustine notes perceptively that the text dealing with the formation of Eve from Adam's rib speaks of the rib 'being built up' into Eve. He indicates that the Church is analogously 'built up' by the sacraments flowing from Christ's side.[89] He asks, too, what groom gives his beloved bride his own blood as her wedding gift, yet this is what Christ does for the Church.[90] Similarly he asks: 'What patient is cured by the death of his physician?' Once again, it is Christ who accomplished this mysterious deed through the cross, motivated by love for his bride.[91] He is truly the wounded-healer.

In St Ephrem's *Armenian Hymn* 49, he encourages the faithful to 'gaze with the inner eye' at the blood flowing from Christ's wounded side on the cross. A peculiarity of the Syriac tradition, found not only in St Ephrem, is the idea that the soldier's spear, by wounding Christ's side, reverses the plight of the entrance to the Garden of Eden being blocked by the cherub with a flaming sword (cf. Gn 3:24). The soldier's lance, by wounding Christ's side, effectively opens the gates of paradise:

> From the rock water gushed forth for the Jewish people who drank and were strengthened. From the wood of Golgotha the fountain of life gushed forth for the gentiles.
>
> By the edge of the sword was the way to the Tree of Life guarded, but now the Lord of the Tree has given himself as food for the gentiles.
>
> Whereas the first Adam was given the trees of Eden as food, to us the Planter of Eden has himself become food for our souls.
>
> We went forth from Paradise with Adam, when he left it, but now, that that lance is removed by the other, let us gird ourselves and enter.[92]

Christ's wounded side becomes the key unlocking the gates of paradise. Ephrem describes not only water and blood flowing from Christ's side, but also 'oil', intended for the sick. The crucified Lord is the source of all the sacraments through which the members of the Church are initiated, nourished and healed.[93]

CONCLUSION

While celebrating the 50th International Eucharistic Congress this year we are also marking the fiftieth anniversary of the opening of the Second Vatican Council. In his opening speech at the Council, John XXIII urged the participants to adopt a policy and a methodology in their deliberation and debates that combined *ressourcement* and *aggiornamento*. He advocated the return to the nourishing study of scripture, the Fathers and the early liturgies of the Church in addition to an attentive reading of the signs of the times. The Church must engage in a Janus-like exercise of looking back and looking forward.

This paper has been an exercise in *ressourcement*, engaging with varied texts from the Patristic tradition in the hope of gleaning some fresh inspiration and insight from the rich patrimony of the past. One of the great fruits of Vatican II was the recovery of a greater sense of the mystery of the Church understood as a *communio* of worship and service. Rooted in the mystery of the Trinity itself, in whose mission she actively shares, the Church is invited to be an icon of the Trinitarian fellowship itself in her constitution, her liturgical celebrations, her pastoral outreach and her doctrinal role. At the heart of the *communio* of the Church is the Eucharist, the source and summit of the Church's life and mission.

Attentive to the theme of the Eucharistic Congress, this paper sought to look at some Patristic insights into the understanding of the Eucharist as communion. We began by looking at the unitive significance of the eucharistic elements of bread and wine used in the celebration of the Eucharist. Building on Paul's teaching in 1 Corinthians 10:16-17, we saw how several Fathers made regular appeal to this theme in seeking to overcome divisions in their communities and foster greater harmony, concord and unanimity. Similarly, Cyprian's explanation of the liturgical significance of mixing water and wine in the chalice reminds us of the inseparability of Christ and our selves in the offering of the Eucharist.

Two further sections of the paper explored the twin themes of the Eucharistic Congress, 'communion with Christ' and 'communion with one another'. We saw how the Fathers used a rich array of language and metaphors to describe our union with Christ, often appealing to the metaphor of food and nourishment, but also speaking of growing in the divine life, anticipating the resurrection, bearing the image of our King and sharing his divine nature. Holy things were destined for holy people and helped fashion this holiness. Union with each other stressed the need for and practice of reconciliation among Church members, so that the right atmosphere characterised the offering of the Eucharist and that the liturgical kiss of peace was a meaningful sign. The Eucharist was clearly seen by the Fathers as a privileged locus for praying for others, the sick, the dead, and all who were in need. Making a collection for those in need was another concrete expression of 'communion'. Likewise, the powerful and challenging statements of someone like John Chrysostom, on the ethical imperative of caring for the poor, stressed the close link between the Eucharist and social outreach to others. We can never share the bread of the Eucharist with others and yet 'rush past the poor and the hungry', ignoring the pearl and the golden coin on the side of the road.

An exploration of the theme of sacrifice, so commonly associated with discourse about the Eucharist, led us to understand with Augustine the deeper meaning of the term and its relevance for a two-fold union, involving the community's cleaving to God and the establishment of a holy fellowship among its members. Augustine also stressed the union of the Church's offering and Christ's offering in the Eucharist. Building on Pauline ecclesiology, he loved to dwell on the union of head and members, constituting the *totus Christus*, in offering the Eucharist. It is through this communal offering that the Church learns to offer herself with Christ. It is no wonder that he addressed the *neophytes* in Hippo on Easter morning with the eloquent and crisp phrase: 'Be what you see, receive what you are.' Their own mystery was placed before them on the altar, inviting a meaningful response in their *Amen*. Finally, we looked at Patristic exegesis of John 19:34, noting the close links between the wounded Christ on the cross, the gift of the sacraments and the formation of Christ's bride, the Church. Many mysteries lay hidden in the side of Christ. The Eucharist and the 'perfume of grace', emanating from his pierced side, both invite and enable us to continue to work with zeal and energy to renew and deepen the manifold bonds of communion in the Church today.

NOTES

1 *Didache* 9. The English translation is taken from Maxwell Staniforth and Andrew Louth's *Early Christian Writings: The Apostolic Fathers*, Penguin: Harmondsworth, 1987, pp. 194–5.

2 Ibid.,10 (*Early Christian Writings*, p. 195).

3 Cyprian, *Ep*.69.5 (CSEL, 3.2,754; FOTC, 51, 247–8).

4 Idem, *Ep*.63.13 (CSEL, 3.2,712). The English translation is taken from Daniel J. Sheerin, *The Eucharist* (Message of the Fathers of the Church), vol. 7, M. Glazier: Wilmington, Delaware, 1986, 264.

5 Augustine, *Sermo* 227 (PL, 38, 1100; Sheerin, *The Eucharist*, pp. 96–7). See Cor Traets, 'The Eucharist and Christian Community: Some Pauline and Augustinian Evidence', *Louvain Studies* 12 (1987), pp. 152–71.

6 Idem, *Sermo* 272 (PL, 38, 1247–8; Sheerin, *The Eucharist*, 95).

7 Exactly similar sentiments are expressed in a related sermon by Augustine (*Sermo Gurlferbytanus* 7 = *Sermo* 229A.2, also addressed to the *Infantes* on the 'sacrament of unity', MA 1, 462–4; Sheerin, *The Eucharist*, 100–1).

8 Augustine, *In Io. ev. tr.* 26.14 (PL, 35,1613; NPNF, 7,172).

9 Ibid., 26.13 (PL, 35,1613; NPNF, 7,172).

10 Ibid., 26.17 (PL, 35,1614; NPNF, 7,173).

11 Gaudentius of Brescia, *Tractatus* 2 (CSEL, 68, 31–2; Sheerin, *The Eucharist*, 92–3).

12 Ignatius of Antioch, *Ep. ad Rom.* 4 (*Early Christian Writings*, 86).

13 Ibid., 7 (*Early Christian Writings*, 87).

14 Idem, *Ad Eph.* 20 (*Early Christian Writings*, 66). For a fuller analysis of Ignatius' linkage between the Eucharist and martyrdom see Finbarr G. Clancy, 'Imitating the Mysteries that you Celebrate: Eucharist and Martyrdom in the Early Patristic Period', *The Great Persecution: The Proceedings of the Fifth Patristic Conference*, Maynooth, 2003, D. Vincent Twomey & Mark Humphries, eds, Dublin: Four Courts Press, 2009, pp. 106–40, at pp. 107–13.

15 Cyprian, *Ep*.57.2; 58.1; 63.15 (CSEL, 3.2,652, 657, 714; FOTC, 51,159, 163, 213).

16 See Francesca Cocchini 'Aquarii' Angelo Di Berardino, ed., *Encyclopedia of the Early Church,* James Clarke & Co.: Cambridge, 1992, vol. 1, 64.

17 Irenaeus of Lyons, *Adv. Haer.* 5.13 (*Ante Nicene Christian Library*, Vol. 9, 57).

18 Cyprian of Carthage, *Ep*.63.13 (CSEL, 3.2, 711–2; Sheerin, *The Eucharist*, pp. 264).

19 Idem, *De dom. orat.* 23, '*Sacrificium Deo maius est pax nostra et fraterna concordia et de unitate Patris et Filii et Spiritus Sancti plebs adunata*' (CSEL, 3.1,285; FOTC, 36, 148).

20 Tertullian, *De resurr. car.* 8.3 (CCSL, 2, 931).

21 Idem, *De pudicitia* 9.16 (CCSL, 2, 1298).

22 Idem, *De orat.* 6.2, '*Itaque petendo panem quotidianum perpetuitatem postulamus in Christo et individuitatem a corpore eius*' (CCSL, 1,261).

23 Ambrose, *De mysteriis* 9.55, ' ... *quibus animae firmatur substantia*' (CSEL, 73, 113; FOTC, 44, 26).

24 Idem, *De sacr.* 5.4.24, '... *qui animae nostrae substantiam fulcit*' (CSEL, 73,68; FOTC, 44, 316).

25 Ibid., 6.1.4, ' ... *et tu, qui accipis carnem, divinae eius substantiae in illo participaris alimento*' (CSEL, 73,73; FOTC, 44, 320).

26 Idem, *Explan. Ps.XII.*1.33 (CSEL, 64, 29). The English translation is taken from Íde Ní Riain's *Commentary of St Ambrose on Twelve Psalms,* Halcyon Press; Dublin, 2000, 21.

27 Ibid., 43.37, ' ... *cuius cotidie vescimur sacramento*' (CSEL, 64,289; Ní Riain, *Commentary on Twelve Psalms*, 227).

28 Idem, *Expos.Ps.CXVIII.*18.26, ' ... *meus cibus est qui non corpus inpinguat sed confirmat cor hominis*' (CSEL, 62, 411). The English translation is taken from Íde Ní Riain's, *Commentary of St Ambrose on Psalm 118*, Halcyon Press: Dublin, 1998, p. 263.

29 Ibid.,18.28 (CSEL, 62, 411–2; Ní Riain, *Commentary on Ps. 118*, 263).

30 Idem, *Explan. Ps.XII.*1.33; 35.19 (CSEL, 64,29, 63; Ní Riain, *Commentary on Twelve Psalms*, 21, 47); *Expos. Ps.CXVIII.*21.4 (CSEL, 62, 475; Ní Riain, *Commentary on Ps.118*, 305–6).

31 Augustine, *Sermo* 112.5 (PL, 38, 645; WSA III/4, 150).

32 Idem, *Enarr. in Ps.* 100.9, '*Nam et nos de cruce Domini pascimur, quia corpus ipsius manducamus*' (PL, 37, 1290; WSA III/19, 40); *Sermo Denis* 3 = 228B.2, '*Hoc agnoscite in pane, quod pependit in cruce; hoc in calice, quod mandavit ex latere*' (MA 1,18–20 at 19; Sheerin, *The Eucharist*, p. 103). Sheerin notes, as likewise many other scholars, the lack of consensus on whether *Sermo Denis* 3 is an authentic Augustinian text or not.

33 Idem, *Conf.* 7.10.16, '*Cresce, et manducabis me. Nec tu me in te mutabis, sicut cibus carnis tuae; sed tu mutabis in me*' (PL, 32,742). The English translation is taken from R.S. Pine-Coffin, *Confessions of St Augustine*, Penguin: Harmondsworth, 1961, p. 147.

34 Idem, *Sermo* 272 (PL, 38,1247–8). See also *Sermo Denis* 3 = 228B.3 (MA, 1,19; WSA III/6,262).

35 Cyril of Jerusalem, *Myst. Cat.* 4.3 (PG, 33, 1100; FOTC, 64, 182).

36 Ibid., *Myst. Cat.* 4.7 (PG, 33, 1101; FOTC, 64, 183–4).

37 Ibid., *Myst. Cat.* 4.9 (PG, 33, 1104; FOTC, 64, 186). Cyril draws inspiration here from Psalm 103(104):15.

38 Ibid., *Myst. Cat.* 5.19 (PG, 33, 1124; FOTC, 64, 202). See also *Didache* 9–10 (*Early Christian Writings,* 195).

39 Ephrem the Syrian, *Hymns on Virginity* 37.2. The English translation here is taken from Sidney H. Griffith's article '"Spirit in the Bread; Fire in the Wine": The Eucharist as "Living Medicine" in the Thought of Ephraem the Syrian', *Modern Theology* 15.2 (1999, pp. 225–46 at p. 230).

40 Idem, *Hymns on the Nativity* 16.7. See Kathleen McVey, *Ephrem the Syrian: Hymns,* Classics of Western Spirituality series, Paulist Press: New York, Mahwah, 1989, 150.

41 Idem, *Hymns on Faith* 10.18. The English translation is taken from Robert Murray, 'A Hymn of St Ephrem to Christ on the Incarnation, the Holy Spirit, and the Sacraments', *Eastern Churches Review* 3 (1970–1, 142–50 at 144).

42 Idem, *Armenian Hymns* 49.4. The English translation is taken from Sebastian Brock, *The Harp of the Spirit,* Studies Supplementary to *Sobornost* No.4, London: Fellowship of St Alban & St Sergius, 1983, pp. 80–2 at p. 80.

43 Idem, *Hymns on Unleavened Bread* 14.23 (S. Griffith, 'Spirit in the Bread', 237); *Hymns on the Church* 3.21 (see Joseph P. Amar, 'Perspectives on the Eucharist in St Ephrem the Syrian', *Worship* 61 [1987, 441–54 at 445]); *Armenian Hymns* 49.10 (S. Brock, *The Harp of the Spirit,* 81).

44 Idem, *Homily* 3.2.4–5 (see T. J. Lamy, *Sancti Ephrem Syri Hymni et Sermones,* Malines, 1886, 3, 216–22). This is the Patristic text used in the Office of Readings in the *Liturgy of the Hours,* vol.3, 45*–46*, for the memorial of St Ephrem on 9th June.

45 Idem, *Hymns on Unleavened Bread* 17.12 (SC, 502, 150). See Sebastian Brock, 'The Poet as Theologian', *Sobornost* 7.4 (1977, 243–50 at 247).

46 Idem, *Homily on Our Lord* 3.3–4 (FOTC, 91, 279).

47 John Chrysostom, *Homily* 82.5 *on Matthew* (PG, 58, 743–4; Sheerin, *The Eucharist,* pp. 290–1).

48 Idem, *Homily* 24.2 *on 1 Corinthians* (PG, 61, 200; Sheerin, *The Eucharist,* 210).

49 See his *Homily* 24.3 *on 1 Corinthians* (PG, 61, 203; Sheerin, *The Eucharist,* pp. 293–4).

50 Ibid, *Homily* 24.5 *on 1 Corinthians* (PG, 61, 204–5; Sheerin, *The Eucharist,* pp. 296).

51 Idem, *Homily* 46.3 *on John* (PG, 59, 260–1; Sheerin, *The Eucharist*, p. 205).

52 *Didache* 14 (*Early Christian Writings*, p. 197).

53 Cyril of Jerusalem, *Myst. Cat.* 5.3 (PG, 33, 1112; FOTC 64, 192–3).

54 John Chrysostom, *Sermon on the Betrayal of Judas* 6 (PG, 49, 382; Sheerin, *The Eucharist*, pp. 146–7).

55 Ephrem the Syrian, *Hymns on Faith* 10.7 (Murray, 'A Hymn of St Ephrem to Christ', 143).

56 Idem, *Armenian Hymns* 49.15 (Brock, *Harp of the Spirit*, 82); *Hymns on Faith* 10.16 (Murray, 'A Hymn of St Ephrem to Christ', 144).

57 Idem, *Hymns on the Church* 32.2: 'Blessed is the one who granted us freedom with his bread and erased the bill of our debts with his chalice' (J. P. Amar, 'Perspectives on the Eucharist', 450).

58 Idem, *Armenian Hymns* 49.17 (Brock, *Harp of the Spirit*, 82).

59 Justin Martyr, *1 Apol.* 65 (PG, 6, 428; Sheerin, *The Eucharist*, pp. 33–4).

60 Ibid., *I Apol.* 66 (PG, 6, 428–9; Sheerin, *The Eucharist*, p. 34).

61 Ibid., *1 Apol.* 67 (PG, 6, 429; Sheerin, *The Eucharist*, p. 35).

62 Benedict XVI, Encyclical Letter of 2005 – *Deus caritas est, Acta Apostolica Sedis* 98 (2006, 217–52 at 233–7 [no. 20–5]).

63 For good studies on John Chrysostom in this area see William J. Walsh and John P. Langan, 'Patristic Social Consciousness: The Church and the Poor', *The Faith that Does Justice: Examining the Christian Sources of Social Change*, John C. Haughey, ed., New York, Ramsey, Toronto: Paulist Press, 1977, pp. 113–51; Dolores Greeley, 'St John Chrysostom – Prophet of Social Justice', *Studia Patristica* 17.3, 1982, 1163–8; Peter C. Phan, *Social Thought*, Message of the Fathers of the Church, vol. 20, M. Glazier: Wilmington, Delaware, 1984, 135–60; Justo L. González, *Faith and Wealth: A History of Early Christian Ideas on the Origin, Significance and Use of Money*, Harper and Row Publishers: San Francisco, 1990, pp. 200–13.

64 John Chrysostom, *Homily* 27.3 *on 1 Corinthians* (PG, 61, 227–9; Sheerin, *The Eucharist*, pp. 212–13).

65 Ibid., *Homily* 27.4 *on 1 Corinthians* (PG, 61, 229; Sheerin, *The Eucharist*, pp. 213–14).

66 Ibid., *Homily* 27.5 *on 1 Corinthians*, (PG, 61, 230; Sheerin, *The Eucharist*, p. 215).

67 Ibid., PG, 61, 232; Sheerin, *The Eucharist*, p. 217.

68 Idem, *Homily* 50.3 *on Matthew* (PG, 58, 508). Extracts from this famous Homily occur in the Office of Readings on Saturday of week 21 in the *Liturgy of the Hours*, vol.3, 480–2.

69 Ibid., *Homily* 50.4 *on Matthew* (PG, 58, 509).

70 John Chrysostom preached seven homilies on Lazaraus and the rich man (see Lk 16:19-3). The reference to the poor man as pearl and gold coin occurs in *De Lazaro* 6.5. See Catharine P. Roth's translation of six of these homilies in *St John Chrysostom: On Wealth and Poverty,* Crestwood, New York: SVS Press, 1984.

71 Idem, *Homily* 32.7 *on Matthew* (PG, 57, 386; Sheerin, *The Eucharist*, 322).

72 Cyprian, *Ep.*63.17, *'Passio est enim Domini sacrificium quod offerimus'* (CSEL, 3.2,714; Sheerin, *The Eucharist*, 266).

73 Augustine, *Conf.* 10.43.70, 'For the price of my redemption is always in my thoughts. I eat it and I drink it and I minister it to others, and as one of the poor I long to be filled with it' (Pine-Coffin, *Confessions*, 252; PL, 32, 810).

74 Idem, *Contra ep. Parmen.* 2.8.16 (PL, 43, 60); *Contra Faustum* 20.18 (PL, 42, 382).

75 Idem, *Contra Faustum* 20.21 (PL, 42, 385; NPNF, 4, 262).

76 Idem, *De civ. Dei* 10.6, *'Proinde verum sacrificium est omne opus, quo agitur, ut sancta societate inhaereamus Deo, relatum scilicet ad illum finem boni, quo veraciter beati esse possimus'* (CCSL 47, 278). The English translation is taken from Henry Bettenson, *City of God,* Harmondsworth & London: Penguin Classics, 1972, 1987, p. 379.

77 Ibid., *'Hoc est sacrificium Christianorum: 'multi unum corpus in Christo.' Quod etiam sacramento altaris fidelibus noto frequentat ecclesia, ubi ei demonstratur, quod in ea re quam offert, ipsa offeratur'* (CCSL, 47, 279; Bettenson, *City of God*, p. 380).

78 Ibid., *De civ. Dei* 10.20, *'Per hoc et sacerdos est, ipse offerens, ipse et oblatio. Cuius rei sacramentum cotidianum esse voluit ecclesiae sacrificum, quae cum ipsius capitis corpus sit, se ipsam per ipsum discit offerre'* (CCSL, 47, 294; Bettenson, *The City of God,* p. 401).

79 *Martyr. Polyc.,* 15–16 (*Ancient Christian Writings,* 130). For more detailed comment on Polycarp's martyrdom see F.G. Clancy, 'Imitating the Mysteries that you Celebrate', pp. 113–9.

80 Cyprian, *Epp.*57.2; 58.1 (CSEL, 3.2, 651–2, 656–7).

81 Augustine, *In Io. ev. tr.* 27.12; 84.1 (PL 35, 1621, 1846–67; NPNF 7, 178, 349–350); *Sermo* 329.1 (PL 38, 1454–1455; WSA III/9, 182). For the links between Eucharist and martyrdom envisaged by Augustine see F. G. Clancy, 'Imitate the Mysteries that you Celebrate', pp. 127–38.

82 For a detailed early study and compilation of relevant Patristic texts on this theme see Sebastian Tromp SJ, 'De Nativitate Ecclesiae ex Corde Iesu in Cruce', *Gregorianum* 13 (1932, 489–527).

83 John Chrystostom, *Homily* 85.3 *on John* (PG, 59, 463; FOTC, 41, 435).

84 Idem, *Bapt. Cat.* 3.16–18 (ACW, 31, 61–2).

85 Ambrose, *Explan. Ps. XII.*37.32; 45.12 (CSEL, 64, 160, 337–8; Ní Riain, *Commentary on Twelve Psalms*, pp. 124–5, 263–4).

86 Idem, *Expos. Ps.CXVII.*3.8 (CSEL, 62, 45; Ní Riain, *Commentary on Ps.118*, 29). The scripture reference to the vineyard of Engedi is Song of Songs 1:13–14.

87 Ibid., *Expos. Ps. CXVIII.*5.9 (CSEL, 62, 86–7); Ní Riain, *Commentary on Ps.118*, 57). For further commentary on this point see Finbarr G. Clancy, 'Christ the scented apple and the fragrance of the world's redemption: a theme in St Ambrose's *Commentary on Psalm 118'*, *Salvation according to the Fathers of the Church: Proceedings on the Sixth International Patristic Conference, Maynooth/Belfast 2005*, D. Vincent Twomey SVD & Dirk Krausmüller, eds, Dublin: Four Courts Press, 2010, pp. 70–92.

88 See Augustine, *In Io. ev. tr.* 120.2 (PL, 35, 1953); *C. Faust.* 12.16 (PL, 42, 263); *De civ. Dei* 15.26 (CCSL, 48, 493–4).

89 Idem, *De civ. Dei* 22.17 (CCSL, 48, 835–6).

90 Idem, *In Io. ev. tr.* 8.4 (PL, 35, 1452; NPNF, 7,58).

91 Ibid., *In. Io. ev. tr.* 110.7 (PL, 35, 1924; NPNF, 7, 412).

92 Ephrem the Syrian, *Armenian Hymn* 49.8–11. The English translation is taken from Sebastian Brock's article 'The Mysteries Hidden in the Side of Christ', *Sobornost* Series 7, No. 6, 1978, 462–72 at 471, which differs slightly from his translation of the same Hymn in *The Harp of the Spirit*. This article is most valuable for its comparative exploration of the significance of John 19:34 in the exegesis of St Ephrem and other Syriac writers also. On the theme of the two lances in Syriac writers see Robert Murray, 'The Lance which re-opened Paradise', *Orientalia Christiana Periodica* 39, 1973, 224–34, 401.

93 Idem, *Comment. Diat.* 21.11 (SC, 121, 380) where St Ephrem compares the crucified Christ to an olive tree, whence not only water and blood flow from his wounded side, but also oil. The importance and symbolism of oil in the Syriac tradition is eloquently addressed in St Ephrem's *Hymns on Virginity*, 4–7.

'THE DOMESTIC SANCTUARY OF THE CHURCH' (*APOSTOLICAM ACTUOSITATEM*, 11): LIVING EUCHARIST IN THE FAMILY TODAY

DR CLARE WATKINS
Westminister Seminary, London

The argument of this paper is made in response to two related observations on the teaching of the Second Vatican Council and its reception. The first of these is widely recognised: that a central – possibly *the* central – theme of Vatican II is a concern for evangelisation, a renewal of the Church as essentially missionary. My second observation is perhaps more controversial: that, for all its missiological intentions, Vatican II has been largely received as a Council of internal reform, and that the energies around its reception have been predominantly *ad intra,* rather than *ad extra*. The understanding of the Church as essentially missionary is the key to Vatican II's ecclesiology, and so to its eucharistic understanding; but, in practice and in much Catholic theology, evangelisation remains, if not a dead letter, then certainly something of a rather lame post script to more structural and liturgical ecclesial concerns. My argument is that this state of affairs has been especially detrimental to our eucharistic sense of things, and to our understanding of lay living, with damaging implications for the Church as a whole; and that one of the crucial things needed is a retrieval of a living theology of a eucharistically formed 'domestic church'. Living eucharistically in the family as the *ecclesia domestica* can radically renew our response to Vatican II's call to be thoroughly missionary, Church for the world.

In a longer presentation it might be a fruitful exercise to explore the theme of evangelisation and the difficulties in its reception in more detail. Here we just note that the Council's work can be seen in terms of that longer project of envisioning what it might mean to be Church in increasingly secularised, and post-Christendom cultures. In this respect, a certain trajectory of magisterial exhortation to mission can be recognised following on from the Council. One of the first Ordinary General Synods following the Council[1] took as its theme 'Evangelisation in the Modern World', and in the remarkable and influential apostolic exhortation that followed,[2] Paul VI explicitly relates this evangelising concern to the second Vatican Council: 'the objectives of which are definitively summed up in this single one: to make the Church of the twentieth century ever better fitted for proclaiming the gospel to the people of the twentieth century.' [3] It is also clear that it is evangelisation that is *the* leading concern for John Paul II's long pontificate.[4] In a piece of remarkable self-abnegating ecclesiology he writes at the start of his pontificate:

> The Church wishes to serve this single end: that each person may be able to find Christ, in order that Christ may walk with each person the path of life ... Against a background of the ever increasing historical processes ... Jesus Christ becomes, in a way, newly present, in spite of all his apparent absences, in spite of all the limitations of the presence and of the institutional activity of the Church.[5]

It is especially to John Paul II that we can attribute the language and thinking of the 'new evangelisation', on the basis of which the present pope has recently established a new Pontifical Council for Promoting the New Evangelisation.[6]

For all this, the single most significant area of failure with regard to the reception of Vatican II teaching is found in this powerful theme of evangelisation. This is not to say that anyone disagrees with it; it is specifically not one of the areas of polarised controversy that has afflicted the Council's theology over the last fifty years. Rather, for all the magisterial emphasis on mission, and for all its eirenic acceptance in principle, we remain a Christian community whose interpretation of its doctrine and life is almost intractably with regard to the Church *ad intra*.

In this paper I want to show how this failure to be true to the evangelising purposes of the Council has affected two particular areas of theology and life: primarily our celebration of, and catechesis concerning the Eucharist; and secondarily, in related ways, our sense of the apostolate of lay people. Following this, I propose an understanding of the eucharistic living of the 'domestic church' as a remedy, and as a vital contribution to renewing the sacramental-missionary sense of Church.

A. HOW THE FAILURE TO RECEIVE THE EVANGELISING ECCLESIOLOGY OF VATICAN II DEFORMS CHRISTIAN LIVING AND LITURGY

The *ad intra* pull and the deforming of theologies: the Eucharist

Perhaps the most vivid effects of Vatican II were the liturgical reforms it initiated, and the ways in which these have been carried out in the subsequent decades. Alongside this there has been a marked tendency to read the Council's sacramental theology almost exclusively through the lens of *Sacrosanctum Concilium*, a constitution not, in fact, concerned with sacramental theology *per se*, but specifically with liturgical reform.[7] As one contemporary commentator, the Dominican Romanus Cessario, comments:

> In the middle of the first decade of the twenty-first century, the study of sacramental theology remains almost exclusively subordinated to the programs in liturgical studies ... Few would contest that while the majority of the seminarians enrolled in programs of formation in the United States are able to air views on sacramental symbolism, very few are trained to give accounts of sacramental causality or even efficacy.[8]

On an experiential level many of us can witness to the ways in which our parishes expend enormous energies, of laity and clergy alike, on liturgies, far above what might be put to the service of evangelisation or social outreach. Liturgy not only absorbs our energies unduly, but it is – as Cessario suggests – in danger of obscuring a fuller theology of sacrament, beyond the strictly ritual.[9]

Something of this tendency and its questionable *ad intra* pull was recognised quite soon after the Council. As early as 1968, Nicholas Lash was challenging us to think more clearly about what it might mean to say that the Church was also the Church 'in between Masses'.[10] Emphasising those elements of the Second Vatican Council's teaching on the presence of Christ in the eucharistic community, and (significantly) drawing on a Rahnerian understanding of grace and the world, Professor Lash challenges us to think how Eucharist might be lived *in the world, ad extra*:

> ... if we really believe in the universality of the redemption event in Christ, then all our relationships, every form of human community, cries out for eucharistic expression. And the fact that it cannot attain this expression (until the king's great supper of the kingdom), should be a principal source of pain, challenge and longing, for the Christian in the world.[11]

A few years later Juan Luis Segundo holds the very 'success' of the Vatican II liturgical reforms responsible for 'our pagan insistence on the altar',[12] which has, he claims, undermined the ways in which the Eucharist, and the sacraments generally, form us for work towards justice and the Kingdom in the world. Subsequently, voices have been raised periodically to remind us of the prophetic and life-transforming call of the Eucharist in a missiological key, both within the academy,[13] and – increasingly – in documents of the magisterium.[14]

My suggestion is that the liturgical emphases of Vatican II have led to a certain distortion in sacramental theology, one which specifically undermines missiological and evangelising readings of the Eucharist. I would further suggest that this is at odds with the Council itself, whose liturgical reforms are specifically framed by evangelising concerns,[15] and whose expansive reading of the Church as 'the universal sacrament of salvation',[16] and as itself the body of Christ through which the christological missions are carried out,[17] militates against a narrowly ritualised understanding of Eucharist. The oft-quoted passage from *Sacrosanctum Concilium*, which describes the liturgy as 'the summit toward which the activity of the Church is directed ... [and] the font from which all her power flows',[18] speaks not only of the centrality of the Eucharist, but also – and especially in its context – of the 'smallness' of the celebration as 'summit and source' for the evangelising mission of the Church.[19] Yet for all this, the tendency has almost uniformly been toward the liturgical rather than the missionary living of Vatican II's vision of Eucharist. Our eucharistic celebrations too often have forgotten that they have been traditionally named from the place of dismissal – *ite missa est* – which names Mass and mission together as the decisive moment of Christian vocation in the world.

The *ad intra* pull and the deforming of theologies: the lay vocation

A similar – and related – *ad intra* distortion can also be seen in the ways in which Vatican II's theology of laity has been received. The story of the development of theologies of laity in the years preceding the Council, and their powerful influence on the ecclesiology of Vatican II itself,[20] is well documented. Both in the two great constitutions on the Church, and in the Decree on the Laity, there is a striking rediscovery of the baptismal theology, and an unprecedentedly strong theological account given for the basis of the lay Christian vocation. In particular, the description of lay people in terms of their ecclesial and eucharistic identity as members of the body of Christ, and so fully participant in the Lord's priestly, prophetic and sovereign missions, provides a rich, sacramental basis for lay living and holiness.[21]

Vatican II certainly gives a more satisfactory and ecclesiological account of the theology of lay life, which is effectively taken up by the 1983 Code of Canon Law, which allows for a variety of ways in which lay people might properly serve in the Church's ecclesial structures.[22] These theological and structural developments have, together, supported a rich and varied enabling of lay gifts for Church service. Growing formal and informal patterns of lay ministry have shaped the life of the Vatican II Church; indeed, in post-Christendom countries lay people are increasingly being called upon as a necessary part of maintaining structures and works which previously relied on clergy.

In the face of these pastoral developments we are in danger of missing something crucial about Vatican II's vision of lay life: that it is a lay *apostolate*, a sending out into the world, whose identity is 'secular'.[23] For the Council Fathers the primary exercise of the lay christological missions of priesthood, prophecy and sovereignty was envisioned as being 'in the world'. For sure, the priestly function finds a particular expression and source of power in the liturgical celebration, especially of the Eucharist;[24] but the specifically lay vocation to the *consecratio mundi* is given a higher profile. This consecration of the world to God is effected by ordinary living in the Spirit, and through the 'spiritual sacrifices' which, as Christians in the world, we are called upon to make.[25] Lay people are the means by which the gospel can 'permeate' the world, 'a leaven in the world'.[26] It is the particular and prophetic task of lay people, as Church in and for the world, to discern the signs of the times, and bring the light of the Gospel to bear on them.[27] The lay vocation is essentially missionary.

It is in this context that we might helpfully re-read Karl Rahner's much criticised comments concerning lay Church workers, which suggested that such men and women should be considered 'quasi-clerics'.[28] Whatever the clumsiness of this idea (and I'm not at all recommending it!) in it Rahner is struggling to describe the way in which the normative lay vocation is not to do with the *ecclesia ad intra*, which is, rather, a properly limited area of concern traditionally overseen by clerics. The 1997 curial document *Instruction on Certain Questions Regarding Collaboration*,[29] might also be helpfully understood against this background, and informed by the missionary reading of lay life set out in the earlier text, *Christifideles Laici*.[30] It may be that this 1997 text was struggling to sustain a rich theology of lay living 'in ordinary', which has become less and less prevalent since the Council which did so much to promote it. In the academy, too, the post-conciliar years are notable for a sudden and dramatic decrease in thinking about the theology of lay life, when compared with the pre-conciliar years; what has taken its place seems to be ecclesiologies of structural reform on the one hand, and theologies of ministry and community on the other.

The *ad intra* pull of the reception of Vatican II can be seen to have affected our reading of that Council's theologies of laity and of Eucharist. Our inability to be truly free in reading the expansive understandings of grace, the Church and the world in those documents, has resulted in new forms of ritualism and clericalism. The resulting distortions of our understandings of Eucharist and lay vocation are a part of, and contribute to, the widespread failure in our communities to appropriate in lively, instinctive ways the great conciliar message: that the Church is essentially *missionary*. It is at this point that I want to return our thoughts to a particular aspect of Vatican II theology, and outline its potential in offering something of a remedy for this situation. It is through the development of the idea of the Christian household as the 'domestic church' that we might better receive not only an appropriately 'worldly' account of lay mission, but also a renewed sense of the missionary and world-transforming nature of the Eucharist.

B. HOW THE 'DOMESTIC CHURCH' REORIENTATES LIFE AND EUCHARIST TO MISSION

The *ecclesia domestica:* Church in mission

The idea of the 'domestic church' is referred to only twice in the Second Vatican Council, and one of these occasions is by allusion.[31] An attempt is made here, and in later texts,[32] to give the term some weight of tradition by referring to its occurrence in one or two patristic texts; whilst such occurrences are present, it does appear, none the less, as a rather surprising term, lost to much of the tradition. This makes its development and growing currency in the decades since the Council all the more remarkable. 'Domestic church' seems to be a term which speaks in especially resonant and powerful ways to our own time, inspiring as it does not only a particular sense of vocation for the 'ordinary' lay Catholic, but also a renewed sense of what 'Church' is, and where it is to be found.

In both places where Vatican II refers to the domestic church it is striking that the immediate context is *both* missionary *and* explicitly sacramental. In *Lumen Gentium* 11 the sacramental nature of the Christian life is being described, as a reflection on what it is to be baptised into Christ's priesthood. Participation in the Eucharist is seen not only in its liturgical significance, but also as the participative offering of the whole of life, and the place from which the Christian is empowered to witness to the body of Christ in the world. From this reflection flows the idea of the sacramental life of marriage, in which, whilst firmly a part of human secular society, Christians are called to a particular proclamation of the gospel, through their life together as 'domestic church.'

This evangelical-missionary sense of domestic church is even more vivid in A*postolicam Actuositatem*. Here it is the specific lay vocation to marriage and family life that is being spoken of, both in terms of the family as 'the first and vital cell of society' and, simultaneously, as a life shaped by liturgy, spiritual sacrifice, active charity and evangelisation. Through these means the Christian household is revealed as 'the domestic sanctuary of the church'.[33]

What develops from these small conciliar reflections on the *ecclesia domestica*, is an increasing magisterial (papal) use of the term, especially in relation to the missionary vocation of the Church. For Paul VI the Christian family precisely as domestic church has an essential role to play in evangelisation;[34] and this theme is repeated throughout John Paul II's substantial teaching on evangelisation. In turning our attention decisively to the *ad extra* mission of the Church John Paul II reminds us that 'The family is not simply the object of the Church's pastoral care; it is also one of the Church's most effective agents of evangelisation.'[35] His central conviction remains that ... if they live up to the ideal which God places before them, Catholic homes will be true centres of evangelisation.'[36] It is striking, too, that in the *Lineamenta* for the 2012 Synod on the New Evangelisation, 'new ways of "being Church" are spoken of as needed for an appropriate missionary form of ecclesial life; among these forms 'domestic church' is given special mention.[37]

The domestic church is thus formally linked with a missionary ecclesiology; but this exhortatory magisterial teaching is worth probing a little further. In it we catch a glimpse of the possibility of re-imagining Church through centring it on its institutional margins – that is, in the households of ordinary lay Catholics. Such a reorientation is radical in its implications, and, if fully appropriated, demands that our primary ecclesiological focus must always be on ecclesiastical (that is, organisational) edges, rather than on the managerial and governance centre of the hierarchical organisation. The domestic church challenges profoundly the *ad intra* assumptions of our academic and pastoral theologies, and speaks, instead, of a Church thoroughly embedded in human society, with a profound solidarity with our non-Christian neighbours. At the same time, the domestic church is characteristically shaped by the sacramental, both through liturgical celebration (baptism, confirmation, marriage and Eucharist), and through the baptismal offering of spiritual sacrifices which consecrates the world to Christ:

> For all their works, prayers and apostolic endeavours, their ordinary married and family life, their daily occupations, their physical and mental relaxation, if carried out in the Spirit, and even the hardships of life, if patiently borne – all these become 'spiritual sacrifices acceptable to God through Jesus Christ'. Together with the offering of the Lord's body, they are most fittingly offered in

> the celebration of the Eucharist. Thus, as those everywhere who adore in holy activity, the laity consecrate the world itself to God.[38]

As Church in the world, the *ecclesia domestica* is most intractably Church in mission, sacrament in mission.

The *ecclesia domestica:* eucharistic living

The thesis which is beginning to emerge from the argument so far might be expressed something like this: as part of an overall trend in the reception of Vatican II, the theology of Eucharist has been increasingly and unhelpfully focused on the *ad intra* liturgical and ritual aspects of sacrament. As a remedy for this undermining of the Church's essentially missionary nature, the domestic church presents itself as a rich possibility. Through the essentially lay and *ad extra* lens of the domestic church, a missionary ecclesiology can be envisioned, within which our theology and practice of Eucharist might be effectively reoriented towards the *missio Dei*, towards God's loving purposes for the whole of creation.

It remains for this paper to put some flesh on these dry bones, and see to what extent this theological idea of domestic church as eucharistic and missionary might live.

Key to this proposal is the belief that eucharistic celebration is fulfilled only in eucharistic living. This refers us not only to Eastern Christian traditions of 'the liturgy after the liturgy',[39] but also back to those glimpses of eucharistic ethic which we have seen in the documents of Vatican II, and in a particularly powerful way in the writings of liberation theologians. In fact the notion of eucharistic living is also a strong theme in recent magisterial teaching. In *Ecclesia de Eucharistia,* John Paul II not only calls ordained priests to a daily activity which is 'truly eucharistic',[40] but sees such a eucharistic patterning of life as essential to the Church's mission, and as a universal call:

> Proclaiming the death of the Lord 'until he comes' (1 Cor 11:26) entails that all who take part in the Eucharist be committed to changing their lives and making them in a certain way completely 'Eucharistic'.[41]

Significantly this call is especially associated with the eucharistic action of Jesus in his washing the feet of his disciples.[42]

These hints at the non-liturgical fulfilment of the Eucharist in the transformed worldly life of Christians is most explicitly articulated magisterially by Pope Benedict XVI, in an apostolic exhortation whose very structure reflects the living out of Eucharist in the world, as the goal of eucharistic theology and liturgy:

> Christianity's new worship includes and transfigures every aspect of life: 'Whether you eat or drink, or whatever you do, do all to the glory of God' (1 Cor 10:31). Christians, in all their actions, are called to offer true worship to God. Here the intrinsically eucharistic nature of Christian life begins to take shape. The Eucharist, since it embraces the concrete, everyday existence of the believer, makes possible, day by day, the progressive transfiguration of all those called by grace to reflect the image of the Son of God (cf. Rm 8:29ff.). There is nothing authentically human – our thoughts and affections, our words and deeds – that does not find in the sacrament of the Eucharist the form it needs to be lived to the full ... Worship pleasing to God thus becomes a new way of living our whole life ...[43]

It is this notion of eucharistic living, so clearly in tune with the missionary and sacramental thrust of Vatican II's ecclesiology, which finds a particularly powerful embodiment in the living of Christian family life, from where, I believe, it can renew the evangelising vocation of the people of God.

To illustrate what I might mean by this, I will finish by referring to three key aspects of eucharistic theology which can be beautifully informed by, as well as beautifully transform, the routine patterns of domestic living. These are: sacrifice, thanksgiving and eschatology.

Given that most people in the pew have experience of family or shared domestic life of one kind or another, I have often found myself puzzled when priest colleagues adamantly claim that the language of eucharistic sacrifice is incomprehensible to people today. It is, of course, the case that ritual or bloody sacrifice is culturally alien to most of us; and that the language of sacrifice can and has been abused as a way keeping the oppressed in their oppression. What the domestic Church offers us is a living and authentic vision of eucharistic sacrifice, in which the laying down of one's life for one's friends (Jn 15:12-13) –

the giving of one's body as if it were just bread – is given contemporary embodied form. The parental vocation – indeed, the marriage vocation – demands a particular kind of routine of living a 'given up' life, where one's own desires have to give way to the other, and where the 'letting go' of frequent forgiveness and being forgiven forms relationships in self-gift and sacrifice of self. The Eucharist calls us to that daily losing of life which is about taking up our cross and following Christ, in the sure faith that it is only by this way that our life will be found (Mt 10: 38-39). This is a losing of life, a sacrifice, in the context of total love; and it is a form of Eucharist lived moment to moment in the details and ordinary sufferings and graces of domestic relationships.

Naming the eucharistic life of the domestic church in such terms of suffering, cross and sacrifice – whilst true – may give rather a bleak impression! These things are daily lived out in the context of love, and of hope; the eucharistic forms of domestic living are transfigured, like the eucharistic sacrifice itself, by the reality of resurrection. This is why the Mass in not 'just' sacrifice, but a 'thanksgiving sacrifice' – it is Eucharist. And if ever there was a place where the transforming power of saying 'thank you' was powerfully and instinctively known, it is in the intense and complex life of the household. In a place where relationships are lived over many years – even decades – in all the ups and downs, and tedium of daily existence, the mysterious gifts of the other's presence and service are easily (inevitably?) taken for granted. It is here that the love-language of thanks or Eucharist – of 'good gift' or 'good grace' – is heard in all its transforming power.[44] It is a word that recognises gift, and names it as grace – something freely given, and 'graceful' (beautiful); something to which we have no right, and to which we can only fully respond by receiving. Any parent who has ever experienced the spontaneous thank you of the demanding teenager will know something of that eucharistic transforming grace of thanksgiving.

All this joyful and painful living of domestic church takes place in an intractably eschatologically conditioned place. For the domestic church is never a static reality; it never stands still, and its routines are always being broken by the emergence of new needs, new lives, new personalities. The eschatology of the domestic church thus refers to the fragility of the future that is held within family life, where so many lives are inextricably bound up with others, making one's own future and plans always contingent, always open to the event of the other's life. In a particular way this need to entrust the future to God, and learn to be open to his providence, is learnt by parents as they let their children grow into adults, letting them go with all the anxieties of losing control and influence for their happiness and well-being. The wisdom of those who have lived a long vocation in the domestic Church is always characterised by such moments of a hard learning of trust and resting content in the unknowability and uncontrollable nature of what lies ahead. As a eucharistic people we are people turned to God's future in ways which transform our sense of 'hold' on our own time, ways which are embodied in a particular way in this experience of family life.

There are other ways in which the Eucharist and the domestic Church can be seen mutually to inform one another – most obviously, perhaps, as places of nourishment, and of return and sending out. But I hope that enough has been said here to capture our imaginations about the possibilities for the non-liturgical fulfilment of Eucharist in the household setting. If what has been set out in this paper is even a little bit true then it has far-reaching implications for us ecclesiologically, eucharistically, and so pedagogically. For if we are to know the domestic church as that remedy for the ills of an over emphasis on the *ad intra*, with its undermining of the missionary character of the Eucharist, then we can surely no longer be content to teach and preach about the Mass, and about daily lay living in ways which fail to witness to the vital and charismatic integration of these sacramental realities. What is required is a pervasive catechesis, of life and sacrament, and an attendant renewal of both liturgy and Christian domestic living. To learn, in these ways, to live the Eucharist in and from the domestic church would be a powerful reception of the teaching of Vatican II, with its deep concern for the bringing of all people to Christ; for through such a domestic living of Eucharist, Christ's body finds embodiment in and for the world, at the heart of human living and loving.

That is why education is so important in fostering ecclesial communion. Education should deepen people's awareness that there is no standing outside the dialogue and dialectic of text/experience. There is no escaping from one's tradition, but there is a radical challenge to appropriate it authentically through a hermeneutic of retrieval and a hermeneutic of suspicion. The former retrieves what is good and true; the latter lays bare how inauthenticity can clothe itself as authenticity. In this process, the teaching authority of the Church, the Magisterium, and the faithful's sense of what is true both play a significant part. The most important educational contribution to the hermeneutical process is to awaken people to the distanciation between text and experience and to appreciate that this distanciation is, in fact, the foundation on which the text can be re-appropriated and one's identity and self-understanding reinterpreted. In this way the otherness of the text, because it is other, can promote greater understanding. There is no detached presuppositionless starting point from where one can objectively analyse what has been handed on.[5] Indeed, it can be argued that prejudice can even become a precondition for interpretative understanding.[6] Since the texts of one's tradition are already constitutive of one's identity one can only ever begin from the middle: what is required is not an easy claim to objectivity but a continuing historically reflective encounter of text/experience that yields a reinterpretation of one's identity. Ricoeur says: 'The first task is not to begin, but from the midst of speech, to remember, to remember with a view to beginning.'[7]

Given the significance of hermeneutics to our ecclesial communion it is useful to try and formulate a hermeneutical principle that is adequate for the educational task that every generation of Christians must undertake. An educational hermeneutic should textualise experience while contextualising texts. To textualise experience is to weave and craft experience in dialogue with texts. And we must contextualise every text, not just in terms of the author and the world in which the text emerged, but most importantly of all it must be recontextualised in the world of the reader. To recontextualise will demand that one decipher texts, not primarily for the purposes of reductive criticism, but with the aim of ciphering experience anew. Let us analyse one example. The Nicene-Constantinopolitan creed was composed by the Fathers of the first two ecumenical councils at

Nicea in AD 325 and Constantinople in AD 381. This is a classic text of the Magisterium. It was formulated at the two councils based on several centuries of reflection on Christian revelation. It stands as a classic Christian text handed down from one generation to the next and has been received by Christian communities as the authoritative statement of orthodox belief and a key foundation for communion between the particular Churches. We can contextualise it through historical-critical studies of earlier theology, of the participants in the council, of any records of the debates, of the socio-political realities of the Constantinian era. We can do our best to reconstruct what it was that the authors intended by the various affirmations found in the creed. But all of this, while very valuable, is only reductive criticism. We must also allow the text to cipher our experience. As Paul Ricoeur says:

> Ultimately, what I appropriate is a proposed world. The latter is not *behind* the text, as a hidden intention would be, but *in front of* it, as that which the work unfolds, discovers, reveals. Henceforth, to understand is *to understand oneself in front of the text.* It is not a question of imposing upon the text our finite capacity of understanding, but of exposing ourselves to the text and receiving from it an enlarged self.[8]

Thus through liturgy, through teaching, through prayer, through music, through art, through silence, through theological studies, through Christian praxis, through the lives of the saints, our lives are reinterpreted by the Triune God. We stand in front of the creed and it can disclose, reveal, unfold as the possibility emerges of new worlds of meaning disclosed by the text. From an educational perspective the interpretation of living Christian tradition is always complex. But it rewards the effort made with an ever-deeper sense of ecclesial communion.

THE BLESSED 'AND'

The word 'and' is very important in understanding Catholicism: faith *and* reason, scripture *and* tradition, grace *and* nature, religion *and* culture, belief *and* science. Contrast this with more fundamentalist readings of religious texts in Evangelical Protestantism: faith rejects reason, scripture uproots tradition, grace supplants nature, religion replaces culture, belief disparages science. Contrast this also with reductionist readings of religious texts in contemporary atheism: faith ridiculed by reason, scripture and tradition reduced to myth, grace displaced by nature, religion excluded from the public square of culture, belief annihilated by science. There are few more important tasks facing Catholic education today than to retrieve this blessed 'and'. If we fail to do so then there is a real danger that our ecclesial communion might withdraw into an intellectual ghetto.

The whole intellectual history of the Catholic Church involves a critical interaction with human reason. From its encounter with neo-Platonic philosophy in the third, fourth, and fifth centuries to the rediscovery of Aristotle in the twelfth and thirteenth centuries, the dialogue between faith and reason characterises the high intellectual achievement of the Catholic Church. Today, in an era often dominated by religious fundamentalism on the one hand and atheistic science on the other, this commitment to a dialogue between faith and reason was rarely more relevant. We live in an era when science and religion might completely diverge from each other as if it was impossible for the same person to be a rigorous scientist and a sincere religious believer. In the English-speaking world this trend is exacerbated by the restriction of the very term 'science' to empirical study of the natural world. This goes completely against the history of the term which covers all areas of human knowledge. Thus philosophy and theology are just as surely sciences as physics and biology. Faith and reason can live and thrive in the same person: while one cannot be reduced to the other they both play a dynamic role in forming and educating a mature person. There is no contradiction between being a fully educated person and a committed Christian. There are few more important tasks for Christian educators than to revisit and re-imagine the relationship between faith and reason.

Pope Benedict XVI has consistently drawn attention to this fundamental issue. At his meeting with representatives of British society in Westminster Hall he said:

> I would suggest that the world of reason and the world of faith – the world of secular rationality and the world of religious belief – need one another and should not be afraid to enter into a profound and ongoing dialogue, for the good of our civilisation.[9]

He has described the Second Vatican Council as dedicated to finding a new definition of the relationships between the Church and the modern age, between the Church and the modern State and between Christian faith and other religions.[10] All of these tasks demand the utmost respect for the mutual autonomy and the dynamic interaction of both faith and reason. The reflection on these issues initiated at the Council must be continued and deepened for as St Peter famously stated we should always be ready to give an account (*apo-logia*) of the reason (*logos*) for our hope (1 Pt 3:15).

Christian faith is always lived in particular cultures. The dialogue between faith and culture takes place in the heart and mind of the individual believer, in families, in parish communities and, not least, in schools and colleges. Christian schools and colleges stand as a reminder that the Christian faith is not a private, irrational commitment embraced by individuals but it comprises a philosophically justified act of faith in a transcendent, personal God and is an intelligent and reasonable response to what was revealed in the life of Jesus Christ. Furthermore, these educational institutions give expression to the public dimension of Christian faith in their commitment to social solidarity, to outreach to those in need and to promotion of the common good. There will always be a certain tension between religious faith and culture: some people reduce culture to religious faith and so withdraw into a fundamentalist ghetto where everything outside is seen as a threat; others empty culture of all religious reference so that religious belief amounts to nothing more than personal whim and traditional superstition. A true dialogue between faith and culture allows one to inform the other and calls individuals, families, communities, and indeed, our schools and colleges, to an ever greater commitment to human maturity.

THE EUCHARIST: SCHOOL OF COMMUNION

Catechists and teachers make an extraordinary contribution to the life of the Church by explaining the Catholic faith to young and old alike. Nowhere is this more evident than in sacramental preparation where dedicated individuals and teams explain the meaning of the various parts of the ceremony to the candidates and to their parents and sponsors. However, sacraments are not just rituals to be understood but mysteries to be experienced. Indeed, it is in the celebration of these sacred rites that we encounter the Divine and we grow in communion with God and with each other. If an educational hermeneutic is necessary to help us interpret tradition, a liturgical hermeneutic is also needed to awaken us to the Triune God who reveals and communicates life in the ritual actions of the Church, particularly in the celebration of the Eucharist. This is the place where the sick are healed, the deaf hear, the blind see, prisoners are set free and good news is proclaimed to the poor.

Bread and wine are among the most wonderful of human creations. But they are precisely that: human creations. They do not grow on sheaf and vine. From sowing the seeds and tending the vine, to harvesting the wheat and grape, to the sharing of bread and the pouring of wine, human community is created and fostered. Through the work of human hands the fruit of the earth becomes our food and drink. The preparation of bread and wine and the transformation of these two basic realities into the body and blood of Christ are a sign and foretaste of the destiny of all reality. All creation, all human labour and endeavour will be transformed into the new creation. It is the Eucharist that teaches us this great truth.

Christians are called to work with adherents of all faiths and none to build a world of human justice and dignity. In the same way as with our hands we create bread and wine so we must struggle with political ideas and institutions to create a humane world. The Church's sacramental celebration gives shape to a new world and nourishes believers in their efforts to create it. Thus, the Eucharist points the way to overcome the dichotomies that emerge between the sacred and the secular.

The Eucharist is primarily about the future. Though it is rooted in events of close to two thousand years ago its true orientation is towards the future. God has laid hold of human history and has begun to transform it from within. The Eucharist is bread broken for a new world; it is a prayer of praise and thanksgiving; it is a foretaste and a promise. The Eucharist orientates us to the future not as threat but as invitation. In a world that can easily become preoccupied with the present we are invited to open our hearts to the future as God's promise. The Eucharist unites the Church in heaven and on earth in giving praise and thanks to God for the gift of creation, for the even greater gift of redemption and for the pledge of future glory. As the bread and wine are transformed into the Body and Blood of Christ so too we await the transformation of all creation in Christ 'so that God may be all in all' (1 Cor 15:28). The text of theological and pastoral reflections in preparation for the 50th International Eucharistic Congress states:

> In receiving the Eucharist we are called to anticipate a new future through words and actions so that the future can already be grafted onto the present and so that we can already taste what we are to become.[11]

Education provides the key to such a future. Without an enlightened pedagogy we are doomed to revisit the past over and over again. In awakening our sensibilities and disturbing our consciences, education can liberate us from our inherited stereotypes to embrace the future with renewed energy and hope. The Eucharist is a school of communion. It reveals to us the wonderful plan that God has in store for us and it invites us to enter into an ever-deeper communion with the Triune God and with all of creation. As Jesus was the greatest of teachers so the Eucharist remains our most trusted educator.

NOTES

1 There is a good introduction to various hermeneutical thinkers in Richard Kearney, *Modern Movements in European Philosophy*, Manchester: Manchester University Press, 1986.

2 *Address of His Holiness Benedict XVI to the Roman Curia*, 22nd December 2005.

3 Paul Ricoeur, *Hermeneutics and the Human Sciences*, John B. Thompson, ed., Cambridge: Cambridge University Press, 1981, pp. 139–40.

4 Paul Ricoeur, *Hermeneutics and the Human Sciences*, pp. 131–44.

5 Paul Ricoeur, *Interpretation Theory: Discourse and the Surplus of Meaning*, Forth Worth: Texas Christain University Press, 1976, p. 74.

6 Prejudice as a precondition for understanding was an important part of Gadamer's contribution to hermeneutics. See Hans-Georg Gadamer, *Truth and Method*, New York: Seabury Press, 1975, pp. 258ff., 331ff.

7 Paul Ricoeur, *The Symbolism of Evil*, Boston: Beacon Press, 1967, pp. 348–9.

8 Paul Ricoeur, *Hermeneutics and the Human Sciences*, p. 143 (emphasis in the original).

9 Pope Benedict XVI, *Meeting with the Representatives of British Society, including the Diplomatic Corps, Politicians, Academics and Business Leaders*, Westminster Hall, 17th September 2010.

10 *Address of His Holiness Benedict XVI to the Roman Curia*, 22nd December 2005.

11 *The Eucharist: Communion With Christ and With One Another, Theological and Pastoral Reflections in Preparation for the 50th International Eucharistic Congress*, Dublin: Veritas Publications, 2011, no.120.

BEYOND THE BIG BANG:
THE EUCHARIST AT THE HEART OF COSMIC, EVOLUTIONARY AND HUMAN HISTORY

REV. DR BRENDAN PURCELL
Adjunct Professor of Philosophy,
Notre Dame University, Sydney

At least in English-speaking culture, where popular science has magisterial authority, the natural world from here to the edge of the observable universe, forty-six billion light years away, is often presented as ultimately meaningless. As biologist Jonathan Marks puts it, 'The scientist says: "Science has explained many things about the universe. Your life has no meaning. Have a nice day."'[1] Certainly, from a philosophical or theological viewpoint, the natural sciences don't ask the big questions about the meaning of the universe, but as Blessed John Paul II memorably said:

> Science can purify religion from error and superstition; religion can purify science from idolatry and from false absolutes. Each can draw the other into a wider world, where both can flourish ... Only a dynamic relationship between theology and science can reveal those limits which support the integrity of each discipline, so that theology does not profess a pseudo-science and science does not become an unconscious theology.[2]

So the methods of the natural sciences neither nor exclude nor include questions of ultimate meaning. The question of what started the Big Bang itself is a *boundary* question, occurring at the edge of astrophysics, but not answerable by it. Nor is it answered, only postponed, by any variation of the multiverse hypothesis. Since today we're 'Exploring Sources and Ways of Communion', in terms of theology, both natural and revealed, we'll try to go beyond the Big Bang by briefly examining the eucharistic significance of what we'll call cosmos, bios, and anthropos:

1. **COSMOS:** the astrophysical universe from the Big Bang onwards;
2. **BIOS:** the emergence and flourishing of life in its almost four billion-year-long evolution on our planet, including what evolutionary biologist Sean Carroll calls 'the Big Bang of animal evolution';[3] and
3. **ANTHROPOS** what paleontologist Richard Klein calls 'the Big Bang of human consciousness'[4] and the subsequent history of humanity.

Before going into the eucharistic significance of cosmic, evolutionary and human existence, it'll be useful to say something about communion within God, and communion between God and his creation.

INTRODUCTION:
THE POSITIVE NOT-BEING OF LOVE IN THE TRINITY AND IN CREATION

1. In the Trinity: In his recent book on the Trinity, Piero Coda has an interesting section headed 'The positive not-being of love'.[5] He explores the contemporary theological understanding of how, in the analogy of love, 'God's being as *agape* is penetrated and quickened by mutual not-being, through ... the love of each of the divine Persons for the others.'[6] Each of the persons 'loses himself' for the other, so that the three persons in the Trinity, are one because for each of them, their love *is not* and *is* at the same time. Each person, in Aquinas's terms, is a subsistent relation,[7] is love, is a completely other-related person by not being. And it's through this not-being of love that each person dwells in the other in an everlasting gift of self.

Coda points out how this positive not-being of love, this inner life of the Trinity – of the God St John defines as *agape*, love (cf. 1 Jn 4:8,16) – in contemporary Christology has been understood as most dramatically exploding into our space-time universe at the moment St Paul speaks when Christ 'emptied himself' (*ekénosen*, Phil 2,7).[8] Let's see how the act of creation can be seen as an external expression of this divine not-being of love.

2. In the divine act of creation: It's because Coda sees the one divine act of creation as rooted in this Trinitarian not-being that he gives a *positive* meaning to the phrase, 'created out of nothing', *ex nihilo*, as expressing the nothing of love:

> The nothing ... does not only say, negatively, that before creation there was nothing except God. It also says, positively, that God's act of creation is an act of pure love, an act in which he makes himself nothing, in relation to the created, so that the created may exist.[9]

Seen in this way, the act of divine creation requires of God a negation, or 'emptying' of himself, in order to affirm created reality as *other* than himself. The act of creation then, is more clearly seen as a relationship of love between giver and gift. And this notion of creation out of the nothing of love helps us to appreciate the huge drama of all created existence as coming from God-love and returning to God-love through the Eucharist woven into the entire tapestry of cosmic, evolutionary and human history.

3. Creation as gift: This focus on the nothing of love expressed by the act of creation doesn't take away the traditional meaning of 'creation out of nothing', More clearly than Aristotle ever did, in Romans 4: 17, St Paul puts it: 'God ... who ... calls into existence the things that do not exist.' But seeing creation as encounter makes it easier to comprehend its intrinsic giftedness, which contrasts, for example, with Sartre's *La nausée*. There, Roquentin is famously disgusted at the absurd giveness of the roots of a chestnut tree, expressing a modern failure to find any *ultimate* sense in creation.

The rest of our reflection will explore the creation we've summed up as *cosmos, bios* and *anthropos* as participating in the divine not-being of love. This can be articulated in the two interrelated phases of *love* and its *kenosis,* resulting in the third phase of creation as *gift*. It's no harm to remind ourselves here of G. K. Chesterton's wonderful phrase for St Francis, surely the patron saint of cosmic and evolutionary creation, whose eucharistic approach to nature Chesterton called a 'grammar of gratitude'.[10]

COSMOS: THE EUCHARIST AT THE HEART OF COSMIC HISTORY

1) Cosmic *agape* reflecting the Unity and Trinity of God: Because, as Aquinas tells us, creation shares both in the existence and creativity of God-love, we can speak of a cosmic *agape* that mirrors the *unity* of God.[11] For example, astronomers now realise that galaxies are bound together in superclusters spanning from several hundred million light-years to 1 billion light years across, taking in more than 5 per cent of the observable universe. This ever greater symmetry in what seemed a disorganised ocean of space indicates that the morning stars in the Book of Job (38:7) have every reason to sing in harmony.

It's a harmony St Francis' deeply Trinitarian 'Canticle of the Creatures' expressed, lifting Job's and the psalmist's insight into the whole of creation's adoration of God up to a vision of all creation united in mutual love as brothers and sisters of their one Father. Caspar Friedrich recovered something of this vision in paintings like *The Cross in the Mountains* (1807–8), of which he said: 'Jesus Christ, nailed to the tree, is turned here towards the sinking sun, the image of the eternal life-giving Father ... The firs stand around the cross, evergreen, enduring through all ages, like the hopes of man in him, crucified.' A contemporary painter, Gerhard Richter, warns against our losing Friedrich's insight into God's unifying presence in the cosmos: 'For me, what is missing is the spiritual foundation underlying Romantic painting. We have lost the feeling of the ubiquity of God in nature. For us everything is empty. And yet the paintings are still there, and they speak to us. We continue to love them, to use them and to need them.'[12]

Considering its origin, it's hardly surprising that Aquinas also sees the universe as all the more perfect the more diversity it contains.[13] We can see the sheer multiplicity of its estimated one hundred to three hundred billion galaxies as a created echo of the *Trinity*. Coda writes that the created image, spread out in space and time, of that all/nothing of love in God-Trinity that is the Word/Son of the Father ... *Nothing*, because he *receives* his being from the love of the Father; *All*, because the infinite riches of the Father is *fully* reflected and expressed in him ... So that the eschatological goal of the becoming of the created universe is grasped by the apostle Paul as the free and gratuitous indwelling of God in all created realities: 'so that God may *be* all *in* all' (1 Cor 15:28) ... the interconnection of unity and multiplicity in created reality, at its various levels of existence and development, is woven into space and time. The book of creation is written in the Trinitarian grammar of the nothing of love.[14]

The incredible diversity of astrophysical and chemical realities which at the physical level is governed by the four constant laws of gravitation, electromagnetism, and the strong and weak forces, and at the level of chemistry by Paul's exclusion principle governing the periodic classification of elements. Behind these physical and chemical levels, philosopher and theologian Bernard Lonergan provided a framework he called emergent probability to make sense of the entire world process in terms of one dynamic whole, making sense of its (i) enormous spatial distribution, ii) large numbers, and (iii) long intervals of time.[15] Later what's called the anthropic principle and the 'Goldilocks enigma' were formulated, again discerning in and through the immense multiplicity of realities and events a unifying principle that makes sense of them all.[16]

As we've said, this unity in diversity may be understood as a created echo of the beautiful difference in unity of the Trinity of Persons in the One God. However, if *agape* is at the heart of cosmic existence, we shouldn't be surprised if it's linked with the kind of cosmic *agon* or suffering we're calling *kenosis*.

2) Cosmic kenosis: In its co-creative capacity, through the upward dynamism from subatomic particles to humans, created nature has to undergo its own kenosis, where each lower level of existence makes a sacrifice of itself for the sake of the next highest level.

As we now know, the elements necessary for life could only come into existence through the process of nucleosynthesis. The only place hot enough to 'cook' the light element helium into the heavier element carbon, apparently, is the heart of a dying star. Some ten to five billion years ago, the first generation of stars, when their hydrogen cores burnt up at a heat of one hundred million degrees Kelvin, an incredibly finely tuned process, released carbon and the other heavier elements into the universe.[17]

Theologically, this kind of intra-cosmic kenosis can fill out St Paul's famous comment: 'We know that the whole of creation has been groaning with labour pains together until now ... ' (Rm 8:22). So the cosmic drama both reflects and can be assumed into the drama of the Paschal mystery, where in order to be creative and re-creative the creation has itself to participate in the nothingness of the divine act of creation. And because of this *co-creative kenotic love* inbuilt into the cosmos, we may now sketch the eucharistic significance at its heart.

3) The Eucharist at the heart of the cosmos: Nineteenth-century American-based painters like Thomas Cole, Albert Bierstadt and others of the Hudson River School, not to mention twentieth-century artists like Ferdinand Hodler in Switzerland, the Canadian Group of Seven, or Georgia O'Keeffe in the US, found ways of making landscapes luminously transparent for a divine presence that they may have been unable to express in any other way. Nor should it surprise us that a philosopher of history like Eric Voegelin can glimpse more than a hint of the divine in their treatment of matter by an ancient like Lucretius, or a modern like Paul Valéry in a poem like *Cimetière Marin*.[18]

What of the eucharistic meaning of the material cosmos? If the immense space/time of the universe is required for our planet within the solar system to exist in our spiral of the Milky Way,[19] then all those beautiful photos of nebulae and galaxies cascading into view are ordered towards our existence, which itself is ordered towards the incarnation and the Eucharist. Without that material basis there would have been no incarnation and no Eucharist. As nuclear engineer and philosopher Sergio Rondinara puts it, 'the cosmos is our home, our dwelling. Each of us is a being in space-time, living in a given place and at a specific historic period.'[20] At the very heart of the entire universe, with its galaxies, our solar system, and our planet Earth is their being a cosmic preparation not only for man, but for the God-man present through all space and time in the Eucharist.

This is perhaps why, in his 24th July 2009 homily at vespers in the Cathedral of Aosta, Pope Benedict could say that:

> The role of the priesthood is to consecrate the world so that it may become a living host, a liturgy: so that the liturgy may not be something alongside the reality of the world, but that the world itself shall become a living host, a liturgy. This is also the great vision of Teilhard de Chardin: in the end we shall achieve a true cosmic liturgy, where the cosmos becomes a living host.[21]

Not only can the Eucharist be seen to be at the heart of the entire material universe, but very particularly, it's our own bodies' rootedness in the physico-chemical universe that is the material basis for our *uniqueness* as incarnate spirits. Like every creature in this universe, our unique, materially-based existence, isn't necessary, but contingent.

Yet, as David Walsh has written, 'Contingency is not itself contingent. Once we realise that what characterises the flow of things ... cannot necessarily be extended to the whole itself, we are no longer so lost in the cosmos.'[22] For contingency can only be understood in relation to its necessary ground.

The fact is that God loves our time-and-space-bound contingent existence immensely. We can say that from eternity, each of us is loved by the Father, uttered by him as he utters his Son. In a short poem, Gerard Manly Hopkins focuses on the Jesus in us more than we are in ourselves:

As kingfishers catch fire, dragonflies draw flame;
... each hung bell's
Bow swung finds tongue to fling out broad its name;
Each mortal thing does one thing and the same:
Deals out being | indoors each one dwells;
Selves – goes its self: *myself* it speaks and spells,
Crying *What I do is me: for that I came.*

I say more: the just man justices;
Keeps grace: that keeps all his goings graces;
Acts in God's eye what in God's eye he is –
Christ. For Christ plays | in ten thousand places,
Lovely in limbs, and lovely in eyes not his
To the Father through the features of men's faces.[23]

And it's this apparently fragile connection of each one's utter material contingency with utter belovedness as sons in his Son by our Father that underlies the multiplication of the Eucharist into as many materially separate hosts as are needed for each embodied human spirit to personally and physically encounter the Body and Blood, soul and divinity of Jesus Christ.

BIOS: THE EUCHARIST AT THE HEART OF EVOLUTIONARY HISTORY

1) Bios reflecting God's creative love: It's no harm to remind ourselves that despite his hesitant agnosticism, Darwin's closing words to *The Origin of Species* still credited the Creator with the whole evolutionary tapestry:

> There is grandeur in this view of life, with its several powers, having been originally breathed by the creator into a few forms or into one; and that, whilst this planet has gone cycling on according to the fixed law of gravity, from so simple a beginning endless forms most beautiful and most wonderful have been, and are being, evolved.[24]

Of course, as Blessed John Paul II noted, 'evolution presupposes creation. In the light of evolution, creation can be seen as a [single] event extended over time – as a "continuous creation"'.[25] It is with the creation of life that *created creativity* really takes off – with a freedom and inventiveness unmatched by any galactic fireworks no matter how many light-years across. This continuous creativity unleashed an enormous multiplicity of life forms, with thirty-six major families or phyla in the animal kingdom alone. Aquinas, in agreement with Aristotle, held that every agent produces something like itself. So this biodiversity. Governed by the only slowly coming to be understood complementarity of evo-devo's unchanging biogenetic laws with the continual adaptations of Darwinian evolutionary theory, may again be understood as a created expression of the beautiful difference in unity of the Persons in the Trinity.

2) The kenotic drama of life: Let's remind ourselves of St Paul's remark about the groaning of the whole of creation with labour pains together until now (Rm 8:22) because it best expresses nature's participating in the kenosis of the Incarnate Word, through whom 'all things were made' (Jn 1:3). Since life first emerged on earth around 3.8 billion years ago, there have been cycles of destruction and renewal – classically the K-T (or Cretaceous-Paleogene) extinction event 65.5 million years ago. As with the astrophysical universe, this evolutionary drama can be assumed into the drama of the Paschal mystery, where the life-world can be seen to participate in something of the nothingness of the divine act of creation in order itself to be creative and re-creative.

Again and again, the lower levels 'suffer' to make a gift of themselves to the higher ones. We see this in the vital role played by the earliest life forms on earth, the algae. These algae turn water, carbon dioxide and sunlight into their food, with oxygen as a very important by-product, which, from 2.7 billion years to 2.2 billion years ago, changed the earth's atmosphere from lacking oxygen to containing almost 20 per cent oxygen, without which the later plants, animals and ourselves couldn't exist. Most obviously there's the kenosis of providing nourishment for higher-level living things, which brings us to the absolutely highest instance of this. That is when the bread and wine consecrated into the Body and Blood of Christ becomes the living bread by which he nourishes his followers with himself. As with the cosmos, the bios too participates in what we've called *co-creative kenotic love,* allowing us to understand the upward development from bacteria to humans as a sequence of offerings from lower to higher levels of life.

3) Is the Eucharist at the heart of evolutionary history? Yes, because at the centre of evolutionary process is the mystery of life, where from bacteria upwards, we define living things as self-assembling, self-maintaining and self-reproducing. And through what's offered by the plant life of the earth, the Eucharist brings us the one who said of himself, 'I am ... the life.' Piero Coda notes how, from the perspective of the incarnation, creation understood as a whole 'in its diachronic development and in its synchronic convergence, is *Christiform* or, to use Teilhard's phrase, *Christofinalised*'.[26] So, through the incarnation, the entire created universe – physical-chemical-biological-botanical-zoological-anthropological – is assumed into the body of Christ.

Nor is the cosmic-biological-human world's ascension into the Eucharist simply one-way. Chiara Lubich, writing on 'The Eucharist and the Transformation of the Cosmos' suggests that 'if the Eucharist is the cause of the resurrection of man, is it not possible that the body of man, divinised by the Eucharist, may be destined to decay underground in order to contribute to the renewal of the cosmos? We can say, therefore, that after we have died with Jesus we are the Eucharist of the earth. The earth eats us up as we eat the Eucharist, indeed not in order to transform us into the earth but to transform the earth into 'new heavens and a new earth' (Rv 21:1).

The Eucharist redeems us and makes us God. We, after dying, cooperate with Christ in the transformation of nature, so that nature turns out to be like an extension of the body of Jesus ... [who] through the incarnation, took on human nature, which is where all of nature's elements meet.[27]

In this sense, the Eucharist is the heart of cosmic and evolutionary history, where the world offers up its material and living existence to become Eucharist, and through our eucharistified bodies will achieve its final transformation into the 'new heavens and the new earth' (Is 65:17; 2 Pt 3:13; Rv 21:1).

ANTHROPOS: THE EUCHARIST AT THE HEART OF HUMAN HISTORY

1. Each person and each culture as a you-for-God

Human beings are creation's Everest, piercing through the clouds of the space-time universe to limitless Love. Being created in God's image and likeness means each human being is a 'you' for the divine I am. As Etty Hillesum, a Dutch Jewish Auschwitz victim in Westerbork concentration camp puts it: 'My life has become an uninterrupted dialogue with you, oh God, one great dialogue.'[28] Abstract Expressionist Barnett Newman captures this intrinsic dialogicality in his painting, *Covenant* (1949), with two vertical zips as he called them: black for Adam, meaning man as earthen, and gold for God. Yet in the painting, man's mortal 'I' and God's immortal 'I' are parallel, in some sense equal. And the blood red background to the zips indicates the kenotic depth of suffering underlying this pledged faithfulness of God to man and man to God.

Giuseppe Zanghí points out that 'When God enters into relationship with humanity, precisely because he is love, he can only do it by giving himself completely, by 'not being' in order to make the other equal to himself (as Aristotle said, there can't be true love without equality).'[29]

Voegelin notes that what makes us one human family isn't primarily our belonging to the same biological species. Rather, it's our common relationship to God that constitutes humankind:

> Without universality, there would be no mankind other than the aggregate of members of a biological species; there would be no more a history of mankind than there is a history of catkind or horsekind [in 1968 lecture notes he mischievously adds 'monkeykind']. If mankind is to have history, its members must be able to respond to the movement of divine presence in their souls. But if that is the condition, then the mankind who has history is constituted by the God to whom man responds.[30]

Every culture known to us has engaged in a quest towards this ultimate source of existence, from archaic myth, to the great oriental religious experiences – Confucius, Tao, Hinduism, Buddhism, Zoroastrianism – to classic Greek philosophy, Judeo-Christian revelation and Islam. Various substitute divinities emerge during and after the Enlightenment – matter, the nation, race, history, the imagination, reason, the libido, the collective unconscious, or more recently with Stephen Hawking and Lawrence Krauss, the fundamental laws of physics.[31]

In our time there have been profound post-ideological recoveries of experiences of a transcendence apparently eclipsed by ideologies. Philosophers like Levinas and the later Derrida; writers like Solzhenitsyn and Walker Percy; film directors like Andrei Tarkovsky and Kryzsztof Kieslowski; poets like Patrick Kavanagh and Les Murray; painters like Hughie O'Donoghue and Andy Warhol; composers like Arvo Pärt and James MacMillan, not to mention the great religious founders of our time like Blessed Teresa of Calcutta, Jean Vanier, Andrea Riccardi and Chiara Lubich, are all part of this immense recovery and renewal of the experiences at the heart of our humanity.

This entire drama of the one humankind with its agelong cultural diversity, from myth to revelation, philosophy, ideology and art, mirrors the unity and Trinity of God. But that mirroring comes at a price.

2. The kenotic drama of humanity

a) Stone-Age kenosis? Since you're probably more familiar with how later cultures prepare for their encounter with the divine by various forms of asceticism or self-negation, let's have a look at what we can understand as pre-kenotic messages left by our Stone-Age brothers and sisters.

If we make our way through the seventeen-thousand-year-old Stone-Age 'cathedral' of Lascaux, we arrive at the six-metres-deep shaft which is its spiritual centre. Following Marie König's interpretation, its paintings portray a life and death struggle between two figures. On the right is a mortally wounded bison, whose wound seems to have been inflicted by a long spear lying across its body. Facing the bison on its left is a figure of what could be a man with a bird's head, a long narrow rectangle for a body, four fingers on each hand, and an erect phallus. Since the bison's horns are aimed menacingly in his direction, and the male figure is falling backwards, it looks as if he's been gored by the bison. Underneath the man is a complete painting of a bird, perched on a vertical line, facing left, away from the scene of conflict. What the bird is looking towards is the partly completed figure of a powerful rhinoceros, striding further leftwards. Three vertical sets of two dots are painted, leading from the rhinoceros's tail in the direction of the rectangular figure.

Marie König has found bull, mammoth, and other horns frequently used to represent moon-phases, and is inclined to see the dying bison as symbolising the waning moon. Since the earth is often represented by symbolisations of its four directions – four lines, squares, and so on – she interprets the rectangular-bodied figure with its four-fingered hands as symbolising the dying earth. The long vertical line the bird is perched on could represent the sun, moving in a line from east to west across the sky, while bird symbols often represent messengers from the heavens. The kenotic focus for this drama in three acts is on the cosmic struggle between death and life in the depths of winter, with the annunciation of the hope of cosmic rebirth symbolised by the rhinoceros linked to the six moons of the new year.[32]

There's an equivalent cosmic kenosis enacted by the Neolithic people who built Newgrange 5,200 years ago. At the moment of midwinter dawn as the sun entered the long passage grave, there, in and through their loving-suffering struggle for attunement at the centre of the cosmos the Boyne people touched ecstatically for a few boundless timeless moments the divine ground of existence.[33] Seamus Heaney wrote of this event which marks the first moments of the beginning of the New Year:

> Inside the cosmic hill. Who dares say 'love'
> At this cold coming? Who would not dare say it?[34]

We can let Aeschylus summarise the entire range of what we're calling pre-kenotic experiences with his phrase 'wisdom through suffering' (*Agamemnon*, 179). If we were to reinterpret them in terms of our addressing a personal God, we could say each of them seeks to enact in word and action that 'You are everything, I am nothing'.

b) Christian kenosis: But in Christianity, that sacrificial saying, 'You are everything, I am nothing' – common in one form or another to all cultures – is elevated into the cry of Jesus on the cross, 'My God, my God, why have you forsaken me?' As man, Jesus elevates the agon of the human quest for the divine you into the cry of the God-man for his Father. And in the same Jesus, that cry of the human in search of God intersects with the cry of God in search of the human. To the cry of Christ's humanity to God, 'You are everything, I am nothing,' answers the cry of his divinity to the human, 'you are everything, I am nothing.' Jesus as man *is-not* out of love for God, Jesus as God is-not out of love for man.[35] More than anywhere else, human history can be seen as centring here, 'at the still point of a turning world', where in Christ, *agape* and *kenosis* become thanksgiving to the Father. Which is why the Eucharist can be seen as underlying all of human history.

3. The Eucharist at the heart of human history

Aquinas has pointed out that all humans 'from the beginning of the world until its end' potentially belong to the mystical body of the Church with Christ as its head.[36] But the full actualisation of that capacity only occurs in the Church, through graceful participation in the Eucharist. There, each one's thanksgiving shares in the divine gratitude within the Trinity. This is possible because, as Aquinas has said, 'the proper effect of the Eucharist is the transformation of man into God', our divinisation.[37] And since God can only exist in God, the Eucharist brings those who gracefully receive it into the inner life of the Trinity. Our oneness with Jesus in the Eucharist is in fact so profound – St Julian Eymard says it's second only to the hypostatic union[38] – that the communicant, in and with the Son, is led to address the Father as Abba.

Then, all of cosmic, evolutionary and human history achieves its fulfilment in thanksgiving to the Father. As Coda puts it:

> At the end of time all that will remain is God in God: uncreated and created. The ultimate truth of everything is to be itself in relation to God, which means to be itself distinct from God, but as an expression of God. The vocation of all of created reality is to become Eucharist: real presence of God distinct from God. So, at the end, the *eschaton*, the *omega* of creation (as also its origin, *proton, alpha*) is trinitarian. It's the vocation of creation to become the spouse of the lamb.[39]

Voegelin, paraphrasing Plato, remarked, 'History is Christ written large'.[40] In the Church and its eucharistic celebration, the whole fourteen billion years of cosmic and evolutionary history along with all human history has been in St Paul's word, 'recapitulated' in Christ, and we can add, in the Church constituted by the Eucharist.[41]

NOTES

1 Jonathan Marks, *What It Means to Be 98 per cent Chimpanzee: Apes, People, and Their Genes*, Berkeley: University of California Press, 2002, p. 283.

2 John Paul II, 'Message to the Rev George V. Coyne, June 1, 1988', quoted in Mariano Artigas, *The Mind of the Universe: Understanding Science and Religion*, Philadelphia: Templeton Foundation Press, 2001, p. 321.

3 Sean Carroll, *Endless Forms Most Beautiful: The New Science of Evo-devo and the Making of the Animal Kingdom*, New York: Norton, 2005, p. 138.

4 Richard G. Klein with Blake Edgar, *The Dawn of Human Culture: A Bold New Theory on What Sparked the 'Big Bang' of Human Consciousness*, New York: Wiley, 2002.

5 Piero Coda, *Dalla Trinità: l'avvento di Dio tra storia e profezia,* Rome: Città Nuova, 2011, p. 567.

6 Coda, *Dalla Trinità*, p. 570.

7 For example, *Summa Theologiae*, 40, 2, ad. 1.

8 Coda, *Dalla Trinità*, p. 569. See also his *Evento Pasquale: Trinità e Storia*, Rome: Città Nuova, 1984 and *L'altro di Dio: rivelazione e kenosi in Sergei Bulgakov*, Rome: Città Nuova, 1998.

9 Coda, *Dalla Trinità*, p. 572. See also his '*Dio e la creazione, I: Trinità e creazione dal nulla*', *Nuova Umanità*, 115, January–February, 1998, pp. 67–88.

10 Chesterton wrote of Francis in his *St Francis*: 'He was above all things a great giver, and he cared chiefly for the best kind of giving which is called thanksgiving. If another great man wrote a grammar of assent, he may well be considered to have written a grammar of acceptance; a grammar of gratitude. He understood down to its very depths the theory of thanks; and its depths are a bottomless abyss. He knew that the praise of God stands on its strongest ground when it stands on nothing.' Quoted in Ian Ker, *G. K. Chesterton, A Biography*, New York: Oxford University Press, 2011, p. 501.

11 'Nor is it superfluous, even if God can by himself produce all natural effects, for them to be produced by certain natural causes. For this is not a result of the inadequacy of divine power, but of the immensity of his goodness, whereby he also willed to communicate his likeness to things, not only so that they might *exist,* but also that they might be *causes for other things*. Indeed all creatures generally attain the divine likeness in these two ways ... By this, in fact, the beauty of order in created things is evident.' *Summa Contra Gentiles*, III, p. 70.

12 In a 1973 interview, quoted in Jean-Philippe Antoine, Gertrud Koch & Luc Lang, *Gerhard Richter*, Paris: Dis Voir, 1995, p. 82.

13 Aquinas, answering his question, 'Could God Make a Better Universe?' replies: 'The perfection of the universe depends essentially on the diversity

of natures by which the various levels of goodness are fulfilled, rather than on the multiplying of the individuals within one nature.' *In Sent I*, 44.1.2, quoted in Norman Kretzmann, 'The Metaphysics of Creation: Aquinas's Natural Theology', *Summa Contra Gentiles II*, New York: Oxford University Press, 1999, 224, no. 106.

14 Coda, *Dalla Trinità*, pp. 572–3.

15 Bernard Lonergan, *Insight: A Study of Human Understanding*, London: Longmans, 1961, pp. 121–8.

16 See John D. Barrow and Frank J. Tipler, *The Anthropic Cosmological Principle*, Oxford: Oxford University Press, 1986, and Paul Davies, *The Goldilocks Enigma: Why is the Universe Just Right for Life?* Boston: Houghton Mifflin, 2008.

17 See John D. Barrow and Frank J. Tipler, *The Anthropic Cosmological Principle*, Oxford: Oxford University Press, 1986, p. 252f.

18 See Eric Voegelin, *Anamnesis: On the Theory of History and Politics*, David Walsh, ed., Columbia: University of Missouri Press, 2002, p. 81.

19 See for example, Hugh Ross, *Why the Universe is the Way it is*, Grand Rapids, MI: Baker Books, 2008.

20 Sergio Rondinara, '"Dio Amore" e la nostra comprensione del cosmo', unpublished lecture, Rome, 2009.

21 Pope Benedict is recalling Teilhard de Chardin's 'Mass on the World' with its observation that 'mysteriously and in very truth, at the touch of the supersubstantial Word the immense host which is the universe is made flesh. Through your own incarnation, my God, all matter is henceforth incarnate.' Available online, originally published in his *Hymn to the Universe*, New York: Harper & Row, 1961.

22 David Walsh, 'The Turn Toward Existence and Existence in the Turn', *Philosophy, Literature and Politics: Essays Honoring Ellis Sandoz*, Charles R. Embry and Barry Cooper, eds., Columbia: University of Missouri Press, 2005, pp. 3–27, at p. 24.

23 In *Gerard Manley Hopkins: The Major Works*, Catherine Phillips, ed., Oxford: Oxford University Press, 2009, p. 129 (I've added the vertical breaks in the text.)

24 Charles Darwin, *The Origin of Species by Means of Natural Selection or the Preservation of Favoured Races in the Struggle for Life*, London: John Murray, 1902[6], p. 670. Darwin added 'by the Creator' to the 2nd, and retained it right up to the 6th and last edition of the *Origin of Species*.

25 John Paul II, 'Christian Faith and the Theory of Evolution', address to participants at the International Symposium, April 1985, in *Osservatore Romano*, 27 April 1985.

26 Piero Coda, *Il logos e il nulla: Trinità, religioni, mistica,* Rome: Città Nuova, 2003, p. 217.

27 Chiara Lubich, *The Eucharist,* Brooklyn, NY: New City Press, 1977, pp. 61–2.

28 Etty Hillesum, *Etty: The Letters and Diaries of Etty Hillesum, 1941–1943,* Klaas A. D. Smelik, ed., Arnold J. Pomerans, trans., Grand Rapids, MI: Eerdmans, 2002, p. 640.

29 Giuseppe Maria Zanghí, 'Verso una cultura del post-ateismo', *Gen's,* 1, 1997, 10.

30 Eric Voegelin, *The Ecumenic Age,* Baton Rouge: Louisiana State University Press, 1974, p. 305.

31 See Stephen Hawking and Leonard Mlodinow, *The Grand Design,* London: Bantam Press, 2010; Lawrence Krauss, *A Universe From Nothing: Why There Is Something Rather Than Nothing,* New York: Free Press, 2012.

32 Marie König, *Unsere Vergangenheit ist älter,* Frankfurt: Krüger, 1980, pp. 106–11.

33 See Brendan Purcell, 'In Search of Newgrange: Long Night's Journey into Day', *The Irish Mind: Exploring Intellectual Traditions,* Richard Kearney, ed., Dublin: Wolfhound Press, 1985, pp. 39–55.

34 Seamus Heaney, 'A Dream of Solstice', *Irish Times,* 21st December 1999.

35 I've based these last thoughts on a 1993 meditation Giuseppe Maria Zanghí shared with me and a group of priests at the Focolare school of formation for diocesan priests, then located in Frascati, outside Rome.

36 Aquinas, *ST,* III, 8, 3.

37 Thomas Aquinas, *In Sent. IV,* 12. 2. 1.

38 Pierre Julien Eymard, *Le sainte Eucharistie: La presence réele, Tome I,* Paris: Librairie Eucharistique, 1949, p. 303.

39 Coda, *Dalla Trinità,* p. 590.

40 Eric Voegelin, *Published Essays 1966–1985,* Ellis Sandoz, ed., Colombia, MO: University of Missouri Press, 2000, p. 78.

41 See Heinrich Schlier, *Lettera agli Efesini,* Brescia: Paideia, 1965, p. 73.

THE IRREDUCIBLE PARTICULARITY OF CHRIST: BEAUTY, EUCHARIST AND COMMUNION

PROF. GILL GOULDING CJ
University of Toronto

Christ[1] is the radiant impulse of God's revelation arising from the central nexus of the Trinity, endowing every created thing with meaning and value and recapitulating all within himself back to the Father by the irradiating presence of the Spirit. At the heart of all our academic exchanges over these days stands the figure of Christ who brings into dynamic conjunction the reality of beauty, Eucharist and communion within his own person. It is this timeless and eschatological[2] dynamic that enables us to speak of the irreducible particularity of Christ.

Fifty years after the opening of the Second Vatican Council the Eucharistic ecclesiology of Benedict XVI and the spirituality of communion of John Paul II are seen to be rooted in the same person of Christ as an ongoing elaboration of his redemptive mission. Communion ecclesiology has moved in the post-Vatican II years from a focus on the Christological imperative to a more profound awareness of the revelation of the Trinity made known in contemplating the face of Christ. In addition, over these last fifty years the pontiffs have owned their indebtedness for their developments in ecclesiology and spirituality to the work of the redoubtable Swiss theologian Hans Urs von Balthasar.[3] Balthasar, John Paul II and Benedict XVI were all interested in *bildung* – the formation of the soul in its multidimensional complexity. All were offering a hermeneutic of continuity for the interpretation of the documents of the Second Vatican Council.[4] Also Benedict XVI shares with Balthasar an interest in beauty as a transcendental property of being and in love as a theological virtue, and indeed the form of all virtue.[5]

This paper which falls roughly into three parts also draws from the work of Balthasar. It focuses first on Christ as the archetype of beauty. Secondly, it explores the Eucharist as radiant communion with Christ and Trinitarian gift. This involves the Church called to radiate the beauty of Christ which is most powerfully revealed in the celebration of Eucharist. Finally we explore the invitation to respond to the gift of Christ in the Eucharist by living our part as members of the Church in the redemptive mission of Christ. Here we focus on the Church as person and mission and on how living out the mission we receive 'in Christ' means growing into the fullness of the persons we were created to be.

CHRIST THE ARCHETYPE OF BEAUTY

All beauty comes from God. There is no beauty that does not come from the Father through Christ, himself the embodiment of all beauty. St Augustine, in a famous passage from the *Confessions*, addresses God as beauty personified: 'Late have I loved You, O beauty ever ancient, ever new, late have I loved you!' Contrary to popular opinion, true beauty is *objective*. Truth and goodness are beautiful, just as the beautiful is true and good. A wonderful passage from Balthasar's *The Glory of the Lord* says,

> Beauty is the word that shall be our first. Beauty is the last thing which the thinking intellect dares to approach, since only it dances as an uncontained splendour around the double constellation of the true and the good and their inseparable relation to one another. Beauty is the ... one without which the ancient world refused to understand itself, a word which ... has bid farewell to our new world, leaving it to its avarice and sadness.[6]

Balthasar begins his theological aesthetics, *Herrlichkeit*, by lamenting the demise of beauty in theology: it is 'a word from which religion, and theology in particular, have taken their leave and distanced themselves in modern times by a vigorous drawing of the boundaries'.[7] While beauty was central to the vocabulary of antiquity and in the theology of the Fathers, modern theology has turned away from beauty as a transcendental aspect of being. Without beauty, Balthasar argues, 'the good also loses its attractiveness' and 'the proofs of the truth have lost their cogency'.[8]

'*Gestalt* provides a key to the whole (understanding of beauty).'[9] *Gestalt* or 'form' meaning a totality of parts and elements, grasped as such, existing and defined as such, which for its existence requires not only a 'surrounding world' but ultimately being as a whole.[10] Form is more than we see, it is the outer expression of an inner depth. Always here, we need to keep in mind the Fourth Lateran Council's stress that as great as may be the similarity, so much greater must the dissimilarity between Creator and creature be preserved.[11] This is especially the case when the word 'form' is applied to Christ. In his very person lived in the mission of his life, passion, death and resurrection Jesus is 'the form of God'. Jesus Christ is a 'legible' form and not just a sign, but his form can be grasped for what it is only when it is accepted as the appearance of a divine depth transcending all worldly nature. Jesus as the form of God (*Gestalt Gottes*) God's eternal Word become flesh. What appears in Christ by reason of the hypostatic union is 'the becoming visible and experienceable of the God who is himself triune'.[12] This form shows forth and communicates and expresses the form, the beauty and the radiant glory of the triune God.

Because the world into which the form of Jesus the Logos incarnate is sent by the Father is a sinful world, in need of redemption, Jesus' form has to take on suffering, death and even descent into hell in order to save us. This form has to take on the modalities of fallen existence so as to transvalue them by redemptive suffering. Here, God's splendour reveals and authenticates itself definitively precisely in its own antithesis as love selflessly serving out of love. We see this definitively in the salvific action of God on behalf of human beings in the incarnation, passion, death and resurrection of Christ. There are two foundational theological insights operational in Balthasar's project of recovering beauty: the glory of God; and the covenant to which God's glory invites the human person. God is not only glorious-in-Godself, but also glorious-for-us. God is not only love, the eternal act of perichoretic indwelling between the Father and the Son hypostasised as the Spirit who is herself Love, but God also loves the human person on whom he freely chooses to disclose divine love in the fullness of the act of creating. The Trinity is love *ad-intra* and *ad-extra*. Accordingly, God's love is a mutual revelation of the divine Persons in whom they are lover, beloved and love and an external revelation of love as God's nature to each human person.

Human beings always stand in awe of God who is always greater, always mightier, always transcendent, always completely and irrevocably other. The love between Creator and creature is always of the powerful Lord who graciously and mercifully bestows kindness and delight on his servant. Balthasar's extraordinary theological vision attempts to speak words of beauty and honour to reflect the grandeur of the mystery of God's love for human beings made known in Christ. The foundation of his project is the very human experience of being struck by glory, of being penetrated by divine presence, to be elevated to God's own dignity. The *Herrlichkeit* is thus a 'theological aesthetics' that is, a theological reflection on how the enfleshed spirit is moved, is enraptured in seeing the form of God.

The foundation of the God-human covenant is the paradox of God's glory as love – the divine desire to exchange love with human beings and for them to bear fruit.[13] If this is so, then it is not surprising that Balthasar's own theological project is inherently paradoxical. Indeed he excels at accentuating contrary – though not contradictory claims about God and the world, while holding them tenaciously in tension. To draw a musical analogy, if one begins an encounter with a fugue by Bach by analysing in the score the use of rhythms, time and key signature, entry points of the fugal theme and counterpoint, one can hardly be said to have *heard* the fugue. His method is one of 'integration not evolution'.[14] Nevertheless his project comes across as more piercing, incisive and pointed rather than smooth and melodious. Balthasar wants to shock, not invite to complacency, his message is profoundly penetrating and fiery in order to awaken us – twenty-first century Christians, entrapped in our end-of-modernity darkness and emptiness – to wake up to be attentive and to follow the master.

Balthasar was deeply concerned that our own post-Christian times have lost the sense of beauty and glory. We have become desensitised, our affect flattened, our hearts not attuned to God or being. As Nietzsche claimed 'God is dead', because we have killed our inherent desire to be grasped by God. This 'murder' of God, however, is our tragic cultural suicide: the fragmentation of truth to scientism and relativism; the collapse of the good to narcissism and legalism.[15] Balthasar's *Glory of the Lord* is a long lament – in seven volumes – about this loss and this dehumanisation. He recognises that if we are to wake up and bear our Christian responsibility namely to bear the light/*doxa* revealed to the world we must also recognise its continuity yet at the same time discontinuity with the light experienced in the history of the world.[16] It is this paradox of the need for the retrieval of a sense of beauty in history[17] yet at the same time, for remembering and being conformed to the newness that Christ continues to bring to history that is the task of the Christian today.

Balthasar presents a helpful threefold schema that contrasts the Greek experience of *doxa* with the Hebrew biblical *kabod* and Christian *gloria*, while also suggesting a post 'modernity' awakening and synthesis to *doxa-kabod-gloria*. For the Greeks, *doxa* was a cosmic appearance, first as the personified 'gods' and later as the harmonious revealedness of the cosmos itself. This 'book of nature' exposed the world as just and fitting with divine ordinances, and hence as inviting to an ethical ordering of human life in imitation of cosmic life. In turn, this beauty and order of the cosmos was experienced as awakening a sense of gratitude, awe and delight, which expressed itself in poetry, myth and philosophy as natural theology.[18]

If we look at the Hebrew Bible, the most profound experience of the Hebrews of the radiant beauty of God was as the Word of God spoken directly to them as a people, through the voice of mediators: Moses, the judges, kings and prophets. The word was 'an integration from an abstract-sensuous *kabod* reality to the concrete-personal *kabod*',[19] which bound them to the lived experience of God's goodness, grace and blessing, but that called for their radical obedience to the *Torah*, the law of God. The three-fold experience of *doxa-kabod* in the Hebrew bible – as a *call* experienced as *gift* that enraptures and called forth a *conversion* of heart to an ethical living – is therefore unbroken.[20]

It remains unbroken even in the 'totally new' of the Christian *Gloria* where the Word *is* revealed as Divine Person *who* becomes flesh and is emptied on the cross for us. The 'form' and 'splendour' of Christian revelation are one and the same in the one who reveals who God is – self-offering love – while hiding in its antithesis, the cross as symbol of human sin. The revealed law is that which transcends all law – love – while the grace that is experienced is the very Person of the Holy Spirit. In our post-modern times, Balthasar likewise presents the challenge to us: in the final revelation-in-hiddenness of God's love on the cross, we are invited to a new creation, a new right worship in the Spirit that imitates Christ, who is the first-born of God's new eschatological creation. This will be the task of Christian life; this has always been the task of Christian life and it finds its appropriate foundation in the self-emptying of the Son.

The theological task, which is always a scriptural exegesis attentive to the signs of the times continues in the Church through the re-interpretation of its foundational experience/story in the eucharistic tradition of breaking open the word/Word in the prayerful reflection on God. For Balthasar, this theological task also has – together with its 'appropriate foundation' as aesthetics, as attentiveness to divine beauty – a 'proper centre': the kenosis of the Son. This is where Balthasar's Trinitarian theology becomes evident. If for Balthasar the created realm is Christoform, it is because Christ is the mediator par excellence between God and the world. And if Christ in being the Word-made-Flesh is the 'form' of the Father, his very divinity hidden in his humanity was revealed in the glorious act of his resurrection. I emphasise the resurrection first, because it is in the experience of Christ as alive, as glorified flesh, as conqueror of death, that the early Church – in particular as recalled in the earliest witnesses such as Paul – remembers and ponders the cross. As Paul states, 'If Christ has not been raised, then our proclamation has been in vain and your faith has been in vain.'[21] Balthasar continually points to the totality of the *mysterium paschale* – the death on the cross, the descent into hell and resurrection into life.

Accordingly, the resurrection is the ground in contradistinction to which the icon of the cross, and hence divine glory can emerge. And in fact it emerges most profoundly because it synthesises (and is simultaneously iconoclastic of) the Old Testament images of the hoped-for mediator: the political Messiah, the new David who would save the people from their oppressors; the one 'coming from above' the apocalyptic Son of Man who reveals divine power and might; the personification of divine wisdom herself as co-fashioner of the cosmos; and finally the suffering servant, the prophet, whose body and entire being is possessed by God. In the Johannine Gospel's passion drama, the Logos (sapiential wisdom) who comes 'from above' (apocalyptic tradition) is revealed as king of another realm (messianic expectations) raised up on his throne that is the cross (Isaiah's suffering servant). The cross thus becomes the entry point through which humanity encounters a new truth, a new goodness and the most provocative beauty: 'I am the way, and the truth and the life.'[22] Christ on the cross is the 'way' to the Father, the eternal source of 'life' and goodness as the 'truth' of self-emptying love.[23] And as Pope Benedict XVI emphasised in the Mass inaugurating his pontificate in 2005: 'There is nothing more beautiful than to be surprised by ... the encounter with Christ.'

EUCHARIST: RADIANT COMMUNION WITH CHRIST – TRINITARIAN GIFT

In an atmosphere of constant thanksgiving the Christian community feeds on the word and causes to rise towards God, as a song of praise, the word that he himself has given us. And every action, every gesture, every service is accomplished within this profound relationship with God, in the interior movement of Trinitarian love that descends towards us and rises back towards God, a movement that finds its highest expression in the eucharistic sacrifice.[24]

There is an eschatological reality in the Church's celebration of the Eucharist as she embodies within herself in such celebration the end to which she looks forward as well as the means towards that end. In the gift of the real presence of Christ in his Body and Blood made present in the eucharistic celebration and received by the faithful there is both the promise of the final communion to which we all journey and the very present communion of the sustaining presence of Christ nourishing his body the Church to continue his mission until the end of time. And 'precisely as a gift of communion, the Eucharist unveils both the Trinitarian life of God and the ultimate nature of created being in their difference and unity'.[25]

The Eucharist is essentially a Trinitarian gift: 'it is the Father who gives his Son's body for the world through the unitive mediation of the Spirit.'[26] In addition the Eucharist is the expression of the Son's eternal gratitude for the original gift of the Father. Within the Eucharist Christ communicates both his human life and the Trinitarian reality.

The Eucharist implies much more than that (Christ) merely stands before the Father as mediator in virtue of his acquired merits; likewise more than that he merely continues in an unbloody manner in heaven the 'self-giving' he accomplishes in a bloody manner on earth. It ultimately means that the Father's act of self-giving by which, throughout all created space and time, he pours out the Son is the definitive revelation of the Trinitarian act itself in which the 'Persons' are God's 'relations', forms of absolute self-giving and loving fluidity.[27]

There is a word of gratitude and thanksgiving that is in and of the Trinity. This word is taken up and echoed in the human response of believers gathered together in eucharistic Communion. In receiving the Body and Blood of Christ, the faithful are then sent forth back into the world with the imperative of Christ's mission as the determining impulse of service to the world. This action that flows from the contemplation of the eucharistic Christ is the word of unity that draws the body into deeper communion with Christ the Head. 'The word that has given itself as flesh and blood, the Word that has entered the believers and now speaks within the Church, which has her foundation in the Eucharist, as the word of the unity between Head and body, the word in the satisfied hunger of the soul, the word of common thanksgiving.'[28] The very thrust of the incarnation is towards a eucharistic reality in so far as it is grounded in God's gift of self to the world and the outworking of this in the passion, death and resurrection of Christ.[29]

It is in the midst of the suffering of Christ that the Eucharist is brought into being.[30] But this is a suffering freely borne out of love and oriented to that definitive act of love in terms of the salvation of all human persons in and through the ordinary reality of their lives. Accordingly 'every possible detail of the believer's life is caught up, supported and simultaneously enclosed in the Eucharist as an ecclesial, sacramental act'.[31] At the same time it becomes clear that there can be a sharing in the suffering of the Lord by whatever means such suffering enters into human life if it is clearly aligned with the Paschal mystery and thus is part of having eucharistic fellowship with him.[32]

The Church as the mystical body of Christ is instrumental in God's plan of recapitulating all things in Christ. Accordingly, there is a twofold task both to facilitate this movement moment by moment within temporality and to acknowledge the *telos* of this movement in the eschatological reality of the celebration of the Eucharist. Here Christ present in his Body and Blood – by the will of the Father and the work of the Holy Spirit – offers to believers both his real presence and a share in his redemptive mission for the life of the world.[33] 'The unity of the Church has its origin in the participation of the community in his self-emptying: in the Eucharist and at the same time in the active frame of mind which the reception of the Eucharist should effect in us.'[34] Our participation in the Eucharist takes place as a true 'eating and drinking', which is a process of real transformation but it is Christ who transforms us into himself, rather than that we transform him into ourselves. We are drawn to offer our lives so that we might become more and more the one whom we receive by faith. 'Above all, the boundary between oneself disposing (even in faith) and being at God's disposal must disappear.'[35]

Inasmuch as I would argue the Eucharist is inseparable from the Church, 'and the Church is given to "drink" of the Holy Spirit of the Father and the Son', then it is clear that 'a personal relationship of the believer to Christ has already expanded into the Trinitarian sphere'.[36] Kenosis seen from this standpoint is an emptying out to provide a space that can be filled, and the Eucharist is the permeation of the kenosis of Christ with the Triune God's love being poured out across all space and time as flesh given up and blood that is shed.[37] 'Given the plan to bring about creatures endowed with freedom, the ultimate form of this pouring-forth will be that of the Eucharist, which, as we know it, is intimately connected with the passion, *pro nobis*.'[38]

CHURCH, PERSON AND MISSION IN COMMUNION

According to Balthasar we receive Trinitarian life through the death and resurrection of Jesus. Not only does his death take away sin but from the depths of the Paschal mystery flows the gift of the Holy Spirit.[39] If we are in Christ we participate in his Sonship. In this way we offer not just ourselves to the Father but also the Son, by the effective working of the Spirit, this is central to the mystery of the Eucharist. And we are incorporated into the body of Christ – the Church. Here, 'so fruitful is his passion that its grace flows into us and enables us to share in his fecundity'.[40]

The culmination of the drama of divine and human freedom is to be found at the cross. It is here that God's definitive 'yes' overcomes the 'no' of sin across all generations. The willing, loving obedience of the Son even unto death and through death to resurrection enables the possibility of eternal life, life lived by gratuitous divine invitation in the presence of the Trinity. The Spirit, poured out upon humankind from the cross, opens up the new possibility of human existence lived out in a daily act of eucharistic thanksgiving – an act central to the life of the Church – and drawing on the most 'natural' Christian attitude of gratitude. It is this attitude which is both inspired by the Holy Spirit and promoted by those in leadership within the Church.

Ecclesial communion is inspired and sustained by the Holy Spirit and preserved and promoted by the apostolic ministry. And this communion, which we call 'Church', does not only extend to all believers in a specific historical period, but also embraces all the epochs and all the generations. Thus we have a two-fold universality, a synchronic universality – we are united with believers in every part of the world – and also a diachronic universality, that is: all the epochs belong to us and all the believers of the past and of the future from with us a single great communion ... The Church's apostolic tradition consists in the transmission of the goods of salvation which, through the power of the Spirit makes the Christian community the permanent actualisation of the original communion ... Tradition is the communion of the faithful around their legitimate pastors down through history, a communion that the Holy Spirit nurtures, assuring the connection between the experience of the apostolic faith, lived in the original community of the disciples and the actual experience of Christ in his Church.[41]

Balthasar, in his essay on the nature of the Church,[42] asks a provocative question: *who* is the Church? His own answer to the question emphasises that 'to frame the question in this way is to presuppose that the Church is "someone", in other words a person.'[43] Balthasar sees the Church not merely as an institution like other institutions but as a person because she is the body of Christ. The Church is the mystical body of Christ. Therefore this body has a centre of consciousness which resides in the head who is Christ.

So Balthasar explains 'The "body", in the sense of the simile, forms, together with the "Head", one being; that is, (the Church) is a person only "by grace" of the Head.'[44] Therefore in response to the question, who is the Church? Balthasar gives the reply: the Church is 'Christ living on', 'For (Christ) it is no sort of hubris, but a simple statement of fact to make the equation: *L'Église c'est moi*.'[45] This insight is not merely a pertinent theological assertion, but the foundation upon which we stand as a communion in Christ's body. It has radical implications for the life and conduct of those who are members through baptism and particularly those who are called to ordination or to serve in diverse ministries within the Church.

The Church by its very nature is missionary. In like manner we can view Balthasar's *Theo-drama* as a study in missiology. At the centre of this metaphor of 'the drama of existence', in saying there is a relationship between life and theatre, in the claim that there is in dramatic theory 'an *instrumentarium*' from which theology might learn and borrow, is the basic assumption that in life there is a story to be enacted by players fulfilling certain roles.[46] For each of these players, save the divine author who is also the lead player, there stands the questions 'who am I?' and 'what am I to do?' These questions reveal the integrated themes that are the focus of the *Theo-drama* – identity and mission.[47] They are the component parts and the pathway to personhood in Balthasar's theological anthropology, for he has said, it is only 'when God addresses a conscious subject, tells (him/her) who (he/she) is and what (he/she) means to the external God of truth and shows (him/her) the purpose of (his/her) existence – that is, imparts a distinctive and divinely authorised mission – that we can say of a conscious subject that (he/she) is a "person"'.[48]

But for many people in today's world, this pathway to personhood is far from clear. For many people there exists more than just questions and uncertainty regarding ideas such as role, identity, purpose and action in the world. Identity and action have become completely detached from a sense of purpose and from each other and the contemporary world offers little to help define, orient, or integrate them. For Balthasar, mission, which guides and motivates activity in the world, is grounded in and flows from the person whom God made. As Balthasar wrote, 'if the mission is the real core of the personality, it opens up the latter – because it comes from eternity and is destined for eternity – far beyond the dimensions of which it is conscious in the world or which others allot to it.'[49] There is, however, as Balthasar emphasises a communal aspect to the search for personal identity and mission and neither can really be found in isolation from other people. It is only in true inter-subjectivity, in relationship with another, that we will come to know ourselves. Systems and social structures cannot tell us who we are.

This idea of the inter-subjectivity in the search for identity and mission is present also in the theology of Balthasar, not in the sense of human inter-subjectivity, but rather in the interrelationship of divine-human freedom. According to Thomas Dalzell, Balthasar's understanding of the dynamic between human and divine freedom is such that, while God's freedom always has 'priority' in the 'God-creature relationship', we can nevertheless also say that Balthasar's theology 'rescues the positivity of human transcendence in such a way that the human subject can be regarded as a real partner in the relationship'.[50] Despite the utter transcendence of God in Balthasar's theology, there is a claim of genuine inter-subjectivity between humanity and the divine through which each reveals something of the other. The individual human mission, of which the individual's identity is a part, is only fully revealed as it is understood to be related to the divine mission of the Son. It is the interrelationship of the individual's sense of mission to the divine mission of the Son that permits the individual to act in true freedom and to fulfil the identity which they were given by God.

For Balthasar then, the human individual must seek unity of personhood achieved when identity and mission come together (but are not equated) 'at some mysterious point' and become 'a kind of reflection on the mission of Christ'.[51] It is a dramatic mysterious point. Like the union of divine and human freedom, in the interrelationship between the individual human mission and the mission of Christ, there is a dramatic tension. And here, Balthasar's ecclesiology impels us to consider the nature of what it means to be *persons*-in-communion. Not just as biological beings, nor merely as a social group held together by commonly accepted customs, and courtesy, persons in communion means first and foremost persons grounded in love – a love originating from the depths of the Trinity.

The Church does not exist in isolation, but only in relation to her Head. There is a Trinitarian consciousness and disposition that existentially grounds the body. It is the Trinitarian life of God toward which the Church is ever attracted and attracts others, through its participation in Christ. The Church is not the source of her own life. For Balthasar, the Church is not merely an institution or social body, the Church is a person and expressly a 'someone' whom the Lord loved and for whom he died. It is the passionate irreducible love of Christ that the Church is called to reflect.[52]

CONCLUSION

There is a certain beauty in this love of Christ which is the convergence of divine and human freedom. We see this in Christ's obedience and child-like simplicity. His free-loving obedience to the Father's will is also beautiful. His unrestricted 'yes' to the Father, by grace enables a 'yes' from believers a loving 'yes', which has both its origin and its determining consent – it is as it were caught up into the 'yes' of Christ – in the obedience of the Son. No finite freedom can be freer from restrictions than when giving its consent to infinite freedom. Or (which is the same thing) no mission can be more unrestricted and universal than that which gives the yes that God looks for, the yes to his all-embracing plan. The sole condition is the consent that makes no conditions.[53]

The focus of Balthasar's consideration here is on properly ordered love which draws its strength and serenity from union with Christ and is always fruitful. Disordered love by contrast is self-referential and restlessly consuming but is never satiated, rather there is an inbuilt process of decay. Ordered love of Christ in the Church is always radiant and is perceived in lives of authentic service. 'All beings are, in the last analysis, interpreted according to their goal and calling, which, in the human being's case is always love. All else is but means to an end; love alone is the goal.'[54] Love truly becomes rightly ordered and is at its most expansive when focused in Christ who is the supreme example of such love. In becoming so focused in Christ there is an opening to the life of the Trinity where giving and receiving abounds. '(God's nature) is always both what is possessed and what is given away, and we cannot say that a particular hypostasis is rich in possessing and poor in giving away, for the fullness of blessedness lies in both giving and receiving both the gift and the giver.'[55]

The particularity of Christ in his life and Paschal mystery revelatory of divine Trinitarian life draws human persons to a life of giving and receiving in gratitude. The wonder of gratitude and thanksgiving, however, is not perceptible without the experience of the Cross. 'The human being has to accept that he must go through the narrow door of humiliation, of the cross, encountering the infinite precisely in the most finite, in order to arrive at communion with infinite freedom.'[56] Christ shows us what filial self-gift is, and focuses it upon the natural dependency of a child.[57] The transparency of a child is of particular importance if human persons are to be open to the superabundance of God's gift and here the sacramental life of the Church is vital. In the Eucharist, Balthasar states: 'We have primarily the ever-new presence of Christ's physical humanity that has now become pneumatic.'[58] We become changed into Christ through the work of the Spirit. Of primary importance here is participation in the sacrament of the Eucharist where as we receive the eucharistic Christ we are gradually transformed and enabled to radiate his spirit.[59] This is the fruit of remaining in Christ as even the smallest branches remain in the vine. This mystery is a 'reciprocal indwelling that lies beyond all imagination, proceeding from the perception of the "unveiled vision of the glory (of love) of the Lord" to an "ever more glorious reflection through the transformation into the same image, which the Lord works through the power of the Spirit"'.[60]

Christ is the archetype of beauty and the Church as his body is called to radiate the beauty of Christ. This is most significantly seen by the eyes of faith in the Eucharist. The onus then is on the awareness with which human persons come to the Eucharist. Such awareness is a vital dimension of how we live into or become part of the redemptive mission of Christ. Relationship of person and mission is how we truly become persons in and through living our part in the mission of Christ.[61] Therefore Eucharist, communion and beauty in the irreducible particularity of Christ who alone makes the reality of the Trinity and the delightful interplay of beauty, truth and goodness present indicate something of the shared delight of love operative within the Trinity.[62] The mysteries of the Trinity, creation, revelation, incarnation and redemption all include a eucharistic dimension that defines Christian existence. At the heart of the Church the mystery of the Eucharist is the source and centre of mission and the Church's mission is to draw all to participate in the Eucharistic mystery for in doing so we are drawn deeper into the divine human drama of the Word made flesh – the irreducible particularity of Christ.[63]

the gift of love with which God draws near to us.' Pope Benedict XVI, *Deus Caritas Est* (1), 2006.

58 Hans Urs von Balthasar, *Theo-Drama Theological Dramatic Theory III: Dramatis Personae: Persons in Christ,* Graham Harrison, trans., San Francisco: Ignatius Press, 1992, p. 43.

59 Cf. Hans Urs von Balthasar, *Theo-Logic III: The Spirit of Truth,* Graham Harrison, trans., San Francisco: Ignatius Press, 2005, p. 18.

60 Hans Urs von Balthasar, *Love Alone is Credible,* D.C. Schindler, trans., San Francisco: Ignatius Press, 2004, p. 123. Also cf. 2 Cor 3:18.

61 'Balthasar's personal understanding of the Church weaves together the unity and distinction, identity and difference of ecclesial *communion* in the closest possible way.' Stephan Ackermann, 'The Church as Person in the Theology of Hans Urs von Balthasar', *Communio* 29 (summer 2002).

62 'This convertibility of divine love and divine being also implicates the other transcendental in dynamic circumincession with one another inasmuch as the intentional *ecstasies* of one divine *persona* toward repose in the goodness of another is prompted by delight in the other's beauty, and inasmuch as this very *ecstasies* acknowledges the authority of an "evidentiary" claim and therefore affirms the true.' Michael Hanby, 'Trinity, Creation, and Aesthetic Subalternation', *Love Alone is Credible: Hans Urs von Balthasar as Interpreter of the Catholic Tradition volume 1,* David L. Schindler, ed., Grand Rapids, Michigan: William B Eerdmans, 2008, pp. 41–74.

63 'As incarnate, the Son not only provides the measure and norm for the relation between God and the world "from above, by the standard of heaven", so to speak, but also and simultaneously "from beneath and from within, using his humanity, body and soul, as the unit of measurement".' Hans Urs von Balthasr, *A Theology of History,* San Francisco: Ignatius Press, 1994, p. 65. See also 'In this sense Christ can be called the only *concrete* analogy of being, since he constitutes in himself, in the union of his divine and human natures, the measure of every distance between God and man. And this union is his person in both natures. The philosophical formulation of the analogy of being is related to the measure of Christ precisely as is world history to his history – as promise to fulfilment, the preliminary to the definitive.' Ibid., p. 74. Cf. 'The Trinitarian analogy enables the Son, without abolishing the *analogia entis,* simultaneously to do two things: he represents God to the world – but in the mode of the Son who regards the Father as "greater" and to whom he eternally owes all that his is – and he represents the world to God, by being, as man (or rather as the God-man, "humble, lowly, modest, docile of heart" [Mt 11:29]). It is on the basis of these two aspects, united in an abiding analogy, that the Son can take up his one, unitary mission.' Hans Urs von Balthasar, *Theo-Drama Theological Dramatic Theory III: Dramatis Personae: Persons in Christ,* Graham Harrison, trans., San Francisco: Ignatius Press, 1992, p. 230, fn. 68.

THE ANTHROPOLOGICAL ROOTS OF COMMUNION

REV. PROF. PAUL O'CALLAGHAN
Pontifical University of the Holy Cross, Rome

The concept of 'communion' has, in recent decades, been closely and principally associated with ecclesiology, ecumenism and the Eucharist. And rightly so. The 1985 Synod of Bishops, held twenty years after the conclusion of Vatican Council II, spoke insistently of the value and centrality of what came to be called an 'ecclesiology of communion'.[1]

COMMUNION AND ECCLESIOLOGY

Much may be said in favour of an 'ecclesiology of communion'.[2] As a manner of describing the life and action of the Church, the notion of 'communion' links easily both with the Pauline description of the Church as the body of Christ, and with the notion of the people of God to whom God freely communicates his Spirit and gifts.[3] It has deep roots in early Christian centuries[4] and throughout the history of theology, the principal expression being that of *communio sanctorum*, 'the communion of saints (or of holy realities)', found frequently in the symbol of faith[5] and closely associated with the Church. Besides, the notion of communion has the advantage of emphasising the personal relationship established by the Spirit between believers and God, thus emphasising Christian spirituality and prayer-life. Without excluding the role of an institutional Church, an ecclesiology of communion points preferentially to the spontaneous initiatives the Spirit awakens in the lives of Christian believers, 'the glorious freedom of the children of God' (Rm 2:21).[6]

Still, two less positive aspects of an ecclesiology of communion may be noted. First, it does not always provide a satisfactory explanation of the relationship between the spiritual (or charismatic) and institutional sides of the Church. It easily leaves the organisational, visible and hierarchical aspects of the Church in the shade.[7] Second, insistence on communion ecclesiology reveals a tension between the Church as a network of friendly personal relationships between its members and as a mystical communion of grace between the members of the Body of Christ. The term 'communion' is used, sometimes confusingly, to cover both union with God and fellowship with other believers. Many have attempted, not always successfully, to combine the two aspects. The following expression of Arnold Rademacher, in his classic study of communion, is not untypical: 'The more intimate man's relationship to God is, the warmer also will be the relationship of men to one another.'[8] But is this the case? Is communion with God automatically reflected and experienced as communion with others? Or taken in the opposite direction: does human fellowship carry believers by the hand, as it were, to personal union with God?

In this paper I intend to address this issue, considering from a dynamic anthropological standpoint the ways in which communion with God, established by faith and lived in charity, expresses itself and finds support in communion, or fellowship, with other believers, indeed with the rest of humanity.

THE NOTION OF COMMUNION IN SCRIPTURE

The biblical notion of *koinõnia*, a term that is commonly translated as 'communion', has roots that go deeper than issues related to ecclesiology. Semantically, *koinõnia,* and other similar terms used in the New Testament (such as *koinos* and *koinõnos*),[9] is opposed to *idios,* that is what is private and individual, what belongs to the self. Besides, *koinõnia* is related to the term *koinos,* equivalent to the Latin *communis,* 'common', which frequently refers, even in the New Testament,[10] to what is vulgar and impure. More specifically, however, the term *koinõnia* evokes participation, association, common origin.[11] It is therefore a characteristic typical of a religious community.[12]

One question of an etymological or exegetical kind I consider to be of particular interest. Whereas the New Testament term *koinõnia* and its equivalents are translated generally as 'communion', some particularly influential translations of the Bible, such as the Vulgate, render it preferentially as *communicatio,* 'communication'.[13] This is particularly so in Pauline texts,[14] less so for Johannine ones.[15] The Vulgate, in fact, uses the Latin term *communio* only once (Heb 13:16, whereas the revised Vulgate (or Neo-vulgate, second edition, 1979) frequently puts *communio* where the Vulgate has *communicatio.*[16] Likewise, the term *communicatio* is commonly used among early Latin Christian writers and by theologians during the Middle Ages.[17] Conversely, the term *communio* is not particularly frequent. Interestingly, the Roman Canon (or First Eucharistic Prayer) includes the prayer *Communicantes et memoriam venerantes,* which is usually translated as ' ... *in communion* with those whose memory we venerate, especially the glorious ever-Virgin Mary ... '.

The term *communicatio,* which derives from the verb *communicare,* adds to that of *communio* the dynamic aspect of something that is given. Whereas the term *communio* is descriptive and factual, referring to participation in a common reality, *communicatio* is active. The use of *communicatio* expresses God's saving action as a gift, and makes it clear that *communio,* sharing – or common participation – in God's gifts, is the *result* of God's self-giving (*communicatio*) that humans accept and share with others. This is an important, indeed essential, aspect for a dynamic understanding of *communio* that looks to God as the living source of all communion. For *communio* is not merely a sociological category, though it may have sociological connotations; it is a fully and primarily a theological one.

Let us examine how the logic of God's self-communication to humans gives rise to the mystery of communion. First let us consider the question of human equality and difference.

THE MEANING OF HUMAN EQUALITY AND DIFFERENCE

Humans relate to God as inferiors, to material creatures as superiors, to other human beings as equals. Thus they praise God, they use creatures, they relate to, dialogue and share with other persons. Besides, it is undeniable that on the face of things differences between human beings are of greater weight than likenesses. As a result, people feel driven to attempt to detect and overcome differences and discrepancies with others, though for the most part they may not quite manage to do so. This is so much the case in practice that it would seem more reasonable to say that human equality as such is an aspiration, though an unreachable one.

Ancient philosophers for the most part denied human equality. Slaves, what Aristotle called 'living tools', are naturally inferior to 'freedmen'. For him it was 'clear that some are free and others are slaves by nature'.[18] The same concept may be found in Roman Law:

only the *paterfamilias* had full rights, whereas his wife, children and slaves, as well as buildings, lands and herds were considered his disposable property.[19] The Sophist Aristophanes (died 385 BC) thought differently, however, and said that 'by nature we are all created equal in every way, barbarians and Greeks'.[20] So did the Stoic Seneca (died AD 65): all humans are equal, he said, because they have reason in common, 'whether they are slaves or free, freeborn of freed'.[21] But this was the exception among ancient thinkers, not the rule.

It is widely accepted that Christian faith in Jesus Christ as the Saviour of humanity opened the way to a clearer understanding of the fundamental equality of all humans. If all can be saved, if all are the object of God's eternal love, even the less well considered members of society, even sinners, then in their innermost constitution all humans should be considered as fundamentally equal. All humans are present in God's mind and Christ's work. After all, God made them 'in his image and likeness' (Gn 1:27). And St Paul draws the inevitable conclusion: 'There is neither Jew nor Greek, there is neither slave nor free, there is neither male nor female; for you are all one in Christ Jesus' (Gal 3:28; see also 1 Cor 12:13; Col 3:11). The Alexandrine Jew Philo, a contemporary of Christ, wrote: 'we humans are all brothers, because God is our common Father.'[22] Even J. J. Rousseau (died AD 1778), hardly an enthusiast of the Christian view of the world, recognised that Christianity was responsible for introducing into the world the notion, or at least the objective, of the equality of all humans.[23]

However, the fact remains that for many people 'equality' is an unobtainable aspiration, whereas inequality seems more real, more accessible, more definitive; perhaps equality is a straightjacket, whereas the recognition of inequality is a sign of tolerance.

I shall attempt to reflect on the issue following the writings of Thomas Aquinas (died AD 1274) and Catherine of Siena (died AD 1380).

Saint Thomas asks the question openly: *utrum inaequalitas rerum sit a Deo?*,[24] whether the inequality existent among created beings, indeed among humans, derives from God. Did God make creatures unequal? Or are humans responsible for the discrepancies that exist in society? Aquinas rejects the popular understanding of Origen's teaching, according to which the differences existing between human beings derive from the sin of each one. Everyone is situated in the world, says Origen in *De principiis*, according to the greater or lesser intensity of his or her personal misdeeds. Thomas correctly rejects this position, and holds that the variety present among creatures is due not fundamentally to sin, but to God's will, *propter perfectionem universi*,[25] 'for the sake of the perfection of the universe'. In other words, God creates unequally; all creatures are creatures, but not all creatures are the same. God even creates humans different one from the other.

But what does that mean? Did we not say that God creates humans *equal* to one another, made in his image and likeness? Are they equal and unequal at the same time and in the same respect? In a somewhat provocative text, which I intend to quote at length, St Catherine of Siena takes up the same issue in speaking of the gifts God gives to each one and the meaning they have. She places the following words in God's mouth:

> I distribute the virtues quite diversely, I did not give all of them to each person, but some to one, some to others ... I shall give principally charity to one; justice to another; humility to this one, a living faith to that one ... And so I have given many gifts and graces, both spiritual and temporal, with such diversity that I have not given everything to one single person, so that *you may be constrained to practice charity* towards one another ... I have willed that one should need another and that *all should be my ministers in distributing the graces and gifts* they have received from me.[26]

Catherine does not distinguish between gifts of nature and of grace, between human talents and supernatural life, between natural virtues and infused virtues, for all without distinction derive ultimately from God, Creator and Lord of the universe. Yet it is obvious to her that not all humans are in possession of the same gifts and talents. So what does 'equality' mean here? She replies: in the fact that one and all are 'constrained to practice charity'; that each and every person is constituted as God's 'minister in distributing graces and gifts'.

Catherine's intuition is simple and profound: the reason why God provides humans with different gifts and graces is that they may relate to one another in disinterested self-donation.[27] In that sense communion between humans is not just the result of the *static fact* of their being social beings. It is the fruit of the self-donation of humans to one another, of their *communicating* gifts to others which ultimately derive from God. What they give one another is what God has given them in the first place. Thus we may say that human sociality and communion is not just a fact, but primarily a dynamic, finding its *source* in God, its *meaning* in charity, in generous self-giving, and its *opportunity* in inequality, in the God-given diversity present among humans. Aristophanes, as we saw, says we are equal because we all have *nature* in common, Seneca because we have *reason* in common; Christians accept both but add a deeper root in the fact that all humans are constituted in such a way as that they are capable of *receiving and communicating* God's gifts: they can give and receive.

Of course God could have created each and every person exactly as he wished, complete down to the last detail. But he chose not to do so. He wished to communicate his gifts to humans *through the mediation of other humans*, in such a way that we would live in dependence not only on him but also on others. A complicated system, one might say, but an interesting one to say the least.[28]

GIVING AND RECEIVING: A DYNAMIC ANTHROPOLOGY OF COMMUNION

Still, it might be objected that in the heel of the hunt one person will end up giving, while the other will just receive; one is master and the other disciple. And if this is the case, then the giver must be considered superior to the receiver, and thus equality is denied.

This need not be so, however, for two reasons. *Firstly*, because the gifts and talents each one possesses and eventually communicates to others derive always, directly or indirectly, from God. Thus the act of donation to another in real terms is always an act of reception, because what is given was once received, either from other people, or from God, or better, always from God and often through others. Those who give, in other words, are never justified, in real terms, in congratulating themselves for their generosity. *Secondly*, the one who gives may not be considered as superior to the one who receives because the very act of receiving is in itself one of self-giving to the giver, an act of true humanity. One can give something to an animal, but the animal receives it in an animal-like way (see Mt 7:6). But humans, no matter how profoundly in need they may be, receive (or can receive) *humanly*, that is, as the gift of another person; they are capable of recognition and reception. The one who receives is enriched not only by what he obtains in its materiality, but also by the fact that he opens himself to another in an act of grateful love. The receiver *gives* the donor a response, offering a conscious act of acceptance.

In real terms, both the giver and the receiver both receive and give: the giver receives from God and hands on to the other; the receiver receives from the giver and offers in turn his human acceptance. In their fundamental capacity to give and receive, that is in their capacity to love, giver and receiver are equal to one another in the deepest sense of the word. Strictly speaking, creatures do not give, they receive; yet human creatures, besides, willingly offer their acceptance of the gift – they freely 'allow' themselves to be enriched by the other. On the contrary, egoism and individualism may be manifested either in terms of not handing to others what one has received, or of closing oneself off to what is given as a gift.

NEW TESTAMENT TEACHING ON GIVING AND RECEIVING

Several texts from scripture give expression to this dynamic of giving and receiving, and serve as a basis for a better understanding of communion. In real terms they reflect Jesus' own life and action; they correspond to his personal *modus agendi* as the incarnate Son of God, which he attempts to communicate to his followers. Perhaps the most powerful single expression may be found in Matthew's Gospel, chapter 10, as Jesus prepares the disciples for their mission, and says to them: *gratis recipistis, gratis date*: 'you have received freely, give freely' (Mt 10:8), as if to say: all you have is received; the gifts and talents at your disposition are not your own, but come from God; they put you under pressure, as it were, under constraint, to generously communicate those very gifts to the rest of humanity, according to *their* specific needs and not as a favour. 'Charity', notes St Josemaría, 'does not consist so much in "giving" as in "understanding"'.[29] Thus we can understand that the love of neighbour is truly a *commandment* (Mt 22:39), a solemn obligation.

According to Luke, the disciples of Jesus, after having faithfully carried out the task they received, exclaimed: 'We are unworthy servants. We have only done what is our duty' (Lk 17:10): no complacent self-congratulation here, just a realisation they are administrators of divine goods (Lk 12:42). On the contrary, the man who had the fortune of having a rich harvest said to himself: 'What shall I do, for I have nowhere to store my crops?' And he said, 'I will do this: I will pull down my barns, and build larger ones ... And I will say to my soul, Soul, you have ample goods laid up for many years; take your ease, eat, drink, be merry' (Lk 12:17-19). He held on to his God-given possessions as if they were his own. Perhaps the most interesting text is that of Mt 5:16, in which Jesus encourages believers to do good deeds (to others, clearly) while not drawing attention to themselves but *to God*. 'Let your light so shine before men, that they may see your good works and *give glory to your Father* who is in heaven' (Mt 5:16; cf. 1 Pt 2:12).

Let us take stock. God gives humans his gifts, gifts of nature and of grace. Humans are called to accept these gifts in humility and acknowledgment of the giver. As a proof of their grateful acceptance, of recognising that what they have at their disposition is not their own, they are invited to share their gifts generously with others, according to their possibilities and others' true needs, to *communicate* these gifts. On the basis of God's original donation and of humans' grateful reception and generous handing on of the divine gift, it may be said that the shared 'good' produces a 'new good', a 'new creation', that did not exist beforehand, a good shared by God, by the one who receives it from God and hands it on, and by the one who receives it from the latter. The 'good' in question has God as its ultimate source; yet it belongs also to humans insofar as they accept it and communicate it. Humans both glorify God for the gifts they have received, and share them with other creatures as a proof of having done so. This 'new good', that comes from God and is shared by humans, is what gives rise to 'communion': *the fruit of communication is communion.*

Besides, God and humans are united with one another while not being fused with one another, while not forfeiting their personal subjectivity and individuality. Communion thus presents itself as unity but non uniformity. This is a singular and profoundly relevant feature of Christian anthropology, eschatology and spirituality:[30] union does not involve amalgamation; those who are divinised do not become divine. The human person is open, but is not openness; the human being is related, but is not relation. Paradoxically, the more one is enriched, the more one becomes oneself. Speaking of eschatological fullness, we read in the *Catechism of the Catholic Church*: 'To live in heaven is "to be with Christ". The elect live "in Christ", but they retain, or rather find, their true identity, their own name.'[31]

SOME EXISTENTIAL IMPLICATIONS OF A SPIRITUALITY OF COMMUNION

It may be suggested that the process just described seems to come across – if this is the right word – as excessively automatic. It does not take sufficiently into account the personal experience of giving and taking that is so important for humans, the appeal to freedom, the complexity of deliberation, the hesitation over acceptance, the calculation and the risk-taking, the exhilaration of recognition. Apart from the fact that the receiver may have to deal with the perceived humiliation of having to accept what has been given,[32] it might also be asked why and how the giver actually comes to give in the first place. Those who give experience their giving as a losing, in the sense that they hand over to another person the time, the intelligence, the sympathy, the talents, the affection that is at *their* disposal. And the question inevitably arises: who will fill in the gap? Who will give back to me what I have generously given? Would it not be wiser just to hold on to what I have? Perhaps, as the English poet Thomas Gray said, I am just 'wasting my sweetness on the desert air'? Is there anyone 'out there' who will recognise my sacrifice and reward it?

Yet *Gaudium et spes* stated openly that 'Man can fully discover his true self only in a sincere giving of himself',[33] a phrase often commented upon by Blessed John Paul II. How can this dense expression be unpacked?

In the first place, one might say, the receiver *should* by right be grateful to the giver. The giver expects recognition and gratitude from the receiver, to be loved in return (in Cicero's Latin, there is a specific term for this: *redamare*). But he or she may not receive it, or at best may receive it later on. The one who loves expects to be loved in return. But this may not take place when and how one wishes. The giver in his or her very act of giving may thus be left with a sense of solitude, emptiness and sterility. Perhaps this is where Christian spirituality centred on the love God diffuses into our hearts (Rm 5:5) is meant to leave its mark. The act of self-giving that stems from the infused virtue of charity is of course a finite one, for humans are finite beings. However, since it is informed by the divine gift of charity, it is meant to be lived 'in a divine way', as it were, that is, as an unconditioned and faithful self-giving to one's neighbour, loving *as God loves*: 'A new commandment I [Jesus] give you, that you love one another; *even as I have loved you*, that you also love one another' (Jn 13:34). The Christian transformed by charity loves as God loves, in spite of refusals, offences, misunderstandings, lack of recognition on behalf of the person beloved. Recognising the magnanimity of the love of God for oneself, the believer is freely moved to love neighbour generously, magnanimously. 'The cause of the love of God is God himself,' St Bernard says, 'the measure of love is that it has no measure.'[34] The reward for loving, doubtless, is being loved in return, but in this case, principally, it means allowing oneself to be loved by God, and secondarily, being loved in return by our neighbour.

The fact that the giver does not perceive right away the fruit of his or her self-giving means that the latter must be lived as an act of faith or trust, or, as one might crudely put it, of investment in the future. Living by charity the Christian does not seek his or her own benefit as a personal end; he simply intends to allow Christ live in him (Gal 2:20), to act through him; he wishes to be an *alter Christus*, 'another Christ',[35] doing the will of the eternal Father, not letting his left hand know what his right hand is doing (Mt 6:3). The Christian however should also savour the words of Jesus' promise to those who strive to accumulate treasure in heaven (Mt 6:20): 'And every one who has left houses or brothers or sisters or father or mother or children or lands, for my name's sake, will receive a hundredfold, and inherit eternal life' (Mt 19:29; cf. Mk 10:30). The powerful words of St John of the Cross should be kept in mind: 'Think nothing else but that God ordains all, and where there is no love, put love, and you will draw out love.'[36] The fact is that those who, moved by God's grace, dedicate their lives generously though not without difficulty to other people, receive sooner or later from other persons, in God's time and in God's ways, the affection, gratitude and recognition, multiplied many times over, that they deserve. As the psalmist proclaims: 'May those who sow in tears reap with shouts of joy' (Ps 126:5).

CONCLUSION

One of the key issues in properly understanding 'communion' at an anthropological level is how to integrate union with God and human fellowship, how to fully synthesise love of God and love of neighbour. In this paper we have attempted to show, on the basis of a reflection of the meaning of equality and difference among humans, how the dynamic of Christian charity communicated by God to believers induces them to generously communicate to others the gifts they have received. In doing so, their communion with God is reinforced, as is their communion with other creatures. On the basis of God's original self-giving, a common 'good' is at once possessed by God who gives, by humans who both receive and hand on to others what they have received. Thus, in order to fully understand the notion of *communio*, priority should be accorded to 'communication', to God's action and human collaboration, the result of which is 'communion', the common sharing of divine goods.

NOTES

1 The Extraordinary Synod of Bishops took place on occasion of the twentieth anniversary of the Second Vatican Council. See the final report dated 7th December 1985 in '*Enchiridion Vaticanum*', vol. 9.

2 Cf. the classic works of Y.M.J. Congar, *Ministères et communion ecclésiale*, Paris: Cerf, 1971; idem., *Diversity and Communion*, Mystic (CT): Twenty-Third Publications, 1985; A. Acerbi, *Due ecclesiologie: ecclesiologia giuridica ed ecclesiologia di comunione nella 'Lumen Gentium'*, Bologna: Dehoniane, 1975. Cf. also J. Rigal, *L'ecclésiologie de communion: son évolution historique et ses fondements*, Paris: Cerf, 1997; J. M. R. Tillard, 'Communion', *Dictionnaire critique de théologie*, J.Y. Lacoste, ed., Paris: Puf, 1998, pp. 236–42; R. Marangoni, *La Chiesa, mistero di comunione: il contributo di Paolo VI nell'elaborazione dell'ecclesiologia di comunione, 1963–1978*, Roma: Pontificia università Gregoriana, 2001; S. Dianich and S. Noceti, *Trattato sulla Chiesa*, Brescia: Queriniana, 2002, pp. 185–212; G. Calabrese, 'Comunione', *Dizionario di ecclesiologia*, G. Calabrese, P. Goyret and O. F. Piazza, eds, Roma: Città Nuova, 2010, pp. 268–88.

3 See A. R. Dulles, *Models of the Church*, 2 ed., New York: Doubleday, 1987, pp. 58–60; J.M.R. Tillard, 'Communion', pp. 236–42.

4 See especially L. Hertling, *Communio – Church and Papacy in Early Christianity*, Chicago: Loyola University, 1972. This work was first published in 1943.

5 Cf. my study 'Comunión de los santos', *Diccionario de Teología*, C. Izquierdo, J. Burgraff and F. M. Arocena, eds, Pamplona: Eunsa, 2006, pp. 142–6.

6 Different aspects of communion ecclesiology may be found in the New Testament. For example, scripture speaks of a fraternity based on listening to the words of the apostles, on the breaking of bread, on prayer and on having all things in common (Act 2:42-47; 4:32-35; 5:12ff.). This may be considered as the first cell of Church, the ideal to be striven towards. The Eucharist is obviously central: sharing in a common bread, all believers become one body (1 Cor 10:17), which is the Church. This common participation (10:21) makes Christians *koinõnoi* (10:18, 20). The Church thus is a *communitas* rather than a *societas*.

7 This dualism appears to some degree in Lutheran ecclesiology with the distinction between the personalistic *Ekklesia* and the church of law and order (Emil Brunner or Paul Tillich) who contrasts the 'spiritual community' with the Churches. P. Tillich, *Systematic Theology*, Chicago (IL): University of Chicago Press, 1956, vol. 3, pp. 162–72. In a sense, an ecclesiology of communion, rooted in the action of the Holy Spirit, may have the effect of exalting the Church even beyond its due, turning it into an impossible dialogue partner. It may be said that communion ecclesiology does not always offer Christians a clear sense of identity and mission. The sending of the Holy Spirit may leave the motivation for Christian mission obscure. On the topic in Lutheran–Catholic dialogue, see P. O'Callaghan, 'The Mediation of Justification and the Justification of Mediation: Report of the

Lutheran/Catholic Dialogue: "Church and Justification: Understanding the Church in the Light of the Doctrine of Justification" (1993)', *Annales Theologici* 10 (1996), pp. 147–211.

8 A. Rademacher, *Kirche als Gemeinschaft und Gesellschaft. Eine Studie zur Soziologie der Kirche*, Augsburg: Haas und Grabherr, 1931, p. 48.

9 Cf. W. Bauer, F. W. Danker, W. F. Arndt and F. W. Gingrich, eds., *A Greek-English Lexicon of the New Testament and other Early Christian Literature,* 3 ed., Chicago (IL); London: University of Chicago Press, 2000, abbrev. BDAG, 552f., s.v. κοινωνια; 466f., s.v. ἴδιος; J. M. R. Tillard, 'Communion', pp. 236–42.; P. C. Bori, *Koinonia: l'idea della comunione nell'ecclesiologia recente e nel Nuovo Testamento*, Brescia: Paideia, 1972; E. Franco, *Comunione e partecipazione: la koinônia nell'epistolario paolino*, Brescia: Morcelliana, 1986.

10 See for example Mk 7:2-5; Act 10:14-15; 11:8f.; 14:14; 21:27; BDAG, 552, s.v. κοινός, is used most frequently in the sense of making common or impure, defiled in the cultic sense.

11 The expression 'communion' does not derive as is sometimes thought from *cum* (with) and *unio* (union), but from *cum* and *munis*, the latter term deriving from *munus* which means office, task. 'Communion' refers therefore to a shared task, an enterprise carried out in common. In classical Latin the term refers to common possession, common character, perhaps, community; see *Thesaurus Linguae Latinae*, vol. 3, G. Teubneri, Leipzig 1979, 1960–68; A. Ernout, J. André and A. Meillet, eds., *Dictionnaire étymologique de la langue latine: histoire des mots,* 4 ed., Paris: Klincksieck, 1985); P. G. W. Glare, ed., *Oxford Latin Dictionary*, Oxford: University Press, 1984, p. 369. In Patristic Latin the term *communio* refers on the one hand to the goods God communicates to the Church, the Word of God, ministry, sacraments, and especially the Eucharist, and on the other hand, what Christians are meant to communicate to one another, especially mutual support of a material and economic kind. Christians are also said to be 'in communion' on account of the goods communicated by God which belong to all the members of Christ's body. During the Middle Ages the term *communio* becomes restricted, and refers primarily to reception of the Eucharist.

12 Interestingly, *koinõnia* and its root *koinos* have no clear equivalent in Hebrew. The closest is *hbr*, which on several occasions is translated by *koinos, koinõnia,* etc. in the LXX. The principal usage refers to Pharisee communities centred on a master with the will to follow the Law strictly in close fraternity and solidarity: *habūrah.*

13 *Koinõnia* is translated in the New Testament Neo-Vulgate once as *communio*, eight times as *societas*, six as *communicatio*, once as *collatio*, once as *participatio*. See J. M. R. Tillard, 'Communion', p. 237.

14 For example in Acts 2:42; 1 Cor 10:16: 2 Cor 8:4; 9:13; Phil 1:5; Phm 6.

15 For example 1 Jn 1:3, 6, 7.

RESPONDING TO THE GREAT CHALLENGES FACING THE CHURCH TODAY:

BLESSED JOHN PAUL II AND THE ECCLESIOLOGY OF COMMUNION

REV. PROF. SLAWOMIR NOWOSAD
Vice-Rector, John Paul II Catholic University of Lublin, Poland

The world today, though so proud of its scientific and technological progress, is at the same time a restless place. There returns always anew a question whether that 'progress, which has man for its author and promoter, make human life on earth "more human" in every aspect of that life? Does it make it more "worthy of man"?' There can be no doubt that in various aspects it does. But the question keeps coming back with regard to what is most essential – whether in the context of this progress man, as man, is becoming truly better, that is to say more mature spiritually, more aware of the dignity of his humanity, more responsible, more open to others, especially the neediest and the weakest, and readier to give and to aid all.[1] All those questions and concerns, expressed by Blessed John Paul II at the threshold of his pontificate seem to have lost none of their relevance in 2012. Amidst all the restlessness of the modern world the Church of Christ proclaims and gives witness to the truth of God who is communion and therefore calls all men and women to come and share in that same Trinitarian communion. Because 'God so loved the world that he gave his only Son, that whoever believes in him should not perish but have eternal life' (Jn 3:16).

DIVERSE FACES OF THE WORLD

Perceiving man as her *primary and fundamental way*, the Church is called to discern always anew the overall situation and state of the world in which man lives. All that happens, phenomena and trends are to be interpreted *in the light of the gospel* and thus the Church will be able to answer the questions of the men of our time who continue to experience *the joy and hope, the grief and anguish.*[2] It is in almost all John Paul II's documents and in so many speeches that a serious attempt to understand *signa temporum* can be found so that the proclamation of the gospel is not done *in abstracto*, but in the context of man's current situation which is in no way uniform. The Pope does not describe that situation by enumerating sheer facts but rather tries to see them in the perspective of Christian faith as having both roots and consequences for man's life and supernatural vocation.

There are over seven billion people in the world now. Regardless of all aspects of globalisation, its (good and bad) effects and the degree of its advancement, the world remains an 'intricate mosaic' of nations, cultures, languages, traditions and religions. They all, however, comprise the one rich patrimony of the human family. In so diverse a world a common longing for freedom should be noticed: 'an extraordinary global acceleration of that quest for freedom ... is one of the great dynamics of human history.'[3] This shows that the world, though so manifold and mixed, can experience phenomena common to all men and women.

In order to identify more important *signa* as challenges the Church has to face, I will often refer to several documents not so often analysed, namely to the apostolic exhortations which followed continental synods of bishops convoked by John Paul II. They are a valuable source enabling us to understand the panorama of the modern world. Though some of the characteristics relate to some parts of the world more than others, they all in some way allow us to apprehend the complexity of the world.

Though an ever more globalised reality, the world remains deeply divided and marked by many injustices. The globalisation itself is an ambiguous phenomenon with different implications. There are positive consequences like efficiency, increased production, growing economic links between countries and nations – thus bringing greater unity among peoples. But it is also true that ruled merely by the laws of the market, it serves mainly the powerful. Economy is being absolutised, the distance between rich and poor continues to grow (including poor nations, not just parts of a society which find themselves in abject poverty), it brings about unemployment, reduction of public services, little regard for the integrity of the of the environment, etc. Not only in the American context the growing urbanisation is accompanied by external debts, corruption, the drug trade and ecological concern.[4]

Many modern societies undergo all kinds of rapid changes. Like the above mentioned emergence of huge urban conglomerations in which some sectors of society are being exploited and terrorism, organised crime and prostitution thrive in large depressed areas. Another major social event is internal and external migration through which people become vulnerable to uncertain and difficult economic and cultural problems and situations, causing destructive effects on individual and family life.[5] While some nations are highly developed or rapidly developing, others see no hope for a better future living in the persistent reality of poverty and the exploitation of people.

Social and political difficulties like famine, wars, racial tensions and divisions, political instability, social disorientation and despair, the violation of human rights and the threats to the family, including the spread of AIDS and even the survival of the practice of slavery, are in fact true not only in many African nations. The international debt, the arms trade, growing numbers of refugees and displaced persons are too present in Latin American and Asian countries where there is little regard for the safety and dignity of people. Another group of problems are those related to demography where it is often overlooked that the population growth is not merely an economic or political problem but above all a moral one, as it involves the essential issue of human promotion where human dignity and inviolable rights of every person should be respected. It refers also to the problem of poverty and exploitation of women who need their authentic liberation. The awakening of women's consciousness to their dignity and rights is a striking *signum temporis* in the modern world.[6]

A particular question is the vast field of social communication facing an unusually rapid and deep transformation. While the modern information and communication technologies are a true human achievement and can be an important force for good, it happens often that the modern mass media have a negative influence on human and social life being intrusive and manipulative, full of images of violence, hedonism and materialism, imposing 'a distorted vision of life and of man, and thus fail to respond to the demands of true development'.[7]

When referring to Europe and Euro-Atlantic civilisation John Paul II puts stronger emphasis on the philosophical and cultural dimension of the current transformations of society. Not disregarding corruption, ethnic conflicts, the re-emergence of racism or interreligious tensions, the crisis of marriage and family as well as social selfishness, he points out to *signa temporum* which are especially 'clouding the horizon of the European continent'. Among those he draws attention to existential fragmentation, inner emptiness and the loss of the meaning of life, loneliness, practical agnosticism and religious indifference, prevalent concern for personal interests and privileges. All this leads to the emergence of a new culture, largely influenced by the mass media, whose content and character are often in conflict with the gospel and the dignity of the human person. This culture is also marked by a widespread and growing religious agnosticism, connected to a more profound moral and legal relativism rooted in confusion regarding the truth about man as the basis of the inalienable rights of all human beings. At times the signs of a weakening of hope are evident in disturbing forms of what might be called a 'culture of death'.[8] More and more Europeans seem to live in the world closed to transcendence and so European societies – as John Paul II puts it – are 'suffering from horizontalism'. A vision of the world with no spiritual roots is being created where its religious, particularly Christian heritage is ignored. It is all based on a 'vision of man apart from God and apart from Christ'.[9]

This flawed, reductionist concept of man yielding to the temptation of self-sufficiency is sometimes called 'a new cultural model of man' and was for John Paul a major concern. This model would be comprised of radical individualism and subjectivism, secularism, spiritual nomadism, materialistic naturalism accompanied by a perniciously invasive impact of mass media. When speaking to representatives of the Jagiellonian University in Kraków during his pastoral visit to Poland in 1997, the Pope stressed that the crucial debate about man had not been finished with the collapse of communism and Marxist ideology, quite the opposite – it continues to intensify in the contemporary cultural context.[10]

Looking at the world and living one's life *as if God did not exist* leads to secularism, which is characteristic of many parts of modern society. A tendency to live and develop contemporary individual and social life without reference to God seems to be on the rise. Religion is both moved to the margin of public life and regarded as belonging strictly to the private sphere. Consequently, the natural religious sense is being weakened and religious convictions are denied their role in forming people's moral life and consciences. It follows that the Church has a diminished role in public affairs. According to John Paul II, a growing number of people

> are no longer able to integrate the gospel message into their daily experience; living one's faith in Jesus becomes increasingly difficult in a social and cultural setting in which that faith is constantly challenged and threatened. In many social settings it is easier to be identified as an agnostic than a believer. The impression is given that unbelief is self-explanatory, whereas belief needs a sort of social legitimisation which is neither obvious nor taken for granted.[11]

Obviously, all those negative and disturbing realities of the modern world do not exhaust the Pope's description. In many of his documents and addresses he would stress that signs of hope are in no way lacking both in Church life and in the world. Men and women today are ever more conscious of their human dignity and inalienable rights as well as ready to safeguard them. Despite growing secularism and materialism, among many nations in Africa, Asia and Latin America people have preserved a profound sense of the existence of God and of a spiritual dimension of life. A strong sense of community, respect for the family and for human life, a powerful sense of solidarity, as well as of religious tolerance and peaceful co-existence are held dear in many parts of the world. There can often be found openness and new forms of cooperation in the spirit of fraternity accompanied by hard work and discipline. In places like Europe, North America and Australia, while legitimate diversity is being respected and fostered in civil societies, just democratic procedures in administration and government are being introduced leading to the growing unity of the continents. Being very Western in cultural patterns or social structure, often multicultural and technologically developed, those nations refuse to accept structural poverty, reject terrorism and violence as means of political or social change, foster the right to education and health care for all.[12]

Though modern societies are often marked by increasing secularisation and spiritual 'deserts', one cannot leave unnoticed positive and praiseworthy *signa temporum* among Catholics and all Christians. Though in some the sense of God and of his providence has diminished, there are a lot of Catholics with a growing awareness of belonging to the Church and accepting responsibility for her mission in the world. They bear clear witness to the primacy of ethical and spiritual values in daily life. Though restrictions are being imposed on the freedom of religion, so many of Christ's disciples bear daily testimony to the gospel of salvation in Jesus Christ living their lives of authentic holiness and thus leaving a most precious inheritance to the future generations. There are also those who amid situations of hostility or even persecution, are ready to make the supreme sacrifice and shed their blood for the Lord of life, thus proclaiming the gospel of hope in the most radical way.[13]

In all these complex situations of mankind today the Church is to find new effective ways in order to respond to questions of men and women. As in the past, she is now to proclaim and testify to her deepest conviction and faith that Jesus Christ is the way, the truth and the life to man of every age. Though so many people face 'dimming hope' and seem disoriented and uncertain, the Christian message brings new hope to all presenting them with the gift of communion offered in Christ. When the man of today finds himself threatened by the result of the work of his hands, the Church cannot allow 'her voice to be silenced or her witness to be marginalised'.[14]

COMMUNIO ECCLESIALIS – ITS ESSENCE AND ASPECTS

Among the many contributions of Vatican II (1962–5) to the Church's self-understanding the concept of *communio* (Greek: *koinonia*) should be regarded as the central one expressing the very heart of the mystery of the Church established by Christ as his mystical body and as the people of God: '*The reality of the Church as Communion is,* then, the integrating aspect, indeed *the central content of the "mystery"*, or rather, the divine plan for the salvation of humanity.'[15] These two other concepts make the necessary context for a proper understanding of the Church as *communio*. It was in 1985 that the Catholic bishops gathered at the extraordinary synod declared that 'the Church is essentially a mystery of communion, a people made one with the unity of the Father, the Son and the Holy Spirit. This sharing of the life of the Blessed Trinity is the source and inspiration of all Christian relationships and every form of Christian community.'[16]

In his early study of the post-conciliar years *At the Foundations of the Renewal,* the young cardinal Wojtyła stressed *communio* as a notion and reality that would most explicitly reveal the Catholicity of the Church, referring to *Gaudium et spes*: in *communio personarum,* which the Church is in her deepest nature, all men and women can fully discover their true selves in the sincere giving of themselves. Hence, through this giving the good belonging to one person is being shared by all, consequently it becomes universal (Catholic). When the good becomes a gift, the community (the Church) becomes universal (Catholic). In this sense *communio* is the foundation of Catholicity.[17] As Vatican II teaches: 'In virtue of this Catholicity each individual part contributes through its special gifts to the good of the other parts and of the whole Church. Through the common sharing of gifts and through the common effort to attain fullness in unity, the whole and each of the parts receive increase.' In this way, the *communio* of the Church bears fruit when the members of the Church share these goods in common. *Communio* is a characteristic bond of the community of the people of God which brings with itself both 'a distinction' and 'a union' among the members of the Church. Its fruit is also the fact that 'all share a true equality with regard to the dignity and to the activity common to all the faithful for the building up of the body of Christ'[18] – all are truly equal in the Church. For this and other reasons it is of utmost significance that all in the Church were conscious of *communio*. The meaning of *communio* is fundamentally theological and ecclesiological, but Wojtyła would also stress its ethical dimension, because it makes it possible to form a truly Christian social morality which would be introduced by the Church both *ad intra* and *ad extra* (introducing *communio* among all people, not just among the faithful).[19]

Basically *communio* signifies union with God brought about by Jesus Christ in the Holy Spirit. Hence, the *communio* of the Church is a gift of the Blessed Trinity. It is the fruit of God's love to mankind which was accomplished by the Saviour in the Paschal mystery and brought to completion by the Holy Spirit on the day of Pentecost. It enabled the Church to share in the divine *communio* of love between the Father and the Son in the Holy Spirit. As St Paul says to the Romans: 'God's love has been poured into our hearts through the Holy Spirit who has been given to us' (5:5). Consequently, the gift of *communio* brings about a double union – the communion of the believer with the Triune God (vertical) and the communion with other believers and the rest of mankind (horizontal). The vocation of the Church in her pilgrimage on earth is to preserve and strengthen communion with God and communion among those who believe in him.[20]

It is the Word of God and the sacraments that make the communion present in the Church while at the same time it is essential to see *communio* in the proper relationship with the mystery of the Church as a sacrament. A person is introduced to the communion of the Church by faith and by baptism. All three sacraments of Christian initiation play a fundamental role here. Baptism is the door to *communio*, it incorporates a believer into the body of Christ. In confirmation, the Christian is more perfectly bound to the Church becoming a true witness of Christ and his communion of love with the Father. In the Holy Eucharist the Church sacramentalises the communion between the Christian and the Triune God and the intimate bonds of communion among all the faithful (cf. 1 Cor 10:16).[21] The Eucharist is 'the supreme sacramental manifestation of communion in the Church', the culmination and perfection of our 'communion with God the Father by identification with his only-begotten Son through the working of the Holy Spirit'.[22] The Eucharist, being a sacrament of sacrifice, communion and presence, is the 'living and lasting centre around which the entire community of the Church gathers'.[23] Since it unites every Christian with Christ, the Eucharist is both the source and force of communion, it manifests and fosters communion (cf. 1 Cor 10:17). Following St Paul's teaching to the Corinthians (1 Cor 11:17-34) it becomes obvious that an authentic communion with Christ taking place in the eucharistic celebration urges everyone to renew fraternal communion with brothers and sisters. This led John Paul II to emphasise the importance of Sunday Mass for each member of the faithful in order to become a true witness and promoter of communion in daily life. The Sunday Eucharist is 'the privileged place where communion is ceaselessly proclaimed and nurtured. Precisely through sharing in the Eucharist, the Lord's Day also becomes the day of the Church, when she can effectively exercise her role as the sacrament of unity.'[24]

Ecclesial communion has both invisible and visible aspects. In the invisible dimension it is Christ himself who unites us to God in the Holy Spirit and among ourselves. In the visible dimension it involves communion in the teaching of the apostles, in the sacraments and in the hierarchical order of the Church which are 'outward bonds of communion'. Full and authentic communion needs both dimensions just as the Church is both an invisible and visible reality and the only sacrament of salvation. Additionally, the invisible aspect of communion extends also to the saints – those who belong to the heavenly Church, who have left this world in God's friendship and his grace. It is on this foundation that the traditional devotion to the saints, and especially to the Blessed Virgin Mary has always been based in Christian piety. This also points to a mutual relationship between the pilgrim Church on earth and the heavenly Church and thus again reflects the mystery of the Church as a *communio* transcending the earthly reality.[25]

Ecclesial communion, being an organic communion, is very diverse and complementary. Just like a living body, it is marked by a *diversity* and a *complementarity* of vocations, ministries, charisms and responsibilities. The Holy Spirit is the principle of diversity and unity in the Church because it is he who distributes his different gifts for the welfare of the one Church: He 'gives life to, unifies and moves the whole body'[26] (cf. 1 Cor 12:1-11). According to John Paul II, 'the universality of the Church involves, on the one hand, a most solid unity, and on the other, a plurality and a diversification, which do not obstruct unity, but rather confer upon it the character of *communion*' (1989). This plurality is about diverse forms and ministries of life as well as traditions in liturgy and culture. All this does not contradict the unity of the one Church but rather enriches it. This *unity in diversity* needs to be safeguarded and fostered and the task belongs to the pope universally, to every bishop in his local Church and to everyone as a member of the one body in daily life by means of charity.[27]

In 1992, John Paul II devoted a series of catecheses to *communio ecclesialis* which can be seen as a review of the topic. First he states that in order to make this communion real and to accomplish the communion of all with Christ, Jesus gives a commandment which he calls *my commandment* – the commandment of love. Jesus speaks of himself not only as the living model of that love ('as I have loved you') but also as the source of that love being the *vine*: 'The members of this community love Christ and in him they love one another. It is a love with which Jesus himself loves them, and it is linked to the source of the God-man's love – the communion of the Trinity'.[28] In fact, it is the intimate *communio* between the Father and the Son which is the supreme model of the *communio* of the Church (and of any *communio*). This love, that Jesus teaches, is the same love with which the Father loved his Son (cf. Jn 17:24) and which is the deepest need of man: 'Man cannot live without love. He remains a being that is incomprehensible for himself, his life is senseless, if love is not revealed to him, if he does not encounter love, if he does not experience it and make it his own, if he does not participate intimately in it.'[29] On this love the Church as *communio* is founded. This implies that she is to bear witness to this love, to practice it and make it visible. Finally, the Eucharist is the sacramental expression of this love and so the Church as *communio* is continually reborn and renewed in the Eucharist.[30]

The first image of the Church as *communio* after the ascension of the Lord is the community devoted to prayer. The Holy Father says that prayer, especially prayer in common, was the basic feature of the Church's *communio* in the beginning and so it will always be. Prayer expresses spiritual communion, creates and deepens it and produces spiritual unity. Also worth noting is the fact that 'Mary was there', thus she was at the origin of that communion of the Church. Since it is the Eucharist which is the supreme sacrament of the unity among the disciples of Christ, it is also the Church's special prayer to the Father for his gift of the Holy Spirit who can make all 'one body, one spirit in Christ'.[31]

Communio ecclesialis has Christ at its centre according to John (cf. 1 Jn 1:1-2). Saint Paul would point to 'sharing in Christ's sufferings', which in fact is sharing in his whole Paschal mystery. Consequently, 'communion in Christ's Passover becomes a source of reciprocal communion: "If one part [of the community] suffers, all the parts suffer with it" (1 Cor 12:26)'.[32] In order to make the *communio ecclesialis* real, nourished and accomplished, the Holy Spirit must intervene, and the fruit is the 'participation in the Spirit' (cf. Phil 2:1).

Saint Peter in his First Letter describes the Church as a 'communion in God's holiness'. As such the Church is realised through 'spiritual sacrifices', which have their source in Christ's own sacrifice and should be offered according to his example. The communion in God's holiness brings about the sanctification accomplished in the faithful by the Holy Spirit in virtue of Christ's sacrifice. On the part of the faithful the communion in holiness leads to a true commitment to the salvation of all men and women.[33] Taking into account the importance of the sacrament of holy orders the pope says the Church 'is and functions as a priestly community'.[34] In his several consecutive catecheses the pope spoke about all the sacraments and their role in the Church as communion.[35] Hence, baptism brings us into the Church the body of Christ, when we are baptised we enter the ecclesial community. The sacrament of confirmation brings to perfection the gift of the Holy Spirit already received in baptism, so that the confirmed Christian is able to witness to Christ in speech and with his life. Ecclesial community comes to fulfilment above all in the Eucharist. If sin is a wound inflicted upon the Church and harms the ecclesial community, reconciliation with God is also reconciliation with the Church and heals the wound on the body of Christ. At the same time in the sacrament of penance the Church shows that she is a priestly community of mercy and forgiveness. The sacrament of anointing of the sick brings not only the personal welfare of the sick person but also the spiritual growth of the whole Church. In this way the suffering members of the Church contribute greatly to the intimate union of the whole ecclesial community with Christ. Through the sacrament of matrimony the married couple participates in the unity and love between Christ and his Church and the whole family is called to bear witness to the life, love and unity which derive from the very nature of the Church as a sacred community: 'The communion of love between God and people ... finds a meaningful expression in the marriage covenant which is established between a man and a woman.'[36] It is also worth noting that when teaching about the sacraments, the sacrament of holy orders and of matrimony are called in the *Catechism of the Catholic Church* 'the sacraments at the service of communion'.[37]

The Church being the witness to God who is *communio* of the Father with the Son in the Spirit, is to be a sign and instrument of that communion before the world. It is rooted in the truth that the members of the Church share the life of Christ just like branches remain part of the vine (cf. Jn 15:1-17). Communion is a part of the plan of God for all men and women. It is willed by God and destined for completion in the fullness of God's kingdom.[38]

It is the bishops in the Church who hold a particular task as builders of ecclesial communion. Since each one of them is the visible principle and foundation of the unity of his particular Church, they are duty-bound to promote communion in their dioceses. Communion in the Church, signifying life, must constantly be nourished and increased. When the local Church is gathered around her bishop, the *communio ecclesialis* is expressed and lived in a special way. Hence, the bishops in their collegiality and in communion with the successor of Peter are those who are called to safeguard and promote the ecclesial communion among all the faithful.[39] The Eucharist, being the supreme manifestation of communion in the Church, when celebrated in a particular local community transcends its borders and participates and co-builds the universal *communio ecclesialis*. In fact, the endeavour of fostering communion needs priests as well as religious and lay women and men as its agents. While the role of priests and religious is rather clear, the lay faithful fulfil their vocation in the service of communion in two areas: intra-ecclesially where they are delegates of the Word, catechists, group leaders, etc. and in the secular world where they evangelise family, social, professional, cultural or political life.[40]

Communio ecclesialis among local Churches is thus based not only on common faith and the sacraments but also upon the unity of the episcopate – the unity of all the bishops united with the Bishop of Rome as the visible head of the Church.[41] The valid celebration of the Eucharist necessitates real communion with the pope who is the source and foundation of the unity of all the bishops and of the faithful. Local Churches, under the guidance of their bishops, are Churches in which the Church of Christ – one, holy, Catholic and apostolic – is present. However, the universal Church is not a sum or a federation of particular Churches. It is then possible to speak of one Church as a communion of Churches only in an analogous fashion. The one Church is not 'the result of the communion of the Churches, but, in its essential mystery, it is a reality ontologically and temporally prior to every individual particular Church'.[42] When a believer is incorporated into the Church through faith and baptism, it does not happen in a mediate way through a particular Church; he becomes a member of the Church in an immediate way. The *communio ecclesialis* between the universal Church and particular Churches is then rooted in the same faith and in one baptism as well as in the Eucharist and in the episcopate. The Church clarifies that 'the universal communion of the faithful and the communion of the Churches are not consequences of one another, but constitute the same reality seen from different viewpoints'.[43]

The Church, being the universal sacrament of salvation (and thus sent to save all mankind) is not closed and cannot be closed on herself, rather it is open to 'ecumenical endeavour', sent to witness to the mystery of communion she had received from God in order to share it with all people and gather them into the one family of God. Though divided among themselves, there exist elements of communion between the Catholic Church and other Christian Churches and ecclesial communities. They should be nourished and promoted through dialogue, cooperation, promotion of justice, common prayer, sharing in the Word of God and in the experience of faith in Christ. Since the Catholic Church does not believe that 'beyond the boundaries of the Catholic community there is an ecclesial vacuum',[44] a certain, albeit imperfect, communion needs to be acknowledged among all those baptised in the name of the Holy Trinity. An ecumenical commitment, being a 'binding imperative' for all those incorporated in Christ, should lead to a new conversion to the Lord. Important priorities for all should be prayer, penance, study, dialogue and collaboration. Although it is not possible to celebrate the same Eucharist where there is no full communion in the profession of faith, in the sacraments and in ecclesiastical governance, all Christians should desire to join in celebrating the one Eucharist of the Lord thus fostering communion among those who are divided.[45]

The Church, being a witness to God who is communion of love between the Father and the Son in the Spirit, is called to become 'the home and the school of communion' for all. Having been sent to the world by the Lord, the Church is to share this gift with the world and thus to invite the world to the common home and the common school. But first, through contemplation and prayer, rather than her pastoral activity, the Church must continually receive the gift of communion from God himself. In this context, John Paul II points out a spirituality of communion which is to be promoted as a guiding principle of education for all who make up the community of the Church. This spirituality of communion indicates four more detailed issues like: 'the heart's contemplation of the mystery of the Trinity dwelling in us'; thinking of brothers and sisters in faith as 'those who are a part of me' (so we can share their joys and sufferings); seeing what is positive in others (which is also a gift for me); bearing each other's burdens (and thus making room for others).[46] The spirituality of communion – being a gift as well as a task – is like blood in the Church's veins which makes her live and bear fruits. Consequently, all the faithful who constitute the Church are invited to renew their baptismal commitments, to make room for the gifts of the Spirit. The spirituality of communion makes all the baptised active members of the body of Christ and promoters of the kingdom of God in the world 'by their work for the evangelisation and the sanctification of people'.[47]

COMMUNIO BRINGING FRUITS

The mystery of *communio ecclesialis* shows that the bond of communion between Christ the bridegroom and all his disciples is at the heart of the mystery of the Church. Being members of the Lord's mystical body they are all united to the Father which – as a consequence – brings about the communion among all Christians who share it with one another through Christ in the Holy Spirit. Hence, the Church of Christ is the sacrament of a double union – of man's *communio* with God and of the unity of the whole human race which flows from people's union with God. Since it is in the Lord Jesus that the communion between God and his people finds its definitive fulfilment, the Church being Christ's body is where man can experience the loving presence of the Saviour himself – the Incarnate Word who said he would remain with his disciples to the end of time (cf. Mt 28:20). The Church as *communio* is then a *place* of encounter of man with Jesus Christ so that He can 'walk with each person the path of life'.[48]

For man this encounter is of indispensable significance. The Church proclaims a fundamental truth of man as being created by God and in his image and likeness. If 'God is love and in himself he lives a mystery of personal loving communion', the human person has the vocation of love and communion. It is his fundamental and innate vocation. Being created through love, man is called to love. In Jesus love is full and to the end (cf. Jn 13:1), without Jesus man cannot live nor love. Hence, the communion of the Church, where man is being incorporated in the communion of the Triune God's love, is a life-giving mystery for all men and women. It is the task of the Church as *communio* to bear witness to the faith in God who is *communio* in love. This is the answer the Church offers to the world with all its problems and challenges and thus offers the world authentic hope.[49] John Paul II expressed that in New York when speaking to members of the UN General Assembly: 'We Christians believe that in his death and resurrection were fully revealed God's love and his care for all creation. *Jesus Christ is for us God made man, and made a part of the history of humanity. Precisely for this reason, Christian hope for the world and its future extends to every human person.*'[50]

Authentic communion, revealing the true dignity of the human person rooted in God the Creator, shows that dignity and protects it in various circumstances of earthly life. It is truly at the service of human promotion and integral development. Authentic development of man and society 'begins and ends with the integrity of the human person created in the image of God and endowed with a God-given dignity and inalienable human rights'.[51] The Redeemer took on human nature and died that all may be free, thus advanced and defended the dignity of man – God's masterpiece which is common to all, without exception.[52]

Living in communion with Christ – true God and true man, allows man understand better who he is and what is his final destiny: ' ... it is only in the mystery of the Word made flesh that the mystery of man truly becomes clear.'[53] Referring many times to this expression John Paul II would strongly emphasise its importance to show the necessity of God-made-man for man to finally know the truth of himself. All the words and actions of Jesus, in a special way his suffering, death and resurrection reveal before every man depths of what it means to be human: 'Jesus' perfectly human life, devoted wholly to the love and service of the Father and of man, reveals that the vocation of every human being is to receive love and give love in return ... Jesus became once and for all both the revelation and the accomplishment of a humanity recreated and renewed according to the plan of God.'[54]

The Church is to proclaim and transmit her own mystery of *communio* so that man, being 'the meeting point of many conflicting forces' and experiencing in his heart symptoms 'of the deeper dichotomy', can find the way amidst 'his real problems, his hopes and sufferings, his achievements and falls'.[55] Therefore, the basic task of Jesus' disciples is the proclamation of the good news, that is, evangelisation – the vocation proper to the Church and her profound identity. It is another fruit of the deep union – *communio* – with God achieved through Christ. In this sense to evangelise is to proclaim the Word of the Lord and share his gift of *communio* so that each man can enter into that communion and renew his life and hope. 'Many are the paths on which each one of us and each of our Churches must travel, but there is no distance between those who are united in the same communion, the communion which is daily nourished at the table of the Eucharistic Bread and the Word of life.'[56]

The main purpose of evangelisation is 'transforming humanity from within and making it new'. The Church believes that the proclamation of the Word and sharing the Lord's grace of *communio* will be able to transform all people of good will who are ready to open their hearts to the Holy Spirit. However, in order to fulfil her mission of evangelisation with credibility, the Church must first evangelise herself and thus make constant conversion and renewal her own path among the paths of the world. It will make the task of evangelisation more profound and more fruitful.[57]

When teaching about the tasks of the Church in the missionary context, the Holy Father would stress that the communion with the Lord is to bring fruits in mission. The communion is not something to accept and keep, rather, it is something to sow and share. The call to mission, rooted in the very identity and vocation of the Church of Christ, is addressed to all the faithful being participants of the ecclesial *communio*.[58] Those who are united with Jesus through faith and baptism should recognise the call to 'go forth from Jesus in his power and with his grace'. The Church is being called by the Lord always anew to 'share in his mission with new energy and creativity'.[59] Spreading the good news of Jesus Christ is a fruit of encountering him in one's life and then accepting his call to 'cast the nets once more' (cf. Lk 5:1-11). 'The way of Jesus is always the path of mission.' He invites his followers to proclaim the gospel so that 'culture and gospel proclamation will meet in a mutually enriching way and the good news will be heard, believed and lived more deeply. This mission is rooted in the mystery of communion'.[60] The more difficult and unpromising the times are, the clearer and unambiguous the call of the Lord is. The Church as a sacrament of unity is always open to missionary endeavour so all men and women may come to know Jesus Christ in whom the Father receives all into a communion of love and life.[61]

When, according to St John's Gospel, Jesus tells the parable of the true vine (cf. 15:1ff.) it becomes obvious that entering into the communion with him is to bear fruit, while the opposite is also true – where there is no fruit, there is no real communion there.[62] Hence, real fruitfulness depends upon the communion with Christ and its result which is communion with other people. It is then clear that there exists a crucial union between *communio* and mission: 'They interpenetrate and mutually imply each other, so that communion represents both the source and fruit of mission: communion gives rise to mission and mission is accomplished in communion.'[63]

In the perspective of an encounter of the gospel and culture, there is an essential need for a true and balanced inculturation in order to preserve the integrity of the gospel as well as to avoid cultural confusion. It is based on a double respect – both for the gospel and for the culture. Hence, authentic inculturation becomes a significant fruit of the proclamation of the God-given *communio* to all peoples and is in fact the way leading to the fullness of ecclesial *communio*. It is an insertion of the gospel message into a particular culture. Inculturation has its roots in the mystery of the incarnation when God chose a particular people with a distinctive culture in order to reveal to all humanity and all cultures His gift of love and life. It is necessary to discern carefully among all values of any culture to see what is of the gospel and what is not. The Church accepts that a culture can offer its values and forms with which the gospel can be preached more fruitfully, while at the same time the gospel challenges and transforms some values or forms. It is in the light of the mystery of the incarnation and of the redemption that all values and counter-values can be discerned and then those authentic values will be purified and restored to their full meaning. Thus every culture is to be renewed in the light of Christ's Paschal mystery.[64]

Communio is strongly linked to dialogue, in fact they are both 'two essential aspects of the Church's mission which have their infinitely transcendent exemplar in the mystery of the Trinity, from whom all mission comes and to whom it must be directed'.[65] In the above mentioned context of inculturation the dialogue makes the meeting of the gospel and culture effective and leads to identifying the deepest values in any culture. It is also necessary in fostering relations with the followers of other religions, particularly for the sake of peace. Dialogue has to 'be conducted and implemented with the conviction that the Church is the ordinary means of salvation and that she alone possesses the fullness of the means of salvation.'[66]

The salvific mission of the Lord has restored communion between God and people and at the same time established a new communion between all people, divided by sin, who can now live as brothers and sisters.[67] This makes the disciples of Christ aware that they are called to serve and support one another in all needs. Consequently, solidarity and service are another fruit of ecclesial communion which is grounded in the mystery of Trinity and seeks the good of others, first of all of the poorest and thus most in need. In this Christian love is expressed in a 'commitment to reciprocal solidarity and the sharing of the spiritual gifts and material goods ... fostering in individuals a readiness to work where they are needed. Taking the gospel as its starting-point, a culture of solidarity needs to be promoted'.[68]

In the above mentioned concept of the spirituality of communion, John Paul II would stress many particular tasks and effects it is expected to bring. Among those he details: promoting vocations to the priesthood and consecrated life; promotion of various ecclesial associations and movements; pastoral care of the family and the promotion of the vision of marriage as 'a mutual and total bond, unique and indissoluble'; an ecumenical task – fostering reconciliation and communion among divided Christians; respect for the life of every human being; a new commitment to charity and works of mercy with the awareness that 'beginning with intra-ecclesial communion, charity of its nature opens out into a service that is universal'.[69]

To the humanity deeply hurt after the original sin, whose union with the Creator has been broken, God offers his gift of a new and eternal communion. Not disregarding all external individual and social signs of the lost communion John Paul II would see their root in man's heart implicated in sin. Thus the Church, being *communio* of all with the Father in his Son, is the response and the gift offered to the world in all the stages of its history.

When a new millennium was opening before the Church 'like a vast ocean', Blessed John Paul II called all to go forward in hope. *Duc in altum!* The missionary mandate urges and impels us to start out anew and 'our steps must quicken' as we cross the roads of the world we now live in. We believe that 'there is no distance between those who are united in the same communion, the communion that is daily nourished at the table of the Eucharistic Bread and the Word of life'.[70] When expecting the Year of Faith, Pope Benedict XVI reminds us that the door of faith is 'open for us ushering us into the life of communion with God'.[71] This gift of *communio* with God we are to share with all men and women, because we believe all people were touched by God and thus made receptive to the mystery of *communio* offered to all in Christ.[72] We do it by renewing our own faith and Christian life and bearing witness in the world to the Lord who is for ever the only *Redemptor hominis*.

NOTES

1 John Paul II, *Redemptor Hominis*, The Vatican: LEV 1979, no. 15.

2 Cf. Vatican II, Pastoral Constitution on the Church in the Modern World *Gaudium et Spes* (1965), no. 1 and 4; John Paul II, *Redemptor Hominis*, no. 14.

3 'This phenomenon is not limited to any one part of the world; nor is it the expression of any single culture. Men and women throughout the world, even when threatened by violence, *have taken the risk of freedom*, asking to be given a place in social, political, and economic life which is commensurate with their dignity as free human beings.' John Paul II, *Address at UN Headquarters*, New York, 5th October 1995, no. 2. Cf. John Paul II, Apostolic Exhortation, *Ecclesia in Asia*, The Vatican: LEV, 1999, no. 6.

4 Cf. John Paul II, Apostolic Exhortation, *Ecclesia in America*, The Vatican: LEV, 1999, no. 20–5.

5 Cf. John Paul II, *Ecclesia in Asia,* no. 7.

6 Cf. John Paul II, Apostolic Exhortation, *Ecclesia in Africa*, The Vatican: LEV, 1995, nos. 47–51; John Paul II, *Ecclesia in Asia,* no. 7. 'In a world controlled by rich and powerful nations, Africa has practically become an irrelevant appendix, often forgotten and neglected', John Paul II, *Ecclesia in Africa*, no. 40.

7 John Paul II, *Ecclesia in Africa*, no. 52. 'New forms of behaviour are emerging as a result of over-exposure to the mass media and the kinds of literature, music and films that are proliferating on the continent', John Paul II, *Ecclesia in Asia*, no. 7.

8 John Paul II, Apostolic Exhortation, *Ecclesia in Europa*, The Vatican: LEV, 2003, no. 9.

9 Ibid., no. 9 and 34.

10 Cf. S. Nowosad, *Współczesny spór o człowieka*, in: *Ko ciół – pluralizm – Europa*, M. Hintz, ed., Warsaw: KKSFL 2005, pp. 49–53; S. Nowosad, *Man as the Primary Way for the University*, 'Roczniki Teologii Moralnej', Lublin, 1(56): 2009, pp. 93–105.

11 John Paul II, *Ecclesia in Europa*, no. 7. Cf. John Paul II, *Ecclesia in Asia*, no. 29; John Paul II, Apostolic Exhortation *Ecclesia in Oceania*, The Vatican: LEV 2001, no. 7.

12 Cf. Ibid., *Ecclesia in Asia*, no. 6–8; *Ecclesia in Africa*, nos. 42–3, *Ecclesia in Europa*, no. 12; *Ecclesia in Oceania*, no. 7.

13 ' ... they tell us that martyrdom is the supreme incarnation of the gospel of hope: In this way, martyrs proclaim the gospel of hope and bear witnesses to it with their lives to the point of shedding their blood, because they are certain that they cannot live without Christ and are ready to die for him in the conviction that Jesus is the Lord and the Saviour of humanity and that,

therefore, only in him does mankind find true fullness of life', John Paul II, *Ecclesia in Europa*, no. 13. Cf. John Paul II, *Ecclesia in Oceania*, no. 6.

14 John Paul II, *Ecclesia in Oceania*, no. 7. Cf. John Paul II, *Redemptor Hominis*, no. 15; John Paul II, *Ecclesia in Europa*, no. 7.

15 'The ecclesiology of *communion* is a central and fundamental concept in the conciliar documents', John Paul II, Apostolic Exhortation *Christfideles Laici*, The Vatican: LEV, 1984, no. 19.

16 Quoted from: John Paul II, *Ecclesia in Oceania*, no. 10. 'From the beginning, Jesus associated his disciples with his own life ... And he proclaimed a mysterious and real communion between his own body and ours: "He who eats my flesh and drinks my blood abides in me, and I in him".' *Catechism of the Catholic Church*, The Vatican: LEV 1992, no. 787.

17 Cf. K. Wojtyła, *U podstaw odnowy. Studium o realizacji Vaticanum II*, Kraków: PTT 1988, 1st ed. 1972, pp. 116–17; *Gaudium et Spes*, no. 24.

18 Vatican II, Dogmatic Constitution on the Church, *Lumen Gentium*, 1964, no. 13 and 32.

19 Cf. Wojtyła, *U podstaw odnowy*, pp. 120–5; *Lumen Gentium*, no. 32.

20 Cf. Congregation for the Doctrine of the Faith, Letter to the Bishops of the Catholic Church on some Aspects of the Church Understood as Communion *Communionis Notio*, The Vatican: LEV 1992, no. 3; John Paul II, *Christifideles Laici*, no. 19; John Paul II, *Ecclesia in Oceania*, no. 10.

21 Cf. *Lumen Gentium*, no. 11; *Communionis Notio*, no. 1 and 5; John Paul II, *Christifideles Laici*, no. 19.

22 John Paul II, Encyclical Letter *Ecclesia de Eucharistia*, The Vatican: LEV, 2003, respectively no. 38 and 34.

23 John Paul II, *Ecclesia in America*, no. 35.

24 John Paul II, Apostolic Letter *Novo Millennio Ineunte*, The Vatican: LEV, 2000, no. 36; cf. John Paul II, *Ecclesia de Eucharistia*, nos. 40–1.

25 Cf. John Paul II, *Ecclesia de Eucharistia*, nos. 35–6; *Communionis Notio*, no. 4–6; *Lumen Gentium*, no. 14. 'This Assembly ... was of profound significance for the universal Church ... because of the very nature of ecclesial communion which transcends all boundaries of time and space. In fact the Special Assembly inspired many prayers and good works through which individuals and communities of the Church in the other continents accompanied the Synodal process. And how can we doubt that through the mystery of ecclesial communion the Synod was also supported by the prayers of the Saints in heaven?', John Paul II, *Ecclesia in Africa*, no. 19.

26 *Lumen Gentium*, no. 7.

27 *Christifideles Laici*, no. 20; *Communionis Notio*, nos. 15–16.

28 John Paul II, Cat. *The Church Is a Communio of Love*, 15th January 1992, cf. www.vatican.va.

29 John Paul II, *Redemptor Hominis*, no. 10.

30 'Communion is the fruit and demonstration of that love which springs from the heart of the Eternal Father and is poured out upon us through the Spirit which Jesus gives us (cf. Rm 5:5), to make us all "one heart and one soul" (Acts 4:32). It is in building this communion of love that the Church appears as "sacrament", as the "sign and instrument of intimate union with God and of the unity of the human race"', John Paul II, *Novo Millennio Ineunte*, no. 42.

31 *The Eucharistic Prayer III*; cf. John Paul II, Cat. *The Church: A Communio of Prayer*, 29 January 1992; John Paul II, *Ecclesia de Eucharistia*, no. 43.

32 John Paul II, Cat. *The Church Lives in the Mystery of Communio*, 5th February 1992.

33 Cf. John Paul II, Cat. *The Call to Holiness Is Essential for the Church*, 12th February 1992.

34 John Paul II, Cat. *The Church Is a Priestly Community*, 18th March 1992.

35 What follows cf. catecheses from 18th March through 6th May 1992.

36 John Paul II, Apostolic Exhortation *Familiaris consortio*, The Vatican: LEV 1981, no. 12. Cf. John Paul II, *Ecclesia in America*, no. 46.

37 Cf. *Catechism of the Catholic Church*, no. 1533ff.

38 'We must proclaim that this communion is the magnificent plan of God the Father; that Jesus Christ, the Incarnate Lord, is the heart of this communion, and that the Holy Spirit works ceaselessly to create communion and to restore it when it is broken', John Paul II, *Ecclesia in America*, no. 33. Cf. *Catechism of the Catholic Church*, no. 775.

39 John Paul II, *Ecclesia de Eucharistia*, no. 39 and no. 42; John Paul II, John Paul II, *Ecclesia in America*, nos. 36–8; John Paul II, *Novo Millennio Ineunte*, no. 44; John Paul II, *Ecclesia in Oceania*, nos. 9–11.

40 'The presence and mission of the Church in the world is realised in a special way in the variety of charisms and ministries which belong to the laity ... lay people are called to embody deeply evangelical values such as mercy, forgiveness, honesty, transparency of heart and patience in difficult situations. What is expected from the laity is a great creative effort in activities and works demonstrating a life in harmony with the gospel', John Paul II, *Ecclesia in America*, no. 44.

41 'Gathered around the Successor of Peter, praying and working together, the Bishops of the Special Assembly for Asia personified as it were the communion of the Church in all the rich diversity of the particular Churches over which they preside in charity', John Paul II, *Ecclesia in Asia*, no. 25.

42 *Communionis Notio*, no. 9. Cf. John Paul II, *Ecclesia in Oceania*, no. 11.

43 *Communionis Notio*, no. 10. Cf. *Lumen Gentium*, no. 23; John Paul II, *Ecclesia de Eucharistia*, no. 39; John Paul II, *Ecclesia in Asia*, no. 25. Every Eucharist celebrated in a local community is the one Eucharistic Sacrifice offered by Christ for all. The same applies to the unity of the Episcopate with its head – the Roman Pontiff being the head of the Body of College of Bishops. Cf. *Communionis Notio*, nos. 11–14.

44 John Paul II, Encyclical Letter *Ut Unum Sint*, The Vatican: LEV, 1995, no. 13.

45 Cf. John Paul II, *Ecclesia de Eucharistia*, no. 44; John Paul II, *Ut Unum Sint*, no. 45; John Paul II, *Ecclesia in America*, no. 49; John Paul II, *Novo Millennio Ineunte*, no. 48; *Communionis Notio*, nos. 17–18.

46 Cf. John Paul II, *Novo Millennio Ineunte*, no. 43.

47 'Therefore the Church of the Third Millennium will need to encourage all the baptised and confirmed to be aware of their active responsibility in the Church's life', John Paul II, *Novo Millennio Ineunte*, no. 46.

48 'The Church therefore sees its fundamental task in enabling that union to be brought about and renewed continually. The Church wishes to serve this single end: that each person may be able to find Christ, in order that Christ may walk with each person the path of life, with the power of the truth about man and the world that is contained in the mystery of the incarnation and the Redemption and with the power of the love that is radiated by that truth', John Paul II, *Redemptor Hominis*, no. 13. Cf. John Paul II, *Familiaris Consortio*, no. 13; John Paul II, *Ecclesia in Asia*, no. 24.

49 'The Church "is not entitled to express preferences for this or that institutional or constitutional solution" for Europe, and for this reason she consistently desires to respect the legitimate autonomy of the civil order. Nevertheless, she has the task of reviving faith in the Trinity among the Christians of Europe, knowing full well that this faith is the herald of authentic hope for the continent', John Paul II, *Ecclesia in Europa*, no. 19. Cf. John Paul II, *Familiaris Consortio*, no. 11.

50 John Paul II, *Address at UN Headquarters*, no. 17.

51 'The various international declarations on human rights and the many initiatives which these have inspired are a sign of growing attention on a worldwide level to the dignity of the human person', John Paul II, *Ecclesia in Asia*, no. 33.

52 Cf. John Paul II, *Ecclesia in America*, no. 57.

53 *Gaudium et Spes*, no. 22.

54 'In Jesus then, we discover the greatness and dignity of each person in the heart of God who created man in his own image (cf. Gn 1:26), and we find the origin of the new creation which we have become through his grace', John Paul II, *Ecclesia in Asia*, no. 13.

55 Respectively *Gaudium et Spes*, no. 10 and John Paul II, *Redemptor Hominis*, no. 18.

56 John Paul II, *Novo Millennio Ineunte*, no. 58. Cf. John Paul II, *Ecclesia in America*, no. 66.

57 Cf. John Paul II, *Ecclesia in Africa*, no. 55 and 47–8.

58 'Some members of the Church are sent to people who have not heard of Jesus Christ, and their mission remains as vital as ever. But many more are sent to the world closer to home, and the Synod Fathers were keen to stress the mission of the lay members of the Church. In the family, in the workplace, in the schools, in community activities, all Christians can help to bring the good news to the world in which they live', John Paul II, *Ecclesia in Oceania*, no. 13.

59 John Paul II, *Ecclesia in Oceania*, no. 3.

60 Ibid.

61 'From this sacramentality it follows that the Church is not a reality closed in on herself; rather, she is permanently open to missionary and ecumenical endeavour, for she is sent to the world to announce and witness, to make present and spread the mystery of communion which is essential to her: to gather together all people and all things into Christ; so as to be for all an "inseparable sacrament of unity"', *Communionis Notio*, no. 4.

62 Jn 15:5: 'He who abides in me, and I in him, he it is that bears much fruit'; Jn 15:2: 'Each branch of mine that bears no fruit [my Father] takes away.'

63 John Paul II, *Ecclesia in Asia*, no. 24.

64 '"Every culture needs to be transformed by gospel values in the light of the Paschal mystery." It is by looking at the mystery of the incarnation and of the redemption that the values and counter-values of cultures are to be discerned. Just as the Word of God became like us in everything but sin, so too the inculturation of the good news takes on all authentic human values, purifying them from sin and restoring to them their full meaning.' John Paul II, *Ecclesia in Africa*, no. 61. Cf. John Paul II, *Ecclesia in Asia*, nos. 21–2; John Paul II, *Ecclesia in Oceania*, no 16.

65 John Paul II, *Ecclesia in Asia*, no. 31.

66 John Paul II, Encyclical Letter *Redemptoris Missio*, The Vatican: LEV, 1990, no. 55. Cf. John Paul II, *Novo Millennio Ineunte*, nos. 54–6.

67 'There is neither Jew nor Greek, there is neither slave nor free, there is neither male nor female; for you are all one in Christ Jesus', Gal 3:28.

68 John Paul II, *Ecclesia in America*, no. 52.

69 Cf. John Paul II, *Novo Millennio Ineunte*, nos. 46–51.

70 Ibid., no. 58.

71 Benedict XVI, Apostolic Letter *Porta Fidei*, The Vatican: LEV, 2011, no. 1.

72 Cf. John Paul II, *Ecclesia in Oceania*, no. 7.

BECOMING EUCHARIST FOR ONE ANOTHER THROUGH FORGIVING

PROF. ROBERT D. ENRIGHT
Department of Educational Psychology, University of Wisconsin-Madison and International Forgiveness Institute, Madison, Wisconsin, USA

The purpose of this presentation is to explore what it means to forgive another person who has acted unjustly. In my twenty-six years as a university professor examining the topic of forgiveness, I have grown slowly into the understanding that to forgive is intimately tied to Jesus Christ's sacrifice for us on the cross. To make this point as clearly as I can, I would like to begin by first discussing what most people think forgiveness is when they read books or journal articles on this topic. Once we have this foundation in place, I would then like to take us higher, into a much richer realm of understanding what forgiveness is.

A TYPICAL UNDERSTANDING OF THE TERM 'TO FORGIVE'

Were you to consult the numerous books on the topic, you would find that to forgive encompasses three parts: 1) There has been an injustice against the one who is contemplating forgiveness; 2) The forgiver then gives up something negative within, resentment; 3) The forgiver gives something positive of him – or herself to the offending party. What is given can range from patience to respect to moral (*agape*) love in which the forgiver wishes the other well and has his best interest at heart.

At the heart of forgiveness is a virtuous act of mercy. As a virtue, forgiveness comes alongside justice, kindness, respect and other acts of goodness in that it possesses the following characteristics: forgiveness differs from such concepts as excusing, forgetting, and reconciling because the latter three are not moral virtues. For example, reconciliation does not originate inside one person, but instead is a negotiation between two or more people for the purpose of mutual harmony in a relationship.

Because it is a virtue, forgiveness, like all other virtues, is not contingent on accidental external situations for its expression (forgiveness is contingent essentially on someone acting unjustly because such unjust acts by another are part of the essence of what forgiveness is). Examples of accidental external situations are the other's repentance or apology, encouragement from others to forgive, the trustworthiness of the other, and the other's willingness to reconcile.

In essence, then, we can say that forgiveness is a moral virtue, unconditionally expressed as an act of mercy toward those who have acted unjustly toward the forgiver. There are at least three end-points to forgiveness that I am able to see:

1) to express *agape* love as an end in itself because this is a moral good regardless of what follows from its expression;
2) to help change the offending other's behaviour so that he or she grows in the moral virtues (such as patience, kindness, and love); and
3) to unite in moral love with an offending other or others.

GOING MORE DEEPLY

Sacred scripture challenges us to look more deeply at this virtue of forgiveness in ways that are veiled to the typical academic discussion of the topic. For example, when we examine the parable of the prodigal son (Lk 15:11-32), we realise that to forgive is an unconditional act of love, given freely to others for their benefit. We realise further in Jesus' commentary on the Lord's Prayer in Matthew (6:14-15) that our forgiving others is intimately tied to our being forgiven by the heavenly Father. There is an inextricable link here. God forgives us, we forgive others. As God forgives us, we realise the seriousness of our now going forth and doing likewise. The sacrament of penance and our forgiving others are joined. We need the grace from the sacraments, all that are available to us if we are to forgive well. After all, which other virtue asks us to love those who have been cruel to us?

As we continue to explore sacred scripture, we find the exact kind of love with which we are to love those who are cruel to us. In Jesus' upper-room discourse, right before he is to experience his passion, crucifixion and resurrection, he teaches his disciples about the love we are to offer. Greater love has no man than to lay down his life for his friends (Jn 15:13). Jesus is about to lay down his life in forgiving love for us. We are to go and do likewise by laying down our lives in love for, yes, even those who are cruel to us.

Part of this self-giving love involves praying for those who hurt us, as it is explained in Matthew (5:43-47). Yet, there is more as Peter explains in his first epistle (1 Pt 4:12-14, 19). We are to *share* in Christ's suffering. He suffered for the unjust. We are to do the same, and in a *shared* context with him. Yet, what does it mean to 'share in Christ's sufferings' and what does this have to do with forgiving a person who has been unfair? The answer, I think, is in Colossians 1:24 where Paul writes the potentially theologically perplexing statement that he (Paul) fills up 'what is lacking in Christ's afflictions for the sake of his body, that is, the Church' (Revised Standard Version). This is a perplexing statement in our first look at it because it seems to be implying that the perfect God-man is lacking something. Being God, Christ can lack nothing. The perplexity is eliminated when we look more closely at the words. Paul is not saying that Christ lacks anything. Instead, he says that Christ's *afflictions* lack something.

So, we must ask the question: what is the nature of Christ's afflictions? Then we must ask: how are those afflictions lacking? When we ask, 'what is the nature of Christ's afflictions?' we already know the answer in John 15 because Jesus already told us. His sufferings involve *agape* love: no great love has a man than to lay down his life for his friends. Jesus suffered precisely *in love* for us.

What, then, is the nature of *agape* love? Love given by one person to another surely is virtuous and even heroic, but it is lacking something. All love by its nature requires a 'yes' from the other for its completion. On the cross, Jesus' love is not completed until the one who is loved says yes and joins Jesus. The love on the cross is not completed until the one who is loved joins Jesus on the cross and does so out of love for Jesus himself. How do we know that we are to share this love with Jesus on the cross? Why cannot we join him from a safer distance? We have already seen in 1 Peter that we are to share in the suffering (*pathema*, a form of *pathos*, or The passion) of Christ, not just admire this or imitate this. Imitation and union are not the same thing. First Jesus tells us in John to love as he does and then Peter tells us to share Jesus' suffering and then Paul in Colossians 1:24 tells us to rejoice in our suffering as we join with Jesus. Three writers and three common themes: love as Jesus loved and do so with him on the cross to complete the nature of *agape* love.[1]

CRUCIFIED LOVE AND FORGIVENESS

It is time now to tie all of this to your forgiving those who have been unjust to you. The Biblical teachings are clear.

- We are not only to be imitators of Christ but also united to him.
- Not only are we to be united to him but also we are united to him specifically in mutual self-giving love.
- Not only are we to be united to him in self-giving love but also we are to accomplish this on his cross with him.
- Not only are we to accomplish this on the cross with him but also we are to do so for the sake of others, as he has done on the cross.
- And we are to do so not only for the sake of general others, for the world, but also precisely for specific individuals, those who have been unjust to us.
- Is this not what Jesus did on the cross, die for specific people who committed specific offences against him? We are to do likewise.

What, then, does it mean to forgive another who has hurt you? It means that you first are to unite in love with Jesus on his cross out of love for him. From that position of united love with the Saviour, you are to offer that love precisely to your offenders. You are to lay down your life in love for those who have offended you.

Surely this cannot be accomplished without divine grace and this is why there has to be an intimate connection between being forgiven by God and offering unconditional love with Jesus for those who have crucified us by their actions against us. Jesus' one and only commentary on the Lord's Prayer in Matthew drives this point home. Person-to-person forgiving is tied to God-to-person forgiving.

HOW ARE WE 'EUCHARIST' FOR ONE ANOTHER WHEN WE FORGIVE?

First, let us understand the term 'Eucharist'. At the Council of Trent, begun in 1545, the Eucharist was defined as the 'true and proper sacrifice' of Jesus Christ on the altar at Mass. This was reaffirmed by Pope Leo XIII in 1896 in his dogmatic Bull, 'Apostolicae Curae', that the Eucharist is the 'sacrifice of the true Body and Blood of Christ' on the altar. Jesus Himself is the sacrificial gift, offered by a qualified person, the priest, as voluntarily surrendering of His life for the forgiveness of sins. We, then, are eucharist (with a small 'e') as we unite in love with Eucharist himself. As we participate as (small 'e') eucharist, we, too, become voluntary gift of love, with Jesus as Eucharist, for those who have sinned against God and who have offended us. If Jesus' passion lacks nothing, then why does he allow us to participate in this? It is not because his passion lacks anything and therefore needs us to complete an act. It is because he loves us and is giving meaning to our suffering:

As Jesus redemptively suffered for the forgiveness of others, we play a part in this redemption as we voluntarily give ourselves in love first to Jesus on his cross and then with him for those who have offended us. We are giving not only our prayers or our fasting as sacrifice but more importantly we are giving *ourselves* in all of our suffering for the other. Consider Blessed John Paul II's words on this in his Apostolic Letter, *Salvifici Doloris:*

> The Redeemer suffered in place of man and for man. Every man has *his own share in the redemption*. Each one is also *called to share in that suffering* through which the redemption was accomplished. He is called to share in that suffering through which all human suffering has also been redeemed. In bringing about the redemption through suffering, Christ *has* also *raised human suffering to the level of redemption*. Thus each man, in his suffering, can also become a sharer in the redemptive suffering of Christ. (19)

This is not grim suffering at all. Paul in Colossians 1:24 rejoices in his sufferings and Peter (1 Pt 4:13) tells us to do the same: rejoice in so far as we share Christ's sufferings. We rejoice because, as Blessed John Paul II says, human suffering has been linked to love, for Christ and, in the case of forgiveness, for those who have caused our suffering. Linking suffering to love manifests 'the moral greatness of man, his *spiritual maturity*'. (SD, 22; italics in original)[2]

That redemptive love, as Blessed John Paul II says, continues each day through the Church and her sacraments. Christ forgives us through the sacrament of penance and unites with us in his suffering in the Eucharist. It is precisely in the Church where the redemptive suffering is understood, manifested, appropriated, fulfilled and continued throughout human history. It is from this centre, the Church, where we as persons go forth to bring redemptive suffering in love to the world.

PRACTICAL APPLICATIONS

I would like to recommend two spiritual exercises which relate directly to this understanding of forgiving as being Eucharist for others. One centres on time spent in eucharistic adoration. The other centres on the reception of the Holy Eucharist during Mass.

While in prayer in front of the Blessed Sacrament, recall that this is the exact same Jesus who has been sacrificed on the cross both for the one who hurt you and for you. First meditate on Jesus' profound love to suffer in this way for both of you. Second, abide in the loving union with Jesus. Third, then join your wounds to Jesus' wounds and ask him to save this person who hurt you. Eventually, over days or weeks or months, the emotional pain in your heart is likely to lessen.

When at Mass, particularly when the priest begins the consecration, place your woundedness, received from one particular person for one particular injustice against you, on the altar with Jesus. Abide in the love that you share with him. You both share being wounded by people's injustices. As he is broken for you and for the one who hurt you, allow yourself to be broken with Jesus for this person. As you go up to receive Holy Communion, pray for this person. As you take in the Body, Blood, soul and divinity of Jesus, broken for us all, unite your wounds, your suffering, with the crucified Christ for this specific intention: that the one who hurt you is saved by Jesus. When you return to your seat, meditate on the fact that Jesus is now inside of you and that you are now united in love with Jesus. From this position of love, meditate on the fact that both Jesus' wounds and your wounds are efficacious in helping this person.

FORGIVENESS BETWEEN CREATED WISDOM AND RECONCILING GRACE

DR GERALDINE SMYTH OP
Associate Professor and Head of Irish School of Ecumenics, Trinity College, Dublin

FORGIVENESS BETWEEN THE THEOLOGICAL AND THE SECULAR

Dietrich Bonhoeffer, writing about forgiveness and justification, suggests that these are closely related and that they live in the middle ground between secular wisdom and Christ's atoning grace. Christians are thus called to stand in the gap between the historical realities that mould the destiny of states and nations, and the possible impossibility of the forgiveness of sin as the gift and call of Christian discipleship. Thus, according to Bonhoeffer:

> [f]or the Church and for the individual believer there can only be a complete breach with guilt and a new beginning which is granted through the forgiveness of sin, but in the historical life of the nations, there can always be only the gradual process of healing ... It is recognised that what is past cannot be restored by any human might, and that the wheel of history cannot be turned back. Not all the wounds inflicted can be healed, but what matters is that there shall be no further wounds.[1]

Such words may seem a hard saying for the Church, setting the ideal high for Christians, even as they recognise in the political realm the possibility of 'a faint shadow' of the kind of forgiveness offered by Christ. Christians and Churches cannot escape the historical fact that they too have often been in the front line of inflicting wounds and grievously slow to forgive as Christ forgave. Wherever Churches have become trapped in cultural accommodation or political compromise, or wherever a theology of forgiveness becomes fixed in juridical frameworks, the fullness of the forgiveness embodied and taught by Christ has been defaced.

Through biblical revelation, Christians know that forgiveness finds its origin in divine wisdom and grace. The grace of forgiveness may be encountered in the promise of the prophets, in the dramatic portrayal of God's love in the parable of the prodigal son (Lk 15:11-32), or in Christ's dying prayer for forgiveness of his oppressors (Lk 23:34). The signs of divine forgiveness may be disclosed in the world of human culture and in other belief systems. The grace of forgiveness may also be encountered within the texts of a violently bereaved person's struggle to transcend the impulse to revenge, or it may conceal or reveal itself in the shape of poem.

POETRY, POLITICS AND PHILOSOPHY

Michael Longley is one among a number of Irish poets who, through the medium of symbolic imagination, reflects on the ethical dissonance of a largely Christian society enmeshed in sectarian violence, managing over decades to accommodate itself to enmity and retaliation and to resist any social idea of forgiveness as 'a complete breach with guilt and a new beginning'. In a context where sectarian violence claimed at least 3,700 lives, left 40,000 others gravely injured, and marked thousands more with hidden scars of trauma, Longley finds analogues in Homer's epic of the Greek-Trojan wars.[2] In his poem 'Ceasefire' he dramatises the conflict between the unhinged reflex for revenge and the possibility of being forgiven in analogously impossible circumstances. It is noteworthy how many writers have felt drawn to delve into the imaginative Homeric landscape and indeed into this particular ethico-tragic episode. It perhaps intimates the unceasing human preoccupation with the ambiguities of human choice and destiny that pervade the world of warfare – the claims and counter-claims inherent in notions of honour, legitimate cause, guilt, revenge and reconciliation.[3] Longley's poem opens with the face-to-face encounter of war-enemies, Achilles, the greatest warrior of Greece and Priam, King of Troy, whose son, Hector, has been slain in a clash with Achilles and left to rot dishonoured. Priam approaches Achilles to ask for the body so as to perform the mourning rituals. It is a dangerous encounter. Yet, strangely, both become transported beyond vengeance as each of them discovers their desperate need co-implicated in the other's. Enmity is deflected by empathy when Achilles recognises in Priam's grief-wracked face, a mirror image of his own Father, and Priam responds. Long parley ensues, each opening his tortured heart to the other, 'till their sadness filled the building'. Then they share a meal. It is as if Longley deliberately renders his account of the (classical) story into the local (Christian) context. The meal shared in the shadow of loss and death, signifies even before the Priam pronounces it in word that vengeance must finally yield to forgiveness and reconciliation:

> I get down on my knees and do what must be done
> And kiss Achilles' hand, the killer of my son.[4]

Intertextuality is at work here, evoking a moral challenge at once ancient and new. In Longley's poem, Homer's words are charged with the verbal echoes of Christ's choice of forgiving over vengeance even in the throes of a most brutal death. Classical and Christian worlds intersect and are interposed into the contemporary Irish world of revenge killings. For this vicious world has also been the site of self-surpassing self-transcending forbearance and forgivingness amid seas of bitterness.

Christians should not fail to expect a disclosure of the Holy Spirit present and active in such manifestly human acts of self-surpassing forgiveness. Edward Schillebeeckx rightly asserts that Christian visions of forgiveness fail the test of incarnational faith as long as they remain disembodied from the reality of human desolation and human love. Rather, they are to be embodied in such sacramental rituals as washing with water, bodily anointing and celebrations of the eucharistic meal.[5] He insists there is nothing abstract or disembodied about grace at work in human experiences of suffering and empathy. Such grace, its origins in divine mercy, has the power to break the wheel of revenge through gestures of solidarity.

Today it is possible to witness on the global stage of international relations and international justice dramas and rituals of apology and forgiveness. Days of pardon and reconciliation between once violent enemies have been enacted, adding texture, breadth and interconnectedness to the personal, political and religious understandings of forgiveness. From the time Christian theology was making a 'turn' to the social in the 1960s, so too, world figures in Church and State often in unaccustomed ritual gesture have brought forgiveness into public prominence.[6] One might name Konrad

Adenauer, Anwar Sadat, Nelson Mandela, Blessed John Paul II and Ang San Suu Kyi. The emergence of post-conflict truth and reconciliation commissions from South Africa to Latin America, has brought legal system and ethical standard to such discourses, paving the way for enemies to engage with the past in ways that eschew vengeance in favour of an approach that is interrelational, educative and open to a future where past wrongs are acknowledged and a reconciling of memories tentatively begun.[7]

So too, the insights of the human and social sciences have challenged and assisted theologians to rethink and broaden the understanding of reconciliation, and to re-examine the theological categories of forgiveness, reconciliation and restorative justice. Much can be learned from the disciplinary fields of psychology, memory studies, trauma studies, peace studies and war studies, for example. Recent experiences, nationally and internationally teach that politics alone cannot deliver peace, and reconciliation is not born of a signed treaty. It comes also in opening to an inclusive just way of living together; with concern for the most vulnerable; it is linked to the assurance of human rights and social justice; it needs to be actualised in reconciled relationships. In this public sphere are there not traces and hints of the biblical vision of *Shalom* – of God's all-embracing peace and justice for the earth and its peoples? Christians do well to recollect that theology commands no monopoly on the language of forgiveness and reconciliation.

This notwithstanding, ideas and practices of forgiveness are saturated with religious experience and shaped by Christian theology, and secular philosophy has been scant in its engagement with forgiveness.[8] Most often, moral philosophy and social sciences are less than open to the deep structure and power of religious traditions, zoning in on religious violence and the history of effects of theological legitimisation of the refusal of reconciliation, failing at the same time to apply due hermeneutical method to such religious sources and histories.[9] We need to take account of the growing body of thematised discourse and construct appropriate methods of mutually critical correlation, taking care to dialogue also with insights from other world faiths and diverse cultures. There is need for much more in depth and critical conversation at the crossroads of faith and culture.

Interestingly, Hannah Arendt, writing as a Jewish philosopher, claimed that the 'discoverer of the role of forgiveness in the realm of human affairs was Jesus of Nazareth',[10] seeing no disjunction between the theological and secular horizons. In both spheres, there are times when only mutual release and dismissal of wrongs committed unknowingly can free people to begin afresh. That Jesus 'made this discovery in a religious context and articulated it in religious language,' she claimed, '[w]as no reason to take any less account of it in the secular context of socio-political transformation.'[11] Clearly then, the theology of forgiveness can be enriched through dialectical engagement with other discourses, taking constructive account of human experience, the insights of created wisdom and contextual praxis.

A BROADENING METHODOLOGY AND CHANGING CONTEXT

For Christian theology, the reality of God's gracious mystery must be affirmed, though without disengaging from interdisciplinary elucidation nor from the particularities of context and experience. Schillebeeckx, echoing Aquinas, speaks of grace making humans more human and more than human.[12] He insists that Churches and theologians must engage with the socio-political and ecumenical context in their iterations of dialogues, reconciliation and forgiveness, while never forgetting that it is God's grace which is always the originating source and ultimate fulfilment of human visions of peace. Theology is called to constant reappraisal and renewal of its own sources. Certainly in post-conflict civil society in Northern Ireland, secular colleagues do still look to Christian ministers and theologians to draw from their own wells and share the refreshment with them – even if sometimes there is a need for a liming out of the wells, to ensure that the Churches' multi-faceted theological understandings and pastoral approaches to reconciliation are both deep and accessible to culturally divided, politically complex societies both as context and object. Such contributions also need to be appropriately modest, sensitive and capable of shaping a needed vision of spiritual and moral reconciliation in its interaction with secular culture.[13]

Schillebeeckx's insistence remained apposite in the second half of the twentieth century. From that time, many theologians and official Church documents were marked by a more critical and inclusive methodology firmly grounded in biblical tradition, attentive to personalist accounts of the moral life (philosophically and anthropologically) and to a radical consciousness of the social – in explicating social responsibility, in a language that harked to the structural dimensions of sin, and to the need for faith that connected with the deep structure of grace.[14] As hermeneutical advances associated with historical and critical method made their way into the mainstream of biblical theology, theologians like Schillebeeckx, Metz, Sölle and Moltmann typically spoke of the Christian call in terms of an intentional praxis of the kingdom of God. Christians were thus called to a living out of grace through socio-political virtue and action as a corrective to the preceding emphasis on individual salvation and on the privatisation of sin and the spiritual life.

The gradually diminishing popularity of individual auricular confession and of the ominous rhetoric against sins of the flesh emanating from preachers of parish missions may be an outward signal of a cultural rejection in Ireland of Jansenist severity, and of its austere antecedents in the old penitentialism.[15] The Planter Churches repudiated excessive moral striving and pious display as the rotten fruit of 'works', but evangelistic 'home missions', and 'tent missions' also re-inscribed a Puritanical fear of God, evoking born-again conversion in wrathful warnings against backsliding sin. A Pelagian ethic and individualistic piety remained a keynote in Irish Catholicism and Protestantism alike.[16]

There can be no gaping ditch between the spiritual and the secular, or between creation and redemption in Christian reflection on forgiveness. Theology can provide a fine-tuned syntax and proven language whereby to contribute wisdom to the public discourse of reconciliation. As well as providing believers with a potentially integrating rationale and inspirational narratives, theological reflection must be able to communicate its message in context and to those who live by other narratives and beliefs about what it is to be human and social in relation to the healing of histories.

THEOLOGICAL MEANINGS OF FORGIVENESS AND RECONCILIATION

A reliable dictionary exposition of forgiveness uncovers its deeper religious structure. With semantic roots in the old English *for-giefan*, the prefix *for* suggests an intensiveness in giving, as in overlooking an offence or debt, the showing of mercy that relinquishes one's own rights.[17] This relational dynamic in overcoming inflicted harm is grounded in the sense of a gratuitous gift. Existentially the implication is of a giving away of oneself in a superlative reach that opens the possibility of reorientation and new start. There are encouraging signs here for a dynamic relational theological anthropology of forgiveness.

This more explicitly theological part of this paper continues in two steps: it will explore the mutually enriching understandings of Christian forgiveness in dialogue with its own tradition, with context, and with other discourses. It stresses the pre-eminence of God's grace and the utter newness of Christ's salvation, remembering that creeds are not closed cognitive systems,[18] but narratives and patterns of deep and whole ways of life, open to the face of God and to the face of 'the other', bearing social witness, *ad extra* to the way of Jesus Christ and his offer of salvation for all. This assumes acute significance when the context is fractured by politico-religious fault-lines. Northern Ireland is such a place where the dominant divergent theologies cut across secular and Church domains. In a further step, the essay will correlate different Christian understandings of forgiveness with actual experiences and histories in an island emerging from four decades of violence.[19]

Here arises the critical challenge as to how a divided Christian community might realise reconciliation in identification with Jesus Christ who, in the Johannine tradition, speaks of himself as the way the truth and the life. It is intrinsic to the Church's trinitarian mission to encourage divided communities to live into the truth, attending to the wounds of 'the other', and in their mutual relationships to build trust in a future structured by respect and regard for the other rather than by sectarian isolation. From such a vision, Churches will discover together or not at all a lived *koinonia* ethic that is self-limiting and self-giving in a reconciliation of God's people that is sealed by the Holy Spirit, in promise of its eschatological fullness: 'In him you also ... were marked with the seal of the promised Holy Spirit; this is the pledge of our inheritance toward redemption as God's own people, to the praise of his glory (Eph 1:13-15) – tellingly, the Greek 'marked with the seal' – *hesphragistheté* – bears similarity to the word for a betrothal ring, again conveying a sense of interrelationship of trust and hope beyond our own capabilities.

FORGIVENESS AND RECONCILIATION – A WAY OF PARADOX

'Forgiveness' is a recurring biblical term of polyvalent meaning in regard to the forgiving of sin. Three words stand out: *kaphar* – to cover up or cover over, to atone; to purge, to forgive (for example, Ps 78:38). So too, *naga* with its various suggestions of forgiveness as bearing, lifting or taking away a burden (for example, Hos 14:2); and *salach* which represents divine pardon – never forgiveness between people – the idea of forgiveness as sparing and restoring, if not atoning (Ex 34:9; 1 Kgs 8:30).[20]

So too, forgiveness is central in Jesus' ministry most often in association with liberation or deliverance from some form of bondage, illness, guilt or punishment (for example, Mt 9:10-13; Lk 2:1-12; Lk 4:1820). In his life and teaching, forgiveness is often contextualised in terms of a reconciled and reconciling relationship between those lost, estranged or at enmity (Mt 18:10-22; Lk 7:36-50). In his parable of the unforgiving servant, Jesus issues a harsh warning about those who refuse to forgive debts, when they have been shown such divine patience and generosity themselves (Mt 18:23-35). Repeatedly in the New Testament, this relational experience of forgiving and being forgiven constitutes the core of the Church's resurrection faith in the person of Jesus Christ and at the heart of the continuing mission and ministry of the Church through the power of the Holy Spirit.

Reconciliation in soteriological perspective is a model favoured by Paul who speaks of reconciliation (*katallasso, katallagé*) in its various forms, thirteen times – for example, Rm 5 and 2 Cor 5, denoting the reconciliation coming from God in Christ and among the followers and ambassadors of Christ. Paul, too, is a classic exponent of the interplay and sometimes interchangeable meaning of forgiveness and reconciliation, his teaching forged from his personal experience of the in-breaking grace of forgiveness, at the very time when he was persecuting the early Christian communities and in the light of his vision of the Risen Christ (Acts 9). In the narrative of the conversion of Saul, the double pattern stands out: the first moment describes how, in one blinding flash, without any expressed commitment to change, he experiences Christ's forgiveness. The second movement of repentance *followed* that experience (Acts 9:3-30). The first singular dramatic event is one moment within a larger sequence involving Ananias and the wider community of reconciliation. Reconciliation, in this perspective, is the graced matrix of forgiveness. Paul's blinding conversion finds its personal core in his experience of Christ's unconditional forgiveness that is also a call that opened his life to a dynamic *koinonia* in its universal, cosmic fullness.

Gabriel Daly, writing of forgiveness and reconciliation in the context of reconciling memories in Ireland, elucidates these soteriological connections between forgiveness and reconciliation. He construes reconciliation as the broader, generative term while forgiveness is 'the personally significant core' of reconciliation.[21] They are thus co-implicated and interdependent. Whether seen in the Irish or in other contexts of ecclesial division, such an interrelationship between forgiveness and reconciliation point to a *koinonia* faith and ethic that is irreducibly personal, ecumenical and eschatological.[22]

In Christian faith and theology, forgiveness and reconciliation are paradoxically related. Often at the knot of the tension one finds a further complex aspect. This is perhaps best seen in the troubling connection between repentance and forgiveness. Here too, one must wrestle with claims and counter-claims of forgiveness being tied to prior repentance. In the field of post-conflict justice and in the face of the lived anguish of victims and survivors, one confronts inexorable questions of alleged cause and effect, guilt and innocence, and the sheer difficulty of forgiveness. This was never more severely contested than in 2000 when, through the early release terms of the 1998 Good Friday Agreement, eighty-nine convicted prisoners were released on licence without requirement of contrition or acknowledgement of wrong, in the interests of breaking the Gordian knot of past wrong-doing on every side.

Theologically, one must tread carefully, not least in the face of so many broken lives, resisting simplistic reductions of forgiveness to repentance which could cancel the utter gratuity of divine grace. Equally, grace must not be cheapened through the opposite tendency of positing available forgiveness as a quick fix that wipes the slate clean and sends the offenders on their way, untouched by the claim of God or neighbour and detached from responsibility for the healing of relationships.

Paul Ricoeur, writing from a French Reformed perspective, cogently questions the persistence in theological discourse of confusing cause and effect *vis à vis* forgiveness and repentance. In the necessarily paradoxical relationship between forgiveness and reconciliation, repentance is the human response and therefore it is contingent and precarious. Forgiveness is not tied to one instant. Rather, 'it is the meaning of a whole life with its ups and downs, its crises but also its quiet display'.[23] Thus, it is a conversion to relationship and to life within the horizon of *koinonia*.

From a Catholic perspective, Schillebeeckx likewise calls attention frequently to the synoptic theme of conversion (*metanoia*) at the core of Jesus' preaching and *praxis* of the kingdom of God. In this context, such *metanoia* was not constrained by conditionality but came with the gift of forgiveness, inviting those to whom it was offered to decide for a different future of grace, healing and newness that characterised life in the kingdom of God here on earth.[24]

For these contemporaneous theologians, repentance in the context of forgiveness implies a *turning away from sin*, but also a *turning towards* relationship – with God and with others (reflecting the Jewish pattern of *Teshuvah* and the liturgy associated with *Rosh Hashanah*, the Day of Atonement). Schillebeeckx speaking of deliverance and the implied relationship between forgiveness and *metanoia* asserts: 'Deliverance, redemption, consists in so being reconciled to one's past that confidence in the future is again made possible.'[25] Although the latter is not possible without the former, forgiveness does not require repentance in advance, it does invite a new orientation to life with others as an empowering gift, amid the contingencies of history, and entering into the realities of human frailty and flourishing, a call beyond isolation. Also denoted is the actual possibility of full, conscious, and active participation in the transcendent nature of forgiveness.[26]

In Jesus' own teaching, God's forgiveness of us is correlated with our forgiving others (Mt 6:12). In the Christic pattern of reconciliation, Christ's disciples are to show mercy as God shows mercy (Lk 6:36-37). Forgiveness opens the door to a fullness of life, the healing of relationship and the inclusion within one community of sinner and sinned against, as symbolised in the eschatological gathering at the meal of God's reign (Mt 22:10). Here is a new community in which just and unjust distinctions are overcome and apparently irreconcilable moral opposites are reconciled within the abundance of divine hospitality.

THEOLOGY EAST AND WEST – 'BREATHING WITH BOTH LUNGS'

Problems of formalism and issues associated with predestination can arise if theological forgiveness and reconciliation are disjoined from this Christ-centred interrelational context and eschatological horizon. Here we confront the dominance of legal modes of soteriology associated with some Augustinian writings.[27] When locked in metaphors of the lawcourt – stringent penalties for sin and depersonalised exacting of restitution – divine justice is cast in a mode worlds apart from the tender, forgiving God we glimpse in the same author's *Commentaries on the Psalms*, for example, or in *The Confessions*.[28] It was, however, Augustine's penal, forensic account that came to represent what has been called, 'the majority report' on sin and forgiveness in the West.[29] The 'minority report' on the other hand reflected the trajectory associated with Irenaeus and the Eastern Fathers, whose intrinsically relational model of salvation, is expressed in metaphors of God's compassion and forbearance for sinning creatures, and the divine plan to circumvent sin and evil by gentle understanding and recapitulation of humanity into Christ through the incarnation.[30] Metaphors here are not about being in the dock nor primarily ethical in orientation. They are couched in a medicinal mode of reference in compassionate terms of cleansing from sin and healing from sickness and God's response to the human yearning for wholeness. Thus portrayed, salvation is implicit in the incarnation as part of the divine plan whereby Christ became the second Adam. In thus taking on human nature in every phase and way, Christ gathers humanity and all creation into the divine.[31]

It would be untrue to suggest a simple bifurcation of Eastern and Western traditions. Nevertheless, Christianity in the West did veer towards a trend of systematisation of law and centralisation of ecclesiastical governance, notwithstanding the periodic and betimes prophetic counter-cultural challenges to the Church's Constantinian and Carolingian investiture with pomp and power, as from monastic or later reform movements. In the twentieth century, some theologians in the West sought to recover more dynamic, interrelational constructions of nature, sin and forgiveness, deliberately invoking the

Eastern Orthodox tradition, Yves Congar among them, asserting that the Church needed to 'breathe with both lungs'.

Thus, a truly ecumenical renewal will hark towards this 'both-and', seeking to overcome disunity and grow in relationship, eschewing fragmentation and assimilation.[32] The renewal of the Church was the vision of Vatican II with its teaching that theology draw from the wells of biblical, patristic and liturgical studies. With the emergence of liberation, feminist and other contextual theologies contemporary faith found a language which reconnected faith and revelation with the realities of history and the world of suffering. In contexts of social injustice, salvation was portrayed as liberation, healing and the fulfilment of hope.[33] Jesus' call to unity is a personal call to conversion of heart[34] and for the Churches a call to ecumenical dialogue. John Paul II speaks of this in radical terms as a 'dialogue of conversion'.[35] This poses questions as to how far Christian theology and sacramental celebration of reconciliation and forgiveness represent release from sin and death *and* the birth of relationships of new creation within and across Christian communities. If Christian reconciliation is to be transparent of the good news of the gospel in ecumenical and cross-cultural contexts, it needs a linguistic and symbolic register not centred axiomatically on mortality and sin disjoined from the life of nature and grace, rooted in natality and humility.

Repeatedly, in the gospel accounts, in Jesus's parables, table-fellowship, and miracles of healing are revealed the inextricable link between the kingdom as already 'in your midst', and its first fruits as sign of human transformation, anticipating a promise to be fulfilled in glory. Theological explanations of salvation must never disengage from actual signs of God's forgiving mercy as it is longed for, lamented or celebrated in the embodied lives of people in time of affliction and of liberation.[36]

FORGIVENESS AND RECONCILIATION IN NORTHERN IRELAND

When relationship is ruptured, the possibility of being forgiven offers hope of a way back through the healing of the injury and the possibility of a new start. In this transitional context in Ireland – and here the focus will be mainly the North of Ireland – Christian symbols of reconciliation and forgiveness need to find connection and significance within the life world of people's experience, whether of the lack of or longing for reconciliation. Such symbols will sustain hope and enliven love as they, in sign and actuality, break down the enmity and open a path to relationships sealed by Christ and the Holy Spirit. A properly soteriological account of forgiveness can fruitfully affirm its Chalcedonian horizon without pitching camp there in ahistorical abstraction. Christian forgiveness and reconciliation needs to embody what Schillebeeckx terms 'a searching Christology', one that lifts us out of where we are hopelessly wedged and manifests good news for those who cry out now in pain and hope.[37] Where there is no imagination, there is no empathy. In human terms, where there is no empathy, forgiveness falters. Without forgiveness where can hope be found?

Yet, often in divided societies and Churches, stubborn attachment to history and to our own grievance or sense of righteousness paralyses imagination and empathy, and thus the cycle of blame and self-exoneration is fruitlessly repeated, and within that macro-history, communities in the present re-stage the patterns of prejudice that cripple hope. Churches too are burdened by history with its legacy of catastrophe and loss. Christologically, the incarnation of Jesus becomes key and the memory of his passion and violent death crosses the histories and horizons of present-day violence, sin and suffering, thus transforming them with hope. In widening the space of our habitual tent (Is 54:2), we find Christ taking flesh among us in diverse places and communities where new signs of God's kingdom of love are made manifest, in the ongoing search for healing, and in experiences of boundary-crossing through which Christ's gift of forgiveness is being poured out in lives filled with the Spirit of hope and new birth.

REMEMBRANCE AS MOURNING AND HOPE FOR FORGIVENESS

In the North of Ireland, the search for reconciliation dramatises the struggle with that stubborn historicity at every level, but also, the movement of grace in the Church's tentative dialogue across old divisions and in *orthopraxis* – actual involvement with groups from zones of political violence, in cooperative projects of conflict resolution, the mending of memory and trust in the 'promise' of newness – construed as co-remembering and 'com-promise'.

The journey out of violence towards peace in Ireland has been painful, slow. Competing claims of the primacy of justice over reconciliation and on whether forgiving demands forgetting,[38] that double bind that bedevils so many societies in transition out of mass violence: 'Too much memory or not enough; too much enshrinement of victimhood or insufficient memorialising of victims and survivors; too much past or too little acknowledgement of the past's staging of the present.'[39]

Forgiveness is complicated and difficult. Where memory is as an unpayable debt to the past or 'duty' to the ancestors it becomes a wheel of no release. One can surely agree with Ricoeur's avowal that within memory 'lies the most secret resistance to forgiveness', when we are bound by 'a duty to remember' rather than embarking on 'the work of memory' as a journey of working through loss by mourning until we find the capacity to accept our situation.[40] The sharing of some stories from the crucible of the Irish conflict may be salutary here, whose protagonist have in different ways struggled to work through their loss by mourning. Thereafter these will be brought into conversation with analogous theological reflections on forgiveness as grace.

Some of us have been blessed to encounter folk who, in their bereavement thorough sectarian violence, have stood out and said, 'Enough. No more killing. No revenge in my name.' Many have indeed managed in a context where life was cheap and acts of retaliation evinced a rhetoric of self-justifying vengeance, to turn themselves inside out and become signs of a radical dependence of God and of a different way of living together. Some even found words of forgiveness – not by denying their affliction, but out of its very depths. Michael McGoldrick was one such, whose son Michael was murdered in a random Loyalist attack, days after his graduation. Speaking at his son's burial he said, 'How can I *not* forgive the people that killed my son? If I did not, I could no longer pray the "Our Father", and then, I might as well go down there into that grave with my son.' He dedicated the next ten years of his life organising missions of solidarity to Romania and caring for orphans there over several visits a year. It was on such a mission of mercy in *remembrance* of his son that he died in 2010. Michael was a sign and witness of Christ's kingdom in our midst.

There are, of course, others similarly bereaved for whom mourning involves a long night's journey into the day of being able to let go of loss and open to *the possibility* of forgiving. There are some who cannot find their way to the daylight – the ones who find that forgiveness poses insurmountable psychological, ethical and religious difficulties. Still others maintain that forgiveness is God's business – 'Who can forgive sins but God alone?' (Mk 2:7b; Mt 9:6-8 and Lk 5:20-26). Forgiveness cannot be prescribed, however psychologically and spiritually freeing it might be for all concerned. Christ's teaching and example must be used caringly and certainly should not be used prematurely to force the issue. Who knows, but even behind a person's unreadiness or unwillingness, some trace of transcendence may yet flicker, as if in hint of the self-transcending divine grace that inheres in the act of forgiving – for that is not so much duty as always gift. True forgiveness is not cheap and its cost is counted in human suffering, as it is in the suffering of Jesus.[41]

Another man I came to know lost several family members in separate assassinations by a militants fighting for a United Ireland. On a TV panel with him I was moved by his response to the interviewer's question, 'Are such sins too heinous to forgive?' Such questions cannot be answered in the abstract. He spoke deliberatively of his struggle with loss and grief over many years often in the company of the suffering Christ. One could say that for him 'work of memory' had lasted more than twenty years and was still incomplete. He shared that now he could forgive in part the people who had murdered his father and uncle, robbed him of his youth and destroyed his family: 'I can possibly forgive them for what they did to me, but it is not for me to forgive them what they did to my mother and family.' Yet, this young man remained open to the possibility of a fuller forgiveness at some time.

The existential experience of loss was disempowering. There are many in the victims-survivors community who also speak of this impotence of not knowing; of not being able to challenge the perpetrators, ask them why or hear their answer; of being denied a just trial. No face and so no potential for a conversation that might lead to reconciliation. So many fractured lives are denied access to a whole meaning, to an apprehension of the totality of the political context, or deliverance from a faceless sinister system of identity-in-enmity. The source of forgiveness and reconciliation must be sought elsewhere. And this was the discovery of my friend, whose story as it unfolded told of his own sense of being called into a new ministry of reconciliation with others. It told of knowing himself to be forgiven, and in ways not clear to him, of his desire to participate in God's forgiveness, now through his priestly pastoral ministry among traumatised communities, accompanying them in their own mourning, helping them to find Christ's peace, justice and reconciliation. Over an evening meal we spent some hours talking and walking together through experiences and memories of our divided painful history and of the part faith played in working through the bitterness of loss. It was an Emmaus moment where we felt drawn into the mystery of eucharistic hope in communion with Christ, the table-companion of those who have lost their way. In this shared memory of rupture and long mourning, I glimpsed into the paradox that although my companion could not find a concrete access to forgiving those men without face or and name, he seemed to me as one who knew himself to be participating in the mystery of Christ's reconciling grace, in its self-limiting, self-giving power.

THE *MEMORIA PASSIONIS* RENEWED IN EUCHARISTIC HOPE

Theologians need to be wary of any facile spiritualising of such human suffering in the face of those who are close to violent deaths. Douglas J. Davies, Anglican priest and anthropologist, proposes that these 'offending deaths' do often fuel the cycle of retaliation. He also highlights the paradox that the blatant offence against social and moral values that pervade the public mourning of such deaths, may, however, evoke the sacrificial aspect, exposing the failures of those with political responsibility, and awakening public resistance and protest for fundamental change.[42]

I have contended elsewhere that it was acts of mourning-as-civic-protest which helped finally turn the tide of violence and the demand for a peaceful future for our children: one thinks of the massive mourning of such 'offending deaths' following the Shankill bomb in 1993, or that in Omagh in 1998 which killed twenty-nine women, men, children and unborn twins; or following the arson attack that killed the three Quinn children asleep in bed, during the

Orange Order stand-off at Drumcree in 2001; or again in Omagh in 2011 at the funeral of Constable Ronan Kerr, where shared rituals of mourning this 'offending death' manifested a tangible solidarity among leaders of our divided Churches and political parties, and among citizens from opposing cultures, standing alongside one another in town squares, churches and at gravesides. I would suggest that it was when divided communities recovered the human capacity to share the other community's unfathomable sorrow that they could finally stand in the breach together and demand an end to any more wounds. It was in such sites of grace that sundered histories began to be healed, with the possibility of forgiveness, repentance and reconciliation held in trust.

At a theological level, the way God makes forgiveness real is both revealed to us and concealed from us, but it surely draws our experience and history into the transcendent realm of grace, in a way that human nature alone cannot account for, involving the work of healing that only God can do. It is salutary in this regard, to cross over from the theological framework of forgiveness within our own denomination, and see it through the eyes of 'the other'. We may find ourselves surprised in the discovery of insights familiar or hitherto concealed.

Reformed theologian, H. R. Mackintosh, exploring those attributes in God revealed to the forgiven person, identifies three. The sacramental and sacrificial dimensions of eucharistic love and forgiveness are in clear profile when he notes the experience of God 'disclosed as personal, and as the doer of a miracle ... [and] *the insight also reached by way of pardon that his very nature is sacrificial love*'.[43] In crossing the breach, Jesus so utterly identifies with human misery that he is 'numbered among the transgressors'. Yet, as Churches and communities confront one another across historical religious divides, is it not the beginning of repentance to acknowledge ourselves also as 'numbered among the transgressors' rather than accounting ourselves among righteous? Acknowledgement can be the beginning of repentance and invites deeper communion in the other's suffering in Christ who gave over his life for the forgiveness of sin.[44]

Mackintosh points to those experiences of unfathomable human suffering ('voyages of anguish'), which are analogous with the forgiveness Christ imparts, 'flowing from unmeasured expenditures of grief and will', not as some 'changeless absolute, but one who shares our grief and shame'.[45] Most significantly, he calls for a supreme act of imaginative remembrance of an experience of a deep treachery at the hands of another, to drive home the idea that human forgiveness is never painless or cheap but a call into encounter with 'sacrificial agony' with a need for *cleansing* from the 'repulsive evil'.[46] Here, the grammar of Irenaean soteriology is unmistakable.

It is remarkable that Schillebeeckx, writing from a more fundamentally Catholic eucharistic perspective on the forgiveness of sins and appealing to the notion of *anamnesis*, accents these very same realities of experiential, personal and sacrificial love.[47] Thus, according to the Dominican, Christ's presence in the Eucharist is not isolated from the rest of life, but is

> as *one who gave himself in death 'for our sins'* and was brought to life for us by God. Our personal relationship with the Lord is also as essentially an *anamnesis*, a calling to mind of the historical event of salvation on the cross ... insofar as it endures eternally in its completion. The eternity is, however, not situated behind history, but accomplished in history ... bestowing a lasting validity on this history, namely in its completion.[48]

In insisting upon the utter gratuitousness of this gift of salvation, as 'not our handiwork' and 'always beyond our grasp'.[49] Schillebeeckx is equally clear that it needs to be given substance and concrete form in the Church's life through 'human religious symbolic activity' that meets the actuality of people's struggle and hope for healing and reconciliation, through such actions as the anointing with oil, or the washing with water or the laying on of hands:[50]

> Thus, in the Eucharist, the food, the meal and the community of believers at table, all essentially belong to each other – they are the human matter, which becomes the sacrament.[51]

THE CHURCHES' ROLE IN FORGIVENESS AND RECONCILIATION

To many in Ireland, whether in the light of persisting inter-church division or following the scandalous involvement in and cover-up by the Catholic Church in abuse of children, the raising of the Church's profile in forgiveness and reconciliation may seem ironic and dubious. And yet the Church is the custodian of the *memoria passionis Christi* – the memory of divine forgiveness that is renewed in the Eucharist – Christ's giving up his life so that we might be reconciled to God. Its mission is to be a sacramental embodiment of Christ's invitation to saving grace, though it belongs to the Holy Spirit to effect this transforming work and to awaken faith in the community of the faithful.

Yet, how far can the Churches bear witness to forgiveness and contribute to social reconciliation, without more fully addressing the challenges of ecumenical relationship and the visible effects of broken communion in their ecclesial life? For howsoever they fail to confront this reality honestly, their witness will lack inner substance and outer credibility. Christian communities are called by Jesus to cross over to the other side, and to be reconciled with one another, ready to bear one another's burdens, learning to pardon and forgive in symbolic gestures of atonement. Like Lazarus (Jn 11:44), none can unbind themselves, but in self-surrender can allow themselves to be unbound by the other.

Churches have long experience in tending the weak and in the 'the cure of souls' through the transforming power of symbolic and sacramental rituals of darkness and light, sin and forgiveness, reconciliation and atonement, death and resurrection. Even where Churches have witnessed weakly to the prophetic, priestly, pastoral Christ, in word and action,[52] the Holy Spirit has continued to raise up in their midst friends of God and prophets who lived the gospel of forgiveness, showing comfort to the afflicted and bearing witness to Christ the reconciler – wise mediators who stayed the hand of retaliation wherever they could, courageous peacemakers who stood in the breach or who risked building bridges across it through prayer or preaching, the countless, quiet bearers of hope when in times of despair.[53] While we await and work for the day of full Eucharistic sharing rooted in 'one Lord, one faith, one baptism' (Eph 4:5) that communion draws us even now to live the fullness of Christ's mystery of forgiveness in a new life of grace and hope shared and made manifest. Christ's new creation, as Schillebeeckx reminds us, will always be 'beyond our grasp'.

With Bonhoeffer we recall that radical discipleship demands 'a complete breach with guilt and a new beginning which is granted through the forgiveness of sin', and that in the slower processes nations and history, what matters is that even when what is past cannot be restored or healed, 'what matters is that there shall be no more wounds ... [and that this] forgiveness within history can come only when the wound of guilt is healed, when violence has become justice ... and war has become peace'.[54] Forgiveness is both grace and responsibility, gift and call.

In fulfilling that responsibility for forgiveness within history, political and religious leaders become a catalyst for change when they act towards their counterparts no longer out of their sense of moral righteousness or power, but in humility towards one another. Such a stance is *more than* ethical. Ricoeur coins the term, 'hyper-ethical', echoing Jesus' extravagant call to go the extra mile, and to bless those who curse us and love our enemies (Lk 6:27-28); and Paul's call to the Corinthians to live Christ's reconciliation with it logic and economy not of 'strict equivalence' but of 'superabundant grace'.[55] This is all the more important for Christian leaders who would exercise the ministry of forgiveness and reconciliation in the person and pattern of Jesus who 'counted himself among the transgressors', and pleaded from a transgressor's cross, 'Father forgive them, for they know not what they do' (Lk 22:34). This will demand the letting go of selective memory and doctrinal self-sufficiency, cultural collusion and forms of social witness stubbornly maintained in isolation from one another. Living into Christ's forgiveness draws us to keep truth connected to lives of suffering, beauty and gracious justice, so that once more steadfast love and faithfulness will meet; righteousness and peace will kiss (Ps 85:10).

Sent out in vulnerability, Christ's professed followers are to be one with him in 'being counted among the transgressors'. Through the unifying love of the Holy Spirit, even though enmired in still unrepented divisions, they may still participate in the fullness of the divine *koinonia*, rising up with Christ in the grace of their baptismal and eucharistic calling. Living the ecumenical charism in reciprocal commitment to witnessing together to God's reign of forgiveness and reconciliation, Churches can make their own the prayer of Christ for the oneness of his Church – 'so that the world may believe that you have sent me' (Jn 17:21). Would this not be a graced sign in our world of power over others of Christ's power made perfect in weakness? Thus, united with the whole creation in its groaning (Rm 8:22), the whole Church, which already enjoys 'the first fruits of the Spirit' (Rm 8:23), can be transformed into the Christ who makes all one through the dynamic power in weakness that is the Holy Spirit. Such vulnerable eucharistic love is the hermeneutical key to understanding the divine spirit of forgiveness in its hidden and manifest disclosure between created wisdom and reconciling grace.

NOTES

1 Dietrich Bonhoeffer, *Ethics,* Eberhard Bethge, ed., Neville Horton Smith, trans., London: Fontana, Collins, 1970 (order of 6th German edition, 1963, pp. 118).

2 Cf. Frank Fagles, Homer, *The Iliad,* NY: Penguin Books, 1990. This epic poet of eighth-century BCE recounts the stories of these twelveth-century BCE wars in Bk 2.

3 Chaucer and Shakespeare are among the earliest English treatments. More recently, David Malouf's novel, *Ransom,* NY: Vintage Books, 2011; and Eliza Cook's Achilles, NY: Picador, 2001 testify to the perennial appeal of this classic text.

4 Michael Longley, *Collected Poems,* London: Jonathan Cape, 2006, p. 225.

5 Edward Schillebeeckx, *The Eucharist,* Stagbooks, London: Sheed and Ward, 1968: 'Thus, in the Eucharist, the food, the meal and the community of believers at table all essentially belong to each other – they are the human matter which becomes sacrament', pp. 134–5.

6 Gregory Jones, *Embodying Forgiveness: A Theological Analysis,* Grand Rapids: Eerdmans, 1995, pp. 73–118; Martha Minow, *Between Vengeance and Forgiveness: Facing History after Genocide and Mass Violence,* Boston: Beacon Press, 1998, offers an international law perspective; also the Roman Catholic Church International Theological Commission Report, *Memory and Reconciliation: the Church and the Faults of the Past,* in *Origins,* no. 48, 16 March, 2000, whose publication virtually coincided with a special Day of Pardon. Hereby, Church leaders, politicians and erstwhile combatants assumed the spirit of dialogue, reconciliation and forgiveness, par 5.1.

7 See, Robert I. Rotberg and Dennis Thompson, eds, *Truth v. Justice: The Morality of Truth Commissions*, Princeton, NJ: Princeton University Press, 2000; also, Russell Daye, *Political Forgiveness: Lessons from South Africa,* NY: Orbis Books, 2004.

8 H.R. Mackintosh, *Christian Experience of Forgiveness,* London: Nisbet & Co., Ltd, 1954 (1927), p. 187.

9 Hans-Georg Gadamer, *Truth and Method,* 2nd Revised Edition, NY: Crossroads, 1989, p. 360. The author rightly stresses the living interplay between a tradition and its interpreters through active reception.

10 Hannah Arendt, *The Human Condition: A Study of the Central Conditions Facing Modern Man,* Chicago: Chicago University Press, 1959 (1958), p. 240.

11 Hannah Arendt, *The Human Condition*, pp. 238–9.

12 Schillebeeckx's early theology of grace was worked out in the context of his dialogue with the writings of Karl Adam, whose strong affirmation of creation and culture, however, laid him open to the ideology of Nationalist

framed by the dualistic terms of Manichaeism and his argumentation against Pelagius: *Creation and Redemption,* Dublin: Gill and Macmillan, 1988, p. 13, pp. 117–19. Daly argues that a demythologisation of the excesses of metaphor and literalisation is hermeneutically necessary to a more balanced construal of Augustine's soteriology.

29 John Hick, *Evil and the God of Love,* London: Macmillan, 1985 (1966). Hick identifies the Irenaean tradition as the 'minority report' contrasting with the 'majority report' which won out in Western theology, pp. 253, also, pp. 205–18.

30 Cf., St Irenaeus, *Against the Heresies: The Writings of Irenaeus: Ante-Nicene,* Christian Library; Translations of the Writings of the Fathers Down to AD 325, Vol. V (vol. 1), Rev. Alexander F Roberts DD and James Donaldson LLD, eds, Alexander Roberts and WH Rambaut, trans., Edinburgh: T&T Clark, 1910, Book III.12.3–5.

31 St Irenaeus, *Against the Heresies,* Vol. V (vol. 2), *Irenaeus to Hippolytus,* Fragments *of the Third Century,* ed. Alexander Roberts and James Donaldson, Edinburgh: T and T Clark, MDCCCLXIX, Book IV.xxxviii.1–3; also, 'Against the Heresies', in *The Writings of Irenaeus,* Vol. V (vol. 1), Book IV. xiv, 2. See also Vladimir Lossky, *In the Image and Likeness of God,* John Erickson and Thomas Bird eds, NY: SVS Press, 1985, pp. 97–110, where Lossky contrasts the Western understanding of the ultimate human goal in terms of 'redemption' (with sin as point of departure) and 'the more positive definition of the same mystery' of the Eastern Church in terms of 'deification' as 'the ultimate vocation of created beings' (p. 110). Although Augustine strove – against Pelagius – to underline the gratuitousness of grace, against reducing faith to an ethic of striving, the penal influence dominated in Christian history. Combining with the subsequent Celtic penitential approach to sin, this resulted in an overemphasis on individualised repentance and on human expiation. See also, John Mahoney, *The Making of Moral Theology: A Study of the Roman Catholic Tradition,* Oxford: Clarendon Press, 1987, pp. 224–31.

32 See, Gabriel Daly O.S.A., *One Church: Two Indispensable Values: Protestant Principle and Catholic Substance,* Irish School of Ecumenics Occasional Papers 4, Dublin: Dominican Publications, 1998, pp. 11–13.

33 See, for example, Sallie McFague, *The Body of God: An Ecological Theology,* London: SCM Press, 1993, p. 133; also Susan Frank Parsons, ed., *The Cambridge Companion to Feminist Theology,* Cambridge: Cambridge University Press, 2002, esp., idem, ch. 12, 'Redeeming Ethics' on the realigning of care, justice and the common good (pp. 206–3); Peter Atkins, *Memory and Liturgy: the Place of Memory in the Composition and Practice of Liturgy*, Aldershot: Ashgate, 2004, for example, ch. 7, 'Memories of Sin and Pain' (pp. 83–97) and ch. 10, 'Memory, Imagination and Hope' (pp. 126–39).

34 The Documents of Vatican II: 'The Decree on Ecumenism': 'There can be no ecumenism worthy of the name without a change of heart' (no. 4).

35 *Ut Unum Sint:* Encyclical Letter of the Holy Father John Paul II on Commitment to Ecumenism, London: CTS, 1995, nos. 34, 35. The pope is explicit in his association of a necessary 'dialogue of consciences' with conversion and with Christ's forgiveness and expiation of our sins. Thus, 'Christian unity is possible, provided that we are humbly conscious of having sinned against unity and are convinced of our need for conversion. Not only personal sins must be forgiven and left behind, but also social sins, which is to say the sinful "structures" themselves which have contributed and still can contribute to division and to the reinforcing of division' (no. 34).

36 Schillebeeckx makes this point trenchantly in Part II of *Jesus*, with the author's exegesis of the 'praxis of the kingdom of God' in terms of bringing good news and making others glad. Particular focus is brought to the narration of gospel parables, and the table fellowship and healings, associated with sinners, pp. 124–5, 140ff. 153–4, 156ff., 185ff. The hermeneutical baseline is clear: that 'through this community alone did it prove possible for the experience of salvation in Jesus with God as its source to develop after his death from a soteriological recognition of Jesus into a Christological conversion to Jesus the Christ' (p. 219). It can be no different for his community of disciples today.

37 Schillebeeckx, *Jesus*, pp. 124–7, p. 169. Although this was an area on which he was criticised the absence of focus on sin and guilt, for example, or Walter Kasper's remonstrance that it led to a reductionism of salvation to mere human well-being and liberation, the Dominican theologian mounts a redoubtable defence: Cf., his 'Interim Report on the Books *Jesus* and *Christ'*, pp. 99–102. Directing 'doubters' to his second book *Christ*, and unequivocally avowing 'objective redemption', he asserts that, 'redemption which has been achieved in Jesus needs to be presented in such a way that our history in fact remains ongoing human history ... Christians believe in and through Jesus, that despite everything, the kingdom of God, as salvation for mankind, is still coming and will come; what has been achieved in Jesus Christ is the guarantee of this' (pp. 101–2).

38 On different ways of remembering, see, Geraldine Smyth, 'Sabbath and Jubilee', *The Jubilee Challenge: Utopia or Possibility,* Hans Ucko, ed., WCC, Geneva, 1997, pp. 59–76, particularly re the Jewish tradition of the Sabbath of Remembrance, Shabbat Zachor, p. 72; also Interchurch Group on Faith and Politics, *Remembrance and Forgetting: Building a Future in Northern Ireland,* The Faith and Politics Group, 8, Upper Crescent, Belfast, 1998 which examines the interplay of such issues as memory in a contested space, memory and power, selective memory, the Churches and memory, memory and biblical faith; also, Interchurch Group on Faith and Politics, *Forgive Us Our Trespasses: Reconciliation and Political Healing in Northern Ireland,* Belfast, 1996, p. 8 and passim.

39 Martha Minow, op. cit., p. 2.

40 Paul Ricoeur, 'The Difficulty to Forgive', op. cit, p. 15 (italics mine). He continues, stressing the need to let go of the claim to construct a story of our life without lacks or gaps, or of any expectation that we can repair all wounds (15). This has overtones of the Christian call to relinquish self-sufficiency in favour of actively opening one's life to salvation as gift.

41 Cf., Mackintosh, op. cit: In seeking to understand how God forgives and how we forgive, there are some questions which should not yield easy answers '... questions to which no reply is possible, and which it is difficult even to clothe in words without an appearance of folly. We possess no psychology of God.' Mackintosh reflects on the unbridgeable gap between knowing that we are pardoned and not knowing how our forgiveness is made real. This 'is hidden from us, and no enlargement of human faculty is conceivable for which the mystery would be resolved' (pp. 183–4).

42 Douglas J. Davies, 'Offending Death, Grief and Religions', *Sociology of Religion*, Richard K. Fenn, ed., Oxford: Blackwell Companion Series, 2001, 2003, pp. 404–17, p. 412.

43 Mackintosh, op. cit., pp. 184–91, p. 185 (italics mine). This pain-filled human intercourse becomes a window on God's agonising exchange with us. Thus, does Jesus enter into communion with human misery, crossing the unbreachable gulf, numbered among the transgressors. Thus, 'face to face with Jesus, we become aware ... that the love in virtue of which he does this amazing and redeeming thing is positively the love of God himself' (p. 189). This is the 'only conceivable medium of forgiveness', for in both instances, human-to-human and divine-to-human, the costing, saving grace confronts 'the tragedy for both sides – pain forming the necessary vehicle for forgiveness in an experience in which nature is rent asunder' (p. 189). It is from the depths of this self-abandoning 'divine-human passion' that God forgives the world, and 'to see into the unchanging heart of things, we must gaze upon the travail of the cross' (p. 190).

44 Some examination of the traditional structure of the sacrament of reconciliation is also apposite here, though limits of space prevent a fuller treatment – contrition; confession (acknowledgement) and penance (satisfaction) – the matter of the sacrament and the acts of the penitent, and absolution, the form of the sacrament and the action of the priest. See, James J. Walter, 'Reconciliation', *The New Dictionary of Theology*, Joseph J. Komonchak, Mary Collins, and Dermot A. Lane, eds, Dublin: Gill and Macmillan, 1987, pp. 830–6, p. 834; also, Joseph Martos, 'The Sacrament of Reconciliation', Michael Glazier and Monika K. Hellwig, eds, *The Modern Catholic Encyclopedia,* Dublin: Gill and Macmillan, 1994, pp. 771–5, p. 772.

45 Mackintosh, op. cit., p. 187.

46 Ibid., p. 188.

47 Edward Schillebeeckx, *The Eucharist,* Sheed and Ward, London, 1995 (1968), 99, 103, 126ff.

48 Ibid., p. 126.

49 Ibid., p. 128.

50 Ibid., p. 134.

51 Ibid., pp. 134–5.

52 Terence P. McCaughey, *Memory and Redemption: Church, Politics and Prophetic Theology in Ireland*, Dublin: Gill and Macmillan, 1993, pp . 67–71, pp. 97–102 and passim.

53 Cf. John D. Brewer, Gareth L. Higgins and Francis Teeney, *Religion, Civil Society, and Peace in Northern Ireland,* Oxford: OUP, 2011, 29ff. and passim, though the authors also bemoan the Churches' failures, and the relative lack of accessible 'spiritual capital' in Church-society and interchurch relationships (pp. 172ff. & 214ff.).

54 Dietrich Bonhoeffer, *Ethics*, Eberhard Bethge, ed., p. 118.

55 See, Paul Ricoeur, 'Love and Justice', *Figuring the Sacred: Religion, Narrative, and Imagination*, David Pellauer, trans., Mark I. Wallace, ed., Philadelphia: Fortress, pp. 324–5.

THE CHURCH'S MARIAN PROFILE AND THE RECEPTION OF VATICAN II'S ECCLESIOLOGY

REV. PROF. THOMAS NORRIS
International Theological Commission

INTRODUCTION

The emergence of Mary, 'the mother of Jesus', as St John prefers to call her (2:1; 19:25), in the early centuries of the Church is an intriguing phenomenon. Not mentioned by name in St Mark and only anonymously in the Pauline corpus (Gal 4:4), she is called *Theotokos* by the third century. Saint Athanasius (AD 296–373) mentions her and spells out the meaning of the august title.[1] However, there is no sign that he had a devotion to her such as was to be the case by the early second millennium. However, what is most striking in the early centuries, particularly in the fourth and fifth centuries when the Church was elaborating the contours of her own doctrinal landscape, and doing so generally in the teeth of pulverising heresy, is the fact that a doctrinal profile of Mary also emerged with clarity and in depth.

And there is more. It was the very heresies that attacked the identity of the Redeemer that were the occasion, if not the very cause, of the mother's emergence. It is worth our time to look, even if only briefly, at the history of dogma in the decisive fourth and fifth centuries. At the beginning of the fourth century, the Church had to face the shock of Arianism. The Church had come out of the catacombs, as it were, having endured the appalling persecution of Diocletian (AD 307–12). With the denial of the unequivocal divinity of the Son, trouble moved from outside the house of God to within the house of God. The first ecumenical Council of Nicaea (325) faced the burgeoning heresy with its famous Creed in which the 318 Fathers thundered out the truth of the Saviour's divinity in a creedal crescendo that has resonated down the centuries in the Church's worship.

The issue of Jesus' true humanity now arose. Apollinarius and his school put forward a grotesque position: Jesus had a body but no human soul, since the place of the soul was occupied by the divine Son and task of the soul was fulfilled by the same Son. The incarnation had not occurred since the Son had not taken up our integral humanity. The second ecumenical Council at Constantinople, fifty-six years after Nicaea, affirmed the full and authentic humanity of the Son.

It was inevitable that the Church would now have to address the manner of the relationship of divinity and humanity in the Redeemer. The first magister in the field was Patriarch Nestorius of Constantinople. Nestorius kept divinity and humanity somewhat apart. His Christology peeped out in his rejection of two frequently occurring faith-statements of the time. The first was that 'the Son of God was crucified', the second that 'Mary is mother of God'. Nestorius's opposition to both statements revealed his Christology according to which the union of divinity and humanity in Jesus is 'moral' and not metaphysical. The Son of God had not died for us, but the man Jesus had!

Now the response of the Third Ecumenical Council, held at Ephesus in AD 431, was striking. It affirmed vigorously the fact that the Son of the Father had joined himself 'according to the *hypostasis*' to his humanity, the Son of the Father in heaven becoming the Son of a woman on earth. The corollary had to follow that Mary is not *Christotokos* but *Theotokos*, the very begetter of God according to the flesh.

What is striking in this rapid overview is that all the attacks of heresy on Jesus Christ led to one outcome – the exaltation of the Mother.[2] When heretics said that her Son was not God, as Arius did, or that he was not truly Man, as Apollinarius did, or that he had not shed his blood for us on the cross, as Nestorius did, it was then that an ecumenical council proclaimed Mary as *Theotokos*, Mother of God. The title affirms that her Son is God, it implies his authentic humanity, and it insinuates the manner of their union. Thus all the heresies that dishonoured the Son tended inexorably towards the exaltation of the Mother. And just as Mary was once instrumental in protecting the Holy Child against the murderous designs of Herod, (Mt 2:13-15) so now she protected him again against the heretics who would dismember the mystery and crucify the Redeemer of humanity a second time! Little wonder, then, that we find in the Church's prayer the ancient antiphon, *Gaude, Maria Virgo, cunctas haereses sola interemisti in universe mundo* ('Rejoice, Virgin Mary, for alone you have destroyed all heresies in the world'). Thus Mary 'has grown into her place in the Church by a tranquil influence and a natural process'.[3] As her place in the Church in the first centuries was lowly, so now her influence is pervasive.

The emergence of Mary in the early centuries, and, in particular, the doctrinal clarification of her place in the mystery of Christ, is an instructive theological paradigm. Perhaps another council might have to deal, not with foundational Christological and Trinitarian questions, but with questions regarding our access to the mystery of God in the sacraments, as well as issues regarding the mystery of the Church. Perhaps there would be a *kairos* moment when a development of major importance for the Church's identity, as well as for her mission to the men and women of the third millennium, could come into view. The twenty-first ecumenical Council, Vatican II, is such a Council: it occurred in a scenario of vast scientific, cultural and technical change, change frequently bringing with it a serious disturbance of our access to the living God of Jesus Christ. Little surprise, then, that this Council should have turned its attention to the mystery of God, the mystery of the Church, and the drama of the Church in the modern world. Could it be that the challenges of our times could have called forth a fresh realisation of Mary's role in the mystery of Christ and his Church? It is the thesis of this paper that a 'Marian profile' of the Church is a key hermeneutic for the reading of the ecclesiology of Vatican II, and its 'reception'. 'At the dawn of the new millennium,' writes Blessed John Paul II, 'we notice with joy the emergence of the Marian profile of the Church that summarises the deepest contents of the conciliar renewal.'[4]

DEFINING OUR TERMS

A key principle of Christianity is that of the incarnation such that 'the flesh is the very hinge of salvation' (Tertullian). In Johannine language, 'The word became flesh and pitched his tent among us and we saw his glory' (Jn 1:14). 'Here the impossible union of spheres of existence is actual.'[5] From this key and foundational principle other principles unfold like the colours emanating from the prism. They include principles such as dogma, faith, theology, sacraments, mystical sense of scripture, grace, asceticism, the malignity of sin and matter's capability of sanctification.[6]

As a religion in which the eternal Son of God became flesh, one should be on the alert for that 'constellation of characters' which constitutes the warp and the woof of Jesus' concrete existence and ministry. Saint Augustine stresses the point in these words, 'God could give no greater gift to men than to make his Word, through whom he created all things, their head and to join them to him as his members, so that the Word might be both Son of God and son of man, one God with the Father, and one man with all men ... Let us then recognise both our voice in his, and his voice in ours.'[7] Among the characters constituting the constellation of agents around the incarnate Son one may name the following. There is Peter, always listed as the first of 'the Twelve', who is the most frequently encountered name in the whole of the New Testament. He seems to personify office and ministry as Jesus renames him (Jn 1:42) and gives him 'the keys of the kingdom of heaven' (Mt 16:19) as well as the task of strengthening his brothers in faith (Lk 22:31-32). Then there is John the Apostle who seems to embody the principle of love which leads to community and to the building up of the Church in faith and love (13:34–35,17). As for Paul, he personifies the novelty of grace, the energy of evangelisation and freedom in the spirit. James, the Bishop of Jerusalem and the writer of the *Letter*, personifies the principle of 'tradition' and so of continuity, order and stability.

On an occasion, Hans Urs von Balthasar, who is the principal protagonist of these principles or profiles,[8] portrayed their interaction as follows. To do so ' ... he drew a shape on the chalkboard distributing each of these in four different points in the shape of a cross – Peter to the right, John to the left, James above and Paul below.' But the most obvious person in the constellation of characters constituting 'the concreteness of incarnation' was not so far mentioned. Who is this? It is she who not only:

Gave God's infinity
dwindled to infancy
welcome ...
But mothers each new grace
That does now reach our race.[9]

She precedes the other personalities, not only in time but also in dignity and in depth. To highlight the fact of this pre-eminence, von Balthasar continued the lesson with master pedagogy: 'He then traced an ellipse around them by way of indicating Mary who embraces everyone.'[10] Not only is Mary the most pre-eminent profile or principle, she is also the one that connects all of the others in an unrivalled proportion that allows the works of God to shine out in all their beauty or *claritas*.[11]

An Irish theologian comments on this interrelationship in these terms. 'The ontology of the Church is such that there is a mutual indwelling (circumincession) in Mary of the Church's principles, dimensions and states of life. If any one of the four major principles should be separated or made absolute, the Marian profile of the Church would suffer.' Thus, to take two instances, 'Should the Petrine-institutional dimension loom large, the Church's visage becomes distorted in organisation and administration. If the Pauline characteristic of freedom in the Spirit is unilaterally highlighted, the result is rationalism and dogmaticism, a diplomatic updating following what is popular and fashionable.'[12]

THE MARIAN PROFILE OF THE CHURCH

This pre-eminence of the Marian profile may not be so obvious. It is certainly more interior than the others. It is also more subtly rich, just as a mother's place in a family is both imperceptible and influential. The best method to follow in search of its outline is to follow out Mary's faith-experience. The scriptures narrate that experience generously. There one sees that 'each of her life situations is history at its most fulfilled'.[13] The central pattern of those situations is clear as we follow through Mary's involvement in God's self-revelation to humanity. That involvement is both personal and archetypal. 'Mary's faith experience revolves around being virgin, bride and mother ... There is a Marian transparency with three distinctive features – virginal openness to God's mystery, bridal response to the Word's self-emptying that creates communion, and maternal missionary activity linked to the Holy Spirit.'[14] These features deserve a brief unfolding with a view to gaining a realisation of Mary's involvement with the content and drama of divine revelation and faith. As Vatican II puts it, 'having entered deeply into the history of salvation, Mary, in a way, unites in her person and re-echoes the most important doctrines of the faith'.[15]

First, the angel Gabriel approaches the virgin of Nazareth with the news that God has an eternal Son who wishes to become her Son on earth. Initially deeply troubled by this offer, Mary asks how this is to be possible since she is a virgin. This leads to the identification of the Holy Spirit as the very agent of the enfleshment of the Son in Mary's flesh. Here is a radically new revelation from the God of Jacob and of David. It is in fact a revelation of the three Persons whose 'roles' are suggested. Mary's response enables the incarnation of the Son so that she becomes the beloved daughter of the Father and the temple of the Holy Spirit (Lk 1:26-38). This is the scriptural mystery that St Paul often writes about (Rm 16:25; Eph 1:9:3:3-4; Col 1:26).

Mary enters into this mystery profoundly by virtue of her radical 'Yes'. The event begins to manifest the unique design which God has for Mary. That design 'originates within the trinitarian dialogue of love that "decided" on creation and redemption. Contemporaneous with the Son's offer of himself to the Father, and the Father's acceptance and mandate of the Son, and with the Spirit's readiness to mediate between heaven and earth, God included Mary's word of assent as an indispensable part of his plan to unite all things under Christ' (Eph 1:10; cf. Jn 17).[16] Here we see Mary's virginal openness to the mystery and the secret or plan of the God of Abraham, Isaac and Jacob, now in the course of being revealed as the economic Trinity.

Mary's journey into and with the unfolding divine plan or mystery continues, however. It will stand out in a very particular way on Calvary. John captures the scene powerfully, albeit with characteristic brevity (19:25-27). The Word who has become flesh reaches the summit of his love for sinful humanity, showing forth his 'grace and his truth', and, in a particular way, the truth of his love for the Father and for us (1:18; 3:16; 14:31a). The 'hour' of the divine Son of Mary arrives as he climbs the cross (Jn 2:4). In that hour of his passion we see the hour of Mary's compassion.[17] It is the hour when the Word's self-emptying reaches its summit. It is also the hour when we see the Mother's bridal response to that sacrifice. Saint Bernard wrote, 'No soul could penetrate your Son's flesh without piercing your soul.'[18]

Here there occurs a unique communion between the Redeemer and the woman who is his bride. From this communion there is born the first cell of the Church. The Son's appointment of Mary to be Mother of the beloved disciple and he to be her son establishes the first 'cell' of the Church. In 'losing' her motherhood of the Word made flesh, she gains a second motherhood of which John is a first fruit. 'And from that hour the disciple took her into his house' (19:29). Mary's journey continues after the death and the resurrection of the divine Son. For the ascended *Kyrios* and the Father now pour out the promised Holy Spirit (Lk 24:49). Saint Luke in his second volume, the *Acts of the Apostles*, highlights the presence of Mary in the cenacle together with the Twelve and the disciples persevering in prayer for the Holy Spirit. (1:14). 'The Holy Spirit had first descended upon her, and now she prays in the midst of the community that what occurred in her may occur again. And this is fulfilled at Pentecost.'[19] As at the annunciation in Nazareth, the Holy Spirit effected Mary's motherhood of the eternal Son, so now at Pentecost her maternal mediation is instrumental in an analogous 'incarnation' of her crucified and resurrected Son in the early Church thanks to the same Holy Spirit. Mary's motherhood of the Church as her Son's mystical body (Gal 3:28), a body spreading out in space and time in preparation for the glory of the world to come, now comes into view. This is her motherhood in the missionary activity of the Church where, in total dependence on her glorified Son and the Holy Spirit,

> She holds high motherhood
> Towards all our ghostly good. (Hopkins)

Hans Urs von Balthasar explains that the Holy Spirit illuminates Mary's experience for Mary. 'What is unique about her is that the Spirit of Pentecost basically does nothing other than to present to her the content of her own experience as her memory had retained it, a memory that contains all the natural dogmas of revelation in their complete unity and interwovenness.'[20]

THE ECCLESIOLOGY OF VATICAN II

Among the greatest achievements of the Second Vatican Council is the Dogmatic Constitution on the Church, *Lumen Gentium*. It contains many of the deepest contents of the conciliar renewal. Its slow methodical elaboration throughout the first three sessions of Vatican II,[21] an elaboration drawing upon the riches of *ressourcement,* called forth a text unprecedented in the history of the Church's twenty-one ecumenical councils. At the twenty-first council, the Church had come of age, as it were, enough in fact to be able to offer her members, as well as the men and women of goodwill, this exciting and original self-profile. However, the riches of this exceptional text are a challenge to our understanding of the Church *as a mystery of faith*. They state a task that has scarcely been noticed so far! It is not our categories that are competent to assess this text, but rather this text is both challenge – and correction – for our habitual Church categories. To appreciate the text, a moment of immediate pre-history is worthwhile, particularly in order to appreciate the conciliar context.

Shortly after World War I, Romano Guardini noticed a development.[22] 'An event of incalculable importance is happening: the Church is awakening in the souls of people.' Until that time, the ecclesiology of the Counter-Reformation held sway in the minds of people. Vatican I had very largely concentrated on the Petrine dimension of the Church. Johann A. Moehler, the famous Tubingen theologian, put it like this, 'In the beginning, God created the hierarchy and had thus set up the Church.' But now an insight emerges, coming directly from the scriptures, and, in particular, from the Fathers who saw in the Persons of the Trinity the very 'fountainheads' of the Church (St Jerome). It was the Pauline revelation that the Church is the body of Christ, in fact, his mystical body. Now 'body' in the New Testament does not have a Platonic meaning as the ignoble prison of the noble soul. Rather, it has its own meaning of the spirit's way of being in the world. Accordingly, to call the Church the 'body of Christ' is to highlight the truth that the Church is a living entity: it is the crucified and living Lord's way of being in the world. Christ had found a Body for himself, and in this body he continued in the world (cf. Acts 9; 22;26). This means that Christ is not confined to the past but lives now and invites his members towards a life that is full (Jn 10:10) and that grows into eschatological completion (Mt 25:30-45; Col 1:26-29; 1 Cor 15:50-57).[23]

This body both grows and develops. Besides, it does so in order to remain itself. Already in the first half of the nineteenth century, Cardinal Newman had discovered this truth when, as leader of the

Oxford Movement, he noticed how in the first millennium there was a sequence of Councils that struck off the dogmas of faith generally in response to the heresies of the times. As an Anglican, he accepted this doctrinal history. But the addition of fresh dogmas in the second millennium was not only unacceptable, it was a major corruption of the apostolic faith. This was his mind until a sequence of theological discoveries came his way. He was transfixed by the realisation that *living bodies must develop in order to remain themselves*. This vigorous development was the outward sign of the interior vitality of word, sacrament and office. In his epoch-making, *An Essay on the Development of Christian Doctrine*, he came to realise that a doctrinal development, far from introducing corruption into the apostolic faith, was the proof of that faith's vitality. Development, he concluded, was one of the constitutive first principles of Christianity.

Around the time of the Second World War, Henri de Lubac opens up the notion of 'eucharistic ecclesiology'.[24] He learns that in the first millennium there was a bond of cause and effect between the Eucharist and the Church. He discovers, for example, that the term, *Corpus Mysticum*, was the name given to the sacred species, and that it made Christians into the *Corpus Reale*, the real body of Christ. Saint Augustine, he argued, could write, 'We receive the Body of Christ to become the body of Christ', and again, 'Be what you see, and receive what you are'.[25] The Eucharist makes the Church! The Church exists fully in all properly constituted local 'eucharistic communities', a topic developed with particular vigour by the emigrant Russian orthodox theologians fleeing persecution. The Church abandoned this terminology only upon the heresy of Berengarius at the close of the eleventh century.

Eucharistic ecclesiology threw up the further insight that Jesus' Last Supper is an event that actually founded the Church. There the Paschal Christ gives a liturgy of life and death in fulfilment of the earlier covenants (1 Cor 11: 23-26). The Fathers of the Church advance to the insight that the Church is actually a creature of the Last Supper and the passion, for she is born from the pierced side of Christ from which the Eucharist and baptism emerge (Jn 19:34-37).[26]

The Church, however, has a history that precedes the event of Christ and that reaches outside the visible confines of the Church.

We can say, in other words, where the Church is but we cannot say where she is not. That is why the idea of 'the people of God' had to emerge. In the Old Covenant, God formed a people. This was the case from the very election of Abraham whom God promised to make into a great nation in order to bless all the nations of the earth (Gn 12:3). This dimension of the pre-conciliar ecclesiology favoured and facilitated a fresh understanding of the Orthodox Churches as well as of the communities emanating from the Reformation. The imperative of ecumenism comes on to the horizon, and with it the Church's special rapport with the people of the first covenant and even with the great religions.

'ECCLESIOLOGY OF COMMUNION'

Now if a 'eucharistic ecclesiology' has begun to emerge, an 'ecclesiology of communion' cannot be far behind. This is what happened in fact. Though the word 'communion' is not central in the texts of the Council, the idea is. Thus the opening words of the *First Letter of John* provide the ouverture for the Council's scintillating constitution on Divine Revelation, *Dei Verbum*. '... that which we have seen and heard we proclaim also to you, so that you may have fellowship (communion – *koinonia*) with us; and our *koinonia* is with the Father and with his Son Jesus Christ' (1:3). The upshot of the life of the Trinity communicated to humanity is described in the next verse, 'We are writing these things so that our joy may be complete.' However, it took until the Extraordinary Synod of 1985 for the reality of communion actually to be named as the central organising category of the Second Vatican Council. It had stolen into the Council, as it were, through the inspiration of the Holy Spirit and – as we have been at pains to point out – through the labours of theologians, Church historians and scripture scholars for more than a century before the Council.

THE ENACTMENT OF THE ECCLESIOLOGY OF VATICAN II

Now if one picks up the Council's masterpiece on the Church, *Lumen Gentium*, one will immediately see how the insights of this *ressourcement* have entered Catholic theology. It is enough to look at the sequence of chapters of that Constitution. Chapter one presents the Church as mystery. In doing so, it combines the riches of scripture, the insight of the Fathers and the elaborated doctrine of sacramentology. Thus the Church is described there as 'a sacrament – a sign and instrument, that is, of communion with God and of the unity of the entire human race'.[27] Participating in Christ the sacrament, the result is that 'the Church is a people made one from the unity of the Father, the Son, and the Holy Spirit'.[28] Thirdly, she is the historical embodiment of God's design for creation and the 'new creation' of the cosmos and humanity, showing forth 'the plan of God hidden throughout the ages and the generations' (Col 1:26).

Chapter two changes our perspective in order to present the Church as the 'people of God'. God 'has willed to make women and men holy and to save them, not as individuals without any bond between them, but rather to make them into a people who might acknowledge him and serve him in holiness'.[29] The Church is the event of unity, a unity begun in the old covenant, fulfilled in the new covenant (1 Cor 11:25), and aimed at in the sacrifice and prayer of the one Redeemer (Jn 17:21f.). Jesus' prayer that all be one is a prayer spoken over the whole of history by the *Kyrios* and Lord of history, to the Father to whom all ages belong, and in the unity of the Holy Spirit who makes creation itself groan for the final arrival of the liberty of the Spirit (Rm 8:18-21).

The third chapter presents the Petrine profile of the Church. This profile underlines the objectivity of the Church's holiness in Word, sacrament and ministry. At Vatican II, however, the Council presents the doctrine of the collegiality of the bishops with the pope. It completes Vatican I's teaching on the pope's primacy and infallibility. God is one and God is three. The Founder of the Church imprints his image and likeness, as one and three, on his Church. 'The pope calls to mind the mystery of God's unity. The college, which consists of many people, calls to mind, by analogy, the Trinity.'[30] Collegiality is the principle of communion as it affects the apostolic college.

The chapter on the lay faithful is unique, not only for its being the first time a Council has ever spoken about them in such fashion, but also for the beauty of its teaching. They are prophets, priests and pastors in virtue of baptism and confirmation. Consequently '... they are called by God to contribute to the sanctification of the world from within, like leaven, in the spirit of the gospel, by fulfilling their own particular duties.'[31] Their field of action is as broad as the great occupations and projects that constitute the whole secular world. The witness of their lives is an evangelisation of the world.

Chapter five addresses the universal call to holiness. The Gospel calls all the baptised to holiness of life in the particular vocation of each. Christianity, in fact, is a call to, and a method of attaining, holiness. The ontological holiness of grace given in the sacraments is to become the existential holiness of the every day. The next chapter speaks of the religious as those consecrated to God. They live publicly by the evangelical counsels, thereby manifesting the tension towards the future and witnessing to the fact that 'the world as we know it is passing away' (1 Cor 7:31) and that 'we have not here a lasting city but we look for the city that is to come' (Heb 13:14).

The seventh chapter addresses the topic of the pilgrim Church which 'will receive its perfection only in the glory of heaven, when the time for the renewal of all things will have come' (Act 3:21).[32] Christianity is in fact an eschatology in that the crucified and risen Lord calls us to forget the things that lie behind and to strain forward to the things that are to come (Phil 3:13). There is a deep communion between the pilgrim Church and the Church already in glory in heaven to which 'the prize of the heavenly call of God in Christ Jesus' (Phil 3:14) beckons all believers. The communion of saints is both constitutive of the Church's being as well as the omega point of her pilgrimage in time and space.

HOW THE MARIAN PROFILE FLOWS INTO THE CHURCH

Thus far we have examined Mary's place in the mystery, in the communion of the Church, and in the mission of the fledgling nascent Church. She is located there according to the eternal design and plan of God the Holy Trinity. The revelation of that mystery, communion and mission involves Mary, as the scriptures amply testify. The net result is that we have perceived an *embedding* of Mary in the mystery of Faith according as she is virgin, bride and mother. As virgin, she had a total readiness for the design of the Father, facilitating the incarnation of the Son and cooperating with the Holy Spirit. As bride, she responded to the self-offering and self-emptying of the redeeming

Son on Calvary, having followed him to Jerusalem and Golgotha. Her response facilitates the emergence of the Church as the communion of those baptised into her divine's Son's death and resurrection. As mother, she prayed with the disoriented community in the Upper Room for the 'gift of God' and the unpacking of the riches of the mystery of revelation for humanity (Eph 3:7-13). That prayer and availability are rewarded with the irruption of the grace of the Holy Spirit on the community that now goes towards the nations, becoming a 'Church from Jews and gentiles' (Acts 9:32-10; Eph 2:14-18).

The question now arises and necessarily, how does this Marian profile flow *into* the Church of all times and of the eschatological aeon? God the Holy Trinity had located this creature in the mystery of the creation, redemption and divinisation of humanity. This location occurred, or rather unfolded, at the birth of the Church, but it is to continue in the life of the Church for time and for eternity. Is it possible to appreciate the mystery of the Church for all times without appreciating Mary?

The answer is given at the Council: the Council Fathers opted to write about the Mother of God, not apart from the Church, but as the concluding and final chapter of its profiling of the Church! It is as if they could not conclude *Lumen Gentium* without the *Theotokos*: it is Christ who is the light of the world indeed, but it is his Mother who spreads his light to suit our sight. She would, in fact, enable us to perceive the mystery of her divine Son's Church, and, understanding her, enable us to 'receive' the Church. Theology speaks of the 'reception' of Church doctrines: it is the process by which the people of God assent to, and assimilate, the teaching of the pastors under the grace of the Holy Spirit. In Mary we glimpse the fact that she has already received the mystery, the communion and the mission of the Church in both a personal *and* archetypal fashion. Her personal reception, however, is more than a reception: 'it is in truth an *actualisation* of the Church of the Trinity'. This makes her the keeper of the secrets of God, *Runai De [The Secretary of God]*, as the ancient Gaelic title puts it with its vivid Pauline resonance. If the time of the Church on earth, the time between the foundation of the Church and the Second Coming, is a time between the dimension of the mysteries of divine revelation and our reception-actualisation of them, then Mary is both type and agent

NOTES

1 See St Athanasius, *Orationes contra Arianos*, iii, 14, 29, 33; also iv, 32.

2 I am indebted to John Henry Newman for this insight, see *Discourses to Mixed Congregations*, London, 1921, pp. 346–9, p. 357; *Sermons on Subjects of the Day*, London 1871, 36–7.

3 John Henry Newman, *Discourses to Mixed Congregations*, London, 1921, 357.

4 Pope John Paul II, *Catechesis on Signs of Hope in the Church*, 23rd November 1998.

5 T. S. Eliot, *Four Quartets*: *The Dry Salvages*, V.

6 See John Henry Newman, *Essay on the Development of Christian Doctrine*, Part 2, chapter 6, section 1.

7 St Augustine, *Enarrationes in Psalmos* 85, 1: CCL 39, 1176.

8 Hans Urs von Balthasar, *The Office of Peter and the Structure of the Church*, San Francisco: Ignatius Press, 1986 .

9 Gerard Manley Hopkins, 'The Blessed Virgin compared to the Air we Breathe', *Poems and Prose*, London, 1986.

10 Marisa Cerini, 'Dimensione mariana', *Unita e Carismi* 8 (1998/1, 2–4).

11 Compare with St Thomas Aquinas' classical definition of beauty as requiring the threefold of fullness, proportion and radiance or *claritas*, Summa, I, q.39, a.8.

12 Brendan Leahy, *The Marian Profile in the Ecclesiology of Hans Urs von Balthasar*, New York: New City Press, 2000, p. 138. One should notice here John Henry Newman's 'final' ecclesiology in 'The Preface to the Third Edition of the *Via Media*', London, 1878 where Newman portrays the interaction of the sacramental, dogmatic and institutional dimensions of the Church. For a study, see H. D. Weidner, ed., *The Via Media of the Anglican Church*, Oxford: Clarendon Press, 1990.

13 Ibid., 69; see St Thomas Aquinas, *Summa*, III, q. 30, a. 1.

14 Leahy, ibid., 160.

15 *Lumen Gentium*, 65; see Thomas J. Norris, 'Mariology a Key to the Faith', *Irish Theological Quarterly*, 55 (1989, 193–205).

16 Leahy, ibid., 72.

17 See Ignace de la Potterie, *Mary in the Mystery of the Covenant*, New York: Alba House, 1992.

18 St Bernard, *Roman Breviary*, III, 262–3.

19 B. Leahy, op. cit., 96.

20 Hans Urs von Balthasar, *Mary for Today*, Slough: St Pauls Publications, 1987, p. 39.

21 For history and commentary on the text, see Gerard Philips, *L'Eglise et son Mystere au Deuxieme Concile du Vatican*, Paris, 1967.

22 For a useful overview of the ecclesiology of Vatican II see Joseph Ratzinger, 'The Ecclesiology of Vatican II', *L'Osservatore Romano*, weekly edition in English, 23rd January 2002, p. 5.

23 See G.K. Chesterton's, *The Everlasting Man,* for a vivid depiction of the Church as the chariot of God careering down the ages.

24 See Henri de Lubac, *Corpus Mysticum. The Eucharist and the Church in the Middle Ages*: many editions.

25 St Augustine, *Sermon* 272.

26 See, to take but one example, St John Chrysostom, *Cat.* 13–19: SC, 50, 174–7.

27 LG, 1; see LG, 48 and Henri de Lubac, *Catholicism*, San Francisco 199, Chapter 1, 'Dogma', for an overview of the Fathers' teaching on the heart of Christianity as the mystery of 'reunification'.

28 St Cyprian, *De oratione dominica*, 64, 4: PL, 3, 1017.

29 LG, 9.

30 Chiara Lubich, *Servants of All*, London 1979, p. 98.

31 LG, 31.

32 LG, 48.

33 The Liturgy of the Roman Rite.

34 Klaus Hemmerle, 'Trinitarische Kirche – Kirche als Communio', *Gemeinsam fuer die Menscheit*, Neue Stadt Dokumentation 2, Muenchen, 1988, 53.

35 Piero Coda, 'Imparare la vita trinitaria guardando a Maria', *Il pianto di Maria*, Giuseppe Greco, ed., Roma, 2003, p. 256, quoting Dante's *La divina commedia*, Il Paradiso, Canto XXXIII.

36 Pope John Paul II, Apostolic Letter for the Third Millennium, *Novo Millennio Ineunte*, paragraph 43.

37 Pope John Paul II, 'Mary's relationship with the Trinity', *Insegnamenti di Giovanni Paolo II*, XIX (1996) I, Vatican City, 1998, 47.

38 See St Irenaeus, *Adversus Haereses*, III, 22, 4: PG 7, 959A.

39 See my 'The Jewish People at Vatican II: The Drama of a Development in Ecclesiology and its subsequent Reception in Ireland and Britain', *Jesus Christ and the Jewish People Today. New Explorations of Theological Interrelationships*, Philip A. Cunningham, Joseph Sievers, Mary C. Boys,

Hans Hermann Henrix & Jesper Svartvik, eds, foreword by Walter Cardinal Kasper, Grand Rapids: Eerdmons Publishing Company, 2011, pp. 251–67.

40 LG, 68.

41 Brendan Leahy, op. cit., 163, referring to Hans Urs von Balthasar, *New Elucidations*, San Francisco: Ignatius Press, 1986, p. 196 and to Pope John Paul II citing of this idea in *Mulieris Dignitatem* (15th August 1988), 27: AAS 80 (1988) II, 1653–1729, especially 1718.

42 See John Paul II, Encyclical *Redemptoris Mater*, 18, Rome 1987.

43 Chiara Lubich, *Essential Writings*, New York: New York City Press, 2007, p. 299.

44 Gerard Manley Hopkins, ibid.

45 LG, 48.

46 LG, 50.

47 Gerard Manley Hopkins, 'That Nature is a Heraclitean Fire and on the Comfort of the Resurrection', *Poems and Prose*, London, 1986.

48 Eugenio Zolli, *Why I Became a Catholic*, New York, 1953, p. 199.

'WITH REVERENCE AND LOVE': BEING A PRIEST IN A DETRADITIONALISED CULTURAL CONTEXT

REV. PROF. EAMONN CONWAY
Mary Immaculate College, University of Limerick

INTRODUCTION

As leaders of parish communities, priests are to the fore in dealing with secularisation. The aim of this paper is to help in assessing the nature and scope of secularisation, with particular though not exclusive reference to the Irish context. In doing so, I will focus on how secularisation impacts especially on the life and work of the priest.

In my title I have referred to the cultural context as 'detraditionalised'. This concept, which I first came across in the work of the KU Leuven theologian, Lieven Boeve, represents an important nuance in the conversation concerning secularisation, especially for countries which, in the past, were as traditionally Catholic as Ireland. I find it particularly helpful, in trying to map secularisation, to relate Boeve's emphasis on detraditionalisation to Charles Taylor's third category of secularisation which he refers to as 'the social imaginary'. After a brief treatment of Taylor's first two understandings of secularisation, this latter third understanding will be the focus of the first part of my paper.

The remainder of the paper will reflect more specifically on the impact of secularisation on priests' lives and work. The third part will attempt to draw some conclusions.

1. MAPPING SECULARISATION

Charles Taylor provides a helpful threefold categorisation of secularisation. With regard to each form I intend to describe it briefly, comment on how pervasive I consider it to be with particular to the Irish context, and then make some observations about its impact, as I see it, on priestly ministry.

Secularisation as exclusion of religion from the public sphere, and purse

In the first instance, Taylor speaks of secularisation in terms of the retreat of religion from the public square and the declining authority and influence of religion in public discourse. As a society's confidence in science, technology and rationality grows, a religious worldview seems unsustainable and incompatible, and over time, is expected to disappear.

In Ireland, we can see a gathering momentum with regard to efforts to exclude religion from the public sphere, and, significantly, also from the public purse. Two 'battlegrounds' over the next few years will clearly be Catholic education, and the reform of the Irish Constitution, which still begins with an invocation of the Trinity.

The Irish Constitution does not allow for any State 'endowment' of religion. Nonetheless, hospitals, schools and colleges, for instance, owned and administered by Church bodies, have been publicly funded. These have already become the flashpoints for this first kind of secularisation as political bodies and interests seek more control over how they operate. A case in point: equality legislation in this country provides for an exemption for religious, educational or medical institutions under the direction or control of a body established for religious purposes; there is momentum gathering to have this exemption removed.

In terms of the official relationship of the State towards religious bodies, we can note that the tendency at least in Ireland is not to exclude them but rather be equally inclusive of religions and atheist perspectives. We saw this, for instance, at the inauguration of our new President when, along with prayers being offered by the various religious leaders, a representative of atheistic humanism also offered a reflection. This is consonant with the structured dialogue with the Churches and faiths which also included humanists and atheists, a forum established by the previous Fianna Fáil-led government

How does this kind of secularisation impact on priests? In parishes, especially rural and small urban areas where the local civil community and the ecclesial parish community still overlap, priests generally still have both public respect and influence. This is in spite of scandals in the Church, where in any case we often hear of people's ability to distinguish between the failings of leadership and the valuable service provided by their local clergy whom they still support.

Generally, in fact, secularisation understood as the exclusion of religion from the public sphere is not progressing as rapidly as many secularists would like. The reality is that post 9/11 there is a recognition that religion remains a potent force in society. In addition, even some secularists regard the loss of the values system and ethics which religion provided as leaving an undesirable moral vacuum, and have called for religions to retain some public role and influence.

A few years ago, the ombudsman for children, Emily O'Reilly famously suggested in a speech to the Ceifin Conference series that we need to 'tiptoe back to the churches' to be reminded of the universal truths about charity and decency and how to lead a good life, and to regain a sense of the magic of ritual.[1]

I remember this quite distinctly because in particular I was surprised at how many priests at the time took solace from this remark and felt heartened by it. I actually felt that this was quite dangerous.

It seems to me, and this is my main point with regard to this first type of secularisation, that the dynamic that is at work here is to exclude religion from the public sphere except for the aspects of it that are considered 'useful' from a public perspective. This, it seems to me, is more dangerous than outright exclusion because it represents *an appropriation* of religion in the public sphere on the State's terms, and not its own.

We see this happening at a macro perspective. After 9/11, for instance, European Union member states were recommended to make provision for the training of Imams within their own countries in an effort to prevent radicalised Islamic leaders being trained overseas. Insofar as there is a public sphere interest in religion, it is based upon the fear that it remains a potent force even in modern societies and it needs to be 'managed' and controlled.

So, with regard to this type of secularisation it seems to me that the main lesson to be learned is to carefully discern the public openness to and appeal of religion in the public sphere.

Decline in adherence to religious beliefs and practices

In the second instance, Taylor speaks of secularisation in terms of the decline in adherence to religious beliefs and practices, which is taken as a measurement of decline in levels of belongingness to religious institutions.

Hardly a week goes by without some survey of religious beliefs and attitudes, producing statistics with regard to religious practice rates. In recent months in Ireland we have seen various figures from the European Values Study, the Census, and the *Amarach* agency as commissioned by the Association of Catholic Priests. I am not going to delay upon the figures themselves here – these are widely available elsewhere. The reality is that while the majority of Irish people still self-describe as Catholic, regular practice rates vary between one tenth and one half of the population, depending on whether one is looking at rural or urban areas.

There are, however, a few points worth noting with regard to this form of secularisation.

The basis for a creative minority

When one views statistics longitudinally, for example, using the EVS data from 1991–2008, decline in Church practice would seem to be levelling off even across age cohorts. In fact, practice rates are marginally higher among the current eighteen to twenty-nine year olds than the current thirty to forty-six year olds. Speaking very generally, it would seem that one fifth of the Catholic population in Ireland will continue to practice regularly, and this is true even of younger cohorts. One fifth of those who self-describe as Catholic will probably never darken a Church door; for them the term coined by Grace Davie, 'believing without belonging', seems apt. The remaining three-fifths will be occasionally practicing, semi-attached Catholics. In terms of adherence to Church beliefs, the pattern would seem similar, with only a minority accepting 'the full package', and a majority adopting a 'pick and mix' approach.

This landscape raises a number of questions for priests and those engaged in Church renewal. At one level, the expectation of a relatively sizeable practicing minority is quite positive. It means that there will continue to be a core group of committed Catholics.

Pope Benedict XVI, for instance, speaks of a creative minority, a phrase apparently originally used by the English historian Arnold Toynbee. How this core group views itself, and how it is led, will be very important. The emphasis among such a minority, it seems to me must be upon being an outward-looking, inviting and evangelising presence rather than a smug and self-contained sect that is entrenched and feels threatened by the wider secularist milieu. It is important that it does not see itself as a diminished faithful remnant, defining itself in terms of the exaggerated and idealised grandeur of what was (Rahner's vision in *The Shape of the Church to Come* is helpful here). Rather, if it is to be genuinely Catholic then it will understand itself as a sacramental presence, providing a confident witness and exercising a sanctifying role on behalf of all of humanity. Priests will need to have both the skills and the vision to lead such communities accordingly.

The need for a shared strategy for ministering to the semi-attached

At the same time, priests will have to continue to minister to what we might call, and I don't mean the terms pejoratively, 'occasional Catholics', or the semi-attached. This is already a major source of frustration for priests. Part of the frustration is that there does not seem to be any coherent strategy for relating to this category not only at a national level but even within dioceses, for instance with regard to admitting children who are from non-practicing families to the sacraments of initiation, and providing for sacramental marriage.

It is a cultural reality that people are adopting *á la carte* attitude to institutions generally. This means that the occasionally practicing semi-attached Catholic is a phenomenon that is likely to remain. Therefore, there is an urgent need to review the stance the Irish Church takes towards such believers and ensure this is established upon a solid theological foundation. In this regard getting the balance right between providing pastoral care, on the one hand, and genuine invitation into fuller communion and conversion, on the other, will be the challenge.

The real struggle faced by priests ministering to people who only occasionally practise must also be acknowledged. It is a very difficult challenge to administer the sacraments and to preach to people who are not really catechised and at the same time ensure that such liturgies are experienced as genuine joyful celebrations of faith. The situation is complex also because in addition to dealing with people who have never been properly catechised, we also have older generations who experienced a form of Catholicism that in some respects was alienating and oppressive.

From inadequate 'subtraction' theories to the 'social imaginary'
Taylor uses the terms 'recession' and 'subtraction' to describe these first two understandings of secularisation because of their focus on decline in religious practices and public influence.

Helpful as reflecting upon secularisation in both of these ways seem, Taylor urges us to understand them as inadequate to the complexity of religious experience. They focus on 'visible and measurable changes in social practice', in the words of Michael Paul Gallagher, rather than 'deeper movements of spiritual sensibility'.[2]

The understanding of secularisation underpinning both of these forms of secularisation was known as the 'zero sum theory', on the basis that modernisation and religion were considered incompatible with each other and effectively cancelled each other out; a society could not be both modern and religious at the same time. Frequently, for example, sociologists point to the fact that, the more educated people are, the less likely they are to adhere to religious beliefs and practices.

As Taylor notes, there are two problems with this approach to secularisation. The first is a pragmatic one. Modernity has not eliminated religion from the equation as many, often wishfully, predicted. In reality, the two understandings of secularisation described above do not accurately interpret what is happening even with regard to Europe, and former proponents of the secularisation thesis have had to seriously change tack. Taylor's observations in this regard are confirmed *inter alia* by those who speak of 'the new visibility for religion in Europe' and the shift in the institutional location of religion but not its disappearance.[3] In fact, we note that adherence to non-institutional forms of spirituality and religiosity seem to remain relatively constant.

The second problem with these theories centres around their basic assumption that modernity as we know it and define it in the West is the form of life to which all cultures aspire and will eventually converge, bringing with it the consequent demise of religion. Taylor argues that this approach is unacceptably 'acultural' and again does not allow for the complexity of what is happening both in Europe and elsewhere.[4]

This brings us to his third understanding. What we are dealing with in the West is best understood, in his view, as a radically transformed cultural context where the impact of the 'whole', of technology, science, philosophy, rationality, and religion as well, is more than 'the sum of the parts'. The effect of these taken together is a transfigured understanding of the self which is not susceptible to superficial descriptors or scales of measurement. We are dealing with the emergence of a certain complex set of conditions which effectively, one might say pejoratively, 'blinker', or, more neutrally, shape or pre-determine, how we view ourselves, others, God, and so on. Taylor uses the term 'social imaginary' to describe 'the (complex) ways people imagine their existence'.

To put this another way: secularisation, in this third sense, means the emergence of a complex set of conditions in our culture, what he calls a social imaginary, that leads us to understand, relate and respond to religion in ways that can truncate or short-circuit authentic religious experience.

Key among this altered set of conditions key is the stance or disposition we adopt towards the authority of a religious tradition. Taylor contends that there are fundamentally two different kinds of religious sensibility operative in the West today. On the one hand there are those who are engaged in spiritual seeking without the navigational systems which authority provides.[5] On the other, there are those who believe they must search 'beyond (their) own sense of the direction in which God is to be found'.[6] These latter people will still place authority first, and hence 'are suspicious of contemporary modes of quest'.[7]

Just to bring home the point Taylor is making here: in the past, he says, 'no one ever thought that (their) own intimations were valid against the whole weight of Christian doctrine'.[8] However, the modern transformation in spiritual sensibility makes this entirely possible today.

How does this specific issue of the postmodern sensibility with regard to authority impact on priests? Hugely, and in several ways we don't have time to develop here. Just to give a few examples: the priest is no longer necessarily respected as the representative of a tradition. He has to stand far more on the basis of his personal authority, and his personality, than his role authority which is considerably diminished. This in turn can lead to an unhealthy cult of the personality.

It also means that there is a felt need, a kind of latent pressure in ministry to have to 'prove' the validity of Christian truth claims, and this can take from the simple joy of being able to celebrate them and live from and out of them. In the spiritual marketplace, all truth claims are considered equally valid, regardless of the weight of tradition that may lie behind them. This places the priest in the position of being like a purveyor of fine spiritual products in with all the stress that having to be a competitor for people's attention entails. But I am rushing ahead a little here.

For now, however, I want to map further the transformation in spiritual sensibility by drawing in particular upon the work of Lieven Boeve (Leuven).

Fleshing out the 'social imaginary': detraditionalisation and pluralisation

Lieven Boeve opts for the terms detraditionalisation and pluralisation to describe the transformation in spiritual sensibility to which Taylor refers.

Boeve describes our cultural context as one of detraditionalisation because religious traditions, as living embodiments and communities of faith, no longer steer the process of constructing people's personal or religious identity.[9] This occurs in a context of pluralisation where competing worldviews and values are presented as equally valid life options.

Instead, the cultural context in which we live provides what Boeve calls 'an all inclusive consumer culture that presents itself as the intermediary par excellence between us and our cultural context'. In this context it has been noted that 'bonds and partnerships are viewed as things to be consumed'.[10]

What Boeve and, in the USA, Vince Miller, author of *Consuming Religion: Religious Belief and Practice in a Consumer Culture*, demonstrate, is that increasingly people see religious beliefs and rituals, symbols and icons, as commodities to be assimilated into their lives and lifestyle, divorced from or devoid of the meaning and impact that they are meant to have in the context of the tradition in which they originate. Faced with a plurality of life views and options such as a 'pick and mix' approach seems sensible and normal.

A living tradition in which these religious artefacts have meaning is missing but not missed. There is no felt need or desire for a coherent 'package' of religious beliefs that would guide and at times challenge one's life rather than merely offer momentary consolation and reassurance.

There is a need to explore whether self-constructed and highly personalised spiritualities provide any genuine encounter with otherness, with the transcendent, and to this aspect of contemporary culture I now want to turn.[11]

Responding to the contemporary openness to spirituality; the role of pilgrimages

As we have seen, the statistics show that while there is a decline in Church practice, there is no comparable decline with regard to belief in God, however understood, and in adherence to non-institutional forms of religiosity and spirituality. At the same time, our consideration of the transformation in terms of people's spiritual sensibility means that the contemporary spiritual quest may be predicated upon what Taylor calls 'flattened' forms of authenticity, that is, upon truncated understandings of what it is to be human.

Research in the USA has found that 'Moralistic Therapeutic Deism' is *de facto* the 'new mainstream American religious faith for (our) culturally post-Catholic, individualistic mass-consumer society'.[12]

Nicholas Lash has commented that a lot of what sells as contemporary spirituality does so because it 'smoothes rather than subverts our well-heeled complacency'. These comments would support and explain the frustration which as priests we experience in the pastoral context of relating to people who are engaged in such spiritual quests.

Indeed, one of the difficulties is that an authentically Catholic spirituality is not, and cannot be, a series of superficially gratifying spiritual experiences. It cannot feed what in German is called the *Glückssucher* or *Grenzgänger* (perhaps we would say 'thrillseeker') mentality which thrives on so-called 'highs'. Catholic spirituality is far more characterised by what Karl Rahner once called the 'sober intoxication of the Spirit'.

So how, as priests, are we to relate to the contemporary spiritual quest?

Michael Paul Gallagher has suggested that there is merit in seeing the contemporary spiritual quest in a cautiously positive light, possibly as a postmodern openness to the Gospel which, while 'sub-Christian', should not be entirely dismissed.[13] This might go against the grain for many of us who would perhaps have a knee-jerk reaction to much of what passes for contemporary spirituality but it is an important call to a more careful and deliberate discernment of contemporary spiritual quests.

The point Gallagher stresses, following on from Taylor, is that whether we like it or not, the starting point for many people today in terms of their journey into faith is not going to be on the level of concepts or ideas. Nor is it going to be in an overt sense institutional. It will not necessarily be impressed by institutional claims to authority or truth claims; it will not privilege institutional practices such as rituals and sacraments.

Given that faith journeys today tend to take the form of a more personal and individual seeking and searching that is innately suspicious of invitations to travel tried-and-trusted spiritual paths, we must learn new ways of engaging with people. The challenge is to join the dots on their faith maps with the radical and gratuitous love of Christ, of which the Church is the sacrament, which alone can fulfil and satisfy the spiritual quest.

Contemporary spiritual journeying can be lonely and isolating experiences. This is why it is so important that our efforts at evangelisation today invite people into a vibrant community of faith, and not merely a system of ideas. It is a sign of the times for us that so many quite evangelical communities are thriving, not only in Africa and Latin America, but in Europe and the USA as well.

Key, it seems to me, is that we are also attentive to our own spiritual journey, and especially the contours of our own interiority and spiritual sensibility. If our personal Christian conviction remains merely at the level of ideas and of service of a 'system' then in the present context we will convince very few. It is the quality of our personal relationship with Christ that will communicate in the present context and how we allow this to draw us to new depths of self-giving presence to God and others.

I find the contemporary popularity of pilgrimages pastorally significant. On the one hand, they engage people in the Christian tradition in an authentic way; they connect people with a praying community going back over several generations. At the same time, pilgrimages are transient experiences, and this appeals to the semi-attached who do not wish to become committed or, to be less judgmental, may not yet have found a faith community they experience as sufficiently welcoming to which to belong more permanently.

Pilgrimages can also be peak emotional moments; this also appeals to many people today. The more arduous pilgrimages such as Lough Derg also provide a sense of achievement and self-fulfilment.

In viewing pilgrimages in this way I do not intend in anyway to be cynical about them; the opposite, in fact. I think that they can be key pastoral moments of intersection with many people engaged on their spiritual quest. The challenge is to discern how to engage with people on pilgrimage, and, where needed, to deepen or maybe even redefine their search, broaden their horizons, and maybe even burst open what may be a very limited understanding of the beauty, grace and love of God that awaits them.

The test of an authentic spirituality according to Taylor is the willingness 'to deny or sacrifice oneself' instead of merely 'to find oneself or fulfil oneself'. In the wake of the incarnation, Von Balthasar says we are not just satisfied, but awestruck by a love we could never have properly anticipated or imagined. The task is to liberate people from narrow purposeful spiritualities arising from a constricted understanding of the self so that they can encounter the God who is.

2. BEING A PRIEST IN A DETRADITIONALISED CULTURAL CONTEXT

We have been reflecting as we went along upon the implications for priests working in a detraditionalised cultural context, considering for the most part, in light of secularisation aspects of priestly ministry, that need to be prioritised and directed.

In what follows, I want to consider the impact of secularisation, and in particular detraditionalisation and pluralisation, on the understanding and exercise of priesthood itself.

Priesthood in crisis?

Almost every serious theological reflection written on priesthood over the past forty years has referred to priestly ministry as being in crisis. Cardinal Walter Kasper says, 'In the last few decades, the priestly ministry in virtually all the Western European Churches has been in a crisis'. Karl Rahner begins his book *Meditations on Priestly Life* by speaking of 'the crisis which the priest has to endure today, in his self-understanding and way of life'. Gilbert Greshake begins his *Priester sein in dieser Zeit* by saying that the subject of priests has become like a wailing wall against which not only many priests themselves but also helpless bishops and confused laity bang their heads to a pulp (my translation).

These theologians are in broad agreement about manifestations of this crisis: the declining number of priests; aging priests being given heavier responsibilities; priests leaving the active ministry. Kasper speaks in particular about 'a mood of resignation and frustration, which in turn can lead to aggression' and an excessive form of activism among priests.

They are also in broad agreement regarding its causes and sources, some of which we might call 'internal', but others which relate more directly to the cultural context we have been reflecting upon.

Kasper speaks of a 'superficial and one-sided reception of the ecclesiology of the Second Vatican Council, which emphasised the "people of God" and *communio*, and the associated doctrine of the common priesthood of all the baptised', which called into question how the *proprium* and *specificum* of priestly ministry are to be defined.

He also points to what he calls the 'transposition of democratic ideas to the Church without any attempt at differentiation', and how these issues touch the very essence of the Church. Greshake also speaks of how the democratisation of all forms of life has become accepted as a sign of the times but which at the same time undermines the spiritual authority of the priest. Rahner also talks of the impact of the Council's transformation in the Church's self-understanding with a resultant disregard for authority.

Greshake speaks of the Church's new orientation to the world, especially the de-emphasis on how the divine manifests itself though the cultic-sacral, in favour of an understanding of the whole cosmos as imbued with divine presence. This has caused a crisis in terms of an understanding of the sacraments and also robbed a more traditional understanding of priesthood of its plausibility.

Greshake also speaks of the way in which superficial metrics of efficiency, of inputs and outputs, have been used to measure the work of priests in parishes; metrics that actually do a disservice to the integrity of ministry. Indeed, teachers and others who work in the caring professions can identify with this frustration.

Rahner notes that the priestly vocation is sometimes perceived more as that of a 'social worker'. He also sees as significant the impact of increased social mobility on our sense of community, and of increasing secularisation which has reduced 'love of God' to 'purely human fellow-feeling'.

I should balance this emphasis on a priesthood in crisis by referring to the research of Paul Zulehner, Emeritus Professor of Pastoral Theology at the University of Vienna, who conducted extensive empirical research on the priesthood in 2000. He surveyed bishops, priests, and deacons in a number of mainland European countries: Austria, Germany, Switzerland, Croatia, and Poland.[14] Over 2,500 clergy responded (40 per cent of those surveyed; apparently a good result). Of these, two-thirds indicated that they were generally content in their priesthood; that the rewards outweighed the burdens; that they did not regret their decision to become priests, and that if they were beginning their lives again they would make the same decision to become priests.

A plurality of priestly perspectives

At the same time, almost all of the respondents spoke about what Zulehner summarised as *Modernisierungsstress*, a term which hardly needs translation (the stress caused by modernising).

Within the priesthood he noticed a plurality of perspectives through which priests come to deal with this tension. Some become what he calls 'advocates of the tradition', and others, 'advocates of the situation', and others still seek to build bridges between both extremes.

Greshake spoke about two operative theologies of priesthood, each with differing emphases: the one 'from above', or 'vertical', which understands priesthood as a consecration and mission from Christ; the other, which views priesthood primarily as an ecclesial service to fellow Christians and thus more orientated and authorised 'horizontally' or 'from below'. These operative theologies are also reflected in the findings of Zulehner's research and predictably give rise to whether priests are primarily 'advocates of the tradition' or 'advocates of the situation'.

A dangerous polarisation

Such a plurality of theological perspectives and responses to secularisation is unavoidable in a pluralised cultural context, and arguably might even be a grace if it is underpinned by a deeper *communio*.

Yet, as we know from the reality of life in parishes and religious communities, there is a real danger that this plurality of perspectives could lead to a damaging polarisation within priesthood. Greshake remarks: 'there exists within the clergy itself a decisive polarisation in the priestly self-understanding which has more than a little to do with furthering mutual insecurity within the priesthood.'[15] Recent developments in the Austrian Church, the *Pfarrer Initiative*, but also here in Ireland, are evidence of this.

This point is underscored by research from the USA which identified a 'growing chasm between younger and older priests' who have very different views on priestly identity.[16]

According to Katherina Schuth, 'more disquieting and challenging than the differences are the antipathy of one group for the other ...' and that 'the growing chasm between younger and older priests is one of the most distressing indicators of the condition of the priesthood'.[17]

Priests themselves and detraditionalisation

Reference has been made by Kasper, Rahner and Greshake to a decline in the respect for authority; to an appropriation of a cultural critique and distrust of all institutions into the Church; to the pervasiveness of democratic principles which undermine belief in the hierarchical nature of the Church. Is all of this evidence that priests are themselves influenced by detraditionalisation, and in their approach to priesthood are adopting a 'pick and mix' consumer-type approach to priesthood? There is probably some truth in this.

At the same time, God's grace works in and through contemporary culture. The Christian faith is about the Word taking flesh; it is about incarnation. The Church and its ministers must serve as effective signs and instruments of divine grace in the world and therefore be visible and perceptible as such in contemporary culture, even though no level of perception will ever fully grasp or exhaust their meaning. That said, there should not be a naïve appropriation of secular theories or perspectives into the ministry and life of the priest.

3. SOME CONCLUDING REMARKS

The God of Jesus Christ, whom priests represent and seek to mediate to people in contemporary culture, is far from self-evident. Aspects of priestly life, such as celibacy and life-long commitment, which we have not discussed here, are profoundly counter-cultural, and are all the more valuable and important for being so.

As priests, as ministers of Christ, we are called not just to live and work within the cultural context in which we find ourselves but in fact to be agents of culture. Our vocation makes us responsible for shaping spiritual sensibility and not merely reacting or responding to it. In order to do this our own lives have to be clearly and confidently rooted in the culture of the Gospel.

It would be relatively easy to present the Gospel of Christ as one ideology among others to which people could 'opt in', as they see fit and on their own terms. But Christianity is not an ideology; it is an invitation to committed relationship and companionship in community. Only those themselves in relationship with Christ can witness to and communicate Christianity as such.

Our own lives as priests must therefore be lived with unambiguous reverence and love for that which we seek to represent if the contemporary spiritual sensibility is to become truly inhabited by Christ.

NOTES

1 'It would be good if we recognised the new religions of sex and drink and shopping for what they are and tiptoed back to the churches. It may not even be necessary to believe, it may be sufficient just to remind ourselves of some of the universal truths about charity and decency and how to live a good life, all of which are contained in the teachings of the major religions. It would be good to regain our sense of the magic of ritual, of the year marked by rites and rituals, not the seamless, joyless blending of undifferentiated weekdays. It would be nice to get the summer over before the Christmas displays begin', http://www.ceifin.com/resources/paper/Address_to_Ceifin_Conference_by_Ms_Emily_OReilly_1.pdf (accessed 5th July 2012).

2 Michael Paul Gallagher, 'Charles Taylor's Critique of "Secularisation"', *Studies*, Vol. 97, No. 388, 433.

3 See for instance: Michael Hoelzl and Graham Ward, eds, *The New Visibility of Religion: Studies in Religion and Cultural Hermeneutics*, Studies in Religion & Political Culture, NY: Continuum, 2008.

4 Charles Taylor, 'Two theories of modernity', *Hastings Center Report*, March – April 1995, 24 ff.

5 Charles Taylor, *A Secular Age*, Harvard: Belknap Press, 2007, p. 512, hereafter ASA.

6 ASA, 511.

7 ASA, 510.

8 ASA, 511.

9 Lieven Boeve, *God Interrupts History: Theology in a Time of Upheaval*, London: Continuum, 2007, p. 22 ff.

10 Z. Bauman, 'Europe and North America', M. Junker-Kenny and M. Tomka, *Faith in a Society of Gratification*, Concilium 35 (1999/4), 6.

11 See Eamonn Conway, 'The Commodification of Religion and the Challenges for Theology: Reflections from the Irish Experience', *Bulletin ET* Volume 17 (1), 2006. Special Issue, 'Consuming Religion in Europe? Christian Faith Challenged by Consumer Culture', Lieven Boeve & Kristien Justaert, eds, Peeters: Leuven, pp. 142–63.

12 Thomas Rausch, *Educating for Faith and Justice: Catholic Higher Education Today*, Minnesota: Liturgical Press, 2010, p. 146.

13 Michael Paul Gallagher, 'Christian Identity in a Postmodern Age: A Perspective from Lonergan', *Christian Identity in a Postmodern Age*, Declan Marmion, ed., Dublin: Veritas Publications, 2005, p. 153.

14 See P. Zulehner u. A. Hennersperger (2001) *'Sie gehen und werden nicht matt' (Jes 40,31, Priester in heutiger Kultur,* Ostfildern: Schwabenverlag).

15 Gilbert Greshake, *Priester sein in dieser Zeit,* Freiburg: Herder, 2000, p. 23.

16 Katherina Schuth, 'A View of the State of the Priesthood in the US', *Sacerdos in Aeternum: Reflections on Priesthood Today,* special edition of *Louvain Studies*, Vol. 30 spring–summer 2005, Nos. 1–2, 8–24.

17 Schuth, 19.

EUCHARIST AS SACRAMENT OF THE ESCHATON: A FAILURE OF THE IMAGINATION?

REV. DR DERMOT A. LANE
Mater Dei Institute of Education,
Dublin City University

The celebration of the Eucharist is at the heart of Catholic identity, and that alone is a good reason for having a Eucharistic Congress, so that a review and assessment of how we celebrate the Eucharist in theory and practice might take place.

My thesis in this paper is that our celebration of the Eucharist is about two-thirds right. However, there is a missing one-third which though present in theory is absent in practice. There are different ways of expressing what is missing. Basically it comes down to a neglect of eschatology, or another way of saying this is to suggest that there is too much about the past and not enough about the future in the way we celebrate the Eucharist; or yet again, one could talk about a certain forgetfulness of the role of the Spirit within eucharistic *praxis*, that is, a forgetfulness of the Spirit who completes what the Spirit has initiated in creation and history.

One of the significant developments in twentieth-century theology was the rediscovery of the centrality of eschatology to the whole of Christian faith. Prior to the twentieth century, eschatology was seen as dealing with the four 'last things' and then this treatment of the 'last things' usually came at the end of theology, appearing as an appendix to the rest of theology. In contrast, through the influence of the renewal of biblical studies in the twentieth century, eschatology was rediscovered as central to Christianity. Further, the advent of the end of time, that is of the *eschaton*, in the life of Christ was perceived as pivotal to Christian identity. Eschatology in the twentieth century rediscovered its pneumatological and Christological foundations with strong emphases on the advent of the *eschaton* in the Paschal mystery of Christ and the Pentecostal event. Christ, crucified and risen, is presented as the first fruits of God's eschatological harvest, as the beginning of the end, as the arrival of a new creation, and as the realisation, at least *in embryo*, of the Kingdom of God. Part of this renewal of eschatology in the twentieth century also included a new emphasis on eschatology as both realised and futurist, sometimes summed up in the more inclusive statement that the Christ-event inaugurated a new era in the history of salvation.

This renewal of eschatology in the twentieth century, however, did not have much impact on the theology of the Eucharist or on our understanding of the Eucharist or on the way we celebrate the Eucharist. Textbooks on the Eucharist did not have much to say about eschatology and indeed textbooks on eschatology did not have much to say about the Eucharist as such (see for example the otherwise fine book on *Eschatology* by H. Schwarz, 2000). However, there are notable exceptions to these observations which can be found in the writings of Jürgen Moltmann and Joseph Ratzinger/Benedict XVI to mention just two examples.

The purpose of this paper is, first of all, to sketch the eschatological dimensions of the Eucharist within the New Testament and throughout the Christian tradition; and then to ask why is it that Eucharist and eschatology have, by and large, gone their own separate ways, in spite of strong evidence in the scriptures and tradition for a close relationship. Secondly, the paper will look at some of the reasons for the neglect of eschatology within eucharistic theology. The paper will then propose an alternative vision of reality that might reconnect eucharist theology and eschatology. The paper will conclude with an outline of how the recovery of the link between Eucharist and eschatology could enrich our eucharistic theory and praxis.

ESCHATOLOGICAL ASPECTS OF THE EUCHARIST IN THE NEW TESTAMENT AND TRADITION

In looking at eschatological aspects of the Eucharist in the New Testament, one should begin not with the Last Supper but with the meals that Jesus celebrated throughout his ministry. A striking feature of the life of Jesus is the number of times he is found having meals with outsiders:

> Why does he eat with tax collectors and sinners? (Mk 2:6; cf. also Lk 15:2)
>
> He has gone to be a guest of one who is a sinner (Lk 19:7)
>
> Look, a glutton and a drunkard, a friend of tax collectors and sinners (Lk 7:34).

In many instances, these meals were what we today would call 'counter-cultural' experiences, offering an alternative vision to people on the margins of life. Further, these meals were linked symbolically by Jesus to his preaching about the coming reign of God and so were often understood as messianic meals (e.g. Mt 22; Lk 14:16ff.).

It is against this background that we should look at the Last Supper, seeing it as the supper that comes at the end of a series of suppers. It should be noted that the Last Supper took place around the time of Passover and, therefore, would have taken place in an atmosphere charged with eschatological expectations.

Accounts of the Last Supper can be found in Paul in his First Letter to the Corinthians and in the synoptic gospels.

In Paul's Letter to the Corinthians, there is an institution narrative in which Jesus says, quite explicitly: 'For as often as you eat this bread and drink the cup, you proclaim the Lord's death until he comes' (1 Cor 11:26) – a clear association of the Eucharist with the eschatological expectation of the second coming of Christ. A similar connection between the Eucharist and the coming of the kingdom of God can be found in the synoptics where Jesus states: 'Truly I tell you from now on I shall not drink the fruit of the vine until that day when I drink it new with you in the kingdom of God' (Mt 26:29; Mk 14:26; Lk 22:15). Further, at the Last Supper, Paul and Luke associate the cup poured out for you with the establishment of 'the new covenant in my blood' (1 Cor 11:25; Lk 22:20) – a reference that resonates with Jeremiah 31.

It is also significant that in Matthew's Gospel, immediately after the Last Supper, we are told, Christ and his disciples sang a hymn as they went out to the Mount of Olives. This is a reference to the hymn which followed the Jewish Paschal meal, namely the singing of Psalms 114–18, psalms that had a messianic connection and an eschatological orientation for the Jews.[1] In that context, it should be noted that the celebration of the Eucharist in the early Church was often accompanied by the response: 'Come, Lord Jesus' (*Maranatha*, as found in Paul in Corinthians, and in the Book of the Apocalypse, and in the *Didache* known as The Teaching of the Apostles).[2] In addition, in John's discourse about the bread of life in chapter 6, eating the bread and drinking the blood of the Son of Man is connected to the resurrection of the individual on the last day.

There is general agreement among exegetes that there is an eschatological dimension present in the institutional narratives of the Eucharist.[3] This link between the Eucharist and eschatology is also found explicitly in the eucharistic Prayers of St Basil and St John Chrysostom in the Patristic era, prayers that are still in use in the Orthodox Church.

Further, references to the Eucharist as 'the seed of resurrection' in Justin Martyr and as 'the medicine of immortality' by Ignatius of Antioch also highlight a link between Eucharist and eschatology in the Patristic period. In addition, there are others references in the Patristic period to the Eucharist as the anticipation and foretaste of the coming reign of God, especially in the theology of Maximus the Conferssor.

This tradition is developed explicitly in Aquinas's theology of the sacraments in general, and of the Eucharist in particular. According to Aquinas, each sacrament is 'at once commemorative of that which has gone before, namely the passion of Christ, and demonstrative of that which is brought about in us through the passion of Christ, namely grace, and prognostic, that is, a foretelling of glory'.[4]

This sacramental principle of Aquinas is applied in particular to the Eucharist and is summed up in a hymn attributed to Aquinas on the occasion of the institution of the Feast of Corpus Christi, a hymn often described as a synthesis of his eucharistic theology:

O sacred banquet in which Christ is received
The memory of his passion is recalled
The mind is filled with grace
And a pledge of future glory is given to us.

This eschatological emphasis on the Eucharist fades from consciousness after Aquinas and then reappears at the Council of Trent which describes the Eucharist as 'a pledge of future glory and everlasting happiness'.[5]

In the *Constitution on the Sacred Liturgy* (1963) of the Second Vatican Council the Eucharist is described as 'a foretaste of that heavenly liturgy which is celebrated in the holy city of Jerusalem'.[6]

The Catechism of the Catholic Church (1994) refers to the Eucharist as 'an anticipation of heavenly glory' and 'a sign of ... hope in the new heavens and the new earth'.[7]

Equally significant is the presence of this theme of the Eucharist as a foretaste of the future in recent ecumenical statements. One good example is the document published by the World Council of Churches in 1982 entitled *Baptism, Eucharist and Ministry*: in a section entitled 'The Eucharist as Meal of the Kingdom', it points out:

> The Eucharist opens up the vision of the divine rule which has been promised as the final renewal of creation, and is a foretaste of it ... The Eucharist is the feast at which the Church gives thanks to God for these signs and joyfully celebrates and anticipates the coming of the kingdom in Christ. (1 Cor 11:26; Mt 26:29)[8]

In an earlier section the same document notes: The Holy Spirit through the Eucharist gives a foretaste of the kingdom of God: the Church receives the life of the new creation and the assurance of the Lord's return.[9]

Given this connection between Eucharist and eschatology in the New Testament and in the tradition, we must ask: why is it that the Eucharist and eschatology have become so disconnected? Why is the presence of eschatology eclipsed within eucharistic *praxis*? How is it that this eschatological dimension of the Eucharist is present only in theory and not in *praxis*?

REASONS FOR NEGLECT OF ESCHATOLOGY WITHIN EUCHARISTIC THEOLOGY

There are a number of reasons why eschatology has faded from Eucharistic consciousness.

The first reason is that the eucharist is understood as a memorial of the past, a memorial of the saving death of Jesus. The Eucharist is about recalling and remembering the sacrifice of Christ on the cross. The Eucharist makes present once again, or better represents the one

Upon all flesh, And your sons and your daughters, shall prophesy,
And your young men shall see visions
And your old men shall dream dreams.[12]

Pentecost marks the inauguration of a new eschatological era, and the creation of a new Spirit-filled community.[13] The early Church understood itself as a new, Spirit-endowed messianic community. Different expressions of this Spirit-centred eschatological consciousness can be found in the early decades of Christianity. One such expression is the refrain: 'God has given us the Spirit.'[14] Another expression is the refrain: 'You have received the Spirit.'[15] A third expression is the refrain: 'The Spirit of God dwells within you.'[16] There is a deep ecclesial awareness of the gift of the Spirit of the end times as present and active within this newly constituted, messianic community of hope.

This outpouring of the Spirit at Pentecost is experienced and understood as eschatological, as heralding the end of the time. This link between the Spirit and eschatology prompts the American theologian, Kilian McDonnell, to formulate the following principle: 'To do pneumatology is to do eschatology.'[17] It is the Spirit who creates, as in the Book of Genesis chapter one, but it is also the same Spirit who completes, the one Spirit who initiates and fulfils, as for example in the conception of Jesus and in his resurrection from the dead. It is this much-needed recovery of the importance of the *Epiclesis* in the Eucharist that captures the eschatological dimension of the Eucharist. At present, too many eucharistic assemblies appear lifeless because they are experienced as Spiritless. Reconnecting the Eucharist with the Spirit will give new life and energy to the celebration of the Eucharist, and will help with the recovery of the eschatological aspects of Eucharist.[18]

A third explanation of why the Eucharist and eschatology have grown apart relates to the tension that exists between the past and the future, between time and eternity, between *chronos* and *Kairos*. This particular tension is described by Charles Taylor as a feature of the modern world in which we now live. We have moved into an era of homogenised, empty time (W. Benjamin).

One author describes this new situation as an impasse between memory and imagination.[19] We have become limited by and imprisoned in the past, unable to move forward, disabled to go beyond who we are and what we have been to who we might be and what we could become. This does not mean we have to abandon memory, but it does imply we need what is often referred to as a purification of memory. This purification of memory can only come about through the power of imagination. Imagination is essential to the purification of memory and to the possibility of moving from the homogenised, empty time of *chronos* to a different type of time, to a revelatory time of insight and freedom which we call *Kairos*.

This tension between the past and the future, between memory and imagination, between *chronos* and *Kairos* is a feature of the modern, secular world, affecting the whole of theology, and in particular our celebration of the Eucharist. Our inability to overcome this impasse is fundamentally a failure of imagination. The US literary critic and theologian, Amos Wilder, sums up this problem insightfully in the following way:

> When imagination fails, doctrines become ossified,
> witness and proclamation wooden, doxologies and litanies empty,
> consolation hollow, and ethics legalistic.[20]

This quotation will resonate with a lot of people's experience just now in the Catholic Church. My focus here is on the Eucharist and I want to suggest that it is a failure of imagination that helps explain the neglect of eschatology within our *praxis* of Eucharist.

This separation between Eucharist and eschatology, between the past and the future, cannot be overcome at the expense of memory, by simply rushing off to imagination. We need to note and emphasise that imagination lives in and through memory. According to Mary Warnock there is a relationship of deep dependency between memory and imagination. Imagination is able to complete what may be lacking in memory, or fill in what is missing in memory, or recover what is forgotten in memory.[21] Patrick Kavanagh, the Irish poet, captures succinctly this relation between memory and imagination in the following way:

> On the stem
> Of memory imaginations blossom.[22]

Applying these principles to the Eucharist, we are faced with a two-fold task. On the one hand we are challenged to remember faithfully what happened in the Christ-event and at Pentecost. The role of imagination is to recover from memory what may have been forgotten, which in this case is that the future has appeared in the Paschal mystery of Christ, that the Christ-event gives us a preview of the future, a preview made up of both darkness and light. The memory of this particular breakthrough from *chronos* into *Kairos*, from history into eternity, is at the centre of Christian faith, and is best summed up in terms of the inauguration of the reign of God. Images used in the New Testament to describe this breakthrough include accounts of the death and resurrection of Jesus as the advent of 'the fullness of time',[23] 'the beginning, the first born from the dead',[24] 'the first fruits' of God's eschatological harvest'[25] and the initiation of a 'new creation'.[26]

The second task facing imagination yoked to Christian memory is how to translate this breakthrough, this experience of the *novum* that took place in the Christ-event, into our celebration of the Eucharist. The imaginative framework used by Jesus is that of the coming reign of God and this must be also the imaginative framework for us today. Jesus used stories to get across this vision of the reign of God and again we would do well to follow Jesus in this regard. Further, Jesus used carefully chosen, prophetic rituals such as the washing of the feet to communicate imaginatively the coming reign of God. A further symbol imagining the reign of God employed by Jesus was the use of food, of feeding and nourishing the hungry multitudes, the offer of table hospitality to outsiders, as ways of imagining the reign of God.

AN ALTERNATIVE UNDERSTANDING OF REALITY

If this recovery of the complete memory of the Christ-event, and if this retrieval of the centrality of the Spirit to the Eucharist, and if this exercise of imagination linked to memory is to succeed, then this will require a new paradigm of reality, described by some as a new 'metaphysics of the future'[27] and others as a new 'eschatological ontology'.[28] Within this new paradigm priority is given not to the past, but to the future. It is the power of the future that shapes the present and not the past; more specifically, it is the power of God as the future of the world, revealed in the Christ-event as the hope of humanity, that influences the present. It is the advent of the reign of God as given in the Paschal mystery of Christ that impacts on the present in the here and now.

It is the gift of the Spirit at Pentecost invoked within the eucharistic assembly that enables the community to imagine a new future.

This way of looking at life calls for a radical reversal of the way we understand reality. In the conventional view of things, it is the past that influences our understanding of the present and it is the past that causes the shape of things in the present. In this proposed new paradigm, this outlook is reversed. It is the power of the future that shapes the present, beckoning humanity to the transformation and fulfilment introduced into the world by the reign of God, given in the Christ-event and the gift of the Spirit. The truth of reality is to be found in its future fulfilment, and the meaning of things is given not only in their origins, but also in their completion at the end of time.

The justification for this reversal, given by Pannenberg and Zizioulas, is the Christian claim that the *Eschaton* has arrived in the Christ-event. More particularly, it is pointed out that the resurrection of Jesus from the dead reorders the outward appearances of history, showing that evil and justice do not have the last word. Further, the resurrection of Jesus is a reinterpretation of the meaning of life, revealing that death is not the end, but the beginning of new life. If the future has been given already *in embryo* in the death and resurrection of Jesus, and if the advent of the reign of God has already come in the Paschal mystery, then it is that future as given in the Paschal Christ and that gift of the reign of God in the Spirit that shapes the present and reconfigures the meaning of existence.

While this view of the power of the future on the present as outlined by Pannenberg and Zizioulas may seem somewhat inflated, it is hard to deny that the future as given and prefigured in the Christ-event reveals not so much who we are, but what we are called to be in the reign of God. Reality looks different when viewed from the end, rather than from its beginning. The celebration of the Eucharist and especially the eschatological aspects of the Eucharist remind us provocatively of that future as given in the Christ-event.

CONSEQUENCES ARISING FROM AN ESCHATOLOGICAL UNDERSTANDING OF THE EUCHARIST

A number of consequences flow from this emphasis on the Eucharist as a celebration of the *Eschaton* as given in the Christ-event. These include an understanding of the Eucharist as counter-cultural, as pointing towards the embodied nature of the future of the world, and as providing a new context for approaching ecumenical questions about Church unity.

The celebration of the Eucharist as the sacrament of the *Eschaton* is a counter-cultural experience. As counter-cultural, the Eucharist interrupts the tedious flow of homogenised empty time, putting people in touch with another form of time that we call *Kairos*, opening up another world, a future world, already prefigured in Christ, which breaks through and disrupts the tedium of *chronos* from time to time. The Eucharist as the sacrament of the *Eschaton* reminds us that the future is not about some measurable outcome, or some predictable *telos*, but rather it is about a future that comes from God in surprising and transformative ways, like an oak tree from an acorn or a butterfly from a chrysalis or the new creation from the broken body of Christ on the cross. As counter-cultural, the sacrament of the *Eschaton* stands out as a protest against the *status quo*, celebrating equality in a world of inequality, promising justice in a world of injustices, remembering the dead in a world that too easily forgets its dead, offering food, nourishment and hospitality in a world that chooses to ignore and neglect the hunger of millions of people.

However, in being counter-cultural the Eucharist should not be construed as something over and against the world and culture. Instead, the Eucharist as God's gift in Christ is given for the transformation of the world and its culture and, therefore, every celebration of the Eucharist seeks at the same time to engage constructively with the world and its cultures as the *loci* of the coming reign of God. The Eucharist can only be counter-cultural by being immersed in the ways of the world and contemporary cultures. Without this involvement with the needs of the world and 'the liturgy of life', the Eucharist would lose its theological and eschatological edge.

Secondly, the Eucharist as the sacrament of the *Eschaton* gives us a window into the future. The nature of the Eucharist as the transformation of bread and wine into the body and blood of Christ reminds us that the future is an embodied future, and not 'the beatitude of pure spirits'.[29] The *Eschaton* celebrated in the Eucharist points to a future that embraces the embodied character of humanity and the corporeality of creation itself. As Rahner points out on more than one occasion, we Christians are out and out 'materialists', affirming a future that is embodied, following the bodily resurrection of Christ from the dead. In this context, the celebration of the Eucharist as a celebration of the body of Christ should be a reminder of the unity of spirit and matter, body and soul, which is a vital part of the new creation in Christ. In view of this many now make a link between the Eucharist and respect for the integrity of creation and the support of the environment.

A third and concluding consequence arising from an appreciation of the Eucharist as the sacrament of the *Eschaton* concerns the quest for unity among the Churches. If there is a unity between Eucharist and eschatology as we have suggested, and if this gives us a new way of looking at reality, pointing towards what we have called an 'eschatological ontology', or a new metaphysics of the future, then we have a new perspective, a different perspective in which to discuss the search for unity among the Churches. In the quest for Christian unity, we should not proceed simply from past historical divisions and theological differences in our attempt to arrive at a new communion in and with Christ. Instead, we could proceed from the shared gift of the *Eschaton,* already given in Christ, and the outpouring of the Spirit at Pentecost, both of which should inform and drive the search for visible unity much more than is the practice at present. We must allow the future as given in the Christ event and the gift of the Spirit as given in baptism to influence the search for unity among the Churches. This search for unity must be shaped as much by the power of the future on the present as the influence of the past-divisions on the present.

More specifically, the balance between the influence of the future and the influence of the past on the present should be applied to difficult questions around the possibility of occasional eucharistic hospitality and the goal of eucharistic-communion among the Churches. This means that the vision of an eschatological ontology or a metaphysics of the future must also be brought to bear on these contentious issues. If it is true that it is only from the perspective of the end that meaning emerges, and if it is accurate to say that unity is and should be shaped by the impact of the advent of the *Eschaton* as already given in Christ, then we must approach questions about Church unity and eucharistic sharing from the future as much as from the past. There is an important sense in which it seems that history divides the Churches and that eschatology has the capacity to unite them.

The ultimate criterion for Church unity must be what best serves the reign of God as given in Christ and present as Spirit poured out at Pentecost, and what best promotes the reign of God as a task for all of the Churches working together. If that is the case, then greater emphasis must be placed within the ecumenical movement on becoming kingdom-centred Christians, witnessing together to a future already given in Christ as the Sacrament of the *Eschaton*.

To sum up, we are proposing that every celebration of the Eucharist should seek to highlight one or other eschatological aspect of the Eucharist: announcing the advent of the *Eschaton* in Christ, proclaiming Christ will come again to complete the work he has set in train, offering the Eucharist as a foretaste of the reign of God, remembering the future as well as the past. In this way every celebration of the Eucharist should be 'an icon of the kingdom which is to come'[30] and an expression of eschatological art.[31] The Eucharist as an eschatological art-form has the potential to give new life to the way we celebrate the Lord's Supper. This eschatological focus could be incorporated into the penitential rite, or the prayers of the faithful, or the communion reflection or the selection of music. The purpose of this eschatological emphasis is to deepen, not diminish or distract, the responsibility of the Eucharistic community to work for a more just and peaceful world in the present in anticipation and preparation for the future coming reign of God – an emphasis that was to the fore at the forty-second International Eucharistic Congress in Lourdes in 1981 which had the theme 'Jesus Christ, Bread Broken for a New World'.

NOTES

1 See John Zizoulas, 'The Eucharist and the Kingdom of God', p. 17, section viii, available online and accessed on 15th May 2012.

2 See 1 Cor 16:22; Rv 22:20.

3 See Raymond Maloney, *The Eucharist*, London: Chapman,1995, pp. 12 and 14, no. 16

4 Saint Thomas Aquinas, *Summa Theologiae*, III, Question 60, article 3. For an enlightened commentary on this aspect of Aquinas's theology, see the valuable work of Liam Bergin, *O Propheticum Lavacrum: Baptism as Symbolic Act of Eschatological Salvation,* Rome: Editrice Pontificia Universita Gregoriana, 1999, pp. 11–41.

5 Council of Trent, 13th Session, chapter 2, available in J. Neuner and J. Dupuis, eds, *The Christian Faith in Doctrinal Documents of the Catholic Church*, revised edition, London: Collins, 1983, p. 416

6 SC, a, 8. See also GS, 38 and UR, 15.

7 *Catechism of the Catholic Church,* Dublin: Veritas Publications, 1994, a. 1402 and 1405.

8 *Baptism, Eucharist and Ministry*, Faith and Order Paper no. 111, Geneva: World Council of Churches, 1982: a. 22; see also a. 6 and a. 18 of the section on the Eucharist.

9 Ibid, a.18.

10 See John P. Mannoussakis, 'The Anarchic Principle of Christian Eschatology in the Eucharistic Tradition of the Eastern Church', *Harvard Theological Review*, 2007,1: 29–46.

11 Paul Bradshaw, 'The Rediscovery of the Holy Spirit in Modern Eucharistic Theology and Practice', *The Spirit in Worship – Worship in the Spirit*, Minnesota: Liturgical Press, 2009, pp. 79–96 at p. 79.

12 See Acts 2:16-21.

13 See Dermot A. Lane, *Stepping Stones to Other Religions: A Christian Theology of Interreligious Dialogue*, Dublin: Veritas Publications, 2011, pp. 262–3.

14 Acts 5:32, 38:18; Rm 5; 2 Cor 1:22; 1 Th 4:8; 1 Jn 3:24, 4:13.

15 Jn 20:22; Acts 2:33, 38, 8:15, 17, 19, 10:47; 19:2; Rm 8:15; Gal 3:2, 14.

16 1 Cor 3:6, 6:19; Rm 8:9, 11.

17 Kilian McDonnell, *The Other Hand of God: The Holy Spirit as the Universal Touch and Goal,* Minnesota: Liturgical Press, 2003, p. 33.

18 It may come as a surprise to some to note that the Holy See approved the Eucharistic Prayer of Adai and Mari of the Assyrian Church which

has no formal institutional narrative and therefore no formal words of consecration, but does have a clear and explicit emphasis on the role of the Spirit.

19 Constance Fitzgerald, 'From Impasse to Prophetic Hope: Crisis of Memory', *Proceedings of the Sixty-fourth Annual Convention of the Catholic Theological Society of America,* 4th–7th June 2009, 22.

20 Amos Wilder, *Theopoetic: Theology and the Religious Imagination,* Philadelphia: Fortress Press, 1976, p. 2.

21 See Dermot A. Lane, 'Imagination and Theology: The *Status Quaestionis, Louvain Studies,* summer – fall, 2009–2010, 119–145 at 133–134.

22 Patrick Kavanagh, line from 'Father Mat', taken from *Patrick Kavanagh: Collected Poems,* edited by Antoinette Quinn, London: Allen Lane, 2004, p. 126. Used with the permission of the Trustees of the Estate of the late Katherine B. Kavanagh, through the Jonathan Williams Literary Agency.

23 Gal 4:4; Ep 1:10.

24 Col 1 18; Rm 8:29.

25 1 Cor 15:20.

26 2 Cor 5:17.

27 John F. Haught, *God After Darwin: A Theology of Evolution,* Colorado: Westview Press, 2000, pp. 88–9.

28 See John Zizioulas, 'Towards an Eschatological Ontology', unpublished paper delivered at King's College, 1999. A similar ontology is found in the work of Wolfhart Pannenberg.

29 Karl Rahner, 'The Resurrection of the Body', *Theological Investigations,* vol. 2: London: DLT, 1963, pp. 203–16 at p. 215.

30 John Zizoulas, 'The Eucharist and the Kingdom of God', p. 9, section iii.

31 The idea of the Eucharist as an eschatological art-form is inspired by Don Saliers, 'Worship as Christian Eschatological Art: Word and Grace come to life', *Uniting Church Studies,* 9th March 2003, pp. 4–21.

CIVILIZZARE L'ECONOMIA: COMUNIONE E GRATUITÀ NELL'AGIRE ECONOMICO ALLA LUCE DELLA DOTTRINA SOCIALE DELLA CHIESA

PROF. STEFANO ZAMAGNI
Department of Economics, University of Bologna

INTRODUZIONE

C'è posto per la categoria del dono come gratuità entro il discorso e la pratica dell'economia? O quest'ultima è 'condannata' a parlare il linguaggio e quindi ad occuparsi solamente di efficienza, profitto, competitività, sviluppo e, tuttal'più, di giustizia distributiva? La domanda è tutt'altro che retorica se si considera che l'agire caritativo è oggi sotto attacco, sebbene con intenti diversi, da un duplice fronte, quello dei neoliberisti e quello dei neostatalisti. I primi si 'accontentano' della filantropia e delle varie pratiche del conservatorismo compassionevole per assicurare un livello minimo di assistenza sociale ai segmenti deboli e emarginati della popolazione. Ma che non sia questo il senso del dono ci viene dalla considerazione che l'attenzione a chi è portatore di bisogni non ha da essere oggettuale, ma personale. L'umiliazione di essere considerati 'oggetti' delle attenzioni altrui, sia pure di tipo compassionevole, è il limite grave della concezione liberal-individualista, che non riesce a comprendere il valore della empatia nelle relazioni interpersonali. Come si legge nella *Deus Caritas Est*: 'L'intima partecipazione personale al bisogno e alla sofferenza dell'altro, diventa così un parteciparli me stesso: perché il dono non umili l'altro, devo dargli non soltanto qualcosa di mio, ma me stesso, devo essere presente nel dono come persona' (no. 34).

Anche la logica neostatalista non coglie affatto il significato profondo della carità. Insistendo unicamente sul principio di solidarietà, lo Stato si fa carico di assicurare a tutti i cittadini livelli essenziali di assistenza. Ma in tal modo esso spiazza il principio di gratuità negando, al livello della sfera *pubblica*, ogni spazio alla carità intesa come dono gratuito. Se si riconosce che la carità svolge una funzione profetica, perché porta con sé una 'benedizione nascosta', ma non si consente che questa funzione si manifesti nella sfera pubblica, perché a tutto e a tutti pensa lo Stato, è chiaro che lo spirito del dono – da non confondere con lo spirito del regalo – andrà soggetto a lenta atrofia. L'aiuto per via esclusivamente statuale tende a produrre individui bensì assistiti ma non rispettati nella loro dignità, perché non riesce ad evitare la trappola della dipendenza riprodotta.

La sfida da raccogliere, oggi, è quella di battersi per restituire il principio di gratuità alla sfera pubblica. Il dono, affermando il primato della relazione interpersonale sul suo esonero, del legame intersoggettivo sul bene donato, dell'identità personale sull'utile, deve poter trovare spazio di espressione ovunque, in qualunque ambito dell'agire umano, ivi compresa l'economia e la politica. Il messaggio centrale è dunque quello di pensare la carità, e quindi la fraternità, come cifra della condizione umana, vedendo nell'esercizio del dono gratuito il presupposto indispensabile affinché Stato e mercato possano funzionare avendo di mira il bene comune. Senza pratiche estese di dono si potrà anche edificare un mercato efficiente ed uno Stato autorevole (e perfino giusto), ma non si riuscirà certo a risolvere quel 'disagio di civiltà', di cui parla S. Freud nel suo saggio famoso.

Due infatti sono le categorie di beni di cui avvertiamo la necessità: di giustizia e di gratuità. I primi – si pensi ai beni erogati dal welfare state – fissano un preciso *dovere* in capo ad un soggetto – tipicamente l'ente pubblico – affinché i diritti dei cittadini su quei beni vengano soddisfatti. I beni di gratuità, invece – quali sono ad esempio i beni relazionali – fissano un'*obbligazione* che discende dal legame che ci unisce l'un l'altro. Infatti, è il riconoscimento di una mutua *ligatio* tra persone a fondare l'*ob-ligatio*. E dunque mentre per difendere un diritto si può, e si deve, ricorrere alla legge, si adempie ad un'obbligazione per via di gratuità reciprocante. Mai nessuna legge potrà imporre la reciprocità e mai nessun incentivo potrà far fiorire la gratuità. Eppure non v'è chi non veda quanto i beni di gratuità siano importanti per il bisogno di felicità che ciascun uomo si porta dentro. Efficienza e giustizia, anche se unite, non valgono a renderci felici.

BENE COMUNE: PERCHÉ RESISTERE ALLO SFINIMENTO DI UNA CATEGORIA

Cosa comporta, nella pratica, l'accoglimento della prospettiva dell'amore entro l'agire economico? Di due conseguenze desidero qui dire. La prima concerne la messa al centro dell'azione economica della categoria di bene comune. Perché nell'ultimo quarto di secolo la prospettiva di discorso del bene comune, dopo almeno un paio di secoli durante i quali essa era di fatto uscita di scena, sta oggi riemergendo al modo di fiume carsico? Perché il passaggio dai mercati nazionali al mercato globale, consumatosi nel corso dell'ultimo quarto di secolo, va rendendo di nuovo attuale il discorso sul bene comune?

Per rispondere, giova osservare che a partire dalla prima metà dell'Ottocento, la visione civile del mercato e, più in generale, dell'economia scompare sia dalla ricerca scientifica sia dal dibattito politico-culturale. Parecchie e di diversa natura le ragioni di tale arresto. Ci limitiamo ad indicare le due più rilevanti. Per un verso, la diffusione a macchia d'olio, negli ambienti dell'alta cultura europea, della filosofia utilitarista di Jeremy Bentham, la cui opera principale, che è del 1789, impiegherà parecchi decenni prima di entrare, in posizione egemone, nel discorso economico. É con la morale utilitaristica e non già con l'etica protestante – come taluno ritiene ancora – che prende piede dentro la scienza economica l'antropologia iper-minimalista dell'*homo oeconomicus* e con essa la metodologia dell'atomismo sociale. Notevole per chiarezza e per profondità di significato il seguente passo di Bentham: 'La comunità è un corpo fittizio, composto di persone individuali che si considera come se costituissero le sue membra. L'interesse della comunità è cosa? – la somma degli interessi dei parecchi membri che la compongono' (1789 [1823], I, IV).

Per l'altro verso, l'affermazione piena della società industriale a seguito della rivoluzione industriale. Quella industriale è una società che produce merci. La macchina predomina ovunque e i ritmi della vita sono meccanicamente cadenzati. L'energia sostituisce, in gran parte, la forza muscolare e da' conto degli enormi incrementi di produttività, che a loro volta si accompagnano alla produzione di massa. Energia e macchina trasformano la natura del lavoro: le abilità personali sono scomposte in componenti elementari. Di qui l'esigenza del coordinamento e dell'organizzazione. Si fa avanti così un mondo in cui gli uomini sono visualizzati come 'cose', perché è più facile coordinare 'cose' che non uomini, e nel quale la persona è separata dal ruolo che svolge. Le organizzazioni, *in primis* le imprese, si occupano dei ruoli, non tanto delle persone. E ciò avviene non solamente all'interno della fabbrica, ma nella società intera. É in ciò il senso profondo del ford-taylorismo come tentativo (riuscito) di teorizzare e di tradurre in pratica questo modello di ordine sociale. L'affermazione della 'catena di montaggio' trova il suo correlato nella diffusione del consumismo; donde la schizofrenia tipica dei 'tempi moderni': da un lato, si esaspera la perdita di senso del lavoro (l'alienazione dovuta alla spersonalizzazione della figura del lavoratore); dall'altro lato, a mo' di compensazione, si rende il consumo opulento. Il pensiero marxista e le sue articolazioni politiche nel corso del Novecento si adopereranno, con alterni ma modesti successi, per offrire vie d'uscita ad un tale modello di società.

Dal complesso intrecciarsi e scontrarsi di questi due insiemi di ragioni è derivata una conseguenza importante ai fini del nostro discorso: l'affermazione, tuttora presente nelle nostre società, di due opposte concezioni del mercato. L'una è quella che lo vede come un 'male necessario', cioè come un'istituzione di cui non si può fare a meno, perché garanzia di progresso economico, ma pur sempre un 'male' da cui guardarsi e pertanto da tenere sotto controllo. L'altra è quella che considera il mercato come luogo idealtipico per risolvere il problema politico, proprio come sostiene la posizione liberal-individualistica, secondo cui la 'logica' del mercato deve potersi estendere, sia pure con gli adattamenti del caso, a tutti gli ambiti della vita associata – dalla famiglia, alla scuola, alla politica, alle stesse pratiche religiose.

Non è difficile cogliere gli elementi di debolezza di queste due concezioni tra loro speculari. La prima – stupendamente resa dall'aforisma: 'Lo Stato non deve remare, ma stare al timone' – si appoggia sull'argomento della lotta alle ineguaglianze: solo interventi dello Stato in chiave redistributiva possono ridurre la forbice fra individui e fra gruppi sociali. Le cose però non stanno in questi termini. Le disuguaglianze nei paesi avanzati dell'Occidente, che erano diminuite dal 1945 in poi, sono tornate scandalosamente a crescere negli ultimi vent'anni e ciò nonostante i massicci interventi dello Stato in economia. Conosciamo certamente le ragioni per le quali ciò avviene, ragioni che hanno a che vedere con la transizione alla società post-industriale. Si pensi a fenomeni quali l'ingresso nei processi produttivi delle nuove tecnologie infotelematiche e la creazione di mercati del lavoro e del capitale globale; ma il punto è capire perché la ridistribuzione in chiave perequatrice non può essere un compito *esclusivo* dello Stato. Il fatto è che la stabilità politica è un obiettivo che, stante l'attuale modello di democrazia – quello elitistico-competitivo di Max Weber e di Joseph Schumpeter – non si raggiunge con misure di riduzione delle ineguaglianze, ma con la crescita economica. La durata e la reputazione dei governi democratici sono assai più determinate dalla loro capacità di accrescere il livello della ricchezza che non dalla loro abilità di ridistribuirla equamente tra i cittadini. E ciò per la semplice, seppure triste, ragione che i 'poveri' non partecipano al gioco democratico, e dunque non costituiscono una classe di *stakeholders* capace di impensierire la ragion politica. Se dunque si vuole contrastare l'aumento endemico delle disuguaglianze, perché foriero di pericoli seri sul fronte sia della pace sia della democrazia, occorre intervenire prima di tutto sul momento della produzione della ricchezza e non solo su quello della sua ridistribuzione.

Cosa c'è che non regge nell'altra concezione del mercato, oggi efficacemente veicolata dal pensiero unico della *one best way*? Che non è vero che la massima estensione possibile della logica del mercato (acivile) accresce il benessere per tutti. Non è vera, cioè, la metafora secondo cui 'una marea che sale solleva tutte le barche'. Il ragionamento che sorregge la metafora è basicamente il seguente: poiché il benessere dei cittadini dipende dalla prosperità economica e poiché questa è causalmente associata alle relazioni di mercato, la vera priorità dell'azione politica deve essere quella di assicurare le condizioni per la fioritura massima possibile della cultura del mercato. Il *welfare state,* dunque, quanto più è generoso tanto più agisce come vincolo alla crescita economica e quindi è contrario alla diffusione del benessere. Donde la raccomandazione di un *welfare* selettivista che si occupi solamente di coloro che la gara di mercato lascia ai margini. Gli altri, quelli che riescono a rimanere entro il circuito virtuoso della crescita, provvederanno da sé alla propria tutela. Ebbene, è la semplice osservazione dei fatti a svelarci l'aporia che sta alla base di tale linea di pensiero: crescita economica (cioè aumenti sostenuti di ricchezza) e progresso civile (cioè allargamento degli spazi di libertà delle persone) non marciano più insieme. Come dire che all'aumento del benessere materiale (*welfare*) non si accompagna più un aumento della felicità (*well-being*): ridurre la capacità di inclusione di chi, per una ragione o l'altra, resta ai margini del mercato, mentre non aggiunge nulla a chi vi è già inserito, produce un razionamento della libertà, che è sempre deleterio per la 'pubblica felicità'.

Queste due concezioni del mercato, tra loro diversissime quanto a presupposti filosofici e a conseguenze politiche, hanno finito col generare, a livello in primo luogo culturale, un risultato forse inatteso: l'affermazione di un'idea di mercato antitetica a quella della tradizione di pensiero dell'economia civile – una tradizione di pensiero tipicamente italiana che inizia all'epoca dell'Umenesimo civile e si protrae fino a verso la fine del XVIII secolo quando viene surclassata dal paradigma dell'economia politica. Un' idea, cioè, che vede il mercato come istituzione fondata su una duplice norma: l'*impersonalità* delle relazioni di scambio (tanto meno conosco la mia controparte tanto maggiore sarà il mio vantaggio, perché gli affari riescono meglio con gli sconosciuti!); la motivazione *esclusivamente auto-interessata* di coloro che vi partecipano, con il che 'sentimenti morali' quali la simpatia, la reciprocità, la fraternità etc., non giocano alcun ruolo significativo nell'arena del mercato. É così accaduto che la progressiva e maestosa espansione delle relazioni di mercato nel corso dell'ultimo secolo e mezzo ha finito con il rafforzare quell'interpretazione pessimistica del carattere degli esseri umani che già era stata teorizzata da Hobbes e da Mandeville, secondo i quali solo le dure leggi del mercato riuscirebbero a domarne gli impulsi perversi e le pulsioni di tipo anarchico. La visione caricaturale della natura umana che così si è imposta ha contribuito ad accreditare un duplice errore: che la sfera del mercato coincide con quella dell'egoismo, con il luogo in cui ognuno persegue, al meglio, i propri interessi individuali e, simmetricamente, che la sfera dello Stato coincide con quella della solidarietà, del perseguimento cioè degli interessi collettivi. É su tale fondamento che è stato eretto il ben noto, modello dicotomico Stato-mercato: un modello in forza del quale lo Stato viene identificato con la sfera del pubblico e il mercato con la sfera del privato.

Di una conseguenza importante dell'uscita di scena della prospettiva dell'economia civile, conviene qui fare rapido cenno. Tale uscita ha costretto quelle organizzazioni della società civile oggi note come non profit o terzo settore, a definire la propria identità *in negativo* rispetto ai termini di quella dicotomia: come 'non Stato' oppure come 'non mercato', a seconda dei contesti. Non vi è chi non veda come questa concettualizzazione lasci insoddisfatti. Non solamente perché da essa discende che il terzo settore può tutt'al più aspirare ad un ruolo residuale e di nicchia, ma anche perché tale ruolo sarebbe comunque transitorio. Come è stato affermato, quelle non profit sarebbero organizzazioni transitorie che nascono per soddisfare nuovi bisogni non ancora raggiunti dal mercato capitalistico, destinate, col tempo, a scomparire oppure a trasformarsi nella forma capitalistica di impresa. Su cosa poggia una 'certezza' del genere? Sulla acritica accettazione del presupposto secondo cui la forma *naturale* di fare impresa è quella capitalistica e dunque che ogni altra forma di impresa deve la propria ragione di esistere o a un 'fallimento del mercato' oppure a un 'fallimento dello Stato'. Quanto a dire che se si potessero rimuovere le cause generatrici di quei fallimenti (le asimmetrie informative; le esternalità; l'incompletezza dei contratti; i mal funzionamenti della burocrazia e così via) si potrebbe tranquillamente fare a meno delle organizzazioni della società civile. In definitiva, una volta supinamente accolto il principio della naturalità dell'individualismo ontologico, e in particolare dell'*homo oeconomicus,* si ha che l'unico banco di prova per il soggetto non profit è quello dell'efficienza: solamente se dimostra di essere più efficiente dell'impresa privata e/o dell'impresa pubblica esso ha titolo per meritare rispetto. (Si badi che quella di efficienza non è, in economia, una nozione assiologicamente neutrale: solo dopo che si è dichiarato il fine dell'azione economica si può definire l'efficienza.)

Non è difficile a questo punto spiegarsi il ritorno nel dibattito culturale contemporaneo della categoria del bene comune. Dinnanzi allo squallore della tendenziale riduzione dei rapporti umani allo scambio di prodotti equivalenti, lo spirito dell'uomo contemporaneo insorge e domanda un'altra storia. La parola chiave che oggi meglio di ogni altra esprime questa esigenza è quella di fraternità, parola già presente nella bandiera della Rivoluzione Francese, ma che l'ordine post-rivoluzionario ha poi abbandonato – per le note ragioni – fino alla sua cancellazione dal lessico politico-economico. É stata la scuola di pensiero francescana a dare a questo termine il significato che esso ha conservato nel corso del tempo. Che è quello di costituire, ad un tempo, il complemento e il superamento del principio di solidarietà. Infatti mentre la solidarietà è il principio di organizzazione sociale che consente ai diseguali di diventare eguali, il principio di fraternità è quel principio di organizzazione sociale che consente agli eguali di esser diversi. La fraternità consente a persone che sono eguali nella loro dignità e nei loro diritti fondamentali di esprimere diversamente il loro piano di vita, o il loro carisma. Le stagioni che abbiamo lasciato alle spalle, l'800 e soprattutto il '900, sono state caratterizzate da grosse battaglie, sia culturali sia politiche, in nome della solidarietà e questa è stata cosa buona; si pensi alla storia del movimento sindacale e alla lotta per la conquista dei diritti civili. Il punto è che la buona società in cui vivere non può accontentarsi dell'orizzonte della solidarietà, perché una società che fosse solo solidale, e non anche fraterna, sarebbe una società dalla quale ognuno cercherebbe di allontanarsi. Il fatto è che mentre la società fraterna è anche una società solidale, il viceversa non è necessariamente vero.

Aver dimenticato il fatto che non è sostenibile una società di umani in cui si estingue il senso di fraternità e in cui tutto si riduce, per un verso, a migliorare le transazioni basate sullo scambio di equivalenti e, per l'altro verso, a aumentare i trasferimenti attuati da strutture assistenziali di natura pubblica , ci dà conto del perché, nonostante la qualità delle forze intellettuali in campo, non si sia ancora addivenuti ad una soluzione credibile del grande trade-off tra efficienza ed equità. Non è capace di futuro la società in cui si dissolve il principio di fraternità; non è cioè capace di progredire quella società in cui esiste solamente il 'dare per avere' oppure il 'dare per dovere'. Ecco perché, né la visione liberal-individualista del mondo, in cui tutto (o quasi) è scambio, né la visione statocentrica della società, in cui tutto (o quasi) è doverosità, sono guide sicure per farci uscire dalle secche in cui le nostre società sono oggi impantanate.

Che fare per consentire che il mercato possa tornare ad essere – come lo fu nella stagione dell'Umanesimo – strumento di civilizzazione e mezzo per rafforzare il vincolo sociale è la grossa sfida che oggi è di fronte a tutti noi. Che la sfida sia di quelle di portata epocale ci viene confermato da un interrogativo su tutti: nel contesto attuale dominato da economie di mercato di tipo capitalistico, è possibile che soggetti il cui *modus operandi* è ispirato al principio di reciprocità riescano, non solamente ad emergere, ma anche ad espandersi?

Cosa può far pensare che il progetto tendente a restituire il principio del bene comune alla sfera pubblica – a quella economica, in particolare – non sia solo una consolatoria utopia? Due considerazioni, entrambe verificabili. La prima ha a che vedere con la presa d'atto che alla base dell'economia capitalistica è presente una seria contraddizione di tipo pragmatico – non logico, beninteso. Quella capitalistica è certamente un'economia di mercato, cioè un assetto istituzionale in cui sono presenti e operativi i due principi basilari della modernità: la libertà di agire e di fare impresa, per un verso; l'eguaglianza di tutti di fronte alla legge per l'altro verso. Al tempo stesso, però, l'istituzione principe del capitalismo – l'impresa capitalistica, appunto – è andata edificandosi nel corso degli ultimi tre secoli sul principio di gerarchia. Ha preso così corpo un sistema di produzione in cui vi è una struttura centralizzata alla quale un certo numero di individui cedono, volontariamente, in cambio di un prezzo (il salario, di lavoro), che una volta entrati nell'impresa sfuggono poi al controllo di coloro che li forniscono.

Sappiamo bene, dalla storia economica come ciò sia avvenuto e conosciamo anche i notevoli progressi sul fronte economico che tale assetto istituzionale ha garantito. Ma il fatto è che nell'attuale passaggio d'epoca – dalla modernità alla dopomodernità – sempre più frequenti sono le voci che si levano ad indicare le difficoltà di far marciare assieme principio democratico e principio capitalistico. Il fenomeno della cosiddetta privatizzazione del pubblico è ciò che soprattutto fa problema: le imprese dell'economia capitalistica vanno assumendo sempre più il controllo del comportamento degli individui – i quali, si badi, trascorrono ben oltre la metà del loro tempo di vita sul luogo di lavoro – sottraendolo allo Stato o ad altre agenzie, prima fra tutte la famiglia. Nozioni come libertà di scelta, tolleranza, eguaglianza di fronte alla legge, partecipazione ed altre simili, coniate e diffuse all'epoca dell'Umanesimo civile e rafforzate poi al tempo dell'Illuminismo, come antidoto al potere assoluto (o quasi) del sovrano, vengono fatte proprie, opportunamente ricalibrate, dalle imprese capitalistiche per trasformare gli individui, non più sudditi, in acquirenti di quei beni e servizi che esse stesso producono.

La discrasia di cui sopra sta in ciò che, se si hanno ragioni cogenti per considerare meritoria l'estensione massima possibile del principio democratico, allora occorre cominciare a guardare quel che avviene *dentro* l'impresa e non solamente quel che avviene nei rapporti tra imprese che interagiscono nel mercato. 'Se la democrazia – scrive Dahl (41) – è giustificata nel governo dello Stato, allora essa è pure giustificata nel governo dell'impresa' (p. 57). Mai sarà compiutamente democratica la società nella quale il principio democratico trova concreta applicazione nella sola sfera politica. La buona società in cui vivere non costringe i suoi membri ad imbarazzanti dissociazioni: democratici in quanto cittadini elettori; non democratici in quanto lavoratori o consumatori.

La seconda considerazione riguarda l'insoddisfazione, sempre più diffusa, circa il modo di interpretare il principio di libertà. Come è noto, tre sono le dimensioni costitutive della libertà: l'autonomia, l'immunità, la capacitazione. L'autonomia dice della libertà di scelta: non si è liberi se non si è posti nella condizione di scegliere. L'immunità dice, invece, dell'assenza di coercizione da parte di un qualche agente esterno. É, in buona sostanza, la libertà negativa (ovvero la 'libertà da') di cui ha parlato I. Berlin. La capacitazione, nel senso di A. Sen, infine, dice della capacità di scelta, di conseguire cioè gli obiettivi, almeno in parte o in qualche misura, che il soggetto si pone. Non si è liberi se mai (o almeno in parte) si riesce a realizzare il proprio piano di vita. Ebbene, mentre l'approccio liberal-liberista vale ad assicurare la prima e la seconda dimensione della libertà a scapito della terza, l'approccio stato-centrico,vuoi nella versione dell'economia mista vuoi in quella del socialismo di mercato, tende a privilegiare la seconda e la terza dimensione a scapito della prima. Il liberismo è bensì capace di far da volano del mutamento, ma non è altrettanto capace di gestirne le conseguenze negative, dovute all'elevata asimmetria temporale tra la distribuzione dei costi del mutamento e quella dei benefici. I primi sono immediati e tendono a ricadere sui segmenti più sprovveduti della popolazione; i secondi si verificano in seguito nel tempo e vanno a beneficiare i soggetti con maggiore talento. Come J. Schumpeter fu tra i primi a riconoscere, è il meccanismo della distruzione creatrice il cuore del sistema capitalistico – il quale distrugge 'il vecchio' per creare 'il nuovo' e crea 'il nuovo' per distruggere 'il vecchio'– ma anche il suo tallone d'Achille. D'altro canto, il socialismo di mercato – nelle sue plurime versioni – se propone lo Stato come soggetto incaricato di far fronte alle asincronie di cui si è detto, non intacca la logica del mercato capitalistico; ma restringe solamente l'area di operatività e di incidenza. Il *proprium* del paradigma del bene comune, invece, è il tentativo di fare stare insieme tutte e tre le dimensioni della libertà. Ecco perché esso appare come una prospettiva quanto meno interessante da esplorare e per la quale è ragionevole impegnarsi con la realizzazione di opere.

FRATERNITÀ E BENI DI GRATUITÀ

La seconda conseguenza pratica dell'ingresso dell'amore nella vita economica riguarda la ripresa di un antico principio, quello di fraternità. Per fissare le idee, la fraternità è il principio di organizzazione sociale che consente agli uguali di essere diversi, consentendo loro di realizzare il proprio piano di vita ovvero la propria vocazione. (Si badi a non confondere differenza con diversità: la prima si oppone a eguaglianza; la seconda si oppone a uniformità. Ecco perché si può essere eguali e diversi; mentre non si potrebbe essere eguali e diseguali.)

É merito grande della cultura europea quello di aver saputo declinare, in termini sia istituzionali sia economici, il principio di fraternità facendolo diventare un asse portante dell'ordine sociale. É stata la scuola di pensiero francescana a dare a questo termine il significato che essa ha conservato nel corso del tempo. Ci sono pagine della Regola di Francesco che aiutano bene a comprendere il senso proprio del principio di fraternità. Che è quello di costituire, ad un tempo, il complemento e il superamento del principio di solidarietà. Infatti mentre la solidarietà è il principio di organizzazione sociale che consente ai diseguali di diventare eguali, il principio di fraternità è quel principio di organizzazione sociale che consente – come detto – agli eguali di esser diversi. La fraternità consente a persone che sono eguali nella loro dignità e nei loro diritti fondamentali di esprimere diversamente il loro piano di vita, o il loro carisma. Le stagioni che abbiamo lasciato alle spalle, l'800 e soprattutto il '900, sono state caratterizzate da grosse battaglie, sia culturali sia politiche, in nome della solidarietà e questa è stata cosa buona; si pensi alla storia del movimento sindacale e alla lotta per la conquista dei diritti civili. Il punto è che la buona società non può accontentarsi dell'orizzonte della solidarietà, perché una società che fosse solo solidale, e non anche fraterna, sarebbe una società dalla quale ognuno cercherebbe di allontanarsi. Il fatto è che mentre la società fraterna è anche una società solidale, il viceversa non è vero.

Non solo, ma dove non c'è gratuità non può esserci speranza. La gratuità, infatti, non è una virtù etica, come lo è la giustizia. Essa riguarda la dimensione sovraetica dell'agire umano; la sua logica è quella della sovrabbondanza. La logica della giustizia, invece, è quella dell'equivalenza, come già Aristotele insegnava. Capiamo allora perché la speranza non possa ancorarsi alla giustizia. In una società, per ipotesi, solo perfettamente giusta non vi sarebbe spazio per la speranza. Cosa potrebbero mai sperare i suoi cittadini? Non così in una società dove il principio di fraternità fosse riuscito a mettere radici profonde, proprio perché la speranza si nutre di sovrabbondanza.

Si pensi, per considerare un solo esempio, all'ampio dibattito, ancora lungi dall'essere concluso, sul 'big trade-off' – per richiamare il titolo del celebre libro di Arthur Okun del 1975 – tra efficienza e equità (o giustizia distributiva). É preferibile favorire l'una o l'altra; vale a dire, è meglio dilatare lo spazio di azione del principio dello scambio di equivalenti, che mira appunto all'efficienza, oppure attribuire più poteri di intervento allo Stato affinché questi migliori la distribuzione del reddito? Ancora: a quanta efficienza si deve rinunciare per migliorare i risultati sul fronte dell'equità? E così via. Interrogativi del genere hanno riempito (e riempiono) le agende di studio di schiere di economisti e di scienziati sociali, con risultati pratici piuttosto modesti, a dire il vero. La ragione principale di ciò non è certo nella carenza dei dati empirici o nell'inadeguatezza degli strumenti di analisi a disposizione. Piuttosto, la ragione è che questa letteratura si è dimenticata del principio di reciprocità, del principio cioè il cui fine proprio è quello di tradurre in pratica la cultura della fraternità. Aver dimenticato il fatto che non è sostenibile una società di umani in cui si estingue il senso di fraternità e in cui tutto si riduce, per un verso, a migliorare le transazioni basate sullo scambio di equivalenti e, per l'altro verso, a aumentare i trasferimenti attuati da strutture assistenziali di natura pubblica , ci dà conto del perché, nonostante la qualità delle forze intellettuali in campo, non si sia ancora addivenuti ad una soluzione credibile di quel trade-off. Non è capace di futuro la società in cui si dissolve il principio di fraternità; non è cioè capace di progredire quella società in cui esiste solamente il 'dare per avere' oppure il 'dare per dovere'. Ecco perché, né la visione liberal-individualista del mondo, in cui tutto (o quasi) è scambio, né la visione statocentrica della società, in cui tutto (o quasi) è doverosità, sono guide sicure per farci uscire dalle secche in cui le nostre società sono oggi impantanate. (Per un allargamento di discorso rinvio al mio *L'economia del bene comune*, Roma, Città Nuova, 2007.)

Cosa comporta, a livello pratico, l'accoglimento del principio di fraternità entro l'agire economico? Una risposta, sia pure piuttosto indiretta, ci viene dalla considerazione della natura profonda della crisi economico-finanziaria in atto. Due sono i tipi di crisi che, grosso modo, è possibile identificare nella storia delle nostre società: dialettica l'una, entropica l'altra. Dialettica è la crisi che nasce da un conflitto fondamentale che prende corpo entro una determinata società e che contiene, al proprio interno, i germi o le forze del proprio superamento. (Va da sé che non necessariamente l'uscita dalla crisi rappresenta un progresso rispetto alla situazione precedente). Esempi storici e famosi di crisi dialettica sono quelli della rivoluzione americana, della rivoluzione francese, della rivoluzione di ottobre in Russia nel 1917. Entropica, invece, è la crisi che tende a far collassare il sistema, per implosione, senza modificarlo. Questo tipo di crisi si sviluppa ogniqualvolta la società perde il senso – cioè, letteralmente, la direzione – del proprio incedere. Anche di tale tipo di crisi la storia ci offre esempi notevoli: la caduta dell'impero romano; la transizione dal feudalesimo alla modernità; il crollo del muro di Berlino e dell'impero sovietico.

Perchè è importante tale distinzione? Perché sono diverse le strategie di uscita dai due tipi di crisi. Non si esce da una crisi entropica con aggiustamenti di natura tecnica o con provvedimenti solo legislativi e regolamentari – pure necessari – ma affrontando di petto, risolvendola, la questione del senso. Ecco perché sono indispensabili a tale scopo minoranze profetiche che sappiano indicare alla società la nuova direzione verso cui muovere mediante un supplemento di pensiero e soprattutto la testimonianza delle opere. Così è stato quando Benedetto, lanciando il suo celebre 'ora et labora', inaugurò la nuova era, quella delle cattedrali.

Ebbene, la grande crisi economico-finanziaria tuttora in atto è di tipo basicamente entropico. E dunque non è corretto assimilare – se non per gli aspetti meramente quantitativi – la presente crisi a quella del 1929 che fu, piuttosto, di natura dialettica. Quest'ultima, infatti, fu dovuta ad errori umani commessi, soprattutto dalle autorità di

secolo, si afferma gradualmente l'idea del lavoro artigianale, che realizza l'unità tra attività e conoscenza, tra processo produttivo e *mestiere* – termine quest'ultimo che rinvia a maestria. Con l'avvento della rivoluzione industriale prima e del fordismo-taylarismo poi, avanza l'idea della *mansione* (segno di attività parcellizzate), non più del mestiere, e con essa la centralità della libertà *dal* lavoro, come emancipazione dal 'regno della necessità'. E oggi, che siamo entrati nella società post-fordista, che idea abbiamo del lavoro? La civiltà occidentale poggia su una idea forte, l'idea della 'vita buona', da cui il diritto-dovere per ciascuno di progettare la propria vita in vista di una *civile felicità*. Ma da dove partire per conseguire un tale obiettivo se non dal lavoro inteso quale luogo di una buona esistenza? La fioritura umana – cioè l'*eudaimonia* nel senso di Aristotele – non va cercata *dopo* il lavoro, come accadeva ieri, perché l'essere umano incontra la sua umanità *mentre* lavora. Di qui l'urgenza di iniziare ad elaborare il concetto di eudaimonia lavorativa che per un verso vada oltre l'ipertrofia lavorativa tipica dei tempi nostri (il lavoro che riempie un vuoto antropologico crescente) e per l'altro verso valga a declinare l'idea di libertà *del* lavoro (la libertà di scegliere quelle attività che sono in grado di arricchire la mente e il cuore di coloro che sono impegnati nel processo lavorativo).

Chiaramente, l'accoglimento del paradigma eudaimonico implica che i fini dell'impresa – quali che ne sia la forma giuridica – sono irriducibili al solo profitto, pur non escludendolo. Implica dunque che possano nascere e svilupparsi imprese a vocazione civile in grado di superare la propria autoreferenzialità, dilatando così lo spazio della possibilità effettiva di scelta lavorativa da parte delle persone. Non si dimentichi, infatti, che scegliere l'opzione migliore tra quelle di un 'cattivo' insieme di scelta non significa affatto che un individuo si merita ciò che ha scelto. La libertà di scelta fonda il consenso solamente se chi sceglie è posto nella condizione di concorrere alla definizione dell'insieme di scelta stesso. Aver dimenticato il fatto che non è sostenibile una società di umani in cui tutto si riduce, per un verso, a migliorare le transazioni basate sul principio dello scambio di equivalenti e, per l'altro verso, ad agire su trasferimenti di tipo assistenzialistico di natura pubblica, ci dà conto del perché sia così difficile passare dall'idea del lavoro come attività a quella del lavoro come opera.

Infine, di una terza separazione al fondo della crisi attuale mette conto dire. Si tratta di questo. Da sempre la teoria economica sostiene che il successo e il progresso di una società dipendono crucialmente dalla sua capacità di mobilizzare e gestire la conoscenza che esiste, dispersa, tra tutti coloro che ne fanno parte. Infatti, il merito principale del mercato, inteso come istituzione socio-economica, è proprio quello di fornire una soluzione ottimale al problema della conoscenza. Come già F. von Hayek ebbe a chiarire nel suo celebre (e celebrato) saggio del 1937, al fine di incanalare in modo efficace la conoscenza locale, quella cioè di cui sono portatori i cittadini di una società, è necessario un meccanismo decentralizzato di coordinamento, e il sistema dei prezzi di cui il mercato basicamente consta è esattamente quel che serve alla bisogna. Questo modo di vedere le cose, assai comune tra gli economisti, tende tuttavia ad oscurare un elemento di centrale rilevanza.

Invero, il funzionamento del meccanismo dei prezzi come strumento di coordinamento presuppone che i soggetti economici condividano e perciò comprendano la 'lingua' del mercato. Valga un'analogia. Pedoni e automobilisti si fermano di fronte al semaforo che segna il rosso perché condividono il medesimo significato della luce rossa. Se quest'ultima evocasse, per alcuni, l'adesione ad una particolare posizione politica e, per altri, un segnale di pericolo è evidente che nessun coordinamento sarebbe possibile, con le conseguenze che è facile immaginare. L'esempio suggerisce che non uno, ma due, sono i tipi di conoscenza di cui il mercato ha bisogno per assolvere al compito principale di cui sopra si è detto. Il primo tipo è la conoscenza individuale che depositata in ciascun individuo ed è quello che – come bene chiarito dallo stesso F. von Hayek – può essere gestito dai normali meccanismi del mercato. Il secondo tipo di conoscenza, invece, è quella istituzionale ed ha a che vedere con la lingua comune che consente ad una pluralità di individui di condividere i significati delle categorie di discorso che vengono utilizzate e di intendersi reciprocamente quando vengono in contatto.

É un fatto che in qualsiasi società coesistono molti linguaggi diversi, e il linguaggio del mercato è solamente uno di questi. Se questo fosse l'unico, non ci sarebbero problemi: per mobilizzare in modo efficiente la conoscenza locale di tipo individuale basterebbero gli usuali strumenti di mercato. Ma così non è, per la semplice ragione che le società contemporanee sono contesti multi-culturali nei quali la conoscenza di tipo individuale deve viaggiare attraverso confini linguistici ed è questo che pone difficoltà formidabili. Un certo pensiero economico ha potuto prescindere da tale difficoltà assumendo, implicitamente, che il problema della conoscenza di tipo istituzionale di fatto non esistesse, ad esempio perché tutti i membri della società condividono il medesimo sistema di valori e accettano gli stessi principi di organizzazione sociale. Ma quando così non è, come la realtà ci obbliga a prendere atto, si ha che per governare una società 'multi-linguistica' è necessaria un'altra istituzione, diversa dal mercato, che faccia emergere quella lingua di contatto capace di far dialogare i membri appartenenti a diverse comunità linguistiche. Ebbene, questa istituzione è la democrazia. Questo ci aiuta a comprendere perchè il problema della gestione della conoscenza nelle nostre società di oggi, e quindi in definitiva il problema dello sviluppo, postula che due istituzioni – la democrazia e il mercato – siano poste nella condizione di operare congiuntamente, fianco a fianco. Invece, la separazione tra mercato e democrazia che si è andata consumando nel corso dell'ultimo quarto di secolo sull'onda dell'esaltazione di un certo relativismo culturale e di una esasperata mentalità individualistica ha fatto credere – anche a studiosi avvertiti – che fosse possibile espandere l'area del mercato senza preoccuparsi di fare i conti con l'intensificazione della democrazia.

Due le principali implicazioni che ne sono derivate. Primo, l'idea perniciosa secondo cui il mercato sarebbe una zona moralmente neutra che non avrebbe bisogno di sottoporsi ad alcun giudizio etico perché già conterrebbe nel proprio nucleo duro (*hard core*) quei principi morali che sono sufficienti alla sua legittimazione sociale. Al contrario, non essendo in grado di autofondarsi, il mercato per venire in esistenza presuppone che già sia stata elaborata la 'lingua di contatto'. E tale considerazione basterebbe a sconfiggere da sola ogni pretesa di autoreferenzialità. Secondo, se la democrazia, che è un bene fragile, va soggetta a lento degrado, può accadere che il mercato sia impedito di raccogliere e gestire in modo efficiente la conoscenza, e quindi può accadere che la società cessi di progredire, senza che ciò avvenga per un qualche difetto dei meccanismi del mercato, bensì per un deficit di democrazia. Ebbene, la crisi economico-finanziaria in corso – una crisi di natura appunto entropica e non dialettica – è la migliore e più cocente conferma empirica di tale proposizione. Se le preposizioni del mercato sono *senza – contro – sopra* (senza gli altri; contro gli altri; sopra gli altri), quelle della democrazia sono *con-per-in* (con gli altri; per gli altri; negli altri). In definitiva, abbiamo bisogno di ricongiungere mercato e democrazia per scongiurare il duplice pericolo dell'individualismo e dello statalismo centralistico. Si ha individualismo quando ogni membro della società vuol essere il tutto; si ha centralismo quando a voler essere il tutto è un singolo componente. Nell'un caso si esalta a tal punto la diversità da far morire l'unità del consorzio umano; nell'altro caso, per affermare l'uniformità si sacrifica la diversità. Comprendiamo ora perché il principio di fraternità, vero e proprio asse portante dell'identità europea, rivesta un ruolo così centrale per il progresso morale e civile della società.

L'ETICA DELLE VIRTÙ MESSA ALLA PROVA

Un modo di apprezzare la fecondità dei principi del bene comune e di fraternità, di cui si è sopra scritto, è quello di metterli su un particolare banco di prova, quello riguardante il ruolo delle virtù nel disegno dell'assetto istituzionale della società.

Come noto, tre sono i tipi di norme di cui le società, di ogni tempo e luogo, abbisognano per la loro sostenibilità: le norme legali, espressione del potere coercitivo dello stato, la cui esecutorietà è legata a ben definiti sistemi di punizioni; le norme sociali, che sono il precipitato di convenzioni e tradizioni più o meno antiche, e la cui esecutorietà dipende dalla vergogna che sempre accompagna la stigmatizzazione di comportamenti devianti (perdita di status e discriminazione sociale); le norme morali, associate alla prevalenza di ben definiti matrici culturali (di tipo religioso) e non, la cui violazione fa scattare negli individui il senso di colpa. É all'antropologa americana Ruth Benedict che si deve la distinzione tra civiltà della vergogna e civiltà della colpa[1] e l'affermazione del pensiero per cui il passaggio dalla prima alla seconda ha rappresentato un autentico progresso morale. Ce ne dà ragione il ben noto filosofo american Bernard Williams, quando scrive che mentre 'le esperienze primitive della vergogna hanno a che fare con la vista e con l'essere visto', la colpa pone 'le sue radici nell'ascolto', nel sentir 'risuonare in se stessi la voce del giudizio'.[2]

Quale il nesso fra le tre tipologie di norme? Che se le leggi che vengono promulgate 'marciano contro' le norme sociali e, ancor più, contro le norme morali prevalenti nella società, non solamente le prime non produrranno i risultati desiderati, in quanto non saranno rispettate per la semplice ragione che non è certo possibile sanzionare tutti i loro violatori, ma quel che è peggio andranno a minare le credibilità e/o l'accettabilità delle altre due categorie di norme, minacciando così la stabilità dell'ordine sociale stesso. É quel che succede con quelle che oggi si chiamano 'inexpressive laws', cioè leggi che non riescono ad esprimere quei valori che sorreggono l'architettura di una determinata società. Ancor oggi purtroppo la teoria economica è muta circa le relazioni esistenti fra i tre tipi di norme. Salvo rarissime occasioni, la divisione del lavoro intellettuale è tale che economisti e giuristi si occupano solo di leggi; i sociologi soltanto di norme sociali e gli eticisti di norme morali. Non è allora difficile darsi conto del perché gran parte delle norme giuridiche siano così 'inexpressive'.

Volgendo ora l'attenzione ai sistemi motivazionali che presiedono ai comportamenti degli individui, si è soliti distinguere tra motivazioni estrinseche (compio una certa azione per il vantaggio, monetario o di altro tipo, che ne ricavo); intrinseche (la mia azione ha per me un valore non strumentale e quindi mi assicura una remunerazione appunto intrinseca); trascendenti (realizzo una certa opera perché desidero che altri ne traggano vantaggio; in altro modo, perché voglio coscientemente produrre esternalità positive). Dalla prevalenza nelle persone dell'uno o dell'altro tipo di motivazione discendono i comportamenti che si osservano nella realtà: antisociali (è tale, ad esempio, il comportamento dell'invidioso che trae vantaggio dalle disgrazie altrui e che è pertanto disposto a sostenere costi specifici per conseguire questo scopo); asociali (quello dell'*homo oeconomicus* che si propone né di danneggiare né di avvantaggiare gli altri, avendo preferenze individualistiche, è interessato solamente al proprio io); prosociali (l'altruista più o meno razionale; l'*homo reciprocans*; colui che pratica il dono come gratuità e così via).

Come la storia insegna e l'esperienza quotidiana conferma, i tre tratti comportamentali sono sempre presenti nelle società di umani, quale che essa sia. Quel che muta da una società all'altra è la combinazione: in alcune fasi storiche prevalgono comportamenti antisociali e/o asociali, in altre quelli prosociali, con esiti sul piano economico e su quello del progresso civile che è facile immaginare. (Per fare un esempio di grande attualità, si pensi al modello della *commons-based peer production*, di cui la forma più nota è quella del progetto Wikepedia, un fenomeno di cooperazione sociale il cui successo sarebbe stato impossibile immaginare ancora una decina di anni fa. La produzione tra pari è un modello sociale di produzione caratterizzato da due elementi. Il primo è la decentralizzazione; il secondo è che non sono i prezzi né i comandi ad indurre all'azione una pluralità di soggetti partecipanti, ma le motivazioni intrinseche e trascendenti.) Si pone la domanda: da cosa dipende che in una data società, in una data epoca storica, la composizione organica dei tratti comportamentali sia dell'un tipo o dell'altro? Ebbene, è quando si giunge a porsi interrogativi del genere che si riesce ad apprezzare il grande merito dell'intuizione di Giacinto Dragonetti illuminista napoletano, autore nel 1766 del celebre *Delle virtù e dei premi:* il fattore decisivo, anche se non unico, è il modo in cui si arriva alla costruzione dell'apparato legislativo. Se il legislatore, facendo propria una antropologia di tipo hobbesiano, secondo cui l'uomo è un ente malvagio fin nello stato di natura e quindi è un soggetto tendenzialmente antisociale, confeziona norme che caricano sulle spalle di tutti i cittadini pesanti sanzioni e punizioni allo scopo di assicurarne la esecutorietà, è evidente che i cittadini prosociali (e anche quelli asociali), che non avrebbero certo bisogno di quei deterrenti, non riusciranno a sopportare a lungo il peso conseguente e quindi, sia pure *obtorto collo*, tenderanno a modificare per via endogena il proprio sistema motivazionale.

É questo il cosiddetto meccanismo del *crowding out* (spiazzamento): leggi di marca hobbesiana tendono a far aumentare nella popolazione la percentuale delle motivazioni estrinseche e quindi ad accrescere la diffusione dei comportamenti di tipo antisociale. Un'idea questa che già Platone aveva anticipato quando scriveva: 'Le persone buone non hanno bisogno delle leggi che dicano loro di agire in modo responsabile; mentre le persone cattive troveranno sempre un modo per eludere le leggi'. Proprio perchè i tipi antisociali non sono poi così tanto disturbati dal costo dell'*enforcement* delle norme legali, dal momento che cercheranno in tutti i modi di eluderle. Nella celebre opera *Memorie di Adriano* di Marguerite Yourcenar si legge:

> Credo poco alle leggi. Se troppo dure, si trasgrediscono e con ragione. Se troppo complicate, l'ingegnosità umana riesce facilmente ad insinuarsi entro le maglie di questa massa fragile ... La maggior parte delle nostre leggi penali – e forse è un bene – non raggiungono che un'esigua parte dei colpevoli; quelle civili non saranno mai tanto duttili da adattarsi all'immensa e fluida varietà dei fatti. Esse mutano meno rapidamente dei costumi; pericolose quando sono in ritardo, ancor più quando presumono di anticiparli.

Possiamo ora apprezzare appieno la posizione di Dragonetti quando scrive:

> Un altro mezzo di prevenire i delitti è quello di ricompensare le virtù. Su di questo proposito osservo un silenzio universale nelle leggi di tutte le nazioni del dì d'oggi. Se i premi proposti dalle Accademie ai discopritori di utili verità hanno moltiplicato e le cognizioni e i buoni libri, perché i premi distribuiti dalla benefica mano del sovrano non moltiplicherebbero altresì le azioni virtuose? La moneta dell'onore è sempre inesausta e fruttifera nelle mani del saggio distributore.

É difficile trovare, nel XVIII secolo, pensatori più chiari e lungimiranti del Nostro sul tema in discussione. Si confronti tale brano con quello corrispondente di Beccaria in *Dei delitti e delle pene* del 1765: 'Le leggi sono condizioni colle quali uomini indipendenti e isolati si unirono in società, stanchi di vivere in un continuo stato di guerra, e di godere una libertà resa inutile dall'incertezza di conservarla. Essi ne sacrificarono una parte per goderne il restante con sicurezza e tranquillità'. É agevole constatare l'applicazione, in tale brano,della linea di pensiero hobbesiana quale emerge sia dal *De Cive* (1642) sia dal *Leviatano* (1651), le due grandi opere del filosofo inglese. In definitiva, il punto importante è che una società che offre opportunità per esercitare il comportamento virtuoso è una società che rende possibile la proliferazione di soggetti virtuosi.

L'argomentazione di cui sopra abbisogna tuttavia di una qualificazione importante, che concerne la distinzione tra premio e incentivo. Nonostante la confusione di pensiero che, complice la manualistica corrente di economia, continua a circolare, notevoli sono le differenze tra questi due concetti che vengono presi come sinonimi. (Si tenga presente che una sanzione o una punizione sono un incentivo col segno meno, cioè un disincentivo.) Ne indico alcune, quelle più significative ai fini del presente discorso. Primo, con l'incentivo il principale di una qualsivoglia relazione di agenzia induce il suo agente – si pensi al rapporto tra impresa e dirigenti; tra il responsabile di una organizzazione e i suoi stretti collaboratori; tra un genitore e il figlio – ad operare nell'interesse *privato* del principale. In altro modo, fine ultimo dello schema di incentivo è quello di allineare l'interesse dell'agente con quello del principale. Nel caso dell'impresa, questo significa assumere che l'interesse personale dell'amministratore coincide con quello di coloro per conto dei quali agisce (gli azionisti). Non così con il premio, che, invece, mira al *bene comune*. 'Il premio – scrive Dragonetti – è il vincolo necessario per legare l'interesse particolare col generale, e per tenere gli uomini sempre intenti al bene'.

In secondo luogo, la struttura formale dell'incentivo è quella di un contratto che, una volta sottoscritto dalle due parti di una relazione di agenzia, diviene vincolante per entrambe anche se è empiricamente accertata la manipolabilità degli incentivi da parte dell'agente. Esso è dunque ex-ante rispetto allo svolgimento dell'azione, e ciò nel senso che i termini contrattuali devono essere noti all'agente prima ancora che questi si ponga all'opera. Al contrario, il premio è ex-post, essendo un atto volontario del principale che, in quanto tale, non istituisce un'obbligazione in capo alle parti. L'essenza del premio è dunque quella del dono come gratuità, mentre l'essenza dell'incentivo è l'attribuzione all'agente di parte del valore aggiunto creato da questi a favore del principale. Ne deriva che la pratica, su larga scala, degli schemi di incentivo, nei più svariati ambiti della vita sociale, tende a lungo andare ad affievolire nella comunità lo spirito del dono, in seguito appunto all'operare di un meccanismo come quello dello spiazzamento.

Terzo, uno degli effetti maggiormente indesiderati dell'impiego degli incentivi è l'erosione del rapporto di fiducia tra principale e agente. Pensiamo ad un qualsiasi esempio di contratto incentivante. É inevitabile che, prima o poi, l'agente si chieda perché mai il suo principale gli offre l'incentivo. Infatti, delle due l'una: se quel che viene chiesto all'agente rientra nei compiti specificati nel contratto di lavoro (o nel contratto d'opera), l'offerta dell'incentivo costituisce il prezzo che il principale paga per la mancata fiducia nell'integrità morale del suo agente; se invece all'agente si chiede di fare di più rispetto a quanto previsto dal contratto oppure di fare qualcosa che viola il codice di moralità mercantile, allora l'incentivo si configura o come forma di parziale sfruttamento dello sforzo extra compiuto dall'agente – nel primo caso – oppure come il pagamento versato per indurre l'agente a vincere le sue resistenze morali – nel secondo caso, che è quello oggi più frequente. (Si pensi all'incentivo rappresentato dalla concessione di stock options al top manager delle grandi imprese finanziarie per indurre quest'ultimo a fare ciò che diversamente mai farebbe, come la recente crisi ha dimostrato *ad abundantiam.*) In entrambi i casi, quel che si va a produrre è una perdita dell'autostima (la *self-esteem* di cui parlava Adam Smith nella sua *Teoria dei sentimenti morali* del 1759) da parte dell'agente – il manager di una banca che per incassare l'incentivo inganna il cliente che gli chiede consiglio circa l'acquisto di prodotti finanziari, perde la stima in sé e alla fine il proprio benessere spirituale – e soprattutto l'erosione del capitale fiduciario. E come si sa, senza fiducia non può esserci sopravvivenza dell'economia di mercato. Nulla di tutto ciò accade col premio che, invece, accrescendo l'autostima, rafforza il legame sociale. (Il figlio che, impegnandosi molto nello studio, riceve, alla fine del percorso scolastico, il premio del genitore rafforza la fiducia in sé e quindi sarà pronto per ulteriori sfide.) Non così, invece, il giovane che 'negozia' col genitore l'incentivo in una forma del tipo 'se sarai promosso con una certa media, otterrai *X*; con un'altra media, otterrai *Y*'. Il giovane attribuirà verosimilmente l'offerta dell'incentivo al fatto che il proprio genitore conosce la sua indole pigra oppure la sua modesta capacità di apprendimento. In situazioni del genere, l'effetto indiretto negativo dell'incentivo, che opera sul sistema motivazionale del giovane oppure sulla sua costituzione morale, dominerà l'effetto diretto positivo che invece opera sullo sforzo profuso nello studio: il giovane studia di più, ma impara di meno, perché come ricordava Goëthe 'si apprende solo ciò che si ama'.

Di un'ultima differenza tra incentivi e premi mette conto di dire. É vero che nel breve periodo l'uso di incentivi può aumentare la produttività e può comportare un abbassamento dei costi di gestione. Un esempio proposto da Dari-Mattiacci e De Greet in un recente raffinato studio[3] fa al caso in questione. Un dittatore tiene sotto scacco la popolazione del suo paese con la minaccia (incentivo negativo) assicurata da un solo proiettile: il primo che oserà ribellarsi verrà ucciso. Con il costo di un solo proiettile, il dittatore riesce pertanto a conservare il proprio potere. Cosa succederebbe, invece, se, anziché l'incentivo (negativo), il dittatore volesse adottare un sistema di premi a favore di tutti coloro che, non ribellandosi, accettano la perdita della democrazia? Che il costo di implementazione di un tale sistema diverrebbe proibitivo. Di qui la conclusione sopra riferita: i premi sono troppo costosi da gestire. Il che è quanto la teoria economica *mainstream* insegna ancora oggi.

Cosa contesterebbe un Dragonetti agli autori dell'esempio? Per un verso, che il modello da loro elaborato si regge sull'assunto antropologico secondo cui tutti i soggetti sono individualisti ed edonisti. Il che non è, perché, come sopra indicato, non è empiricamente vero che tutti i soggetti che operano nel mercato sono mossi all'azione da motivazioni estrinseche; ci sono infatti anche i prosociali che, avendo motivazioni trascendenti, sono pronti a sacrificarsi per gli altri o per un'ideale. Solo chi non conosce la storia degli uomini potrebbe negare questo. Per l'altro verso, che è proprio l'impiego a lungo andare di incentivi a modificare, in una certa direzione, la struttura motivazionale delle persone, cambiandone il sistema di valori. L'uomo, ci confermano le neuro-scienze, è l'animale più capace di adattamento all'ambiente in cui vive: se questo è 'tenuto su' con gli incentivi è ovvio che, a lungo andare, anche la sua mente comincerà a funzionare secondo un meccanismo omeostatico di adattamento. Un punto questo che il grande economista Alfred Marshall aveva già compreso alla fine dell'Ottocento, quando osservava che l'impresa, prima ancora di essere luogo di produzione di beni e servizi, è luogo di formazione del carattere di chi in essa lavora: a seconda di come l'impresa viene organizzata, si formeranno uomini di un tipo o dell'altro.

Gli incentivi creano sempre, tanto o poco, dipendenza – ed è per questo che sono inflazionistici: basti guardare alle remunerazioni del top management di oggi e confrontarle con quelle del top management di alcuni decenni fa – e abbassano i costi personali della tentazione – ed è per questo che generano effetti perversi. Non è così con i premi. Ecco perché Dragonetti può scrivere: 'Essendo le virtù un prodotto non del comando della legge [né del contratto], ma della libera nostra volontà, non ha su di esse la società diritto veruno. La virtù per verun conto non entra nel contratto sociale; e se si lascia senza premio, la società *commette un'ingiustizia* simile a quella di chi defrauda l'altrui sudore' (corsivo aggiunto).

L'EMERGENZA, OGGI, DELLA PROSPETTIVA DELL'ECONOMIA CIVILE

Quanto sono venuto fin qui dicendo mi porta, in conclusione, ad abbozzare i tratti di differenziazione tra il programma di ricerca dell'economia politica – oggi ancora dominante – e quello dell'economia civile – oggi in costante ascesa.

É alla sintesi smithiana – l'Adam Smith sia della *Teoria dei sentimenti morali* (1759) sia della *Ricchezza delle Nazioni* (1776) – che si deve la prima e più compiuta elaborazione del paradigma dell'economia politica. Dei tre principi regolativi che stanno a fondamento di ogni ordine sociale, il programma di ricerca scientifica dell'economia politica prende in considerazione solamente i primi due: il principio dello scambio di equivalenti (di valore) che ha come fine ultimo quello di assicurare l'efficiente allocazione delle risorse e il principio di redistribuzione la cui mira è l'equità sociale (da non confondersi con l'egualitarismo). Efficienza significa che le risorse produttive, sia esse quelle del capitale o del lavoro, non vengono sprecate (come accade nel caso della disoccupazione) né male utilizzate. Equità significa dare a tutti la possibilità di partecipare al gioco economico di mercato, il che avviene dotando ciascuno di un adeguato potere d'acquisto. Un'economia di mercato, infatti, non è sostenibile nella prospettiva della durata se è capace solamente di produrre ricchezza; deve anche saperla distribuire tra tutti coloro che hanno preso parte al processo della sua creazione.

É da questa concettualizzazione che discende il cosiddetto modello dicotomico Stato-mercato. Al mercato si chiede di provvedere all'efficienza massima nell'uso delle risorse, cioè di produrre quanta più ricchezza possibile, date le condizioni di contesto: a ciò deve mirare il processo di libero scambio che, proprio per questo, deve sottostare ai canoni della *giustizia commutativa*. Allo Stato si chiede di intervenire sia per porre rimedio ai cosiddetti 'fallimenti del mercato' sia per assicurare la *giustizia distributiva* nel momento in cui si pone mano al taglio della torta (il PIL). Se l'accento o le preoccupazioni vengono poste, in prevalenza, sul momento della produzione della ricchezza si sarà liberali, secondo una versione o l'altra del liberalismo; se invece l'accento è principalmente sulla distribuzione della ricchezza si sarà socialisti o riformisti, anche qui in forme e gradi diversi a seconda delle propensioni ideologiche.

Ciò che accomuna tutte le molteplici scuole di pensiero del programma di ricerca dell'economia politica – da quella classica a quella neoclassica, da quella keynesiana a quella neo-istituzionalista o a quella austriaca – è la trascuranza del terzo principio di un ordine sociale cui sopra alludevo: quello di reciprocità, un principio che mira a tradurre in pratica il principio di fraternità. Ebbene, il programma di ricerca dell'economia civile si caratterizza proprio per la sua capacità di tenere insieme tutti e tre i principi di cui ho detto e ciò sia nella fase costituzionale – la fase cioè in cui si pone mano al disegno istituzionale dell'organizzazione economica della società – sia nella fase post-costituzionale, quella in cui concretamente si svolge il gioco economico. A scanso di equivoci, conviene precisare che anche agli studiosi dell'economia politica non sfugge la rilevanza nella pratica del principio di reciprocità. Tuttavia, il punto da sottolineare è che per costoro la pratica della reciprocità nulla ha a che vedere con la sfera economica, al cui buon funzionamento basterebbero i contratti (possibilmente completi) e le norme giuridiche (possibilmente ben fatte). Lo spazio per la pratica della reciprocità è quello della famiglia, dell'associazionismo, del mondo del non profit. I corpi intermedi della società – come sono indicati all'art. 2 della nostra Carta Costituzionale – sono considerati da tali studiosi tanto importanti per il progresso culturale e morale del paese, quanto irrilevanti per il suo successo economico.

Altrove mi sono occupato di chiarire a fondo le differenze tra i due programmi di ricerca e di indicarne le rispettive matrici storiche.[4] Qui mi limito a ricordare che quella dell'economia civile è una linea di pensiero esclusivamente italiana che nasce nell'età dell'Umanesimo Civile (XV secolo), quando l'economia di mercato, come oggi la conosciamo, inizia a prendere forma e prosegue fino alla prima metà del secolo XVIII con i contributi, veramente notevoli, degli illuministi della scuola sia napoletana (Antonio Genovesi – cui si deve l'invenzione dell'espressione 'economia civile' nel 1753 – Ferdinando Galiani, Giacinto Dragonetti) sia milanese (Pietro Verri, Cesare Beccaria, Giandomenico Romagnosi, Melchorre Gioja). A partire dalla fine del Settecento, grazie all'enorme influenza del pensiero smithiano, l'economia civile viene soppiantata e totalmente emarginata dall'economia politica. É solo nell'ultimo ventennio che, per tutta una serie di ragioni che ho illustrato altrove, si assiste ad una lenta ma robusta ripresa, nella ricerca scientifica e soprattutto nell'agire economico, della prospettiva dell'economia civile.

Invero, se all'agire di mercato si toglie la dimensione della reciprocità (e dunque il principio del dono, che è il *primum movens* della relazione di reciprocità), così che quello economico diventa un gigantesco gioco del dilemma del prigioniero, è ovvio che nelle fasi avverse del ciclo economico non vi sia altra soluzione per spezzare il circolo vizioso che quella di ricorrere alla potenza dello Stato. Il quale diviene il surrogatore della mancanza di fiducia generalizzata mediante l'attivazione di ben precisi programmi di spesa pubblica. Esemplare a tale riguardo l'atteggiamento di Roosevelt, che pur non essendo affatto un keynesiano convinto, nel suo primo discorso presidenziale del marzo 1933, allo scopo di rimettere in moto la macchina che la crisi del '29 aveva bloccato, deve promettere che lo Stato in persona si assumerà il compito 'di dare un lavoro alla gente ... Questo compito può essere assolto grazie a un reclutamento da parte dello Stato stesso'.[5] Ma sono le pratiche di reciprocità a creare, dal basso e per via endogena, i legami fiduciari senza i quali il mercato non può funzionare; non certo lo Stato. Ecco perché lo statalismo è una 'mala bestia', secondo la celebre espressione sturziana.

Una specifica circostanza ha contribuito non poco a riammettere nell'universo del discorso economico il principio di reciprocità e quindi la categoria dell'amore. Si tratta del cosiddetto paradosso della felicità, noto anche come paradosso di Easterlin, dal nome dello studioso americano che per primo ne diffuse la conoscenza a metà degli anni Settanta. Già Pascal aveva ricordato: 'Tutti gli uomini cercano di essere felici, senza eccezioni, e tutti tendono a questo fine, sebbene diversi siano i mezzi che usano ... Ecco, questo è il motivo di tutte le azioni di tutti gli uomini, finanche di quelli che s'immpiccano' (*Pensieri*, n. 425). Ora, fintanto che la teoria economica ha potuto far credere che 'essere' felici fosse la stessa cosa che 'avere' la felicità, essa è riuscita a contrabbandare l'utilità per la felicità e dunque a persuadere che massimizzare l'utilità fosse operazione non solo razionale, ma anche ragionevole, espressione cioè di saggezza.

I nodi sono giunti al pettine quando si è scoperto, per via empirica e non già per via deduttiva, che la relazione tra reddito pro capite – quale indicatore sintetico, sia pur rozzo, del livello di utilità – e benessere soggettivo è rappresentabile mediante una curva a forma di *U* rovesciata (una parabola con la concavità verso l'alto): oltre un certo livello, l'aumento del reddito pro capite diminuisce il benessere soggettivo. Non intendo qui soffermarmi sulle spiegazioni – che ormai sono tante – del paradosso in questione, da quelle psicologiche, basate sugli effetti di *treadmill*, a quelle economiche, centrate sulle esternalità posizionali, a quelle sociologiche, focalizzate sulla nozione di bene relazionale. La letteratura è assai ampia e rinvio per tutti a Bruni (2004), che opportunamente non manca di annotare come già Aristotele aveva associato la vita buona (*eudaimonia*) alla vita di relazione e cioè alla disponibilità di beni relazionali (amicizia, amore, impegno civile, fiducia, etc.).

PER CONCLUDERE

Altrove mi sono occupato delle caratteristiche peculiari del bene relazionale e del suo significato nelle nostre società avanzate (Zamagni, 2005). Qui desidero aggiungere che la ragione principale per la quale il paradigma individualista mai riuscirà a trattare in modo adeguato la categoria dei beni relazionali è che, per tali beni, è il rapporto in sé a costituire il bene e dunque la relazione intersoggettiva non esiste indipendentemente dal bene che si produce *e* si consuma al tempo stesso. Ciò significa che la conoscenza dell'identità dell'altro con cui mi rapporto è indispensabile perché si abbia il bene relazionale. Al contrario, il presupposto della relazione di scambio di equivalenti – che è la sola relazione, oltre a quella di filantropia, di cui può trattare l'approccio individualista – è che sia *sempre* possibile sostituire colui o coloro dai quali dipende il mio star bene. (Posso sempre cambiare macellaio tutte le volte in cui non sono soddisfatto di quello abituale. Ma non posso certo sostituire il soggetto che mi fornisce un servizio personale con altro soggetto senza registrare una variazione del mio indice di felicità.) Come Wicksteed (1910) aveva lucidamente compreso, è il non tuismo (*non-tuism*) più ancora che il *self-interest*, il fondamento primo del mercato capitalistico, perché gli affari si fanno al meglio con coloro di cui non si conosce l'identità personale! Nella prospettiva relazionale, invece, il rapporto con l'altro presuppone un movimento di riconoscimento e di accoglienza: si tratta di accogliere una presenza che, nella sua umanità è a me comune e nella sua alterità è da me distinta. Compito non facile, certo – 'L'inferno sono gli altri' diceva a proposito J. P. Sartre – ma indispensabile se si vuole superare la grave scarsità di beni relazionali, tipica della nostra società. L'individualismo è un'ottima guida per l'utilità che dipende da beni e servizi che possono esser fruiti anche in isolamento; ma un cattivo maestro per la felicità, dato che bisogna *essere* almeno in due per sperimentare la felicità. Proprio come ci rammenta il testo biblico: 'Non è *bene* che l'uomo sia solo'.

Ciò significa che ho bisogno dell'altro per scoprire che vale la pena che io mi conservi; anzi che fiorisca nel senso dell'*eudamonia* aristotelica. Ma anche l'altro ha bisogno di essere da me riconosciuto come qualcuno che è bene che fiorisca. Poiché abbiamo bisogno del medesimo riconoscimento, io agirò nei confronti dell'altro come davanti ad uno specchio. La realizzazione del sé è il risultato di tale interazione. La risorsa originale che posso mettere a disposizione di chi mi sta di fronte è la capacità di riconoscere il valore dell'altro all'esistenza, una risorsa che non può essere prodotta se non viene condivisa. É importante prendere atto di ciò che implica il riconoscimento dell'altro: non solo del suo *diritto* ad esistere ma anche della *necessità* che esista perché possa esistere io, in relazione con lui. Riconoscere l'altro come fine in sé e riconoscerlo come mezzo rispetto al fine della propria realizzazione tornano così ad essere unificati. Con il che viene risolto il dualismo riduzionista fra una moralità, di marca kantiana, che esige che l'altro venga visto come fine in sé e basta e una teoria della razionaltà strumentale che invece vede nell'altro il mezzo per il proprio fine. Il bene dell'autorealizzazione è raggiunto quando il riconoscimento reciproco tra persone è assicurato. Si badi – a scanso di equivoci – che il fatto che il riconoscimento dell'altro porti con sé il riconoscimento reciproco di cui io pure abbisogno non rende tale disposizione meramente strumentale. Infatti, il sé è costituito anche dal riconoscimento che l'altro gli conferisce. Alla luce di ciò, la stessa relazione mezzi-fini si svuota di significato, perché la capacità che un soggetto ha di calcolare i mezzi richiesti per conseguire un determinato fine dipende dalla relazione di reciproco riconoscimento che si è instaurata tra quel soggetto e gli altri.

NOTES

1 R. Benedict, *Il crisantemo e la spada*, Dedalo, Bari, 1968 (1946).

2 B. Williams, *Vergogna e necessità*, Bologna, Il Mulino, 2007.

3 Citato in E. Carbonara, 'Incentivi e premi', *Dizionario di Economia Civile*, L. Bruni e S. Zamagni, cit.

4 Si veda L. Bruni e S. Zamagni, *Civil Economy,* Oxford: P. Long, 2007; Bologna, Il Mulino, 2004; L. Bruni e S. Zamagni, a cura di, *Dizionario di economia civile*, Roma, Città Nuova, 2009; L. Bruni, L. Becchetti, S. Zamagni, *Microeconomia. Un testo di economia civile*, Bologna: Il Mulino, 2010.

5 F. D. Roosevelt, *The Roosevelt Reader*, a cura di B. Rauch, New York, Winston, 1957, p. 92. Si pensi alla creazione della Civil Works Administration, alla Federal Emergency Relief Administration, alla Works Progress Administration, ecc.

THE EUCHARIST: APOSTOLICITY OF COMMUNION

REV. DR OLIVER TREANOR
St Patrick's College, Maynooth

Recent magisterial statements give reason for renewed interest in the idea of apostolicity by coupling it with Eucharist.[1] Normally we predicate apostolicity of the Church as the creed does, or of ministry or ecclesiastical structures. But to focus on the apostolic nature of the Eucharist as a consideration in itself is something of a directional innovation. Even if the papal intention was to underscore the requirement of ordination for the celebration of the Mass, the Eucharist's specific apostolicity is still worth reflecting on for its own sake. Not only is this aspect of the faith interwoven with every other (the *nexus mysteriorum*); not only, therefore, does it shed light on the whole (as every article of faith does); it brings to the deposit of faith a unifying clarity that emanates from the Eucharist's central and constitutive place in the revelation of Christ, Church and salvation. In particular, we might ask how the notion of eucharistic apostolicity illuminates the nature of the Church's relationship to the sacrament of Christ's Body and Blood in terms of the Paschal mystery as a manifestation of the Trinity; and consequently if it has anything to tell us about the nature of that communion which is presupposed by eucharistic sharing and underlies the Church's pastoral mission and motivates it as the universal sacrament of salvation. The aim of this paper then is to investigate what is meant when we speak of the Eucharist in apostolic terms and what implications this may well have for our perception of the Church's apostolicity, both in its local and universal dimensions as the efficacious instrument of the kingdom in its service to the world in this provisional, last age before the final resurrection.

APOSTOLICITY

When we speak of apostolicity we are speaking primarily of tradition, the *process of transmitting* the original first-century witness to the event of salvation, particularly that of the Twelve who formed Jesus' closest band of disciples, including Matthias and not excluding Paul of Tarsus, and those other New Testament authors whose writings are considered inspired and are accepted by the Church. It also refers to the *content* of faith as they passed it on to successive generations, the good news of Jesus Christ. Both aspects are evident in Paul's words to the Christians at Corinth, 'Let me remind you brothers in what terms I preached to you the gospel, which you received ... For I delivered to you as of first importance what I also received, that Christ died ... was buried ... was raised on the third day ... and that he appeared to Cephas, then to the twelve, etc.' (1 Cor 15:1-5). Already – a quarter-century after the Christ event – both the *kerygma* (content) and its transmission (process) are firmly established. It is moreover a *living* tradition: it gives life to people and establishes its own life in the ground that propagates its roots and disseminates its seed. The language used by Paul is that of *personal* giving and receiving: 'You received ... what I preached to you; I delivered to you ... what I also received.' The personal pronouns abound. He is one who has 'received'; he speaks as one who 'delivers', as an original witness to the resurrection, grafted onto the apostolic stock and on par with the Twelve. So the reliability of the gospel is tied to his personal authority as an apostle and is accepted as such by those who acknowledge his apostleship. Henceforth, the originality of what was preached will be preserved by a succession of witnesses faithful to that message and entrusted with its entire transmission through the laying-on of hands as attested by New Testament practice.

Succession therefore ensures continuity, continuity assures authenticity and authenticity guarantees integrity. In other words, the full dynamic of salvation is rendered accessible to those who receive what has been transmitted intact from the first. While this is not additional to *Dei Verbum*'s presentation of revelation, what *is* of interest is that the three key terms which interact with one another in this understanding of apostolicity – content, transmission and person-witness – all lead *directly* to the Eucharist.

APOSTOLICITY AS CONTENT AND TRANSMISSION

Let's take a closer look then at the first two terms, 'content' and 'transmission'. The saving content of Christian faith was never an esoteric body of knowledge, a secret *gnosis* (1 Cor 8:1b-3), but rather the person of the Son of God made flesh. Salvation comes through unity with him who gives access to the Father in the Holy Spirit. Therefore the good news that comprises the gospel is nothing but the Father's gratuitous gift to the world of the incarnation, life, death and resurrection of Jesus Christ. John's Gospel expresses the message with the succinctness of evangelising repetition: 'God so loved the world that he *gave* (*édoken* = as a gift) his only Son, that whoever believes in him should not perish but have eternal life' (3:16). The Letter to the Romans makes the same point, but stronger. Contrasting God's gift with the testing of Abraham (whose son was not required in sacrifice) Paul measures the cost of a love that 'did not spare his own Son but *gave him up* [*parédoken* = delivered up, abandoned him] for us all' (8:32). Furthermore the apostle recognised in Christ's obedience the Son's acceptance of this abandonment and his fullest collaboration in it: 'the Son of God ... loved me and *gave himself* [*paradóntos* = giving himself up] for me' (Gal 2:20c).[2]

Two points emerge from an examination of the language here. First, the verb used for the yielding up of Jesus – *paradidonai* – is the same as the term used for tradition – *paradosis*. In the former instance the Son is delivered into the hands of his enemies (abandoned)[3] for suffering; in the latter he is delivered to the faithful (preached) for their redemption ('for I delivered to you ... '). Christ was handed over *in order* to be handed on; what has been *handed down* is the *Handed-over* One; he was *delivered to* death that all generations might be *delivered from* death. Thus transmission and content are one. Together the content of tradition and the purpose of its transmission constitute a single plan which Paul bears witness to elsewhere as the 'mystery hidden for ages but now revealed *to his holy apostles and prophets* by the Spirit' (Eph 3:5. Cf. Col 1:26-27). This mystery then could not be accomplished without the apostolic tradition any more than it could be accomplished without Christ. His being-handed-down is part of his being-handed-over: it consummates the Father's donation of his Son to all people and completes the Son's cooperation in the giving of himself for all time.

Secondly, the verb *parédoka* (I delivered) is repeated by Paul with reference to the Lord's Supper, the efficacious memorial of the mystery revealed. As before it is part of a fixed formula: 'I received from the Lord what I also delivered to you, that the Lord Jesus on the night when he was betrayed ...' (1 Cor 11:2). 'Betrayed' announces the start of the passion which is commemorated in the Eucharist as the proclamation of 'the Lord's death until he comes' (v. 26). The tradition brought by Paul to Corinth, therefore, is no mere reportage of an incident lost in the past; it is the gospel event itself activated in the form of worship. What was handed down as *kerygma* – the handing over of Jesus, his deliverance up to the cross – is now delivered sacramentally to the evangelised that they might *receive in their hands* the gift handed-over-to-be-handed-on and so participate in the fruits of his sacrifice.[4] It is a process that will continue on into an indeterminate future reaching right up to the eschaton, 'until he comes'; for that final coming is always anticipated and indeed brought about by his many intermediate comings through the ongoing mystery of the eucharistic anamnesis.

What is preached has to be *enacted* for the proclamation to be complete and the fullness of the mystery made present. Christ has to be delivered in every sense – in his handing himself over to the Father's will, in his abandonment by the Father to Calvary *and* in his being passed down from one generation to the next in the form of the Church. Since the Eucharist is the sacrament of his total self-giving, and word and sacrament are inseparable, the *kerygma* finds its realisation in the Church's liturgical action just as Jesus' kenosis found its fullest expression in the breaking of bread and sharing of the cup at the Last Supper, the hermeneutic of his whole life and death. In other words what the gospel promises the Eucharist delivers, vindicating the word and conferring its saving effect wherever the Sacrament is celebrated. Passed down through time it delivers time from its limitations, infiltrating it with the Father's gift and placing the whole of history under the influence of Christ's eternal act. In this way the Spirit of the Paschal mystery is released with power to redeem the past and shape the future and does so in a continuous present that is potent with the victory of the resurrection.

Therefore, it is in the very nature of the Eucharist to be apostolic. It *constitutes the tradition* that extends the one eternal sacrifice and generates communion, particularises[5] the salvation gratuitously offered to all and so substantiates the unifying and saving truth of the gospel. At the same time it preserves down through the Church's many historical manifestations the unique ecclesial reality that is Christ's body, identical in them all. Even more, the Eucharist constitutes *the Church's* apostolicity through which her unity, holiness and Catholicity are revealed existentially and ontologically. *Existentially* the one whom the Church distributes through history is the source of her unity through bodily communion with him; he is the Holy One who sanctifies the Church in the very process of being handed over in the sacramental life; and it is he who provides her with the fullness of the means to salvation by his universal self-giving wherever she is found. Consequently the Church is one, holy and Catholic *in being apostolic* and is apostolic *because* she is eucharistic.[6] To understand better how this is so *ontologically* however, we need to consider the third dimension linking apostolicity directly to the Eucharist, that of person-witness.

APOSTOLICITY AS SUCCESSION

To speak of apostolic tradition – both the content of salvation and the process of handing it on – is to speak ultimately of a succession of historical persons down through the generations in whom the content lives and through whom it is faithfully transmitted. This personal *succession,* however, begins with personal *procession* – that is the procession of the second and third divine persons within the immanent being of the Trinity. Here is the proper starting-point for any attempt to understand what apostolicity means.

Within the inner life of the three-personed God, the Son proceeds from the Father in a timeless process of being generated, as the Father pours out on his beloved Son his own unique substance, the whole divine nature by which the Son is equal to the Father who begets him. In his turn, the Son surrenders back to the Father all that he is in the perfect harmony of filial love. The Holy Spirit too proceeds from the Father and the Son in the manner of spiration, as their mutual breathing as it were, being the intimate bond of charity that unites them in a unity so complete that we profess belief in one God and not three. The mutual indwelling of the three distinct persons, proceeding from and returning to one another in selfless self-emptying, we call *circumincessio* or *perichoresis*, a choreographic movement of eternal giving and receiving, separation and reunion in the joy of their distinctness and inseparability. It is this triune ontology that creates the possibility and is the source of the temporal missions of the second and third persons in God's loving outreach to the world: the Son's mission, sent to bridge the divide between God and sinful humanity as mediator of salvation, and the Spirit's mission to be the mediation of salvation.[7]

Through the passion Christ fulfilled his role by total fidelity to God and total fidelity to sinners without compromising his love for either, *and the Eucharist is the efficacious sign of this*. The effect, as Jean Daniélou puts it, was the death-agony of Calvary, the tearing asunder of the only-begotten 'who bore this division within himself in order to abolish it' so that on the cross 'without leaving the bosom of the Trinity he stretches out to the ultimate limit of human misery and fills the whole space in between'.[8] *The breaking of bread and the pouring of the cup had already anticipated this in prophetic action as a promise which the cross delivered in full.* In this way he brought God and man together, reconciling the difference in the unity of his own person. *Hence the alternative name for the Eucharist – Holy Communion.* What the self-sacrifice of the cross therefore displays in human form before the eyes of the world is both the Son's separation from the Father, which his proceeding from him involves, and his return to the Father in the unbreakable cycle of Trinitarian love – *a truth reflected in the materiality of the eucharistic species and their subsequent disappearance in being consumed.* By manifesting his self-giving in the flesh he obviated the disobedience of fallen mortal nature as the new Adam, the corporate representative of all Adam's sons who, inserted by the Spirit into Christ's Paschal mystery, would now truly become sons of God. And so the historical-horizontal dimension of this event could now be intersected vertically by the outpouring of the Spirit on all humankind. For having offered exiled humanity to God on the cross, Christ had taken humanity back with him, like a true prodigal, to the Father in his perichoretic return as the risen and glorified man in whom all the obstacles to communion had now been overcome, namely time and space, sin and death.

It is in the eucharistic action and eucharistic presence (since Christ's action and being are one) that the future of God's plan is guaranteed and its implicit dependence on an apostolic succession revealed, given the universality of God's salvific will. The Eucharist contains and actualises the personal missions of the Son and the Spirit – the horizontal mission of Christ, the vertical mission of the Paraclete. It represents and activates their missionary purpose: the communion of humanity with the Triune God. By its very definition communion means a history of persons, a body of pilgrims processing through time. Since it is the Spirit's task to unite pilgrims under Christ as head, and Christ's to unite them with the Father, then the Eucharist, superlatively, is where this is done, being the sacrament of the divine self-gift and self-giving: the gift from the Father of his Son *for* the world, the giving by the Son of himself *through* the world, the giving by both of their Spirit *to* the world. And also because it is the sacrament in which the world itself is made to be a gift for God, from God, through God, so that the whole of creation's inter-relational being might be drawn up into the heart of the Trinity, into the life-giving circumincessio of the divine hypostases in whose nature it shares by adoption. This is primarily how the Second Vatican Council, following the Fathers of old, understood the Church: 'A people united in the unity of the Father, the Son and the Holy Spirit':[9] an apostolic people generated and proceeding through history as a communion through the Eucharist, the apostolic fruit of the apostolic missions of God himself.

To carry this project forward to the ends of the earth and the end of time as Jesus intended at the Supper with his significant instruction, 'Do this in remembrance of me' (Lk 22:19; 1 Cor 11:24, 25), a succession of subjects ontologically infused with his life, the life of the Spirit, is necessary – as the Church itself is necessary – and inevitable: first the Twelve, then those who would replace them in time, apostolic witnesses called and chosen from above, anointed and sent by the Spirit, entrusted with the mystery encapsulated by the Eucharist, and empowered to confect the sacrament *in persona Christi* as ministers in service of the New Covenant. For just as the Word of God and the Spirit of God proceed by nature from the Father as divine persons, so this same Word and same Spirit succeed in the work they were sent to do only through a succession of created persons who will act as apostle-witnesses. Neither by human initiative,[10] therefore, nor by fortuitous chance do they become such; but rather by participating in the witness-apostleship of Christ and the Spirit who alone can bear testimony to the truth that the Eucharist contains as the sacrament of salvation.

The New Testament clearly recognised Christ the Word as the proto-typical apostle (meaning One-who-is-sent), the unique witness to truth at its divine source, origin of all the Church's missionary proclamation and eucharistic worship. The Letter to the Hebrews for example describes Jesus as '*the* apostle and High Priest of our confession' who 'was faithful to him who appointed him (that is, who sent him)' (3:1), while the Apocalypse identifies him as 'Jesus Christ *the* faithful witness (from the Greek word *martus* comes our word *martyr*) the first-born from the dead and ruler of the kings on earth' (1:5). In each case Christ's Apostleship and authority as witness occur within the context of his priestly sacrifice ('He has freed us from our sins by his blood': Rv 1:5) or the sacerdotal nature of the people he redeemed – ('He made us a kingdom, priests to his God and Father': Rv 1:6). Both texts would have had a eucharistic resonance for the early Christian community, as did the passage in the First Letter of St John, where the eucharistic-sacramental implication of the witness given by Christ and his Spirit in the Church is very clear indeed: 'This is he who came by water and blood, Jesus Christ, not with water only but with the water and the blood. And the Spirit is the witness, because the Spirit is the truth. There are three witnesses; the Spirit, the water and the blood; and these three agree' (5:6-8). From a consideration of these New Testament texts what is apparent is that *apostleship, sacrifice* and *Eucharist* are themselves a perichoresis: a mutual indwelling of distinct ideas that flow from and back to one another to form a single reality.

For Joseph Ratzinger, the economic nature of the mystery revealed – its sacramental character – depends on its being linked to personal witness. Opposing the Reformers' contention that succession applies only to the word as such and not to its appointed servants and the sacramental structures of ecclesial ministry, he observes that, according to

> the form of tradition in the New Testament ... the word is tied to the witness, who guarantees it an unambiguous sense, which it

Jesus summoned these disciples who were to be with him and to be sent, 'He then went home' (3:19b).

Would it be stretching exegesis too far to see in this an oblique reference to Christ's future return home to his Father, the ascension? Might we deduce a theological hint here that once an apostolic college has been pre-formed, the essential means towards salvation have, in anticipation, already been put in place: the preaching of the word, the healing authority over the demons of sin and death, and eventually the eucharistic celebration of the Paschal mystery? So that when Christ in the flesh should pass from sight his mission and purpose would continue through which his personal presence would be assured in sacramental-doctrinal form until the end of time. Whether that was Mark's intention, this in fact is what happened. The word that gives life, the healing that is reconciliation, the body broken on the cross, the resurrection of the truth – are all contained in the fullness of the eucharistic mystery. It stands at the centre of the Trinitarian processions in eternity, the divine missions in time, the apostolic succession of history and the eschatological climax of salvation.

APOSTOLICITY AS COMMUNION

The centrality of the Eucharist as the apostolic sacrament of communion was one of the key teachings of the Second Vatican Council nearly fifty years ago. While it may not have used the term 'apostolic' of the Eucharist specifically, that is what the Council's teaching amounted to. It is the constitutive sacrament of the apostolic Church; it is the dynamic means towards, and manifestation of, that Catholic unity, that unity in its fullness that Jesus desired for his disciples and that subsists in the Catholic Church as something she can never lose (UR, 3, 4). For it is in the sacrament of the eucharistic bread that 'the unity of believers, who form one body in Christ, is both expressed and brought about' (LG, 3). This Church today, as in the time of the New Testament, is really present in all local eucharistic communities united with their pastors and bishop, above all in the Eucharist where Christ is truly present through whose power the apostolic Church is constituted (LG, 26). Not only is Christ present objectively in the Church's apostolic liturgy; he is present there actively in his ongoing mission from the Father. Hence, 'It is through the liturgy, especially in the divine sacrifice of the Eucharist, that "the work of our redemption is accomplished" (SC, 2)', 'is continually carried out' (LG, 3; PO, 13). For 'Christ always associates the Church with himself in this great work (of the Mass) in which God is perfectly glorified, and people are made holy' (SC, 7).

In this brief synopsis of conciliar eucharistic ecclesiology, the Eucharist – as the foundation of mission, and of the transmission of redemption, of ecclesial reality, and of fullness of communion – has re-vitalised contemporary appreciation of the apostolic inheritance, which the Council helped us retrieve through its return to the sources of the scriptures and Patristics with the help of the *nouvelle théologie*. But this is not exactly the aspect of Vatican II's teaching that I want to explore as regards the Eucharist's apostolic nature. Rather it is another point that the Council Fathers made that really gives us a way into our theme.

It is the concept of Eucharist as source and summit of all the means given for salvation. Thus, 'in the Eucharist is contained the whole spiritual good of the Church' (PO, 5). This is because while the other sacraments and instruments of grace channel the fruits of Christ's redemptive work, the Eucharist *is* Christ himself and the eucharistic liturgy *is* the one sacrifice of Calvary rendered present in the form of the Supper. Therefore, 'it is a sacred action surpassing all others' (SC, 7), unique in its efficacy (Ibid.). It is 'the source and summit of all the preaching of the gospel' (PO, 5), of the Christian life (LG, 11); 'all the ecclesiastical ministries and works of the apostolate are bound up with the Eucharist and directed towards it' (PO, 5); it is the peak towards which all the activity of the Church is directed (and) the fount from which all its power flows (SC, 10). Pope John Paul, taking up the theme in his 2003 encyclical, *Ecclesia de Eucharistia*, concludes that 'the Church draws her life from the Eucharist' (EE, 1, 6, 7, 12) – an affirmation he repeats no less than four times – so that 'the Eucharist stands at the centre of the Church's life' (EE, 3). Perhaps in this last statement the pope was thinking of the Bethlehem prophecy of the prophet Micah, which envisages the good shepherd of Israel standing in the midst of his sheep, gathering them to himself and nourishing them: 'And he shall stand and feed his flock in the strength of the Lord … and they shall dwell secure for he shall be great to the ends of the earth' (Mic 5:4).

Putting all of this together – this eucharist-centred ecclesiology of Vatican II, with the Eucharist in its static and dynamic dimensions as the fount and peak of communion, its very source and summit, its origin and end, the *terminus a quo* and the *terminus ad quem*, the pivotal point from which all good flows and to which all good returns – putting all of this together, one can only describe this sacrament as God's maelstrom of love. Filling the universe it centres and stabilises the creation, lavishly expending the Trinitarian gifts for salvation through the Church and then gathering into itself the fruits of its own generosity. The Eucharist is a two-directional dynamism: a centrifugal force that jettisons and distributes all the self-giving that is personhood in God, and a centripetal force that draws all human personhood into the communion of the Trinity. A spiralling out and a spiralling in, a reaching towards and a bringing back again all that was lost or unloved or dead.

The language of the Eucharist is the language of the Trinitarian relations *ad intra*: the breathing out and breathing in of the Father and the Son in the Holy Spirit, the processional distinction, the inseparable union. It is the language too of the divine missions: the sending forth of the Son and the Spirit and their return home to the Father, their witness complete, the redemption accomplished. It is, finally, the language of apostolicity: the appointment and commissioning of disciples, sent to gather the new Israel into the one body of Christ, the Temple of the Holy Spirit, before returning as the twelve so often did, and the seventy-two, to him who sent them, rejoicing that even the demons obeyed them and that their names were written in heaven (Lk 10:17-20).

The nature of the apostolic communion which the Eucharist expresses, and which it pre-supposes in those who seek hospitality and fellowship as communicants, is full ecclesial communion. It is unity in and with the Church on the level of one's being and of one's life. Since Christ's body is undivided, and that body is the Eucharist and is also the Church, then though the modes of *Corpus Christi* may differ yet in the unique person of Christ they are one. No man after all can have more than one body, not even the glorified Jesus. What the Eucharist is substantially, the Church is mystically so that it has even been said that the Church is the Eucharist extended, while the

Eucharist is the Church condensed.[12] Both can be called the universal sacrament of salvation and are so by dint of their inter-relatedness, the Eucharist generating the Church, the Church making the Eucharist. It is from the sacrament of Christ's Body and Blood that fellowship in the Church flows since the Eucharist is the source and fount of the Church's entire spiritual good, being the sacrament of the cross and the actualisation of Christ's risen presence. And it is back to the Eucharist that all ecclesial fellowship must return since, as we have seen, it is also the summit of the Church's saving activity and the end to which that activity is directed. From a worthy participation in the Eucharist comes a perfecting of ontological communion; and through belonging to the Church, a deepening of existential communion. Since what we are and what we do are intimately connected, it is unthinkable that either form of communicating with Christ should be divorced from the other. To countenance such a situation would not only vacate the very meaning of communion but would hold in contempt the integrity Christ had in mind when he prayed to his Father that 'they should be one as we are one'. Nothing less than the mutual indwelling of the body's head and members, in fidelity to Christ, in fidelity to each other, can mirror the circumincessio between God and his Son and convince the world that – in Jesus' words – 'it was you who sent me' (Jn 17:21). In other words, the apostolicity of Christ is witnessed to by the full apostolicity of his eucharistic Church. For in this apostolic fullness is the Catholicity of the message and the mission, and in its fullness of communion is the holiness of unity with God and one another.

The elements of the ecclesial communion pre-required for authentic eucharistic sharing are, to cite *Lumen Gentium* (art. 14), an acceptance of all the means of salvation bequeathed to the Church with her entire organisation – since the mystical body, like Christ's incarnate, historical form, is a complex reality that expresses its human and divine aspects through visible social structures and hierarchical organs that serve the Holy Spirit's purpose as the principle of the body's life and growth. Secondly: oneness with Christ in the bonds of profession of faith, the sacraments, and a sharing in the common life under the teaching authority and pastoral jurisdiction of the Pontiff and bishops. In addition, there is the requirement of genuine invisible communion which is the state of grace that manifests itself in charity. Reiterating the Council's teaching in his 2003 encyclical, Pope John Paul observed that 'the profound relationship between the invisible and visible communion is constitutive of the Church as the sacrament of salvation', and stressed that the maintenance of this relationship provides the only context in which 'there can be a legitimate celebration of the Eucharist and true participation in it' (EE, 35).

What the encyclical envisages – and the Council forty years before it, and the many other Magisterial documents since, including the Irish and British Bishops' Statement, *One Bread, One Body* (1998) – is nothing short of what the primitive Church was practising as a matter of course two millennia ago. In the Acts of the Apostles, the very same criteria decided who belonged to Christ's body and who it was that would partake of Christ's body at the *agape* celebrations of the Lord's Supper. And so, from the time of Pentecost, 'the disciples devoted themselves to the apostles' teaching and fellowship, to the breaking of bread and the prayers' (2:42) – a way of life they called by the richly textured term, *koinonia*. From the first century to the twenty-first, the apostolic Eucharist has been the bench-mark of the Church as envisaged by Christ, just as apostolic communion has been the bench-mark of the Eucharist as intended by the Holy Spirit.

CONCLUSION

It has been the aim of this paper to explore some aspects of the relationship between the Church the Eucharist in terms of the apostolicity of communion. Many aspects have not been dealt with that could have been considered, such as the vertical intersection by the Holy Spirit's mission of the horizontal, Christological dimension of the Church in history. But what we have discussed is meant to focus attention on the importance of the Eucharist within the community of faith at a time when Pope Benedict has called for a spiritual renewal of the Church in Ireland. Coinciding with the recent new translation of the Roman Missal, his call makes this an appropriate moment for reflecting on the centrality of the Eucharist in any process of renewal. Appropriate too because we are on the threshold of the 50th International Eucharistic Congress in Dublin, *and* in the year that marks a half-century since the opening of the Second Vatican

Council, which gave official status to ecclesiology as a discipline in its own right, and emphasised the eucharistic nature of the Church's sacramental identity.

With *rinnovamento* in mind, as Pope John XXIII had when he called the Council, how might a theology of the Eucharist's apostolic character as constitutive sacrament of unity help us approach those obstacles to the Church's mission which we come across in the culture we live in today? How, for example, can Catholics celebrate the Mass as a communion in faith if they do not know the faith? What kind of fellowship do the faithful expect at the Eucharist if attendance at Mass is largely a matter of convention – going to weddings and funerals, or at State occasions in a predominantly Catholic country? How important any more are the contours of the moral map when it comes to receiving communion at Mass? If an isolated conscience is one's only judge, what has become of the pastoral and moral authority of the Church's teaching office which St Paul, for example, insisted was an intrinsic part of Christian *koinonia* in his letters to the Churches in Asia Minor and Greece?

We tend in Ireland to avoid these problems, to by-pass the awkward issues. But as recent sad history here has shown this tendency is precisely why the Church here is in need of renewal. Part of the problem perhaps has been an inadequate theology, the lack of an appropriate intellectual means to deal with the challenges to faith that a proper faith-understanding could provide. It is my hope that the opportunities afforded by the Eucharistic Congress and by this Symposium of Theology might go some way towards a new appreciation of the rich inheritance we have received in the Church and the Eucharist, since here we have most assuredly been given all that we need for life and salvation.

NOTES

1 Chapter three of Pope John Paul II's 2003 encyclical, *Ecclesia de Eucharistia*, is entitled 'The Apostolicity of the Eucharist and of the Church'. The following year he again drew attention to the theme which he acknowledged as his own in his 'Letter to Priests for Holy Thursday'; speaking of the Eucharist's connection with the sacrament of ordination he writes, 'Here we touch on what I have called the *Apostolicity of the Eucharist* (no. 3). Only a month before (25th February 2004), the *Lineamenta* in preparation for the XI Ordinary General Synod of Bishops, *The Eucharist: Source and Summit of the Life and Mission of the Church,* devoted a section of its second chapter (nos. 17–18) to an elaboration of the topic under the sub-title 'The Apostolicity of the Eucharist'.

2 Cf. also Eph 5:2, 'Walk in love, as Christ loved us and gave himself up (*parédoken*) for us, a fragrant offering and sacrifice to God.'

3 The full extent of Jesus' abandonment is presented in the gospels as a confrontation between divine love and human sinfulness. The same verb, *paradidonai,* formerly used of the Father and of Christ is now attributed also to sinners as if to show God's Son as the confrontational point where the conflict will be resolved. Thus Judas asks the chief priests 'What will you give me if I deliver (*paradóso*) him to you?' (Mt 26:15), and the Fourth Gospel records that Pilate 'then handed him over (*parédoken*) to them to be crucified' (Jn 19:16). It is this that Jesus accepts, his being utterly surrendered, given up, delivered unto, handed over by all – Jews and Gentiles, compatriots and foreigners, friend and stranger, as well as by heaven itself (Mk 15:34).

4 The sheer giftedness of Christ's broken body is emphasised in the text by the personalist phrase, *úpèr úmôn* (for you, v. 11). In Luke's account which follows the Pauline tradition the sacrificial nature of this personal giving is rendered even more explicit: úpèr úmôn *didómenon* (being given for you, 22:19).

5 That is, personally and individually.

6 What the Eucharist is, the Church is: the body of Christ emanating from the body of Christ. As the Church is generated from the Eucharist so the defining marks of Christ's body ecclesial are the consequence of its natural relationship with the Lord's eucharistic body. In this way the mystery of Christ's body is seen to have embraced the Church and through her the whole of the universe in whose nature the Church's created nature also shares. Inserted into Christ, assumed by him, the Church is the first-fruits of the new creation, transformed by communion with Christ, beginning with the eucharistic change of the elements of bread and wine and continuing in those who themselves are changed in Christ's Body by becoming what they receive.

7 Von Balthasar maintains that 'everything that can be thought and imagined where God is concerned' – that is, in the economy of revelation and salvation – 'is, in advance, included and transcended in this self-destitution which constitutes the person of the Father, and, at the same time, those of the Son and the Spirit'. For, he explains, 'God as the "gulf" of absolute Love contains in advance, eternally, all the modalities of love, compassion, and even of "separation" motivated by love and founded on the infinite distinction between the hypostases', Hans Urs von Balthasar, *Mysterium Paschale*, Edinburgh: T&T Clark, 1993, viii–ix.

8 *Essai sur le mystère de l'histoire*, Paris, 1953, cited by Joseph Ratzinger, *Introduction to Christianity*, San Francisco: Ignatius Press, 1990, pp. 220–1.

9 *Lumen Gentium*, 4. Cf. St Cyprian of Carthage, *De Orat. Dom.* 23: PL, 4, 553; St Augustine, *Serm.* 71, 20,33: *PL* 38,463; St John Damascene, *Adv. Iconocl.* 12: *PG* 96, 1358D.

10 2 Cor 3:5-6; Gal 1:15-16; 2:7; Heb 5:4-5.

11 *Called to Communion. Understanding the Church Today*, San Francisco: Ignatius Press, 1996, pp. 67–8.

12 J. Hamer, 'Stages on the Road to Unity. The Problem of Intercommunion', *One in Christ* 4 (1968), pp. 235–49, at p. 241; see also, by the same writer, 'Why Not Intercommunion?', *America* 118 (1968), pp. 734–7 at p. 735.

LAITY AND MINISTRY IN THE CHURCH AS COMMUNION: CANONICAL PERSPECTIVES

REV. PROF. MICHAEL MULLANEY
St Patrick's College, Maynooth

INTRODUCTION

The Church is the communion of all the baptised sharing in the priestly, prophetic and kingly mission of Christ. There is a true equality of all the baptised by virtue of baptism but difference in mission. Baptism is the source of shared obligations and rights of all the baptised which are exercised and fulfilled in the Church in a different way according to the mission of each. While baptism is one, the participation in the priesthood of Christ and his work varies according to the diversity of charisms and ministries bestowed by the Holy Spirit. The Church, the communion of the baptised, is made up of different orders, according to the various charisms and ministries flowing from them. But all diversity and variety of functions or ministries must first be anchored in the essential and fundamental equal status of baptism. For all the baptised have the equal task or co-responsibility in building up the communion which is the Church, each collaborating differently, according to the function, charism, ministry given to them by the Holy Spirit.

Just as the life of the Trinity which the Church as the sacrament of salvation leads us to, is a communion in the substantial nature of the divine union, but simultaneously in the distinctions of the appropriations and of the missions of each of the divine persons, likewise, by analogy, the Church, is the structured and visible sign of communion of charity of the Holy Spirit given by Christ, but at the same time in the distinctions of missions through the diversity of charismatic and hierarchical gifts and ministries which enrich the life of the Church. This unity in charity, this communion, must be expressed visibly in the life of the Church in ministries and vocations which reflect the divinely instituted structures of the institutional-charismatic Church. Canon law is in the service of this communion when it explains and clarifies the different missions and ministries for the building up of the body of Christ.[1]

In this presentation we look specifically at the relationship between the laity the call to ministry or exercise an office or function in the Church.

SECULAR CHARACTER OF LAY APOSTOLATE

The Second Vatican Council was the first Council to treat the laity from a theological, rather than exclusively canonical point of view.[2] The Council wrestled with the question of how to define the lay faithful. From a canonical point of view, they were baptised Christians who had not received the sacrament of orders. Seeking a more positive definition, the Council taught that lay Christians were incorporated in the body of Christ by virtue of their baptism and therefore shared in their own way in Christ's threefold office as priest, prophet and king. As a result they partook in the mission of the Church.

The mission of the Church was described differently in various documents, but in all of them, consistently and clearly, the mission of the Church is entrusted to all the baptised. The Council highlighted and underlined the 'secular' characterisation of the mission of the laity; however, it was not a rigorous definition of the lay mission. Nor did it apply to all members of the laity or exclusively to them. Together with laypersons, some priests and religious were engaged in the temporal sphere and thus were doing what the council depicted as proper to the laity.

The laity had a specific role in the world where the Church can be salt of the earth in a way distinct from that of priests or religious. The laity are the Church in the world and the witnesses of its mission in their engagement and transformation of the temporal and secular order in accordance with the will of God (LG, 31, 33; AA, 2, 7). 'They live in the world,' said the Council, 'that is, in each and in all of the secular professions and occupations. They live in the ordinary circumstances of family and social life, from which the very web of their existence is woven' (LG, 31). From this it followed that they 'are called in a special

offered 'a description of a type, that is, of what typifies a layperson's situation and activity. A layperson typically is married, has a job, lives in the world, etc.' To absolutise the secular dimension of the laity or to transform it into an essential definition of the layperson goes beyond the Council's more modest intent. The descriptive should not be read as prescriptive. The fact that most lay people work 'in the world' does not mean that it is inappropriate for lay ministers to work in the Church. But there is a larger theological issue here. The responsibility to transform the secular world according to the light of Christ does not belong to the laity alone. It is the responsibility of the whole Church.

CONCILIAR AND POST-CONCILIAR MAGISTERIUM AND LAY MINISTRY

While the *Instruction* was necessary to correct abuses, it does not undo, indeed it cannot reverse, the emergence and growth of ministries that express the conciliar ecclesiology of communion and participation. The documents of Vatican II did extend the word 'ministry' to the laity. These instances, though few in number, are significant. By virtue of the common priesthood of all the baptised are called to the apostolate/mission in the world, the further call of some persons to the ministry of laity by which the Holy Spirit 'makes them fit and ready to undertake various tasks and offices for the renewal and building up of the Church' (LG, 12). But it also entails – as we shall see – an explicit relationship of mutual accountability to and collaboration with the Church hierarchy or the competent ecclesiastical authority.[6]

The possibility for the laity to undertake ministries in the Church is grounded in numerous affirmations of conciliar documents: LG, 33, 37; AA, 24; PO, 9.[7] It must be still noted, however, that while these documents supported the recognition of the ministry of the laity in the Church, they still emphasised the apostolate of the laity in the world, that is, their secular character.[8] Nevertheless, these texts demonstrate that it was no longer possible to presuppose to tie the exercise of ministry and participation in the mission of the Church to the power of orders and in these texts we see the Council opens the way for the laity to have legitimate access to the ministries according to the needs of the Church and in response to the call of the shepherds.[9] It is, therefore, with the help of priests, deacons and other ministers, that the apostolic ministry of the bishop contributes to the building up of the ecclesial body of Christ and realises its mission. For according to LG, 30: 'For the pastors know how much the laity contribute to the welfare of the Church. They also know that they are not ordained by Christ to take upon themselves alone the entire salvific mission of the Church toward the world. On the contrary, they understand that it is their noble duty to shepherd the faithful and to recognise their ministries and charisms, so that all, according to their proper roles may cooperate in this common undertaking with one mind.'

Paul VI also developed the theme of ministry in the *motu proprio Ministeria quaedam*[10] in which he affirmed there were ministries for the laity (non-ordained). Lector and acolyte were not longer referred to minor orders, but ministries which not only those who are preparing for diaconate or priestly ministry could receive, but also the laity who would remain so and for whom it was a means of living their co-responsibility in the Church. This ministry is not just in response to a shortage of priests, but because of baptism, which rendered all the faithful an active subject of the mission of the Church. This has been received in can. 230, §1, and because these ministries are given only to men who are preparing for the permanent diaconate and priesthood they are looked at with some suspicion and perplexity by those who promote the autonomy of the lay vocation and has not had much application or response.

Nevertheless, the *motu proprio* did not just confine itself to these two ministries, but was open to the emergence and recognition of other ministries, inviting episcopal conferences to approve them for their regions. And later Paul VI returned to the question of the flourishing and widening of ministries in his apostolic exhortation, *Evangelii nuntiandi* and specifically repeated in the *Catechism of the Catholic Church*: 'The laity can also feel called, or in fact are called, to cooperate with their pastors in the service of the ecclesial community, for the sake of growth and life. This can be done through the exercise of different ministries according to the grace and charisms which the Lord has been pleased to bestow on them' (EN, 73; CCC, 910).[11] It is for the service of communion and mission of all that some receive a ministry in and for the Church.

In his apostolic exhortation *Christifideles Laici* on the laity (1988), Pope John Paul expressed satisfaction with the progress made since

Vatican II in achieving greater collaboration among priests, religious and lay faithful in the proclamation of the Word of God, in catechesis and in the great variety of services entrusted to the lay faithful. In a special section on lay ministries the pope strongly urged pastors to 'acknowledge and foster the ministries, offices and roles of the lay faithful that find their foundation in the sacraments of baptism and confirmation' (CL, 23).

But at the same time he cautioned against 'a too-indiscriminate use of the word ministry', which is sometimes overextended to include merely casual or occasional activities. The exhortation also warns against 'clericalisation' of the lay faithful, which would overlook the distinction between their functions and those of the ordained.

The conciliar and post-conciliar documents did not propose that ministry is for all laity but for some, working with priests and deacons subject to the bishop, which guarantees that their ministry expresses and build ecclesial communion. Not all the faithful are, on the basis of their participation in the common priesthood of Christ, or by baptism and confirmation in themselves, entitled *a fortiori* to exercise ministry in the Church. The exercise of any such ministry also requires of the laity the necessary qualities, gifts and qualifications, and to be entrusted with the task or office by the competent ecclesiastical authority. We can speak of ministries 'entrusted' to the laity.

But if lay people are called to ministry, it is because, in virtue of the grace of their baptism and confirmation, their charisms and gifts, the Church or the competent ecclesiastical authority judges it necessary to call them to participate in the mission of the Church.[12] The ministry of the laity is sacramental because its basis is the sacraments of baptism and confirmation; it is ecclesial because it has a place within the community of the Church, whose communion and mission it serves, and because it is submitted to the discernment, authorisation and supervision of the hierarchy. Finally, it is ministry because it is a participation in the threefold ministry of Christ, who is prophet, priest and king.[13] While all the baptised have a right to co-responsibility in the life and mission of the Church, collaboration is 'entrusted' to laity.

LAY MINISTRY IN THE CODE OF 1983

While there is a section in the Code on 'offices', it does not have a specific chapter on 'ministry', in fact, it does not make many references to ministry. And while the Code explicitly recognises the capacity of the lay faithful to exercise a function (*munus*) or task or an ecclesial office (except in the case of can. 150, that is, the office that requires the care of souls and for whose fulfilment the exercise of the priestly order is required) it avoids the term 'ministry'. The most significant references to 'ministry' are found in can. 230, §1 – mentioned above; can. 230, §3: 'When the need of the Church warrants it and ministers are lacking, lay persons, even if they are not lectors or acolytes, can also supply certain of their duties, namely to exercise the ministry of the Word, preside over liturgical prayers, to confer baptism, and to distribute Holy Communion, according to the precepts of the law.' Can. 759 states that the laity can be called to cooperate with the bishop and with priests in the exercise of the ministry of the Word. Can. 230, §3 refers therefore to a supply in case of necessity and because of a shortage of ordained ministers, for example, in the case of parish communities without a resident priest to celebrate the Sunday Eucharist every weekend.

Can. 228, §1–2: 'Lay persons who are found suitable are qualified to be admitted by the sacred pastors to those ecclesiastical offices and functions for which they are able to exercise according to the precepts of the law.' This is rooted in LG, 33: the laity 'have the capacity to assume from the hierarchy certain ecclesiastical functions, which are to be performed for a spiritual purpose'. The exercise of an ecclesiastical office no longer presupposes the exercise of the power of governance or orders (even though some offices still require them). An interesting development, echoing also the mind of the Council, can. 145, §2 foresaw the possibility of a competent ecclesiastical authority, other that the Roman Pontiff, establishing ecclesiastical offices. This opens the possibility for a diocesan bishop or episcopal conference (or an ordinary of a clerical religious institute of pontifical right) to do so. Some commentators see this canon as a reference to the availability of administrative offices for laity, primarily on the diocesan level, while offices involving the *plena cura animarum* at the parish level remain supplementary.[14]

The legislation reflects the position that no one can make themselves a minister but must be entrusted with it by the competent authority (can. 157). Baptism and confirmation in themselves do not qualify the laity for ministry. If that were the case, all the baptised, by virtue of their baptism, would be capable of ministry. In other words, all the baptised would be 'ministers'. While baptism renders all the faithful capable of participating in the mission of the Church, *only some* – those who are suitable and having been admitted by the competent ecclesiastical authority – have the capacity for ministry.[15] *Co-Workers in the Vineyard of the Lord* refers to this as 'authorisation for lay ecclesial ministry': 'Authorisation is the process by which properly prepared lay men and women are given responsibilities for ecclesial ministry by the competent Church authority. This process includes the following elements: acknowledgement of the competence of an individual to a specific position ... along with the delineation of the obligations, responsibilities, and authority of that position ...'[16]

Can. 519 (echoing CD, 30; AA, 10, 24) foresees the entrusting of the pastoral care of parish priests/pastors and invokes the collaboration and the cooperation of other priests, deacons and laity according to the norm of the law. The invocation of the collaboration of the laity is innovative and significant and a recognition of the place of the laity in the service of the community (as called for in can. 275, §2). In affirming the principle of collaboration of the other faithful, the Code recognises that the parish priest may not have all the gifts required to carry out all his pastoral responsibilities. His ministry is essentially a priestly ministry of presiding. Although he possesses the title *plena cura animarum* (can. 521), he does not exercise this ministry of parish priest alone. For this reason the Code also foresees the establishments of parish pastoral councils (can. 536) over which the parish priest presides and in which the Christian faithful, together with those who share in pastoral care by virtue of their office in the parish, assist in fostering pastoral action.

The laity can participate in something less than the *plena cura animarum*, something less than the richness of the conciliar documents. Nevertheless, it is a canonical way of recognising the participation of the laity in the exercise of pastoral care: a duly authorised and perfectly legitimate participation, but partial rather than full. Distinguishing lay participation in the exercise of pastoral care as partial rather than full does not minimise or denigrate that exercise, it simply differentiates it as based on the sacraments of baptism and confirmation rather than the sacrament of orders. 'Partial' does not imply a small or minor participation, nor does it imply that the sharing is temporary or an emergency situation. Indeed, a partial sharing can be the major share, all except the sacramental roles reserved to priests as well as the homiletic role that is part of the liturgy itself (can. 767, §1). And it can be quite permanent and stable.[17]

Can. 517, §2 refers, we presume implicitly, to the laity when it states: 'If, because of a lack of priests, the diocesan bishop has decided that participation in the exercise of pastoral care of the parish is to be entrusted to a deacon, or another person who is not a priest, or to a community of persons, he is to appoint some priest who, provided with the powers and faculties of a pastor, is to direct the pastoral care.' However, the canon has the tone of an exception in the case of a shortage of priests.

Overall, the Code applies the term 'ministry' to laity in only seven canons. Taking the seven together, it is clear that the Code has a narrower use of the word 'ministry' and 'service' than the conciliar and post-concililar documents. Laity may be invited into ministry only by hierarchical invitation, but there is no ministry which belongs to laity through baptism. There is no ministry which is fulfilled in the secular sphere, and there is no ministry which the laity can carry out on their own initiative. This can be explained by the Commission's desire to highlight the difference between the ordained priesthood and the common priesthood.[18] While there is a greater recognition for the ministry of the laity in the Code, in the words of Elizabeth McDonagh: 'it is also true that there is no position, role, function, office or status in the Church that is open to the laity that is not either heavily conditioned (cc. 204, §1, 208, 210, 216); carefully qualified (cc. 212, § 3, 218); institutionally circumscribed (cc. 226, §2, 229, §1, 230); or hierarchically controlled (cc. 223, §2, 228).'[19] In addition, there are various interpretations and understanding about what qualifies as ministry of the laity.

Canonists and commentators can sometimes focus too much on certain limitations or drawbacks of a particular canon and fail to appreciate the overall positive effect of the Code's renewal. However, the Code does much to further the role of laypersons, not only 'in the world' but in the interior life of the Church as well. The 1917 code had only 43 canons on the laity, and all but two were about associations. The 1983 code, following on Vatican II, contains a whole title on the lay faithful's rights and obligations. And the code contains many other canons clarifying the role of laypersons internally in the Church:

- To hold ecclesiastical offices (for example, in the tribunal)
- To carry out many administrative roles in the chancery
- To serve as official missionaries and catechists
- To teach in every level of ecclesiastical academic institutions, including those of higher education with a canonical mandatum
- To participate in diocesan synods
- To preach under certain circumstances
- To baptise and officiate at marriages with appropriate authorisation
- To conduct benedictions and funeral rites.

There is still, however, ambivalence in the code: are laity true lay ministers or are they only supplementary ministers? Are they in fact developing into a *tertium quid,* a third branch of status in the Church (as religious once were viewed)? Perhaps. If so, the conciliar developments that were included in the code laid the groundwork for ecclesial practice, as it often does, to alter the law in the future.[20]

INSTRUCTION ECCLESIAE DE MYSTERIO (1997)

In 1997, eight Roman dicastries issued an instruction expressing concern about the developments in lay ministry and drew a sharp distinction between the priesthood of the ordained and the priesthood of the baptised and the activities proper to each. The *Instruction* has exposed the tension between practice and law in the area of the ministry of the laity. While some authors and commentators felt the *Instruction* was long overdue, others interpreted it as a new obstacle to the participation and collaboration of the laity in the mission and life of the Church. According to Aymans, the *Instruction* is a legislative text in view of the manner of its promulgation (*in forma specifica* by the pope). It has a limited purpose and it should be read as such. Its subject is not the collaboration between priests and lay people but the priestly ministry in so far as lay people can collaborate in it. The *Instruction* will seem restrictive only to those who consider the supplementary tasks as a desirable field for the activity of the laity.[21]

The document is not concerned with all the apostolate of lay people in the Church. While it did address abuses in collaboration, it also indirectly shed light on lawful collaboration of lay people in the ministry of the priest. Indeed, the document does list eleven possibilities whereby lay people collaborate in the ministry of the priest. According to Cardinal Ratzinger's commentary, the *Instruction* was not a limitation on the authentic and genuine promotion of lay participation in the evangelical and ecclesial apostolate, which, on the contrary, is strengthened and encouraged in the right direction consistent with Catholic ecclesiology. However – following what was said in the text of *Christifideles laici* – it intends to rebut and prevent 'the tendency towards a "clericalisation" of the lay faithful, and the risk of creating, in reality, an ecclesial structure of parallel service to that founded on the sacrament of Orders' (*Christifideles laici*, 23, §6).

The Instruction is made up of two parts:
The first part is entitled the Theological Principles.

- The first focuses on the distinction between the common priesthood and ministerial priesthood
- The second on the unity and diversity of ministerial functions
- The third recognises the indispensability of the Ordained Ministry
- Fourthly, the collaboration of the non-ordained faithful in pastoral ministry.

The second part is entitled Practical Provisions, that is, thirteen articles that address different matters or areas of lay participation in the Church, which have lead to particular abuses in certain parts of the world.

The document calls on bishops to check abuses that have arisen in the collaboration of lay people in the life of the Church. It draws attention to the unique ministry of the ordained. It holds that the services of lay people should only be engaged when there is a shortage of priests, and not just for the sake of convenience or to promote the 'ambiguous advancement of the laity'. The *Instruction* restates the laws governing the Sunday celebrations in the absence of a priest, lay distribution of communion, defining the roles of diocesan and parish pastoral councils as consultative. It revoked any particular laws or faculties allowed for experimental purposes, which are contrary to these norms.

Pope John Paul II, speaking to the American bishops on their *ad limina* (2nd July 1993), stated that: 'It is not a wise pastoral strategy to adopt plans which would assume that it is normal, let alone desirable, that a parish community would be without a priest pastor. To interpret the decrease in the number of priests ... as a providential sign that lay persons are to replace priests is irreconcilable with the mind of Christ and the Church.'[22]

HAS THE INSTRUCTION MADE ANY CONTRIBUTION TO THE MINISTRY OF THE LAITY?

Some argue that the *Instruction* has implemented the teaching of the Council.[23] The *Instruction* was given to clarify ambiguities that have crept into the use of some terms, particularly 'ministry'. According to the *Instruction*, ministry has always referred only to the ministry exercised by ordained ministers. Because of a shortage of priests, lay people can be called according to the law by the competent ecclesiastical authority to supply for some offices to which they enjoy no right. Only then can the term 'ministry' be permitted and even then they are designated 'extra-ordinary' ministers. The term 'extra-ordinary' minister can only be applied to those to whom functions have been entrusted canonically (catechist, lector, acolytes, etc.). For this reason, one of the more controversial demands of the *Instruction* is to avoid this confusion by not conferring titles like 'pastor', 'chaplain', etc. to the laity.

While the *Instruction* clearly called for a recovery of the secular nature of the mission of the laity, it did list possibilities where collaboration of the faithful is possible in eleven practical provisions. In any case, these are only supplementary while there is a shortage of priests exists. The matters dealt with regarded: homily, preaching in non-eucharistic settings, the participation of laity in the pastoral care of he parish, the collaboration of the laity in diocesan and parish pastoral councils, laity at liturgical celebrations, leading the Sunday celebration in the absence of a priest, distribution of Holy Communion as extraordinary ministers, assistance to the sick, assisting at the celebration of marriages, extraordinary ministers of baptism.

Nevertheless, the *Instruction* and has not exhausted all the variations of participation of the laity. And while it may not seem like it, there are a lot more ministries that laity are involved in which are not mentioned here. While some might argue it is a restrictive document, it does no more than insist that the current legislation be observed.

THE POWER OF GOVERNANCE

A significant difference between the current Code and previous one is that the 1917 Code, in can. 118, stated that 'only' clergy are able to obtain the power of ecclesiastical jurisdiction. The omission of the word 'only' in the current legislation implies that, while clergy are indeed capable of the power of governance, they are not the only ones who are capable of exercising it.[24] Ghirlanda argues that the words 'only clergy' in can. 274, §1 are to be taken to mean that in virtue of ordination, only clerics are *ipso facto* able to receive offices which involve the exercise of power of governance and require orders (can. 129, §1).

Yet, we also said that a lay person may hold an ecclesiastical office that does not involve power of orders and the power of governance (can. 145, §1, 228, 274, §1). The combination of these laws leaves a number of offices in universal law open to the laity or other offices that might be established by the competent ecclesiastical authority. All this is very clear, but what gives rise to the question of whether the laity can participate in the power of governance is the existence of can. 1421, §2. The canon allows a lay person to be appointed an ecclesiastical judge in an ecclesiastical tribunal. The issue is that judicial power is a form of the power of governance. The issue is joined at the apparent contradiction of can. 274, §1, which restricts offices and which exercise the power of governance to clergy, and can. 1421, §2, which includes the laity in one of those such offices. But this is not an issue restricted to these canons, but that of power, its source and subject in the Church.[25]

This question was intensely debated by the Commission during the revision of the Code and still *doctores disputant*. The problem is rooted in a theological question relating to the source of power in the Church. Is ordination/orders necessary to exercise the power of governance. Or do orders and power enjoy a certain independence, in the sense that power can be transmitted by the law (canonical mandate/mission) and the sacrament confers ontological capacities required for certain acts of power? Or rather is orders or baptism the source of power?

There are two schools of thought (these schools are called different names by different authors: sacramental/non-sacramental; first/second theory/doctrine; German/Roman). In this paper we will adopt the later. Firstly, the German school (partly because of one of its main champions – Klaus Morsdoff), which holds that the source of the power of governance is sacramental. There is an intrinsic unity between the sacrament of order and the power of jurisdiction. Canonical mission or mandate only specifies the legitimate ambit of its exercise. This would explain the requirement in the apostolic constitution *Romano Pontifici eligendo* that anyone elected pope without episcopal character has only a right to become pope, but must immediately be consecrated bishop and only then can he exercise his full and supreme power over the universal Church. This theory excluded the laity from any kind of exercise of ecclesiastical power.

The second school, or the Roman school, holds that the source of governance is both orders and canonical mandate. They affirmed that jurisdiction cannot be seen as a mere *sine qua non* for the exercise of a power already substantially received in ordination. Jurisdiction granted through canonical mission had its own proper content, that is, it is not the unshackling of powers already received in ordination, nor the assigning of subjects over which jurisdiction already received is going to be exercised. According to those who hold this position, sacred ordination confers not only the power of orders, but also the function of teaching and governing, these require the power of governance given by the canonical mission. This school of thought referred to the many historical examples where non-consecrated men and women exercised the power of governance legitimately in the Church. Indeed, Alfons Stickler, who pointed out that it was not until 882 that a bishop was elected pope, they were either priests or deacons.[26] This historical evidence demonstrates that orders and jurisdiction are separate.

Except in the case of the Roman Pontiff, canonical mission from the competent ecclesiastical authority confers on the ordained a fuller share in the power of jurisdiction and specifies the sphere within which that power can be exercised. Since according to this school of thought, the power of order and the power of jurisdiction can be separated, as for example in the case of the Roman Pontiff receives jurisdiction directly from the Lord on the acceptance of his legitimate election even if he is not yet ordained a bishop. He is subsequently consecrated bishop in order to give this power an episcopal character.

Depending on which school of thought one subscribed to, the interpretation and application of the canons can take very diverging paths. In the example to hand, the German school, the canon allowing a lay person to be a judge is an error since the power of governance is rooted in orders. The lay judge doesn't participate in the power of governance, but the college does. The lay judge is only 'cooperating' in the ecclesiastical power but this is ontologically only possible because of the two other members of the college of judges are priests. This argument is not sustainable, as in canonical doctrine judges – even in a college of judges – have power in their own right. A college presumes all members are equal, therefore, if a lay judge did not have judicial power in his or her own right, then the lay judge would not be equal to the other two priest judges. Furthermore, the power of judges comes from their appointment by the bishop – it is the ordinary power of office – not from being a member of a college of judges. A lay person can exercise judicial power, the power of governance in their own right. There are ample examples of when the supreme moderator (for example can. 686, §1 – an indult/rescripts of exclaustration; can. 647, §1 – decree of erection, suppression, transfer of a novitiate house), major superior (can issue a singular precept of warning), lay brothers in their participation of chapters, superiors of institutes of consecrated life and societies of apostolic life (permissions which are acts of executive power). The Code does not say that collegial bodies and superiors in lay institutes of consecrated life and societies of apostolic life exercise the power of governance. Nevertheless, if the act is acknowledged as the power of governance when performed by a cleric, it follows the same act, when lawfully performed by a lay person, is also an act of governance by the law itself.[27]

In contrast, the Roman school holds that orders renders clergy capable to possess and the right to exercise both orders and jurisdiction, even though jurisdiction requires the further juridical specification of a canonical mission/mandate in order to be able to exercise that power. Nevertheless, baptism renders a lay person capable to receive and exercise the power of jurisdiction from the supreme authority of the Church.

Therefore, while can. 274, §1 states that only clerics can obtain offices for which exercise the power of ecclesiastical governance is required, this does not refer to all offices which involve the exercise of the power of governance, but only 'capital' offices that require sacred orders in which the sacred minister acts 'in the person of Christ the Head', for example, the primatial office of the pope, the office of bishop or equivalent functions (can. 1008). There are some cases where the power of order and the power of governance are so close that the power of governance cannot be exercised unless by someone who has the power of orders: for example, sacramental absolution (can. 966, §1); confirmation (can. 882). While the laity cannot exercise these 'capital' offices, they may be called to cooperate with the pastors of the Church in subordinate offices of governance, exercising judicial and executive power in offices open to them in the universal law. Also the location of can. 274 among the rights of clerics provides the context to understanding what the canon means, a cleric has a right to receive an office which requires the office of orders and the power of governance. In this case, when two equally qualified candidates present themselves for the same office requiring the exercise of governance, and one is a lay person and the other a priest, the bishop would be obliged to choose the priest. However, not if the priest's ministry was required in the pastoral ministry or another office.

Furthermore, can. 230, §3: when the need of the Church warrants it and ministers are lacking, lay persons can fulfil the certain duties of the ordained. In situations where there is a shortage of priests who would normally hold an office requiring the exercise of the power of governance, a lay person can be appointed to it.

Clearly, in discussing who may exercise the power of governance, we are not in the realm of immutable divine law, but merely ecclesiastical law that can change, has changed, and is very likely to see other developments.[28] But the lack of solution is a major impediment to progressing the question of assigning offices which require the exercise of the power of governance to the laity. No easy solution seems in sight any time soon as the arguments presented by both sides do not present any easy compromise or reconciliation. Nevertheless, some offices are open to the laity, a growing practice of appointing lay people to offices implies what direction this is moving albeit slowly.

Also it is worth noting, for even priests, orders is not enough for the exercise of governance. The intervention of a competent ecclesiastical authority is always required through a canonical mission. Perhaps an official line from the Pontifical Council for the Interpretation of the Texts or another *Instruction* or a clarification from CDF might help. But in this case, it might also be argued that we should allow practice to lead and see where this will bring us.

NOTES

1 G. Ghirlanda, *Il Diritto nella Chiesa: Mistero di Communione*, Roma: Edizioni San Paolo, 2000, pp. 58–9.

2 A. Hagstorm, 'The Secular Character of the Vocation and Mission of the Laity', *Ordering the Baptismal Priesthood: Theologies of Lay and Ordained Ministries*, S. Wood, ed., Collegeville: Liturgical Press, 2003, p. 154; D. Astigueta, 'Los Laicos en la Discusión Teológico-Canónico desde el Concilio al CIC 83', *Periodica* 90, 2001, pp. 559–63.

3 Ibid., pp. 161–5.

4 Ibid., p. 167.

5 'The Instruction: An Explanatory Note', *Origins* 27/24, 27th November, 1997, p. 409.

6 United States Conference of Catholic Bishops, *Co-Workers in the Vineyard of the Lord: A Resource for Guiding the Development of Lay Ecclesial Ministry*, Washington: USCCB, 2005, p. 26.

7 'Besides the apostolate that certainly pertains to all Christians, the laity can also be called in various ways to a more direct form of cooperation in the apostolate of the hierarchy ... they have the capacity to assume from the hierarchy certain ecclesiastical functions, which are to be performed for a spiritual purpose' (LG, 33c); 'Let the spiritual shepherds recognise and promote the dignity as well as the responsibility of the laity in the Church. ... Let them confidently assign duties to them in the service of the Church' (LG, 37c). '... the hierarchy entrusts to the laity certain functions which are more closely connected with pastoral duties, such as the teaching of social doctrine, certain liturgical actions, and the care of souls.', (AA, 24); 'Priests must sincerely acknowledge and promote the role of the laity and the part proper to them in the mission of the Church' (PO, 9).

8 E. Zanetti, 'I "Ministri Laicali" nel Post-Concilio: Cifra di una Chance e di un Disagio', *Periodica* 90, (2001), p. 594.

9 A. Borras, 'Quelle Régulation Canonique pour les Ministères de Laïcs? Du Code au Droit Particulier', *Studia Canonica* 40 (2006), p. 357.

10 M.P. Ministeria quaedam, 15th August 1972.

11 E. Zanetti, 'I "Ministri Laicali" nel Post-Concilio: Cifra di una Chance e di un Disagio', *Periodica* 90 (2001), pp. 596–9.

12 A. Borras, 'Quelle Régulation Canonique pour les Ministères de Laïcs? Du Code au Droit Particulier', *Studia Canonica* 40 (2006), p. 353.

13 United States Conference of Catholic Bishops, *Co-Workers in the Vineyard of the Lord: A Resource for Guiding the Development of Lay Ecclesial Ministry*, Washington: USCCB, 2005, p. 12.

14 E. Rinere, 'The Exercise of Cura Animarum through the Twentieth Century and Beyond', *The Jurist* 65 (2005), p. 43.

15 A. Borras, 'Quelle Régulation Canonique pour les Ministères de Laïcs? Du Code au Droit Particulier', *Studia Canonica* 40, (2006), pp. 357–8.

16 *Co-Workers in the Vineyard of the Lord*, USCCB, 2006, p. 54.

17 J. Coriden, 'Parish Pastoral Leaders: Canonical Structures and Practical Questions', *The Jurist* 67 (2007), p. 469.

18 E, Rinere, 'Conciliar and Canonical Applications of "Ministry" to the Laity', *The Jurist* 47 (1987), pp. 219–20.

19 E. McDonagh, 'Laity and the Inner Working of the Church', *The Jurist* 47, (1987), pp. 240–1.

20 J. Alesandro, 'The Code of Canon Law: Past, Present and Future', *Origins* 37/23 (2007).

21 W. Aymans, 'Instruction calls for necessary change in attitude and practice', *L'Osservatore Romano*, English Version, no. 7 (18th February 1998), pp. 10–11.

22 AAS, 86 (1994), p. 406.

23 L. Kizito, Lay *People and the Tria Munera Christi: A Study from can. 204, §1 to Instructio Ecclesiae de Mysterio*, Rome: UUP, 2002, pp. 138–9. Here the author refers to H. Schwendenwein, D. Castrillon Hoyos, F. Moraglia.

24 J. Huels, 'The Power of Governance and its Exercise by Lay Persons: A Juridical Approach', *Studia Canonica* 35 (2001), p. 80.

25 E. McDonagh, 'Laity and the Inner Working of the Church', *The Jurist,* 47 (1987), pp. 230–1.

26 Gregory the Great was elected pope in February 590 and ordained bishop 3rd September 590; Gregory VII was elected pope 22nd April 1073, ordained a priest 22nd May and consecrated bishop 20th May 1073; Innocent III was elected pope 8th January 1198, ordained a priest 21st January and consecrated bishop 22nd February

27 J. Huels, 'The Power of Governance and its Exercisc by Lay Persons: A Juridical Approach', *Studia Canonica* 35 (2001), pp. 74–8.

28 Ibid., 72.

HOMILY
THURSDAY OF THE NINTH WEEK OF ORDINARY TIME

MOST REV. PIERO MARINI
President, Pontifical Committee for International Eucharistic Congresses

READINGS: 2 TM 2:8-15; MK 12:28-34

The first of the Commandments
At that time, one of the scribes asked Jesus: 'Which commandment is the first of all?' This is no idle, abstract question. All of us who consider ourselves experts in the law have to ask ourselves the same question. Bishops, priests, committed lay men and women, all of us have to ask: What is at the heart of my religious life, at the heart of my moral life? What is the value around which I am building my life?

Hear, O Israel
This is the answer which Jesus continues to give to each of us. We have to start by listening. Attentive listening is already a movement: in the act of hearing, I open myself to another person and I allow him or her to become present in me. Hearing establishes a bond, a relationship, in which I step out of my isolation and enter into a relationship with another person. Jesus tells us that hearing leads to knowledge: 'The Lord is one', and then that hearing leads to love: 'You shall love the Lord.' Hearing thus brings about an exodus from ourselves, an exodus that springs from God and his Word. Hear, O Israel ...

You shall love the Lord with all your heart
To love the Lord with all our heart, with all our mind and with all our strength, and to love our neighbour as ourselves, means that we express our love with our bodies. Love needs to be 'embodied', not only in my physical body, but also in the body of the family and the body of the Church. Hearing the Word of God tends to make the divine Word a part of our bodies, a part of our whole person and of all our relationships. Hearing thus belongs to the dynamism of the incarnation: 'The Word was made flesh and dwelt among us.' The

words: 'Hear, O Israel', do not only refer, then, to hearing; they also refer to seeing and receiving.

A gesture of love

We have listened to Jesus' words about loving God and loving our neighbour during our celebration of the Eucharist. It has been written that the Eucharist is completely enclosed in an act of love. 'Having loved his own who were in the world, he loved them to the end; and while they were at supper, he took bread and broke it, saying: "Take this, all of you and eat of it, for this is my body, which will be given up for you."' The Eucharist is the entire life of Jesus. He alone lived to perfection the one commandment: love for God and love for us led him to death on the cross. Whenever we celebrate the Eucharist, he tell us once more: 'Love one another, as I have loved you.' For us, every celebration of the Eucharist is a school of love. Let us never forget that the authenticity of our eucharistic celebrations is not measured simply by how meticulously we respect the Church's rules and celebrate her rites, but also by the extent to which those celebrations bear fruit, in ourselves and in our eucharistic communities, in mutual listening, in communion, concord, forgiveness and the common effort to know and to do God's will.

You are not far from the Kingdom of God

'You are not far from the Kingdom of God.' This is the compliment that Jesus pays to the scribe; it is also a compliment he pays to us today. But his words make it clear that more remains to be done. True, we have seen what is at the heart of our lives of faith, but we have not yet followed the Master to the end. It is Jesus, Jesus alone, who teaches us fully, ever anew, who God is and what it means to love him; who our neighbour is and what it means to love him or her. Like the scribe in the gospel, we too still need to follow Jesus fully, even unto the cross.

Friday 8th June 2012

LEARNING FROM ECUMENISM

KEYNOTE SPEAKERS

at the International Symposium of Theology 50TH INTERNATIONAL EUCHARISTIC CONGRESS

• • 1 • •

CHAIR: **MOST REV. THOMAS DABRE DD** (Bishop of Pune, India)

SPEAKER: **HIS EMINENCE KURT CARDINAL KOCH**
President, Pontifical Council for Promoting Christian Unity
The Relation between the Eucharist and Ecclesial Communion: An Ecumenical View

• • 2 • •

CHAIR: **MOST REV. RICHARD CLARKE**
(Church of Ireland, Bishop of Meath and Kildare)

SPEAKER: **REV. PROF. NICHOLAS SAGOVSKY**
Member of ARCIC III
Ut Unum Simus: *What I Learnt from Jean-Marie Tillard*

SPEAKER: **DR JULIE CANLIS** University of Aberdeen
Reforming Ascent: Calvin's Communion Motif

• • 3 • •

CHAIR: **MOST REV. ANTHONY FARQUHAR DD** (Chairman of the Council for Ecumenism of the Irish Catholic Bishops' Conference) and **SR ELIZABETH COTTER IBVM** (Vicar for Religious, Archdiocese of Dublin)

SPEAKER: **REV. PROF. GEOFFREY WAINWRIGHT**
Duke University Divinity School, Durham, North Carolina
From Communio Imperfecta *through* Communio in Via *to*
'Full Communion in Faith, Mission and Sacramental Life'?

SPEAKER: **HIS EMINENCE METROPOLITAN EMMANUEL ADAMAKIS OF FRANCE**
President of the Conference of European Churches
Dialogue and Communion: An Orthodox Perspective

THE RELATION BETWEEN THE EUCHARIST AND ECCLESIAL COMMUNION: AN ECUMENICAL VIEW[1]

HIS EMINENCE KURT CARDINAL KOCH
President, Pontifical Council for Promoting Christian Unity

'That which we have seen and heard we proclaim also to you, so that you too may have fellowship with us; and indeed, our fellowship is with the Father and with his Son Jesus Christ' (1 Jn 1:3). In this profoundly significant sentence from the First Letter of John we find all the essential dimensions of the Christian understanding of *communio*. This key theological concept has in the reception of the Second Vatican Council constantly been applied to describe more clearly the essential nature of the Christian Church.[2] The extraordinary Bishops' Synod of 1985 above all, which undertook to evaluate the position of the Church twenty years after the Council, took up the conciliar initiatives towards a renewed *communio* ecclesiology and followed them to their logical conclusion by merging conciliar ecclesiology with the fundamental concept of *communio*.[3] This term can therefore serve as a synthesis of conciliar ecclesiology, to the extent that in it one can discern its new and at the same time totally original thrust, the 'real heart of Vatican II on the Church'.[4]

According to this conciliar view, based on John, the point of departure for all *communio* is the encounter with Jesus Christ as the Son of God become flesh. In this encounter, *communio* also emerges between human beings, grounded in the *communio* with the Triune God. Both meanings of *communio* receive their clearest expression and realisation at the same time in the celebration of the Eucharist, as is very beautifully expressed in the subject of this year's Eucharistic Congress: 'The Eucharist: Communion with Christ and with One Another.' In the Eucharist not only the individual Christian is united with the resurrected Christ himself, present as the body of Christ in the form of bread: those participating in the Eucharist are also united in communion with one another through the shared reception of the body of Christ. Eucharistic *communio* is not only to be understood and enacted *personally* as the participation of the faithful in the resurrected Christ, but also *ecclesially* as communion of the faithful with one another in Christ. Therefore it has a profound significance that the current expression for the reception of the eucharistic gift in the Roman Catholic tradition is 'Communion'. The Church arises and exists through the resurrected Christ communicating himself to human beings, entering into communion with them and thus bringing them into *communio* with one another: 'The Church is the communication of the Lord with us, which at the same time creates the true communication of human beings with one another. Therefore Church in each instance comes into being around an altar.'[5]

Ecclesial *communio* is most profoundly eucharistic *communio*, and the Eucharist is quintessentially the sacrament of *communio*. Conciliar communion ecclesiology is therefore intrinsically eucharistic ecclesiology. At its core it signifies that the 'body of Christ' as the eucharistic gift, and the 'body of Christ' as ecclesial communion between the baptised, form a single indivisible sacrament. This indivisible unity of Church and Eucharist has deep biblical roots which already at Jesus' Last Supper become clearly apparent. The communion character of the Last Supper, and with it the root of the ecclesial dimension of the Eucharist, finds expression firstly in the rite of breaking bread, which refers back to the then common praxis of opening the meal each time with the breaking of bread. Since by the breaking of bread all who receive a piece of the broken bread are bonded into a communion, the broken bread is a sign of the communion of those sharing the meal. Whoever receives a piece of bread belongs to God's *communio* of blessing. In this tradition Jesus' breaking of bread signifies and lays the foundation of the new *Chabura*, and with it the Church in *nuce* of the Israel gathered by Jesus. This intention of Jesus' Last Supper becomes even more apparent in the rite of sharing the one cup, which is the image of the painful destiny of one individual. Accordingly, drinking from the common cup is the sign of profound solidarity in the communion of destiny. It is above all on the basis of the interpretive words of Jesus of the 'blood of the covenant' that is 'shed for many', as preserved in the Markan–Matthian tradition, that Jesus' Last Supper is comprehensible as 'making a covenant: it is the prolongation of the Sinai covenant, which is not abrogated but renewed'.[6] As the conclusion of the covenant, Jesus' Last Supper is the foundation of God's covenant relationship with the disciples of Jesus, with whom he is in blood communion, which is at the same time communion with God.

In the New Testament it is Paul above all who substantially deepens the indivisible vital connection between eucharistic and ecclesial communion. In the tenth chapter of the First Letter to the Corinthians he found a succinct expression for this by applying the term 'Christ's body' to both the eucharistic gift and ecclesial communion: 'The cup of blessing that we bless, is it not a participation in the blood of Christ? The bread that we break, is it not a participation in the body of Christ? Because there is *one* bread, we who are many are one body, for we all partake of the one bread' (1 Cor 10:16-17). How important the indissoluble link between Eucharist and ecclesial communion is for Paul can be inferred above all from the fact that he – in contrast to all other New Testament Lord's Supper traditions – reverses the order of the words about the bread and the cup, or more precisely, places the word about cup before the word about bread. The reason for this striking and individual procedure can only lie in the fact that Paul can thereby express more clearly the connection between Eucharist and ecclesial communion. He switches immediately from 'the body of Christ', in which the eucharistic bread grants participation, to the 'body of Christ' which is the Church. Thus he makes it intelligible that the building up of the Church occurs through the eucharist, and the unity of the many faithful in the one Church comes from the one eucharistic bread and thus from the one Christ: because Christ is one, the eucharistic bread is also only one; and because the faithful partake of communion with the one Christ through this one bread, the Church too can only be one.

This emphatic stress by Paul on the ecclesial dimension of the Eucharist found its natural continuation with the Church Fathers. This is true above all of Augustine, who apprehended the vital connection between the Eucharist and the Church so profoundly that he was able to condense it into the incisive formula: 'If you therefore are Christ's body and members, it is your own mystery that is placed on the Lord's table! It is your own mystery that you are receiving! ... You should be what you see and should receive what you are.'[7] The Eucharist is therefore for Augustine the 'sign of unity and the bond of charity'.[8] In the same sense Pope Leo the Great also declared: 'We are assimilated into that which we receive.'[9] Thus it is absolutely clear that one cannot dissociate the nature of the eucharistic sacrament as Christ's body from the nature of ecclesial *communio* as Christ's body, without at the same time effecting the dissolution of both the Church and the eucharistic sacrament.

In view of this great biblical and patristic tradition, one cannot of course deny that this character of the Eucharist as ecclesial *communio* has regrettably not always been maintained in the history of the Church, but was instead allowed to fade out and sink into oblivion. It was above all the great French theologian Henri de Lubac who demonstrated persuasively that the connection between the sacramental body of Christ and the ecclesial body of Christ was largely lost during the second Lord's Supper controversy in the eleventh century.[10] The consequences of this development must be perceived in the fateful individualisation or even privatisation of the understanding and enactment of the Eucharist, which is still in effect today in the general consciousness of not a few Catholics. By contrast we owe it to the Second Vatican Council that it was able to overcome this one-sided development and once more root ecclesial communion in eucharistic communion, as the Dogmatic Constitution on the Church emphasises: 'Truly partaking in the body of the Lord in the breaking of the Eucharistic bread, we are taken up into communion with him and with one another.'[11]

LITURGICAL CONCENTRATION OF THE UNDERSTANDING OF THE CHURCH

When one observes the fundamental significance of this revitalisation of the ecclesial dimension of the Eucharist, in the first instance it seems logical in regard to eucharistic *communio* to speak above all of a threefold *communio*, as summed up in the liturgical language of the Eucharistic Prayer, and surely most clearly in the third Eucharistic Prayer, which the Catholic theologian Medard Kehl rightly termed 'the liturgical celebration of hope'.[12]

of the people. When the nascent Church defined itself as *ekklesia* against the background of this tradition, it gave expression to its faith conviction that Jesus Christ is the new and true Sinai, and all who gather around him form the final gathering of God's people, which of course becomes Church only through being gathered anew by Christ and by the Spirit in the Eucharist, and is therefore God's people only because it is constantly renewed through the body of Christ. On the basis of the Eucharist, *ekklesia* is 'not only *like* the body of Christ, it *is* the body of Christ because it owes its existence to the salvific working of the re-awakened crucified One, is filled with his pneumatic presence and placed by him in the service of reconciliation'.[17]

EUCHARISTIC ECCLESIOLOGY IN ECUMENICAL DIALOGUE

The Christian understanding of the Church is characterised by a liturgical or more precisely a eucharistic concentration. There is a broad ecumenical consensus on this. Eucharistic ecclesiology has of course been given a distinctive individual stamp by each of the various Christian churches and ecclesial communities, and one must bear these in mind in order that the existing ecumenical consensus can be extended and deepened.

A eucharistic ecclesiology was in the first instance developed by Russian Orthodox theologians in exile in Paris after the First World War, in fact in deliberate opposition to what they claimed to be the centralism of the papacy in the Roman Catholic Church. In this Orthodox view the Church of Jesus Christ is present and realised in each local Church, gathered around its bishop, where the Eucharist is celebrated. Because the local Church celebrating the Eucharist with its bishop is understood as the representation, actualisation and realisation of the one Church in its concrete location, each eucharistic community is wholly Church and lacks nothing beyond itself. Therefore the unity of the eucharistic community with other communities celebrating the Eucharist is ultimately an extrinsic dimension, and the horizontal unity of local Churches between one another is not considered constitutive for being Church, at least not in the sense that it must necessarily exist. Such a unity is indeed recognised as beautiful and certainly pertaining to the fullness of the Church, but is in the end not constitutive. This applies a *fortiori* to a potential unity of the individual eucharistic communities with the Bishop of Rome, because on principle there can on no account be any priority of the universal Church over the local Churches.

The Reformation tradition also takes the liturgical concentration as the starting point of its understanding of the Church, taking its classical form in the definition of the *Confessio Augustana*, according to which the Church is the assembly of the faithful in which the gospel is preached in its purity and the sacraments are administered according to the gospel. Since this occurs concretely in the local congregation, according to the Protestant concept the Church of Jesus Christ not only subsists in the concrete individual congregation, but the congregation is in fact considered the prototypical realisation of the Church. Herein lies the principal reason why the Protestant understanding of the church too is totally focused on the congregation in its specific location, as can be demonstrated already in the thinking of the Reformer Martin Luther. In the desolation of the times he was no longer able to discern the spirit of Christ in the whole of the Catholic Church. Nor did he of course perceive 'Church' in the theological sense of the word in the Protestant state Churches which gradually formed during his lifetime. Instead he considered them sociological–political entities necessary for specific purposes and under the leadership of political powers, in the absence of other authorities. He declared the term 'Church' as such a negative concept, and used the word 'congregation' (*Gemeinde*) to give expression to its essential theological nature. Following the line of this tradition, the Protestant understanding of Church today finds its unequivocal focus and its centre of gravity in the concrete local congregation: the Church of Jesus Christ in its fullest sense is present in the concrete congregation assembled in worship around the word and sacrament. The individual communities do in fact also engage in exchange with one another according to Protestant understanding, and to that extent the supra-congregational aspect of the Church exists implicitly, but it is of an external nature and therefore secondary, and that applies absolutely also to the dimension of the universal Church.

Both the Orthodox and the Protestant ecclesiologies, oriented in worship, do not in principle stand in opposition to the Catholic understanding of Church in any way; they can in fact be integrated into a broader Catholic view. Catholic theology undoubtedly shares with the Orthodox a eucharistic ecclesiology which 'includes the individual responsibility of each community'; it is differentiated from it in the emphasis on a eucharistic ecclesiology which 'excludes self-sufficiency and requires the location within the whole'.[18] With Protestant theology too the Catholic understanding of Church shares the conviction that the Church is wholly present in the specific eucharistic community; but it is differentiated from it in the conviction that the individual eucharistic community is not the whole Church.

In the Catholic view, the unity of the individual eucharistic communities with one another and in communion with the respective bishop and the Bishop of Rome as the Pontiff of the universal Church is constitutive for being Church. The basis of this view is the Christological and eucharistic theological conviction that the body of Christ, present in the Eucharist of the individual local community, unites the participants with all others who believe in Jesus Christ and are joined with his body through baptism and eucharist, as Cardinal Joseph Ratzinger emphatically highlighted: 'Christ is everywhere whole ... At the same time Christ is everywhere only one, so I can have the one Lord only in the unity he is, in the unity of all those who are also his Body and through the Eucharist must evermore become it. Therefore, the reciprocal unity of all those communities who celebrate the Eucharist is not something external added to eucharistic ecclesiology but rather its internal condition.'[19]

This 'internal condition' also applies with regard to the connection with the Bishop of Rome,[20] since his primacy is not simply a juridical and certainly not purely an external supplement to eucharistic ecclesiology, but is grounded in that ecclesiology itself, in so far as the Church which represents and realises itself as a worldwide network of eucharistic communities also requires at the universal level a ministry of unity with full authority. The papacy can ultimately only be understood from the perspective of this worldwide eucharistic network. It is therefore an abiding essential element of the Church, because it stands in the service of the eucharistic unity of the Church and bears the responsibility for the Church as it continually takes its measure from the Eucharist. This interconnectedness of the Petrine office and the Eucharist was expressed already in early times by St Ignatius of Antioch, when, in his Letter to the Romans in the year

110, he designated the cathedra of the Bishop of Rome as that Church which has 'the primacy in love'. Since in the early Church the word 'love' – *agape* – was also a term for the mystery of the Eucharist, through which Christ's love for his Church can be experienced with particular intensity, it becomes apparent that the Bishop of Rome exercises his special responsibility above all in living 'the primacy in love', and binding all the local Churches of the whole world with one another into a universal Church in the Eucharist.

It is only from the perspective of the Eucharist that the deepest essence of the Church becomes visible: each local Church that celebrates the Eucharist is *wholly* Church, but no local Church is the *whole* Church. It is in fact only really Church when it stands in relationship with all local Churches celebrating the Eucharist, and in unity with the primacy in love. This Catholic – in its original sense – dimension of the Eucharist found clear expression in the early Church in the so-called 'Communion letters', which were known as *litterae communicatoriae* and *litterae pacis:* any Christian who went travelling carried with him such a certificate from his Eucharistic community, made out by his bishop. With it he not only found refuge with every Christian community, but also nurtured the communion in the body of Christ as the centre of eucharistic hospitality. On the basis of the Eucharist the Christian is at home in every Christian community, and on the same basis the belonging to the eucharistic communion – which is the belonging to the Church – is universal: anyone who belongs to *one* local Church belongs at the same time to *all*. Partaking of the Eucharist implies incorporation into the one Christ and therewith the becoming one of all communicants in the universal *communio* of the Church.

ECCLESIAL AND EUCHARISTIC COMMUNION IN ECUMENICAL PERSPECTIVE

That perspective also illuminates the ecumenically thorny problem of eucharistic *communio,* which represents a sore point in every eucharistic ecclesiology. Because for the Roman Catholic Church the intrinsic relationship of Eucharist and Church is fundamental, she holds fast – like the majority of Christian Churches – to the principle of the indissoluble unity of ecclesial communion and eucharistic communion,[21] which at one time, until the middle of the twentieth century, represented a broad ecumenical consensus. The Churches and ecclesial communities that emerged from the Reformation also shared this consensus, which can readily be inferred from the fact that there was no fellowship in the Lord's Supper between the Lutheran and Reformed Churches despite the already existing unity in the doctrine of justification. The Churches of the Reformation only departed from this ecumenical consensus in the seventies of the previous century, or more precisely with the Leuenberger Concord of 1973. For not a few Protestant communities it was possible to gain the impression that the ecumenical goal does not consist in the restoration of ecclesial *communio* but in eucharistic inter*communio*, and 'if this is achieved, all the rest could remain as it was'.[22]

By contrast, the Roman Catholic Church holds firmly to the conviction, alive already in the early Church, that there can be no true eucharistic fellowship without ecclesial communion, and without the Eucharist no full ecclesial communion. In the light of the sacramental understanding of the Church it is not possible to separate from one another communion with Christ, ecclesial communion, and eucharistic communion; they must instead be apprehended in their intrinsic unity. This is the most profound reason that in the Catholic view the goal of all ecumenical endeavours cannot consist in the first instance in so-called intercommunion, but only in the restoration of ecclesial *communio*, 'within which the communion in the Lord's Supper also has its place'.[23] Cardinal Karl Lehmann has therefore rightly warned against 'dissolving and as it were dismembering a certain harmony and cohesion of ecclesial unity and communion in the Lord's Supper'; and he draws from that the conclusion: 'The shared Supper belongs as a whole at the end and not at the beginning of ecumenical endeavours.'[24]

This view becomes intelligible only against the background of the relationship between baptism and Eucharist in the view of the Second Vatican Council. The *Decree on Ecumenism* sees, on the one hand, the foundation of the affiliation of all Christians with the Church in baptism, which constitutes 'the sacramental bond of unity linking all who have been reborn by means of it'. On the other hand, baptism is however, 'only a beginning, a point of departure, for it is wholly directed toward the acquiring of fullness of life in Christ' and 'oriented toward a complete profession of faith, a complete incorporation into the system of salvation such as Christ himself willed it to be, and finally toward a complete participation in eucharistic communion'.[25] Whereas baptism grants a fundamental but incomplete communion between Christians and is to that extent the sacramental bond of unity, it remains, on the other hand, oriented toward the shared profession of faith and the celebration of the Eucharist as the fullness and climax of ecclesial unity.

This definition of the relationship between baptism and Eucharist provides a precise definition of the position of ecumenism today, located between the fundamental communion of the sacramental bond of baptism on the one hand, and the not-yet-possible full communion in the Eucharist on the other. This location obligates all Christians and Churches to take baptism seriously and on the basis of this shared foundation mature in ecumenical rapprochement, so that the hour can approach in which we can take our place together at the table of the Lord. Only then would an ecumenical eucharistic ecclesiology be possible. It would then no longer be a wounded but a healed and hallowed eucharistic ecclesiology, towards which our ecumenical path must remain directed.

there was always an extraordinary depth of research and an unfailing focus on the task in hand.

One of the most creative moves in *The Gift of Authority* is to begin from the recognition of the authority of Christ by an individual believer. The 'Yes' of the individual to Christ and the 'Amen' of Christ to the individual as described in *The Gift of Authority* began life in a preliminary paper by Tillard[4] as a 'double yes' on the part of the individual to Christ and the Church. It was his generative insight that this 'double yes' should be contextualised within the life of a local Church and that the authority of scripture and Tradition immanent within the local Church could then be related to the ministry of episcopacy (oversight) – before going on to relate this to collegiality, synodality and ultimately to the ministry of the Bishop of Rome. This was vintage Tillard. He published his book on *The Bishop of Rome* in 1982, and his magisterial study of *The Local Church* in 1995.[5] He had thought out his position in a way that was deeply true to his own Catholic tradition, but open to Anglicans as well. He knew what would be the sticking points for Anglicans and thus, for example, repeatedly emphasised the way that the authority of the Bishop of Rome is exercised *within* the body of bishops, and not independently of them.

In the same way, before anyone else on ARCIC had begun seriously to think about how to approach the work on Mary, Tillard presented a paper on Mary as 'icon of the Church'. He wanted to steer us away from taking the defined dogmas about the Immaculate Conception and bodily assumption of Mary 'head on', just as he had steered us away from taking papal infallibility 'head on'. As always, he was determined to ensure that the words which defined our differences would be subsumed within a wider understanding of communion and of ecclesiology. Tillard had an extraordinarily clear sense as to where consensus lay, in terms of the scriptures and of the tradition of the early centuries, both Eastern and Western. It was on this consensus that he wanted to build.

At ARCIC meetings, Tillard didn't stay around for small talk. Behind the dazzling smile one sensed his mind was already at work on something you hadn't yet thought of – but you knew that the fruits of his research would become evident at the strategic moment. He was a sharp operator, with a touch of theological genius.

TILLARD AND THE EUCHARIST

Tillard was thirty-seven when in 1964 his first major book, *L'Eucharistie, Pâque de l'Eglise*[6] appeared. This was during the time he was a *peritus* at Vatican II, advising the Canadian episcopate on the religious life. This study of the Eucharist was central to all his later concerns. Sharing of the Eucharist was indispensable for the *communion de vie* (we might say, 'living communion') in Jesus. The book was number forty-four in the *Unam Sanctam* series of the Dominican *Editions du Cerf*. The same series already included four books by its founder,Yves Congar, de Lubac's *Catholicisme* and Hamer's *L'Église est une Communion,* so the lineage is clear. Tillard's work was embedded within the *Ressourcement*[7] associated with names such as these. His opening words are that 'This book attempts simply to bring to the light the roots of a truth that is traditional in ecclesiology and in sacramental theology: 'The Eucharist makes the Church.'[8] In his book he does two things of huge importance for his future work: first, he relates the Eucharist to its Jewish roots in the narrative of the Passover and the memorial narrative of the Jewish Passover meal. With that, he relates the Eucharist to the future hope of the Church, the hope of salvation. Central to his study is the notion of *anamnesis* as a living memorial of the past and as a remembrance before God of the future.

Tillard's understanding of the term *anamnesis* helped ARCIC find a way through the deadlock set up by simplistic understandings on both sides of the 'once-for-all' sacrifice of Christ and of the Eucharist as a repeated sacrifice. He helped to change the way Anglicans like myself understood the Lord's words, 'Do this in memory of me',[9] to break down rigid divisions between past, present and future when thinking about the meaning of 'living communion'. It was from this reflection on *anamnesis,* I guess, that Tillard developed his commitment to the need for a 'ministry of memory' within the Church, something he attributed not so much to theologians as to bishops. For him, apostolic succession was linked to communion in the apostolic tradition, which was based upon the faithful witness of the apostles (the 'deposit of faith'). Teaching that is faithful to apostolic tradition is thus in itself an *anamnesis*: it is a 'sharing' in the teaching of the apostles in their witness to Christ and also a 'sharing' in the full knowledge of Christ that is to come. 'Memory' – calling to mind – is an exploration both of the past and of the future.

Tillard's knowledge of patristic theology was vital to his whole project. It enabled him to see how Greek terms could often 'go behind' the Latin terms that had been made the subject of minute analysis and distinction by the theologians of the medieval schools. Terms like *anamnesis* and *koinonia* could be used with a flexibility indebted to the New Testament and the Fathers of the early Church. In *L'Eucharistie,* he notes that 'communion' has been used to translate the Greek term *koinonia,* which he calls 'one of the key terms of the theology of the Church, of salvation and of grace'.[10] Increasingly, *koinonia* became a keyword for ecumenical theology. It was used as the central, integrating motif for the work of ARCIC I.[11]

Something else that is striking about *L'Eucharistie* is the depth of Tillard's scholarship in the study of the Bible, the Fathers and the liturgy of the early Church. For him, these were the resources of the 'undivided Church', shared by Roman Catholics, Orthodox and Anglicans alike. As a Dominican, he readily turned to Aquinas for further illumination, but to few other medieval writers. His way of reading scripture and the Fathers was alert to the best critical scholarship, but it was more akin to *Lectio Divina.* He read these texts with the trust of one who believed that here are the riches of the Apostolic Tradition and within the Apostolic Tradition are to be found the entire resources needed for the Christian life. For him, there were still many things for the Church to learn from Apostolic Tradition, but in essence everything has already been revealed.

TILLARD, THE BISHOP OF ROME AND THE ECCLESIOLOGY OF COMMUNION

Through the years that followed Vatican II, Tillard wrote extensively on religious life. I shall not comment on this aspect of his work, important though it is, because I did not engage with it directly. It was, however, essential to his identity: I was conscious that he was a Dominican through and through. In any rounded account of his achievement this would have to be explored. Alongside his reflections on holiness and religious life, as his experience of the ecumenical movement grew, he was in these years developing and deepening his ecclesiology of communion. Not, however, till 1985 did he lay out his ecclesiology of communion systematically – in Église *d'Églises.*[12]

This provided essential background for ARCIC's work on *Church as Communion* (1990), which was a short agreed statement of the ecclesiology of communion that underlay all the work of ARCIC to that point. Needless to say, it drew heavily on Tillard's expertise.

Three years earlier Tillard published his groundbreaking study of *The Bishop of Rome*, the one book of his that was well translated into English. *The Bishop of Rome* (1982) was essential to *The Gift of Authority* (1999), ARCIC's third statement on authority. The two earlier statements of ARCIC I on authority had left unresolved questions around the Petrine texts, the use of the term *jus divinum* to describe the universal papacy (was it according to the specific will of God?), the universal jurisdiction of the Pope, and also papal infallibility.[13] At precisely this time Tillard was working on his own study of the papacy in the context of an ecclesiology of communion which made it possible to address these questions afresh.

Tillard's vision of the Church as a 'communion of communions' was for me one of his most important and liberating insights. For him, the identity of the Church was in the proper sense a *mystery*: what makes the Church the Church is not its institutional continuity but its participation in the life of God. Tillard showed me that the Catholic Church is not a monolith: it is constituted of local Churches in communion with one another.[14] Through his scholarly work and his ecumenical engagement he reminded me of the diversity of communities, rites and canon law within the Roman Catholic Church and especially of the importance of Eastern Rite Catholicism. For an Anglican, this mirrors the diversity within the Anglican Communion, whilst at the same time raising the question as to whether Anglican Churches could ever constitute a communion or 'communion of communions' within the Roman Catholic Church – in the famous words of Dom Lambert Beauduin at the Malines Conversations 'united not absorbed'.

Language about 'a communion of communions' of course raises the question as to what holds the local Churches together. For Tillard, it must be participation in the one Eucharist, shared with all the bishops and, in particular, with the Bishop of Rome. Anything else is not truly communion. It also raises the question as to the role of the college of bishops and the papacy within the whole body of the Church. Tillard extended my imagination to see that Anglicans can and should, for excellent historical and theological reasons, long to accord to the Pope the 'primacy of honour' accorded to the Bishop of Rome in the first millennium, something we can approach through our experience of the Archbishop of Canterbury as *primus inter pares* amongst the bishops of the Anglican communion.

WHAT TILLARD DID NOT TEACH ME

Jean Tillard died on 13th November 2000. Towards the end of his life, the provinces of the Anglican communion began to ordain women as priests and bishops. He could see that things would get markedly more difficult ecumenically. In the last months of his life, he had a series of conversations – conversations in Winter – with the theological journalist Francesco Strazzari. They began by discussing words supposed to have been uttered by Yossel Rakover from within the Warsaw ghetto: 'I believe in the God of Israel, although he has done everything to shatter the faith which I have in him.'[15] For Tillard, the convergence of the Churches for which he had worked throughout his life and in which he had believed seemed to have been reversed. He didn't say that his faith had been shattered, but he did, in a late paper, put the question, 'Are we the last Christians?' Since the time of his death the process of divergence has accelerated.

Tillard would be the first to say that what has been achieved through fifty years of ecumenical dialogue since Vatican II has been achieved through the concerted efforts of many contributors. His contribution was that of a theological visionary who was able to inspire others and draw them with him. The problem was that his vision only partially corresponded to the reality, and the reality has now to a considerable degree overtaken the vision. I believe the fundamental difficulty was this. Tillard's view of *koinonia* never gave full weight to the reality of conflict and its place in the development of *koinonia*.[16] His account of *koinonia* was, in the end, entirely positive. One key text for him was Acts 4:32: 'Now the whole group of those who believed were of one heart and soul, and no one claimed private ownership of any possessions, but everything they owned was held in common.' Common ownership was of course something Tillard practised as a Dominican. 'Consensus' was, for him, characteristic of the life of the monastery and of the early Church.

Tillard was increasingly troubled by the lack of consensus within the Churches that he had so longed to see reunited. I do not think his theological equipment allowed him to recognise persistent and unresolved conflict within the life of the Church as something that could be brought about by the Holy Spirit.[17] Yet, without such conflict it is impossible to see how the Church can be brought to face new challenges and, in effect, to change its mind, as it has done, for example, in its teaching on slavery. This 're-reception' involved a radical rereading of scripture and the tradition of the Church, which until the nineteenth century was entirely accepting of slavery. The same could be argued of human rights.

Tillard's reading of history was, then, in this sense idealistic. He tended to view the struggles and disagreements of the Church through the lens of the conciliar process by which they were resolved. He spoke of the *sensus fidei* as a kind of olfactory sense by which the believer is able to intuit sound doctrine, the lay person perhaps in advance of the bishop.[18] He had a high regard for the *sensus fidelium* or the *consensus fidelium* which was vital for the Church's discernment of the truth. What troubled him were instances where there has evidently been no such *sensus* or *consensus*, or the consensus has been opposed to the official teaching of the Church. One example might be the widespread lack of reception within the Roman Catholic Church for its teaching on birth control. Tillard wasn't sympathetic to the reading of history from the perspective of the marginalised or the excluded. For him, the life of the Church was situated within the great Tradition of the undivided Church: one, holy, Catholic and apostolic. It allowed little space for the darkness of not knowing, for conscientious dissent and prophetic adventure. When ARCIC II turned to the moral teaching of the Church, having outlined our common vision of human flourishing within *koinonia,* we discussed the differing teaching of Anglicans and Roman Catholics on marriage after divorce, contraception, abortion and homosexual relations. I think the discussion troubled him. On the relation between communion and dogmatic teaching he had absolute clarity; on the relation between communion and moral teaching he was outside his comfort zone.[19]

The trouble was that the ecclesiology of communion had been developed *over against* an ecclesiology of the Church as institution.

Tillard wrote about the friction of the two theologies in *Lumen Gentium*.[20] So strongly did he want to emphasise the Church as in its essence communion in the Holy Trinity that he had little time for the canon law which undergirds the institutional life of the Church. This came home to me not so long ago, when I was asked to reflect on 'The Contribution of canon law to ecumenism' for a colloquium of Roman Catholic and Anglican canon lawyers.[21] Up to that point, I had simply not thought about the facilitative role played by canon law in protecting space for ecumenical activity and regulating that activity for the good of the Church. The awkwardness around the creation of the ordinariate shows very clearly that if and when there is to be a renewed sharing of eucharistic communion, the structures within which this takes place have to be very carefully thought out. This is a task for canon lawyers and ecumenically alert theologians to work on together.

This links with a further problem. Tillard did not know Anglicanism (or English!) as well as he thought he did. He found affirmation and encouragement in Anglican friends who could see the immense resonances for Anglicans in all that he stood for. In his friendships with Anglicans, I think he also found relief from the pressures of his high-profile position as a leading Roman Catholic ecumenist. His approach was immensely attractive to any Anglican nurtured in the tradition of Michael Ramsey or the participants in the Malines Conversations. Tillard refreshed our sense of the Catholicity and apostolicity of Anglicanism, circumventing the divisive legacy of the Oxford Movement. But there are many Anglicans worldwide to whom these things mean little. They would not agree to the notion of a 'double yes': that a 'yes' to Christ means a 'yes' to Christ's Church. For many Anglicans, both evangelical and liberal, the imperative of mission means that the Church must be prepared to grow and change far more that Tillard would have accepted – for instance by recognising the ministry of women as priests and bishops. For many Anglicans also, decisions about the evolving identity of the Church can be safely taken at provincial level. They see no need for appellate jurisdiction beyond the level of provincial or national Churches. It is not that they do not recognise the exercise of authority by the Bishop of Rome; they do not want it.

WHERE ARE WE NOW?

If Tillard were alive today, he would be in a difficult position. It has become increasingly clear that concern for the theology of communion must be balanced by a concern for the juridical structures which undergird it. At a time when it is difficult to see what further progress can be made in areas such as ministry and authority, when we may seem to be moving further away from, rather than nearer to, sharing the eucharist, it is clear that the ecumenical agenda has changed. ARCIC III has begun its exploration of 'The Local Church and the Church Universal' and of 'the discernment of moral teaching within the local church'. These themes are well chosen to take us to the heart of our current ecumenical difficulties, but I do not think they would have appealed to Tillard. Here, there are no clear communion-dividing issues like those listed in paragraph 79 of *Ut Unum Sint*.

Tillard, of course, contributed massively to our understanding of the local Church, and he never lost his concern for its authentic Catholicity of the local Church. As he told Francesco Strazzari, 'I have never said or written that the Church of God comes about from the sum or addition of local churches ... I make quite a different point: that the Church of God is the communion (the *koinonia*) of local Churches that exist, have existed, or will exist.'[22] Though, prompted for example by *Lumen Gentium* to reflect on the role of the apostles (19), the bishops (22) and the Pope within 'The universal Church', for him the local Church had priority. He describes the shift from the ecclesiology of Vatican I to that of Vatican II as 'the movement from an ecclesiology starting with the idea of the universal Church divided into portions called dioceses, to an ecclesiology which understands the Church as the communion of all the local Churches: the universal Church', he says, 'arises from the communion of Churches.'[23]

One promising development in the post-Tillard era has been the appearance of 'Receptive ecumenism'.[24] This has been defined in a number of different ways but it seems to me two ideas are central. One is that ecumenism consists in the receiving and giving of 'gifts' within the (impaired) communion of the Churches. The second is that it is within the actual life of the Churches that we discover what those gifts may be. This second perspective leads into study of the Churches as they really are, something that is needed as a complement to the somewhat idealistic functioning of the life of the Church as described by Tillard. The first is something for which Tillard's theology prepares the way. From his early work on the *epiclesis* in the Eucharist, he was profoundly interested in the gifts that are given by the Spirit within the communion of the Churches and how they may be used to build up the Church as a whole. He often returned to Ephesians chapter 4 as a key ecumenical text. He was himself an extraordinarily gifted person. As an Anglican, it is easy to see how he points to gifts within the tradition of the Church, both East and West that can and must be re-received to enrich the life of the Church today. Perhaps the most important of these gifts is his deep awareness that 'The Eucharist makes the Church' and that we cannot rest until we have reached that point of full, visible unity in which Christians of divided traditions are reunited in communion at the Eucharist. In his time, by his commitment to the ecumenical movement and to bilateral dialogue, he was a pioneer and an explorer. Without his extraordinary contribution to what we might call 'the practical ecclesiology of communion', the Churches would be far farther apart than we are today. He was a man 'restless for unity' and from that restlessness I learnt more than I can say.

NOTES

1 I must record my thanks to Dame Mary Tanner, who knew Jean Tillard well. She read this paper in full, making several suggestions for its improvement.

2 See, for example, C. Ruddy, *The Local Church: Tillard and the Future of Catholic Ecclesiology*, New York: Herder and Herder, 2006, p. 5.

3 *The Bishop of Rome*, London: SPCK, 1983, e.g., pp. 77–86.

4 Published as 'Faith: The Believer and the Church', *Mid-Stream* 94, 1995, 45–60.

5 *L'Église locale, Ecclésiologie de Communion et Catholicité*, Paris: Éditions du Cerf, 1995.

6 *L'Eucharistie, Pâque de l'Eglise, Unam Sanctam* 44, Paris: Éditions du Cerf, 1964.

7 Cf. the recent study edited by Gabriel Flynn and Paul Murray, *Ressourcement, A Movement for Renewal in Twentieth-Century Catholic Theology*, Oxford: Oxford University Press, 2012.

8 For the background to the phrase 'The Eucharist makes the Church', see P. McPartlan, *The Eucharist Makes the Church: Henri de Lubac and John Zizioulas in Dialogue*, Edinburgh: T&T Clark, 1993.

9 Tillard was not alone in this. He himself refers to J. Jeremias's groundbreaking *The Eucharistic Words of Jesus*, Oxford: SCM, 1955, which interprets the words of Jesus as, in effect, a prayer to the Father, pleading his coming sacrifice and in faith anticipating the Father's response, cf. *L'Eucharistie*, p. 179.

10 *L'Eucharistie*, p. 244.

11 See, *The Final Report*, London: SPCK/CTS, 1982, Introduction: 'Fundamental to all our Statements is the concept of *koinonia*', p. 5.

12 Église *d'Églises, L'ecclésiologie de communion*, Paris: Éditions du Cerf, 1987.

13 *The Final Report*, 'Authority in the Church II', pp. 81–100.

14 See the excellent study by Christopher Ruddy on Tillard's understanding of *The Local Church*.

15 William Rusch ed., *I Believe, Despite Everything, Reflections of an Ecumenist*, Collegeville, Minn.: Liturgical Press, 2003, p. 1.

16 I have discussed this in *Ecumenism, Christian Origins and the Practice of Communion*, Cambridge: Cambridge University Press, 2000, pp. 206–7.

17 Brian T. Flanagan argues in *Community, Diversity and Salvation, the Contribution of Jean-Marie Tillard to Systematic Ecclesiology*, London/New York: T&T Clark, 2011, pp. 119–33, that one major lacuna in his thought is his lack of a direct connection between his understanding of communion and the concrete reality of the Church.

18 *L'Église locale,* pp. 314–16.

19 For a splendid discussion of *koinonia* and the moral teaching of the Roman Catholic Church, see John Mahoney, *The Making of Moral Theology: A Study of the Roman Catholic Tradition,* Oxford: Clarendon, 1987.

20 See, for example, 'The Church of God is a Communion. The Ecclesiological Perspective of Vatican II', *One in Christ* 17, 1981, 117–31.

21 'The Contribution of Canon Law to Anglican-Roman Catholic Ecumenism', *Ecclesiastical Law Journal* 13:1, 2011, 4–14.

22 J. M. R Tillard and William G. Rusch, eds, *I Believe, Despite Everything,* Minnesota: Liturgical Press, 2003, p. 24. In *The Local Church,* Ruddy discusses in depth the debate between Benedict XVI and Cardinal Kasper about the priority of the universal or the local Church. He stresses that for Tillard there is a 'simultaneity' of the local and universal Church, pp. 100–9, which stems from the creation of the Jerusalem Church on the Day of Pentecost as described in Acts, cf. *L'Église locale,* pp. 29–37.

23 *The Bishop of Rome,* p. 37.

24 Paul Murray ed., *Receptive Ecumenism and the Call to Catholic Learning,* Oxford: Oxford University Press, 2010.

REFORMING ASCENT: CALVIN'S COMMUNION MOTIF

DR JULIE CANLIS
University of Aberdeen

Calvin's writings are rich in theological insight and spiritual depth, particularly in regards to communion. His writings are both about communion – with communion with God as a constant theme – but they are also acts of communion themselves. It shows humility and grace to hear these insights from one who himself broke communion with the Catholic Church five hundred years ago, though that was not his initial intent. I consider it a tremendous honour to speak to you today, and to be in communion with you through, with, and (above all) in Jesus Christ.

Many recent documents and treatises about communion begin with communion as a fundamental human longing, which (theologically) I believe is true. Calvin would agree wholeheartedly with this. He writes, 'And, indeed, there is nothing in which man excels the lower animals unless it be his spiritual communion with God in the hope of a blessed eternity.'[1] But after much pondering, rewriting, and rearranging, Calvin's final edition of the *Institutes* does not begin with communion as a fundamental human longing or as an anthropological principle, even as his work radiates its reality. He, instead, restructures it around God's own communion, as it is revealed in Christ.[2]

When the exiled Calvin first penned his *Institutes of the Christian Religion* from Basle, at the tender age of twenty-seven, his mission was to encourage reforming Christians in his own country, France. His work followed the same structure as Luther's catechism, designed to give persecuted Christians a mini-tutorial on the ten commandments, the confession of faith, the Lord's prayer, and the sacraments. Over all the years that it grew (from six chapters to eighty), over all the years that it matured (from 1536–59), Calvin's original purpose never wavered. The 'systematic' Calvin who was later to be admired is more of an anachronism, for he viewed doctrine not as the communication of beliefs about God but as a personal experience of communion with God and others. It must not be forgotten that Calvin was first and foremost a pastor who was intent on forming a people for and by union with Christ.

As Calvin's *Institutes* grew, the project changed – and Calvin finally abandoned its catechetical structure in favour of a Trinitarian one comprised of four books: Father, Son, Spirit, and Church. In so doing, we begin to see a subtle shift in Calvin's approach to theology – perhaps even a shift in his spirituality. Calvin restructured the *Institutes* such that God's triune communion sets the stage. It is not scripture, or God's unity, or the chronology of predestination that is dealt with first (although later redactors of Calvin would unfortunately restructure this), but for Calvin, it is the story of God triunely relating *to us* that frames his theological vision. Let me explain why I think this is of such significance: in Reformation times, catechisms functioned to personalise one's faith. (For example, the 1549 *Catechism of the Church of England* begins with the question, 'what is your name?' suggesting that catechisms have very much to do with the personalisation of the faith.) They had their rough origins in the medieval Church, but were pioneered by the Reformers in order that Protestants could know what they believed, why they believed it, and to have this make a difference to their daily life and practice. (The benefit of catechesis was ironically noted at Trent, in the preface to the Roman catechism which reports, 'the mischief which the Protestants have done the Catholic Church, not only by their tongues, but especially by their writings called catechisms'.) And yet Calvin abandons this as the framework for his *Institutes* (he does not abandon catechisms); his motivation for doing so remains a mystery to us, even as his delight in his new Trinitarian structure is evident.

I have a theory, which may or may not have motivated Calvin, but is certainly an unintended consequence with significant implications for communion. In his move from catechetical structure to a Trinitarian one, the central player is no longer the human being attempting to 'personalise' faith, but rather God personalising us. It is God, not the human being, who sets the communion stage. We enter into a drama already well under way. The doctrine of the Trinity is a way of reminding us that everything God does it personal, because

God is *three persons* who can only be received in a personal way. It is not we who make the good news personal; rather, it is God who is eternally personal – who is himself a communion of love – who offers his gospel to us. So from the very beginning, before the first page is turned, Calvin's challenge is for us to wake up to the personalness (the communion) of God all around us. And it is in this personal, relational manner that we are led in to the *Institutes*.[3]

When it comes to communion, Calvin knows himself to be working with shadows and figures. We cannot truly know what communion is by looking at the Bible's description of the first humans. Calvin remarks, 'that original excellence and nobility which we have recounted would be of no profit to us ... until God ... appeared as Redeemer in the person of the only begotten Son.'[4] Neither can we peer behind the veil and discern the communion of the godhead itself. Calvin warns, 'when they indulge their curiosity, they enter into a labyrinth'.[5] So if we cannot look at humans to understand communion aright, nor can we penetrate the ineffable mystery of the godhead to understand communion, where shall we go?

Although the Trinitarian communion will always be a mystery, Calvin is emphatic that there are aspects of it which have been flung open to us in Christ. He says, 'Christ alone is the mirror in which we can contemplate that which [we cannot clearly see for] ourselves.'[6]And this is where I get to the heart of Calvin's contribution to the ecumenical discussion of communion: communion must take as its starting point Christ's earthly relation with his Father. This is the ontological entry-point to our experience of communion – whether it be our communion with God, with one another, or within the structures of the *ecclesia*. Calvin understands this primary relationship – that of Father and Son – to be at the root of all reality. It took me multiple reads of the *Institutes* and commentaries to realise what Calvin is doing: he is painting the whole biblical story in terms of a *father and son*. We humans fit into this prior dynamic. T. F. Torrance, that famed Scottish theologian who was a student of Calvin, notes much the same thing when he says that 'God was not always eternally creator but he was always and eternally *Father*'.[7] The human story does not unfold within God generally, but the story of humanity unfolds within a particular aspect of God's *koinonia*, of Father and Son.

THE OLD TESTAMENT: THE FATHERHOOD OF GOD

Indulge me for a moment, by allowing me to paint in broad brushstrokes just how pervasive this Father–Son communion is for Calvin, colouring everything he has to say about the human story. In Calvin's *Institutes*, Adam is called a 'son' who is surrounded with signs of the 'paternal goodness'[8] of God. Adam's glory lies not in his superhuman perfections but rather that he is a 'partaker' of God for everything he enjoys in the garden. Human perfection, in other words, lay in communion with God. To be human, Adam needs God. This is Adam's glory – the way he was designed – not a deficiency due to sin.

So what is broken in the Fall? Communion with God, specifically as children with their Father. Calvin emphasises over and over again is that humanity can no longer (and I quote) 'from a mere survey of the world, infer that he is father' (II.6.1). In fact, worse – we now feel *terror* at the sight of God.[9] Whereas Adam was surrounded by signs of paternity that he can no longer discern, the future of humanity is to know God intimately as Father once again. Calvin sketches the story in broad brushstrokes familiar to us all: Adam refused to be the loving son, but a promise is given to his seed.[10] The story gains complexity as a new son is raised up through the seed of Abraham, and expands to include the nation of Israel, who is portrayed as this son. But here is a unique twist, particularly for one seen as a founder of the Protestant movement: Calvin emphasises that Abraham was not justified by the promise or 'a word', but 'because he embraced God as his Father'.[11] Even here, we find Calvin orienting that famous or (in) famous Protestant emphasis upon justification toward its ontological basis: communion.[12]

This, for Calvin, is the story of the Old Testament. It is the story of a Father who is trying to adopt his son, trying to bless his son, trying to protect his son. Calvin pays exquisite attention to the filial, father-child dimension found throughout the Old Testament because he believes that this is the pattern of God's communion with us. Even the cult and the law, those often opaque and downright difficult portions of scripture to understand, receive this familial interpretation: they are to shape the people of God into sons. Calvin portrays the law not as the primary mode of relationship that God has with his people, but more like a 'tutor' for a child, until the time 'appointed by the father, after which [the child] enjoys his freedom.'[13] The ceremonies are given the same treatment – they are 'little external observances,' akin to 'rules for children's instruction'[14] that testify to the children that God alone can expiate guilt, forgive sin, and bring about communion. As Israel could not believe that God was a gracious Father, God had to institute a system to remind them of it![15] Through all of these strange and foreign and sometimes off-putting practices, Calvin believes that God was attempting 'to attest that he was Father, and to set apart for himself a chosen people'.[16]

But the son would have none of it. Calvin, through the mouth of Hosea, portrays the Father as lamenting the loss of communion with his children. 'I have not otherwise governed them than as a father his own children; I have been bountiful towards them. I indeed wished to do them good, and, as it was right, required obedience from them.'[17] It is in the framework of the faithful Father, and the disobedient children, that Calvin most clearly articulates the work of Christ's salvation.

THE GOSPELS: THE SONSHIP OF CHRIST

(For) at last, in the fullness of time, God brings forth *the* Son.[18] Calvin writes, 'Our Lord came forth as true man and took the person and the name of Adam in order to take Adam's place in obeying the Father ...'[19] The son in the garden failed; the son in the covenanted nation failed; but this Son does not fail. Here, at last, is a human fully in communion with God; here is a human rendering faithful filial obedience to the Father, and in this is our salvation. The quality of that life of Christ to which Calvin is most attuned is to his lived Sonship – his life lived in listening and attentive fidelity to the Father. In places where the text does not even warrant it, Calvin interprets the primary dynamic as between Father and Son. In his baptism, Calvin does not see Christ as fulfilling the law (as do his contemporaries), so much as rendering obedience to the Father. In his atoning sacrifice, 'his willing obedience is the important thing'.[20] Calvin even goes so far as to paint Christ as crying out 'Father, Father, why hast thou forsaken me?' – instead of the text's 'my God, my God ...'[21] Pope John Paul II evokes the same truth in *Dives in Misericordia*, when he speaks that it is the 'vision of the Father', which 'constituted the central content of the messianic mission of the Son of Man'.

But Christ does not just do this *for* us. He invites us into this very relation – the communion of Father and Son. The filial story of God and humanity is not that of Adam – then Israel – and then Christ. It keeps going. It moves forward to *sons*. Calvin is convinced that there is so much that God desires to give to humanity, but now what God wants to give will take on a Christ-shape, a Son-shape. For this Christ walked the earth – breaking the power of sin, disease, and destruction – so that his Sonship can become ours. 'Christ has [no] thing, which may not be applied to our benefit,'[22] says Calvin. As such, the humble life of Jesus of Nazareth is not a self-enclosed story, at least not in Calvin's version. It does not intrude into the present in the sense that it is a moral pattern for us to follow, but because it was lived deliberately for us to share in by the Spirit. Every event in Jesus' life was done with the intent that humanity be able to draw from it and be made new by it. This has always been the momentum of the triune love.

OUR ADOPTION INTO THE FATHER-SON RELATION

For Calvin, God becoming our Father is perhaps the best summary of the gospel.[23] He writes in his *Commentary on John*, 'There are innumerable other ways, indeed, in which God daily testifies his fatherly love toward us, but the mark of adoption is justly preferred to them all.'[24] It reveals that it is not only the pardon, but the life of communion that is now ours. For this, Calvin has no words – he gropes and fumbles, calling it the 'mystical union' or in shorthand, 'our adoption'. He writes, 'We must understand that as long as Christ remains outside of us, and we are separated from him, all that he has done for the salvation of the human race remains useless and of no value for us. Therefore, to share with us what he has received from the Father, he had to become ours and to dwell within us.'[25] And what is the primary thing that Christ has come to give to humanity? It is communion with his Father.

Calvin rarely, if ever, speaks of union with God. (Calvin notes that even Plato spoke of union with God.) For Calvin, our union with God takes the shape of Christ: we are joined, by the Spirit, to Jesus who in turn *opens up to us his earthly relationship to his Father*. In union with Christ, Jesus' Father becomes our Father, we become children, and we enter the family dynamic. We move from being orphans to suddenly sitting around a table, eating the family food, being included in the Father's legacy, and getting in on everything in this family economy.

This comes across most strikingly in Calvin's analysis of Christ's own baptism. When God rends the sky and thunders his blessing over Jesus – calling him *beloved* – Calvin reminds us that this is not just a private and personal emotion God felt for his only-begotten Son. This was God's declaration of *our belovedness as well*, for those of us who would be engrafted into Christ.[26] Even our belovedness is anchored in Christ and his baptism, for Calvin's point is that God has a Trinitarian, *personal* way of doing things. He refuses to give us gifts in which he himself is not personally involved.

If Christ's life on earth as the *Son* is the foundation for our adoption, then Calvin saw Christ's ascension as that which grounds our ongoing communion with the Father as the goal of the Christian life. Ascension is not so much that which establishes the physical Church, but rather – with a human at the right hand of the Father – ascension is that which secures our future as communion with God. Ascent is primarily Christ's, yet his mission was to include us in his ascending return to the Father – for being with the Father is 'the ultimate object at which you ought to aim'.[27] Calvin is clear that Christ's descent to us would be cut short if it did not also result in our ascent with him, to communion with the Father. 'Lift up your hearts' was Calvin's favourite saying of Origen, meaning the whole orientation of our heart, soul, and minds to communion with the Father, in the Son, by the Spirit.

So now we are ready to understand Calvin's unique understanding of communion: it has been flung open to us in Christ. Communion is not an amorphous quality of God, an anthropological tendency in humanity, or a mere counter to individualism. It has a peculiar shape – that of Father and Son. It is perhaps for this reason that Calvin's pneumatology retained its non-instrumentalist flavour, for the Spirit is the one who brings the human into the heart of the Father-Son relation. It is entirely the domain of the Spirit, whose work is to bring us to live out of our new reality. Without the Spirit, Calvin says, 'no one can taste either the fatherly favour of God or the beneficence of Christ'.[28]

But the history of various denominations within Protestantism has perhaps borne out that it is difficult for us humans to begin 'above' (with the spiritual, revealed reality) without being tempted to some strain of Gnosticism, in which the 'below' (incarnate life on earth) is not in some way downgraded, or seen as unnecessary for one's private spiritual union. For some Protestants, I candidly admit, are uncertain as to why the Church matters if they already have union with Christ, and they are not certain why the physicality of bread and wine can truly nourish their bodies and their faith, and they are confused as to what role other Christians play in their communion with God. For when you do theology 'from above', it threatens to remain 'above' and never have an organic connection to 'below'. Calvin, though, does not fall into such a dualistic trap – for he sees the divine and human as inextricably linked. Furthermore, there is clearly strength to Calvin's structure: communion is not limited to the institutional Church. It is pre-eminently a reality within the Godhead itself, as revealed and flung open to us in the person of the Son. Church structures can no more than bear testimony to this, by witnessing to it in the personal manner in which they conduct themselves.

The challenge to both Protestant ministers and Catholic priests is the same – how do we ourselves live out of our communion with the Father, in the Son, by the Spirit? Can we transform the impersonal structures of the Church into a school of communion (as Pope John Paul II says, in *Novo Millennio Ineunte*), if we are not first participating in the source of communion itself? It is at this point that Calvin's gentle words are of utmost importance: this is the territory of the Spirit whose ongoing work is to draw us, and all of reality, into the uniqueness of the relation of the Father and Son. It is ours to respond; it is ours to discipline ourselves to live into this reality, and to – as a result – move from being individuals to becoming *persons*. It is ours to hear the Father calling us 'beloved' in the desert of our identity, and from this place, to move forward into an identity as a person-in-communion, in Christ, in his Church. When we are living this communion, the Church can then, as Pope John Paul II says, 'reveal God, that Father, who allows us to "see" him in Christ' (*Dives in Misericordia*).

NOTES

1 John Calvin, *A Reformation Debate: Sadoleto's Letter to the Genevans and Calvin's Reply*, John C. Olin, ed., New York: Harper & Row, 1966, p. 59.

2 While Barth took Calvin's emphasis, and made it into a hermeneutical principle to do theology 'from above' rather than 'from below', we do not find Calvin so oppositional. Barth himself noted this about Calvin, *The Theology of the Reformed Confessions*, 1923, p. 94.

As remarkable as it may sound when I say this about Calvin, he thinks initially not from God but from the human person and his situation. Yet the situation of humanity cannot be considered with any seriousness at all without thinking immediately of God. For what purpose is the human created?

To begin with the Trinity is not a denial of human experience but is *precisely Calvin's way to approach human experience*. Even his opening sentences of the *Institutes* reflect his desire to do justice to both human experience and divine revelation concurrently. Calvin says:

> Our wisdom, in so far as it ought to be deemed true and solid Wisdom, consists almost entirely of two parts: the knowledge of God and of ourselves. But as these are connected together by many ties, it is not easy to determine which of the two precedes and gives birth to the other. For, in the first place, no man can survey himself without forthwith turning his thoughts towards the God in whom he lives and moves; because it is perfectly obvious, that the endowments which we possess cannot possibly be from ourselves; nay, that our very being is nothing else than subsistence in God alone. In the second place, those blessings which unceasingly distil to us from heaven, are like streams conducting us to the fountain. Here, again, the infinitude of good which resides in God becomes more apparent from our poverty. (*Institutes* I.1.1)

3 This is reflective of the Protestant 'reticence' to start with nature and ascend to God, but Calvin is not averse to doing so – as long as it is not turned into an anthropological principle. Speaking generally, the Protestant fear is that if one begins with common human experience, depending on one's century and culture, it is all too easy to pour one's expectations, qualifications, and preconceived notions into this. For example, it has been said that the history of theological interpretation of the *imago dei* is better seen as a cultural history, than as a theological one. We can't help it: we are incarnate people, shaped by our relationships, and context, and the glorious gift of life in a particular place, in a particular time on earth. So perhaps it is not too surprising that the *imago dei* was perceived as rational capacity in the fourth century, Augustine, free choice in the twelfth, Bernard, vitiated and near-absent in the sixteenth, Reformers, and today, I have seen it construed as our capacity to be ecological caretakers. As a result of this, for better and for worse, the Protestant instinct is to be reticent about nature, experience,

and all things 'human', such as the longing for communion) without first taking one's bearings from God's revelation in Christ. But the question remains, can this really be done at all? Can we pretend to be people of the Word and not also of the world we inhabit? Can this not easily lead into a Gnosticism of its own? This is, perhaps, the Protestant predicament.

4 All references to Calvin's *Institutes of the Christian Religion* are to the 1559 edition. I am working from the two-volume Library of Christian Classics, 20–21) edition, John T. McNeil, ed., Ford Lewis Battles, trans., Philadelphia: Westminster, 1960. This passage is from *Institutes* II.6.1.

5 *Institutes* I.13.21

6 Calvin's *Commentary on Ephesians* 1:20.

7 T. F. Torrance, *The Trinitarian Faith*, London/New York: T&T Clark, p. 88.

8 *Institutes* I.14.2.

9 'But who might reach to him? Any one of Adam's children? No, like their father, all of them were terrified at the sight of God (Gn 3:8)', *Institutes* II.12.1.

10 'For we must hold fast to that statement of St Paul, that the blessing of Abraham was not promised to his seeds, but to his seed', *Commentary on Exodus* 4:22.

11 *Commentary on Genesis* 15:16. This is no isolated case, for having embraced God as Father, Abraham is now the one with whom God enters into covenant – 'and the adoption of his people was founded upon it', *Commentary on Ezekiel* 16:8, Lecture 43. Circumcision, Calvin is quick to note, is Abraham's 'pledge of adoption', *Commentary on Genesis* 17:8.

12 In the 1999 *Joint Declaration on Justification*, we see that it is through the category of 'love' (which is, of course, ordered to communion) that Lutheran and Catholic theologians approached a rapprochement over the subject.

13 *Commentary on Galatians* 4:1, my emphasis. 'The pupil, although he is free and even lord of all his father's family, is still like a slave, for he is under the government of tutors. But this subjection under a guardian lasts only until the time appointed by the father, after which he enjoys his freedom. In this respect the fathers under the old covenant, being the sons of God, were free. But they were not in possession of freedom, since the law like a tutor kept them under its yoke. The slavery of the law lasted as long as God pleased and He put an end to it at the coming of Christ. Lawyers enumerate various methods by which guardianship is brought to a close; but of them all, the only one that fits this comparison is that which Paul puts here, the appointment by the father.'

14 'Until Christ should shine forth', *Institutes* II.6.5.

15 Calvin's whole context of election keeps this from being an if/then conditional covenant. *Commentary on Genesis* 17:6, 'See how kindly I indulge thee!'

16 *Institutes* II.9.1.

17 *Commentary on Hosea* 11:4.

18 Jesus is the true seed, *Institutes* II.6.2.

19 The quotation continues, 'to present our flesh as the price of satisfaction to God's righteous judgment, and, in the same flesh, to pay the penalty that we had deserved', *Institutes* II.12.3.

20 *Institutes* II.16.5.

21 *Institutes 1536*, II.15.

22 *Commentary on Hebrews* 7:25.

23 '[Paul] proves that our salvation consists in having God as our Father', *Commentary on Romans* 8:17.

24 *Commentary on John* 17:23.

25 *Institutes* III.1.1.

26 'It was rather the design of Christ to lay, as it were, in our bosom, a sure pledge of God's love toward us', *Commentary on John* 15:9.

27 *Commentary on John* 14:28.

28 *Institutes* III.1.2.

29 *Institutes* IV.1.1.

30 *Institutes* IV.1.1.

31 *Commentary 1 Corinthians* 10:16.

32 *Institutes* IV.17.9.

33 Calvin's Letter to Peter Martyr, 8th August 1555.

FROM *COMMUNIO IMPERFECTA* THROUGH *COMMUNIO IN VIA* TO 'FULL COMMUNION IN FAITH, MISSION AND SACRAMENTAL LIFE'?

REV. PROF. GEOFFREY WAINWRIGHT
Duke University Divinity School, Durham, North Carolina

Let me from the start indicate the three stages of the track along which I hope to lead my hearers or readers. The first chapter treats the Second Vatican Council and the way in which the notion of 'communion' became the principal category in the ecclesial self-understanding of the Roman Catholic Church, allowing also for a more flexible and expanded appreciation of other Christian communities. Second will come an examination of 'communion' in the multilateral context of the World Council of Churches (WCC), remembering that while the Roman Catholic Church is not a member of the WCC, it has since 1968 contributed officially appointed theologians to the Council's Faith and Order Commission, and that a Joint Working Group operates between the Roman Catholic Church and the World Council of Churches. Thirdly we shall look at the repeatedly stated goal of the post-Vatican II bilateral dialogue between the World Methodist Council and the Roman Catholic Church in terms of 'full communion in faith, mission and sacramental life'. At each of our three stages we shall pay particular attention to eucharistic communion in its focal or iconic role within the broader question and reality of ecclesial communion.

EUCHARISTIC COMMUNION AND (IM)PERFECT ECCLESIAL COMMUNION

Already in its first constitution – that on the sacred liturgy – the Second Vatican Council located the 'preeminent manifestation of the Church (*praecipua manifestatio Ecclesiae*)' in the eucharistic celebration under the presidency of the bishop:

> The bishop is to be considered as the High Priest of his flock from whom the life in Christ of his faithful is in some way derived and upon whom it in some way depends. Therefore all should hold in the greatest esteem the liturgical life of the diocese centred around the bishop in his cathedral church. They must be convinced that the principal manifestation of the Church consists in the full, active participation of all God's holy people in the same liturgical celebrations, especially in the same Eucharist, in one prayer, at one altar, at which the bishop presides, surrounded by his college of priests and by his ministers.
>
> But since it is impossible for the bishop always and everywhere to preside over the whole flock in his church, he must of necessity establish groupings of the faithful; and among these, parishes, set up locally under a pastor who takes the place of the bishop, are the most important, for in some way they represent the visible Church constituted throughout the world ... Efforts must also be made to encourage a sense of community within the parish, above all in the common celebration of the Sunday Mass (*et adlaborandum [est] ut sensus communitatis paroecialis, imprimis vero in communi celebratione Missae dominicalis, floreat*).[1]

Arriving at its dogmatic constitution on the Church, the Second Vatican Council resumed the sacramental theme in order to expound the nature of the Church as a communion in Christ:

> By communicating his Spirit, Christ mystically constitutes as his body those brothers of his who are called together from every nation. In the body the life of Christ is communicated to those who believe and who, through the sacraments, are united in a hidden and real way to Christ in his passion and glorification. Through baptism we are formed in the likeness of Christ: 'For in one Spirit we were all baptised into one body' (1 Cor 12:13). In this sacred rite fellowship in Christ's death and resurrection is symbolised and is brought about: 'For we were buried with him by means of baptism into death'; and if 'we have been united with him in the likeness of his death, we shall be so in the likeness of his resurrection also'

separated communities, and perhaps with the Catholic Church. The ecumenical decree of Vatican II immediately goes on to give positive appreciation, in a nuanced way, to the worship practices of the separated communities:

> The brethren divided from us also carry out many liturgical actions of the Christian religion. In ways that vary according to the condition of each Church or community, these liturgical actions most certainly can truly engender a life of grace, and, one must say, can aptly give access to the communion of salvation. It follows that the separated Churches and communities as such, though we believe they suffer from the defects already mentioned, have been by no means deprived of significance and importance in the mystery of salvation. For the Spirit of Christ has not refrained from using them as means of salvation which derive their efficacy from the very fullness of grace and truth entrusted to the Catholic Church …
>
> Little by little, as the obstacles to perfect ecclesiastical communion are overcome, all Christians will be gathered, in a common celebration of the Eucharist, into the unity of the one and only Church, which Christ bestowed on his Church from the beginning. This unity, we believe, subsists in the Catholic Church as something she can never lose, and we hope that it will continue to increase until the end of time.[6]

But, to insist: what meanwhile of the Eucharist within and between the separated communities, and even in relation to the Catholic Church? The cases vary. The Eastern and Oriental Orthodox Churches occupy a 'special position':

> Everyone knows with what love the Eastern Christians celebrate the sacred liturgy, especially the eucharistic mystery, source of the Church's life and pledge of future glory … Through the celebration of the Eucharist of the Lord in each of these Churches, the Church of God is built up and grows in stature, and through concelebration, their communion with one another is made manifest … These Churches, although separated from us, yet possess true sacraments, above all – by apostolic succession – the priesthood and the Eucharist, whereby they are still joined to us in closest intimacy. Therefore some worship in common (*communicatio in sacris*), given

> suitable circumstances and the approval of Church authority, is not merely possible but is encouraged.[7]

The case of 'the separated Churches and ecclesial communities in the West' is historically and theologically different. Limiting our attention to recognisably Protestant Churches (which include the Methodists to which I belong):

> We rejoice that our separated brethren look to Christ as the source and centre of ecclesiastical communion. Their longing for union with Christ impels them ever more to seek unity, and also to bear witness to their faith among the peoples of the earth. A love and reverence – almost a cult – of Holy Scripture leads our brethren to a constant and diligent study of the sacred text ... While invoking the Holy Spirit, they seek in these very scriptures God as he speaks to them in Christ, the one whom the prophets foretold, the Word of God made flesh for us. In the scriptures they contemplate the life of Christ, as well as the teachings and the actions of the Divine Master for the salvation of men, in particular the mysteries of his death and resurrection ... Although the ecclesial communities separated from us lack the fullness of unity with us that flows from baptism, and although we believe they have not preserved the proper reality of the eucharistic mystery in its fullness, especially because of the sacrament of Orders, nevertheless when they commemorate the Lord's death and resurrection in the Holy Supper, they profess that it signifies life in communion with Christ and await his coming in glory. For these reasons, the doctrine about the Lord's Supper, about the other sacraments, worship, and ministry in the Church, should form subjects of dialogue.[8]

Such dialogues have certainly resulted from the Second Vatican Council, and we shall say more about them in the second and third chapters of this address, but the rest of this first chapter will be devoted to examining Roman Catholic attitudes and practices towards eucharistic communion in the circumstances of an ecclesial '*communio imperfecta*'. We shall draw chiefly on Pope John Paul II's Encyclical of Holy Thursday 2003, *Ecclesia de Eucharistia vivit*, both for what it reveals of some tendencies within the Roman Catholic Church and for the teaching – positive as well as corrective – given there by the Pope.[9]

Pope John Paul II formulated his warnings and rebukes thus in paragraph 10 of his encyclical:

> In various parts of the Church abuses have occurred, leading to confusion with regard to sound faith and Catholic doctrine concerning this wonderful sacrament. At times one encounters an extremely reductive understanding of the eucharistic mystery. Stripped of its sacrificial meaning, it is celebrated as if it were simply a fraternal banquet. Furthermore, the necessity of the ministerial priesthood, grounded in apostolic succession, is at times obscured and the sacramental nature of the Eucharist is reduced to its mere effectiveness as a form of proclamation. This has led here and there to ecumenical initiatives which, albeit well-intentioned, indulge in eucharistic practices contrary to the discipline by which the Church expresses her faith. How can we not express profound grief at all this? The Eucharist is too great a gift to tolerate ambiguity and depreciation.

Yet the Eucharist certainly is 'a true banquet, in which Christ offers himself as our nourishment' (*Ecclesia de Eucharistia,* 16). That is what 'elevates the experience of fraternity already present in our common sharing at the same eucharistic table to a degree which far surpasses that of the simple human experience of sharing a meal' (*Ecclesia de Eucharistia,* 24).

Pope John Paul II viewed positively some of the developments in ecumenical doctrinal dialogue, and notably in the 'convergence text' dating from the Faith and Order Commission in Lima 1982, *Baptism, Eucharist and Ministry*, to which we shall ourselves come in our second chapter. The Pope welcomed the growing ecumenical consensus on the pneumatological dimension of the Eucharist, which owes much to the Eastern Churches (*Ecclesia de Eucharistia,* 17 and 23; cf. *BEM*: E 14–18). He recognised 'the eschatological thrust which marks the celebration of the Eucharist': 'The Eucharist is a straining towards the goal, a foretaste of the fullness of joy promised by Christ (cf. Jn 15:11); it is in some way the anticipation of heaven, the "pledge of future glory"'(*Ecclesia de Eucharistia,* 18; cf. *BEM*:E 22–6, 'The Meal of the Kingdom'). While rejecting any reduction of the Eucharist to its 'mere effectiveness as a form of proclamation', the Pope's interpretation of the eucharistic sacrifice – 'the memorial of the Lord's death and resurrection', 'a commemorative celebration' (*Ecclesia de Eucharistia,* 11–16) – draws at least in part on the twentieth-century 'rediscovery' of the biblical and sacramental category of 'anamnesis', which funds the Lima text in its exposition of 'The Eucharist as Anamnesis or Memorial of Christ' (*BEM:* E 5–13).

Approaching the end of our first chapter, we must finally look at the question of the pastoral sharing of eucharistic communion as it has been viewed by Roman Catholic authorities since the Second Vatican Council. The Second Vatican Council offered hospitality, in exceptional circumstances, to Orthodox Christians in the sacraments of penance, Eucharist, and the anointing of the sick (*Orientalium Ecclesiarum,* 26–9; *Ecumenical Directory*, 1967, 39–45; 1993, 122–8), and would have liked the faculty to be reciprocated by the Orthodox Churches towards individual Catholics; but with the temporary exception of the Moscow patriarchate for some years after 1969, this has not occurred. In 1984, however, Pope John Paul II and Oriental Orthodox Syrian Patriarch Ignatius Zakka I entered into such a mutual pastoral agreement for the sake of their faithful who have no access to their respective priests. Similar arrangements have followed, on the basis of sufficient consensus in Christology, between Rome and other non-Chalcedonian churches (including the Assyrian Church of the East).

Protestants have been included in the provisions made in the Ecumenical Directories of 1967 (55) and 1993 (129–31) – and endorsed by Pope John Paul II in both the 1995 Encyclical *Ut Unum Sint* (46) and the Encyclical *Ecclesia de Eucharistia* (46) – for rightly disposed non-Catholics to receive, upon request, the Catholic Eucharist in the emergency circumstances of mortal danger, persecution, imprisonment, or serious spiritual need. A condition is that the sacramental faith of such seekers be consonant with the Catholic faith. That pastoral opening may have hitherto unexplored implications for the way in which the Catholic Church might view the sacramental and ecclesial reality of Protestant bodies, for where else would such communicants have come to their faith except in their own communities? Consonance with Catholic faith regarding the sacraments urgently necessary to salvific health is, however, rather stringently defined by Pope John Paul II in *Ecclesia de Eucharistia*: 'Denial of one or more truths of the faith regarding these sacraments and, among these, the truth regarding the need of the ministerial priesthood for their validity, renders the person asking improperly disposed to legitimately receiving them.'

In the other direction, the encyclical repeats the injunction that 'Catholics may not receive communion in those communities which lack a valid sacrament of Orders' (*Ecclesia de Eucharistia,* 46; cf. 30). In the same context, Pope John Paul II repeats the prohibition against any Catholic involvement in 'concelebration' or 'intercommunion' before 'the visible bonds of ecclesial communion are fully re-established' (*Ecclesia de Eucharistia,* 44–5). Such actions, he warns, 'might well prove instead to be *an obstacle to the attainment of full communion,* by weakening the sense of how far we remain from this goal and by introducing or exacerbating ambiguities with regard to one or another truth of the faith. The path towards full unity can only be undertaken in truth.'

Undoubtedly the Pope's warning against any premature mutuality of communion, or any acquiescence in inadequate forms of unity, is both authoritative for Catholics and salutary for the broader ecumenical movement. Yet one may still wonder whether John Paul II has exhausted the ecumenical potential of the axiom of his early-thirteenth-century predecessor Pope Innocent III – that the Eucharist '*significat et efficit unitatem ecclesiasticam*' (*De sacro altaris mysterio,* IV, 36; PL, 217:879) – when John Paul writes that 'the celebration of the Eucharist cannot be the starting-point for [ecclesial] communion; it presupposes that communion already exists, a communion which it seeks to consolidate and bring to perfection' (*Ecclesia de Eucharistia,* 35). John Paul II himself a little later in the encyclical puts the emphasis on the effective power of the Eucharist: 'The Eucharist creates communion and fosters communion' (40). The question therefore remains legitimate: How far do we have to be advanced in the unity which the celebration of the Eucharist 'signifies' before we can draw on the sacramental grace to 'effect' the fullness of that unity? Ongoing ecumenical exploration is appropriate in the determination and achievement both of what is required and what is sufficient for shared eucharistic communion to further ecclesial unity (*quod requiritur et sufficit*).

And with that, we arrive at our second chapter.

THE WORLD COUNCIL OF CHURCHES AND THE QUESTION OF 'INTERCOMMUNION'

The Eucharist and eucharistic communion have been matters of doctrinal and practical concern from the early days of the modern, multilateral ecumenical movement. Historically controversial matters of eucharistic doctrine began to be explored at the Lausanne conference of Faith and Order in 1927 and at the Edinburgh conference in 1937, and studies and dialogue have continued ever since. Faced by the fears of some that the World Council of Churches – founded at its Amsterdam Assembly in 1948 – might be turned into a 'Super-Church', the WCC's central committee declared in its Toronto Statement of 1950 that membership in the Council did not require any church to surrender its own ecclesial self-understanding or to recognise the churchly claims of fellow members. The principal practical issue turned on the relation between ecclesial communion and eucharistic communion, and this found its most poignant manifestation in connection with the liturgical events as celebrated at ecumenical gatherings.[10]

For much of the twentieth century, 'intercommunion' was the slogan around which the ecumenical debate turned regarding the point at which Churches might properly enter into eucharistic fellowship with one another. The Orthodox rejected altogether the notion of *inter*communion – name and thing – on the ground that there is either 'communion' in the one Church or no communion at all. A similar substantive position was held by the Roman Catholic Church, some Anglicans, some Lutherans, and some Baptists, although these all differed on what was required for the unity of which eucharistic communion was or would be the sacramental expression. On the other hand, those Churches which accepted a 'federal' model of unity used the word 'intercommunion' without any pejorative intent or sense of provisionality, to describe their sacramental sharing across persisting denominational boundaries.

Between those two positions stood those ecumenists who had most at stake in the notion of intercommunion. At some point along the road to an ever-fuller unity, they argued, it becomes appropriate – both possible and desirable – for Churches to practice intercommunion as both a sign of the unity they already enjoy and a means towards a more perfect unity. Sometimes adopting an eschatological perspective (for the Lord's Supper prefigures the banquet of the final Kingdom, where a divided fellowship is unthinkable), they argued that the goal of unity could become proleptically effective through the active anticipation of it in the sacrament. At the time of the Faith and Order Conference in Lund in 1952, T. F. Torrance spoke of the Eucharist as 'the divinely given sacrament of unity, the *medicine for our divisions*'.[11]

Now as to liturgical practice, especially at meetings in the multilateral versions of the ecumenical movement: In a custom dating from the early years of the modern ecumenical movement, an occasional 'open' Communion was included in its meetings; it was the Anglicans who most often acted as hosts, since this usually ensured a maximum number of communicants (if only because Anglicans themselves were ready to receive at the hands of an Anglican presider, whereas they were not sure to do so in the case of a Methodist or a Presbyterian). In the heyday of the World Council of Churches, the practice became established – formalised by the Central Committee in 1963 upon recommendation of the World Conference on Faith and Order at Montreal – of including on the official programme of big ecumenical conferences both a Eucharist, 'according to the liturgy of a Church which cannot conscientiously offer an invitation to members of all other Churches to partake of the elements' and one, 'in which a Church or group of Churches can invite members of other Churches to participate and partake'. This dual practice witnessed to disagreements among the Churches about whether eucharistic communion was a means on the road to unity or rather the goal of the journey; and more will be said about that in a moment. In the ecumenical case, 'occasional communion' was not understood on an individualistic basis, as though participants took part as 'private persons'. Rather, all who figured in the celebration, in whatever liturgical role, acted and received in some sense as representatives of the Churches or ecclesial communities to which they belonged.

The dual pattern was abandoned at the Eighth Assembly of the WCC, held at Harare (Zimbabwe) in 1998. At the previous instigation of the Orthodox, there was to be no Eucharist in the general programme of the meeting, but rather a vigil of 'confession and repentance for our brokenness', of penitence for the inability to eat together at the Lord's Table; and on the Sunday morning of 13th December delegates dispersed freely to participate in the communion of local Churches as denominationally or confessionally appropriate, to be followed by an Assembly 'service of recommitment' on the Sunday afternoon.[12] An amendment to the constitution of the WCC, under 'purposes and functions', placed the responsibility more directly on the Churches themselves, 'to call one another to visible unity in one faith and in one eucharistic fellowship, expressed in worship and common life in Christ, through witness and service to the world, and to advance towards that unity in order that the world may believe'.[13]

In some of its contemporary work on ecclesiology, the Faith and Order Commission of the WCC floated the idea of a structural correspondence between the eucharistic assembly and the constitution of the universal Church:

> Most Churches accept that a Eucharist needs a president. Among these there are some who would go on to say that it follows that a gathering of eucharistic communities at a regional and world level similarly need a president in the service of communion.

Admittedly, this thought occurs only in a 'problem box' in the draft *Nature and Purpose of the Church* (Faith and Order Paper No. 181, Geneva: WCC, 1998, p. 55); regrettably, it disappeared from the revised *Nature and Mission of the Church: A Stage on the Way to a Common Statement* (Faith and Order Paper No. 198, Geneva: WCC, 2005).

Meanwhile there had appeared the most significant contribution towards ecumenical doctrinal agreement on sacramental matters in the shape of the so-called 'Lima document' under the title *Baptism, Eucharist and Ministry* (quickly abbreviated to 'BEM').[14] Over fifty years in the long-term making, and a couple of decades in more proximate composition, this text attained a content and phrasing that was unanimously agreed – at the meeting of the Faith and Order Commission in Lima (Peru) in January 1982 – to be apt for sending to the Churches as its best presently achievable formulation.[15] The text claimed to represent a noteworthy 'convergence', not yet a complete consensus; and it was submitted to the Churches for their evaluation and for possible use in their own particular dialogues and educational processes. From the viewpoint of our present thematic interest in eucharistic and ecclesial communion, the most important doctrinal paragraphs in 'Eucharist' are no. 2 and then the section on 'The Eucharist as Communion of the Faithful' (nos. 19–21) in the five-part creedally structured 'The Meaning of the Eucharist'.

The second paragraph reads as follows:

> The Eucharist is essentially the sacrament of the gift which God makes to us in Christ through the power of the Holy Spirit. Every Christian receives this gift of salvation through communion in the Body and Blood of Christ. In the eucharistic meal, in the eating and drinking of the bread and wine, Christ grants communion with himself. God himself acts, giving life to the body of Christ and renewing each member. In accordance with Christ's promise, each baptised member of the body of Christ receives in the Eucharist the assurance of the forgiveness of sins (Mt 26:28) and the pledge of eternal life (Jn 6:51-58). Although the Eucharist is essentially one complete act, it will be considered here under the following aspects: thanksgiving to the Father, memorial of Christ, invocation of the Spirit, communion of the faithful, meal of the Kingdom.

Concerning the more ecclesiological paragraphs on 'The Eucharist as Communion of the Faithful', we find the following:

> The eucharistic communion with Christ who nourishes the life of the Church is at the same time communion within the body of Christ which is the Church. The sharing in one bread and the common cup in a given place demonstrates and effects the oneness of the sharers with Christ and with their fellow sharers in all times and places. It is in the Eucharist that the community of God's people is fully manifested. Eucharistic celebrations always have to do with the whole Church, and the whole Church is involved in each local eucharistic celebration. In so far as a church claims to be a manifestation of the whole Church, it will take care to order its own life in ways which take seriously the interests and concerns of other churches. (19)
>
> The Eucharist embraces all aspects of life. It is a representative act of thanksgiving and offering on behalf of the whole world. The eucharistic celebration demands reconciliation and sharing among all those regarded as brothers and sisters in the one family of God and is a constant challenge for appropriate relationships in social,

> economic and political life (Mt 5:23f.; 1 Cor 10:16f.; 1 Cor 11: 20-22; Gal 3:28) … As participants in the Eucharist, therefore, we prove inconsistent if we are not actively participating in this ongoing restoration of the world's situation and the human condition. The Eucharist shows us that our behaviour is inconsistent in face of the reconciling presence of God in human history: we are placed under continual judgement by the persistence of unjust relationships of all kinds in our society, the manifold divisions on account of human pride, material interest and power politics and, above all, the obstinacy of unjustifiable confessional oppositions within the body of Christ. (20)
>
> Solidarity in the eucharistic communion of the body of Christ and responsible care of Christians for one another and the world find specific expression in the liturgies: in the mutual forgiveness of sins; the sign of peace; intercession for all; the eating and drinking together; the taking of the elements to the sick and those in prison or the celebration of the Eucharist with them. All these manifestations of love in the Eucharist are directly related to Christ's own testimony as a servant, in whose servanthood Christians themselves participate … (21)

And continuing on into 'The Eucharist as Meal of the Kingdom' (22–6):

> … The Eucharist is precious food for missionaries, bread and wine for pilgrims on their apostolic journey … Insofar as Christians cannot unite in full fellowship around the same table to eat the same loaf and drink from the same cup, their missionary witness is weakened at both the individual and the corporate levels. (26)

Going into the final chapter on 'The Celebration of the Eucharist' (27–33), our document makes several proposals to help bring eucharistic communion closer to its proper role in ecclesial communion. Thus:

> The best way towards unity in eucharistic celebration and communion is the renewal of the Eucharist itself in the different Churches in regard to teaching and liturgy. The Churches should test their liturgies in the light of the eucharistic agreement now in process of attainment. The liturgical reform movement has brought the Churches closer together in the manner of celebrating the Lord's Supper. However, a certain liturgical diversity compatible

> with our common eucharistic faith is recognised as a healthy and enriching fact ... (28)
>
> Christian faith is deepened by the celebration of the Lord's Supper. Hence the Eucharist should be celebrated frequently. Many differences of theology, liturgy and practice are connected with the varying frequency with which the Holy Communion is celebrated. (30)
>
> As the Eucharist celebrates the resurrection of Christ, it is appropriate that it should take place at least every Sunday. As it is the new sacramental meal of the people of God, every Christian should be encouraged to receive communion frequently. (31)
>
> The increased mutual understanding expressed in the present statement may allow some Churches to attain a greater measure of eucharistic communion among themselves and so bring closer the day when Christ's divided people will be visibly reunited around the Lord's Table. (33)

Naturally, some criticisms were addressed by the Churches to the 'Eucharist' text (sometimes from mutually opposite angles!), but the official ecclesiastical responses were, on the whole, remarkably positive; and many Churches drew on the statement in making revisions to their own liturgical and teaching texts and practices, and some were thereby enabled to enter into closer ecclesial relations.[16]

The Lima meeting itself closed with a celebration of the Eucharist according to a liturgical text largely prepared beforehand by Frère Max Thurian. The chief presider was the Rev. Dr J. Robert Wright of the Episcopal Church in the USA, and the range of concelebrants and communicants was stretched to the canonical limits. The Roman Catholic and Orthodox members of the Commission, by their own Church discipline and to their openly expressed sorrow, did not receive Communion. The rite itself was heavily thematised in favour of 'baptism, Eucharist and ministry', but 'The Lima Liturgy' soon showed itself amenable to adaptation towards other principal topics and in different circumstances. It was celebrated at the Sixth Assembly of the World Council of Churches at Vancouver (Canada) in 1983, where the general theme was: 'Jesus Christ, the Life of the

World.' Presiding at that eucharistic service, framed as 'The Feast of Life', was Dr Robert Runcie, then Archbishop of Canterbury, and the event was regarded by many as a highlight of the Assembly. That the rite has often been adapted since for other occasions is a sign of the widespread desire for a common eucharistic liturgy that can be employed when doctrinal and ecclesiological conditions permit.[17]

This, our second chapter, may be concluded by listening to the words of the Ninth Assembly of the WCC, meeting at Porto Alegre (Brazil) in 2006. 'Called to be the One Church' was issued as 'an invitation to the Churches to renew their commitment to the search for unity and to deepen their dialogue'.[18] In reading that text, we shall, of course, pay particular attention to our interactive themes of eucharistic communion and ecclesial communion. It may first be noted that the text is firmly Trinitarian: 'The Church's oneness is an image of the unity of the Triune God in the communion of the divine Persons', it is said, thereby matching the fundamental statement of the Second Vatican Council: 'The universal Church is seen to be brought into unity from the unity of the Father, the Son and the Holy Spirit' (*Lumen Gentium*, 4). 'Churches in the fellowship of the WCC remain committed to one another on the way towards *full visible unity*. This commitment is a gift from our gracious Lord. Unity is both a divine gift and calling':

> Our churches have affirmed that the unity for which we pray, hope, and work is 'a *koinonia* given and expressed in the common confession of the apostolic faith; a common sacramental life entered by the one baptism and celebrated together in one eucharistic fellowship; a common life in which members and ministries are mutually recognised and reconciled; and a common mission witnessing to the gospel of God's grace to all people and serving the whole of creation' ['The Unity of the Church as *koinonia*: Gift and calling' – The Canberra Statement, 2.1]. Such *koinonia* is to be expressed in each place, and through a conciliar relationship of churches in different places.

It is acknowledged that 'there are different ecclesiological starting points, and a range of views on the relation of the Church to the Churches. Some differences express God's grace and goodness; they must be discerned in God's grace through the Holy Spirit. Other differences divide the Church; these must be overcome through the Spirit's gifts of faith, hope, and love so that separation and exclusion do not have the last word.'

As to the Church and the Churches: 'Each Church is the Church Catholic, and not simply a part of it. Each Church is the Church Catholic, but not the whole of it. Each Church fulfils its catholicity when it is in communion with the other Churches. We affirm that the Catholicity of the Church is expressed most visibly in sharing holy Communion and in a mutually recognised and reconciled ministry.' In particular, 'baptism bestows upon the Churches both the freedom and the responsibility to journey toward common proclamation of the Word, confession of the one faith, celebration of one Eucharist, and full sharing in one ministry'. In the meantime, each Church is challenged to 'articulate the judgments that shape, and even qualify, its relationship to the others. The honest sharing of commonalities, divergences, and differences will help all Churches to pursue the things that make for peace and build up the common life.' A series of questions is proposed that the Churches should continually address concerning their own life and that of other Churches, including these: 'To what extent can your church discern the faithful expression of the apostolic faith in its own life, prayer and witness and in that of other Churches? Does your Church recognise a common pattern of Christian initiation, grounded in baptism, in the life of other Churches? Why does your Church believe that it is necessary, or permissible, or not possible to share the Lord's Supper with those of other churches? In what ways is your Church able to recognise the ordered ministries of other Churches?'

The invitation ends with a picture of the churches along the way ('*in via*', we might say, towards a 'more perfect communion'):

Our Churches *journey together* in conversation and common action, confident that the risen Christ will continue to disclose himself as he did in the breaking of bread at Emmaus, and that he will unveil the deeper meaning of fellowship and communion (Lk 24:13-35). Noting the progress made in the ecumenical movement, we encourage our Churches to continue on this arduous yet joyous path, trusting in God the Father, Son and Holy Spirit, whose grace transforms our struggles for unity into the fruits of communion.

'FULL COMMUNION IN FAITH, MISSION AND SACRAMENTAL LIFE'

From the multilateral and multifarious scene typified by the World Council of Churches we narrow our focus in this third chapter to one particular bilateral dialogue, namely that between the Roman Catholic Church and the World Methodist Council. The figure of the journey is maintained, and the goal is now more precisely phrased as 'full communion in faith, mission and sacramental life'. We shall look for what theological categories, and even practical steps, are here being proposed to assist progress along the road from 'some degree of communion, albeit imperfect, with the Catholic Church' to an ecclesiastical relation between Methodists and Roman Catholics that embraces a 'full communion in faith, mission and sacramental life'.[19]

That the international dialogue takes place between 'the (Roman) Catholic Church' (RCC) and 'the World Methodist Council' (WMC), points already to the fundamental issue to be negotiated – or problem to be solved: ecclesiology. The RCC and the WMC are two different kinds of entity. Simply put: on the one hand, the RCC, as we have seen, understands that the Church *subsists in* the Catholic Church, and is governed by the successor of Peter and by the bishops in communion with him. On the other hand, Methodists declare themselves to 'form a family of Churches', which 'claim and cherish our true place in the one holy, Catholic and apostolic Church'. Thus, the RCC makes a close identification of itself with 'the one Church of Jesus Christ', while Methodism has never had more than a 'denominational' view of itself – though claiming to be 'part of' what is confessed as 'the Holy Catholic Church', 'the Church universal', 'the body of Christ' (and being committed, since the earliest days of the modern ecumenical movement, to the cause of Christian unity). The crucial questions for the dialogue concern the sense and ways in which each partner can (come to) recognise the churchly character of the other and thus make possible their ecclesial reconciliation and unity.

First, a little history as to the start and the procedures of the dialogue: at its meeting in London (England) in August 1966, the World Methodist Council – on whose behalf several senior figures had been present at Vatican II as delegated observers – responded enthusiastically to the Roman invitation to set up a 'bilateral dialogue' of the kind to which the Catholic Church was also inviting other 'world confessional families', as they were then called, later to be named 'Christian world communions'. The first meeting of the Methodist–Roman Catholic dialogue, in fact, took place at Ariccia, near Rome, in October 1967. From the start, the Commission has operated in periods of five years, in order to be able to present a report of its work simultaneously to the Holy See and to the World Methodist Council according to the quinquennial rhythm of the latter body's plenary sessions. That last procedure has led to the practice of citing the documents (informally also on the Catholic side!) by the venue and date of their presentation to the WMC. Typically, the WMC 'receives with gratitude' the reports and authorises the continuation of the dialogue. In Rome, the reports are examined by the Congregation for the Doctrine of the Faith and then are published by the Pontifical Council for Promoting Christian Unity in company with an essay by a respected theologian that summarises their strengths and weaknesses from a Catholic point of view. Over the years, there has naturally been some renewal in the Commission's composition, but the general sense is that of consistency in the work done.

Already in its first report – 'Denver 1971' – the Joint Commission called attention to a most remarkable document from the hand of John Wesley himself, the principal founder – under God – of the Methodist movement. That was his 'Letter to a Roman Catholic', written from Dublin in July 1749 in an effort to allay Catholic opposition to the evangelistic work of the Methodists in Ireland. Wesley begins with the 'tenderest regard' in which he must hold his addressee on account of their being creatures of the same God and their both being redeemed by God's own Son and 'studying to have a conscience void of offence towards God and towards man'. In the two main sections of the Letter, Wesley then sets out 'the belief of a true Protestant' and 'the practice of a true Protestant', making the most of the commonalities between Protestants and Catholics. The *fides quae creditur* is presented in terms of an exposition of the Nicene-Constantinopolitan creed (including an affirmation of the perpetual virginity of Blessed Mary), and Wesley expands on the creed in order to bring out the Chalcedonian teaching concerning the person and natures of Christ and the traditional understanding of Christ's 'threefold office' as prophet, priest and king. The *fides quâ creditur* gets embodied in love towards God and neighbour, 'works of piety' and 'works of mercy'. Together these constitute 'the old religion', 'true, primitive Christianity'. And on that shared basis, Wesley says to his Catholic reader: 'If we cannot as yet think alike in all things, at least we may love alike'; and so they should be kind to one another in thought, word, and deed, and finally 'endeavour to help each other on in whatever we are agreed leads to the kingdom': 'So far as we can, let us always rejoice to strengthen each other's hands in God.' It may certainly be hoped that not only the 'union in affection' but even the 'entire external union', which Wesley – in a related sermon entitled 'Catholic Spirit' (1750) – deemed unattainable in his own day on account of 'smaller differences' in theological 'opinions', 'modes of worship' and 'Church government', has been brought closer by the agreements and convergences recorded by the Joint Commission.[20]

It was the Nairobi report of 1986 which brought ecclesiology thematically to the front in the Commission's work. 'Towards a Statement on the Church' falls into two parts: a general consideration of 'the nature of the Church' – its 'sacramental' character and its 'vocation to unity' – elides by way of 'structures of ministry' into an exploration of 'the Petrine office' that really constitutes the second half of the document.

By virtue of its precision and its biblical foundation, the opening paragraph of the Nairobi report was reckoned by Jean-Marie Tillard, in an official Roman Catholic evaluation of the text, to belong 'among the most beautiful definitions of the Church'. It reads: 'Because God so loved the world, he sent his Son and the Holy Spirit to draw us into communion with himself. This sharing in God's life, which resulted from the mission of the Son and the Holy Spirit, found expression in a visible *koinonia* of Christ's disciples, the Church.'

The Nairobi Report introduced the term 'sacrament' to designate the Church. By the Spirit, the Church 'is enabled to serve as sign, sacrament and harbinger of the kingdom of God in the time between the times' (8). Or Christologically: 'Christ works through his Church, and it is for this reason that Vatican II speaks of the Church as a kind of sacrament, both as an outward sign of God's grace among us and as signifying in some way the grace and call to salvation addressed by God to the whole human race (cf. *Lumen Gentium,* 1)' (9). This is a perspective that many Methodists, after initial tentativeness, also found helpful. On the sacramental character of the Church, broadly understood, the Nairobi report suggests that 'the Mystery of the Word made flesh and the sacramental mystery of the eucharist point towards a view of the Church based upon the sacramental idea, i.e., the Church takes its shape from the incarnation from which it originated and the eucharistic action by which its life is constantly being renewed' (10). Declaring that Methodists and Catholics 'are committed to a vision that includes the goal of full communion in faith, mission and sacramental life' (20), the Nairobi report introduced what would time and time again be stated as the goal of the dialogue.

Admitting that no 'ecclesiology shaped in a time of division [can be] entirely satisfactory' (22), the Commission declared that 'in obedience to him who will bring about this unity, we are committed to a vision that includes the goal of full communion in faith, mission and sacramental life. Such communion, which is the gift of the Spirit, must be expressed visibly. This visible unity need not imply uniformity, nor the suppression of the gifts with which God has graced each of our communities' (20–21 The *koinonia* that was intended and envisaged received a fuller description thus in paragraph 23:

> For believers it involves both communion and community. It includes participation in God through Christ in the Spirit by which believers become adopted children of the same Father and members of the one Body of Christ sharing in the same Spirit. And it includes deep fellowship among participants, a fellowship which is both visible and invisible, finding expression in faith and order, in prayer and sacrament, in mission and service. Many different gifts have been developed in our traditions, even in separation. Although we already share some of our riches with one another, we look forward to a greater sharing as we come closer together in full unity (cf. Vatican II, Decree on Ecumenism, *Unitatis Redintegratio*, n. 4).

In exploring, with a view to 'a reunited Church', various possible 'ways of being one Church', the Nairobi report (24) named two that would retain their attraction: first, the notion, originally proposed by Cardinal Willebrands, of 'typoi', whereby, given 'basic agreement in faith, doctrine, and structure essential for mission', there may be 'room for various "ecclesial traditions", each characterised by a particular style of theology, worship, spirituality and discipline'; second, the analogy of 'religious orders' within the Roman Catholic Church, which, 'while fully in communion with the Pope and the bishops, relate in different ways to the authority of Pope and bishops', whereby 'such relative autonomy has a recognised place within the unity of the Church'. Two decades earlier, Albert Outler – a Methodist observer at Vatican II – had described Methodism as *une église manquée*, 'an evangelical order' needing 'a church catholic' within which to function.[21]

Regarding what may perhaps be called the 'topography' of ecclesial unity, the Commission 'broached the question' of whether the 'varying needs' of historically developed 'spiritual traditions' could be 'provided for within the framework of the local congregation, and how far a particular tradition or form of prayer and worship may require special provisions (parishes, ministries, other organisations). How far would the pastoral care of such groups require separate, possibly overlapping jurisdictions, or could it be provided by one, single, local form of *episkopé* (supervision or oversight)?' (27). A provisional conclusion in principle was that 'there have to be limits to variety; some arise from the need to promote cohesion and cooperation, but the basic structures of the Church also set limits that exclude whatever would disrupt communion in faith, order and sacramental life' (28).

With the ecumenical goal in view, Methodists are declared to 'accept that whatever is properly required for the unity of the whole of Christ's Church must by that very fact be God's will for his Church' (58). In that light, 'a universal primacy might well serve as focus of, and ministry for, the unity of the whole Church' (ibid.), and 'it would not be inconceivable that at some date in a restored unity, Roman Catholic and Methodist bishops might be linked in one episcopal college and that the whole body would recognise some kind of effective leadership and primacy in the bishop of Rome. In that case, Methodists might justify such an acceptance on different grounds from those that now prevail in the Roman Catholic Church' (62).

The Commission and its sponsors recognised that further work on the Church would require attention to some themes of 'fundamental theology' and their incidences on ecclesiology. That explains the approach adopted in the following three rounds of the dialogue: thus 'Singapore 1991' treated 'The Apostolic Tradition'; 'Rio de Janeiro 1996' viewed 'Revelation and Faith' under the title 'The Word of Life'; and

> succession, the assurance asserted of certain authoritative acts of teaching, and the place and role of the Petrine Ministry. (92)

Despite these differences, the claim is made that 'Catholics and Methodists do, in fact, hold in common many beliefs and priorities regarding the Church' (97).

In light of the 'very considerable' (97) or 'extensive' (141) agreement on the nature and mission of the Church thus established through the exchange of ideas in a dialogue of truth, the Joint Commission considered the moment had come to face directly the question of the Church's identity and concrete location. The Report states (97):

> It is time now to return to the concrete reality of one another, to look one another in the eye, and with love and esteem to acknowledge what we see to be truly of Christ and of the gospel, and thereby *of the Church*, in one another. Doing so will highlight the gifts we truly have to offer one another in the service of Christ in the world, and will open the way for an exchange of gifts which is what ecumenical dialogue, in some way, always is. In our striving for full communion, 'we dare not lose any of the gifts with which the Holy Spirit has endowed our communities in their separation'. The Holy Spirit is the true giver of the gifts we are seeking to exchange.

The Catholic partners in the Joint Commission in fact express in the Seoul Report openness to the list of potential gifts from the side of Methodism. Catholics find and respect in Methodism a 'vigorous Trinitarian faith', a 'great attachment to the person of the Word incarnate', a 'quest for holiness', a 'commitment to mission and to social responsibility', a form of 'unity in communion' expressed as 'watching over one another in love'. Further: 'Much Methodist music and hymnody is already benefiting Catholics. Likewise, Catholics have much to learn from the Methodist understanding and practice of lay ministry, based on Baptism and the priesthood of all believers, and they have much to ponder with regard to the place of lay people in the governance of the Church' (126). As to the transgenerational communion of the saints, 'the gift of John and Charles Wesley themselves, outstanding and godly men, to be shared as heroes of Christian faith, would be a cause of joy and thanksgiving' (127). In turn, Catholics invite Methodists to consider as possible gifts from the Catholic Church a more 'articulated ecclesiology', with its 'visible manifestation' of 'communion across space, expressed by the collegiality of the bishops, and communion across history, served by the apostolic succession of the bishops', and 'within the framework of the college of bishops ... the Petrine ministry as a service of love' (128–129). Catholics also invite Methodists to 'look afresh at those doctrines which, in the turmoil of the Reformation, became obscured in Protestant life instead of simply being reformed of their excesses' – and notably 'the sacrificial aspect of the Eucharist and the understanding of the ordained ministry as priesthood' (130). Catholics likewise wish to share with Methodists 'the absolute confidence in Christ's action through the ministry of word and sacrament' (134), taking this approach also to 'the disputed issue of "infallibility"': 'Just as Catholics believe that Christ can unfailingly wash, feed and forgive his people through the sacramental ministrations of the Church and its ministers, so too they believe that he can unfailingly *teach* his people' (135).

The Joint Commission summed up the potential benefits of reconciliation between Methodists and Catholics as 'the mutual enhancement of each other's oneness, holiness, Catholicity and apostolicity' (137). The chapter on 'deepening and extending our recognition of one another' thus concludes that, 'in an important sense, two uniting churches [would] give to one another the gift of *unity*', reinforce their shared sense of *holiness* in the Church, augment the shared desire for ever greater *catholicity*, and gain a vital sign of *apostolicity* in providing Methodists with the apostolic succession of bishops and Catholics with a rich Methodist sense of apostolic mission.[22]

Finally, the Seoul Report offered some practical proposals that include concrete gestures such as those that Pope Benedict XVI has seen as necessary to the 'inner conversion that is the prerequisite for all ecumenical progress'. The proposals fall into three categories: (1) making more evident in practice the existing degree of shared belief between Catholics and Methodists about the nature and mission of the Church; (2) proposals based on what Catholics and Methodists already recognise in each other as being truly of the Church; (3) proposals for the sake of the mutual exchange of ecclesial gifts and endowments between Catholics and Methodists. They are 'specific recommendations to help us attain the next stage on the way to the full visible unity of apostles, the saints, prayer and nature. God speaks! From the first hours of his revelation, he is a being of relation, awaiting the consecration of his chosen people. If we, indeed, stick to a broad definition of dialogue as an exchange of words, God dialogues with his people in a diversity of ways. While some dialogues are real conversations, others are callings, appeals, and elections. The dimension of the conversion of the hearts within the people of God becomes the privileged field of a prophetic action. Indeed, from the announcement of misfortunes to the proclamation of God's judgement, the centre of the prophetic message is a call to communion through conversion.

Perhaps the most prominent expression of dialogue and communion is found in John 1: 'In the beginning was the Word, and the Word was with God, and the Word was God. He was in the beginning with God ... And the Word became flesh and dwelt among us, and we beheld his glory, the glory as of the only begotten of the Father, full of grace and truth.

This passage illustrates both the transcendence and immanence of a God who has given himself to the world through the incarnation. The incarnation of the divine Logos, the Christ, the second Person of the Holy Trinity, changed everything. The mystery of the incarnation concentrates all the theological representations of the development between dialogue and communion. The Word became flesh – the Logos is revealed in knowledge – in a world made new through the incarnation. Christ, fully God, became fully human in a union that the ecumenical councils attempt to explain. Thus, rising against the duality of hypostases as proposed by Nestorius – for whom the incarnation was limited to the indwelling of the Logos – united not only to a human nature, but also to a human being. The deeper Chalcedonian examination (451) of the controversy over the hypostatic union of Christ emphasises fundamental soteriological tenants, while considering the poverty of the language before the mystery of the incarnation. This clarification focuses on the union, the perfect communion between humanity and divinity in the person, the hypostasis, of Christ: 'Only one nature of God incarnated the Logos.'

It is of this hypostatic union in the Logos – of the humanity and the divinity – that the conditions for a radical change of the soteriological perspective arise. In the fourth century, recalling the words of St Irenaeus of Lyon, St Athanasius the Great said: 'God became man so that man might become God.' The exchange of words becomes a communion with the Word, and the possibility is granted by the incarnation of the Logos. The Christian vocation becomes the acquisition of the Logos, a union with Christ and salvation in deification, namely theosis. We are walking along the same path in this generation as the layman Nicolas walked in St Seraphim's time.

Because dialogue brings us into communion with God and transforms us through his divine presence, dialogue is therefore a theological paradigm through which communion becomes not only the starting point of repentance, but also that of salvation as a union between God and man. I will examine certain of these aspects in greater depth in the latter part of this presentation; however I should state here that Orthodox theology, based on the mystery of the incarnation, affirms the possibility of participating in the divine nature through grace. This deification constitutes partaking in what God is as he allows us to approach him. For the Cappadocian fathers, and for St Gregory Palamas in the fourteenth century, it is the uncreated energies that allow the participation. In the words of Olivier Clément: 'in the mystery of God himself, of the unity in the otherness and of the otherness in the unity.'

According to Metropolitan John of Pergamon, 'the Eucharist is the only occasion in history when the body of Jesus and the body of the Church are identified. The Body of Christ, which is the body of the Eucharist and simultaneously of the Church, is the body of the risen, the eschatological Christ.'[1]

We have looked individually at dialogue and at the inter-relatedness of dialogue and communion to bring us into a state of conversion. Let us now turn our attention to the role of the sacraments in this paradigm.

2. COMMUNION, DIALOGUE AND SACRAMENTS

Humanity's response to Christ's word of salvation includes participation and adherence. The word of the believer is expressed in a confession of faith attached to a sacramental act, incorporating it into the ecclesial community. Therefore, adherence to Christianity is

3. MYSTICAL ASPECT OF COMMUNION OR THE APORIA OF EVERY WORD

In this section, I will continue my reflection and will consider the limits of any dialogue inside the mystery of communion.

a) Communion in the ascetic discourse

The ascetic and monastic tradition to which Orthodox theology remains committed will also allow us to consider a new description of the link between dialogue and communion. Indeed, it is understood by many that in the monasticism of the desert fathers, we find over and over again this introductory phrase which is almost a ritual in every discussion, 'Father, give me a word of salvation'. The envisioned exchange – this dialogue – becomes the starting point for a state of communion understood as *metanoia*. The dialogue that is desired is between master and disciple. The hierarchical dimension which must be underlined at this point is primarily a search for a didactic perspective. The words of the Elder, often enigmatic, will not, however, take form until the disciple has implemented them. The conversion is that of the heart, but it is only possible in the practice of repentance and confession of sins, prayer, and asceticism. Generally, *metanoia* is considered a synonym for repentance when it engages the whole spiritual life in humility, patience and tears. It comes as an act of contrition after the completion of an action considered sinful, and is usually related to the practice of the sacrament of confession. Along this same line of understanding, *metanoia* is not only repentance, but it is also reconciliation.

Repentance and reconciliation are the fruits found in communion, along with salvation, forgiveness of sins, purification, eternal life and even deification. Communion engages the participant in a complete change from the way one lives his or her life as one turns toward God. This change generally involves dialogue with an elder who becomes the key to any transmission of spiritual experience as illustrated by St Seraphim's relationship with Nicolas. For two millennia, many letters and books have been filled with ascetic writings involving this type of meeting, so the value of seeking to dialogue with a wise leader who can guide us to fruitful communion with God and humanity is well documented.

b) The power of the name of Jesus to initiate communion

Ecumenical Patriarch Bartholomew has noted that 'Prayer is always a dialogue'. Like the relationship with a wise teacher, prayer involves sharing your heart with God and pausing in silence to listen for his counsel. One simple invocation called the Jesus Prayer goes like this: 'Lord Jesus Christ Son of God have mercy on me.' Within this ten-word utterance, a theological universe has been developed by numerous Russian, Greek, patristic and monastic authors. In a very detailed study on the subject entitled *The Great and Glorious Name*, Metropolitan Hilarion Alfeyev, currently President of the Department of External Church Relations of the Moscow Patriarchate, analyses the introduction, use and meaning of the name of Jesus in the context of this simple prayer. Building on the foundation of Diadochus of Photicée (fifth century), the author insists that 'the invocation of the name of Jesus Christ [has] an inherent power in the name in itself. There is an echo of the ancient Christian understanding of the name of Jesus, which possesses in itself a special miraculous force, as shown in particular in the book of Acts of the Apostles.' The power evoked by the Metropolitan of Volokolamsk does not cease to be a force which brings the person invoked, the Christ, into the very presence of the one praying. Consider that in the invocation of the name lays not only the power, but also the mystery of the whole person.

The repetition of the name of Jesus derives its meaning from the Person, whose name is invoked, creating in the intimacy of the heart a meeting point, and by saying meeting one can also say an exchange between the creature and his Creator. Indeed, more than just a prayer, the prayer of Jesus is also a confession of faith in which the attributes of the divinity joined to humanity are recognised in Christ. As the intimate dialogue develops, it transforms, polishes, and converts the heart and the intellect in order to allow a human to encounter God. Dialogue, communion, conversion of the intellect and the heart, and the patristic thought does not consider them as two separate members, but as one single organ: a meeting place. The conversion constitutes purification in view of the illumination. Moreover, it is not just the intellect alone that engages in the participation in the prayer; the entire body is called to participate by psychophysical codified methods.

leading to the highest aims of Christianity. In the final analysis, the work of every Christian is to obtain more of the Holy Spirit, and we should pursue dialogue and communion, realising these higher goals are attainable only in the encounter. I will close with this revelation from St Seraphim: 'We have become so inattentive to the work of our salvation that we misinterpret many other words in Holy Scripture as well, all because we do not seek the grace of God and in the pride of our minds do not allow it to dwell in our souls. That is why we are without true enlightenment from the Lord, which he sends into the hearts of men who hunger and thirst wholeheartedly for God's righteousness.'

NOTES

1 John D. Zizioulas, The ecclesiological presuppositions of the Holy Eucharist at www.resourcesforchristiantheology.org

2 John D. Zizioulas, *Being as Communion: Studies in Personhood and the Church*, London: Darton, Longman and Todd, 1985, p. 81.

MISSION: CLIMAX AND CONSUMMATION OF THE EUCHARIST

REV. PROF. MICHAEL McCABE SMA
Head of the Mission Studies Department,
Tangaza College, Nairobi

One of the major contributions of the Second Vatican Council (1962–65) to the renewal of the Catholic Church was its emphasis on the centrality of both the Eucharist and mission to the life of the Church and on the inseparable bond between them. The Eucharist is not only the source and nourishment for the Church's mission; it also determines its content and method. Mission is not only the conclusion of the Eucharist but the concrete living out of that mystery of divine love that it symbolises and celebrates. My presentation will attempt to explore the relationship between the Eucharist and mission, highlighting especially the common theme which connects them: communion with God and with one another.

GATHERED TO BE SENT

The Eucharist is the central expression and celebration of the Church's identity as the sacrament of God's universal and unconditional love, made manifest in Christ. Born of a love that is measureless (cf. Eph 3:18-19), the Church is rooted in a liberating truth it must communicate to others. It is possessed by a vision of life that embraces all peoples and indeed the whole of creation. It is energised by a life it is impelled to share. In its first approved document, *Sacrasanctum Concilium*, the Second Vatican Council stated that the Eucharist strengthens the faithful in order 'to preach Christ, and thus show forth, to those who are outside, the Church as a sign lifted up among the nations under which the scattered children of God may be gathered into one' (SC, 2).

In his Post-Synodal Apostolic Exhortation on the Eucharist (2007) Pope Benedict XVI underlined this missionary imperative of the

Eucharist in even more emphatic terms in the following words: 'The love that we celebrate in the sacrament [Eucharist] is not something we can keep to ourselves. By its very nature it demands to be shared with all ... We cannot approach the Eucharistic table without being drawn into the mission which, beginning in the very heart of God, is meant to reach all people. Missionary outreach is thus an essential part of the eucharistic form of the Christian life' (*Sacramentum Caritatis*, 84). The Eucharist has a double movement: a drawing in and a sending out. Timothy Radcliffe says that 'this rhythm of gathering the community around the altar and then sending it away belongs to the oxygenation of the Church's life-blood. Without it the Church would stop breathing and die.'[1] Hence, every Eucharist climaxes in a sending forth of the assembly on mission: *Ite, Missa est.*

If the Eucharist is the central statement of the Church's identity as the universal sacrament of salvation, this is as much a statement of commitment as an affirmation of identity. It is an expression of the Church's essential vocation. To be true to this vocation, the Church cannot limit its outreach to one group of people. It must reach out to every corner of the globe and bring to all peoples the full riches of Christ. The Church's constant and fundamental challenge is to break through the barriers which separate people from one another – the barriers of race, colour and creed – and draw them towards unity through the reconciling power of Christ. As missionary, the Church strives for a unity which will express more comprehensively its inherent Catholicity as expressed in the Eucharist. For the Church to close in on itself and cease to reach out to others would be to turn its back on its essential vocation and deny its very *raison d'etre*. If the Church ceases to be missionary, it is no longer the Church that celebrates its Catholic identity in the Eucharist.

ON GOD'S MISSION

As a eucharistic community gathered into one through the action of the Holy Spirit by the gift of Christ's Body and Blood, the Church is sent forth on a mission that comes from God and belongs to God. The Church is not the proprietor of mission. God is. Mission is, first and foremost, God's turning towards the world in creative love, redemptive healing and transforming power. God's mission, as expressed in the Eucharist, embraces the entire human race and, indeed, all of creation. The Third Eucharistic Prayer gives praise to the Father in these words: 'You are indeed Holy, O Lord, and all you have created rightly gives you praise, for through your Son, our Lord Jesus Christ, by the power and working of the Holy Spirit, you give life to all things and make them holy.'

While the Church is the supreme and indispensable sacrament of this divine outreach, it does not exhaust it. Pope John Paul II's great encyclical letter on the Church's mission, *Redemptoris Missio,* states that the presence and activity of God's Spirit 'are universal, limited neither by space nor time' and that this presence and action of the Spirit 'affect not only individuals but also society and history, peoples, cultures and religions' (RM, 28). This universal outreach of God's mission is the context within which the Church's mission must be situated. Its mission is not to take over from this divine mission but rather to serve and promote it. Moreover, in participating in God's mission, the Church encounters human beings and a world in which God's Spirit is already present and active. Mission is an encounter with a mystery: the mystery of a missionary God whose love embraces the world and all its inhabitants; the mystery of the Spirit's power present in unexpected places and unsuspected ways; the mystery of people's participation in the Paschal mystery in ways we have not known or imagined (cf. GS, 22). This realisation has enormous implications for all who are involved in the Church's mission, especially those with the special calling to serve its mission *ad gentes,* namely, those we call missionaries. They must be what *Redemptoris Missio* calls 'contemplatives in action'. [2]

CONTEMPLATION AND MISSION

God's presence among peoples can be gleaned only from a profound listening to the Spirit who has plumbed the depth of God and knows God's ways. In the past, missionaries were encouraged to develop an apostolic rather than a contemplative spirituality, a spirituality which put the accent on action and loving service of others rather than on one's personal journey into the heart of God. Contemplation was viewed as a rather esoteric form of prayer appropriate for those who had withdrawn themselves 'from the world' and lived in monasteries.

There is, to be sure, nothing wrong with an apostolic spirituality. However, unless this spirituality is rooted in a profound life of prayer, it can and indeed has often led to activism and even arrogance – an activism and arrogance that unfortunately at times marred the modern missionary movement.

It is only in prayerful contemplation of the mystery of God manifested in their own lives and in the lives of others that missionaries can ever hope to attune themselves to God's missionary agenda. It is vitally important for missionaries today to retrieve something of that unity of contemplation and apostolic action that marked the great monastic missionary movement of the Middle Ages. In the judgement of the renowned mission theologian, David Bosch, 'it was because of monasticism that so much authentic Christianity evolved in the course of Europe's dark ages and beyond ... In the midst of a world ruled by the love of self, the monastic communities were a visible sign and preliminary realisation of a world ruled by the love of God.'[3] Fortunately, *Redemptoris Missio* has gone some way to correcting the divorce between the missionary and contemplative apostolates by describing the missionary as a 'contemplative in action' (RM, 91), thus underlining the intimate relationship between action and contemplation in the life of the missionary.

TO GATHER INTO ONE THE SCATTERED CHILDREN OF GOD

The Church, as the Second Vatican Council affirmed, is 'kind of sacrament – a sign and instrument of communion with God and of unity among all people' (LG, 1). But what kind of unity? The Eucharist manifests and celebrates a unity which embraces diversity. In the words of Pope Benedict XVI's post-synodal apostolic exhortation, *Africae Munus*: 'The table of the Lord gathers together men and women of different origins, cultures, races, languages and ethnic groups. Thanks to the Body and Blood of Christ, they become truly one. In the eucharistic Christ, they become blood relations and thus true brothers and sisters, thanks to the word and to the Body and Blood of the same Jesus Christ. This bond of fraternity is stronger than that of human families, than that of our tribes' (AM, 152).

The Church's outreach then to other peoples and cultures has nothing in common with any form of cultural or religious imperialism.

To quote Timothy Radcliffe: 'Preaching the gospel is not a matter of turning other people into Christians just like ourselves. We are not recruiting people to adopt our view and our identity ... We are sent on mission to discover who we are in and for those other people ... Christian identity is both given and always to be discovered with one's unknown brothers and sisters.'[4] The Church's mission is not to simply transplant the Church from one location to another. It is charged with creating something new, by incarnating the gospel among the peoples and cultures of the world. The way of mission, then, must to be the way of inculturation and dialogue, following the example of Christ who, by his incarnation, committed himself to doing the Father's will within the particular social and cultural context of the people among whom he lived.

Many outstanding missionaries in the past opposed any artificial transplanting of the Western forms of Christianity on foreign soil. They expected the Gospel to take on new forms as it found a home among new peoples with their unique cultures. Mission, they insisted, was not about cloning a mature product, but about bringing something new to birth. This principle which was somewhat overshadowed in the modern missionary movement has been happily re-affirmed by the Second Vatican Council. Its implementation, however, still remains the fundamental challenge for mission today, a task now more urgent than ever, given the dominance of a globalised technological culture which is doing irreparable damage to the traditional cultures of many peoples.

One of today's leading African theologians, Laurenti Magesa, views inculturation as the fundamental challenge facing the Church and its mission in Africa today. The Church, he insists, must help African peoples resist the forces of globalisation and regain the ability and power of self-definition, thus affirming their dignity and self-respect. For Magesa, the issue of self-definition is critical, for this is precisely what globalisation, following on the heels of colonisation, is taking away from Africans.[5] Africans must be accorded the right to live their Christian commitment and express the Church's doctrines in accordance with their own cultural forms of expression, without of course diluting those doctrines. As the post-synodal exhortation *Africae Munus* puts it: 'It is imperative ... [for the Church] to make a commitment to transmit the values the Creator has instilled in the hearts of Africans since the dawn of time. These have served as a matrix for fashioning societies marked by a degree of harmony, since they embody traditional formulae for peaceful coexistence' (AM, 38). This approach calls for humility as well as sensitivity from the Church. It must allow people the space and the time for the seed of God's Word 'to grow in its own soil, obeying its own embryonic urges, and shaping its own blades of new life'.[6]

However, if the unity manifested in the Eucharist and willed by Christ (cf. Jn 17:21) is to be realised, the integration of cultural values into the life of the Church must be accompanied and complemented by the evangelisation of cultures since 'Christ himself is the truth for every man and women, and for all human history. The Eucharist becomes a criterion for our evaluation of everything that Christianity encounters in different cultures' (*Sacramentum Caritatis* 78). In light of the ethnic, tribal and regional divisions which today afflict many parts of the African continent and are evident even within some African ecclesial communities, Pope Benedict XVI, in his post-apostolic exhortation *Africae Munus* calls the Church in Africa to 'a profound and permanent conversion of life' (AM, 32), and to live what he calls a 'spirituality of communion' (AM, 34).

Borrowing from a speech of Pope John Paul II, on the eve of the third millennium, Pope Benedict XVI then goes on to give a striking description of what is involved in this spirituality of communion:

> the ability to perceive the light of the mystery of the Trinity shining on the faces of brothers and sisters around us ... ; the ability as well to recognise all that is positive in the other and to welcome it and prize it as a gift that God gives me through that person ... ; and finally, the ability to make room for our brothers and sisters, bearing 'each other's burdens' (Gal 6:2) and resisting the selfish temptations which constantly beset us and provoke competition, careerism, distrust and jealousy. (AM, 35)

This is as good a description as you are likely to come across of what it means for the Church to be *communio,* to be 'family-of-God'.

I would like to highlight here the important witness of international missionary and religious communities to what is concretely involved in this spirituality of communion. These communities represent people (including many Africans) from very different ethnic, cultural and linguistic backgrounds who leave their homelands to make a home among strangers. They are committed to learning the language of the people to whom they are sent, eating the local food and adapting themselves to their culture. Perhaps more significantly, they embrace a wide range of cultural and ethnic differences within their communities as they live and work together in the service of the gospel. Thus, by their very existence, these communities give clear and prophetic witness to what Timothy Radcliffe calls, 'God's vast home, the wide openness of the kingdom in which all may belong and be at ease'.[7]

FOR THE TRANSFORMATION OF THE WORLD

'Each celebration of the Eucharist makes sacramentally present the gift that the crucified Lord made of his life, for us and for the whole world. In the Eucharist Jesus also makes us witnesses of God's compassion towards all our brothers and sisters' (*Sacramentum Caritatis*, 88). However, we celebrate this gift of Christ's life in a world that is torn apart by violent conflicts, defaced by unjust socio-economic structures, mired in selfishness and greed – a world that is far from that vision of *communio* embodied in the Eucharist. The Eucharist thus impels us to continue Jesus' mission of proclaiming and inaugurating God's kingdom of justice, peace and love. Jesus has shown us what the kingdom of God is like. As the Anglican biblical scholar, N.T. Wright puts it:

> In Jesus we see the biblical portrait of God come to life: the loving God, rolling up his sleeves (Is 52:10) to do in person the job that no one else could do, the creator God giving new life; the God who works through his created world, and supremely through his human creatures; the faithful God dwelling in the midst of his people; the stern and tender God relentlessly opposed to all that destroys or distorts the good creation, and especially human beings, but recklessly loving all those in need and distress.[8]

Wright uses a striking image to capture the relationship between Jesus and the members of his Church. 'We are,' he says, 'like musicians called to play and sing the unique and once-only-written musical score. We don't have to write it again, but we have to play it.'[9] We are called, not so much to repeat what Christ has done but to live by his Spirit and reflect his light to the world, so that God's kingdom may come and his will be done on earth as it is in heaven.

All mission in Christ's name is directed towards the integral transformation of this world in which we live. There was nothing escapist or private about the message and ministry of Jesus. He lived and died and rose again in order to establish God's kingdom on earth and, as disciples of Jesus, our task is to announce in word and deed that God's kingdom has indeed come and, by the power of the Spirit, to act boldly to shape our world in accordance with it. However, the way we act in the world, and for the sake of the world, must be the way of Jesus, the way of suffering love, the way of the cross. 'Christ does not propose a revolution of a social or political kind, but a revolution of love, brought about by his complete self-giving through his death on the Cross and his resurrection' (AM 26).

John Fuellenbach reminds us that the words 'success' and 'optimism' are not part of our tool kit as witnesses, signs and instruments of God's kingdom: 'Our faith tells us that it is hope against hope that keeps us going and gives us the necessary courage and even the audacity to believe that the kingdom will win.'[10] Jürgen Moltmann expresses this profound conviction of our faith in these words: 'Where people suffer because they love, God suffers in them and they suffer in God ... Where God suffers the death of Jesus and thereby demonstrates the power of his love, these people also find the power to remain in love despite pain and death, becoming neither bitter nor superficial.'[11] The way of suffering love is certainly not easy but is profoundly hope-filled. Its hope is grounded in the experience of God's power made perfect in the utter vulnerability of compassionate loving, releasing men and women from fear and apathy to live new purposeful lives – lives that are compassionate, joyful and free and that bring the life of Christ to others. And it is this hope which is celebrated and consummated in the Eucharistic banquet to which all are invited.

Iglesia un espacio de comunión y comunicación de pueblos y culturas. Toda la vida de nuestros pueblos fundada en Cristo y redimida por Él puede mirar al futuro con esperanza y alegría acogiendo el llamado del Papa Benedicto XVI: '¡Sólo de la Eucaristía brotará la civilización del amor que nos capacitará para que además de ser el continente de la esperanza, sea también el continente del amor!'[12] (cfr. DA, 127).

El llamamiento que hace Jesús, el Maestro, y la invitación a 'hacer esto en conmemoración mía', conlleva una gran novedad. En la antigüedad los maestros invitaban a sus discípulos a vincularse con algo trascendente, y los maestros de la Ley les proponían la adhesión a la Ley de Moisés. Jesús invita a encontrarnos con Él y a que nos vinculemos estrechamente a Él porque es la fuente de la vida (cf. Jn 15:5-15) y sólo Él tiene palabras de vida eterna (cf. Jn 6:68). En la convivencia cotidiana con Jesús y en la confrontación con los seguidores de otros maestros, los discípulos pronto descubrieron dos cosas del todo originales en la relación con Jesús:

Por una parte, no fueron ellos los que escogieron a su maestro. Fue Cristo quien los eligió. Por otra parte, ellos no fueron convocados para algo (purificarse, aprender la Ley ...), sino para Alguien, elegidos para vincularse íntimamente su Persona (cf. Mc 1:17; 2:14). Jesús los eligió para 'que estuvieran con Él y enviarlos a predicar' (Mc 3:14), para que lo siguieran con la finalidad de 'ser de Él' y formar parte 'de los suyos' y participar de su misión. El discípulo experimenta que la vinculación íntima con Jesús en el grupo de los suyos es participación de la Vida salida de las entrañas del Padre; es formarse para asumir su mismo estilo de vida y sus mismas motivaciones (cf. Lc 6:40b); correr su misma suerte y hacerse cargo de su misión de hacer nuevas todas las cosas.

En la celebración de la Eucaristía, cada bautizado es configurado con el Maestro. La admiración por la persona de Jesús, su llamada y su mirada de amor buscan suscitar una respuesta consciente y libre desde lo más íntimo del corazón del discípulo, una adhesión de toda su persona al saber que Cristo lo llama por su nombre (cf. Jn 10:3). Es un 'sí' que compromete radicalmente la libertad del discípulo a entregarse a Jesucristo, Camino, Verdad y Vida (cf. Jn 14:6). Es una respuesta de amor a quien lo amó primero 'hasta el extremo' (cf. Jn 13:1) como lo hizo en la Última Cena. En este amor de Jesús madura la respuesta del discípulo: 'Te seguiré adondequiera que vayas' (Lc 9:57).

Para configurarse verdaderamente con el Maestro es necesario asumir la centralidad del mandamiento del amor, que Él quiso llamar suyo y nuevo: 'Ámense los unos a los otros, como yo los he amado' (Jn 15:12), hasta el extremo de dar la vida por sus amigos, como ocurre en su entrega personal cada vez que 'hacemos esto en conmemoración' suya. Este amor, con la medida de Jesús, de total don de sí, además de ser el distintivo de cada cristiano no puede dejar de ser la característica de su Iglesia, comunidad discípula de Cristo, cuyo testimonio de caridad fraterna será el primero y principal anuncio, 'reconocerán todos que son discípulos míos' (Jn 13:35).

En el seguimiento de Jesucristo, aprendemos y practicamos las bienaventuranzas del Reino, el estilo de vida del mismo Jesucristo: su amor y obediencia filial al Padre, su compasión entrañable ante el dolor humano, su cercanía a los pobres y a los pequeños, su fidelidad a la misión encomendada, su amor servicial hasta el don de su vida.

Hoy contemplamos a Jesucristo tal como nos lo transmiten los evangelios para conocer lo que Él hizo y para discernir lo que nosotros debemos hacer en las actuales circunstancias.

Identificarse con Jesucristo es también compartir su destino: 'Donde yo esté estará también el que me sirve' (Jn 12:26), y el mayor servicio nos lo dejó en la Última Cena, lavando los pies de sus discípulos. El cristiano corre la misma suerte del Señor, incluso hasta la cruz: 'Si alguno quiere venir detrás de mí, que renuncie a sí mismo, que cargue con su cruz y que me siga' (Mc 8:34).

En nuestra Iglesia, innumerables cristianos buscan configurarse con el Señor al encontrarlo en la escucha orante de la Palabra, recibir su perdón en el sacramento de la reconciliación, y su vida en la celebración de la Eucaristía y de los demás sacramentos, en la entrega solidaria a los hermanos más necesitados y en la vida de muchas comunidades que reconocen con gozo al Señor en medio de ellos. (cfr. DA, 136–142)

LA CELEBRACIÓN EUCARÍSTICA NOS HA DE LLEVAR A SER ENVIADOS A ANUNCIAR EL EVANGELIO DEL REINO DE VIDA

Jesucristo, por su sacrificio voluntario, como Cordero de Dios pone su vida ofrecida en las manos del Padre (cf. Lc 23:46), quien lo hace

hace miembros del mismo cuerpo (cf. 1 Cor 10:17). Ella es fuente y culmen de la vida cristiana,[16] su expresión más perfecta y el alimento de la vida en comunión. En la Eucaristía se nutren las nuevas relaciones evangélicas que surgen de ser hijos e hijas del Padre y hermanos y hermanas en Cristo. La Iglesia que la celebra es 'casa y escuela de comunión'[17] donde los discípulos comparten la misma fe, esperanza y amor al servicio de la misión evangelizadora.

La Iglesia que celebra la Eucaristía, como 'comunidad de amor',[18] está llamada a reflejar la gloria del amor de Dios que es comunión y así atraer a las personas y a los pueblos hacia Cristo. En el ejercicio de la unidad querida por Jesús, los hombres y mujeres de nuestro tiempo se sienten convocados y recorren la hermosa aventura de la fe. 'Que también ellos vivan unidos a nosotros para que el mundo crea' (Jn 17:21). La Iglesia crece no por proselitismo sino 'por 'atracción': como Cristo 'atrae todo a sí' con la fuerza de su amor'.[19] La Iglesia 'atrae' cuando vive en comunión, pues los discípulos de Jesús serán reconocidos si se aman los unos a los otros como Él nos amó (cf. Rom 12:4-13; Jn 13:34).

Reunida y alimentada por la Palabra y la Eucaristía, la Iglesia católica existe y se manifiesta en cada Iglesia particular en comunión con el Obispo de Roma.[20] Esta es, como lo afirma el Concilio 'una porción del pueblo de Dios confiada a un obispo para que la apaciente con su presbiterio'.[21]

Siguiendo el ejemplo de la primera comunidad cristiana (cf. Hch 2:46-47), la comunidad parroquial se reúne para partir el pan de la Palabra y de la Eucaristía y perseverar en la catequesis, en la vida sacramental y la práctica de la caridad.[22] En la celebración eucarística ella renueva su vida en Cristo. La Eucaristía, en la cual se fortalece la comunidad de los discípulos, es para la parroquia una escuela de vida cristiana. En ella, juntamente con la adoración eucarística y con la práctica del sacramento de la reconciliación para acercarse dignamente a comulgar, se preparan sus miembros en orden a dar frutos permanentes de caridad, reconciliación y justicia para la vida del mundo. La Eucaristía, fuente y culmen de la vida cristiana, hace que nuestras parroquias sean siempre comunidades eucarísticas que viven sacramentalmente el encuentro con Cristo Salvador. Ellas también celebran con alegría:

La Eucaristía, signo de la unidad con todos, que prolonga y hace presente el misterio del Hijo de Dios hecho hombre (cf. Fil 2:6-8), nos plantea la exigencia de una evangelización integral. La inmensa mayoría de los católicos de nuestro continente viven bajo el flagelo de la pobreza. Esta tiene diversas expresiones: económica, física, espiritual, moral, etc. Si Jesús vino para que todos tengamos vida en plenitud, la parroquia tiene la hermosa ocasión de responder a las grandes necesidades de nuestros pueblos. Para ello tiene que seguir el camino de Jesús y llegar a ser buena samaritana como Él. Cada parroquia debe llegar a concretar en signos solidarios su compromiso social en los diversos medios en que ella se mueve, con toda 'la imaginación de la caridad'.[23] No puede ser ajena a los grandes sufrimientos que vive la mayoría de nuestra gente y que con mucha frecuencia son pobrezas escondidas. Toda auténtica misión unifica la preocupación por la dimensión trascendente del ser humano y por todas sus necesidades concretas, para que todos alcancen la plenitud que Jesucristo ofrece.

Benedicto XVI nos recuerda que 'el amor a la Eucaristía lleva también a apreciar cada vez más el Sacramento de la Reconciliación'.[24] Vivimos en una cultura marcada por un fuerte relativismo y una pérdida del sentido del pecado que nos lleva a olvidar la necesidad del sacramento de la reconciliación para acercarnos dignamente a recibir la Eucaristía (cfr. DA, 175–7).

Valoramos y agradecemos con gozo que la inmensa mayoría de los presbíteros vivan su ministerio con fidelidad y sean modelo para los demás, que saquen tiempo para su formación permanente, que cultiven una vida espiritual que estimula a los demás presbíteros, centrada en la escucha de la Palabra de Dios y en la celebración diaria de la Eucaristía: '¡Mi Misa es mi vida y mi vida es una Misa prolongada!'[25] Agradecemos también a aquellos que han sido enviados a otras Iglesias motivados por un auténtico sentido misionero.

El Pueblo de Dios siente la necesidad de presbíteros-discípulos: que tengan una profunda experiencia de Dios, configurados con el corazón del Buen Pastor, dóciles a las mociones del Espíritu, que se nutran de la Palabra de Dios, de la Eucaristía y de la oración; de presbíteros-misioneros: movidos por la caridad pastoral, que los lleve a cuidar del rebaño a ellos confiados y a buscar a los más alejados predicando la Palabra de Dios, siempre en profunda comunión con

La Iglesia en sus inicios se formó en las grandes ciudades de su tiempo y se sirvió de ellas para extenderse. Por eso, podemos realizar con alegría y valentía la evangelización de la ciudad actual. Ante la nueva realidad de la ciudad se realizan en la Iglesia nuevas experiencias, tales como la renovación de las parroquias, sectorización, nuevos ministerios, nuevas asociaciones, grupos, comunidades y movimientos. Pero se notan actitudes de miedo a la pastoral urbana; tendencias a encerrarse en los métodos antiguos y de tomar una actitud de defensa ante la nueva cultura, de sentimientos de impotencia ante las grandes dificultades de las ciudades.

La fe nos enseña que Dios vive en la ciudad, en medio de sus alegrías, anhelos y esperanzas, como también en sus dolores y sufrimientos. Las sombras que marcan lo cotidiano de las ciudades, como por ejemplo, violencia, pobreza, individualismo y exclusión, no pueden impedirnos que busquemos y contemplemos al Dios de la vida también en los ambientes urbanos. Las ciudades son lugares de libertad y oportunidad. En ellas las personas tienen la posibilidad de conocer a más personas, interactuar y convivir con ellas. En las ciudades es posible experimentar vínculos de fraternidad, solidaridad y universalidad. En ellas el ser humano es llamado constantemente a caminar siempre más al encuentro del otro, convivir con el diferente, aceptarlo y ser aceptado por él.

El proyecto de Dios es 'la Ciudad Santa, la nueva Jerusalén', que baja del cielo, junto a Dios, 'engalanada como una novia que se adorna para su esposo', que es 'la tienda de campaña que Dios ha instalado entre los hombres. Acampará con ellos; ellos serán su pueblo y Dios mismo estará con ellos. Enjugará las lágrimas de sus ojos y no habrá ya muerte ni luto, ni llanto, ni dolor, porque todo lo antiguo ha desaparecido' (Ap 21:2-4). Este proyecto en su plenitud es futuro, pero ya está realizándose en Jesucristo, 'el Alfa y la Omega, el Principio y el Fin' (Ap 21:6), que nos dice 'Yo hago nuevas todas las cosas' (Ap 21:5).

La Iglesia está al servicio de la realización de esta Ciudad Santa, a través de la proclamación y vivencia de la Palabra, de la celebración de la Liturgia, de la comunión fraterna y del servicio, especialmente, a los más pobres y a los que más sufren, y así va transformando en Cristo, como fermento del Reino, la ciudad actual.

Al servicio de la unidad y de la fraternidad

En la nueva situación cultural afirmamos que el proyecto del Reino está presente y es posible, y por ello aspiramos a un mundo unido, reconciliado e integrado. Esta casa común está habitada por un complejo mestizaje y una pluralidad étnica y cultural, 'en el que el Evangelio se ha transformado ... en el elemento clave de una síntesis dinámica que, con matices diversos según las naciones, expresa de todas formas la identidad de los pueblos latinoamericanos'.[42]

Los desafíos que enfrentamos hoy en el mundo tienen una característica peculiar. Ellos no sólo afectan a todos nuestros pueblos de manera similar sino que, para ser enfrentados, requieren una comprensión global y una acción conjunta. Creemos que 'un factor que puede contribuir notablemente a superar los apremiantes problemas que hoy afectan a nuestro mundo es la integración ...'[43]

Por una parte, se va configurando una realidad global que hace posibles nuevos modos de conocer, aprender y comunicarse, que nos coloca en contacto diario con la diversidad de nuestro mundo y crea posibilidades para una unión y solidaridad más estrechas a niveles regionales y a nivel mundial. Por otra parte, se generan nuevas formas de empobrecimiento, exclusión e injusticia. Nuestro mundo puede y debe lograr su integración sobre los cimientos de la vida, el amor y la paz.

La Iglesia de Dios es sacramento de comunión de sus pueblos. Es morada de sus pueblos; es casa de los pobres de Dios. Convoca y congrega todos en su misterio de comunión, sin discriminaciones ni exclusiones por motivos de sexo, raza, condición social y pertenencia nacional. Cuanto más la Iglesia refleja, vive y comunica ese don de inaudita unidad, que encuentra en la comunión trinitaria su fuente, modelo y destino, resulta más significativo e incisivo su operar como sujeto de reconciliación y comunión en la vida de nuestros pueblos. María Santísima es la presencia materna indispensable y decisiva en la gestación de un pueblo de hijos y hermanos, de discípulos y misioneros de su Hijo.

La dignidad de reconocernos como una familia implica una experiencia singular de proximidad, fraternidad y solidaridad. No somos un mero continente, apenas un hecho geográfico con un mosaico ininteligible de contenidos. Tampoco somos una suma de pueblos y de etnias que se yuxtaponen. Una y plural, la sociedad actual es la casa común, la gran patria de hermanos 'de unos pueblos – como afirmó S.S. Juan Pablo II en Santo Domingo[44] – a quienes la misma geografía, la fe cristiana, la lengua y la cultura han unido definitivamente en el camino de la historia'. Es, pues, una unidad que está muy lejos de reducirse a uniformidad, sino que se enriquece con muchas diversidades locales, nacionales y culturales.

CONCLUSIÓN
LA EUCARISTÍA, FUENTE QUE NOS CONDUCE A CAMINOS DE RECONCILIACIÓN Y SOLIDARIDAD

La Iglesia tiene que animar a cada pueblo para construir en su patria una casa de hermanos donde todos tengan una morada para vivir y convivir con dignidad. Esa vocación requiere la alegría de querer ser y hacer una nación, un proyecto histórico sugerente de vida en común. La Iglesia ha de educar y conducir cada vez más a la reconciliación con Dios y los hermanos. Hay que sumar y no dividir. Importa cicatrizar heridas, evitar maniqueísmos, peligrosas exasperaciones y polarizaciones. Los dinamismos de integración digna, justa y equitativa en el seno de cada uno de los países favorece la integración regional y, a la vez, es incentivada por ella.

Es necesario educar y favorecer en nuestros pueblos todos los gestos, obras y caminos de reconciliación y amistad social, de cooperación e integración. La comunión alcanzada en la sangre reconciliadora de Cristo nos da la fuerza para ser constructores de puentes, anunciadores de verdad, bálsamo para las heridas. La reconciliación está en el corazón de la vida cristiana. Es iniciativa propia de Dios en busca de nuestra amistad, que comporta consigo la necesaria reconciliación con el hermano. Se trata de una reconciliación que necesitamos en los diversos ámbitos y en todos y entre todos nuestros países. Esta reconciliación fraterna presupone la reconciliación con Dios, fuente única de gracia y de perdón, que alcanza su expresión y realización en el sacramento de la penitencia que Dios nos regala a través de la Iglesia.

EN LA ESPERANZA

En el corazón y la vida de nuestros pueblos late un fuerte sentido de esperanza, no obstante las condiciones de vida que parecen ofuscar toda esperanza. Ella se experimenta y alimenta en el presente, gracias a los dones y signos de vida nueva que se comparte; compromete en la construcción de un futuro de mayor dignidad y justicia y ansía 'los cielos nuevos y la tierra nueva' que Dios nos ha prometido en su morada eterna.

Todas las auténticas transformaciones se fraguan y forjan en el corazón de las personas e irradian en todas las dimensiones de su existencia y convivencia. No hay nuevas estructuras si no hay hombres nuevos y mujeres nuevas que movilicen y hagan converger en los pueblos ideales y poderosas energías morales y religiosas. Formando discípulos y misioneros, la Iglesia da respuesta a esta exigencia.

La Iglesia alienta y favorece la reconstrucción de la persona y de sus vínculos de pertenencia y convivencia, desde un dinamismo de amistad, gratuidad y comunión. De este modo se contrarrestan los procesos de desintegración y atomización sociales. Para ello hay que aplicar el principio de subsidiariedad en todos los niveles y estructuras de la organización social.

Los discípulos y misioneros de Cristo promueven una cultura del compartir en todos los niveles en contraposición de la cultura dominante de acumulación egoísta, asumiendo con seriedad la virtud de la pobreza como estilo de vida sobrio para ir al encuentro y ayudar a las necesidades de los hermanos que viven en la indigencia.

Compete también a la Iglesia colaborar en la consolidación de las frágiles democracias, en el positivo proceso de democratización, aunque existan actualmente graves retos y amenazas de desvíos autoritarios. Urge educar para la paz, dar seriedad y credibilidad a la continuidad de nuestras instituciones civiles, defender y promover los derechos humanos, custodiar en especial la libertad religiosa y cooperar para suscitar los mayores consensos nacionales.

La paz es un bien preciado pero precario que debemos cuidar, educar y promover todos en nuestro continente. Como sabemos, la paz no se reduce a la ausencia de guerras ni a la exclusión de armas nucleares en nuestro espacio común, logros ya significativos, sino a la generación de una 'cultura de paz' que sea fruto de un desarrollo sostenible, equitativo y respetuoso de la creación ('el desarrollo es el nuevo nombre de la paz', decía Pablo VI), y que nos permita enfrentar conjuntamente los ataques del narcotráfico y consumo de drogas, del terrorismo y de las muchas formas de violencia que hoy imperan en nuestra sociedad. La Iglesia, sacramento de reconciliación y de paz, desea que los discípulos y misioneros de Cristo sean también, ahí donde se encuentren, 'constructores de paz' entre los pueblos y naciones de nuestro Continente. La Iglesia está llamada a ser una escuela permanente de verdad y justicia, de perdón y reconciliación para construir una paz auténtica.

Una auténtica evangelización de nuestros pueblos implica asumir plenamente la radicalidad del amor cristiano, que se concreta en el seguimiento de Cristo en la cruz; en el padecer por Cristo a causa de la justicia; en el perdón y amor a los enemigos. Este amor supera al amor humano y participa en el amor divino, único eje cultural capaz de construir una cultura de la vida. En el Dios Trinidad la diversidad de Personas no genera violencia y conflicto, sino que es la misma fuente de amor y de la vida. Una evangelización que pone la redención en el centro, nacida de un amor crucificado, es capaz de purificar las estructuras de la sociedad violenta y generar nuevas. La radicalidad de la violencia sólo se resuelve con la radicalidad del amor redentor. Evangelizar sobre el amor de plena donación, como solución al conflicto, debe ser el eje cultural 'radical' de una nueva sociedad. Sólo así el continente de la esperanza puede llegar a tornarse verdaderamente el continente del amor.

Conscientes de que la misión evangelizadora no puede ir separada de la solidaridad con los pobres y su promoción integral, y sabiendo que hay comunidades eclesiales que carecen de los medios necesarios, es imperativo ayudarlas, a imitación de las primeras comunidades cristianas, para que de verdad se sientan amadas. Urge, pues, la creación de un fondo de solidaridad entre las Iglesias que esté al servicio de las iniciativas pastorales propias.

Al enfrentar tan graves desafíos nos alientan las palabras del Santo Padre: 'No hay duda de que las condiciones para establecer una paz verdadera son la restauración de la justicia, la reconciliación y el perdón. De esta toma de conciencia, nace la voluntad de transformar también las estructuras injustas para establecer respeto de la dignidad del hombre creado a imagen y semejanza de Dios ... Como he tenido ocasión de afirmar, la Iglesia no tiene como tarea propia emprender una batalla política, sin embargo, tampoco puede ni debe quedarse al margen de la lucha por la justicia'.[45]

Es el mismo Papa Benedicto XVI quien nos ha invitado a 'una misión evangelizadora que convoque todas las fuerzas vivas de este inmenso rebaño': 'sacerdotes, religiosos, religiosas y laicos que se prodigan, muchas veces con inmensas dificultades, para la difusión de la verdad evangélica.' Es un afán y anuncio misioneros que tiene que pasar de persona a persona, de casa en casa, de comunidad a comunidad. 'En este esfuerzo evangelizador, prosigue el Santo Padre, la comunidad eclesial se destaca por las iniciativas pastorales, al enviar, sobre todo entre las casas de las periferias urbanas y del interior, sus misioneros, laicos o religiosos, buscando dialogar con todos en espíritu de comprensión y de delicada caridad'. Esa misión evangelizadora abraza con el amor de Dios a todos y especialmente a los pobres y los que sufren. Por eso, no puede separarse de la solidaridad con los necesitados y de su promoción humana integral: 'Pero si las personas encontradas están en una situación de pobreza, nos dice aún el Papa,

> es necesario ayudarlas, como hacían las primeras comunidades cristianas, practicando la solidaridad, para que se sientan amadas de verdad. El pueblo pobre de las periferias urbanas o del campo necesita sentir la proximidad de la Iglesia, sea en el socorro de sus necesidades más urgentes, como también en la defensa de sus derechos y en la promoción común de una sociedad fundamentada en la justicia y en la paz. Los pobres son los destinatarios privilegiados del Evangelio y un Obispo, modelado según la imagen del Buen Pastor, debe estar particularmente atento en ofrecer el divino bálsamo de la fe, sin descuidar el 'pan material'.

Mi mejor augurio es que este importante simposio teológico nos ayude a todos a continuar la labor pastoral como ese muelle en donde la Eucaristía siga siendo punto de partida y de llegada de incansables misioneros para la nueva evangelización.

Muchas Gracias.

NOTES

1 Benedicto XVI, *Homilía en la Eucaristía de inauguración de la V Conferencia General del Episcopado Latinoamericano*, 13 de Mayo de 2007, Aparecida, Brasil.

2 Cf. NMI, 28–9.

3 DCE, 1.

4 Benedicto XVI, *Homilía en la Eucaristía de inauguración de la V Conferencia General del Episcopado Latinoamericano*, 13 de Mayo de 2007, Aparecida, Brasil.

5 DI, 4.

6 Benedicto XVI, *Homilía en la Eucaristía de inauguración de la V Conferencia General del Episcopado Latinoamericano*, 13 de Mayo de 2007, Aparecida, Brasil.

7 Cf. EN, 1.

8 Cf. Benedicto XVI, *Homilía en el solemne inicio del Ministerio Petrino del Obispo de Roma*, 24 de Abril de 2005.

9 Ibid.

10 DI, 3.

11 Cf. NMI 25 y 28.

12 DI, 4.

13 DI, 3.

14 Cf. DI, 3.

15 SC, 17.

16 Cf. LG, 11.

17 NMI, 43.

18 DCE, 19.

19 Benedicto XVI, *Homilía en la Eucaristía de inauguración de la V Conferencia General del Episcopado Latinoamericano*, 13 de Mayo de 2007, Aparecida, Brasil.

20 ChL, 85.

21 ChD, 11.

22 Benedicto XVI, Audiencia General, Viaje Apostólico a Brasil, 23 de Mayo de 2007.

23 NMI, 50.

24 SC, 20.

25 Hurtado, Alberto, *Un fuego que enciende otros fuegos*, pp. 69–70.

26 Cf. Ibid., 6.

27 DI, 4.

28 NMI, 33.

29 AG, 2.

30 Benedicto XVI, Homilía en la inauguración del Pontificado, 24 de Abril de 2005.

31 DCE, 15.

32 San Juan Crisóstomo, *Homilías sobre san Mateo*, L, 3–4, pp. 58, 508–9.

33 NMI, 43.

34 Cf. NMI, 20.

35 Ibid., 12.

36 Ibid., 29.

37 Cf. ChL, 51.

38 RM, 37.

39 Cf. EV, 5.

40 DI, 4.

41 DI, 3.

42 Benedicto XVI, Audiencia General, Viaje Apostólico a Brasil, 23 de Mayo de 2007.

43 SD, 15.

44 Juan Pablo II, Discurso inaugural en la IV Conferencia General del Episcopado Latinoamericano, 12 de Octubre de 1992.

45 SC, 89.

COMMUNION WITH CHRIST: MISSION AND EVANGELISATION IN ASIA

REV. DR THEODORE MASCARENHAS SFX
Member of the Pontifical Council for Culture

'And I have other sheep, that are not of this fold; I must bring them also, and they will heed my voice. So there shall be one flock, one shepherd.'[1]

Dear Brothers and Sisters,

These words of Jesus in the Gospel of John come to our mind, the moment we think of Asia and the huge task of evangelisation before us in this great and vast continent. As we know, this is the largest continent that is home to nearly 60 per cent of the world's population. Christianity was born in Asia but today Christianity is the predominant faith only in four countries: Philippines and East Timor, which are majority Catholic countries, and Armenia and Georgia which are majority Christian (not Catholic) nations. Christianity does exist throughout the continent with very active communities found in Lebanon, South Korea, India, Pakistan, Iraq, Jordan, Israel, China, Taiwan, Japan, Singapore, Vietnam, Sri Lanka, Syria, Kazakhstan, Indonesia, Malaysia and Thailand. Remembering the Asian roots of Christianity, Pope John Paul II called it 'Jesus' little flock on this immense continent'.[2] But this is also a continent with a deep seated religiosity, where hunger and thirst for God pervades all facets of life. As the same Blessed John Paul II speaking to the Sixth Plenary Assembly of the Federation of Asian Bishops' Conferences, in Manila, the Philippines, during the memorable tenth 'World Youth Day' celebrations, reminded the bishops: 'If the Church in Asia is to fulfil its providential destiny, evangelisation as the joyful, patient and progressive preaching of the saving death and resurrection of Jesus Christ must be your absolute priority.'[3] The Apostolic Exhortation, *Ecclesia in Asia* is perhaps the document that speaks most comprehensively of Asia and its Evangelisation. Therefore please pardon me if I keep taking frequent recourse to this important magisterial document. I congratulate the organisers for holding this Symposium and thank them for giving me the opportunity to speak on 'Communion with Christ: Mission and Evangelisation in Asia'. When we talk of evangelisation, I would like to think of it in the terms of the call given by John Paul II, 'open wide to Christ the doors of Asia'.[4] The beginning and the endpoint of 'opening wide the doors to Christ' is communion with him. This vast continent with its plethora of religions, multiplicity of cultures, diversity of ways of life, with its thirst for the truth and for God is ripe for evangelisation and can yield a huge harvest for Christ. I would like to propose my sharing under three points:

1. Communion with Christ is the fount and source of evangelisation
2. Communion in the Eucharist is a witness to the love of Christ
3. Communion within the Church brings Christ to those outside.

COMMUNION WITH CHRIST IS THE FOUNT AND SOURCE OF EVANGELISATION

The Church is essentially missionary and its mission of evangelisation comes from Jesus' own mission. 'As the Father sent me, so I send you.'[5] These words of the Master are linked to the prayer he makes to the heavenly Father before marching towards the culmination of the manifestation of his union to the Father in the passion, death and resurrection: 'I pray also for those who will believe in me through their message, that all of them may be one, Father, just as you are in me and I am in you. May they also be in us so that the world may believe that you have sent me.'[6] Evangelisation means making Christ present to the world. But to make Christ present to the world, it is absolutely necessary that the evangelisers themselves are in close union to the Lord. *Ecclesia in Asia* very clearly exhorted:

> The good news of Jesus Christ can only be proclaimed by those who are taken up and inspired by the love of the Father for his children, manifested in the person of Jesus Christ. This proclamation is a mission needing holy men and women who will make the Saviour known and loved through their lives. A fire can only be lit by something that is itself on fire. So, too, successful proclamation

> in Asia of the good news of salvation can only take place if bishops, clergy, those in the consecrated life and the laity are themselves on fire with the love of Christ and burning with zeal to make him known more widely, loved more deeply and followed more closely.[7]

Three beautiful biblical images come to mind when one thinks of the communion of prayer that flows into evangelisation: Moses before the burning bush, Jesus going up to the mountain to pray and the metaphor of the vine and the branches which Jesus offers to his disciples.

Before Moses is commissioned by God to lead his people out of the slavery of Egypt, to be his earthly representative in the formation of his people and to lead them towards the promised land, God brings Moses to himself in a union that will both consecrate him as the 'one sent' as well as fortify and strengthen him. The dynamics of the episode teaches much about union with God and mission.

God has a plan for his people and this plan is to be actualised through an important role played by Moses. In fact Moses is but a simple shepherd. This story will be repeated time and again in the Bible. God choosing simple people for his work: David the shepherd, Amos the shepherd, Peter, James and John the fishermen are just a few examples of a long series. Before the burning bush, in the call that he receives, Moses is reluctant, frightened and aware of his insufficiency for the mission. It is the union with the Lord that gives Moses the strength. The assurance that God gives him, 'I will be with you', is what will finally give Moses the strength and will to be God's agent. Peter and the other apostles go through the same experience: from inept, weak and unsure men, they are transformed into sturdy, powerful and enterprising proclaimers of the Word. James and John who had asked to be placed at the right and left of Jesus, turn out to become servants of the word, Peter who denied Jesus three times is not afraid of martyrdom and Thomas who doubted the resurrection treads out as far as distant India to proclaim the Lord.

It appears to be a standard biblical tradition that the task of Evangelisation is entrusted to men and women who appear weak before human eyes. And yet it is the communion with the Lord that empowers these apostles of the gospel and enhances their proclamatory powers. As the Lord tells St Paul: 'My grace is sufficient for you, for my power is made perfect in weakness.'[8]

The power of evangelisation comes from a communion with the Lord, the communion that is personified in the celebration of the Eucharist and reaches the climax in the partaking of the Body and Blood of the Lord.

The second image that flashes before the mind is that of Jesus in prayer. Again and again, especially before important decisions that are interwoven with his mission, he goes up to the Father. Mark tells us that, 'very early in the morning, while it was still dark, Jesus got up, left the house and went off to a solitary place, where he prayed' (Mk 1:35). Immediately after that, he expresses his desire to extend his mission as he tells the disciples: 'Let us go somewhere else – to the nearby villages – so I can preach there also. That is why I have come.' Similarly in the Gospel of Luke after a hard day's work, when people were coming in droves to see him and seek his healing touch, Luke tells us, 'But Jesus often withdrew to lonely places and prayed'. He thus teaches us, his disciples, that it is communion that provides strength before we undertake our task, sustains us during our mission and provides us solace and comfort after we have toiled hard.

The third illustration is provided to us by Jesus himself. 'I am the vine; you are the branches. If you remain in me and I in you, you will bear much fruit; apart from me you can do nothing.'[9] Just like a branch feeds and nurtures itself on the sap of the stem, every Christian needs to be in communion with the Lord. This communion, as already stated earlier, is at its peak when we 'eat his body and drink his blood'. *Ecclesia in Asia* would point this out very clearly:

> The more the Christian community is rooted in the experience of God which flows from a living faith, the more credibly it will be able to proclaim to others the fulfilment of God's Kingdom in Jesus Christ. This will result from faithfully listening to the word of God, from prayer and contemplation, from celebrating the mystery of Jesus in the sacraments, above all in the Eucharist, and from giving example of true communion of life and integrity of love.[10]

COMMUNION IN THE EUCHARIST IS A WITNESS TO THE LOVE OF CHRIST

The evangelist John begins the narration of the Last Supper, which we consider the first eucharistic celebration with these words: 'It was just before the Passover Feast. Jesus knew that the time had come for him to leave this world and go to the Father. Having loved his own who were in the world, he now showed them the full extent of his love.'[11] In fact the whole meal turns out to be a testimony to love and a lesson in love as the fundamental principle of Christian life. In a Passover meal that Jesus would transform into an anticipated offering of himself as the 'lamb', Jesus transforms the occasion into an act of love and communion. He first takes on the function of a slave, and washes the feet of his disciple. This 'lowly' act itself is a sign of communion as is evident in the exchange of words between Peter and Jesus. Peter remonstrates with the Lord, unable to accept the fact that the Lord would wash his feet: 'you shall never wash my feet,' he tells the Lord. And Jesus' answer has a deep theological significance, 'Unless I wash you, you have no part with me.'[12] To have part with the Lord one needs to be in the communion of love. The message is then communicated loud and clear in other aspects of the celebrative evening. Jesus exhorts his disciples: 'Now that I, your Lord and Teacher, have washed your feet, you also should wash one another's feet. I have set you an example that you should do as I have done for you.'[13] Communion with the Lord in his meal necessarily implies a communion in service and a witness in love. This is further evident with the instance of Judas Iscariot whose departure from the scene of the first eucharistic meal is described by the evangelist thus: 'As soon as Judas had taken the bread, he went out. And it was night.'[14] If the eucharistic meal of love had led the good-hearted Peter to be part of the Lord, the malice of the betrayer pushes Judas into the night. Peter would head the Church and eventually die for the Lord while Judas Iscariot would bring his life to an untimely death by hanging.

In the evangelisation of Asia, the witness of the Eucharist as a meal of love would be a powerful proclamation. The same Eucharist celebrated without compassion for the poor and imbedded in divisions could be the greatest counter witness to the spread of the gospel. St Paul was very severe on eucharistic celebrations that manifested divisions and conflicts. He tells the Corinthians in the passage in which he teaches them about the eucharistic meal: 'So then, when you come together, it is not the Lord's Supper you eat, for when you are eating, some of you go ahead with your own private suppers. As a result, one person remains hungry and another gets drunk. Don't you have homes to eat and drink in?'[15]

Pope John Paul II calls us in Asia to a real communion of love when he quotes St John Chrysostom to make his point: 'Do you wish to honour the body of Christ? Then do not ignore him when he is naked. Do not pay him silken honours in the temple only then to neglect him when he goes cold and naked outside. He who said, "This is my body" is the One who also said, "You saw me hungry and you gave me no food" ... What good is it if the eucharistic table groans under the weight of golden chalices, when Christ is dying of hunger? Start by satisfying his hunger, and then with what remains you may adorn the altar as well!'[16]

The Catholic Church and its missionaries have been wonderful apostles of compassion and mercy especially through its huge network of schools, hospitals and other social works. But the real leaven will be introduced into the evangelising task when the eucharistic communion that we are called to celebrate becomes a witness of love. Many people recognise Christian teachings in the witness of love. Mahatma Gandhi once described Jesus as:

> the highest example of one who wished to give everything, asking nothing in return, and not caring what creed might happen to be professed by the recipient. I am sure that if he were living here now among men, he would bless the lives of many who perhaps have never even heard his name, if only their lives embodied the virtues of which he was a living example on earth; the virtues of loving one's neighbour as oneself and of doing good and charitable works among one's fellowmen.[17]

Our works among peoples will have the authenticity when they emanate from the eucharistic communion.

COMMUNION WITHIN THE CHURCH BRINGS CHRIST TO THOSE OUTSIDE

The celebration of the Eucharist is principally a communion with

Let me end with the testimony of the blessed Mother Teresa of Calcutta:

> It was not until 1973, when we began our daily Holy Hour that our community started to grow and blossom ... In our congregation, we used to have adoration once a week for one hour, and then in 1973, we decided to have adoration one hour every day. We have much work to do. Our homes for the sick and dying destitute are full everywhere. And from the time we started having adoration every day, our love for Jesus became more intimate, our love for each other more understanding, our love for the poor more compassionate, and we have double the number of vocations. God has blessed us with many wonderful vocations. The time we spend in having our daily audience with God is the most precious part of the whole day.

NOTES

1 Jn 10:6.

2 *Ecclesia in Asia*, 4.

3 *Insegnamenti* XVIII, 1 (1995), 159.

4 *Address to the Sixth Plenary Assembly of the Federation of Asian Bishops' Conferences* (FABC), Manila, 15th January 1995.

5 Jn 20:21.

6 Jn 17:20-21.

7 *Ecclesia in Asia*, 23.

8 2 Cor 12:9.

9 Jn 15:5.

10 *Ecclesia in Asia*, 23.

11 Jn 13:1.

12 Jn 13:9.

13 Jn 13:14.

14 Jn 13:30.

15 1 Cor 11:20-22.

16 *Ecclesia in Asia*, 41.

17 'What Jesus Means to Me', *Modern Review*, New York, October 1941.

18 *Ad Gentes*, 36.

19 *Mysterium Fidei*, 67.

20 Lk 24:30-31.

21 'The Eucharist: Communion With Christ And With One Another'. Theological and Pastoral Reflections in Preparation for the 50th International Eucharistic Congress, 26.

22 Message of the FABC 9th Plenary Assembly, 'Living the Eucharist in Asia', 2009.

23 *Ecclesia in Asia*, 10.

the treasure Christians have the honour and duty to carry through the centuries and pass on to next generations.

SECULARISM AND MODERNITY: SOME FUNDAMENTALS

It is important to propose a working definition of secularism, for not everybody would agree on what this often-used term actually stands for. Several characteristics have been put forward; the way in which they are valued largely depends on the initial stance one takes vis-à-vis secularism. These stances vary according to a continuum between a downright negative and dismissive attitude and an enthusiastically welcoming or positive one. Moreover, some scholars contend that secularism is almost over, or that it has had its best time; others are convinced that it still endures and that it may even intensify.[7] Few, however, would say that it is definitively gone or that we are completely beyond it.[8] One may use the term and like or dislike the use of it, but the reality denoted by the concept is in any case still vibrant among us. One may be pro or contra in different degrees, but one cannot say that secularism is irrelevant or a non-issue.

The Secular and the Profane

The central idea of 'the secular' can probably be best explained in terms of metaphorical spatiality.[9] It is a 'place' where society gains independence from religious dominion, an 'area' or 'domain' where the influence of religion does not play any role (anymore) or where it is no longer allowed to play a role. The idea that the institutions of the Church and the state must operate independently has often been considered similar to the basic meaning of secularism.[10] An important question in this regard is whether the emergence of 'the secular' is to be equated with the breakthrough of modernity, which in its own turn must be situated in intellectual developments in fifteenth-century European culture.[11] In other words, are modernity and secularism basically the same phenomenon, or, if not the same, then at least interdependent phenomena? It seems that this sameness or interdependence is taken for granted in a lot of philosophical and theological literature dealing with the destiny of religion, and in particular of the Christian faith, since the last four centuries.

This is not the only option, however, for one could interpret 'secularism' as a broader phenomenon, which is not necessarily connected to an evolution in the history of Western civilisation. My contention would be that if one reduces secularism to modernity, one risks overlooking profound similarities between the concepts of 'the secular' and 'the profane'. In what follows the term 'profane' will be used in line with the descriptions of renowned twentieth-century anthropologists of religion.[12] In this semantic frame the secular or profane is contrasted with 'the sacred'.

The reason I propose that 'secularism' is interpreted here rather anthropologically than philosophically or historically is a theological one. I think it better serves the goal of trying to make sense of the centre of Christians' cult in contemporary cultures (in the West). This idea needs to be elaborated in some more detail.

It seems that the distinction between 'the sacred' and 'the profane' exists in every culture. Someone like Mircea Eliade has argued that, notwithstanding the often-heard idea that the ultimate result of modernisation is a full desacralisation or disenchantment of people's life-worlds, the sacred even persists in contemporary Western culture, albeit in a different form. It shows itself no longer (exclusively) in religious rites and images but in hidden dreams, myths, and stories which occupy the minds of many people.[13] As a corollary, the profane, like the sacred, exists in every culture, even in the most religious one imaginable. Not everything can be sacred and, in real fact, not everything is as densely sacred. The sacred, so the argument continues, can only be lived as sacred on the condition that there is something non-sacred, or profane.[14] Religions are understood as the realities which make, mark and upkeep those differences.

THE INTERRUPTION OF THE PROFANE AND THE TRANSFORMATION OF THE SACRED

Bearing this argumentation in mind, a challenging idea of Yves Congar is worth mentioning – though I will do more than 'mention', I will build upon it. Relying on the tradition and the New Testament and the Church Fathers in particular, Congar suggests that the novelty of the 'good news' (*euaggelion*) consists in announcing that the old cultic dividing lines have ceased to exist. After and through Christ, there is in fact no 'profane' anymore, as distinct from the 'sacred'.[15] The things that people have held to be sacred or holy have lost the meaning that those who desire concrete demonstrations, whether in the form of tangible signs or invisible wisdom, will be easily served.[25] Cultural evidence is not (always) a blessing, let alone an indication, for the faith's authenticity.[26]

To make the consistent focus on the core of the faith possible I think, moreover, that a certain fundamental shift of emphasis needs to occur. I call it a shift from a primarily *epistemological* framework to an encompassing *soteriological* look at things.[27] Contemporary cultures in the West seem to be biased by a basically epistemological attitude towards reality. On a very large scale, and in many domains of the life-world of people, there is a primacy of knowledge and the desire to know. But the question can be raised whether a cognitive interest and notional outlook are ultimately entirely satisfactory. I think that this is not the case. Cognition is important, even indispensable, and good knowledge is always rationally structured, communicable, accountable, transparent, and well-founded – there is no doubt about that. But knowledge and the corresponding human faculties of intelligence and reason may not touch the deepest layers of existence. Questions of meaning and meaningfulness, of happiness and life-orientation, of the good and its realisability, of hope and trust, of joy and misery and how they are existentially addressed, etc. can only partially be answered through *episteme* and its *logos*.

Something 'more' or something 'else' is needed to complement the prevailing status of the epistemological in secular cultures. That is the soteriological. Soteriology, to be sure, is not diametrically opposed to epistemology but surpasses it both in the downward and upward directions. The questions provoked by it pierce deeper than mere knowledge can surmise or express, and the 'answers' it provides reach higher than the culmination of cognition. The perspective of the soteriological is neither limited by rational standards nor conditioned by the a priori reasoning of autonomous subjects holding on to a methodological atheism. It aims to satisfy the whole existence of real persons, and this both individually and insofar as they are members of communities. If knowledge, science, technology, and reason can help persons live their lives, that's fine, but if for some reason they run ashore, soteriology transcends epistemology's painful silences. Soteriology is all about the life-giving Word spoken by the Father, the Son and the Holy Spirit.

The God-question, which seems to have been generally put aside in secular cultures, although from a theological perspective God continues to be (publicly) relevant,[28] serves indeed as an ideal illustration to explain the distinction between epistemology and soteriology. Inasmuch as secularism is penetrated by epistemological preoccupations, it above all wants to know whether God exists. The decision about this mostly depends on difficult reasonings and arguments, but often does not leave the level of the theoretical.[29] What is worse, however, is that the faith commitment of many secularised people somehow depends on the certitude of whether God exists or not. Correspondingly, a believer is someone for whom the assertion 'God exists' still makes sense, more or less. However, this eagerness to know has somehow reduced faith to a set of convictions or a system of ideas, whereby the subject involved first assesses their truth-value and is only afterwards willing to consider him- or herself a believer, and only on the basis of that personal reflection process, possibly, as a member of a faith community. Both believers and unbelievers, insiders and outsiders, theologians as well as atheists, have actually stepped into this logic. But the real wealth of faith does not lie in a defensive and *a priori* approach.[30] When Christians approach 'the secular' apologetically, they in fact subscribe already to polarising schemes of thought which are at odds with their fundamentally reconciling attitude and peaceful access to reality.

As a mere assertion, 'God exists' is a very meagre, not to say hollow insight, though of course not an unimportant one. What does it mean to predicate 'existence' of God? Is God aptly dealt with in the grammatical and logical structure of a subject to which properties can be attributed? Is existence a property next to other possible properties? It seems that tiring intellectual debates about these and related questions have had their best time – whence the proposal for a shift from an epistemological interest to a soteriological paradigm.[31] That is, one not based on discerning degrees of probability and making judgements, but one inspired by what is really at stake in God's salvific initiative as it is embodied in the Christ event and carried on through the centuries (*saecula*) by the close and mutually fertilising entanglement of Church and Eucharist.[32]

THE DIFFERENCES BETWEEN THE EPISTEMOLOGICAL AND THE SOTERIOLOGICAL

The soteriological differs from the epistemological in several aspects. First, it does not depart from a logic of division. Epistemologies divide, since they want to strictly demarcate what can be known from the unknowable. These divisions, however, not seldom lead to divorces and separations of things which intrinsically (or naturally) belong together. What about the human and the divine, for instance? If one can gather knowledge about the human but cannot know anything whatsoever about the divine, how is one then supposed to understand things like faith, liturgy, and redemption?

Second, the soteriological is interested in *all human beings* beyond the distinctions made to organise human life-worlds and societies (like female-male, master-server, employer-employee, black-white, etc.). Soteriology is likewise interested in the *human being as a whole*, for example, not only in intelligence and the will (as corresponding to Kant's *Critiques* of pure and practical reason), but also in desires, the senses, passions, emotions, impressions, etc., but maybe above all, in the imagination – a human faculty which has, undeservedly, far too little been trusted in the history of Western thought.[33] In the end, moreover, one should always remember that the heart is more important than the head.

Third, soteriology is obviously more directly connected with the centre of Christian faith than epistemology. That centre, I would claim, is constituted by the Eucharist as the symbolic bearer of the Paschal mystery,[34] from which everything Christians do flows forth and towards which everything they do and think is oriented (cf. the above LG and SC quotations). The celebration of the mysteries, trying to realise the good, prayer (both communal and individual), and being continuously (in- and re-) formed by Bible and tradition: those are the pillars of the Christian life of faith.[35] The energetic dynamic between them is held (and meant) to draw women and men always closer to the ultimate reconciliation with God. Doctrines are essentially there to sustain and explain the living faith and customs of the tradition. But the living faith of the tradition (the soteriological) clearly prevails over its explication (the epistemological). It seems to me that secular cultures have reversed this order and that therein lies the fundamental reason they alienate themselves from religion – either willingly or unwillingly, either aggressively or ignorantly.

THE EUCHARIST IN SECULAR CULTURES

The next step of my reflections is the application of the above-said to the Eucharist as the culmination of the liturgy. For I think that the particularity of the (liturgical nature of the) Eucharist is largely misunderstood, both within and outside of theological circles. The secular, immersed as it is by epistemological instead of soteriological concerns, has penetrated religion and faith and is still, continuously, leaving its marks. In other words, it no longer stands at their doors, as some would probably like it to. Secularism cannot possibly be thought of as in direct opposition to Christianity or as antithetical to faith. This is, among other things, clear when we describe a common and widespread understanding of what liturgy actually is.

The Relation between the Eucharist and Culture

Many people, Christians and non-Christians alike, suppose that the Eucharist is a ritual. Evidently, it is not a 'rite of passage' in Arnold von Gennep's sense, but a ritual of the repetitive kind.[36] Such a rite is used for entertaining a positive relation with the godhead and/or for obtaining benefits from it. It aims at the stability of the community and functions as a place where the members of the community can refresh themselves at the source of their religion. This 'epistemological' interpretation of the ritual nature of the Eucharist is not untrue, but it can never attain the profoundest layers of its meanings, unless it opens up itself for what I have called the 'soteriological'. What would this ritual have to do with God's universal salvific will sprouting from his eternal love, if it is nothing more than a contingent and arbitrary instantiation of Christians' unavoidable bent for rituality? How would this ritual mediate God's mercifulness and effectuate grace? How could one think of it as a motor of faith beyond the boundaries of cultures, countries and epochs?

If one adopts and applies a merely epistemological approach, the answer to these questions can only be formulated through the indication of external factors, for example, through mentioning that '*Christians assume* that the saviour of humankind is present at their celebration'. Regardless of whether one treats these factors with disdain or sympathy, one will always need a supplement 'from within'.

Put differently, the Eucharist is not a ritual among rituals. It is not simply one of the elements of a given set or a species belonging to a genus. But one can only see this on the condition that one is willing to leave behind an *a priori* approach and to adopt an *a posteriori* attitude, i.e., if one is *receptive* to what the Eucharist *gives*. In this respect, I tend to make a threefold distinction, whereas many philosophers and anthropologists make a twofold distinction. In doing so, I engage myself in the classical nature-culture debate. How and where does religion emerge in the development from nature to culture? Many thinkers assume that there is no spontaneous evolution from nature to culture, but that at some point the natural development is interrupted. Culture is this interruption of nature, and it is usually connected with the enigmatic origin of language. Language, after all, makes it possible for human societies and cultures to emerge. One usually identifies the emergence of culture with the birthplace of religion; animals, like nature, are a-religious (perhaps more consistently a-religious than many humans). And one presumes that primitive people are 'more religious' than modern people, as if one could measure that.

Interestingly, the distinction between the sacred and the profane reoccurs precisely at the point where culture and religion arise. Religion, inasmuch as it is a 'cultural' phenomenon in the above described sense, is determined by flexible and variegating balances of the sacred and the profane. The Christian faith, however, as the response to God's revelation, interrupts these balances as much as culture interrupts nature.[37] It installs a radically new perspective on reality as a whole, including nature and culture, the sacred as well as the profane. Nature and part of culture become creation; religion and other parts of culture should gradually transform into faith; and societies must be made supportive so that all of this can be realised. Christians, then, are the women and men whom God has called upon to assist him in making this happen; and they should invite literally everyone to join them, but refrain from using power in doing so. Christians moreover remember, experience and promise to participate in God's work of salvation at each and every celebration of the Eucharist. That is why there is neither profane nor secular for them; everything must be sweepingly modified through the most profound re-signification possible. That re-signification passes from the depth of the cross to the heights of the resurrection – it comes as no surprise that the sign of the cross is so essential for Christian worship.

SOME PRACTICAL SUGGESTIONS

If all this – or at least some of it – makes sense, what, then, should (or could) be done to turn the tide? That is probably the most difficult question. Nevertheless, I offer some suggestions to conclude these reflections. First, I think that Christians must not always try to convince, prove, explain, argue and demonstrate. The convincing-mode is doubtlessly modelled after the epistemological and is basically rooted in a defensive strategy. The *testifying-mode* seems more appropriate and is more intimately connected with the soteriological.

Second, I would make a case for renewing a truly *visionary theology*. Especially when confronted with secularism and (post-)modernity, Christians generally testify too less of the great vision they cherish. It is as if they silently agree to have their dreams smashed. A visionary theology, however, keeps the senses and the minds focused on heaven, the *eschaton*, the ultimate horizon, the *parousia*, as the goal of all its endeavours.

Third, I think that a renewed emphasis and focus on the *heavenly liturgy* would be more than welcome. There is not only an 'active participation' of all the members of God's priestly people in the celebration of the sacraments, but also an 'active participation' of the earthly liturgy in the heavenly one.[38] Epistemology is likely to find only difficulties when the liturgy talks of angels and saints, but soteriology can recover the deep sense of addressing them and celebrating the Paschal mystery together with them.

Fourth, Christians steeped in secular cultures should engage in critical self-reflection. They should not only ask themselves whether they are doing, thinking, and saying the right things, but also what their deepest desires are. Do they really long for the Eucharist? Or do they only complain that others don't go to Mass? Is the Eucharist the real 'source and summit' of their individual prayer life? Or do they live in a schizophrenic situation, whereby their individual prayers have, on close inspection, nothing to do with the Eucharist, the liturgical year, and the Church? Does the Eucharist appeal to their imagination? Are they really passionate about it? Or do they only treat it as their 'own (particular) ritual'-mode?

Finally, Christians should enter into a great new pact with the arts, whereby art itself might come to be seen as more than simply ornamental – that is, subordinate to liturgical, pastoral, or theological needs. The kind of art that I am looking for shapes the eucharistic imagination and experience. Austrian composer Peter Jan Marthé's *erdwärtsmesse* is a good example of what I mean.[39] This magnificent piece of music does not eschew the effects used in film scores, and it must be performed by a an organ, wind instruments, percussion, a baritone, a large choir and – in line with the liturgical reforms of Vatican II – the whole gathered assembly. The *erdwärtsmesse* looks secular culture right into the eyes and basically says: come and see, you're wholeheartedly invited to join into what gives us Christians the most perfect joy ...

CONCLUSION: FROM SACRAMENTAL MINIMALISM TO LITURGICAL MAXIMALISM

In other words, the time has come to switch theological attention from a 'sacramental minimalism' to a 'liturgical maximalism'. The history of theology and the liturgy of the past few centuries have been too much preoccupied with epistemological questions. The soteriological ambition of the Eucharist has been obscured. There is no doubt that overcoming the many resistant remnants of this mentality will yet require a great deal of effort, both within and outside of the Church. But secularism has, maybe paradoxically, shaped new conditions under which this work can be done. This work, however, must and will not only be ours. It will be a *leitourgia* in the truest sense of the word: a work *of* God's people, yes, but also a work of God *for* his people. There is no reason not to have great confidence that this work can and will be accomplished.

NOTES

1 Rv 7:9-10. This remarkable biblical quotation arguably influenced the Van Eyck brothers when they painted their famous altarpiece *The Adoration of the Lamb* (see Peter Schmidt, *Het Lam Gods*, Leuven: Davidsfonds, 2005), pp. 34; 51, which is kept in the Cathedral of Ghent. For a Eucharistic interpretation of this triptych, see my contribution 'Van Eyck's Ghent Altarpiece as a Magnificent Representation of the Eucharist', *Assembly. A Journal for Liturgical Theology* 36/2 (2010), 18–23.

2 *Lumen Gentium*, 11 literally states: 'Taking part in the eucharistic sacrifice, which is the fount and apex of the whole Christian life, they [i.e. the faithful] offer the Divine Victim to God, and offer themselves along with It.' The whole section is about the involvement of the Christian faithful as members of God's priestly people in the sacramental life of the Church.

3 *Sacrosanctum Concilium*, 10 reads as follows: '[T]he liturgy is the summit toward which the activity of the Church is directed; at the same time it is the font from which all her power flows. For the aim and object of apostolic works is that all who are made sons of God by faith and baptism should come together to praise God in the midst of his Church, to take part in the sacrifice, and to eat the Lord's supper.'

4 This insight is clearly put forward in the work of John W. O'Malley, *What Happened at Vatican II*, Cambridge: Harvard University Press, 2008.

5 This point of departure seems to be consonant with the findings of a most interesting practical-theological study about 'Sunday' carried out and to be situated in the contemporary French context: François Wernert, *Le Dimanche en déroute. Les pratiques dominicales dans le catholicisme français au début du 3ième millénaire*, Paris: Médiaspaul, 2010.

6 For a theological interpretation of the challenges of the processes of globalisation to Christianity, the work of Robert Schreiter is indispensable. See especially Frans Wijsen & Robert J. Schreiter, eds., *Global Christianity. Contested Claims*, Amsterdam: Rodopi, 2007.

7 Part of this debate are discussions about the so-called secularisation hypothesis. Many scholars and thinkers nowadays assume that the basic assumption of this idea is incorrect, for example, that it is untrue that the ongoing transformation of culture and society through the development of science, technology, and economy would make religion disappear. The secularisation hypothesis is thoroughly provoked in the Canadian philosopher Charles Taylor's seminal study *A Secular Age*, Cambridge: The Belknap Press of Harvard University Press, 2007.

8 This may be evident from the fact that there exist respectable academic institutions which study the phenomenon of secularism from different points of view (sociological, political, philosophical). Worth mentioning is, among others, the work of professor Barry A. Kosmin and the Institute for the Study of Secularism in Society and Culture (ISSSC) at Trinity College,

Hartfort, Connecticut) led by him. Cf. also one of their major publications: Barry A. Kosmin & Ariela Keysar, eds., *Secularism and Secularity: Contemporary International Perspectives*, Hartford: ISSSC, 2007.

9 Etymologically, however, the Latin word *saeculum* refers to something temporal, namely to an era, an epoch, or indeed a period of about one hundred years (whence the word for 'century' in romance languages: *secolo, siècle, siglo, século*, etc.).

10 Cf. an interesting article by Charles Taylor, 'What Does Secularism Mean?' in *Dilemmas and Connections. Selected Essays*, Cambridge, MA – London: The Belknap Press of Harvard University Press, 2011, pp. 303–25, esp. p. 308ff.

11 See in this regard the important work of Louis Dupré, *Passage to Modernity. An Essay in the Hermeneutics of Nature and Culture,* New Haven: Yale University Press, 1993.

12 Crucial in this regard is the work of Mircea Eliade, *Le sacré et le profane,* Paris: Gallimard, 1965. The original version of this book appeared in German in 1957: *Das Heilige und das Profane,* Hamburg: Rowohlt Taschenbuch Verlag, 1957; there also exists an English translation from 1961 *The Sacred and the Profane. The Nature of Religion,* New York: Harper and Row, 1961. Other relevant authors include Rudolf Otto, Gerardus van der Leeuw, and Roger Caillois.

13 Eliade, *Le sacré et le profane,* p. 173. Eliade is convinced that an entirely areligious person is a very rare phenomenon.

14 Elsewhere I have expressed reservations towards the idea that one can distinguish degrees of sacredness, Joris Geldhof, 'Sacré, salut et liturgie. À la rencontre de la theologie et de l'anthropologie', *Transversalités* 112, 2009: 19–37, but these reservations do not affect the point I am making here.

15 Yves Congar, 'Where Does the "Sacred" Fit into a Christian Worldview?', *At the Heart of Christian Worship: Liturgical Essays of Yves Congar,* Paul Philibert, trans. and ed., Collegeville: The Liturgical Press, 2010, pp. 107–32, esp. pp. 117; 121; 128. The original French version of this article was published in a 1967 volume in the renowned *Unam Sanctam* series edited by Congar himself.

16 I quote from the new translation of the third *editio typica* of *The Roman Missal* for use in the dioceses of the USA, Collegeville: Liturgical Press, 2011, p. 646 [nr. 100].

17 Rv 15:4.

18 For the elaboration of this powerful idea, reference must be made to the last encyclical of the former pope John Paul II, which bore exactly this title. See in particular *Ecclesia de Eucharistia*, 21–4. It was especially Henri de Lubac's merit that this idea was put on the theological agenda, again, around the middle of the twentieth century. See his historico-theological study on the Eucharist: *Corpus mysticum: The Eucharist and the Church in the Middle Ages,*

Gemma Simmonds with Richard Price, trans., London: SCM Press, 2006, p. 88 and his profound *Méditation sur l'église*, Paris: Aubier, 1953, pp. 123–37.

19 The German language has the potential of expressing this mutual relationship beautifully: *Der Mensch isst, was er ist*, and the reverse, *Der Mensch ist, was er isst*. This idea can be found in the work of the German romantic thinker Franz von Baader. He referred to it more than once and drew the inspiration for it partly from Paracelsus. See for example, Franz X. von Baader, 'Ueber eine Aeusserung Hegels über die Eucharistie', *Sämtliche Werke*, Franz Hoffmann et al., eds, vol. 7, Aalen: Scientia Verlag, 1963, 247–58, p. 258.

20 This is one of the central theological intuitions of Alexander Schmemann, whose consistently liturgical approach continues to influence and stimulate fundamental theological reflections on liturgy and sacraments in all Christian denominations. See especially his books *For the Life of the World: Sacraments and Orthodoxy*, Crestwood: St Vladimir's Seminary Press, 1973, and the posthumously published *The Eucharist. Sacrament of the Kingdom*, Crestwood: St Vladimir's Seminary Press, 1987.

21 For an elaboration of the tension between modernity and the Christian revelation see my *Revelation, Reason and Reality: Theological Encounters with Jaspers, Schelling and Baader*, Leuven: Peeters, 2007.

22 For this idea I strongly rely on and refer to the analyses of the Belgian philosopher of religion and metaphysician Ignace Verhack in his most recent book *Wat bedoelen wij wanneer wij God zeggen?* [What do we mean when we say God?], Kalmthout & Zoetermeer: Pelckmans & Klement, 2011. This intuition seems also to be shared by Charles Taylor, who defends the idea that modernity has accomplished a lot for humanity which is certainly not against the core of the Christian faith. According to him, one can even argue that some typically modern elements are dependent on a historical evolution within which Christianity was indispensable and to which it hence substantially contributed.

23 I interpret 'ideological' here in a very broad sense, whereby the thought-frames which aim to deconstruct ideologies are also included, for the dismantling of ideologies is never an ideology-free maneuver.

24 For a strong interpretation of what it means to see the liturgy as primary theology, see Aidan Kavanagh, *On Liturgical Theology*, Collegeville: The Liturgical Press, 1992, and David W. Fagerberg, *Theologia Prima: What is Liturgical Theology?*, Chicago: Hillenbrand Books, 2004.

25 Cf. 1 Cor 1:22–23.

26 Or, as Charles Taylor succinctly puts it: 'There can never be a total fusion of the faith and any particular society, and the attempt to achieve it is dangerous for the faith.' Charles Taylor, 'A Catholic Modernity?', *Dilemmas and Connections* [n. 10], 167–87, p. 170.

27 I am aware that I will be stretching the meaning of these terms a bit, but I hope that it will become clear what I mean. In a certain sense, I not only agree with Charles Taylor when he says that 'in Western modernity the obstacles to belief are primarily moral and spiritual, rather than epistemic', 'A Catholic Modernity?' [n. 25], p. 177, but I also want to deepen this observation from a theological point of view.

28 See Jürgen Moltmann, *God for a Secular Society: The Public Relevance of Theology*, Minneapolis: Fortress Press, 1999.

29 In this respect, I think that Verhack's contention is right that it has gradually become useless, not to say ineffective and sometimes even counter-productive, to defend and explain Christianity's claims and belief contents by relying on the kinds of deism and theism which have been developed in the seventeeth and eighteenth centuries, *Wat bedoelen wij wanneer wij God zeggen?* [n. 22], pp. 21–9. This strategy may have proven to be successful for some time but it will certainly not work anymore in the future. For, indeed, there are only very few people who have become Christians solely through admitting that an argument in favour of theism is correct.

30 For suggestions of what, then, a 'speculative a posteriori approach' may be, some inspiration can be drawn from the work of nineteenth century romantic and idealistic thinkers like Friedrich W.J. Schelling and Franz X. von Baader. See my *Revelation, Reason and Reality* [no. 21], pp. 91–5.

31 It should be repeated, however, that I don't think that there is a direct opposition between epistemology and soteriology. Soteriology does not deny, the importance of epistemology; it rather broadens and deepens its scope, or adds to it while retaining the value of what it contributes.

32 One could think here again of the work of Henri de Lubac [cf. n. 18].

33 Cf. Douglas Hedley, *Living Forms of the Imagination*, London: T&T Clark, 2008.

34 It is no coincidence that this concept has increasingly become to be seen as the fundamental category denoting the essence of Christian liturgy. See Winfried Haunerland, 'Mysterium paschale. Schlüsselbegriff liturgietheologischer Erneuerung', *Liturgie als Mitte des christlichen Lebens*, George Agustin and Kurt Kardinal Koch, eds., Theologie im Dialog, vol. 7, Freiburg: Herder, 2012, 189–209.

35 I am referring here to the four major sections of the *Catechism of the Catholic Church*, of which John Paul II said in the apostolic constitution *Fidei Depositum*, which introduces the universal catechism, that they are inextricably connected.

36 Hence it should come as no surprise that, unlike other sacraments, the Eucharist does not really fit into a scheme which smoothly matches Christian sacramentality with the religious life-world of contemporary people inasmuch as the latter is centred around important transitional

moments in their lives, like birth, youth, marriage, and death. See Lambert J. Leijssen, *With the Silent Glimmer of God's Spirit: A Postmodern Look at the Sacraments,* New York: Paulist Press, 2006, pp. 4–6.

37 For a thorough analysis of 'interruption' as a theological category I refer to the work of my colleague Lieven Boeve, *God Interrupts History: Theology in a Time of Upheaval,* New York: Continuum, 2007.

38 The two of them may be woven together. Cf. the intriguing work of Hans Boersma, *Heavenly Participation: The Weaving of a Sacramental Tapestry,* Grand Rapids: Eerdmans, 2011.

39 Peter Jan Marthé, Hg., *Die Heilige Messe. Kultisch – szenisch – sinnlich – mystisch,* Würzburg: Echter, 2011.

50TH INTERNATIONAL EUCHARISTIC CONGRESS 2012

EMERGING SCHOLARS

at the International Symposium of Theology

St Patrick's College, Maynooth, County Kildare, Ireland
6th – 9th June, 2012

Wednesday 6th June 2012

EMERGING SCHOLARS

at the International Symposium of Theology
50TH INTERNATIONAL EUCHARISTIC CONGRESS

• • 1 • •

THE ECCLESIOLOGY OF COMMUNION IN
JOSEPH RATZINGER/POPE BENEDICT XVI

CHAIR: **REV. DR TOM DALZELL SM**
(All Hallows College, Dublin)

SPEAKER: **REV. SEÁN CORKERY**
St Patrick's College, Maynooth
Christological Hermeneutic: Sacrament and Scripture in the Work of Joseph Ratzinger

SPEAKER: **MR ANTHONY VALLE**
Pontifical University of the Holy Cross, Rome
Retrieving the Christological Core of Joseph Ratzinger's Communio Ecclesiology

SPEAKER: **DR MARY McCAUGHEY DD**
St Patrick's College, Maynooth
Joseph Ratzinger's Contextual Understanding of the Church as Communion: Embodied, Existential, Ecstatic Praxis

• • 2 • •

EVANGELISATION TODAY

CHAIR: **DR ANN CODD PBVM**
(Council for Pastoral Renewal and Adult Faith Development, Irish Bishops' Conference)

SPEAKER: **MR MATTHEW HALBACH**
Catholic University of America, Washington DC
The Incarnational Dimension of Catechesis and the Work of the New Evangelisation

SPEAKER: **REV. FR NORLAN JULIA SJ**
Heythrop College, University of London
Beyond Basic Ecclesial Communities (BECs): Challenges to the Reception of Communio Ecclesiology in Asia

SPEAKER: **MS CHRISTINA STRAFACI**
Diocese of Phoenix, USA
'Food Indeed': Consequences of the Americanisation of the Family Table for an Ecclesiology of Communion

• • 3 • •

THE MARIAN PROFILE OF THE CHURCH
CHAIR: **REV. PROF. THOMAS NORRIS**
(International Theological Commission)

SPEAKER: **MR PAUDIE HOLLY**
Mary Immaculate College, Limerick
The All-Embracing Maternal Church: The Communion Ecclesiology of Henri de Lubac

SPEAKER: **SR CHAU NGUYEN OP**
Catholic University of America, Washington DC
Mariological Dimensions of an Ecclesiology of Communion: Reading Lumen Gentium *Anew*

SPEAKER: **DR PAUL O'HARA**
Catholic Theological Union, Chicago
A Lonerganian Analysis of the Marian Profile of the Church in the Theology of Hans Urs Von Balthasar

• •4 • •

LITURGY
CHAIR: **REV. PATRICK JONES**
(National Liturgy Centre, Maynooth)

SPEAKER: **DR JAMES A. WICKMAN**
Georgetown University, Washington DC
Toward a Renewed Understanding of Internal Participation in the Eucharist

SPEAKER: **REV. FR SOJAN KAROTTU**
Catholic University, Leuven
The Communitarian and Social Dimensions of the Liturgy Introduced in the Enarxis of the Eucharistic Liturgy of the Syro-Malabar Church

• • 5 • •

THE ECCLESIOLOGY OF COMMUNION: SACRAMENTAL AND HIERARCHICAL PERSPECTIVES

CHAIR: **REV. DR OLIVER TREANOR**
(St Patrick's College, Maynooth)

SPEAKER: **REV. FR JOHN ANTHONY BERRY**
University of Malta
Communion and Co-responsibility in the Church

SPEAKER: **REV. FR THABANG NKADIMENG OMI**
Catholic University of America, Washington DC
The Sacramental Ecclesiology of Communion and the Hierarchical Ecclesiology of Communion, with Insights from Antonio Acerbi's 'Due Ecclesiologie'

SPEAKER: **MR EDWARD TRENDOWSKI**
Catholic University of America, Washington DC
The Bishop as Servant to Communion: Vatican II Revisited

• • 6 • •

MUSICOLOGY AND COMMUNION

CHAIR: **DR JOHN O'KEEFFE** and **MS GIOVANNA FEELEY**
(St Patrick's College, Maynooth)

SPEAKER: **MS ANNE MARY KEELEY**
University College, Dublin
The Ecclesiology of Communion: A Musicological Perspective

SPEAKER: **DR MAEVE LOUISE HEANEY VDMF**
Santa Clara University
Music as Locus Theologicus*: An Expression of Harmonic Grace*

CHRISTOLOGICAL HERMENEUTIC: SACRAMENT AND SCRIPTURE IN THE WORK OF JOSEPH RATZINGER

REV. SEÁN CORKERY DD Candidate
St Patrick's College, Maynooth

The scenario of a widening gap between exegesis and dogma has exercised Joseph Ratzinger (b. 1927) for years. This impasse, the corollary of which is an increasing polarity between history and faith, has led to a situation of 'isolated biblicism', on the one hand, and 'ecclesio-monism' on the other. [1] This paper identifies six theological writings from Ratzinger's corpus which, between the years of 1967 and 2011, show the gradual shaping of his proposal for a 'Christological hermeneutic' as a way forward.[2] It begins with a lecture from 1978 where, through the examination of the biblical term μυστήριον, Ratzinger seeks a corrective to the strict cultic understanding of sacrament sometimes evident in Christian consciousness. This broader definition of sacrament becomes the basis for his proposal – some thirty years later – for a 'Christological hermeneutic' aimed at reconciling the discontinuity between exegesis and dogma. Ratzinger envisages that this reconciliation will occupy the work of the next generation of exegetes and theologians. Finally the paper describes the ecclesial element of this new synthesis.[3]

THE MEANING OF μυστήριον

In 1978, Ratzinger believed the challenge facing Catholic theology was that the spiritual and intellectual component had, for the most part, separated from typological thinking. Consequently, an exegesis reading texts 'backwards' and 'forwards' in respect of the future was replaced with a literal-historical mindset, reading texts backwards and then fastening them to their earliest foundational sense.[4] A key principle motivating his desire to amend this situation is the unity of scripture: 'to every New Testament inquiry belongs a contemplation of Old Testament roots.'[5]

Making its appearance in the later Old Testament period, Ratzinger discovers that the biblical term μυστήριον in the LXX was not, contrary to popular belief, used in a cultic context.[6] Rabbinic theology, undergoing inner development at the time of Jesus, spoke of the *Geheimnissen der Tora* ('mysterics of Torah'). The Torah shows itself as the veiling of 'all that exists in the mystery of God's creation, to advance its mystical interpretation'.[7] According to the Rabbis, the many words of the law have a hidden centre, a hidden sense that is not easily apparent but which is in fact the unveiling of reality. In relation to the New Testament, only in the Pauline corpus does the term appear with any significant regularity (twenty times).[8] Taking the evidence visible in the New Testament, Ratzinger says, 'Rabbi' Paul draws upon the question of the *Geheimnissen der Tora* as his question too. Ratzinger says Paul's use of μυστήριον in the context of his own conversion reveals an important result: the term *Mysterion* is a question of the right interpretation of scripture. It is a hermeneutical term:

> (Paul) knows (the mysteries of the Torah) are now answered. He has met the *Mysterion*. The *Mysterion* of the Torah and of all the biblical allusions have become visible for him in the crucified Christ. *He* is the heretofore hidden content which is behind the many happenings and words of scripture, all that exists, the underlying mystery of God. In him the where, the why and the what-for of creation and of man is manifest. In him the *Mittelpunkt der Parabel* is revealed, which the scripture strides towards; in him God has laid out himself and has given the authentic hermeneutics of the scriptures, the authentic entrance to them. Therefore then Christ is simply named as 'the *Mysterion* of God' (1 Cor 2:1; cf. 2:7 in connection with 1:23; Col 2:2, cf. 1:27; 4:3).[9]

In light of Paul, Ratzinger says the logical conclusion of one who really reads the Bible is to find that it speaks of the salvation of gentiles and Jews because it speaks of Jesus, who is the salvation of all and the union of creation:

> The *Mysterion* pulls its boundary precisely inversely to human borders. It strikes all 'mysteries' aside, in that it gives what they

> subject which transcends the narrowness of individuals, she is the condition which makes theological activity possible.[45]

A second important presupposition is the ecclesiological frame used to deal with the theologian's mission. Rather than opting for a simplistic Magisterium-theology dualism, Ratzinger says *Donum Veritatis* presented 'the framework of the triangular relationship defined by the people of God, understood as the bearer of the *sensus fidei* and the common locus of all faith, the Magisterium and theology'.[46] This living environment, as it were, means that 'the Church, as a living subject which endures amidst the changes of history, is the vital milieu of the theologian'.[47] It follows that theology remains historically relevant only by acknowledging this triangular matrix. Inserting oneself into it, and participating in the organic structure of it, the 'Church is not an organisation which the theologian must regard as alien and extrinsic to thought'.[48] Understanding the Church as the *konkreten Ort* (concrete location) or subject of theology is a sacramental reality and only within the living community does theology fulfil its task of contemplating the things of God.[49]

CONCLUSION

This paper traces something of Ratzinger's response to the challenge facing theology in the wake of critical exegesis. He looks to the early Church's view of μυστήριον as a helpful entry point to the scriptures. In the Pauline naming of Christ as 'the *Mysterion* of God' (1 Cor 2:1) – as the *Christusgehalt* or Christological content[50] of the Bible – the *oeuvre* of Ratzinger's approach was consolidated from the outset. Through harmonising a hermeneutic of faith and of history, alongside a credible acknowledgement of the Bible's inner *typologisch-sakramental* structure, Ratzinger believes the Jesus of the gospels can be a figure that 'is much more logical and, historically speaking, much more intelligible than the reconstructions we have been presented with in the last decades'.[51] This insufficiently brief look at six major texts from Ratzinger's theology has been incapable of capturing every nuance. Nevertheless, it directs the reader to a network of texts which help explain Ratzinger's rationale for a 'Christological hermeneutic' in theology. Collective listening, guided by this hermeneutic, justifies the transmission of the μυστήριον received and borne within the Church.[52]

NOTES

1 See Joseph Ratzinger, 'Dogmatic Constitution on Divine Revelation', *Commentary on the Documents of Vatican II,* Herbert Vorgrimler, ed., William Glen-Doepel, trans., vol. 3 of *Commentary on the Vatican Documents of Vatican II,* Herbert Vorgrimler, ed.; New York: Crossroads, 1989, 267, 162 (respectively).

2 In chronological order, the writings are his 1967 commentary on *Dei verbum*; his 1978 lecture at the Catholic Theology Faculty of the University of Eichstätt, 'Zum Begriff des Sakraments' ; his 1989 lecture at the Lutheran Centre for Religion and Society in New York, 'Biblical Interpretation in Conflict'; his 1990 presentation at the press conference in Rome which launched the CDF document *Donum Veritatis*, 'On the "Instruction concerning the Ecclesial Vocation of the Theologian"'; and the *Forewords* to the first two volumes of his *Jesus of Nazareth* series. For the purposes of this article, references to these works will be cited from the following sources: Joseph Ratzinger, 'Dogmatic Constitution on Divine Revelation', 155–98, 262–72; 'Zum Begriff des Sakraments', *Theologie der Liturgie*, Rudolf Voderholzer et al., eds, vol. 11 of *Joseph Ratzinger Gesammelte Schriften,* Rudolf Voderholzer, ed.; Freiburg im Breisgau: Herder, 2008, 215–232; 'Biblical Interpretation in Crisis', *God's Word: Scripture-Tradition-Office,* Peter Hünermann and Thomas Söding, ed., Henry Taylor, trans., San Francisco: Ignatius Press, 2008, 91–126; 'On the "Instruction concerning the Ecclesial Vocation of the Theologian"', *The Nature and Mission of Theology: Approaches to Understanding its Role in the Light of Present Controversy,* Adrian Walker, trans., San Francisco: Ignatius, 1995, 101–20; *Jesus of Nazareth: From the Baptism in the Jordan to the Transfiguration,* Adrian J. Walker, trans., London: Bloomsbury, 2007, xi–xxiv; *Jesus of Nazareth. Holy Week: From the Entrance into Jerusalem to the Resurrection,* Philip J. Whitmore, trans., London: Catholic Truth Society, 2011, xiii–xvii.

3 I wish to make a clarification for the reader at this point. While the present paper is looking at Ratzinger's formulation of a theological method over the course of many years from the perspective of 'sacrament', the impression may be unintentionally given of a 'christo-monism' in his approach. This would be unwarranted in Ratzinger's case. There is no dichotomy between Christ and the Spirit *in fact,* even if there can be tension, in *our understanding,* between christomonistic institutionalism or juridicism and pneumatological charism. In Ratzinger's work, for example, he uses the pneumatological logion of 2 Cor 3:17 in *Called to Communion: Understanding the Church Today,* Adrian Walker, trans., San Francisco: Ignatius Press, 1996, 33. Also in this book, Ratzinger can be seen to define sacrament in terms of witness and Spirit. For him the *word* is always 'tied to' the (apostolic) *witness* who is guided by the *Spirit* (cf. ibid., 68). One can say that here is a definition of sacrament which incorporates the message, the messenger and the Spirit of the message.

4 See Joseph Ratzinger, *Die Sakramentale Begründungchristlicher Existenz,*

RETRIEVING THE CHRISTOLOGICAL CORE OF JOSEPH RATZINGER'S COMMUNIO ECCLESIOLOGY[1]

MR ANTHONY VALLE PhD Candidate
Pontifical University of the Holy Cross, Rome

INTRODUCTION: THE CHRISTOLOGICAL PRINCIPIUM

In his benchmark tome on Joseph Ratzinger's ecclesiology, Maximillian Heim states that 'the real problem of the present day, according to Ratzinger, is not an ecclesiological but a christological crisis'.[2] Ratzinger himself stipulates: 'Christology must remain the centre of the teaching about the Church.'[3] Now, I want to ask a question that is, *prima facie*, not directly related to the previous two quotations concerning Christology: is Ratzinger's ecclesiology a *communio* ecclesiology?[4] I think it is but, for reasons different than the ones many theologians would submit. Many, I think, would posit a sacramental ground – the Eucharist – as the reason for which Ratzinger's ecclesiology falls under the theological *genus* of '*communio* ecclesiology'.[5] This reason is not incorrect since the Eucharist makes or builds the Church.[6] However, what is often overlooked or treated tangentially in such answers and in many accounts of *communio* ecclesiology is the 'high' onto-Christological[7] dimension 'from above',[8] which by necessity precedes and engenders the tangible eucharistic body of Christ *hic et nunc* and the visible *communio ecclesiae*. What is often missing or diminished is, in a word, the person of Christ – the incarnate Son or the Logos made flesh – as the *principium quod* of *communio*.

If the Church is an intimate communion with Christ, which grows from the sacramental giving and gift of his body in the Eucharist through which we become one body or communion with and in him, then, logically speaking, Christ's identity – his person – would have to be distinguished by communion. In other words, one cannot give or enact what one does not already have or what one is not; or, to recall the medieval-scholastic axiom: *agere sequitur esse* – actions flow from being. To recast the axiom, Christ's action of eucharistic self-giving and his engendering of the Church as communion flow from and are undergirded by his *being* communion. Christ is communion *in se*. As such, there is a divine and theological communion already behind and operative in Christ's eucharistic self-giving that subsequently incarnates visible ecclesial communion. Ratzinger spells out this theological *a priori* as follows:

> Trinitarian faith and faith in the incarnation guide the idea of communion ... *Communio* must first be understood theologically. Only then can one draw implications for a sacramental notion of *communio*, and only after that for an ecclesiological notion.[9]

Hence, the burden of my paper will be to distil from Ratzinger's writings the precise nature of this theological *principium*, namely the pre-existing Christological communion as found in the incarnation.[10] In doing so, I will show that – to go back to the original question – Ratzinger's ecclesiology is indeed a *communio* ecclesiology, but it is so by virtue of its Christological *principium* or core and not (at least not originally) by any sacramental-ecclesial notion. In brief, I aim to retrieve and clarify the Christological core of Ratzinger's *communio* ecclesiology.[11]

THE INCARNATION: THE UNIQUENESS OF CHRISTIAN COMMUNIO

In the concluding section of the first part of his essay 'Communion: Eucharist – Fellowship – Mission', Ratzinger maintains that, in contrast to the repudiation of the possibility of communion between God and man in the Old Testament and the opposite striving for mystical union between the divine and the human in ancient Greek philosophy,[12] something entirely different confronts us with the Christian *kerygma*:

> In the incarnation of the eternal Word there comes about that communion between God and the being of man, his creature, which had hitherto seemed impossible to reconcile with the transcendence of the one God ... Yet in Jesus occurs the new event, the one God entering into concrete communion with men by incarnating himself in human nature. Divine and human

mode of operation of the human and divine wills within the incarnate Christ vis-à-vis communion:

> The Council's response ran as follows: The ontological *union* of two wills that remain independent within the unity of the person means, on the level of daily life, *communion* (κοινωνία) of the two wills. With this interpretation of the union as communion, the Council was devising an ontology of freedom. The two 'wills' are united in that way in which one will and another can unite: in a common assent to a shared value. To put it another way: Both of these wills are united in the assent of the human will of Christ to the divine will of the Logos. Thus on the practical level – 'existentially' – the two wills become one single will, and yet ontologically they remain two independent entities ... (I)t is a unity in the mode of communion – the unity that love creates and (that) love is. In this fashion, the Logos takes the being of the man Jesus into his own being and talks about it with his own 'I': 'I have come down from heaven, not to do my own will, but the will of him who sent me' (Jn 6:38).[24]

As Ratzinger clarifies here, Constantinople III recognised that Christ's two wills 'remain independent (ontologically) within the unity of the person', but on the existential level of daily life their union is described as a '*communion* (κοινωνία) of the two wills'. The human will of Christ becomes one with the divine will of the Logos because Christ's will freely assents to and recognises the inherent value of what – or whom – the Logos assents to. There is a 'common assent to a shared value' created and motivated by love. Love is the active principle of the 'unity (of Christ's two wills) in the mode of *communion* – the unity that love creates and (that) love is'. In another essay in which he discusses Constantinople III, Ratzinger again accents the primacy of love:

> The metaphysical twoness of a human and a divine will is not abrogated, but in the realm of the *person*, in the realm of freedom, the fusion of both takes place, with the result that they become *one* will, not naturally, but personally. This free unity – a form of unity created by love – is higher and more interior than a merely natural unity ... The Council illustrates this unity by citing ... the Gospel of John: 'I have come down from heaven, not to do my own will, but the will of him who sent me' (Jn 6:38).[25]

In the preceding two passages I quoted, Ratzinger, following the lead of Constantinople III, cites Jn 6:38 to clarify the paradoxical metaphysical or ontological twoness and the existential oneness of Christ's human and divine wills. In this paradigmatic and enigmatic Johannine text, the 'I' of the divine Logos speaks for Jesus' will as his own will, as the personal will of the divine Logos so that, existentially, there is in effect one will. How so? Since each respective will loves and thus assents to the same and inherently higher value, for example, the Father's will, the fusion of both wills takes place into a single and pure Yes to the Father, to 'the will of him who sent me' (Jn 6:38). In other words, the existential fusion of these two wills happens by, as Ratzinger calls it, 'a common assent to a shared value'. Communion in the incarnate Christ is, at bottom, a communion of divinity and humanity, of a human will and a divine will united by one free act of love *for* something and someone higher: the will of the Father.

THE INCARNATION AS COMMUNIO: FOUNDATION OF THE EUCHARIST AND THE CHURCH

Now that we have taken the necessary step of probing and retrieving the Christological core, namely the mystery of the incarnation as the communion of Christ's human and divine wills, or what Ratzinger calls 'the spiritual tension of the divine man',[26] we are ready to make the transition from a 'high' onto-Christology 'from above' into the realm of the Eucharist and the Church. Before we do so, however, it would be worthwhile to examine briefly Ratzinger's reflection on the profound ramifications that ensue from the communion of the human and divine wills in Christ.

It is in the obedience of the Son, in the uniting of both these wills in one assent to the will of the Father, that the communion between human and divine being is consummated. The 'marvellous exchange', the 'alchemy of being': this is here becoming a reality as a liberating and reconciling communication that develops into a communion between Creator and creature. It is in the pain of this exchange, and only here, that the fundamental change in man that can alone redeem him, and that changes the conditioning factors of the world, is achieved; here it is that community is born; here Church comes into being.[27]

As we have seen before and now see again, Christ's human will is conjoined to his divine will in such a way that there is a mutual indwelling or communion of wills 'in one assent to the will of the Father'. Moreover, in Ratzinger's estimation this 'communion between human and divine being' in the incarnate Christ has profound anthropological and soteriological consequences. There is a 'marvellous exchange' or 'alchemy of being', more specifically 'a liberating and reconciling communication that develops into a communion between Creator and creature'. In other words, the communion of humanity and divinity within the incarnate Christ makes possible a further communion of universal and salvifc significance in which the being of man and the being of God can join together, creature and Creator can become one, earth and heaven can unite. But how exactly can this further communion, this 'fundamental change in man that can alone redeem him' transpire?

As Ratzinger says in the above passage, it is in 'the pain of this exchange', namely when man renounces the temptation to do his own will and seeks instead to conjoin it in communion with something higher and greater than himself, that 'the fundamental change in man that can alone redeem him ... is achieved'. More specifically, when man chooses to take the way of the *imitatio Christi*, when like Christ he conforms and conjoins his human will to God's, precisely then is he brought up to his full stature and transformed. In fact, when our freedom is a genuine participation in the Son's own freedom, namely when it is lived as filial obedience to the Father, only then is the path of true freedom found, only then does our genuine liberation come fully into its own. In other words, for Ratzinger, it is only through the personal appropriation and sometimes painful reenactment of 'the obedience of the Son' that we really establish true communion between God and ourselves and thus find true communion with one other. Moreover, when 'the pain of this exchange' happens, Ratzinger says, 'here it is that community is born; here Church comes into being'. At this point, Ratzinger segues into the sacramental and ecclesiological ramifications of the communion that the incarnate Christ creates:

> We had already noted that the incarnation of the Son creates communion between God and man and thus opens up the possibility of a new communion of men with another. This communion between God and man that is realised in the person

of Jesus Christ for its own part becomes communicable to others in the Paschal mystery, that is, in the death and resurrection of the Lord. The Eucharist effects our participation in the Paschal mystery and thus constitutes the Church, the body of Christ ... The inmost mystery of communion between God and man is accessible in the sacrament of the Body of the Risen One.[28]

As we can now see more clearly from this passage, Ratzinger originally took us into the core of Christ's person, into the spiritual tension of the divine man where the communion between God and man transpires, so that once having penetrated these innermost depths of communion in Christ himself we could emerge to see the full stature of the Eucharist reveal itself and thus the mystery of the Church open up. The 'communion between God and man' in the incarnate Christ 'opens up the possibility of a new communion of men with another'. More specifically, 'this communion between God and man that is realised in the person of Jesus Christ', becomes communicable to us in our participation in the Paschal mystery as effected by the Eucharist, a participation that in turn constitutes the Church, which is our communion with one another in Christ.[29]

By now we can see that Ratzinger has taken us on a theological journey traversing the entire spectrum of theology. More specifically, he has led us through the hierarchy of truths vis-à-vis communion:[30] Trinitarian communion (between the Father and the Son), Christological communion (between Christ's human will and divine will), eucharistic communion, and ecclesial communion, each of which hinges on the previous.[31] The cardinal point we are left with is this: the Church and her sacramental life grow from within, from Christ, and never vice-versa. Thus, the *sine qua non* of any ecclesiology worth its money, particularly a *communio* ecclesiology, begins with the inmost mystery of the incarnate Christ, with a 'spiritual Christology' and only then does it work its way outward; to do otherwise is illusory. Without penetrating into the mystery of Christ's person as the incarnate Son, as the God-man, we will never understand or properly partake in either the mystery of the Eucharist or the Church. This is no exaggeration or *faux-gravitas*. I would like to conclude this section with a quotation that encapsulates the Christological core of Ratzinger's *communio* ecclesiology:

> [T]he incarnated Son is the 'communion' between God and men. Being a Christian is in reality nothing other than partaking in the mystery of the incarnation, or, to use St Paul's expression: the Church, insofar as she is the Church, is the 'body of Christ' (that is, in fact, [the Church is] men's partaking of the communion between man and God, which is what the incarnation of the Word is).[32]

CONCLUSION: ECCLESIOLALIÁ, ECHOLALIÁ, AND RATZINGER'S COMMUNIO ECCLESIOLOGY FIFTY YEARS AFTER VATICAN II

Before concluding, a summary of my findings is in order. For Ratzinger, the uniqueness of the Christian concept of *communio* lies in the incarnation of Christ since he *is* the communion between God and man. Given this, Christology, which is the study of the incarnate Christ, becomes indispensable for opening up the core of communion that lies at the heart of the divine man. The communion of divinity and humanity in the incarnate Christ is, at bottom, the existential communion of his human will and divine will, which are united by a common assent *to* and one free act of love *for* the will of the Father. Finally, the communion between God and man in the incarnate Christ becomes communicable to us in our participation in the Paschal mystery as effected by the Eucharist, a participation that in turn constitutes the Church, which is our communion with one another in Christ. In these four sections, I have retrieved the Christological core of Joseph Ratzinger's *communio* ecclesiology.

Having said that, I want to ask this: What practical or pastoral difference can this retrieval make, if any? What relevance does it have for today, for the way the Catholic faith is understood, discussed and lived in Ireland or elsewhere, fifty years after the opening of the Vatican II? Without exaggerating the importance of what I have said, in reality what Ratzinger has said and I only systematised theologically, I would like to answer this question concerning my topic's concrete and contemporary relevance.

The term *ecclesiolaliá* means 'Church chatter, prattle or babble', more specifically 'chatter about the Church'.[33] *Ecclesiolaliá* identifies the incessant and insipid chatter of the mass media, opinion makers, and putative intelligentsia when discussing the Church. Since the eve of Vatican II, these extra ecclesial sectors of society have been fixated on Church matters but they have paid little or no heed to the Church's supernatural essence and *raison d'être*, namely the Church as the divine communion founded by Christ for the salvation of souls. In addition to *ecclesiolaliá*, I would add that *echolaliá*, in short, 'echoed speech',[34] has seeped into and infected the Church herself. *Echolaliá* provokes some from within the Church to speak of her as many do from without: as an institutional structure made by human hands and thus malleable according to one's subjective whims and fancy. So, for example, one hears some disgruntled individuals and certain organised groups within the Church – be it the Appeal to Disobedience of the Pfarrer-Initiative in Austria[35] or the Association of Catholic Priests in Ireland[36] – who echo verbatim and *ad nauseam* the hackneyed media chatter they hear about the need for institutional Church reform.[37]

Having said that, the secondary goal of my paper has been to provide a practical alternative to the *ecclesiolaliá* and *echolaliá* that contaminate contemporary discourse about the Church both *ad extra* and *ad intra*. The immediate and concrete means is an ecclesiology that brings the Church back to her original moorings, namely a supernatural *communio* grounded in Christ. Joseph Ratzinger provides us with such a Christologically grounded ecclesiology, one that all local Churches as well as Ireland are in dire need of retrieving fifty years after Vatican II. To be sure, it was precisely Vatican II that espoused such a Christological ecclesiology. In fact, the mundane claims and inane rhetoric of *ecclesiolaliá*, and of *echolaliá* that repeats the former's lines like a mantra, are entirely out of step with both the letter and the spirit of Vatican II. Conciliar Christocentrism precludes a purely juridical or extrincisist ecclesiology that reifies the Church into a merely man-made institution or worldly entity, into a self-contained reality. In fact, in the very first line of *Lumen Gentium* the Council subsumed ecclesiology under Christology and *ipso facto* under theology and not anthropology, under God and not under man. For Ratzinger, this determinative Christological prefix furnishes not only the correct hermeneutic for *Lumen Gentium* but for the entire Council.

Therefore, I will conclude with Ratzinger's analysis of the opening of Vatican II's ecclesiological constitution, an analysis that serves as a synopsis of my own essay and that also, hopefully, can provide a potent antidote to the cancerous *ecclesiolaliá* and *echolaliá* that still corrupt contemporary Church discourse and ecclesiology fifty years after Vatican II. Ratzinger writes:

> The very first sentence of the Constitution on the Church makes it clear that the Council does not regard the Church as a self-contained reality; rather, it sees her from the perspective of Christ: 'Since Christ is the light of the nations, this Council, which is gathered together in the Holy Spirit, would like to light all men with his splendour, which shines forth from the face of the Church' (LG, 1, 1). We can recognise in the background the image from patristic theology that sees in the Church the moon, which has no light of its own but gives out again the reflected light of Christ the sun. Ecclesiology appears as dependent upon Christology, as belonging to it.[38]

Church is the presence of Christ … (H)er first word is Christ, and not herself; she is healthy in the measure in which all her attention is directed toward him. Vatican II magnificently placed this insight at the very head of its deliberations by beginning the foundational document on the Church with the words: '*Lumen Gentium* cum sit Christus' – Because Christ is the light of the world, there is also the mirror of his glory, the Church, which reflects his radiance. *If you want to understand Vatican II correctly, you must begin again and again with this first sentence …* [39]

Lumen Gentium cum sit Christus …

NOTES

1 I would like to extend my warmest gratitude to Bishop Dr Felix Genn, bishop of the diocese of Münster, Germany, for financially supporting my trip to the Theology Symposium. *Ad multos annos!*

2 Maximillian Heinrich Heim, *Joseph Ratzinger: Life in the Church and Living Theology: Fundamentals of Ecclesiology with Reference to Lumen Gentium*, Michael J. Miller, trans., Joseph Ratzinger fwd., San Francisco: Ignatius Press, 2007, 262. Rev. Prof. Dr Maximillian Heim is the Cistercian Abbot of Heiligenkreuz Monastery in Austria and one of the inaugural winners in 2010 of the prestigious Ratzinger Prize.

3 Joseph Ratzinger, 'The Ecclesiology of the Second Vatican Council', *Church, Ecumenism and Politics: New Endeavors in Ecclesiology*, Michael J. Miller et al., trans., San Francisco: Ignatius Press, 2008, 27/Joseph Ratzinger, 'Die Ekklesiologie des Zweiten Vatikanischen Konzils', *Kirche, Ökumene und Politik: Neue Versuche zur Ekklesiologie*, Einsiedeln: Johannes Verlag, 1987, 26: 'die Christologie [muss] die Mitte der Lehre von der Kirche bleiben.' As I did in this footnote, I refer to Ratzinger's works in the following footnotes by first giving the English translation, followed by a slash, and then the corresponding original in German.

4 Though not entirely satisfactory from a linguistic perspective, as is common practice in theology today I use the English 'communion' and the Latin *communio* interchangeably. From the abundant literature on *communio* ecclesiology, one can begin with the following work by the editor in chief of the English-language edition of the journal *Communio*, David L. Schindler, *Heart of the World, Center of the Church.* Communio *Ecclesiology, Liberalism, and Liberation*, Grand Rapids, MI/Edinburgh: Eerdmans/T&T Clark, 1996; also see the works cited in Joseph Ratzinger, 'The Ecclesiology of the Constitution *Lumen Gentium*', *Pilgrim Fellowship of Faith: The Church as Communion*, Stephan Otto Horn and Vinzenz Pfnür, eds, Henry Taylor, trans., San Francisco: Ignatius Press, 2005, 129, 131/Joseph Ratzinger, 'Die Ekklesiologie der Konstitution *Lumen Gentium*', *Weggemeinschaft des Glaubens: Kirche als Communio*, Stephan Otto Horn and Vinzenz Pfnür, eds, Augsburg: Sankt Ulrich Verlag, 2002, 112, 113. For Ratzinger's own understanding of *communio*, one can start with Joseph Ratzinger, '*Communio*: A Program', *Communio. International Catholic Review,* Peter Casarella, trans., 19.3, Fall 1992: 436–39/Joseph Ratzinger, 'Communio – ein Programm', *Internationale Katholische Zeitschrift Communio* 21, 1992: 454–63. For secondary literature on *communio* in Ratzinger's works, see, for example, James Massa, *The Communion Theme in the Writings of Joseph Ratzinger: Unity in the Church and in the World Through Sacramental Encounter*, PhD, Diss., New York: Fordham Univeristy, 1996, and Wojciech Wójtowicz, *La Chiesa come 'Communio' nell'Ecclesiologia di Joseph Ratzinger,* Roma/ Koszalin: Feniks, 2010. In addition to all these works, see the document *Communionis Notio* issued on 28 May 1992 by the Congregation for the Doctrine of the Faith and the accompanying theological essays as found in

Congregazione per La Dottrina della Fede, *Lettera 'Communionis Notio'. Su Alcuni Aspetti della Chiesa Intesa come Communione*, Documenti e Studi 15, Città del Vaticano: Libreria Editrice Vaticana, 1994.

5 The fact that '*communio* ecclesiology' and 'eucharistic ecclesiology' are often used interchangeably suggests that the Eucharist is the *conditio sine qua non* of *communio* ecclesiology and the Church. See Ratzinger, 'The Ecclesiology of the Second Vatican Council', 17/Ratzinger, 'Die Ekklesiologie des Zweiten Vatikanischen Konzils', 17. On eucharistic ecclesiology, see Paul McPartlan, *Sacrament of Salvation: An Introduction to Eucharistic Ecclesiology,* Edinburgh: T&T Clark, 1995.

6 On this point, see Avery Dulles, S.J., 'Reflections on *Ecclesia de Eucharistia*', *L'Osservatore Romano,* Weekly Edition in English, 30th July 2003, 3, and also, Paul McPartlan, *The Eucharist Makes the Church: Henri de Lubac and John Zizoulas in Dialogue*, Edinburgh: T&T Clark, 1993. The phrase, 'the Eucharist makes the Church', can be found in its nascent form in Augustine, *De civitate Dei*, 22, 17, PL, 41, 779. The phrase itself was coined by Henri de Lubac, *Corpus Mysticum: L'Eucharistie et l'Église au Moyen Âge. Étude Historique*, Paris: Aubier-Montaigne, 1944, 103. Furthermore, the phrase has been used in recent magisterial documents; see, for example, *Catechism of the Catholic Church,* with modifications from the *edition typica,* New York: Image-Doubleday, 1997, n. 1396, and also, Pope John Paul II, *Ecclesia de Eucharistia. Encyclical Letter on the Eucharist in its Relationship to the Church*, Vatican City: Libreria Editrice Vaticana, 2003, nn. 21–6. Finally, the second part of the phrase 'the Eucharist makes the Church' should be kept in mind: 'the Church makes the Eucharist.'

7 I abbreviate 'ontological' as 'onto'. By a 'high' onto-Christology 'from above' I mean a Christology whose immediate object of inquiry is the person of Christ in his dual being: Christ *in se.*

8 Ratzinger points out that – because of the Trinity and the incarnation – an ecclesiology based on *communio* must be one 'from above'; see Ratzinger, '*Communio*: A Program', 445–445/Ratzinger, 'Communio – ein Programm', 460–1. For an examination of the distinction between a 'high' onto-Christology 'from above' and a functional Christology 'from below', see Jean Galot SJ, 'Christology IV: Various Approaches', René Latourelle – Rino Fisichella, ed., *Dictionary of Fundamental Theology*, Robert Barr et al., trans., New York: Crossroad, 1994, 126–31. For an example lacking a 'high' onto-Christological dimension 'from above' in relation to *communio* ecclesiology, see Dennis M. Doyle, *Communion Ecclesiology. Vision and Versions*, Maryknoll, NY: Orbis Books, 2000. Despite the fact that it is thin on this 'high' onto-Christological dimension 'from above', Doyle's book stands second to none on *communio* ecclesiology from a historical perspective. For a study that sees this 'high' onto-Christological dimension 'from above' as integral to *communio* ecclesiology, and thus remains faithful to the spirit and letter of Vatican II, see David L. Schindler, *Heart of the World, Center of the Church*, pp. 7–31. Finally, although Ratzinger often works out of a

'high' Christology from above, like Aquinas his theological ken is wide enough, and thus truly c/Catholic that he also possesses a well-developed 'functional' Christology 'from below'. See, for example, both volumes of his *Jesus of Nazareth*, especially his own comments on the distinction between Christology 'from above' and 'from below' as applied to his *Jesus of Nazareth*, which can be found in Joseph Ratzinger, *Jesus of Nazareth: Part Two: Holy Week. From the Entrance into Jerusalem to the Resurrection*, Vatican Secretariat of State, trans., London: Catholic Truth Society/Ignatius Press, 2011, xv–xvi/Joseph Ratzinger, *Jesus von Nazareth. Zweiter Teil: Vom Einzug in Jerusalem bis zur Auferstehung*, Freiburg: Herder, 2011, 12–13.

9 Ratzinger, '*Communio*: A Program', 444, 446/Ratzinger, 'Communio – ein Programm', 460–1: 'Der trinitarische Glaube und der Glaube an die Menschwerdung führen den Gedanken der Gottesgemeinschaft ... Communio ist zunächst ein theologischer, dann aber auch weitgehend ein sakramentaler und erst so auch ein ekklesiologischer Begriff.'

10 In this essay, I focus on Ratzinger's concept of *communio* from a Christological perspective and choose not to develop the Trinitarian dimension, though in the end I will touch on the relation between the Father and the Son. For more on the Trinitarian and pneumatological dimensions of *communio*, see, for example, Joseph Ratzinger, 'The Holy Spirit as Communion. On the Relationship Between Pneumatology and Spirituality in the Writings of Augustine', *Pilgrim Fellowship of Faith*, 38–59/ Joseph Ratzinger, 'Der Heilige Geist als Communio. Pneumatologie und Spiritualität bei Augustinus,' *Weggemeinschaft des Glaubens*, 34–52. For a *communio* theology in a Trinitarian key, see Thomas J. Norris, *The Trinity: Life of God, Hope for Humanity: Towards a Theology of Communion*, David C. Tracy, fwd., Hyde Park, NY: New City Press, 2009.

11 To this end, I will be relying on two essays by Ratzinger, the first of which makes a concerted effort to develop the Christological foundation of *communio* ecclesiology. The first essay is Joseph Ratzinger, 'Communion: Eucharist – Fellowship – Mission', *Pilgrim Fellowship of Faith*, 60–89/ Joseph Ratzinger, 'Communio: Eucharistie – Gemeinschaft – Sendung', *Weggemeinschaft des Glaubens*, 53–78. The second essay is Joseph Ratzinger, 'Taking Bearings in Christology', *Behold the Pierced One: An Approach to a Spiritual Christology*, Graham Harrison, trans., San Francisco: Ignatius Press, 1986, 13–46/Joseph Ratzinger, 'Christologische Orientierungspunkte', *Schauen auf den Durchbohrten: Versuche zu einer spirituellen Christologie*, Einsiedeln: Johannes Verlag, 1984, 13–40.

12 Ratzinger, 'Communion: Eucharist – Fellowship – Mission', 73–77/ Ratzinger, 'Communio: Eucharistie – Gemeinschaft – Sendung', 64–7.

13 Ibid., 76/Ibid., 67: 'In der Fleischwerdung des ewigen Wortes vollzieht sich jene Kommunion zwischen Gott und dem Sein des Menschen, seiner Kreatur, die vorher mit der Transzendenz des einzigen Gottes unvereinbar schien ... In Jesus aber vollzieht sich das neue Ereignis, daß [*sic*] der einzige Gott real in Kommunion mit den Menschen tritt, indem er sich in der menschlichen

mean that the Church is Christ's spiritual body? There is no reason why this should be given a different meaning than that which is usually spoken of as the Church of the body of Christ. We have to consider that "spiritual" is not spiritual in the modern sense, that is to say, only spiritual but not real, but rather wants to testify to the nature of the new Christian reality, of *pneuma*.' (Translation mine).

29 Ibid., 283, 'Ein gottförmiger Menschen allein ist wirkliches Gottesopfer ... Nur eine gottförmingen Menschen gibt es: Christus.'

30 Ratzinger, *Weg Gemeinschaft des Glauben, Kirche als Communio*, Augsburg: Sankt Ulrich Verlag, 2002, 72 (cited in text as *WGG*); *Pilgrim Fellowship of Faith, The Church as Communion*, Stephan Otto Horn and Vinzenz Pfnür, eds, Henry Taylor, trans., San Francisco: Ignatius, 2002, 82 (cited in text as *PFF*).

31 *PFF*, 82–83; *WGG*, 72.

32 *GS: VHG*, 290–291.'Hier erschient das eucharistische Sakrament tatsächlich als das wahre Opfer der Christen-oder vielmehr: als das, Sakrament' diese Opfers. In einer weiter innen liegenden Schicht erweist sich diese Opfer als das innerer und wahre Leib-Christi-Sein der Heilegen. Und zuinnerst ist dieses Opfer die caritas dieser Heiligen. Denn diese caritas ist schleißlich der Geist Christ selbst, von dem her das ganze Leibgefüge überhaupt wirklich ist. Hier liegt aber zugleich die Umkehrung in die alleräußerste Konkretheit vor, denn caritas ist nicht ein mystisches Innen, das für die menschenliche Verwircklichung nichts sagt, sonderen sie ist Kircheneinheit, mehr: sie ist die reale, nüchterne, wirkende Liebe des christlichen Herzens. 'Here the Eucharistic sacrament appears to actually be the true offering of Christians – or rather, as the "sacrament" of this offering. In a further inner layer, this offering proves to be the internal and true becoming of the body of Christ in the saints. And this sacrifice is the charity of these saints. This charity is finally the Spirit of Christ himself, from which the entire body structure exists at all. Yet here exists, at the same time, the reversal into extreme concreteness, since *caritas* is not a mystical inner reality which says nothing to human realisation, rather it is Church unity, more: it is the real, sober, acting love of the Christian heart' (translation mine).

33 Ibid., 292 (translation mine).'Das heißt: Jede Tat echter christlicher Liebe, jedes Werk des Erbarmens ist in einem wahren und eigentlichen Sinn Opfer, Setzung des einen einzigen sacrificium christianorum. Es gibt nicht auf der einen Seite ein uneigentliches moralisches oder persönliches opfer und daneben ein eigentliches kultisches, sondern das erste ist die *res* des letzten, in dem diese erst seine eigentliche Wirklichkeit hat. Wir stehen hier vor dem, was man die Messeopfertheorie Augustins nennen könnte.'

34 *PFF*, 83; *WGG*, 73. 'Das innerste Geheimnis der Kommunion zwischen Gott und Mensch is zugänglich im Sakrament des Leibes des Auferstadenen; das Mysterium fodert so umgekehrt unseren Leib ein, und verwirklicht sich wiederum in einem Leib.'

35 Jean Marie Chauvet, *Symbol and Sacrament: A Sacramental Reinterpretation of Christian Existence,* Collegeville, Minnesota: The Liturgical Press, Pueblo, 1995, 280.

36 Ratzinger, *Truth and Tolerance*, San Francisco: Ignatius, 1999, 124 (cited in text as *TT*).

37 The word *doxa* was to be understood in the sense of 'glory' or 'glorifying'.

38 *TT,* 124.

39 Ratzinger, *Theologische Prinzipienlehre*, Munich: Eric Wewel Verlag, 1982, 367 (cited in text as *TP*); *Principles of Catholic Theology: Building Stones for a Fundamental Theology,* Mary Frances McCarthy, trans., San Francisco: Ignatius, 1987, 350 (cited in text as *PCT*).

40 *TP*, 69; Ratzinger, 'Faith as Knowledge and as Praxis-the Fundamental Option of the Christian Credo', *PCT,* 67.

41 *TP*, 366; *PCT*, 349. Ratzinger explains that existential experience 'is the experience, which takes on board the spiritual principle ... but which also allows for freedom'. 'Es ist die Erfahrung, die *das geistige Prinzip* aufnimmt, dem wir vorhin begegneten, die aber zugleich auch Freiheit läßt.' Italics and translation mine. Sister Mary Frances McCarthy translates 'geistige Prinzip' as 'intellectual principle', but it could also be translated as 'spiritual principle' since in this way it shows that intellectual reflection is not simply a narrow rationality. Neither is it based on a mystical spiritualism but is based on a deeper ontological participation of human beings in God as our explorations of Ratzinger's eucharistic ecclesiology have testified.

42 *TP*, 366; *PCT*, 349.

43 Ratzinger, *Auf Christus Schauen: Einübung in Glaube, Hoffnung und Liebe*, Freiburg: Herder 1989, 68 (cited in text as *ACS*); Ratzinger, *The Yes of Jesus Christ, Exercises in Faith, Hope, and Love,* New York: Crossroad Publishing Co., 1991, 58 (cited in text as *YJC*). Hence as he explains in *Auf Christus Schauen*: 'Der linearen Bewegung unseres Lebens zum Tod antwortet der Kreis der göttlichen Liebe, die für uns zu einer neuen Linie wird–zur immerwährenden und fortschreitenden Erneuerung des Lebens in uns, je mehr Leben einfach Beziehung wird zwischen mir und der Person gewordenen Wahrheit: Jesus. Die unentrinnbare Linearität unseres Weges zum Tod hin wird umgewandelt durch die Geradlinigkeit unseres Weges zu Jesus.' 'Our life's linear progression towards death is answered by the circle of divine love, which becomes a new line for us – the perpetual and progressive renewal of life in us, with life increasing simply according to the relationship that is established between me and the truth which has become a person, Jesus. The inescapable linearity of our path towards death is transformed by the directness of our path to Jesus ...'

44 Ratzinger, *Das Geheimnis von Tod und Auferstehung,* Leipzig: St Benno-Verlag, 13, 'Jesus ist der wahre, der maßgebende Mensch, auf den unser

of fellow believers and by the mutual help of shared faith and prayer ... Being a Christian also calls for fellowship. God comes to a human being only through other human beings. Even in the realm of the spirit the human person is an *unfinished being*; even in the realm of the spirit the principle holds that we can exist as human beings only with the help of one another and for one another.' This translates 'unverschloessene Wesen' as 'unfinished being'. I would argue that it should be translated as 'unsealed being' in that man through his spirit is always open. However the idea of being 'unfinished' also recognises that human beings are open to new experiences through relationship with others.

64 *ACS*, 45; *YJC*, 37. Wo finde ich die Kirche? Wo wird sie mir über ihre amtliche Lehre und ihre sakramentale Ordnung hinaus erlebbar als das, was sie ist? Diese Frage kann zur echten Not werden. Und trotzdem - heute bieten sich neben der Pfarrei als dem normalen Erlebnisraum der Kirche zusehends auch neugewachsene Gemeinschaften an, die gerade aus dem Miteinander des Glaubens geboren worden sind und ihm wieder die Frische unmittelbarer Erfahrung geben. *Communione e Liberazione* is eine solche Stätte des Erlebens von Kirche und so des Zugangs zu der Gemeinschaft mit Jesus, zur Teilhabe an seiner Schau. 'Where, beyond its official teaching and its sacramental order, will I be able to experience it as it is? This question can become one of genuine and urgent distress. And this, despite the fact that today, newly formed communities offer themselves, communities that have sprung directly out of the sharing of believers and give this the freshness of immediate experience. *Communione e Liberazione* is this kind of place where the Church can be experienced and thus a place of access to fellowship with Jesus, to sharing in his vision.'

65 See Ratzinger, 'Eucharist, Communion and Solidarity,' Address to the Eucharistic Congress to the Bishops at Benevent, 2nd June 2002. http://www.doctrinafidei.va/documents/rc_con_cfaith_doc_20020602_ratzinger-eucharistic-congress_en.html (accessed 5th July 2011).

66 See William Harmless, *Augustine and the Catechumenate*, Minnesota: Liturgical Press, Pueblo Book, 1995 (316–23), 319. See Harmless's summary with references to Augustine's sermons, what Augustine means by 'Be what you see, receive what you are'.

ABBREVIATIONS: JOSEPH RATZINGER

ACS	Auf Christus Schauen. Einübung in Glaube, Hoffnung und Liebe
YJC	The Yes of Jesus Christ: Exercises in Faith, Hope and Love
DGJC	Der Gott Jesu Christ
GJC	The God of Jesus Christ
EC	Einführung in das Christentums
IC	Introduction to Christianity
CCC	Christianity and the Crisis of Cultures
GS:OVGTB	Gessammelte Schriften: Offenbarungs-Verständnis und Geschichts-Theologie Bonaventuras
GS:VHG	Gesammelte Scriften: Volk und Haus Gottes in Augustin's Lehre vonder Kirche
GWT	Glaube-Wahrheit-Toleranz
TT	Truth and Tolerance
KBNG	Kirchliche Bewegungen und Neue Gemeinschaften
NOS	New Outpourings of the Spirit
SAD	Schauen auf den Durchbohrten
BPO	Behold the Pierced One: An Approach to a Spiritual Christology
TP	Theologische Prinzipienlehre
PCT	Principles of Catholic Theology
WNKB	Zwei Plädoyers, Warum ich noch in die Kirche bin
TSW	Two Say Why
VSC	Vom Sinn Des Christseins: Drei Predigten
WMC	What it means to be Christian: three sermons
WGG	Weg Gemeinschaft des Glaubens
PFF	Pilgrim Fellowship of Faith
WAT	Wesen und Auftrag der Theologie
NMT	The Nature and Mission of Theology
ZGG	Zur Gemeinschaft Gerufen
CC	Called to Communion
ZLG	Zur Lage des Glaubens
RR	The Ratzinger Report

future generations of believers. This source is Jesus, the Word made flesh, who was raised from the dead; and who, through the Spirit, extends not only the fruits of the incarnation through time and space but himself. What is the fruit (or the branch) without the vine, after all?

The Eucharist is the means *par excellence* by which believers make contact with the risen Jesus and are informed, reformed and transformed by him.[5] The eucharistic celebration is also the primary source of Christian communion, in which believers play an active role.[6] 'They do not merely stand in his presence,' as Hater notes.[7] In addition, eucharistic communion leads to witness, one not rooted in so many religious propositions but in the person of Jesus.[8]

Furthermore, for early Christian communities, eucharistic communion took on a fleshy realism. Such was the case in the Church at Corinth. Here, evidence suggests that members believed they were actual 'body parts' of the risen Jesus.[9] Literally true or not, regarding *the body of Christ, the Church,* in communion with *the body of Christ Jesus,* John Zizioulas suggests that, post-resurrection, Jesus can no longer be understood apart from the Church and its members.[10]

THE INCARNATIONAL DIMENSION, REVELATION AND FAITH TRANSMISSION

The transmission of faith contains the elements of reception and witness. God reveals[11] and faith is our response. Admittedly, the demarcation between revelation and faith is porous. However, we can say that there is a natural progression: faith stems from revelation and, along with reason, functions as its interpreter.[12]

Ratzinger takes the position, here, that the 'believing subject is the Church, not an individual person'.[13] However, this position approaches a divorcing of the mystical body of Christ from physical believers and their unique experience of the dynamics of communion: for example, revelation, reception, and lived faith. Zizioulas offers us another option. He identifies uniqueness and diversity as not precluding Christian unity: *koinonia*.[14] In fact, unity in diversity finds its home in the Trinitarian life: one nature, three Persons. In either case, faith and revelation cannot be viewed apart from one another.[15] The life of faith begins once revelation has been acknowledged. As de Gaál, writing on the christology of Pope Benedict XVI puts it, 'God's announcement requires a commensurate reception on the part of human beings in order for revelation to come about.'[16]

The scriptures bear out this dialogical dynamic, and the body – the incarnate dimension – takes centre stage. The Bible is, among other things, a history of bodily witness to God's revelation. Revelation is depicted, in the Bible, as breaking in on human cultures, lives, and especially human bodies – 'bodies that have sexual relations, give birth, get sick, heal, eat and drink, get damaged, dance, defecate, sing and die'.[17] As S. Tamar Kamionkowski summarises, 'Biblical characters, as embodied beings, interact with God; furthermore, their relationship with God is very much influenced by the multiple states and activities of their bodies.'[18] Indeed, human bodies play a vital role in the living witness of faith that is our coming to share in the divine life of God.[19] But how do bodies witness to revelation? In other words, how do bodies evince faith?

Bodies in scripture witness to divine revelation *performatively*. The Bible portrays people celebrating and sharing in God's providence and presence in a constellation of ways – performing various bodily-religious acts such as sharing meals, marking the body for religious purposes, speaking and singing God's praises, liturgical dancing, ritual cleansings, fasting and other purifications. In addition, bodies in the New Testament also witness to revelation via their *ontological relationship* with Christ made possible chiefly through the incarnate dimension of the paschal mystery, its reception through the gift of faith, and its celebration in the Eucharist.

Moreover, the whole Christian vision of revelation finds its locus in the incarnation. While it is, indeed, the whole person of Christ who reveals God, it is, however, his body that makes this revelation uniquely visible, tangible and, thus, *full* – fleshed out, as it were. Likewise, it is our tangible, bodily selves that lend to a *full* ontological witness to Christ, expressed in the Church's reception of revelation and the transmission of faith.

THE INCARNATIONAL DIMENSION OF CATECHESIS AND THE WORK OF THE NEW EVANGELISATION

The expansion of the incarnation into time and space[20] is made possible chiefly through evangelisation – which is not, itself, a single instrument of communicating the faith, but the distinct character of all faith transmission. In addition, evangelisation, or the *missio ad gentes,*[21] contains the element of catechesis, which John Paul II later describes as a 'moment – a very remarkable one – in the whole process of evangelisation'.[22] Moreover, both evangelisation and catechesis complement each other in the Church's various pastoral tasks; and both are grounded in personal witness.[23] Yet, a reason for the hope inside oneself must also be communicated.[24] Thus, catechesis also requires the systematic presentation of Christian doctrine.[25]

This being said, catechesis in the new evangelisation cannot remain the mere teaching of religious propositions or 'abstract truths'.[26] Rather, it should be 'the communication of the living mystery of God',[27] which aims, ultimately, at putting people not only in touch with Christ but 'in communion, in real intimacy, with him'.[28] Communicating the person of Christ to others must contain an incarnate dimension, as the Word, indeed, has become flesh.[29] In conformity with this incarnational principle, therefore, alongside proclamation and doctrine, human bodies and the 'existential'[30] must also play a key role in the transmission of the faith.

To 'flesh out' the incarnational dimension of catechesis, we now turn to (then) Cardinal-designate Timothy Dolan's address to the College of Cardinals which took place on 17th February 2012, in which he made two pivotal remarks. First, he stated that 'God does not satisfy the thirst of the human heart with a proposition, but with a Person, whose name is Jesus.'[31] Dolan also said that the new evangelisation demands a more evincible witness of joy and love on the part of the baptised. Interestingly, Dolan described this evincible witness as an expression of 'incarnate love'.[32]

Thus, like Hater advises, what's important for an incarnational catechesis is the appropriation of gospel values and attitudes. However, from Dolan's words we can conclude that to become more intentional and explicit about our faith in Christ, the new evangelisation calls us to emphasise the bodily dimension of faith transmission. Thus, an incarnational catechesis operating in the new evangelisation should seek to foster a personal encounter with Christ, one that is necessarily mediated through bodily witness.[33]

As Dolan alludes, the body speaks its own language.[34] Similarly, in his *Theology of the Body*, Pope John Paul II speaks about body language as a 'prophetism' of sorts.[35] He understands that between two spouses there can be such a unity and synchronicity that bodies seem to communicate of their own accord, with their own volition, and very intelligibly. Indeed, in those deep moments of nuptial love, very little needs to be said. In fact, in those quiet, charged moments, saying anything might garble the transmission, deflate the intensity, and break the mood, as it were.

Certainly, though, we can speak of effective body language outside of marriage. The smile of a friend, or the grimace of an enemy, makes its point with little interpretation needed. Likewise, the sadness on the face of a child was enough to motivate people like Mother Teresa to spend their lives wiping the tears of others. Indeed, she has said in many interview that she was able to serve the poor, sick, and dying of India all her life precisely because she was able to see on their faces the face of Christ – an acute awareness of the incarnational dimension of faith. Thus, the more we can recognise our bodies as active agents in extending the incarnation to those who need the touch or gaze of Christ, the more we recognise the need for catechesis going forward in the new evangelisation to attend to the incarnational dimension.

CONCLUSION

For an incarnational catechesis to effectively apply the gospel into the lives of believers, attention must first be paid to the incarnational dimension of faith. This dimension points to the body as a vehicle for encountering the risen Lord and one another in the fellowship of the Spirit. It can be identified in the communion of the body of Christ Jesus; the body of Christ, the Church; and the body of Christ, the believer – manifesting through revelation, eucharistic celebration, and faith transmission.

Thus, as a proponent of human dignity, a key aspect in educating for a new evangelisation,[36] the incarnational dimension of catechesis draws attention to the need for physical witness as an authenticator of discipleship and communion. It supports a social consciousness that has concern for the welfare of others, not only their souls but their bodies as well. And, so, like the following verses from the apostles Paul and James, an incarnational catechesis combines body, faith, and witness; thus it proclaims and actualises, 'The body ... (is) for the Lord and the Lord for the body', and 'a faith without deeds is useless'.[37]

NOTES

1 Throughout this paper we will focus on the body as an active agent in the reception and transmission of faith. References to 'the body' will connote simultaneous references to the body of *Christ Jesus*; the body of *Christ, the Church*; and the body of *Christ, the individual believer.* This is not to suggest equality or the absence of an ontological priority among them, but a similitude, as the incarnation is the central Christian mystery that forms and informs, at once, the life of the Church and the life of the individual believer.

2 Robert J. Hater, 'Incarnational Catechesis: The Word Becomes Flesh', *Catechetical Leader* 17, no. 6 (November/December 2006), 4.

3 'Incarnational Catechesis: The Word Becomes Flesh', 6.

4 Ibid.

5 Second Vatican Council, Constitution on the Sacred Liturgy, *Sacrosanctum Concilium* (4th December 1963), 2. http://www.vatican.va/archive/hist_councils/ii_vatican_council/documents/vat-ii_const_19631204_sacrosanctum-concilium_en.html (accessed 3rd April 2012).

6 Ibid., 14.

7 'Incarnational Catechesis: The Word Becomes Flesh', 5. See also, Pope Benedict XVI, Encyclical, *Deus Caritas Est* (25th December 2005), no. 13. http://www.vatican.va/holy_father/benedict_xvi/encyclicals/documents/hf_ben-xvi_enc_20051225_deus-caritas-est_en.html (accessed 5th March 2012).

8 Cardinal Timothy Dolan, *Address to the College of Cardinals,* 17th February 2012. http://www.oecumene.radiovaticana.org/en1/Articolo.asp?c=563988 (accessed 3 May 2012). Then Cardinal-designate, Timothy Dolan, noted in his address that, 'the invitation implicit in the *missio ad gentes* and the new evangelisation is not to a doctrine but to know, love, and serve – not a something, but a Someone [italics mine]'.

9 Elizabeth Lewis Hall, 'What are Bodies for? An Integrative Examination of Embodiment' *Christian Scholar's Review* 39, no. 2 (winter 2010), 168–9. Saint Paul tells the community at Corinth that their bodies are 'for the Lord'. Hall suggests that this phrase denotes a striking physical connection between the bodies of community members and the personal body of Christ. She bases her analysis on the popular, ancient Jewish notion, presumably known to Paul, which perceived a 'symbolic correspondence between society and the physical body', where one represented the community and the community represented the one. This symbolism goes well beyond mere metaphor.

10 John Zizioulas, *The One and the Many: Studies on God, Man, the Church, and the World Today,* Alhambra, CA: Sebastian Press, 2010, 68–9. 'The Church is part of the definition of Christ. The body of Christ is not first the body of

the individual Christ and *then* a community of 'many', but simultaneously both together. Thus, you cannot have the body of the individual Christ (the one) without having simultaneously the community of the Church (the many). See also, 80–1, 118–25. Here Zizioulas points out that *koinonia*: the 'fellowship in the spirit' enjoyed by believers, is not only Christ-centred but a pneumatological reality. It is the Spirit who calls believers together for witness and worship (*ecclesia*) to manifest the *body of Christ, the Church* within the *body of Christ Jesus*. This is to say, to use a well-known phrase from Henri de Lubac: 'the Eucharist makes the Church and the Church makes the Eucharist.'

11 Second Vatican Council, Dogmatic Constitution on Divine Revelation, Dei Verbum (18th November 1965), no. 2. http://www.vatican.va/archive/hist_councils/ii_vatican_council/documents/vat-ii_const_19651118_dei-verbum_en.html (accessed 4th March 2012).

12 Emery de Gaál, *The Theology of Pope Benedict XVI: The Christocentric Shift*, New York: Palgrave Macmillan, 2010, 22–3.

13 Ibid., 93.

14 *The One and the Many: Studies on God, Man, the Church, and the World Today*, 53–4.

15 *The Theology of Pope Benedict XVI*, 93.

16 Ibid., 88.

17 S. Tamar Kamionkowski, 'Introduction', *Bodies, Embodiment, and Theology of the Hebrew Bible*. S. Tamar Kamioinkowski and Wonil Kim, eds., New York: T&T Clark, 2010, 2.

18 Ibid.

19 ESV, 2 Pt 1:4.

20 Anthony J. Kelly, '"The Body of Christ: Amen!" The Expanding Incarnation' *Theological Studies* 71 (2010): 792–816. Kelly's notion of an expanded incarnation focuses our attention not only on what the revelation of Jesus *means* to us who believe (i.e., *fides quaerens intellectum*), which is the task of theology, but also the *way* in which Jesus reveals God to humanity – which is through his body. Examining and applying this mode is a pedagogical concern, the work of catechesis. Thus an incarnational dimension of catechesis must consider the body's role in the work of divine revelation and faith transmission.

21 John Paul II, Encyclical, *Redemptoris Missio* (7th December 1990), no. 34 http://www.vatican.va/holy_father/john_paul_ii/encyclicals/documents/hf_jp-ii_enc_07121990_redemptoris-missio_en.html (accessed 10th February 2012). 'Missionary activity proper, namely the *mission ad gentes*, is directed to peoples or groups who do not yet believe in Christ, who are far from Christ, in whom the Church has not yet taken root and whose

culture has not yet been influenced by the gospel. It is distinct from other ecclesial activities inasmuch as it is addressed to groups and settings which are non-Christian because the preaching of the gospel and the presence of the Church are either absent or insufficient [italics mine].' See also, Pope Benedict XVI, *First Vespers Homily at the Basilica of St Paul Outside the Walls,* 28th June 2010. http://www.vatican.va/holy_father/benedict_xvi/homilies/2010/documents/hf_ben-xvi_hom_20100628_vespri-pietro-paolo_en.html (accessed 10th February 2012). The New Evangelisation, targeting those cultures that have become heavily influenced by secularization, necessarily incorporates the *missio ad gentes* as a re-proposal (*ripropore*) of the gospel.

22 John Paul II, Apostolic Exhortation, *Catechesi Tradendae* (16th October 1979), no. 19. http://www.vatican.va/holy_father/john_paul_ii/apost_exhortations/documents/hf_jp-ii_exh_16101979_catechesi-tradendae_en.html (accessed 1st May 2012).

23 For a complete list of mutual tasks, see *General Directory for Catechesis,* nos. 48, 85–6. See also, Paul VI, Apostolic Exhortation, *Evangelii Nuntiandi* (8 December 1975), 21. http://www.vatican.va/holy_father/ paul_vi/apost_exhortations/documents/hf_p-vi_exh_19751208_evangelii-nuntiandi_en.html (accessed 5th March 20120). See also, *Catechesi Tradendae,* 1, 13. Note how John Paul II identifies catechesis with 'the whole of the efforts within the Church to make disciples' and 'intimately bound up with the whole of the Church's life'. This is one of the reasons why evangelisation and catechesis are often perceived as synonymous.

24 1 Pt 3:15.

25 *Evangelii Nuntiandi,* 22; See also *Catechesi Tradendae,* 21.

26 *Catechesi Tradendae,* 7; See also, Emilio Alberich and Jerome Vallabaraj, *Communicating a Faith that Transforms: a Handbook of Fundamental Catechetics,* Bangalore: Kristu Jyoti Publications, 2004, 28, 303. The thorough work is an example of catechetical reform with a view to the new evangelisation. It points to the current need for catechesis to become more a source of personal, ecclesial, and social transformation. What is pertinent, however, is their analysis: that meeting the needs of the new evangelisation requires that catechists give up the 'tridentine pattern'; that is, approaches that overemphasise the cognitive dimension, and broaden their horizons to include 'the *significant,* vital, existential characters of the transmitted message ... '

27 Ibid.

28 Ibid., 5.

29 Jn 1:14.

30 See Louis Erdozain, 'The Evolution of Catechetics: a Survey of Six International Study Weeks on Catechetics', *Sourcebook for Modern Catechetics,* Michael Warren, ed., 97–8, Winnona, MN: St Mary's Press, 1983. See also,

Avery Dulles, *Evangelization for the Third Millennium,* Mahwah, NJ: Paulist Press, 2009, 109–10. Regarding catechesis, the term 'existential' is often associated with a period of modern catechesis, which began in the 1960s, known as the 'anthropological phase'. Unfortunately, the tendency of this phase towards anthropocentrism and, consequently, its de-emphasis of cognitive modes of learning have caused some Church leaders to view the existential component of catechesis as suspect and this period of catechesis, generally speaking, as more or less deficient. See, Cardinal Donald Wuerl, United States Conference of Catholic Bishops Committee on Doctrine (USCCB) News Release (18th April 2011). http://old.usccb.org/comm/archives/2011/11-078.shtml (accessed 24th April 2012). This press release quotes the following comments from Wuerl, which were taken from the USCCB document 'Bishops as Teachers: A Resource for Bishops', dated 18th April 2011. In it, Wuerl stated that 'The background against which the bishops must exercise their teaching responsibility today is the generally recognised catechetical deficiencies of past decades beginning with the 1970s. The result is a generation or more of Catholics, including young adults today, who have little solid intellectual formation in their faith.'

31 http://www.oecumene.radiovaticana.org/en1/Articolo.asp?c=563988.

32 Ibid.

33 *Catechesi Tradendae,* 5.

34 Dolan's address spoke of the simple act of smiling in public as an 'ingredient' for effective witness.

35 John Paul II, *Theology of the Body,* Boston: Pauline Books and Media, 1997, 364.

36 Synod of Bishops, XIII Ordinary General Assembly, *Lineamenta* no. 21. http://www.vatican.va roman_curia/synod/documents/rc_synod_doc_20110202_lineamenta-xiii-assembly_en.html (accessed 3rd April 2012). Beginning to focus more on the incarnate dimension of all life is to discover more the dignity of our bodies, ourselves, and the creation that sustains us. This, in fact, is the supreme educational goal of the new evangelisation, described in the *lineamenta* of the forthcoming Synod as an 'ecology of the human person'. This represents the Church's 'entire educational commitment', one which aims at fostering greater respect for all created life. Becoming more aware of the dignity of life is the motivation behind emphasising the incarnational dimension of catechesis.

37 1 Cor 6:13–20; cf. Jas 2:20.

BEYOND BASIC ECCLESIAL COMMUNITIES (BECS): CHALLENGES TO THE RECEPTION OF COMMUNIO ECCLESIOLOGY IN ASIA

REV. FR NORLAN JULIA SJ
Heythrop College, University of London

Filipino Bishop Francisco Claver (1929–2010), whose writings and episcopal work were dedicated to the realisation of Vatican II's vision, considers the Basic Ecclesial Communities (BECs) as 'the new way of being Church in Asia today'. For him, the BECs are the most effective manifestation of the Council's *communio* ecclesiology as well as the most potent vehicles of the Church's much needed renewal. This paper aims to evaluate Claver's assertion drawn mainly from the Philippine experience of the BECs. The theological contributions of the Federation of Asian Bishops' Conferences (FABC) will serve as framework and tools in the critique. Some of the key assertions of the FABC include the *local Church* as agent of evangelisation, the triple *dialogue* with religions, cultures and the poor, and *participation* as the mode of ecclesial life.

The paper will therefore look at the challenges faced by BECs in the contemporary Philippine and Asian situation and raise some questions such as: how can BECs retain the vibrancy and potency they enjoyed in its early years? What forms can or should BECs take in the multi-cultural and multi-religious, albeit largely poor Asian context? May the name of BECs be lent to new forms of *communio* emerging as a result of modern technology, in Asia as well as in other parts of the world? Far from giving certain and definite answers, this paper simply aims to put these questions forward in order to jumpstart a discussion around these pressing theological and practical questions.

under ninety-three names.[11] The FABC formally acknowledged the significance of BECs and endorsed its implementation in its member countries. No record, however, could be found of and no study has been made on the practise of BECs in Asia.

As Claver explains it, BECs are 'worshipping communities of faith-discernment-and-action at the lower levels of the Church, that try, in a participatory way, and under the guidance of the Holy Spirit, to put life and faith together in an integrated whole'.[12] This definition incorporates what, for Claver, are the elements that distinguish BECs from other Church bodies. First, BECs are communities guided by the pastoral method summarised as 'faith-discernment-action'. In these communities, the members reflect on their experiences in the light of the Word of God and discern together the course of action to which the Holy Spirit is directing them.[13] In the seventies, when the Philippines was under the grip of the Marcos dictatorship and countless innocent civilians were subjected to warrantless arrests, illegal detentions, suspicion of conniving with insurgents, and forced recruitment to paramilitary groups, the BECs provided their members with an avenue through which they could make sense of their experiences of violence and injustice and come up with discerned action in response to their experience.[14]

Second, BECs are led and run by lay people, thus giving them a chance to exercise directly and actively their kingly-prophetic-priestly role. Since BECs emerged in grassroots communities in far-flung villages which see their parish priest only once a month, or worse, once a year for patronal feastday, the lay-leaders take on the priest's role of presiding in the Liturgy of the Word. Not only the lay-presider, but the rest of the community, share their thoughts and reflections on the Word of God. Decisions as to the communal stand and action to be taken on a particular social issue are deliberated upon and made by the entire community, not by one person alone. In this way, the BECs are truly participatory in accordance with Vatican II's *communio* ecclesiology. The co-responsibility which must characterise the Vatican II Church is nowhere more palpable than in the BECs where members are no mere passive spectators in the liturgy, followers of ready-made decisions, or recipients of the Church's charitable works. In the BECs, lay people are actively engaged in all aspects of their Christian community life.

Third, in the BECs, Christians are able 'to put life and faith together into an integrated whole'. Inculturation and dialogue happen in the most profound sense in the BECs. For Claver, inculturation may be seen as 'the ongoing and salvific dialogue between a people and the Holy Spirit in regard to their special way of being human and their culture'. It is in the BECs that the people's faith encounter their concrete situation and circumstances as human beings set in a particular culture. In this encounter, faith and culture mutually influence, support or challenge each other, and in the process, enrich or purify, each other.[15] For instance, the strong family ties which characterise Filipino culture serve as a reliable source of emotional support and a stable foundation of unity among family members. However, the same ties become an obstacle to the maturity of socio-political institutions when it is co-opted to maintain political dynasties and justify the practice of nepotism in government and oligarchy in civil society.[16] This is challenged when, in the BECs, members reflect on Jesus' words on loving family more than him (Mt 10:37) and on the priority of doing God's will over obligation to one's family (Mt 12:48). As the members seriously engage in the experience-reflection-action cycle and actively participate in the life of the community, they set the stage for the Spirit's transformative action which engenders conversion within the culture and impels them to become agents of the same good news to others.

CHALLENGES AND PROSPECTS IN TWENTY-FIRST-CENTURY ASIA

Claver admits to his rather idealised presentation of the BECs, despite the real problems in the formation and conduct of BECs that he sees. Nonetheless, he believes that for all the deficiencies of the BECs in their actual practice, they have to be credited for relentlessly pursuing the vision of Vatican II's *communio* ecclesiology, the new way of being Church, and for being a vehicle of social transformation.[17] So that BECs can continue to be an effective manifestation of a renewed Church, it has to face the challenges of contemporary society. Claver's account of the genesis and growth of the BECs is confined mainly to the rural areas of Southern and Northern Philippines where he served as local ordinary. In its early years in the seventies and in the peak of its growth throughout the Philippines in the eighties and nineties, BECs saw their development from the liturgical to the developmental and liberational which contained an imperative to change the whole Church structurally and attitudinally, with regard to its lifestyle and worship, ministry and theology, so as to be a credible witness and a readable sign before the contemporary world'.[23] Pieris adds: 'The commitment to maintain that momentum of this renewal on the frontiers of the Church is exactly what fidelity to the Council as well as the reception of the Council means for us today.' The Church is being challenged to sharpen its powers of imagination to rethink conventional Church structures and pursue the path of the BECs towards the realisation of a new way of being Church. The local Churches play a crucial role in advancing the vision of Vatican II's *communio* ecclesiology. By taking initiatives to implement the reforms of the Council, the local Churches respond to the movement of the Holy Spirit, the dynamic element in the Church.

But this dynamic element in the Church blows wherever it wills (Jn 3:8). Hence, the Church must always be attentive to the promptings of this Spirit. Can it be that the Spirit is leading the Church towards recognising the new forms of BECs such as the basic human communities (BHCs)? If God is to be found and loved and served in all things, as St Ignatius of Loyola held, could he be actively present in the worldwide web as well, and creating there communities of faith? May we, therefore, speak of basic virtual communities (BVCs)? So that, whether in its traditional form or in its alternative form as BHCs or in its emerging forms ushered in by modern technology, BECs play a crucial role for the continuing reception of Vatican II's *communio* ecclesiology. Claver held that with all the challenges that BECs have to face in twenty-first century Philippines and Asia, 'the reality of the BECs as we have them now is in fact one of people struggling toward those ideals ... (however), the mere struggling is enough in a Church which Vatican II says is in need of continual reformation'.[24] Hence, the struggle to build BECs in whatever form conducive to the promotion of the *communio* ecclesiology must continue with a view towards ensuring the vibrancy of the Asian Churches in the years to come.

NOTES

1 K. Rahner, 'Basic Theological Interpretation of the Second Vatican Council', *Theological Investigations* (*TI*) vol. XX: *Concern for the Church*, Edward Quinn, trans., London: Darton, Longman and Todd, 1981, 78, 82. Cf. in the same volume, 'The Abiding Significance of the Second Vatican Council', 90–102.

2 Catalino Arévalo, '... The Time of the Heirs ...', *For All the Peoples of Asia* (*FAPA*) vol. I, Gaudencio Rosales, D.D. and Catalino Arévalo SJ, eds, Quezon City: Claretian Publications, 1997, xvi. See also Edmund Chia, 'Thirty Years of FABC: History, Foundation, Context and Theology', *FABC Papers* 106 (2003).

3 For a summary of scholarly works on the theology of FABC, see James H. Kroeger, *Theology from the Heart of Asia: FABC Doctoral Dissertations* vols. I (1985–98) and II (1998–2008), Quezon City: Claretian Publications, 2008.

4 Francisco Claver, 'The Church in Asia: Twenty and Forty Years after Vatican II (Personal Reflections: 1985 and 2005)', *FABC Papers* 117 (2005), 74.

5 Felix Wilfred, 'The Federation of Asian Bishops' Conferences (FABC): Orientations, Challenges and Impact', *FAPA* vol. I, xxiv–xxv.

6 Peter Phan, 'Reception of Vatican II in Asia: Historical and Theological Analysis', *FABC Papers* 117 (2005), 107–27, esp. 112–21. See also idem, *Being Religious Interreligiously: Asian Perspectives on Interfaith Dialogue,* Maryknoll, N.Y.: Orbis Books, 2004.

7 Michael Amaladoss, 'Is There an Asian Way of Doing Theology?', *East Asian Pastoral Review* 45 (2008), 10–27.

8 Claver, Francisco, *The Making of the Local Church* (Quezon City: Claretian Publ., 2009), 107. What follows is a summary of Claver's presentation on the BECs in this book. Mary Fitzpatrick examines Claver's vision and theology of the local church in Mary Fitzpatrick, *Bishop Francisco F. Claver, SJ, 1972–90: On the Local Church,* Manila: De la Salle University Press, 1995.

9 Ibid., 41–2.

10 On the history, formation and significance of the *comunidades* in the Latin American experience, see Leonardo Boff, *Ecclesiogenesis: The Base Communities Reinvent the Church*, Robert Barr, trans., Maryknoll: Orbis Books, 1986; Marcello Azevedo, *Basic Ecclesial Communities in Brazil: The Challenge of a New Way of Being Church,* John Drury, trans., Washington: Georgetown University Press, 1987.

11 Claver, *The Making,* 115.

12 Claver, *The Making,* 110. See also Jose Marins et al., *Basic Ecclesial Communities: The Church from the Roots,* Quezon City: Claretian Publ., 1983, 12–20.

'FOOD INDEED': CONSEQUENCES OF THE AMERICANISATION OF THE FAMILY TABLE FOR AN ECCLESIOLOGY OF COMMUNION

MS CHRISTINA STRAFACI
Diocese of Phoenix, USA

'When we return home, let us prepare two tables, one for bodily food, the other for that spiritual food which is the Holy Scripture. Let the husband repeat what has been said in the holy assembly; let the wife learn it and the children listen to it. Let each of you make your home a church. Are you not responsible for the salvation of your children? Are you not likely to have to give an account of their upbringing?'[1]

Saint John Chrysostom's primary command in this homily on marriage and family life directs his audience's attention to the 'two tables' designated for the physical and spiritual nourishment of children. In naming the first, the famed Golden Mouth implicitly relates the altar table of the 'holy assembly' – the universal Church – to the dining table of the 'home' 'Church' – the *ecclesia domestica*.[2] With this gesture, Chrysostom elevates the meaning of *feeding the children* to a sacred task with immediate eucharistic significance and eternal consequences, a responsibility for which husband and wife will be held accountable before God. This directive presumes, however, that the family table for 'bodily food' will enjoy daily activity in the home. Contrary to this assumption by the Doctor of Preachers, the modern collapse of the domestic dining table is a widely acknowledged, albeit lamented, phenomenon in the United States, with its disuse cited as both cause and effect of radical deviations in our human experience of food. Yet statistics revealing the American family table's near-disappearance while billions are spent consuming industrialised food and treating obesity-related 'lifestyle' diseases raise more than blood pressures, scale digits and eyebrows. Just as the visible body reveals the invisible person, the physical dimension is not without spiritual consequence. Thus, the question emerges: *If the Person of Christ gives himself to us through eating and drinking during a shared meal, what are the theological implications of America's distorted food practices?*

The goal of this brief examination is to address the *Americanisation of the family table* – the worldwide adoption of American habits of food provision and consumption; behaviours embodying profound distortions of the 'grammar' of creation, patterns detached from all physical, social, ethical and personal contexts, practices dominated by contemporary liberalism's deficient anthropology.[3] This paper points to the rising international obesity epidemic as a crisis heavily influenced by the globalisation of American food patterns, and as such, poses an unexplored threat to the future of *communio* ecclesiology. Without arguing systematically for the asymmetrical, reciprocal relationship between the domestic dining and eucharistic tables, this study presupposes that the form and content of the family table profoundly influence children's perceptions of the eucharistic table, and therein shape their encounter with Christ.[4] Indeed, this analysis claims that the global spread of America's depersonalised gastronomical and culinary habits has the long-term effect of *obscuring their encounters of the Person of Christ in the Eucharist.* In every way disconnected from the family table, children of the modern age are growing up distanced from authentic reality in creation and the meaning of worship, and disinclined – literally and figuratively – towards communion. In (then) Cardinal Ratzinger's words, the ecclesiology of communion has its 'root and centre' in the Eucharist, 'the creative force and source of *communion* among the members of the Church, precisely because it unites each one of them with Christ himself'.[5] Consequently, if 'to meet Christ' in the Eucharist 'creates communion with him and therefore with the Father in the Holy Spirit' and this 'unites men with one another',[6] the Americanisation of the family table results not only in distraction from and desensitisation to the Real Presence of Christ in the Eucharist, but also in difficulty comprehending the Church as the sacrament of the Trinitarian *communio* revealed in Jesus Christ.

Without reciting statistics of rising obesity rates and declining family meals, it is world-widely recognised that the United States struggles with serious, life-threatening distortions in its relationship to food.[7] Obese Americans have become media icons of instant gratification and over-indulgence as pictures of ballooning stomachs regularly inundate the international news media. But while predictions forecast seventy per cent of the United States to be obese by 2030, 'Only in America' is no longer a humorous or valid claim. Obesity is acknowledged to be a *global epidemic* with rates rising at a disconcerting pace in both developed and developing countries.[8] Worldwide obesity has more than doubled since 1980. In the late 1990s, the World Health Organisation (WHO) warned this 'escalating epidemic' would affect millions of people around the world, and in 2008, statistical data surpassed predictions. Global estimates by the International Obesity Taskforce and the WHO's Collaborating Centre for Obesity Prevention allege about 1.7 billion overweight persons over the age of fifteen (of whom 500 million are obese) and 43 million under the age of five, further projecting that by 2015, approximately 2–3 billion persons around the world will be overweight, more than 700 million obese.[9,10] Experts previously restricted the pandemic to high-income countries until few decades ago when evidence emerged of its penetration into even the poorest nations.

Seen from the other side of the Atlantic, the underlying cause of this crisis is less than surprising. Sources indict the hyper-industrialised food practices of the United States – the 'eat-on-the-run, absent-mindedly feeding, cup-holder culture' increasingly promoted and embraced around the globe.[11] Indeed, the McDonald's Corporation champions the dual titles of being the largest owner of retail property and the most famous brand *in the world*, encouraging non-American industries to adopt similar business methods.[12] While the data on the frequency of family meals is sporadic, international obesity studies all blame 'changes' in diet, eating patterns, and overall lifestyles that occur when cultures experience rapid economic development, exchanging active, agricultural self-sufficiency for sedentary, urban techno-industrialisation. Simply, those countries shifting from growing to predominantly buying paradigms are driven by 'changes' in the global food system and the increased availability of cheap, processed, effectively marketed foods. They are either replicating American patterns of production or simply importing high-fat, high-calorie products never before part of their traditional diets. Acknowledging that obesity is an extremely complex phenomenon, researchers nonetheless have concluded that the dramatic rise in passive consumption of an 'energy dense', 'meat-sweet' diet has caused the epidemic and its related illnesses.[13] Indeed, 'Americanisation' is penetrating to the far corners of the globe, embedding severe distortions into the human experience of eating and drinking.[14] But while popular culture might object that immoderate habits are nothing new, our purpose is to acknowledge that rising obesity and declining mobility rates are not the only consequence. At stake is the message mediated to and literally consumed by our children, forming their nascent perceptions of the eucharistic table and the Person of Christ giving himself as the bread of life.

Granted, this proposed relationship between personal eating habits and receiving the sacrament is not obvious to the average communicant, thus we must return to basic questions: *Why are eating and drinking part of the human experience at all?* The dualistic, *techne*-centred anthropology of modern culture would have us believe that daily nourishment is a burdensome contingency of our physiological nature, but more than mere biological entities, we are *embodied persons* for whom the relation between corporal and spiritual appetites is intrinsic and fundamental to our humanity.[15] The human condition of hunger, of both body and soul, is as ancient as the expulsion of Adam and Eve from the Garden of Eden, when man was destined to work for his bread and long for God to provide salvation. In Luke's beatitude, 'Blessed are you who hunger now, for you shall be satisfied' (6:21), Jesus himself intimates that bodily hunger is a natural sign of our supernatural desire for God, satisfied but not yet satiated by the Bread of Life. Eating and drinking to fulfill our earthly longing points us towards and should remind us of the eternal satisfaction promised by Jesus' self-gift to us in the Eucharist. In light of this correlation, we should also recognise the significance of the family table – the preparation of the table and gifts, the sacrifice, and the self-gift that take place for the meals of the domestic Church. How so?

During his pontificate, Blessed John Paul II introduced new language to better understand the nature of the human person. He taught that God made the family to be the first 'school of love' and 'sanctuary of life' for persons, drawing attention to Christ sanctifying and making the family a way of salvation.[16] If the family 'more than any other human reality' is the place where an individual can exist and is loved for himself, where the person learns to live the sincere gift of self within the familial *communio personarum*,[17] this reality is quintessentially expressed *at the table*. Accomplished through the *work* of the table is the gathering and union of family members around the meal anticipated, the repast thoughtfully prepared, the feast transformed by love.[18] If Jesus' mission – his work – is to give himself, and this takes place at the shared meal of the eucharistic table where his work – in anticipation of the cross – reaches its fulfillment, the same must be said of the family table. In a real, albeit analogous way, all work of the family is realised at the table where the personal gift and reception of each family member is essential, and the life of the family is sustained and nurtured. Thus, radiating quietly from the centre of this 'school of love', the dining table symbolises not only the iconic locus of the family but also a school-in-miniature for the development of authentic personhood and relationship to the universal Church. Indeed, the multivalent experience of family meals is a domestic staging ground, forming children with foundational lessons in *giftedness* – of God, creation, themselves, and the familial *communio personarum* – and as such, preparing them to encounter the *Person of Christ*. Unlike the manna-fed Israelites in the desert, however, young victims of 'Americanisation' suffer from an artificial abundance that dulls all their human sensibilities and deprives them of basic training in the structure of being and shape of reality, embedding at an early age major obstacles to their encounter with Jesus' Real Presence in the Eucharist.[19, 20]

The first obstacles manifest *at the level of Creation* where children distanced from the family table are receiving distorted truths about the mystery of God, the world, and their own being.[21] When over-processed imitations of food constantly substitute for real ingredients, children form a deficient rather than robust, living sense of God's presence and enduring awareness of his creation. Such an 'eclipse' of the sense of God and of creation as 'the wonderful result of God's creative activity'[22] risks happening if children, habitually consuming the simulacra of food, never discover the fruits of the earth for their own surprise and beauty, never pondering: *What is an orange? Why?* When a steady diet of technical manipulation, fragmentation and reformulation are the only principles of logic applied to the fruit of creation, the 'real' itself ceases to have meaning. Instead of an incarnational view of reality, children come to see the world through the eyes of a soulless technology that subjects the richness of the Creator's design to 'the devil's policy of desubstantialisation'.[23] When youth witness the authentic substance of ordinary food routinely emptied without question or hesitation, they inherit a flawed foundation for confronting future questions of substance itself. Children weaned on pre-packaged fast meals also implicitly receive pride-filled lessons in their creaturely relationship to God and creation, instead of the required humility towards the Giver of all (edible) gifts. The very presence of real oranges – as opposed to mass-produced preservatives, dyes and sweeteners simulating the 'orange' – helps to form the child's distinction between Creator and creature; *God* having made the world, not man. Similarly, when profit-driven corporate manufacturers hijack food supply, replacing the Creator's substantive bounty with the less-than-real, blurred becomes any sense of the absolute giftedness of creation, the free act of God's Fatherly love providing for his people. Instead, the love implicit in authentic sustenance becomes contingent upon productivity and status as viable consumers, otherwise breeding (food) insecurity.[24] Lost also becomes the significance of sense experience within the supreme beauty of the physical world.[25] Addicted to industrialised foods 'made in a plant' instead of 'from a plant',[26] children age more rapidly, not only desensitised to creation, but also sense*less* – their senses literally dulled by chemical compounds and excess weight. Such children experience disconnection, even alienation from their own bodies, robbed of basic training in the goodness of their God-given embodied nature. When agri-business manufacturers pulverise natural ingredients into nondescript 'stuff', bereft of any nature and reduced to their measurable dimensionality, while marketing agents speak to consumers solely in terms of numbered calorie counts, vitamin grammes, and protein ounces, youthful minds learn to distinguish food – and by extension, the body – solely in terms of external, material and technical specifications, reducing the subject-person to the status of a mechanised object.

The latter effect brings into focus the second obstacle – for example, the phenomena of depersonalisation and objectification inherent in modern food consumption that attacks *at the level of human dignity*. Steady diets of manufactured junk fare not only strip the universe of its Creator but also human beings the source of their life.[33] Shared meals – especially when anticipated and accomplished through working together – overtly remind everyone of the family's identity and foundation in self-donating love. Simultaneously, each person plays a key role in the preparation and sharing of the meal, while children also learn they are neither the main point nor main character of the event; the meal doesn't exist for them alone but for the union of the family members. For all its banality and chaotic unfolding, mealtime benefits go far beyond better emotional health, fewer risk-taking behaviours, and improved school performance. The family table cements relationships, but on a more fundamental level, it serves as a daily reminder to both child and family of their unique identity *as family*.[34] Having been drawn into a relationship with God on a very basic, filial level, the family lives out its receptive stance toward him and his Creation not only but in large part *at the table* – through the gifts being 'changed' by human hands, made different because of his love for the family, transformed because of the love between family members. Indeed, the preparation of the gifts and the personal sacrifices made for the table synthesise the essence of family life: to give myself while receiving the gift(s) of the other – his story-telling idiosyncrasies, her cooking talents, etc. – while I, myself, am received in love as a person. For the growing child, every detail of the joint work of the family meal affirms basic principles about the gift structure of being and the family as *communio personarum*. Absent these introductory lessons in receptivity, gratitude, and communion, children become less apt to comprehend not only that God lovingly and gratuitously gifted creation to sustain life, but also that he gives us the persons of our family to make our lives flourish.[35]

Contemplating these implications of the loss of the family table brings to mind serious consequences for the universal Church. May and June are months dedicated to First Communions in the United States, and while acknowledging that catechesis should begin at home,[36] we cannot ignore compelling evidence of foundational experiences that alienate children from the eucharistic table. America's transactional nature of food consumption represents one of my country's most popular exports, but unlike Hollywood movies and Levi jeans, the global ramifications of her eating habits are toxic, affecting the human person more deeply than films and clothes. Around the world, real food is increasingly replaced by artifice, artful preparation by utilitarian technology, feasting by efficiency, self-emptying sacrifice by self-centred gluttony. The old adage that 'children learn what they live' rings true. If the substance of ordinary food is insignificant, transubstantiation can be emptied of its meaning. If structured times and places for ordinary eating are inconsequential, liturgical time and space become irrelevant. If regular mealtimes signify inconvenience, the abandonment of Sunday worship appears harmless. If youth comprehend themselves as machines, encountering the flesh and blood of Christ goes unnoticed. If children never experience working for or gratitude at the table, the Eucharist as the ultimate sacrifice and act of thanksgiving make no sense. If receptivity towards the gifts of God, creation, and familial persons is never fostered, understanding the Marian dimension of the Church needed for an adequate ecclesial *communio* suffers. If families never join together at table to celebrate their union brought about from above, true relationship with their Christian brothers and sisters around the altar – communion gifted by the Father uniting his people through Christ in the Holy Spirit – remains unseen. Indeed, the Americanisation of the family table effectively impedes the formation of a child's sacramental understanding of the world and obstructs his approach to the divine mysteries unfolding on the altar table of sacrifice, closing him off from the mysteries that mediate communion with our Trinitarian God. The filling-station attitude of food practices today diverts attention away from the eternal fulfilment for which we long. Rendered oblivious to Christ as our 'true food' and 'true drink' (Jn 6:55, NAB), this limited vision reduces the Church to a grace vending machine, a drive-thru for the Eucharist. These phenomena not only threaten the future of *communio* ecclesiology but also very literally breed a culture of death.

For the upcoming Year of Faith, Pope Benedict XVI encourages us to understand more profoundly the truth of Christianity's foundation, our faith as 'the encounter with an event, a person, which gives life a new horizon and a decisive direction'.[37] If we 'encounter' the Lord in things we eat, reclaiming our relationship with ordinary food is one step towards recovering our sense of human dignity, making us more apt to have faith in the extraordinary – the Real Presence of Jesus Christ in the Eucharist – and preparing us to meet the Person – to approach him, to adore him, to be grateful for his abiding presence.

5 Cardinal Joseph Ratzinger, 'Some Aspects of the Church Understood as Communion', *Congregation for the Doctrine of the Faith* (1992), n. 5.

6 Cardinal Joseph Ratzinger, 'The Ecclesiology of Vatican II', *Pastoral Congress of the Diocese of Aversa (Italy),* 15th September 2001.

7 Research evidence supports that life at the American family table has experienced a sharp decline. Regular sit-down meals have been replaced by incessant, portionless grazing, cars have become mobile dining rooms, and vending machine revenue has surpassed $30 billion per annum. Columbia University's National Center on Addiction and Substance Abuse (CASA) also reports that in the last thirty years of the twentieth century, the frequency of structured family meals has dropped by 33 per cent, citing family members being too busy, still at work, engaged in different activities, or simply not at home to cook or share a meal as top reasons for the decline. Data from recent Gallup Polls confirmed only slightly more than a quarter (28 per cent) of adults with children having family dinners together at home every night, down from 37 per cent in 1997. Combine these numbers with Americans reportedly spending more than $100 billion a year on fast food. The 2011 Center for Disease Control 'Trends' report cites a dramatic increase in obesity rates since 1985, with 36 per cent of adults and 17 per cent of children labelled as not just overweight but *obese*, accounting for 53 per cent of the American population suffering from severe excess weight.

8 Prof. Boyd A Swinburn MD, et al., 'The global obesity pandemic: shaped by global drivers and local environments', *The Lancet* 378.9793 (August 2011): 804–14 (accessed March 2012).

9 'Obesity and Overweight: Fact Sheet No. 311', *World Health Organization,* March 2011 (accessed March 2012). It is worth noting that *The Centre for Obesity Prevention* is less than ten years old, newly designated in 2003.

10 *International Obesity Taskforce,* 'Obesity the Global Epidemic', *International Association for the Study of Obesity* (accessed March 2012).

11 Steven Shapin, 'Eat and Run', *The New Yorker,* 16th January 2006 (accessed March 2012).

12 Eric Schlosser, *Fast Food Nation: The Dark Side of the All American Meal,* New York: Houghton Mifflin, 2001, pp. 5–9.

13 The 'meat-sweet' diet is also known among medical professionals as the *Western Pattern Diet* and refers to the high intake of saturated animal fats and simple sugars in fast food, refined grains, and sweetened carbonated drinks. See also 'Diet, Nutrition and the Prevention of Chronic Diseases', *World Health Organization,* WHO Technical Report Series No. 916, Geneva 2003 (accessed March 2012); 'Preventing Chronic Disease: A Vital Investment', *World Health Organization,* WHO Global Report, Geneva 2005 (accessed March 2012).

14 In the global discussion regarding the 'twin dangers' of malnutrition and obesity, researchers also argue that 'capitalism' (via the American model) shoulders substantial blame for the obesity crisis. Rather than a lack of virtuous self-control:

> capitalism has increasingly driven consumer behaviour inducing widespread over-nutrition, promoted by powerful profit-led manipulations of the global supply and quality of food. Food companies maximize their profits by *restricting* our choices, both at the behavioural level, through advertising, price manipulations and restriction of choice, and at the physiological level through the enhancement of addictive properties of foods (Wells).

See J.C. Wells, 'Obesity as Malnutrition: The Role of Capitalism in the Obesity Global Epidemic', *American Journal of Human Biology* 24.3 (May 2012): 261–76 (accessed April 2012). Harvard Global Health Institute's recent symposium on 'The Double Burden of Over and Under-Nutrition' held on 26th April 2012, also addressed the phenomenon of developing nations acquiring not only information and manufactured goods, but also dietary habits and fast foods.

15 To be sure, another loss incurred by the absence of the family table is the opportunity to increase in virtue, on which I have written in the past ('Recovering Chastity at the Family Table: A Love Affair to Remember', *Notre Dame Center for Ethics and Culture Fall Conference*, November 2008), but cannot address in adequate measure here. It is worth noting, however, that virtuous eating habits are not simply to be understood in terms of proper portion size and reasonable quantity of overall food intake. These 'guidelines' (calculators, scales, etc.) regard the body and desire for fulfilment in objectified, utilitarian terms, divorcing what should be the integration of our bodily and spiritual appetites. In this way, virtuous self-mastery is replaced by an extrinsic authority signalling when to stop eating. This is not authentic freedom (eating in accord with one's desire, with what is Good in all of its dimensions) and undermines the subjectivity and freedom of the integrated person. I will make a related argument on depersonalisation later in the paper.

16 *Familiaris Consortio,* 43; *Evangelium Vitae,* 11.

17 *Letter to Families,* 11.

18 It is beyond the limits of this paper to discuss the full definition, significance, and implications of human *work* and *dominion* for the person and for the family. My application of these terms is informed primarily by *Laborem Exercens* and *Caritas in Veritate.*

19 Indeed, 'victims' is not too strong a word to use here. More capable studies have already made the argument against the totalitarianism of multinational agribusiness corporations that control the world's food supply and profit from making cheap, plentiful, addictive substances. These manufacturers

market most of the food available in America, and as other countries emulate the US model, they are expanding production and spheres of influence. Their goals of substituting technology for labour, diminishing family farms, standardising the food supply and creating synthetic food are part of the long-term goal to establish more international food manufacturing systems controlled by a select number of powerful corporations. These commercial and marketing forces profit from having increasing numbers of the world's population sitting passively in front of screens, overeating the wrong foods, and taking no exercise. In America, corporations have fine-tuned methods of selling food to very young children, conditioning them to bad eating habits, as child psychologists are contracted by marketing departments to develop imagery for food branding and advertising based on detailed studies of children's dreams. Sales continue on school campuses with soft drink and snack vending machines in hallways and fast food in cafeterias. The tactics of such corporations which Blessed John Paul II called 'structures of sin' (systemic defects, unjust attitudes and behaviours that assume institutional form; see *Sollicitudo Rei Socialis*, 36). Pope Benedict continues to address in *Caritas in Veritate* (27, 42, 70).

20 While I have divided my examination into categories, I do not mean to convey a fragmented or disordered view of the ontological receptivity and relationality of the human person. This 'division' and the order of my explanation attempts to hold securely in view that the human person's basic experience is first a *filial* one, marked by a *God-centred* gift-receiving and-giving, and the distorted view of being and reality threatens the child at the most fundamental level. In Schindler's words, 'man's 'original solitude' means not only that man is different from all other creatures of the visible universe, but that man's relationality begins most radically in his 'aloneness' before God. The point is not that man is originally without relation, but that man's relationality, his original being-with, is a being-with God (ontologically) before it is a being-with other human beings. Man's being-with God, as creaturely, is first a being-from, in the manner of a child. It is a filial relation' (174). See David L. Schindler, 'Living and Thinking Reality in Its Integrity: Originary Experience, God, and the Task of Education', *Communio* 37, n. 2 (summer 2010), 167–85.

21 *Evangelium Vitae,* 22.

22 *Evangelium Vitae,* 23; *Caritas in Veritate,* 48.

23 Robert Farrar Capon, *The Supper of the Lamb: A Culinary Reflection,* New York: Doubleday, 1969, xiv.

24 See also *Caritas in Veritate,* 27.

25 According to D.C. Schindler, such a 'mechanistic conception of the natural world evacuates sense experience of meaning ... this stripping of sensible objects precisely of their sensibilia coincides with the elimination of the imagination as part of the soul (522, 533). Unless 'the ontological significance of goodness and beauty' is recovered, 'the effort to cultivate

the Christian imagination will be vain' (522). See D.C. Schindler, 'Truth and the Christian Imagination: The Reformation of Causality and the Iconoclasm of the Spirit', *Communio* 33, n. 4 (winter 2006), 521–39.

26 Michael Pollan, 'How to Eat: Diet Secrets from Michael Pollan (and your great-grandma)', *Houston Chronicle*, 23rd January 2010.

27 Further evidence of technologically-(de)formed self-perceptions also lies in the success of the weight-loss industry, reportedly worth over $61 billion in 2011 in the US. The evolution of dietary habits has led to the proliferation of weight-control centres, liquid diets, and surgical techniques, revealing an overall attempt to change the behaviour of food instead of that of the person as well as to reduce the body through mechanical means, not unlike changing a tire.

28 We usually think of gluttony as the desire to eat *too much* food, whereas an authentic Thomistic understanding defines gluttony as the *inordinate desire* for food, a desire not being regulated by reason. Unlike yesterday's 'constant, excessive' thought about food, thoughtlessness distinguishes today's brand of this deadly sin (CCC 1866). See also Brian Wansink, *Mindless Eating: Why We Eat More Than We Think,* New York: Bantam-Dell, 2006.

29 As I will demonstrate at the end, this liturgical language from the preparation of the gifts during the Mass takes on a significantly different meaning (or indeed, is rendered meaningless) when 'work' is the result of consumerism's technological manipulation rather than personal effort motivated by love.

30 See David L. Schindler, '"Homelessness" and Market Liberalism: Toward an Economic Culture of Gift and Gratitude', *Wealth, Poverty, and Human Destiny*, Doug Bandow and David L. Schindler, eds, Wilmington, Delaware: ISI Books, 2003, 347–413. It is important to clarify that I am not suggesting parents become *sacramentally* present in the food prepared. My discussion of the priestly character of and *person*al love communicated through food preparation and meal sharing seeks to emphasise their enormous sign and experiential value, serving as the child's first steps towards the altar, i.e. the table as the natural manifestation of love pointing us towards the supernatural reality of Christ's Real Presence in the Eucharist. Schindler's explanation of bread-making further explains 'that the things themselves ... differ *in their very character as things* ... such that the things themselves take on the nature of gift' (358) because 'the love of the mother affects the dinner precisely in its reality as food'(359–60). Bread-making 'undertaken for the sake of making what intrinsically is a good loaf of bread and for the sake of the person who will consume it' (361) – that is, undertaken for the sake of love – 'gives interior form, hence order or structure, to the thing made' (362). Therefore, it is not only a matter of receiving the gifts of God's love in creation but also the self-gift of parents in the form of their task-sharing, creativity, etc. contributing to the meal. Their 'preparation of the gifts' (and table, etc.) requires paying attention simultaneously to both the

physical and spiritual dimensions of the person, without considering them as separate. For the rightly-prepared meal, the physical *is* spiritual; not 'tastes good *and* is good for you', but is simply good. Thus, 'fast food' and 'health food' fall into the same trap. Both become means of manipulating human behaviour by marketing to the consumer reasons why they should purchase particular foods. Christopher O'Neill deserves credit for helping me to see this last point.

31 *Gaudium et Spes*, 48; *Letter to Families*, 7, 10–12.

32 To be sure, 'receptivity' to the gifts of creation diminishes when buying food predominates over growing it, for example, no longer being dependent on soil, climate, seasons, etc. for sustenance. In the United States, the number of small farms and 'farm families' fell dramatically following the Second World War after its peak of nearly 7 million in 1935.

33 While I make this distinction regarding the person's 'place' within the home, it is not my intention to diminish the significance of the home itself. Schindler emphasises: 'man is truly at home insofar as he finds his identity inside the *constitutive belonging to others* (God, other creatures) summed up in gift and gratitude ... home is where the creature most truly *belongs*, where the creature comes to realise the richness of the relations that most profoundly and intimately constitute his being as a creature' (357). He further explains, 'the love proper to families, which is to say the life that is constitutive of the familial *communio personarum*, generates a new and distinctive sense of place and indeed of institutional structure: it transforms the space, time, matter, and motion – the very "things" or "material objects" – in and through which personal-familial love is exercised. This transformation may properly be termed a "domestication" of space and time' (413). See David L. Schindler, 'Homelessness and the Modern Condition: The Family, Community, and the Global Economy', *Communio* 27, n. 3 (autumn 2000), 411–30.

34 See also *Familiaris Consortio*, 17 ('Family, become what you are').

35 This is far from an exhaustive analysis of the consequences of a reduced stance of *receptivity*. Indeed, with the overwhelming dependence on technology, the dimensions of masculine initiative exceed their limits to the detriment of the perception and integration of feminine receptivity, including an adequate sense of the domestic communion of persons.

36 *Catechism of the Catholic Church*, 2222–3; *Letter to Families*, 16.

37 *Deus Caritas Est*, 1.

38 *Familiaris Consortio*, 52.

THE ALL-EMBRACING MATERNAL CHURCH: THE COMMUNION ECCLESIOLOGY OF HENRI DE LUBAC

MR PAUDIE HOLLY PhD Candidate
Mary Immaculate College, Limerick

The purpose of this paper is to describe Henri de Lubac's communion ecclesiology with an emphasis on the Church as mother. De Lubac (1896–1991) was one of the twentieth century's greatest theologians; his work contributing significantly to the ecclesiology of the Second Vatican Council. I will discuss de Lubac's communion ecclesiology under four headings: theological anthropology, scripture, sacrament and motherhood of the Church.

THEOLOGICAL ANTHROPOLOGY

De Lubac's communion ecclesiology is based on the idea that humanity is naturally unified. He argues that our unity with God and our unity with each other are related concepts.[1] This means that unity among people is the precursor to unity with Christ. It is the precursor in the sense that unity with the mystical body is first of all grounded at a natural and physical level. This natural unity can be seen around us. We have built our civilisation on the fact that we are social creatures. This statement is so radical because de Lubac argues first from a physical natural level, rather than from an ontological spiritual level as might be expected. In *Catholicism: Christ and the Common Destiny of Man* he states, 'the supernatural dignity of one who has been baptised rests, we know, on the natural dignity of man, though it surpasses it in an infinite manner. Thus the unity of the mystical body of Christ, a supernatural unity, supposes a previous natural unity, the unity of the human race.'[2]

According to de Lubac, there are many aspects of humanity that cause us to be orientated to the divine. One aspect he develops is the

Brendan Leahy, in his *The Marian Profile: In the Ecclesiology of Hans Urs von Balthasar,* remarks that the intuition of de Lubac and von Balthasar, is that the Church and Mary were identical, culminated in a 'spiritual watershed'. As a consequence of this watershed the Second Vatican Council 'inserted' a chapter on Mary into the Constitution of the Church. Leahy states that the Marian chapter of *Lumen Gentium* was important for the Church's renewal.[16] As we have seen, de Lubac draws a comparison between the life of Mary and the life of the Church that suggests we emulate the Blessed Virgin in our interaction with the world.

While it is perfectly adequate to argue that the Church is maternal in the sense that she emulates Mary and is prefigured by the women of the Old Testament, de Lubac often describes the Church's maternity at a more basic level. The Church behaves in a maternal fashion simply because she is our Mother. She cares for us through our life. She, like any mother, educates her children. She guides us through the important stages in our relationship with the Father. She watches over us at the moment of our death and celebrates with us when we are married. She is concerned with our character and aids us when we are weak. The Church has all the characteristics of the primordial mother. She is, as we have seen, 'the new Eve'.

CONCLUSION

De Lubac's communion ecclesiology is a framework built upon a sacramental system. This framework is enriched by an understanding of sacraments as instruments of unity and female paradigms emblematic of motherhood. This maternal model of Church suggests inclusion and universality. The Church at this time needs to show that its systems and organisation are forces for good in the world. What better way to do this than to return to the work of one of the finest minds of Vatican II.

NOTES

1 Henri de Lubac, *Catholicism: Christ and the Common Destiny of Man,* San Francisco: St Ignatius Press, 1988, p. 25.

2 *Catholicism: Christ and the Common Destiny of Man,* p. 25.

3 John van Ruysbroeck, *The Mirror of Eternal Salvation* quoted in *Catholicism: Christ and the Common Destiny of Man,* p. 30.

4 *Catholicism: Christ and the Common Destiny of Man,* p. 141.

5 Henri de Lubac, *Scripture in the Tradition,* Luke O' Neill, trans., New York: Crossroad Publishing, 2000, p. 43.

6 *Scripture in the Tradition,* p. 85.

7 Ibid., pp. 89–90.

8 Ibid., p. 90.

9 *Catholicism: Christ and the Common Destiny of Man,* p. 187.

10 Ibid., p. 188.

11 Henri de Lubac, *The Splendour of the Church,* Michael Mason, trans., New Jersey: Paulist Press, 1963, p. 200.

12 Ibid., p. 200.

13 Henri de Lubac, *The Motherhood of the Church,* San Francisco: Ignatius Press, 1982, p. 77.

14 *The Splendour of the Church,* p. 231.

15 Ibid.

16 Brendan Leahy, *The Marian Profile: In the Ecclesiology of Hans Urs von Balthasar,* New York: New City Press, 2000, p. 164.

traditional and dogmatic basis for Mary's place and role in the mystery of salvation'[9] where she emerges as the first and supereminent member of the Church; she is the archetype of the people of God 'brought into unity from the unity of the Father, Son and Holy Spirit'.[10]

Furthermore, the structure of the chapters of the whole constitution reveals the movement and significance of Mary's placement at the end of *Lumen Gentium.* Joseph Cardinal Ratzinger has asserted that one must correctly grasp this correlation in order to properly understand the image of the Church that the Council wished to portray.[11] Canon Charles Moeller describes the chapters of the constitution as developing first from the inner core of the Church as a mystery of the communion of all persons in God – chapters one and two. Chapters three and four follow with the stratification of the Church: its hierarchical constitution and the laity. Chapters five and six address the finality of holiness as a universal call and a particular vocation. The last dual chapters speak of the eschatological consummation of the pilgrim Church, culminating in *de Beata,* the chapter on the Blessed Virgin Mary, Mother of God in the mystery of Christ and the Church. This macro-structure and inner movement of the constitution reveal Our Lady as the culminating model of the Church. In her, the structure of salvation is discernible; she is not a mere addendum to the Church, but rather, she is the exemplary fulfilment of God's work in humanity.

Furthermore, this eschatological dimension of the Church, illumined in the light of Mariology, converges with the communion ecclesiology presented in *Lumen Gentium.* In Mary, it becomes clear that the Church extends beyond the temporal, earthly dimensions to a communion of the saints who enter into Trinitarian communion through the body of Christ. This is the very purpose for which the Church exists – namely, to draw all peoples into the very life of the Trinity. A foretaste of this eschatological fullness is encountered in every celebration of the Eucharist when the earthly liturgy partakes in the heavenly one.[12] Indeed, this eucharistic faith was both anticipated by and prefigured in her whose virginal womb became the dwelling place of the Incarnate Word. The Church's own final glory, with its foretaste in the Eucharist, is a reality already completed in Mary. With that same eucharistic hope, the pilgrim Church journeys forward in holiness toward her final consummation. Like Mary, she does not exist for her own sake, but is the instrument of God for gathering all peoples, until all things are summed up in Christ (Eph 1:10).[13]

MARIAN COMMUNION ECCLESIOLOGY

Having surveyed the significance of the conciliar debates and the resulting integration of Mary to the final, culminating chapter of the constitution, I now turn to the particular contribution of a Marian perspective to communion ecclesiology to see that the pre-conciliar tensions between the Marian and liturgical movements were not simply reconciled at the Council but, rather, became the impulse to a full-fledged eucharistic ecclesiology – an ecclesiology in which the dynamics of the Marian and liturgical movements converge. Toward this goal of delineating the contours of a Marian communion ecclesiology, it is first necessary to define the communion ecclesiology which drives my work as a specifically *eucharistic*.

For St Paul and the early Church Fathers (as shown in Henri de Lubac's extensive study),[14] *corpus mysticum* referred primarily to the Eucharist, and secondarily to the Church insofar as she is united to Christ in that great sacrament where the Lord is bodily present. Every celebration of the Eucharist, therefore, builds up the Church and unites believers in one body of Christ. As oft-quoted of Vatican II, 'The Eucharist is the source and summit of Christian life',[15] it is the *form* of ecclesial communion and the *goal* of ecclesial existence: 'The (eucharistic) encounter with Christ brings about fellowship with him and, thus, with the Father in the Holy Spirit.'[16] The Council's communion ecclesiology is thus thoroughly eucharistic;[17] the Church is defined by the worship she gives to God.

What, then, does the proposed Marian perspective contribute to eucharistic ecclesiology? The answer is twofold. First, the Council's work in integrating Mariology into ecclesiology proffers a *personal* dimension of the Church which brings her bridal imagery to an ontological perfection. Second, insofar as Mary is the ultimate personal concretisation of the Church, her perfect response to God is the paradigm of grace; the perfect love and receptivity of her *fiat* embodies the heart of eucharistic faith.

To better grasp the significance of Mary to the relationship of the Church and the Eucharist, we begin with two eminently scriptural and she mothers. Her ecclesial motherhood springs from her 'spotless, unrestricted Yes to the whole of God's plan for the salvation of the world'[26] and further defines the way in which the Church similarly participates in the sacrifice of Christ in the Mass. The significance of Mariology for eucharistic ecclesiology lies in the fact that the Church must echo Mary's *fiat* as her own.

It is precisely in this dimension of Marian faith that the Church truly partakes of the sacrifice of the Mass; the Church offers Christ's sacrifice precisely in *receiving* it. In the Eucharist, the greatest participation the Church can take on is to bring to the altar her own poverty in an openness which willingly receives, like Mary, anything and everything the Father gives. God, in turn, gives nothing less than his own Son. In receiving this sacrifice with a Marian disposition of perfect receptivity, the Church allows herself to be drawn into the sacrifice of Christ, and 'grasps that *eucharistia* means thanksgiving to the Father for the departure of the Son and thanksgiving that we are permitted to let him depart'.[27]

This Marian disposition illumines both the inner dynamic of how the bride becomes one with the bridegroom as well as the inner coherence of a eucharistic ecclesiology in which the 'assent of the *Ekklesia* to the sacrifice of the Son must press on until it reaches Mary's perfect selflessness'.[28] This is the remarkable meaning of the eucharistic existence of the Church, an existence which Mary exemplifies. *This* is the gem which lies at the *nexus mysteriorum* of the Church and the Eucharist in the light of Marian communion.

FURTHER CONSIDERATIONS

Because the Marian dimension is co-extensive to all aspects of ecclesial life, there are important implications to a full-fledged Marian ecclesiology of Communion. To take one example, a robust Marian ecclesiology would potentially shed new light on the relationship of the universal and local Church. In embodying both individual and communal dimensions of faith, Mary is the concrete realisation of the Church's own faith and future glory. Nonetheless, she never ceases to be a real historical individual who freely offered her personal *fiat* to God. Hence, insofar as she has preceded the Church in the perfection of faith, the notion of the universal Church can never be a mere abstraction; there is real ontological substance to the idea of the universal Church realized in the person of Mary.

Similarly, many crucial aspects of ecclesiology such as collegiality,[29] ecumenism, hierarchy, gender roles, the common priesthood, and Papal primacy – to name but a few – are ripe for the renewed understanding which Mariology brings. The theological fruitfulness of Mariology ultimately stems from the paradox and power of grace at work within the Virgin's docility and faith-filled receptivity. The paradoxes embodied by Our Lady are brilliantly captured in Dante Alighieri's description of Mary as 'Virgin Mother, daughter of thy Son; high above all others, lowlier is none ...'[30] The paradox of a virgin who is a mother, of a mother who is the daughter of her own son, are all paradoxes of the reality of grace. As such, Mary stands at the *nexus mysteriorum,* a fulcrum of 'the intrinsic interwovenness of the mysteries in their irreducible mutual otherness and unity'.[31] Insofar as the Council's Eucharistic ecclesiology has commenced a fresh understanding of the Church in her episcopacy and ecclesial institutions, so too can the personal, receptive dimension of Mariology deepen the impact of Eucharistic ecclesiology.

In summary, as we continue to reap the riches of the Council's teaching, we discover how the Council's decision to integrate Mariology into a robust ecclesiotypical perspective spoke to the deep impulses of liturgical, biblical and ecumenical renewal. Moreover, a close reading of *Lumen Gentium* has revealed how the structure of the constitution itself underscores the inner life of the pilgrim Church oriented to an eschatological consummate existence which – given as a foretaste in every Eucharist – has already found its preeminent fulfilment in Our Lady. Mariology thus brings to a sharp focus the bridal imagery of the Church who, as Bride, remains distinct from her Bridegroom but also comes into union with him in one body. Mary's *fiat* becomes the archetypal response of perfect faith because, at the cross, it achieves the perfect bridal union of the Bride of Christ to his Body; here, Mary entered most perfectly into communion with the sacrifice of her Son and thus becomes mother to his followers. The Church, too, is called to this receptive disposition which opens unto communion with Christ in his eucharistic sacrifice, and further, in that sacrifice, unto service and communion with others.

22 Hans Urs von Balthasar, 'The Mass, A Sacrifice of the Church?' from *Explorations in Theology III: Creator Spirit,* Brian McNeil, trans., San Francisco: Ignatius Press, 1993, p. 240.

23 Ibid., p. 227, emphasis added.

24 Joseph Ratzinger and Hans Urs von Balthasar, *Mary: The Church at the Source,* San Francisco: Ignatius Press, 1997, p. 110.

25 Ibid., pp. 109–110.

26 Ibid., p. 110.

27 'The Mass, A Sacrifice of the Church?' p. 236.

28 Ibid., p. 240.

29 NB: In the Conciliar debates, it had become apparent that conceiving of Mary as simultaneously member and mother of the Church mirrored the role of the pope who is both in and yet, in some sense, above the episcopal college. Cf. Moeller, 141: 'Two positions confronted each other. Both curiously intervened in the same way regarding the pope and the Blessed Virgin. One group considered the pope as superior to and a part of the episcopal college, like the head of a body. The other considered him as superior to but apart from the college, and felt that papal primacy was diminished, run down, compromised in the other position.'

30 Dante Alighieri, *Paradiso* XIII, lines 1–2.

31 Ratzinger and von Balthasar, *Mary: The Church at the Source*, p. 29.

32 John Paul II, *Ecclesia de Eucharistia* (2003), no. 55.

33 Joseph Ratzinger, 'The Ecclesiology of Vatican II', *L'Osservatore Romano,* 23rd January 2002, weekly English edition, no. 4, p. 7.

A LONERGANIAN ANALYSIS OF THE MARIAN PROFILE OF THE CHURCH IN THE THEOLOGY OF HANS URS VON BALTHASAR

DR PAUL O'HARA
Catholic Theological Union, Chicago (CTU),
Professor and Chair of the Department of Mathematics,
Northeastern Illinois University, Chicago

At the dawn of the new millennium, we notice with joy the emergence of the 'Marian profile' of the Church that summarises the deepest contents of the conciliar renewal.[1]

This essay, as the title suggests, will be a systematic analysis of who Mary is in relationship to the Church. It will try to break new ground by attempting a systematisation based on a methodology suggested by Lonergan but inspired by the writings primarily of von Balthasar and Chiara Lubich. It is my hope that what will emerge will be a deeper understanding of who is Mary and what is the Church from an ontological perspective.

A MARIAN PRINCIPLE

The word profile usually denotes an outline or a sketch of someone. Indeed, to the extent that the essay will not be exhaustive, it will only be an outline of the role of Mary in the Church. At the same time it will be a specific outline in that it will attempt to describe the ontological nature of Mary and her relationship to the Church.

In the history of Catholicism, Mary has always had a special role; but that role has taken on different forms and expressions throughout the centuries. For example, during the Council, Mary's was 'hailed as a pre-eminent and altogether singular member of the Church',[2] the prototype of a Christian. Also, her role as mediatrix in the economy

THE NATURE OF THE MARIAN PRINCIPLE

For von Balthasar there are five operative principles at work within the Church: the Petrine, the Pauline, the Jacobine, the Johannine, and finally the Marian principle of which all of the others are an expression. Indeed, to say something about the Marian principle, we have to first say something about the other four.

'Peter' has always played a centre role in the history of the Church, and in a visible way represents both the unity of the Church as an institution, and in its ministerial expression. In the early Church, we are presented with a Peter, who is both meek and insecure (Mt 26:69-75, Mk 14:66-72, Lk 22:54-62, Jn 18:15-27), leader of the Church (Mt 16:18) but at times overshadowed by Paul (Gal 2:11) who is also symbol of the missionary Church (Acts 2:14). Nevertheless, regardless of his strong or weak points, he is the external sign of the unity of the Church. Since then we have had many popes, both strong and weak, who have left their mark on history: some have been papal monarchs, others simple shepherds of their flock, some have been great saints, others a cause of scandal. But regardless of who they were, they were also a visible sign of the dynamic unity of the Church:

> As the 'outward' principle of unity, the pope's role is 'an impossibility', made possible only by God's will in creating him. As the 'fatherly head' of the Church, he is the one called to 'love more'; his role is 'excentric' in that he is to care for the periphery within the communion of the Church, he has judicial authority rooted in the office of judge that Christ received from the Father, an office exercised in order to seek reconciliation and unity. And since the Petrine office cares for the periphery, it manifests itself as infallible.[15]

The Pauline principle can also be found from the beginning of the early Church. In particular, we might recognise its first real expression on the day of Pentecost, when Peter immediately ran into the street to proclaim the word of God. In fact, it is precisely at Pentecost when the concrete expression of the Petrine and Pauline principles come together in Peter (Acts 2:14-36). Later on this principle becomes more differentiated with the Apostle Paul taking on a leading role as missionary to the gentiles.

The Jacobine principle is the one least developed by von Balthasar. It derives its name from James the brother of John and it expresses 'that dimension of the Church which affirms the historical sense of things, continuity, tradition, canon law'.[16]

The fourth principle, which at times is indistinguishable from the Marian principle, is the Johannine one which expresses the fraternal love that holds the members of the Church together. In a certain way, it unites the other three principles, both in its recognition of the key role of Peter and our loving response to him, and also as a witness of the Christian faith, which mediates and gives meaning to the Pauline and Jacobine principles. Without mutual love, there is nothing to preach or no tradition to preserve, while with this love we can understand the expression of Tertullian in his Apology (XXXIX) when he notes that Christians were identified as those who loved one another.

This leads to the Marian principle as what underlies and unifies all of the others, of which they are an expression. Edward Oakes expresses it this way:

> First of all, the Church as a whole is feminine (2 Cor 11:12), open and dependent on her Bridegroom, while the male hierarchy, by contrast, is only one part, whose vocation is to serve the feminine Marian whole. The Church, von Balthasar would always want to insist, existed in a woman before a single man had been called to be an apostle: 'In Mary the Church already has physical existence before it is organised in Peter.'
>
> Furthermore, the hierarchical Church is most definitely founded and established in the wider reality of Church prior to its consent or even its ability to give its finite Yes, as Peter's many denials so amply testify. It was Mary, and not some apostle, or the Twelve assembled in a 'college', who first believed and made possible, on a human level,the incarnation. And so she has the primacy in a way no 'primate' or prelate could ever have.[17]

In other words, for von Balthasar the Church as 'the feminine Marian whole' unifies the other principles and defines the Marian principle of which they are an expression. It predates the Petrine principle in that he sees the Church being founded not on Pentecost Sunday but rather with Mary receiving John as her Son at the foot of the cross. It was Mary together with Jesus and John who constituted the first cell of the Church, and Mary's role in this first cell as both bride of Christ and Mother of Jesus, and later as Mother of John (so to speak) means that she can be identified as the Mother of the Church. The sorrow she freely accepted and embraced by not only watching her son die, but also in accepting another in his place constituted the second *fiat* of Mary, a *fiat* said in blind faith. For this reason (as noted by Benedict XVI)[18] the Petrine profile is contained in the Marian profile. Mary's second 'yes' made the Church possible, at least as we know it, also on an ontological level that can only be properly understood by analogy in terms of Trinitarian relationships or pericoresis. It is a sacramental unity as described by Paul in his Letter to the Ephesians (Eph 5:21-33), analogous to marriage.

Both Cyril of Alexandria and Scheeben explain this through the language of pericoresis. Cyril speaks of a pericoresis between humanity as a whole and Christ. It is this pericoresis that defines the ontological unity of the Church, in the sense that Christ is the vine and we are the branches; while Scheeben speaks of a pericoresis between Mary and the Church,[19] which suggests an identification of Mary with the Church, as pointed out in the Catechism. It is here that the image of a marriage between Christ and Mary 'becomes a rich metaphor to describe a genuine partnership,' as noted by Oakes.

In reality there was only one act (not multiple acts) of creation, also embracing space-time, in which all of creation was recapitulated in Christ through the consent of Mary. Indeed, as *Lumen Gentium* recognised, Mary was predestined prior to the fall to be Mother of God and without her the incarnation as we know it was not possible. Moreover, with the subsequent identification of Mary with the Church as bride of Christ, the recapitulation of all in Christ became possible, according to divine plan, because of Mary's *fiat*, while the incarnation itself took place not because of our sins but in spite of them. This also reflects the Scotus understanding of creation.[20]

A FOUR-POINT HYPOTHESIS

With this in mind, we now try to integrate our understanding of this principle from a metaphysical and ontological perspective using a methodology first suggested by Bernard Lonergan and further developed by Robert Doran in his book *What Is Systematic Theology?* In particular, I will try to use this four-point hypothesis to better understand Rahner's identification of the economic and immanent Trinity in terms of the Marian profile.

In his *De Deo Trino*, Bernard Lonergan notes that:

> There are four real divine relations, really identical with the divine substance, and so four special ways of grounding an imitation or participation *ad extra* of God's own life. And there are four absolutely supernatural created realities. They are never found in an unformed or indeterminate state. They are: the secondary act of existence of the incarnation, sanctifying grace, the habit of charity and the light of glory.
>
> Thus it can appropriately be maintained that the secondary act of existence of the incarnation is a created participation of paternity, and so that it is has a special relation to the Son; that sanctifying grace is a [created] participation of active spiration, and so that it bears a special relation to the Holy Spirit; that the habit of charity is a [created] participation of passive spiration, and so that it has a special relation to the Father and the Son; and that the light of glory is a [created] participation of filation that leads perfectly the children of adoption back to the Father.[21]

Doran suggests that this four-point hypothesis should serve as the basis of a unified field theory in theology. I agree with this up to a point. The four created realities that are analogous to the four relationships in the Trinity also constitute one God. Consequently, the four supernaturally created realities take on a complete meaning in a Christian sense when they too are seen as constituting one new created reality which we can call Mary but later identify with the Church. In other words, both Doran and Lonergan have overlooked in their unified formulation the integrating Marian element that brings the other four supernaturally created realities together.

Mary too is a supernaturally created reality, but also quite different to the other four. Her existence not only presupposes the other realities but also constitutes them, in much the same way that the Marian profile presupposes and constitutes the other profiles of the Church. In terms of these profiles, the secondary acts of existence in which we all participate in paternity has its visible expression, at least from a Catholic perspective, in the Petrine profile, that is, the papacy and the college of bishops. Sanctifying grace speaks directly of the life of the Holy Spirit in the Church and the Pauline profile of mission. The habit of charity speaks of the Johannine profile and is reflected in our mutual love and service to others. The light of glory stemming from the beatific vision, speaks of the Jacobian profile and is reflected in the light that illuminates the tradition and the contemplative life of the Church. I will argue that none of them can exist as we know them without Mary.

She is the integrator on the side of creation of what God was accomplishing. At the same time, without the four created realities there would be no Mary as immaculate conception or assumption. The two are tightly intertwined. In metaphysical language, we can say that Mary is the higher viewpoint that integrates the four realities into one created reality, and that this integration is accomplished in history through the Church. If Jesus is the mediator between God and man, Mary is the mediatrix between Christ and humanity and both mediations are brought about by the Holy Spirit. Her 'yes' was a turning point in sacred history. God by his/her nature is Trinitatrian and One. Creation in relationship to its creator is also Trinitarian (by analogy) but also one. The Trinitarian elements of this new order are Jesus, Mary – Holy Spirit and John, and the unity of these elements embraces the whole of creation in a reality constitutive of the Church.

MARY AS A CREATED PARTICIPATION OF PATERNITY AND THE PETRINE PROFILE

Just as Jesus, the Word become flesh is a 'created participation of paternity', in an analogous way Mary as 'Mother of God' is also a 'created participation of paternity', and by her designation as Mother has a very 'special relationship to the Son'. Indeed, the paternity of God in creation was accomplished by Mary being *theotokos*. The fact that Jesus emerged from Mary's womb and took his humanity from her enables us to define him as a person with a human nature. Likewise, the fact that he was the Word become incarnate allows us to define him as a person with a divine nature. Moreover, her spiritual motherhood embraces the entire Trinity as noted in the Council of Ephesus.

Numerous mystics have tried to explain this. Saint Louis Marie De Montford for example notes that while God created paradise for us, he created Mary to be his own paradise, while Chiara Lubich captures the greatness of Mary by means of a powerful but simple metaphor:

> In the past, we had seen Mary in relationship to Christ and the saints – to make a comparison – as in the heavens where there is the moon (Mary) in relationship to the sun (Christ) and the stars (the saints). Now, it was no longer so. The Mother of God embraced, like a vast blue sky the sun itself, God himself.
>
> Mary, in fact, is the Mother of God because she is the mother of the humanity of the one person of the Word, who is God and who wished to become man. The Word, however, can never be thought separate from the Father or the Holy Spirit. Jesus himself, the son of Mary, tells Philip when the apostle asks him to show them the Father: 'Whoever has seen me has seen the Father ... I am in the Father and the Father is in me' (Jn 14:9-11).
>
> We had contemplated Mary as being set within the Trinity, but now, because of her Son, in her own particular way, we saw her as containing the Trinity.[22]

In this respect the Petrine profile should be understood in an analogous way. Just as Mary embraces God, the Pope embraces the Church, the entire body of Christ. Just as the Father allowed Mary to participate in paternity through parenthood, by helping Christ grow in wisdom and understanding, likewise by analogy the pope as papa (literally Father) participates in God's paternity through his guidance of the Church (the body of Christ) in wisdom and understanding. If Mary contains the Creator, as mediatrix she also contains within her all of creation and, indeed, is the living symbol of the oneness of creation. In an analogous way, the Petrine profile is a concrete expression within history of the Marian profile in the process of becoming, in that his very position represents the oneness of the Church. The pope serves as a visible sign of the unity of the Church and an expression of the paternity and maternity (expressed through Mary) of God in history. This paternity will be seen as complete when the pope, bishops, priests and laity are united in charity. In terms of Mary and end-times this is already complete, in terms of history as a process of becoming, we seem to be a long way from its fulfilment.

SANCTIFYING GRACE AS A CREATED PARTICIPATION IN ACTIVE SPIRATION OF THE HOLY SPIRIT AND THE PAULINE PROFILE

The fact that Mary is called 'full of grace' and also the Immaculate Conception is the quintessential expression of this active spiration. She represents the ultimate 'dynamic state of being in love',[23] with God. Indeed, as noted earlier, Maximilian Kolbe refers to the Holy Spirit as the 'eternal Immaculate Conception',[24] while he refers to Mary as the created 'Immaculate Conception'. It is also within this context that Mary's role in history in terms of apparitions of Lourdes, Fatima, Guadalupe and others can be better understood. Working in conjunction with the Holy Spirit, she is on a mission to guide the Church towards its proper end and glorious assumption at the end of time when all will be recapitulated in Christ. She is the first to proclaim her Son's message and divinity, and to bear witness to his justice and mercy. Indeed, the missionary nature of the Church should be seen as an expression of her role in reaching out to all of humanity as mother.

It also explains, perhaps, why Leonardo Boff referred to Mary as the incarnation of the Holy Spirit. His language might not have been precise and accurate, but at the same time it is an acknowledgment of the special role of Mary with regard to the Holy Spirit within history and 'her preferential option' for the poor and lowly.

For example, in the 'Blessed One' it is noted[25] that:

> Mary's magnificat is a personal, communal, socioeconomic, and moral statement that praises God and celebrates freedom from injustice. Significantly it recognises that God has direct interest in woman, for God meets Mary in her humiliation and helps her and her child. Interpreted through the lens of womanist wisdom, Mary proclaims a cultural revolution favouring the poor, an economic revolution where the poor can receive good things, and a political revolution where the poor can access power.

Mary's ongoing activity in history, whether visibly (through apparitions) or invisibly, represents an ongoing expression of her role as mediatrix for her Son who himself is the only mediator between God and creation. And like all the things of God, it is perichoretic in nature through the action of the Holy Spirit.

HABIT OF CHARITY AS A CREATED PARTICIPATION IN PASSIVE SPIRATION AND THE JOHANNINE PROFILE

The way of Mary is probably the best way to capture the habit of charity as lived by Mary. Don Mitchell, in his book, speaks of the kenosis of Mary as a model for Christian charity and also as a way of dialoging with the Pure Land Buddhist tradition, in that she is the 'personification of the mercy of God'.[26] He points out, borrowing heavily from Chiara Lubich, that the whole of Mary's life beginning with her 'yes' at the incarnation to her 'yes' at the foot of the cross, can be interpreted as a model of Christian charity. Her first 'yes' was an immediate response to God's love for her. This is then followed by her journey to see Elizabeth and help her with her pregnancy. In the magnificat we are allowed to witness her magnificence in that 'her soul magnifies the lord'. In the birth of Jesus in a manger, in her purification in the temple, in the flight to Egypt we are presented with a strong woman but nonetheless the image of a woman who suffers much to protect her child. Indeed, Mary's motherhood is often held up as a model of who we should become as Christians.

In terms of the language of kenosis, Mitchell points out that:

> Through spiritual kenosis, the negative kenosis of ego-centeredness becomes less and less, and Christ-centredness becomes more and more until it is no longer the person or persons who act but Christ within and among them who acts. Not only the person, but, from a communal point of view, the community of God as its communal centre becomes an instrument of God acting in the world. Through a mutual kenosis, the ministry of Christ can be born from the womb of the community for the liberation of the world. In this way the community lives Mary collectively as it gives birth to a self-determination of the unity of God for the unity of humankind.[27]

This last quote expresses most adequately the meaning behind the Johannine profile of the Church. It is the collective self-emptying of members of community as a witness of the mutual love that binds its members together in unity (Jn 17) that proclaims the Johnine profile of the Church. The historical witness of service that the Church has given through its various congregations and religious orders that serve the sick and the poor, is one instance of this profile at work in a collective sense. Moreover, to the extent that the individual members bear witness in their own lives to love of neighbour, the Marian profile and the habit of charity will continue to be manifested, culminating with the presence of 'Jesus in the midst' as proclaimed by the apostle Matthew (Mt 18:20).

THE LIGHT OF GLORY AND THE JACOBINE PROFILE

'The Light of Glory that is the consequent created contingent condition of the beatific vision is', according to Doran, 'a created participation in the Sonship of the divine Word'.[28] In this regard, Mary's participation in the divine Sonship has no comparison in history, in that the incarnation can be seen:

> ... as an *essentially* cooperative effort between Mary and God. It is impossible to conceive of the incarnation apart from either God's or Mary's involvement. The words self-emptying (*kenosis*) is realised in Mary's God-bearing (*theotokos*) and vice-versa; human creativity is included in the creative work of the creator become creator.[29]

In other words, Mary's designation as 'full of grace' and 'Mother of God' contain within them a lot of implications in terms of her participation in the glory of her Son. She literally gave him his humanity and formed him. In that sense, it was her Son who participated in her humanity and consequently she was directly responsible for the divine Word's participation in his own creation. This fact itself cannot but be the source of much wonder and contemplation.

Secondly, the doctrine of the Immaculate Conception not only proclaims that Mary was born free of original sin but in fact that she could never sin in that she was 'preserved from all stain of original sin' throughout her life. Presented from the perspective of pure logic the statement can give rise to many (unnecessary) debates about whether Mary was free to sin or not. In point of fact, it seems to me that all such discussions miss the point. Mary, as Cynthia Rigby points out, is better understood as an artist who is inseparable from her work. She is so totally in love with God that the [divine] plan in fact quite literally presumes symbiosis with her person, since she will both physically receive into her being the person of God and contribute to the God-human her humanity.[30]

In other words, she so participated in the light of glory on this earth that the idea of her not being in union with God is an absurdity. Mary, although completely free, could no more turn against God than Jesus could have succumbed to the temptations in the desert. Whether or not she merited this is not the issue! The doctrine of the Immaculate Conception is an affirmation that *de facto* she could not have sinned. Moreover, the doctrine of the assumption is a logical consequence of the Immaculate Conception. Mary as the 'new Eve' was already living in end times and represented the new creation.

Finally, we might ask if Mary had the 'beatific vision' while on earth, thus preserving her from all sin. Indeed, the beatific vision would seem to explain why in the next life the story of Adam and Eve cannot be repeated *ad infinitum*, with eternity becoming a nightmare existence like that of Sisyphus. In fact, in terms of the mystical tradition, the Spanish mystic Maria Agreda, wrote a 'biography' of Mary based on her mystical visions in which she affirms that Mary did indeed have the beatific vision at certain times while on earth.[31] Certainly, no one is obligated to accept the validity of her claims, but nevertheless if true it would give a deeper understanding of the doctrine of the Immaculate Conception. Moreover, in this regard Lonergan in his first course on Christology that he taught in 1948 speaks of the unity of consciousness and its relationship to the beatific vision. Frederick Crowe explains it this way:[32]

> How does this [the unity of consciousness] apply to the beatific knowledge Christ had? The different levels of consciousness do not conflict with one another, and neither does the beatific vision conflict with ordinary consciousness. It enlarges the field, and adds a new dimension, as three-dimensional geometry adds a new dimension to two-dimensional, but does not cut out the lower. In a similar way the mystics have a new dimension, the experience of a new order, an awful enlargement of consciousness which they cannot express in terms of the lower level.

Mary as the ultimate mystic, characterised by being the Immaculate Conception experienced this 'awful enlargement of consciousness' in a radically different way, that would be very compatible with having the beatific vision. Her corporality did not block it, no more than Christ's corporality blocked his, and the concupiscence of sin did not affect them directly. The beatific vision is a gift which God was free to give her.

Finally, in terms of the Jacobine profile we note the long mystical tradition in the history of the Church, beginning with the desert fathers, Deny the Areopagite, the monastic traditions exemplified by the Benedictines, the Cistercines, the Carthusians, the Carmelites, not to mention the numerous saints who have experienced deep contemplation and mystical visions related to the light of glory. All of these must be seen as an example of the Jacobine tradition and partakers of the light of glory given to Mary as full of grace.

THE CHURCH AND THE MARIAN PROFILE

At this stage a basic analysis has been completed of the four-point hypothesis as a heuristic for understanding the different aspects of the Marian profile of the Church. All four points of the supernaturally created entities (incarnation, grace, charity and beatific vision) have been interpreted as a way of understanding Mary's role from the perspective of the Petrine, Pauline, Johannine and Jacobine principles. Mary participated in paternity as Mother of God, participated in active spiration as full of grace, participated in passive spiration as spouse of the Holy Spirit, and participated in the light of glory as the person who completely lived the Word of God, as 'the beloved daughter of the Father',[33] and as full of grace fully experienced the life of God as light and glory within her.

Nevertheless, as pointed out previously, if the four-point hypothesis is to function as a unified field theory for systematic theology and, in this case, Mariology, it needs also to recognise that the four heuristics and the four supernaturally created realities are an expression and consequence of one unifying reality. This reality is the Church. At the same time, Mary as Immaculate Conception is also another supernaturally created reality which needs to be incorporated into this unity.

In the language of ontology, one can say that the Church is the integrator of the 'four absolutely supernaturally created realities' associated with the four-point hypothesis and the four ecclesial principles. In terms of eschatology, it has both a historical and a historical dimension as immanent and transcendent respectively. In terms of ecclesiology, the Church can only be fully understood, based on the previous analysis, within the context of Mary as Mother of God embracing God himself (cf. Chiara Lubich), whereby the immanent (as bride of Christ) embraces the transcendent (cf. von Balthasar) and the transcendent embraces the immanent. Moreover, underlying this mutual embracing of the immanent and the transcendent is a *pericoresis* between God and humanity, which we now explore more in depth.

MARY AS THEOTOKOS AND AS BRIDE OF CHRIST

Pope John-Paul II, in his encyclical letter 'Mother of the Redeemer', emphasises Mary as a model of faith and as mediatrix between humankind and Jesus, with this latter point being a consequence of the Father entrusting his Son to her, and also of people's need for a mother. Hers is a mediation of motherhood that comes from her Son allowing her to help him in his redemptive plan.[34] He desires to need her.

Mary *entered, in a way all her own, into the one mediation* 'between God and men', *which is the mediation of the man Christ Jesus*. If she was the first to experience within herself the supernatural consequences of this one mediation – in the annunciation she had been greeted as 'full of grace' – then we must say that through this fullness of grace and supernatural life she was especially predisposed to cooperate with Christ, the one mediator of human salvation. *And such cooperation is precisely this mediation subordinated* to the mediation of Christ.

Indeed, John Paul II's development of Marian thought is very much in harmony with Luther's understating of Mary as 'the model of faith', of a faith that comes to her through her Son and of faith in her son. Mary's role as helper to her Son and as mediatrix stems from her being this model.

However, there is also another point. Implicit in the proclamation of Mary as *Theotokos*, as stated by the Council of Ephesus is the fact that Mary is not only the mother of Jesus' human nature but also of his entire person, which embraces the hypostatic union, and consequently all of the Trinity. To repeat the words of Chiara Lubich:

> In the past, we had seen Mary in relationship to Christ and the saints – to make a comparison – as in the heavens where there is the moon (Mary) in relationship to the sun (Christ) and the stars (the saints). Now, it was no longer so. The Mother of God embraced, like a vast blue sky the sun itself, God himself.
>
> Mary, in fact, is the Mother of God because she is the mother of the humanity of the one person of the Word, who is God and who wished to become man. The Word, however, can never be thought separate from the Father or the Holy Spirit. Jesus himself, the son of Mary, tells Philip when the apostle asks him to show them the Father: 'Whoever has seen me has seen the Father ... I am in the Father and the Father is in me' (Jn 14:9-11).
>
> We had contemplated Mary as being set within the Trinity, but now, because of her Son, in her own particular way, we saw her as containing the Trinity.[35]

Lubich's metaphor of Mary as the vast blue sky that embraced the sun also has an aesthetic and allegorical quality to it. Any student of physics knows that the blueness of the sky is caused by the sun that it appears to contain. Without the sun there is no sky. At the same time without the sky something of the sun's majesty and beauty would not be seen. Mary then as creature embraces God, and reflects the beauty, the feminine qualities of God. It is a perichoretic image.

Intimately connected with Mary, as *theotokos*, is her cooperation in giving birth to the Church and her relationship to the whole of creation. In a theistic understanding of creation (in contrast to a deistic one), God is not just a prime mover who leaves everything to unfold according to the laws of physics. Rather he is immanently present in all of creation by means of a perichoretic relationship. Indeed, the specific event of the incarnation is a particular instance of the immanent presence of God within all of creation, a particular instance of 'the fullness of him who is all in all' (Eph 1:23), a fullness which in the previous Biblical verse is identified with the Church (Eph 1:22). Without the incarnation, God's immanence would have been limited and would not have penetrated all of creation, since the human condition would have been excluded from this 'fullness'.

Moreover, following the model of the Trinity, God's immanence within creation is a particular expression of the perichoretic relationship within the Trinity. As Trinity, God embraces the entire creation, including his bride the Church, because outside of God there is nothing, while at the same time, following Lubich's understanding, Mary contains the Trinity. This offers one explanation of Rahner's identification of the immanent and economic Trinity. It is mediated by the Holy Spirit whose presence in creation culminates with Mary. Through the power of the Holy Spirit, Mary contains God just as creation contains God. Moreover, this perichoretic relationship between the creator and creation, which has been there from the moment of creation, takes on a particular (but universal) meaning with the incarnation and *Theotokos*. They occur simultaneously. Historically, Mary becomes the Mother of God at the moment of his conception in her womb, analogous to the co-penetration of the creator into creation through the perichoretic relationship, but also historically this pericoresis is extended to the entire humanity with Mary's second *fiat* at the foot of the cross, where the Church is conceived.

The universe contains God incarnate, as God embraces the universe. In an analogous way Mary contains the Trinity when God created her and embraced her as 'full of grace'. Seen in this light, one can better understand why Lubich and von Balthasar place the origins of the Church at the foot of the cross when Mary united in sorrow with her Son on the cross in a co-redemptive act, embraces John as her adopted son. Once again it is a perichoretic event initiated by the creator. In his forsakenness on the cross, although Jesus embraces the abyss of darkness as a human being, it is a reality lived out within the Trinity (it is his Abba who appears to have abandoned him), while through the perichoretic relationship with her Son, Mary too experiences the divine separation as part of her embrace of the Trinity. Once again the immanent Trinity is instantly communicated as an economic Trinity. Mary's experience at the foot of the cross as the Mother of Sorrows was how she lived the experience of Jesus Forsaken in union with her Son. To quote Lubich:

> I think those who have received a special mission or calling from God can comprehend something of Mary's mysterious suffering. God often tests these people with a spiritual dark night, when

As a final comment, I think the cosmic vision of Jesus and Mary, as real symbols of the created and uncreated coming together in a dynamic way to form the Church further clarifies Doran's observation that the four-point hypothesis should be grounded both in religiously differentiated consciousness, and by 'locating everything in relation to history'.[42] However, a lot more work needs to be done, and one would hope that the future of Trinitarian theology will explore this in more detail, with the four point hypothesis serving as a heuristic.

THE IMMACULATISATION OF THE CHURCH IN HISTORY

In *Constants in Context*, Bevans and Schroeder point out that 'the Church, as such, is missionary by its very nature, because it itself is the result of the overflowing love of God, expressed in the mission of the Son and the mission of the Holy Spirit'.[43] Moreover, this mission 'is understood fundamentally as rooted in the continual self-giving and self-revelation of God within the history of creation',[44] under the threefold aspect of 'God the Father ... who freely creates the world and calls humanity in particular to share in the fullness of divine life ... by generously pouring out the divine goodness in history (the mission of the Son – AG, 3) and never ceasing to do so in history (the mission of the Spirit – AG, 4).'[45] Adding to this, I would note that the 'self-giving and self-revelation of God within the history of creation' presupposes a creation capable of receiving and reciprocating the love that it has received. This then becomes the role of Mary, and through Mary the entire Church.

It is within this context of history that the Marian profile of the Church is fulfilled and made visible. From an ontological perspective, the Marian profile was in place already at the beginning of creation, as the Immaculate one to whom the immanent life of the Trinitarian God is communicated fully to its creation through the economy of salvation. However, placed within the context of history in many ways it is the last profile to become visible and understood. As noted above, God's mission existed from the beginning as 'the continual self-giving and self-revelation within creation', which broke into human consciousness and history with the people of Israel as heralds of this discovery. Later this mission is conceived as Church at the foot of the cross and then becomes the Church's mission with the outpouring of the Holy Spirit at Pentecost.

With this last development, the Pauline profile comes quickly into light, with Peter proclaiming that Risen Christ to the people of Jerusalem (Acts 2:29-47). The Church then begins its mission with the Pauline profile being expressed through Peter. Later as history progresses, the other profiles, while always existing, are further delineated. The Johannine Profile is expressed through the ongoing works of charity undertaken by the Christian community, the Jacobine profile is more deeply understood through the contemplative tradition, and the Petrine profile is more deeply understood with the documents of Vatican I and Vatican II.

But the mystery remains. In what way is Mary of Nazareth the icon of created reality and in what way does she contain God, and how may we anticipate the future unfolding of the Marian profile in history? Interpreted from the perspective of the Marian profile, Chiara Lubich notes that the history of creation is the history of the Immaculatisation of all of creation, accomplished in some mysterious way through Mary as Immaculate Conception. Indeed, as noted earlier, Maximillian Kolbe referred to the Holy Spirit as the eternal Immaculate Conception and Mary as the created Immaculate Conception.

At the core of this mystery are relationships and especially the relationship of the universal to the particular. Mary, the Virgin Mother of God contains all of God, and yet is not God, although without her God's plan could not be realised. The final recapitulation of all of creation in Christ will be the final act of purification of the cosmos. The world will not only be imbued with the Immaculate One but also transformed by the eternal Immaculate One into the created Immaculate One in a union analogically perichoretic with the Incarnate Word, and through the Incarnate Word with all of the Trinity. The uncreated and created through the beatific vision will be perceived as a created *relatio subsistens* (to borrow from Aquinas)[46] in which the immanent and economic Trinity will be completely identified with each other. Each one of us will be present in this perichoretic relationship and yet will also be aware that we are participating in a eucharistic way in the perichoretic relationship of Mary as Mother of God with the immanent Trinity. We will be aware that she is our Mother and that

The above poem captures in a very beautiful way Mary's participation in paternity, through her maternity. She gives the Word through her nothingness, through her *kenosis*. And as a consequence of her nothingness she is full of grace, which then becomes incarnate in her through the action of the Holy Spirit. Similarly, when we silence our ego the Holy Spirit fills us with grace making us like Mary and allows the Word to speak through us. Moreover, when this reality is lived mutually our nothingness gives birth to Jesus in the midst. It is a collective *kenosis,* in which the mutual embracing of Jesus forsaken expressed as Mary desolate allows us to experience the Risen one in our midst. Lubich, while distinguishing the two, never separates them. Mary will always be the blue sky who embraces the sun.

The Church then characterised by Christ's presence among us is an ontological reality – fruit of our becoming empty like Mary through the action of the Holy Spirit. With the presence of Jesus in the midst we become living churches.

The embrace of Jesus forsaken as spouse corresponds to a participation in paternity by enabling us to become Mother and Father to others; our cooperation with the Holy Spirit enables a *kenotic* participation in passive spiration by allowing him to dwell in us; the reaching out to our neighbour in charity enables a cooperation with the Holy Spirit through participating in active spiration; and finally our embrace of Jesus forsaken through our cooperation with the Holy Spirit, enables us to experience the life and light of God within us with whom we are in relationship. This light is a foretaste of the beatific vision, a sense of completeness within our lives which we identify with living the light of glory. It is the fullness of joy that comes from having Jesus in the midst, an intellectual understanding that comes from making the 'ineffable' effable in our lives. And finally, we give birth to Jesus in the midst when we are collectively Mary.

CONCLUSION

At this juncture we bring the discussion about Mary to a close. The four supernaturally created realities owe their formal existence to the existence of the Church as mystical body, which participates in paternity (and maternity) by being the source of life for others, is sustained in existence by grace, is fount of charity through its service to all, and restores people to the light of glory through its offer of redemption. At the core of this Church is a created *relatio subsistens* characteristic of an analogical perichoretic relationship between Jesus and Mary, between the uncreated and the created, a relationship in which the immanent Trinity is equal to the economic Trinity.

Closely related to this is the understanding of the Church as 'bride of Christ', and consequently as full of grace. Furthermore, in affirming the Church in this way, the sacraments which are themselves supernatural gifts and sources of grace can now be subsumed under the theology of Church, and understood from the perspective of the four-point hypothesis or equivalently from the perspective of the Marian profile of the Church. Indeed they are an expression of the Church's life, for without the Church there are no sacraments.

On a final point, we note that the Catholic understanding of Church is very different to the Protestant one. Indeed, in this sense Catholicism is closer to Pure Land Buddhism in that both have an ontological sense of the oneness of creation and also aware of the underlying role of the feminine in constituting this oneness.

In conclusion, the Marian profile serves to unify the other profiles of the Church. It recognises that in reality the whole created universe symbolised by 'a woman clothed with the sun, with the moon under her feet, and on her head a crown of twelve stars' (Rv 12:12) is intimately connected with the Church, through the presence of the Risen Lord. But 'she kept silent because the two could not speak at once' and 'upon the nothingness of the creature Jesus spoke and said: himself'. Through her 'the Word became flesh and dwelt among us', (Jn 1:14) while at the same time 'in him were created all things ... all things were created through him and for him. He is before all things, and in him all things hold together' (Col 1:15-17), as the created Immaculate One.

40 Ibid.

41 Lubich, *Mary,* p. 39.

42 Doran, *Systematic Theology*, p. 76.

43 Bevans and Schroeder, *Constants in Context,* New York: Orbis, 2005, p. 287.

44 Ibid., p. 287.

45 Ibid., p. 287.

46 *Summa Theologiae,* Ia, q.29, a.4.

47 Chiara Lubich, 'Jesus in Our Midst: To Make Visible The Presence Of The Risen Lord In The Church', *New Humanity Review* 14 (2009), pp. 3–10.

48 Rahner, 'The Spirituality of the Church of the Future', *Theological Investigations*, 20.

49 Lubich, *Essential Writings,* New York: New City Press, 2006, pp. 233–4.

50 Lubich, *Mary*, p. 100.

TOWARD A RENEWED UNDERSTANDING OF INTERNAL PARTICIPATION IN THE EUCHARIST

DR JAMES A. WICKMAN DMIN
Georgetown University, Washington DC

The idea of active participation in the liturgy has been at the forefront of the liturgical renewal since the Second Vatican Council fifty years ago. The activities of implementation of the renewal have included a great deal of development related to the meaning of and place of *actuosa participatio*.[1] The first document promulgated by the Council, *The Constitution on the Sacred Liturgy*, notably called for this renewal in paragraph 14:

> Mother Church earnestly desires that all the faithful should be led to that fully conscious, and active participation in liturgical celebrations which is demanded by the very nature of the liturgy. Such participation by the Christian people as 'a chosen race, a royal priesthood, a holy nation, a redeemed people' (1 Pt 2:9; cf. 2:4-5), is their right and duty by reason of their baptism.
>
> In the restoration and promotion of the sacred liturgy, this full and active participation by all the people is the aim to be considered before all else; for it is the primary and indispensable source from which the faithful are to derive the true Christian spirit.[2]

ROOTED IN BAPTISM

The Second Vatican Council rooted the call to active participation in baptism. It is through baptism that one becomes a member of the body of Christ and receives the summons to live as a member in the world:

> By God's gift, through water and the Holy Spirit, we are reborn to everlasting life. In his goodness, may he continue to pour out his

> blessings upon all present, always, wherever they may be, faithful members of his holy people.[3]

Through water and the Holy Spirit, God's faithful people celebrate the sacraments and take part in the life of the Church. This is especially true for the celebration of the Eucharist, as participation in the sacraments is the realisation of the new life in Christ that is promised in baptism. 'Really partaking of the body of the Lord in the breaking of the eucharistic bread, we are taken up into communion with him and with one another.'[4] The Baptised participate both in the sacraments and in God's grace that is given in the sacraments. Through taking part in the breaking of the bread and coming into communion with each another and Christ, they live differently in the world. Participation in the liturgy is essential to living the Christian life.

What does 'fully conscious and active participation' mean then, and what does it look like? How is baptism the root of participation and what does it signify? Mark Searle has put it this way:

> Baptism creates for those being baptised a new set of relationships to Christ, to the Church, and to the world. Anyone who is baptised, then, assumes the responsibility of taking part in representing God to the world and the world to God because this is the work of Christ that has passed over into the liturgy of the Church.[5]

Taking part in the actions of the liturgy, the ritual of the liturgical act, is essential to the formation of these relationships and doing the work of Christ in the world. Through the actions of the liturgy itself, the members of the body of Christ *become* the body of Christ, more fully, and more actively, more consciously.

EXTERNAL PARTICIPATION

This type of participation is taking part in the 'external' expressions of the liturgy. The ritual actions of the liturgical act are taken up as the activity of those who are gathered in worship. The *Constitution on the Sacred Liturgy* describes the need for this kind of participation:

> The people should be encouraged to take part (in the liturgy) by means of acclamations, responses, psalmody, antiphons and songs,

> as well as by actions, gestures, and bodily attitudes. And at the proper times all should observe a reverent silence.[6]

Mark Searle calls this the 'formal' characteristic of ritual behaviour.[7] This type of formal participation 'calls for conformity rather than uniqueness, practice rather than inventiveness. It puts words into our mouths and assigns us roles to act out'.[8]

Many Catholics who attend Church today have learned that 'fully conscious and active participation' is the goal of the liturgy. Singing, responding, taking part in various gestures such as standing, sitting, and processing are all essential to active participation. Throughout the years since the Second Vatican Council, in normal celebrations of the liturgy at the parish, they are done well. However, formational efforts on the liturgy at the average parish have focused on information about the liturgy. The result is that most catechesis imparts information, rather than teaching how to 'live out' the liturgy. As Kathleen Hughes says: 'What is needed is a way to help us enter the world of the liturgy, not simply to think about it but to dwell inside it, not remaining detached students or spectators but rather allowing ourselves to be captivated and claimed by the mystery that unfolds.'[9]

MOVING BEYOND THE EXTERNAL

The *Constitution on the Sacred Liturgy* speaks of the essential character of the Church as active and contemplative, physical and spiritual:

> It is of the essence of the Church that she be both human and divine, visible and yet invisibly equipped, eager to act and yet intent on contemplation, present in this world and yet not at home in it; and she is all these things in such wise that in her the human is directed and subordinated to the divine, the visible likewise to the invisible, action to contemplation, and this present world to that city yet to come, which we seek.[10]

Participants in the liturgy must learn to move beyond the externals. Sacraments are a deeper experience of God's grace that is already present in the world.[11] As important as the ritual of the liturgical celebration is for our experience of the grace of God, our participation in the sacraments goes beyond taking part in the ritual alone. What is called for is paying attention to both the action of the liturgy and contemplation on that action – both engagement and contemplation. The *Constitution on the Sacred Liturgy* says this in paragraph 48:

> The Church, therefore, earnestly desires that Christ's faithful, when present at this mystery of faith, should not be there as strangers or silent spectators; on the contrary, through a good understanding of the rites and prayers they should take part in the sacred action conscious of what they are doing, with devotion and full collaboration. They should be instructed by God's word and be nourished at the table of the Lord's body; they should give thanks to God; by offering the Immaculate Victim, not only through the hands of the priest, but also with him, they should learn also to offer themselves; through Christ the Mediator, they should be drawn day by day into ever more perfect union with God and with each other, so that finally God may be all in all.[12]

This paragraph encourages those present to go beyond the externals because it calls for involvement of both the mind and the body. Three aspects of moving into the internal are identified: 'conscious ... with devotion and full collaboration.'[13] Each of these three elements implies a *mindfulness* about the actions of the liturgy and reflection on them. This mindfulness goes beyond the ritual elements alone because it carries the participant into the meaning behind the ritual.[14]

The opening paragraphs of the *General Instruction of the Roman Missal* (GIRM) are also helpful in expanding an understanding of interior participation:

> It is therefore of the greatest importance that the celebration of the Mass be so arranged that the sacred ministers and the faithful taking part in it, according to the proper state of each, may derive from it more abundantly those fruits for the sake of which Christ the Lord instituted the eucharistic sacrifice of his body and blood and entrusted it to the Church.[15]

Participation here is a vision not so much of what is done – in action, word or deed – but of the result of action and contemplation. This deeper level of prayerfulness is essential to a development of the interior dimension. As Mark Searle wrote when he examined how participation is understood today, 'participation, it now appears, means much more than getting the assembly to appear more involved'.[16] Participation requires that the people understand what they are doing, why they are doing it, and to whom it is directed. Searle says there are two sides to this expanded understanding:

> On the front side is the gathered assembly and its ritual performance. On the hind side is the mystery of the invisible God. Between the two is the mystery of the Church as the body of Christ. The challenge in liturgical practice is to know how to move from the visible to the invisible, from the human to the divine, from the signifier to the signified. For this, the key word is 'participation'.[17]

There must be an inward dimension of participation equal to the outward. The externals are necessary for entering into the ritual of the liturgy. The interior aspect is not present without ritual efforts. These two dimensions are not only dependent on each other, one can even go so far as to say that fully conscious and active participation *does not exist* without both interior and exterior, with the visible leading to the invisible and then back to the visible again.

The question that now comes to mind is this: what does movement to a renewed reflection on interior participation look like? How does one understand participation that goes beyond the visible to the invisible? I propose that that understanding is rooted in a renewed appreciation of the sacrifice of Christ. Taking part in the sacrifice is essential to moving beyond the experience itself to the deeper meaning. My hope is that an increased awareness of and deeper contemplation on the actions of Christ in the liturgy, and how we take part in those actions, will lead to a deeper involvement.

THE SACRIFICE OF CHRIST

The sacraments are a participation the Paschal mystery, in the passion, death and resurrection of Christ. It is here that we join with Jesus in giving of his very self to God the Father. However, most who come to the liturgy week after week do not consider this as part of active participation. One must remember that the sacrifice of Christ takes place on the altar each time the Eucharist is celebrated, and it is central to participation:

> To carry out the will of the Father, Christ inaugurated the kingdom of heaven on earth and revealed to us the mystery of that kingdom. By his obedience he brought about redemption. The Church, or, in other words, the kingdom of Christ now present in mystery, grows visibly through the power of God in the world ... As often as the sacrifice of the cross, in which Christ our Passover was sacrificed, is celebrated on the altar, the work of our redemption is carried on, and, in the sacrament of the eucharistic bread, the unity of all believers who form one body in Christ is both expressed and brought about. All men are called to this union with Christ, who is the light of the world, from whom we go forth.[18]

Christian sacrifice involves a giving of self. Christ gives of himself to God the Father as gift, out of pure love. This gift of Christ is the true Christian sacrifice that is, according to Edward Kilmartin, grounded in the action of God:

> Sacrifice in the New Testament understanding – and thus in the Christian understanding – is, in the first place, the self-offering of the Father in the gift of his Son, and in the second place the unique response of the Son in his humanity to the Father, and in the third place, the self-offering of believers in union with Christ by which they share in his covenant relation with the Father.[19]

It must also be remembered that the action of God comes first, in the gift of Jesus for the salvation of the world. To that gift, Christ responds in his self-offering to God. Jesus did this once and for all on the cross at Calvary, and in the liturgy that action is *re-presented*. 'The sacrifice of Christ on the cross is represented to the liturgical assembly in the action by which the sacrament of Christ's somatic real presence is constituted.'[20] God the Father gave Christ to the world, Christ returned that gift to the Father on the cross, and in the liturgy that sacrifice is present in a real way.

At that same celebration of the liturgy, those who gather together in praise and thanksgiving join in with the self-gift of Jesus. We respond to the love that we have been given in Christ and give freely of ourselves, as Jesus did. French theologian Louis-Marie Chauvet calls this the 'gift – reception – return-gift' symbolic exchange.[21] An understanding of this exchange will help us understand how those who are gathered at the eucharistic celebration take part in the sacrifice.

Christ is freely given by God the Father as gift to humanity. 'For God so loved the world that he gave his only Son, so that everyone who believes in him might not perish but might have eternal life' (Jn 3:16). This gift is given out of pure love, and it is out of that same love that Christ gave up his life to God the Father. Humanity is then caught up in this gift exchange between Father and Son. Therefore, in the celebration of the Eucharist all who are gathered join in the gift of self to God the Father that is given by the Son. We participate by giving freely of ourselves just as Christ does. In this exchange, it is important to remember two key elements.

First, the gift is not dependent on the actions of humans, but entirely dependent on God. It is freely given. 'In the sacraments, the position of gift is occupied by God's gratuitous action. Under this aspect of gratuitousness, God's grace is not something due.'[22] The gift is given purely out of love, which is God. It is a gift of pure grace, and there is nothing that human beings can do to deserve this pure gift.

Second, the reception of this gift of God's grace requires the return gift of faith. What is this return gift of faith all about? The reception of God's grace requires conversion. It requires a change of heart and a change of the way one lives one's life.[23] Although this is all at God's initiative, and it is not dependent on human faith, the return-gift of a life lived anew in grace and mercy is a given. Chauvet goes so far as to say that if there is no return-gift, grace *as grace* from God is not received: 'The reception of grace as grace (and not as something else which would be more or less magical) never goes without a task; it implies the ethical return-gift of justice and mercy.'[24]

Therefore, an understanding of participation as joining with the sacrifice of Christ in the Eucharist is an essential element of coming to a deeper understanding of participation. Interior participation, then, is found in uniting with Jesus' gift of himself, and in turn giving to others. This is what we celebrate in the Eucharist and it leads to real change in the hearts of people in their daily lives. This gifting is found in how each person lives after they leave Mass. It is a way of carrying the Eucharist beyond the walls of the Church. It is this type of participation that goes beyond the Church on Sunday mornings and into everyday life.

It is through the liturgical celebration that the relationship of salvation is made real and present. Called together by God, the people of God celebrate the reality of the salvation given in Christ, and respond by giving of self. The gift of grace is given by God, received by people, and the only return gift possible is to give to others. Sacrifice as active participation in the liturgy means that a response of self-gift to others is, in a manner of speaking, required. This response 'explicitly commits Christians to emulate and to make their own the virtuous dispositions of the human Jesus in his response to the Father'.[25]

CONCLUSION

The liturgy is the work of the people, and that work is to join in with the work of God. The work of the people is not just to pray and sing, listen and read, give and receive the Eucharist, but also to participate in the interior actions of the celebration. They give thanks and praise to God for having invited all to this banquet and join with Christ in his gift to the Father. The *Constitution on the Sacred Liturgy* says this:

> The liturgy is the summit toward which the activity of the Church is directed; at the same time it is the font from which all her power flows. For the aim and object of apostolic works is that all who are made sons of God by faith and baptism should come together to praise God in the midst of his Church, to take part in the sacrifice, and to eat the Lord's supper.[26]

In this movement toward a renewed understanding of interior participation, we see a progression from the visible to the invisible and then back to the visible once again. We are seeking to develop a new appreciation of participation that would foster deeper understanding of the liturgy and lead to greater personal engagement in the event of the liturgy. The ultimate meaning is found in the living out of the sacrament in daily life. It is all about what happens when one leaves the Church on Sunday morning. This is where the love and mercy of God are made visible in the world through the actions of the people who have been renewed in Christ at the sacramental celebration.

NOTES

1 The phrase *actuosa participatio* first appeared in *Tra le Sollecitudini,* the 1903 Motu Proprio of Pius X. In the introduction to this document, the Holy Father expressed the need for an instruction on sacred music.

2 Second Vatican Council, *Sacrosanctum Concilium: Constitution on the Sacred Liturgy,* Vatican: Libreria Editrice Vaticana, 1963, 14.

3 International Committee on English in the Liturgy, 'Rite of Baptism for Children', *The Rites of the Catholic Church*, Collegeville, MN: The Liturgical Press, 1990, 1:70.

4 Second Vatican Council, *Lumen Gentium: Dogmatic Constitution on the Church,* Vatican: Libreria Editrice Vaticana, 1964, 7.

5 Mark Searle, *Called to Participate: Theological, Ritual, and Social Perspectives,* Barbara Searle and Anne Y. Koester, eds, Collegeville: Liturgical Press, 2006, p. 31.

6 *Sacrosanctum Concilium,* 30.

7 Searle, *Called to Participate,* pp. 20–2. Formal is one of four characteristics of ritual Searle identifies here, the others being collective, performance, and formative.

8 Ibid., p. 20.

9 Kathleen Hughes, *Saying Amen: A Mystagogy of Sacrament*, Chicago: Liturgy Training Publications, 1999, p. 7.

10 *Sacrosanctum Concilium,* 2.

11 For a full exploration of sacramentality as the general framework for celebrating the sacraments in the world, see Kevin Irwin, 'A Sacramental World: Sacramentality as the Primary Language for Sacraments', *Worship* 76:3 (May 2002), pp. 197–211.

12 *Sacrosanctum Concilium,* 48.

13 Ibid., 48.

14 See Hughes, *Saying Amen*, 25–8, for a complete explanation of the process of liturgical contemplation that Hughes proposes.

15 United States Conference of Catholic Bishops, *General Instruction of the Roman Missal,* Washington DC, United States Conference of Catholic Bishops, 2002, 17.

16 Searle, *Called to Participate*, p. 44.

17 Ibid., p. 44.

18 *Lumen Gentium,* 3.

OPENING WORDS OF THE SYRO-MALABAR LITURGY

The celebrant begins the liturgy singing or saying the solemn formula '*Puqdankon*' (*Mandatum Vestrum*) to which the assembly responds '*Puqdane Da-Mesiha*' (*Mandatum Christi*). The literary translation of these Syriac words is 'Your Command' and 'The Command of Christ'. The English translation given in the liturgical text is as follows: The celebrant says, 'Let us begin this *Qurbana* in accordance with the command given to you' and people respond, 'We do this in accordance with the command of Christ.'[2] The beginning of this formula and its incorporation into the Syro-Malabar liturgy are apparently obscure.[3] Nevertheless, for the very opening of the liturgy, it has deep theological importance.

Philological studies show that the Syriac term *Puqdana* originates from the verb *Pqad* which means command, designate, entrust, last will, testament, etc.[4] *Puqdana* has its meaning of 'to be bound by a testament' or 'to have the command of'. If so, *Puqdanakon* may mean: 'to whom do you adhere?' 'with whom are you in communion?' 'whose faith do you profess?' The answer is: 'we adhere to Christ', 'we have faith in Christ', 'we come together as Jesus commanded'.[5] Philological study of the Syriac words *Puqdankon/Puqdaneh Da-Mesiha* brings out the social and communitarian aspects of the Syro-Malabar Eucharistic liturgy.

QURBANA AS A SOCIAL FUNCTION

It is customary among St Thomas Christians to ask permission of the assembled to begin a social function. There are many social customs among them preceeded by asking permission of the assembly to begin the function. According to such custom, someone elicits the approval of the assembly before a ceremonial action which is of social and communitarian character.

For example, the marriage customs, such as *Antham Charthal,*[6] *Mylanchiyidal,*[7] *Maduramkodukkal,*[8] come under such communitarian customs. All these ceremonies are performed only after getting the approval of the assembly. Therefore some authors trace the origin of the formula *Puqdanakon* to these social and communitarian customs of Malabar. The resemblance of this usage with the social and communitarian events in the life of the Thomas Christians of Malabar and the use of the plural form of the word confirm the communitarian origin and character of the formula.[9] Holy *Qurbana* is the official act of the whole Church and this seeking of permission from the gathered assembly indicates the communitarian aspect of *Qurbana*. Therefore, this seeking of permission which is not asking authorisation of the assembly but invitation to take part in it actively reflects the social nature of the liturgy.[10]

COMMAND OF CHRIST

These introductory words remind us of various commands of Christ in relation with worship and liturgical celebration, namely, the command to reconcile, the command to love, the command to gather in his name, command to do what he has done, etc. The Church always acts in accordance with the command of Christ and this is the source of her belief in the Eucharist.[11] The Church as such has the power, to gather and to do what it must do in that gathering, only on God's command alone.[12] The intoning of the Syro-Malabar *Qurbana* itself is with a reflection on the command of the Lord. This fact is recalled to the participants at the beginning of the *Qurbana*, as is evident from the response of the community: 'We do this in accordance with the command of Christ.'

All we can say about the eucharistic celebration is that it is because we do here and now what Christ commanded us. It is by the celebration of the Eucharist that we carry out the command of Christ.[13] As Nicolas Cabasilas explains, 'Eucharistic consecration takes place not because the priest recites what Christ has done and commanded to be done but because we fulfil the will of Christ, in accordance with his command.'[14]

COMMAND TO GATHER IN HIS NAME

'Where two or three are gathered in my name, I am there among them' (Mt 18:20). It is the desire of Christ that his followers gather together in his name. Whenever they are gathered together, they have to do in his memory what he has done, that is, the Eucharist (Lk 22:19; 1 Cor 11:23-26).[15]

The command to gather together in his name is recalled in the introductory words of the Syro-Malabar liturgy. The first important and fundamental action of the Eucharist is the gathering in Christ's name. In such a liturgical assembly there is the special presence of him.

The fact that liturgy is the celebration of a gathered assembly is well brought out in the rites and prayers of the *Qurbana*. The fourth *G'hantha*[16] says: 'We are gathered together in your name commemorating and celebrating this awesome mystery.'[17] This prayer is connected with the third *G'hantha*: 'We also, your weak, frail and miserable servants are gathered together.'[18] 'We' here means the liturgical assembly. The prayers present the participants of the liturgy as a congregation assembled in the Church before the holy altar in the name of Christ to celebrate his redemptive mystery.[19]

The phrase in the third *G'hantha* 'when you are gathered together in my name, do this in remembrance of me' is inspired by Mt 18:20. The whole worshipping community is gathered in the name of Christ and by this very fact the congregation enjoys the presence of Christ amidst its members.

The phrase 'who are gathered together' or 'when you are gathered together' is not found in the biblical sources. Nevertheless, a similar phrase we see in St Ephrem: 'When you are gathered together in my name as a Church, wherever it is, do what I did, in remembrance of me.'[20]

As Judith M. Kubicki observes, the act of gathering is not simply a preliminary to the eucharist. Rather, it is in itself a Eucharistic act. Our act of gathering enables us to become mindful again of who we really are: the body of Christ, the Church, gathered in the Word to give thanks and praise and to share the bread of life and the cup of salvation.[21]

DO THIS IN REMEMBRANCE OF ME

The introductory words of the Syro-Malabar liturgy also contain the notion of remembrance and responds to the command of Jesus 'do this in memory of me' (Lk 22:19). Every celebration of the Eucharist is inspired by the command of the Lord and consequently it is a commemoration or memorial of the Christ event.[22]

The idea of commemoration is basic to the understanding of eucharistic theology. 'Do this in remembrance of me', the command of Christ to the apostles at the Last Supper (Lk 22:19; 1 Cor 11:24), reminds us of the memorial aspect of Passover celebration (Ex 13:9). Christ gave a new meaning to the paschal rite and the emphasis was on doing it henceforth in his.[23]

Jesus' command to celebrate his memory becomes a salutary norm for the Church to be earnestly followed. In 1 Cor 11:25, the commandment is that the community should celebrate this as anamnesis and repetition of the Lord's Supper. It is primarily a command to repeat the rite in the future as a remembrance of Jesus.[24]

Besides the opening verses, the prayer of the presentation of the gifts and the prayer immediately following the institution narrative recall this command as coming from him to be followed time and again.[25] We have at the end of the fourth *G'hantha*, a portion often qualified as anamnesis, which gives us a clear picture of the celebration of the paschal mystery of Christ as the fulfilment of the command of Christ: 'And we also are gathered together in your name, and stand before you at this time and have received by tradition the example which is from you, rejoicing and glorifying, commemorating and celebrating this great mystery of the passion, death, burial and resurrection of our Lord and saviour Jesus Christ.'[26]

The liturgical assembly is gathered together according to the command of the Lord to thank and praise for the great favours which God has done to the humanity. After the institution narratives, the theme of memorial goes along with the act of thanksgiving: 'As we have been commanded, O my Lord, we are gathered together because you have done great favours which cannot be compensated.'[27] The Church ceases to be what she is when she does not become the anamnesis of the salvation history. She exists to commemorate and celebrate and to live the salvation and life in Christ.[28]

RECONCILIATION

When Christians gather together for the celebration of the Eucharist, they form a community which shares in Christ's redemption. It is not a perfect community and since its members are sinful, it has to undergo the process of purification and sanctification before celebrating the mystery of love.[29] The ecclesial character of reconciliation with God and humanity is very well brought out in the very initial rite of the Syro-Malabar *Qurbana*. By reciting 'Your command', the celebrant enquires whether the faithful have come before achieving reconciliation in accordance with the command of Christ. That is because reconciliation with others is a necessary condition to offer the sacrifice (Mt 5:25).[30]

Liturgy is the means to reconciliation with God and others. This spirit of reconciliation is evident in the very structure of the Syro-Malabar *Qurbana*. The first penitential rite in the post-anaphora part of the *Qurbana* aims at reconciliation between God and humanity, whereas the second penitential rite is intended to seek reconciliation between the members of the community. We find several prayers which request for pardon of offences and remission of sins. Washing of hands and incensing are specially meant for forgiveness of sins.[31]

The East-Syrian liturgy, through its prayers, often reminds the participants that the communion in the Eucharist effects primarily the remission of sins. The Church being the sacrament and dispenser of salvation, and considering the social and communitarian dimensions of sin, the liturgical assembly becomes the best context for the reconciliation.[32]

COMMAND TO LOVE ONE ANOTHER

The root *pqad* has also the derivative meaning such as last will, the testament, etc.[33] The root *pqad* is used in John 13:14 in the *Peshitta* version of the Bible. This helps us to see the liturgical assembly as a community united to the person of Christ and among themselves by Christ's command of love. The formula said by the priest can also, therefore, be interpreted as asking the assembly for their readiness to be united in love to Christ and fellow beings and to be reconciled with the Church, the mystical body of Christ.[34] In this sense, the formula points to the purity of the faith of the community. Love and faith are intimately related to each other and one depends on the other. The response of the community, then, would be the profession of true and pure faith in Christ and the love and reconciliation with the Church.

The opening words of the liturgy bring to mind the commandments given to us by Jesus: 'You shall love the Lord, your God, with all your heart with all your soul, and with all your mind. You shall love your neighbour as yourself' (Mt 22:37-39). We should be able not only to pardon but also to love our offenders because love is the characterising mark of Christians (Jn 13:34-35).

In the prayer of the faithful of the Syro-Malabar liturgy we find: 'For the concord of love, which is the bond of perfection in the fullness of the Holy Spirit, we ask from you O Lord.'[35] Before the second *G'hantha*, the priest prays for the entire community: 'Sow in us, O my Lord, love and concord with one another and with all, by your grace and mercies.'[36]

Jesus commands us not only to love God but also our neighbour with all our being. It follows then, that as we seek reconciliation with God, we must also seek to be reconciled with our brothers and sisters. In fact Jesus teaches us that when we have caused an offence against another person, it is unacceptable to come to worship God. 'So when you are offering your gift at the altar, if you remember that your brother or sister has something against you, leave your gift there before the altar and go; first be reconciled to your brother or sister, and then come and offer your gift' (Mt 5:23-24).

INVITATION TO ACTIVE PARTICIPATION

The eucharistic celebration is of a profoundly communitarian nature since all the members collaborate for its performance. The Church is very conscious of the need of the active participation of the faithful.[37] The Second Vatican Council instructs that a communal celebration involving the presence and active participation of the faithful is to be preferred to a celebration that is individual.[38]

The liturgy calls for the involvement of the whole community in celebration. Therefore, active participation must be promoted by means of response, hymns, attitudes and gestures etc. The liturgy is not merely the affair of the clergy alone; it is not a clerical concern, but something that concerns the entire Church community. The Church as a whole is a cultic community, and the whole community, not merely the priest, has the cultic task to perform.[39]

In the Syro-Malabar *Qurbana*, the liturgical assembly is actively involved and contributes their share in the liturgy as a corporate action in the celebration. The fact that liturgy is really the 'people's prayer' is indicated by the invitation given by the celebrant and the reply from the community, namely, 'your command' and 'the command of Christ'. Syro-Malabar *Qurbana* keeps the hierarchical distinction of the assembled quite clearly, but allows for constant communication between them and for the united action of all.

The structure of the Syro-Malabar *Qurbana* demands for a meaningful celebration – the active involvement of all the participants. There are prayers and rites reserved to the main celebrant, concelebrants, assisting deacons, other servers and faithful.

Coming to the concrete analysis of the prayers of the Syro-Malabar eucharistic liturgy, the number of the prayers to be recited by each section in the liturgical assembly manifests the extent of the possibility of the active participation: for the celebrant seventy-five prayers, servers nineteen prayers, priest and the community together three prayers, community and the servers together two prayers and the community alone forty prayers. Besides, there are thirteen propers to be sung or recited by the choir and the community during the celebration. The celebrant addresses the congregation several times to evoke replies from them. The liturgical text also prescribes the participation of the deacon whose principal function is to strengthen the contact between the priest at the altar and the congregation. Thus the active communal participation is included in the very nature of the Syro-Malabar *Qurbana*.[40]

COMMUNITARIAN DIMENSIONS OF THE LITURGY

The Syro-Malabar liturgy promotes by all means the involvement of the gathered community for the fruitful celebration and the introductory words of the *Qurbana* highlight the importance of the communitarian and the social dimensions of the liturgy and Christian life.[41]

Salvation which is offered to the faithful is basically communitarian and ecclesial. The Council throws light on this fact in the following words: 'It has pleased God to make humans holy and save them not merely as individuals without any mutual bonds, but by making them into a single people.'[42] Liturgy is always community worship, not that of an isolated individual. It is the whole community that prays together. The dialogical nature of the liturgy deepens the communitarian character of The Syro-Malabar Church. For example, the first and second person plural used so frequently in the prayers of the Syro-Malabar liturgy emphatically underline the togetherness of the gathered assembly.[43]

The structure and content of the prayers abundantly demonstrate the collective character of the liturgy.[44] The participation of each member of the congregation strengthens the bond of the ecclesial community. The liturgy is so communitarian in nature that all the participants have their own active parts to play in the liturgical service.[45] 'Liturgical services are not private functions, but are celebrations of the Church, and therefore, liturgical services pertain to the whole body of the Church.'[46] In the liturgy, the whole public worship is performed by the mystical body of Jesus Christ, that is, by the head and the members.[47] Therefore, it is the action of the whole Church.[48]

The faithful gather as God's children when they come together to the Eucharist. At the Eucharist, they are not mere individuals coming there for direct personal experience of God. They have met God personally and now come to share that experience with their fellow-Christians. They have gathered together not merely as individuals but as Christians, and the community proclaims this fearlessly and proudly right at the start of the Syro-Malabar *Qurbana*. By this invitation and answer, the gathered assembly is reminded of the communitarian dimensions of this sacrament and the role they have to play in making it a reality.

RESPONSE TO THE DIVINE CALL

The liturgy announces the message of salvation to a worshipping community. The Church as a liturgical assembly is convoked to hear and to respond to God who speaks to them in the Word and sacrament. This response to the divine address comes naturally from the people of God, the gathered community for worship. We can rightly say, from the dynamism and content of the prayers of the Church, that the ecclesial celebration is the place where God communicates himself to his people and awaits from them a response.[49] Our impulse to gather for worship is itself a response to an invitation that God gestures to humanity through the life, death and resurrection of Jesus Christ.[50]

Apart from the descending dimensions, the liturgy has its ascending dimensions too. Besides God reaching down to humanity, human beings also ascend to God through their positive response. This response is devised in the Liturgy of the Word by a variety of means which calls for active participation and leads to an experience enriching to the worshipping community. All the prayers and symbolic rituals performed in the course of the liturgy manifest the whole of responses of the community. The very introductory words of the liturgy emphasise this fact.[51]

40 Mannooramparampil, 'Horizontal Dimension of the Syro-Malabar *Qurbana*', 99–100.

41 Ibid, 99.

42 LG, 9. Mannooramparampil, 'Ecclesiology of the Syro-Malabar *Qurbana*', 18.

43 Joseph Powathil, 'The Vertical and Horizontal Dimensions in the *Qurbana*', *A Study on the Syro-Malabar Liturgy*, George Vavanikunnel, ed., Changanacheery: Sandesanilayam, 1976, p. 101.

44 Cyrus Velamparampil, 'The Ecclesial Dimension of the Liturgy of the Word in the Syro-Malabar *Qurbana*', *Christian Orient* 20 (1999), 127.

45 Ibid, 129.

46 SC, 26.

47 SC, 7.

48 Mannooramparampil, 'Ecclesiology of the Syro-Malabar *Qurbana*', 18.

49 Velamparampil, *The Celebration of the Liturgy of the Word in the Syro-Malabar Qurbana: A Biblico-Theological Analysis*, p. 248.

50 Kubicki, The Presence of Christ, 37.

51 Velamparampil, *The Celebration of the Liturgy of the Word in the Syro-Malabar Qurbana: A Biblico-Theological Analysis*, p. 299.

52 Verheul, *Introduction to the Liturgy*, p. 81.

53 Thaksa, 35.

54 George Mangalapilly, *The Church in Syro-Malabar Eucharistic Theology: A Systamatic Study of Current Positions*, Rome: Pontificia Universitas Gregoriana, 2006, p. 75.

55 Arangassery, *Ecclesial Diamansions*, p. 57.

56 Velamparampil, *The Celebration of the Liturgy of the Word in the Syro-Malabar Qurbana: A Biblico-Theological Analysis*, 122.

57 Mannooramparampil, 'Enarxis and Liturgy of the Word in the Syro Malabar *Qurbana*', p. 59.

COMMUNION AND CO-RESPONSIBILITY IN THE CHURCH

REV. FR JOHN ANTHONY BERRY DD Candidate
University of Malta

The involvement of the laity within the life of the Church is a theological issue that has witnessed a series of rapid transformations. The laity has not encountered an easy life in the community of faith. In the course of history, the Church came to recognise a rigid division of the *ordines*, wherein the clergy occupied a hierarchical status compared to the 'simple baptised' who were in complete dependence and left to be guided.

This paper seeks to appraise the current status of the lay people in the Church and their mission in the world. How should one speak of the lay presence in an ecclesiology of communion? This shall be done in three steps:

a) it will be argued that *communion* provides the space for the process of identification and integration of the laity in the life of the Church;
b) it will be seen how the Eucharist not only finds its fundamental expression and significance in communion, but is equally a piercing call to 'shared responsibility' in the Church and in the world;
c) the paper proposes five concrete actions as to better understand the co-responsibility of the laity in the ecclesiology of communion.

THE LOGIC OF COMMUNION

The road towards a renewed theology of the laity has been long and winding. For centuries, the Church has witnessed a long tradition of an exaggerated distinction between the clergy and the laity. The persistence of such a model appears in the encyclical of Pius X promulgated in 1906, *Vehementer Nos* when it says that 'with the pastoral body only rests the necessary right and authority for promoting the end of the society and directing all its members towards that end; the one duty of the multitude is to allow themselves to be led, and, like a docile flock, to follow the Pastors'.[1]

The figure of the priest emerges as the only protagonist in terms of ministry and responsibility in the Church, while the prevailing image of the laity is that of being subject to the centralisation of the pastoral life as well as the strong hierarchical relationships within the Church. This reality is grasped in the words of the Dominican theologian Yves Congar (1904–95) who says: 'The job of priests with respect to lay people is not to make them the *longa manus* of the clergy, telling them what they've got to do; but to make them believing men and women, adult Christians, leaving them to meet and fulfil the concrete demands of their Christianity on their own responsibility and in accordance with their own consciences.'[2]

Paradoxically, it was the same pope who, with the introduction of the term 'participation' in the motu proprio *Tra le Sollecitudini*[3] (22nd November 1903), led to determining steps towards an initial opening of the theological reality of communion in the Church culminating with the Second Vatican Council. The language and logic of 'communion' is unmistakably clear by its emphasis on the notion of the people of God, the baptismal dignity, the call to universal holiness as well as the application of the application of the *tria munera* to the laity as to the priests.[4] The 'pray, pay and obey' mentality of the bygone days has been irrevocably subverted.

The *ecclesiology of communion* promoted at Vatican II not only recognised the full ecclesiality of the laity, but also emphasised the notable shift from being objects to subjects in the life of the Church. Inasmuch as they are baptised, the laity does not simply 'belong' to the Church or are in it as followers, but they actually *are* and *make* the Church. The Italian theologian Giovanni Tangorra (1955) suggests that through the categories of *being* and *doing*, or that of *being in communion* and *engaged in mission*, the proper responsible role of every baptised person within the community of faith is demonstrated.[5]

Through an ecclesiology of communion, the laity discovered themselves as active members in the Church as the new people of God. The language of communion empowered the laity with personal responsibility as well as a renewed enthusiasm to effectively fulfil their mission. 'The laity,' *Lumen Gentium* 33 says, 'can also be called in various ways to a more direct form of cooperation in the apostolate of the hierarchy ... zealously participat(ing) in the saving work of the Church.' The laity is therefore making the Church more present and active, and decidedly contributing to its vitality.

Moreover, in the ecclesiology of communion of the Second Vatican Council, there are further privileged theological categories, including 'participation', 'cooperation', 'collaboration' and 'responsibility'. These are used interchangeably and the use of one term instead of another intends to highlight the mutual exchange between all the protagonists, priests and the laity, rather than simply affirming one's autonomy or commitment.

The favoured term in the area of the liturgy is that of 'participation', while that in reference to actions to be taken in the apostolate is that of 'cooperation'. For instance, *Apostolicam Actuositatem* 10 states that: 'strengthened by active participation in the liturgical life of their community, they ... earnestly *cooperate* in presenting the word of God especially by means of catechetical instruction, and offer their special skills to make the care of souls and the administration of the temporalities of the Church more efficient and effective.'[6] The term 'responsibility' appears particularly in *Lumen Gentium* 37, where it speaks of the task of the spiritual shepherds who are to 'recognise and promote the dignity as well as the responsibility of the laity in the Church'. The ecclesiology of communion favours then the laity, ever more conscious of their own *responsibility* in living as responsible adults while enhancing their action in the world and their messianic vocation of the Church.[7]

The 'ecclesiology of communion' is once again manifest in the 1985 extraordinary synod. This synod chooses to emphasise the missionary aspect of the Church, bringing in the idea of responsibility necessarily linked to the role each single baptised has in the Church. Let us refer to the final repost of this synod: 'Each and every one of us baptised, according to his or her state in the world and in the Church receives the mission to proclaim the good news of salvation in Jesus Christ. Each and every one is therefore called upon to exercise his or her responsibility.'[8]

Recovered from ancient Christianity and in the writings of the New Testament as well as the doctrine of the Fathers, communion is then a central category in theology inasmuch it helps to resolve the tension between unity and plurality. Communion assumes a central role in determining the identity of the Church.

There are four dimensions of communion. In the first place, to speak of communion is to speak of its *Trinitarian* foundation. The Holy Trinity is the origin of all communion between all people through the self-manifestation of God in Christ and in the Holy Spirit. Secondly, there is an *ethical* dimension. This refers in particular to the structures of communion wherein the organisation and style in the life of the Church should reflect above all its dogmatic origin. Thirdly, communion is also *ecclesial*. As shall be seen, the ecclesiology of communion overcomes the dialectical relationship between priests and laity and instead makes room for the new charisms in the Church. Lastly, communion is *sacramental*. Communion finds its fundamental expression in the Eucharist as the sacrament of the presence and the martyrdom of Christ. It is to this subject that we now turn.

EUCHARIST AND CO-RESPONSIBILITY

We are now interested in examining both the true significance of the Eucharist in the life of the Christian as well as the relationship between the Eucharist and co-responsibility in the Church. The recent magisterium – particularly the interventions of Benedict XVI but also John Paul II's *Ecclesia de Eucharistia* (2003) – has several times emphasised the fruit of the Eucharist in terms of communion and mission. Avoiding any bias in favour of the devotional side of the eucharistic tradition, the recent magisterium of the Church recuperates the meaning of nature of this great sacrament in the light of its fruitful liaison with the public orthopractical dimension be it ecclesial and social.

The Eucharist fosters communion and brings in the limelight the values of *sharing* and co-responsibility. This is particularly clear when related to the gesture which Christ, on the night before he died, gave his disciples the extreme *delivery*, that of himself (as a gift *par excellence*). The lived communion with Christ and the Christians among themselves is expressed in a clear manner by the apostle Paul in his *paradosis* of the Eucharist. He says: 'the cup of blessing which we bless is a communion with the blood of Christ? The bread which we break is a communion with the body of Christ? Because there is one bread, we who are many are one body, for we all partake of one bread.'[9] Once again, this is in common resonance with the Acts of the Apostles.

Let us now refer to the recent magisterium on the Eucharist. In the first place we refer to *Sacramentum Caritatis* (2007), which synthesises and re-proposes the main ideas discussed at the World Synod of Bishops taking place in 2005 and which focused its reflection on the Eucharist. There is then *Deus Caritas est* (2005), which underlines the strict relationship which runs between the love of God – of which the Eucharist represents the emblematic sign – and the *energetic zeal* in history. Analogously, in *Spe Salvi* (2007) there is a huge emphasis to bind together eschatological and historical hope. Those who work for the coming of the kingdom are called to act not out of consciences but also manifestly through just structures. The circle of encyclicals ends with *Caritas in Veritate* (2009), wherein the Christian love towards the neighbour, which finds its origin in the Eucharist, commits itself to promote human dignity.

In this sense, 'love – *caritas* – is an extraordinary force which leads people to opt for courageous and generous engagement in the field of justice and peace'. This is again mentioned in the conclusion, where it states that: 'God's love calls us to move beyond the limited and the ephemeral, it gives us the courage to continue seeking and working for the benefit of all', and that 'development needs Christians with their arms raised towards God in prayer'.[10]

But the highest prayer, the most prominent form of 'arms raised' is precisely that of the Eucharist. The Eucharist is the most obvious sign of God's will to share his deepest being with humanity, up to provide them with its own body. We refer to both the mysteries of the incarnation and the Eucharist since although they present two different faces, they belong to the same reality of a God who decidedly shares in the history of mankind. The presence of the Eucharist is then the climax of this sharing since Christ allowed himself to be truly present to humanity across the times.

The Eucharist points to a 'shared responsibility'. The common life of the early Christians, as described in the Acts of the Apostles, is

To speak of co-responsibility, we need to speak of ministries.[15] This should not be limited to that of the liturgy. We speak of a 'new ministry' that does not replace the old one, but rather integrates and completes it in terms of the world and the Church. This has taken place with the ministries of lector and acolyte, reserved only for men. New lay ministries extend to the vast field of the world, work and culture, politics and health, through forms of 'popular ministry', not necessarily formalised, such as to enable the believers to be present, on an ongoing basis and with appropriate ways of learning. Rather than simply filling up the pews in church, the laity are called to renew and identify evangelisation with all the people of God.

Another important feature is rethinking *co-responsibility in terms of evangelisation within the parish*. We are here speaking of the urgency to shift from a pastoral ministry of conserving things to the daring and outward-looking one of evangelisation. What is of importance is not the restructuring or revising of the boundaries of the parishes according to the new cultural and social challenges, but rather to rethink the parish within the perspective of the 'new evangelisation'. This does not mean a *theoretical conversion*, but a *conversion of practice* because most energies and pastoral forces are consumed centripetally *ad intra*. The new evangelisers are the priests, the religious and the laity – men and women all engaged centrifugally *ad extra*. In this sense the Christian community must learn to breathe, to use the famous expression of John Paul II, 'with two lungs', that of the strong parochial roots and that of the strong local presence in the living environment. Evangelisation in a parish cannot take place if it is simply focused on the figure of the priest. This leaves room, certainly, for the religious to resume their traditional and partly forgotten work of itinerant evangelism.

The preferential option for the poor and its daily praxis is another important area of shared responsibility. Co-responsibility depends on rediscovering a renewed commitment to real poverty in the Church.[16] This evangelical turn will be determined by the rôle of the laity. For a long time, poverty was a virtue for religious. But in the post-conciliar Church, in the season of a Church that wants to be poor in its totality and in its members, the issue of poverty becomes central to the laity. The lifestyles of the laity become the 'mirror' of the true image of a Church. Co-responsibility means remembering and practising the essential and necessary in the same manner as the gospel in holy men and women have done like Francis and Clare of Assisi, Vincent de Paul, Charles de Foucauld, Teresa of Calcutta, Oscar Romero, Dorothy Day, Abbé Pierre and the murdered monks of the Algerian desert. The responsibility to witness poverty points above all to an abiding fidelity to the gospel in the form of service and sharing.

Lastly, to speak of an ecclesiology of communion in terms of co-responsibility, there is the need of an adult faith. What matters is whether the Christian lives in an authentic way or not. There can be no new evangelisation without the total presence of real and genuine Christian lay lifestyles. It is the laity who permeate the social fabric. Men and women of faith look at the Church and world with the eyes of faith.

The call of the whole people of God is not only to personal holiness, but that edified by the Eucharist. Indeed, we are called to be architects with Christ in building this school of co-responsibility. This is an ongoing challenge. It is a challenge to the master builder as well as to the ordinary bricklayer. It is challenge cemented by communion.

eloquently written ecclesiological books in the Italian language, not yet translated into English. Owing to limited time and space, I will not elaborate extensively Acerbi's thesis, though I consider the Anglophone theological world would do well at this time to translate, study and develop these writings, with a view to arriving at a correct interpretation of the Second Vatican Council.

This book, which is a composition of the historical documents and acts of the Second Vatican Council – especially around the dogmatic document *Lumen Gentium* – offers methods and an approach which links the ecclesiology of the Church of the Patristic era with that of the Second Vatican Council. This supports the contention that one should never see hierarchical communion as divorced from sacramental communion. Bishops, therefore, are accordingly to be spiritual leaders who have a sacramental responsibility urging them to be holy and to govern in holiness within the holy Catholic Church. To govern without holiness is to govern in an imperfect way and this in the face of a secularised society makes the Church appear indistinguishable and therefore false and not credible in her audacious claims.

The Church is by her very nature a gift of the salvific act of the One and Triune God; she is the primordial sacrament of the Trinity on earth. She is a visible entity, but when viewed with the eyes of faith is also the body of Christ, the bride of Christ, the new Israel and the people of God.[1]

It is a truism that the Church finds her true and proper expression as a communion of all the baptised in the sacred liturgy. It is similarly in the liturgy that the sacramental ecclesiology of communion is understood and effected, and it is equally in the sacred liturgy that the hierarchical ecclesiology of communion can be understood and treasured.

The Fathers of the Church understood the Church as a moon that does not shine of its own light but receives the light from the sun.[2] In the same way the ecclesiological dimension cannot be understood without the Christological dimension. Christ is the light that shines and illumines all people. Analogically, the hierarchical ecclesiology of communion finds its proper expression from the sacramental ecclesiology of communion.

SECTION I: SACRAMENTAL ECCLESIOLOGY

The Church celebrates her birth on the day of Pentecost, and speaking by appropriation we say that the Church is born of the Holy Spirit. However, properly speaking, her supreme cause is the Blessed Trinity.[3] The ecclesial communion is factually a manifestation of the communion which exists between the Father and the Son in the Holy Spirit. On Pentecost day, the Holy Spirit descended upon the apostles who were united, forming but one body. Therefore the Church born of the Holy Spirit is called to that same apostolic communion.

Certain Fathers of the Church emphasised the presence of the Church as being inseparable from the presence of the Spirit. As if to say that where the Church was, the Spirit was of necessity present too. St Irenaeus, for example, maintains that: 'Where the Church is, there is the Spirit of God; and where the Spirit of God is, there is the Church and every grace, and the Spirit is truth.'[4]

The ecclesiology of the first millennium finds its place during the time of the 'undivided' Church up until the schism with the East in 1054. The Church of Rome which presides in charity persists as the centre and exemplar of the other local churches. It is the Church that is built on the tombs of the apostles Peter and Paul. The Bishop of Rome, being the successor of St Peter, is the head and chief shepherd of the universal Church. He is the head and point of reference for all bishops who together with him form but one body.

Only when there is communion between ecclesial communities can there be a clear manifestation of unity at the eucharistic banquet. However, if the communities cannot partake of the same Eucharist this reveals a lack of communion.

The Church during the first millennium was perhaps more appreciative of the mysterious or miraculous properties or marks of the Church. During that era she also enjoyed more fully the truth and reality of the marks of the Church – one, holy, Catholic and apostolic Church. Whereas schisms and heresies were not lacking, the Church strove more successfully to maintain her unity and bring the lost and separated back to the full communion of the Church. As Origen stated so poetically: 'Where there are sins, there are also divisions, schisms, heresies, and disputes. Where there is virtue, however, there also are harmony and unity, from which arise the one heart and one soul of all believers.'[5]

The word *koinonia* had an important place in the infant Church that was rapidly growing. The proper understanding of this same word *koinonia* can be said to be contained in 1 John 1:3 which states: 'That which we have seen and heard we proclaim also to you, so that you also may have fellowship with us; and our fellowship is with the Father and with his Son Jesus Christ. And we are writing this that our joy may be complete.'[6] The apostles wanted to share with their brethren what they had received: faith in the Christ, whose anointing effected in them the communion shared in the bosom of the Trinity.

The early Christians manifested their unity with God and with one another at the celebration of the Holy Eucharist where they partook of the Body and Blood of Christ. It is by participating in the Body and Blood of Christ himself that the Church in all ages manifests and will continue to manifest unity, for Christ has promised to be with his Church until the end of time. Those who do not participate in this communion deprive themselves of the spiritual benefits that the Lord thereby effects, and those who do partake at the same table are signs of the ecclesial communion manifested at the eucharistic table. Therefore the sacramental ecclesiology of communion can be said to manifest itself properly in the celebration of the Holy Eucharist.[7]

This sacramental ecclesiology of communion, therefore, is said to be sacramental because it has the Eucharist as both its visible expression and cause. Saint Paul instructs the Corinthians: 'The cup of blessing which we bless, is it not a participation in the blood of Christ? The bread which we break, is it not a participation in the body of Christ? Because there is one bread, we who are many are one body.'[8]

Saint Ignatius of Antioch speaks of the bishop as he who exercises supreme power over each local Church: 'Take care, then, to partake of one Eucharist; for, one is the flesh of our Lord Jesus Christ, one the cup to unite us in his blood, and one the altar, just as there is one bishop assisted by the presbytery and the deacons.'[9] The bishop is the hierarch in his local Church and it is around the Eucharist that the unity of the ecclesial community is manifested.

SECTION II: THE CHURCH AS A VISIBLE BODY

The Church is a juridically structured society whose members receive charisms which are to be juridically exercised. The charismatic nature of the Church is a gift of God for the mission undertaken within the Church. Charisms are gifts received within the Church and for the Church, therefore possess an immanent structure that determines how they are to be used in the Church. Consequently, from the reception of charisms there flows, of necessity, rights and duties which are of themselves morally obliging. A professor of theology, for example, who holds a canonical mandate to teach theology in a Catholic institute, is necessarily bound by rights and duties by which he has to abide, since the gift of teaching is a charism that must serve other parts of the ecclesial body. Lay persons, for example, receive different charisms to those in the clerical state, since they participate in distinct yet complementary juridical states – royal priesthood and the ministerial priesthood, respectively.

The Church as a sacrament and an ecclesial society with its exterior expression constituted and organised as a society is visible and can therefore be understood as a juridically structured entity. The Church as communion puts the focus more on its charismatic definition which is her interior being, rather than on the exterior expression which exists so that the interior life may reach full flower.[10]

Those united to Peter as visible head of Christ's Church, especially members of the college of bishops, are everything in him and are null when separated from him, for in him is the authority of Christ, head and chief shepherd. Peter remains a man, but his ministry is of divine origin – it is a charism. The ministry entrusted to the prince of the apostles is that of authority, and from Peter up to his current successor, Jesus continues to say the same words '*Tu es Petrus ... tibi dabo claves*'.[11]

The Church possesses, by her very nature a 'public nature' constituted of an organic complex means to salvation. The nature of the Church, in as much as it is public, is human and divine, just as her head and founder is fully human and fully divine. Since all the members of the hierarchy are ordained ministers, by virtue of their sacerdotal ordination they act in *persona Christi capitis*. Therefore, the hierarchy manifests the dimension of priests being *Alter Christus* where Christ continues his saving work of redemption in the world.

As Pope Benedict XVI rightly points out: 'The clear distinction between the "lay person" and the hierarchy in no way signifies opposition ... The Church, in fact, is not a place of confusion and anarchy where one can do what one likes all the time: each one in this organism, with an articulated structure, exercises his ministry in accordance with the vocation he has received.'[12] There is, therefore, a need to be fully united to Christ and to his Church. The temptation to define members of the Church as either 'conservative' or 'liberal' does great harm to the very nature of the Church. Communion with God, with the Church, and with one another is essential for the wellbeing of the Church in the world today.

SECTION III: COMMUNIO HIERARCHICA

Acerbi's *Due Ecclesiologie* demonstrates how *Lumen Gentium* is characterised by two ecclesiologies, each 'incomplete', namely: the sacramental ecclesiology of communion and the juridical ecclesiology of communion. The hierarchical ecclesiology of communion is an innovative means proposed by the Council for mediating between the two ecclesiologies mentioned. From a linguistic point of view, the terminology may seem incompatible, but when seen in the light of what communion means, especially in the Eucharist, then its meaning becomes clearer.

The hierarchical ecclesiology is the visible reality of the structured Church which can be traced back to the appointment of Peter as the chief shepherd. This ecclesiology finds its proper expression when the bishops are united in communion with one another and the Bishop of Rome as the head of the episcopal college. The Supreme Pontiff is the head of the college because he is the successor of St Peter. The bishops succeed to apostolic college although not by immediate succession as in the case of the head of the college.

Lumen Gentium, the Conciliar Constitution on the nature of the Church includes both ecclesiologies which Acerbi mentions. Cardinal Walter Kasper considers *communio hierarchica*, on the other hand, as a typical formula of compromise indicating the juxtaposition between the sacramental ecclesiology of communion and the juridical ecclesiology of unity.[13] What Kasper highlights is an important exegesis of the conciliar texts. However, to interpret *communio hierarchica* as a formula of compromise could mistakenly suggest that there were problems in the preparation of the formula.

To have a 'hermeneutic of continuity' of the tradition of the Church calls for a faithful synthesis of the ecclesiologies present since the beginning of the Church. It is equally true that if the ecclesiology prevailing during the first millennium is stressed more than that prevailing during the second millennium, then this might be interpreted with a 'hermeneutic of rupture' – that is, the first is favoured over the second. The same could be said where the ecclesiology of the second millennium is favoured over that of the first millennium. This is why the new formula *communio hierarchica* comes into the conciliar documents as a synthesis ecclesiology that will merge the two ecclesiologies.

The new formula did not fully serve to integrate the two ecclesiologies in a creative way, while retaining its fidelity to the tradition of the Church of the first and second millennium. More could probably still be done in this regard.

The Second Vatican Council clearly moves from the juridical ecclesiology of the second millennium to that of the first millennium by a renewed liturgical understanding of the Church and the bishop as high priest. However, it does this in the spirit of continuity.

The new formula used, 'hierarchical communion',[14] serves as mediation between the two ecclesiologies. Hierarchical communion also implies reference to the Roman Pontiff with whom every bishop is united in faith and episcopal office; the *missio canonica* of the bishop is received directly from papal authority. The First Vatican Council solemnly defined the primacy of the Roman Pontiff in terms of authority of jurisdiction over the universal Church, including over all bishops and the faithful.[15] The Roman Pontiff's authority extends over all in matters of doctrine and discipline because he receives this authority from Jesus himself, who calls the shepherd to 'feed the sheep'.[16]

Collegiality was the central theme and an important outcome of the Second Vatican Council. The concept of collegiality according to the then-Cardinal Joseph Ratzinger 'serves to illustrate the interior unity of the episcopal ministry'. He later adds that 'The bishop is not a bishop as an individual, but by belonging to a body, a college, which in turn represents the historical continuity of the *collegium apostolorum*.'[17]

The hierarchy should be understood as having the Roman Pontiff as the visible Vicar of Christ himself within history, and cannot be seen as divorced from Christ's immanent presence in his office.

'College' is not understood in a strictly juridical sense, that is as a group of equals who entrust their power to their president, but as a stable group whose structure and authority must be learned from revelation. For this reason, in reply to Modus 12 it is expressly said of the Twelve that the Lord set them up 'as a college or stable group'.[18]

Our understanding of the episcopal college derives directly from the apostolic college, called together by Jesus for ministry. The act of the college is that of the whole united body (*corpus*). However, this does not mean that the college votes unanimously on issues or that the act of the college is that of the majority – it is that of the college taken as a wholly integrated moral body.

The twelve apostles, together with their head, formed a college – *collegium Apostolicum*. The Bishop of Rome directly succeeds St Peter as head and member of the episcopal college. The college is always one and never plural because the members of the one college, together with its head, comprise a single reality.

It can become difficult to understand hierarchical ecclesiology if this is taken to mean a 'closed-circle' kind of authority. It is not purely the question of authority but the service rendered on account of a particular charism that each bishop possesses by virtue of the fullness of holy orders and the *missio canonica*. He is given this to respond to the salvific needs of the people and to confirm them in the truth, in continuation of the apostolic age. Apostolic succession signifies and effects continuity of the charismatic mission that the Church received from her founder.

CONCLUSION

The centre of all the ecclesiologies, be it sacramental, juridical or hierarchical has communion as its focal point. It is this communion that makes visible the catholicity of the universal Church in every local Church. It is also the communion that finds its origin in the Trinity and therefore leads the Church to be a sacrament of salvation and unity. Therefore, as much as the Second Vatican Council did not fully explain the insertion of the new formula, *communio hierarchica*, it strove to reconcile the two ecclesiologies without favouring one over the other.

The hierarchical communion should, first of all, elaborate the mystical reality present in the person and office of its head who is the pope. The pope then, as the successor of St Peter, called to confirm his brothers in the truth, invites his fellow brothers into communion to share in the *corpus mysticum*. To consider hierarchical communion only under its juridical aspect, disregarding the sacramental aspect, would be deficient. The juridical and sacramental dimensions make only one body which is inseparable. It is not possible to act juridically as if the sacramental was not present or vice-versa.

One should, according to this argument, seek to unite the two ecclesiologies, sacramental and hierarchical, so that together they may form one *corpus mysticum*.

As mentioned already, bishops are accordingly to be spiritual leaders who have a sacramental responsibility urging them to be holy and to govern in holiness within the holy Catholic Church. To govern without holiness, is to govern in an imperfect way and this in the face of a secularised society makes the Church to appear indistinguishable and therefore false and not credible in her audacious claims. A helpful ecclesiological distinction should be made between the visible and the invisible. Today, Peter is invisible to us as Peter, likewise the handing over of the keys by Jesus to him is invisible to us. However in the person of the pope, we see Peter. In his office as pope the handing over of the keys by Jesus is made visible. Therefore, we cannot collapse office and person.

It is clear especially after reading the *nota explicativa praevia*, that *communio hierarchica* actually does reconcile the two ecclesiologies of the first and second millennium; it becomes the mediator without doing away with any of the two, but emphasises the ecclesiology of communion. We can say that there is a progression from the patristic understanding of the Church as communion and back to the same theme that was partly lost in the scholastic era. Cardinal Journet reminds us that, 'Jesus leaves in our midst the mediation of the hierarchical powers and the sacramental rites, which prolong his *sensible contact* with the whole world … "Behold I am with you always, to the close of the age" (Mt 28:19-20).'[19]

NOTES

1 LG, 7 and *Catechism of the Catholic Church* (CCC), 770.

2 Cf. Ibid., 748.

3 Jn 15:26.

4 *Adversus Haereses,* bk. 3, chap. 24.

5 Origen, *Hom. in Ezech.,* 9, 1: PG, 13, 732. Cf. CCC, 817.

6 1 Jn 1:3.

7 Cf. Acts 2:42.

8 1 Cor 10:16.

9 Journet, C. *Theology of the Church,* Ignatius Press: 2004, p. 133. Cf. *Letter to the Philadelphians,* chap. 4.

10 Cf. LG, 8.

11 Cf. Mt 16:13-19.

12 Benedict XVI, General Audience, 7th March 2007.

13 Cf. Kasper, W., *Teologia e Chiesa,* Queriniana: 1989, p. 295. 'Il concetto di comunione gerarchica è una tipica formula di compromesso che sta ad indicare una giustapposizione tra l'ecclesiologia sacramentale della *communio* e l'ecclesiologia giuridica dell'unità. Per cui si è parlato di due ecclesiologie presenti nei testi del Vaticano II. Il compromesso è servito ad ottenere l'assenso della minoranza, ma non soddisfa del tutto, perché il problema che esso cela è profondo. Il principio cattolico della tradizione viva non consente di eliminare semplicemente la tradizione del secondo millennio: la continuità della tradizione esige piuttosto una sintesi creativa fra le tradizioni del primo e del secondo millennio. E questa sintesi l'ultimo concilio non è riuscito a compiere. Il che non significa che sarebbe poi compito dei concili sviluppare sintesi teologiche. Un concilio stabilisce dei "dati di fondo", mentre spetta alla successiva teologia operare le sintesi richieste.'

14 LG, 21, 22; NEP, 2.

15 LG, 22.

16 Cf. Mt 16:13-19.

17 Thornton & Varenne, eds, *The Essential Pope Benedict XVI: His Central Writings & Speeches,* New York: Harper Collins, 2008, p. 97.

18 *Notificationes given by the secretary general of the Council at the 123rd general congregation,* 16th November 1964.

19 Journet, C., *The Theology of the Church,* Szczurek, V., trans., San Francisco: Ignatius Press, 2004, p. 25.

THE BISHOP AS SERVANT TO COMMUNION: VATICAN II REVISITED

MR EDWARD J. TRENDOWSKI PhD Candidate
Religious Education and Catechetics
Catholic University of America, Washington DC

The Second Vatican Council referred to a 'diocese' as a particular Church. In a particular Church, the one, holy, Catholic, and apostolic Church is present: 'A diocese is a section of the People of God entrusted to a bishop to be guided by him with the assistance of his clergy so that, loyal to its pastor and formed by him into one community in the Holy Spirit through the Gospel and the Eucharist, it constitutes one particular church in which the one, holy, catholic and apostolic Church of Christ is truly present and active.'[1]

Therefore, in a particular Church the people of God, lay and clerics united with the bishop, are drawn into communion with other particular Churches. As *Gaudium et Spes* states, 'this is the communion of (Christ's) own body, the Church, in which everyone as members ... (renders) mutual service in the measure of the different gifts bestowed on each'.[2] These gifts of the Holy Spirit, or charisms, contribute to the mission of the Church, which is proclaiming the gospel of salvation in Jesus Christ (Jn 3:16-17).[3] One such gift is given to bishops who, 'have been designated by the Holy Spirit to take the place of the apostles as pastors of souls ...'[4]

Bishops share with all members of the Church the mission to proclaim the gospel. Yet, bishops have a distinct ministry.[5] Bishops, through episcopal consecration by the laying on of hands and with an *epiclesis* prayer,[6] receive the office of teaching, sanctifying and governing.[7] This essay examines the bishop as teacher, sanctifier and governor of a particular Church entrusted to his care. As a member of the College of Bishops, an individual bishop can act as a servant to communion for a particular Church which concurrently impacts communion in the universal Church.[8]

MUNUS DOCENDI: THE BISHOP AS 'TEACHER'

Jesus Christ begins his public ministry by announcing: 'This is the time of fulfilment. The kingdom of God is at hand. Repent, and believe in the gospel' (Mk 1:15, NAB). Christ makes the kingdom of God present in his person and offers the invitation for repentance which can lead to belief in the gospel. When Jesus gives his apostles the mandate to 'teach', it is so that they can continue his original message of repentance and gospel (cf. Mt 28:16-20; Lk 4:42-44). Yet, conscious of their own mortality and, '(i)n order that the full and living gospel might always be preserved in the Church the apostles left bishops as their successors. They gave them "their own position of teaching authority"'.[9]

Pope John Paul II stressed that, 'the living centre of the preaching of the Gospel is Christ, crucified and risen for the salvation of all peoples'.[10] This preaching, centred on Christ, is authentically handed on by bishops, 'who have received, along with their right of succession in the episcopate, the sure charism of truth'.[11] The charism of truth is a gift of the Holy Spirit conferred upon bishops by Christ and it is inherent to their office of teaching: 'Jesus Christ promised the assistance of the Holy Spirit to the Church's Pastors so that they could fulfil their assigned task of teaching the Gospel and authentically interpreting Revelation.'[12]

Because bishops receive the charism of truth from the Holy Spirit to teach the gospel and interpret revelation, their teaching requires a response by the rest of the faithful members of the Church. *Lumen Gentium* explains the response due to bishops: 'Bishops who teach in communion with the Roman Pontiff are to be revered by all as witnesses of divine and Catholic truth; the faithful, for their part, are obliged to submit to their bishop's decision, made in the name of Christ, in matters of faith and morals, and to adhere to it with a ready and respectful allegiance of mind.'[13]

Cardinal Donald Wuerl explains that the authentic teaching of the bishops in communion with the pope is inherent to the nature of the Church as *apostolic*: 'The Church is called *apostolic* precisely because she alone can trace her *Origins* to the deposit of faith entrusted to the apostles, the Twelve chosen by Jesus and charged, together with their successors, with the responsibility of teaching the true faith, making sure that it is presented clearly and applying it to the problems and needs of every age.'[14] Therefore, a bishop is responsible for overseeing everyone who hands on the faith in his diocese, including 'teachers of theology and teachers of the ecclesiastical sciences and religious education'.[15] The bishop serves communion in his particular Church by ensuring that an authentic gospel message is being announced.

In their office of teaching, bishops must be fearless in proclaiming the gospel whether it is 'favourable' or 'unfavourable' in an effort to, 'convince, rebuke, and encourage, with the utmost patience in teaching' (2 Tm 4:1-2). Bishops can set an example for the rest of the faithful by internalising the words of St Paul, 'woe to me if I do not proclaim the gospel' (1 Cor 9:16)!

As it was examined above in the words of Christ, repentance is a catalyst for belief in the gospel. The prophet Ezekiel announces that when sinful people turn from their sins, 'they shall surely live' (Ez 18:21-22; 33:7-9). The grace of conversion is granted by the Holy Spirit, leading toward the Person of Christ who manifests the divine *truth* which illuminates the *way* that leads to everlasting *life* (see Jn 14:6).

Pope Benedict XVI warned that 'the faithful are surrounded by a culture that tends to eliminate the sense of sin and to promote a superficial approach that overlooks the need to be in a state of grace in order to approach sacramental communion worthily'.[16] The reality of sin affects the individual and it affects their communion with others. Benedict XVI also points out, 'sin is never a purely individual affair; it always damages the ecclesial communion that we have entered through baptism'.[17]

Therefore, in a particular Church, a bishop is 'charged with offering a kerygmatic invitation to conversion and penance. It is his duty to proclaim with evangelical freedom the sad and destructive power of sin in the lives of individuals and in the history of communities'.[18] Saint Augustine exclaims, 'the sinner is dead, especially he whom the load of sinful habit presses down, who is buried as it were like Lazarus'.[19] But a bishop, as a vicar of Jesus Christ,[20] with prophetic teaching, by the power of the Holy Spirit, can raise sinners from spiritual death in sin to experience new life in Christ (Jn 11:25-27, 44; Rm 6:7-8).

MUNUS SANTIFICANDI: THE BISHOP AS 'SANCTIFIER'

John Paul II has commented that, '(t)he individual Bishop ... in the exercise of his office of sanctifying contributes greatly to the Church's work of glorifying God and making men holy'.[21] The bishop's 'ministry of sanctification' is 'ordered' to the holiness of the people of God.[22] All people are called to holiness.[23] Since this call is aided by the sacraments, especially the Eucharist,[24] it follows that, '(a)mong all the responsibilities of the Bishop's pastoral ministry, that of celebrating the Eucharist is the most compelling and important'.[25]

Because of Christ's presence in the Eucharist, which both manifests and efficaciously creates communion, heaven and earth are united in Christ. Cardinal Ratzinger explains that, 'the Eucharist, again, is for each local Church the point at which people are drawn into the one Christ; this is the process of all communicants becoming one in that universal communion which binds together heaven and earth; the living and the dead; past, present, and future; and opens up toward eternity.'[26] The 'universal' Church is not limited to earthly pilgrims; the universal Church also includes Christ's disciples who are in a state of purgatory and the saints in heaven.[27] The 'principle manifestation' of the universal Church occurs when the bishop celebrates the Eucharist in his particular Church.[28]

Bishops are the visible source of unity in their particular Church,[29] and '(i)t is therefore bishops who are the principal dispensers of the mysteries of God, and it is their function to control, promote and protect the entire liturgical life of the Church entrusted to them'.[30] The bishop safeguards the celebration of the sacred Liturgy for a particular Church entrusted to his care, and acts as a servant to communion by promoting a liturgical life which sanctifies. Also relevant for today, the bishop has a duty to witness to the dignity of the sacrament of marriage because of its relationship to the Eucharist.

Benedict XVI has expressed the following: 'The Eucharist, as the sacrament of charity, has a particular relationship with the love of man and woman united in marriage. A deeper understanding of this relationship is needed at the present time.'[31] The following is a humble attempt at observing a relationship between the two sacraments.

One cannot discuss the relationship between marriage and the Eucharist without beginning with baptism. The sacrament of baptism, 'is a nuptial mystery',[32] through which individuals become members of the body of Christ (cf. 1 Cor 12:12-13). In other words, when someone is baptised, they enter the new Covenant of Christ's love; sometimes imaged as a *marriage* covenant (Rv 19:5-10). Now, sacramentally, as a marriage covenant between two spouses is consummated through uniting in one flesh (Mt 19:5), the new covenant in Christ is consummated through uniting with his flesh in the Eucharist.

While contemplating the eucharistic mystery, observe how Pope John Paul II describes conjugal love between two spouses:

> Conjugal love involves a totality, in which all the elements of the person enter – appeal of the body and instinct, power of feeling and affectivity, aspiration of the spirit and of will. It aims at a deeply personal unity, the unity that, *beyond union in one flesh, leads to forming one heart and soul*; it demands indissolubility and faithfulness in definitive mutual giving; and it is open to fertility.[33]

> Authentic conjugal love, when two spouses become one flesh, aims at a deeper personal unity which ontologically aims at the formation of one heart and soul: the conjugal relationship demands indissolubility and faithfulness. Authentic married conjugal love is *both* mutually self-giving and open to new life. The *unitive* and *procreative* properties remain intact.[34]

To further illustrate the connection between marriage and the Eucharist, it helps to think of, 'the nature of Eucharist as a gift…'[35] 'In the Eucharist Jesus does not give us a "thing", but himself; he offers his own body … He thus gives us the totality of his life and reveals the ultimate origin of this love.'[36] Jesus presents the totality of his life to us in the Eucharist. As members of the 'bride of Christ', we in turn are invited to totally 'offer ourselves'[37] in an act of self-giving love. Through our free response of total self-gift with Christ, new life is possible: our personal new life in Christ (2 Cor 5:17) as well as new life for those to whom we witness who also accept Christ through grace. This communal relationship is a 'constant process of begetting new life in the Spirit …'[38] Analogically speaking, as one consummates the marriage covenant with Christ through mutual self-gift in the Eucharist, both the *unitive* and *procreative* properties must be maintained for authentic love to be realised. Otherwise,

The one, holy, Catholic, and apostolic Church is present in each particular Church. The communion of that Church with the universal Church is principally manifested when a bishop celebrates the Eucharist. As such, the bishop must foster genuine communion in his particular Church, amongst all the parishes, which concurrently fosters communion with the universal Church. Yet, since 'bishops have the obligation of fostering and safeguarding the unity of the faith and of upholding the discipline which is common to the whole Church',[51] bishops must be responsive to the needs of their fellow bishops. 'A particular church that is closed in upon itself and on its own problems and is closed to the mission outside its own boundaries does not live in communion.'[52]

The need for bishops to stand united as one college, with its head the successor of St Peter, is essential today. Christ's gift of self in the Eucharist is an invitation into the love of God which reorients our lives. In the Eucharist, 'the Christian partakes of Christ's self-giving love and is equipped and committed to live this same charity in all his thoughts and deeds'.[53] Bishops in communion with each other and the faithful can respond to Christ with self-giving love, which ultimately manifests the love of God for the world (see Jn 17:20–23). Christ's prayer for unity in his Church begins with him praying for the unity of the apostles (Jn 17:11), which continues today to inspire the successors of the apostles, the bishops. 'God is a perfect communion of love between Father, Son and Holy Spirit',[54] and bishops lead the flock entrusted to their care towards that Trinitarian communion like the good shepherd.

NOTES

1 Second Vatican Council (SVC), *Christus Dominus,* no. 11, in Vatican Council II: *The Conciliar and Post Conciliar Documents,* new rev., Austin Flannery, ed., fourth printing (1998). Northport, NY: Costello Publishing Company, 1996.

2 SVC, *Gaudium et Spes,* 32 in Flannery.

3 John Paul II, *Pastores Gregis,* no. 44, www.vatican.va, http://www.vatican.va/holy_father/john_paul_ii/apost_exhortations/documents/hf_jp-ii_exh_20031016_pastores-gregis_en.html (accessed 6th May 2012). All scriptures citations from NRSV unless otherwise noted.

4 CD, 2.

5 SVC, *Apostolicam Actuositatem,* no. 2, in Flannery.

6 LG, 21.

7 Ibid., 21. The Latin: *docendi, santificandi et regendi.*

8 Ibid., 23.

9 SVC, Dei Verbum, 7, in Flannery; See Irenaeus, *Against Heresies,* 3.3.1, www.newadvent.org, http://www.newadvent.org/fathers/0103303.htm (accessed 29th June 2012).

10 *Pastores Gregis,* 27.

11 DV, 8; Irenaeus, *Against Heresies,* 4.26.2.

12 Congregation for the Doctrine of the Faith, *Donum Veritatis,* no. 15, www.vatican.va, http://www.doctrinafidei.va/documents/rc_con_cfaith_doc_19900524_theologian-vocation_en.html (accessed 28th April 2012).

13 Ibid., 25.

14 Donald Cardinal W. Wuerl, 'Bishops as Teachers: A Resource for Bishops', *Origins* vol. 41, 2 (19th May 2011), 20.

15 *Pastores Gregis,* 29.

16 Benedict XVI, *Sacramentum Caritatis,* www.vatican.va. http://www.vatican.va/holy_father/benedict_xvi/apost_exhortations/documents/hf_ben-xvi_exh_20070222_sacramentum-caritatis_en.html (accessed 6th May 2012), no. 20; See 1 Corinthians 11:27-29.

17 *Sacramentum Caritatis,* 20.

18 *Pastores Gregis,* 39.

19 Augustine, Sermon 17.2, *Nicene and Ante-Nicene Fathers,* 1st series, vol. 6, Philip Schaff, ed., Peabody, MA: Hendrickson Publishing Inc., 1994.

20 LG, 27.

21 John Paul II, *Apostolos Suos*, no. 11, www.vatican.va, http://www.vatican.va/holy_father/john_paul_ii/motu_proprio/documents/hf_jp-ii_motu-proprio_22071998_apostolos-suos_en.html (accessed 7th May 2012).

22 *Pastores Gregis*, 41.

23 LG, 39.

24 LG, 42.

25 *Pastores Gregis*, 37.

26 Joseph Cardinal Ratzinger, *Pilgrim Fellowship of Faith: The Church as Communion,* Stephen Otto Horn and Vinzenz Pfnür, eds, Henry Taylor trans., San Francisco: Ignatius Press, 2005, pp. 142–3.

27 LG, 49.

28 SVC, *Sacrosanctum Concilium*, 41, in Flannery.

29 LG, 23.

30 CD, 15.

31 *Sacramentum Caritatis*, 27.

32 Catechism of the Catholic Church, mod. ed., New York: Bantam Doubleday Dell Publishing Group, Inc., 1995, no. 1617.

33 John Paul II, *Familiaris Consortio,* no. 13, www.vatican.va, http://www.vatican.va/holy_father/john_paul_ii/apost_exhortations/documents/hf_jp-ii_exh_19811122_familiaris-consortio_en.html (accessed 7th May 2012). Emphasis added.

34 Paul VI, *Humanae Vitae,* no. 12, *Humanae Vitae: A Challenge to Love,* Janet E. Smith, trans., New Hope, KY: New Hope Publications, nd.

35 *Sacramentum Caritatis*, 40.

36 *Sacramentum Caritatis*, 7

37 SC, 48.

38 *Pastores Gregis*, 26.

39 John Paul II, *Evangelium Vitae,* no. 13, www.vatican.va., http://www.vatican.va/holy_father/john_paul_ii/encyclicals/documents/hf_jp-ii_enc_25031995_evangelium-vitae_en.html (accessed 2nd May 2012).

40 Jacques Jullien, Archbishop of Rennes, 'The Bishop as the Instrument of Communion in the Particular Churches', *The Bishop and His Ministry*, Vatican City: Urbaniana University Press, 1998, p. 45.

41 LG, 27.

42 Ibid., 18.

43 CD, 25.

44 Jérôme Cardinal Hamer, 'Salient Points on the Munus Docendi', *The Bishop and his Ministry*, p. 54.

45 CD, 8a.

46 LG, 37.

47 CD, 35.1.

48 Ibid., 35.4.

49 LG, 23.

50 *Pastores Gregis*, 7.

51 LG, 23.

52 Jullien, 48.

53 John Paul II, *Veritatis Splendor,* no. 107, Boston: Pauline Books & Media, 2003.

54 *Sacramentum Caritatis*, 8.

THE ECCLESIOLOGY OF COMMUNION: A MUSICOLOGICAL PERSPECTIVE

MS ANNE MARY KEELEY PhD Candidate
University College, Dublin

In his encyclical letter *Ecclesia de Eucharistia,* Pope John Paul II observed that 'the Eucharist, while shaping the Church and her spirituality, has also powerfully affected "culture" and the arts in particular'.[1] The influence can also be said to flow in the opposite direction. Culture, in particular the arts, can influence our relationship with the Eucharist. While there is ample evidence that such influence may often be negative rather than positive, my paper today draws attention to the enormously positive influence that has been exercised by one composer, Olivier Messiaen (1908–92), who devoted much artistic energy to presenting the public with aspects of eucharistic devotion and theology through the medium of his distinctly modernist music. The paper is in three parts. Part one looks briefly at Messiaen the composer. Part two examines the role of the Eucharist in Messiaen's music with reference to several key works. Part three considers the work which is arguably his most important statement on the Eucharist. The paper concludes by pondering what we may be able to learn from Messiaen's music as we reflect on the ecclesiology of communion since Vatican Council II.

PART ONE: MESSIAEN THE COMPOSER

Messiaen was one of France's leading twentieth-century composers. A devout Catholic, his understanding of himself as a composer was distinctly ecclesial. He once said, 'A number of my works are dedicated to shedding light on the theological truths of the Catholic faith. That is the most important aspect of my music.'[2] Much of Messiaen's musical inspiration was rooted in his role as organist at La Trinité Church in Paris and in his deep, personal engagement with the liturgies for which he provided a musical dimension. One of his main preoccupations as a composer was attempting to communicate the theology underpinning those liturgies to an audience beyond the physical boundaries of La Trinité and the ritual boundaries of liturgy.

Messiaen has rightly earned a place in the pantheon of modernist composers. In the field of musicology he is remembered as a composer who paved the way to integral serialism with his iconic 'Modes des valeurs et d'intensités'.[3] As a teacher, he numbered among his students several future leaders of the European musical avant garde.[4] Messiaen was a technical innovator whose principal contributions to the music of the twentieth century were his system of pitch modes, which represents 'both an extension and a codification of Debussian chromaticism', and his novel conception of rhythm as 'an extension of durations in time' rather than a division of time.[5] Arnold Whittall has judged that modernism in Messiaen's music resides in 'the balance between stratified textures and juxtaposed formal segments on the one hand, and the coherence of consistent stylistic qualities and harmonic procedures on the other'.[6] This assessment refers, of course, to the composer's musical materials. But in many of Messiaen's compositions, the idea of a balance of contrasting elements extends further to, on the one hand, his inspirational sources in the teachings and traditions of the Catholic Church and, on the other hand, the striking modernity of the music which seeks to give expression to his inspiration.

PART TWO: THE EUCHARIST IN MESSIAEN'S MUSIC

From the outset of his career, Messiaen emphasised the importance of his faith as an influence in his music composition and this influence included a notable focus on the Eucharist. In an interview given shortly after his appointment as titular organist at La Sainte Trinité, at the remarkably young age of twenty-two, he said: 'Since my second work, *Diptyque*, I have wanted to contrast the earthly life and the life beyond. I wrote a *Banquet eucharistique* which I have now disowned ... This "Banquet" was inspired entirely, as is *Les offrandes oubliées*, by the mystery of the Eucharist.'[7]

Considered a failure by Messiaen, *Le Banquet eucharistique* (1928) for orchestra was soon transformed into *Le Banquet céleste* for organ. This organ work and *Les offrandes oubliées* (for orchestra) endure today. In these and later works, Messiaen usually provided a title and/or a quotation from scripture, the liturgy or well-known spiritual writers at the beginning of a work, or each movement of a work, which act as theological epigraphs. For example, the score of the short organ work *Le banquet céleste* bears one quotation: 'Whoever eats my bread composer's commentaries on his own works and the characteristic traits of the music itself, including the question of whether or not the sound world of Messiaen's compositions was appropriate to 'religious' music. For an entire year, argument raged across the pages of various newspapers and cultural publications. Near the end of the controversy in April 1946, a couple of articles appeared in *Le Figaro littéraire,* which included contributions on the matter from several leading composers and critics. Almost all contributors described Messiaen as 'a very great musician of our time'. But most were 'in agreement about rejecting all the literature and commentaries which the composer or certain bumbling exegetes place around his works, and concur that these do the music a disservice'.[15] *Le Figaro littéraire* claimed to draw a line under the controversy, but opinion will always be divided on these aspects of Messiaen's music.

Characteristically, Messiaen remained true to his ideals. As late as 1977, when commenting on his own aesthetic approach, he observed that the sumptuously-coloured frescoes and paintings of Fra Angelico, Michelangelo, Tintoretto and Rembrandt, are a legacy in the visual arts that is both voluptuous and contemplative.[16] For Messiaen the composer, then, a synthesis of the beauty of sound and the truth of theology was entirely appropriate.

Messiaen remained true to his ideals in other respects. Following a break from sacred music in the 1950s, he resumed composing music inspired by 'the theological truths of the Catholic faith': *Coleurs de la cité Céleste* (1963); *Et expecto resurrectionem mortuorum* (1964); *La Transfiguration de Notre Seigneur Jésus-Christ* (1969); *Méditations sur le mystère de la Sainte Trinité* (1969); *Saint François d'Assise* (1983); *Live du Saint Sacrement* (1984). While all of these later works are notable for their sheer monumentality, they are perhaps most distinguished by an intensification of Messiaen's theological focus. The final section of this paper examines the structure of and theological background to *Livre du Saint Sacrement.*

PART THREE: LIVRE DU SAINT SACREMENT

This organ work is a cycle of eighteen pieces of varying length (see this paper's appendix). Messiaen's characteristic quotations at the start of each piece serve as theological epigraphs. These epigraphs and Messiaen's comments in the introduction to the score present the theological structure of the work. Pieces I to IV are acts of adoration and faith. Pieces V to XI are based on moments in the life of Christ. Messiaen explains here that he has taken his cue from Blessed Columba Marmion: 'All the graces that Christ earned for us at various times in his earthly life still retain their virtue, which apply to us at every liturgical feast. This idea has been developed at length in the very fine book by Dom Columba Marmion, *Christ in His Mysteries*. It is particularly through the Eucharist that the graces of Christ's Mysteries are given to us.'[17]

Pieces XII to XVI are based on the Liturgy of the Eucharist in the Mass, while the seventeenth presents a final point in eucharistic theology. The work concludes with the eighteenth piece.

Several important aspects of eucharistic theology are highlighted in the theological programme of this work, including:

- The Eucharist as banquet and sacrifice
- The Trinitarian context of the Eucharist
- The Eucharist as ecclesial communion
- The Eucharist as banquet and sacrifice.

Raymond Moloney, in his study of the Eucharist published in 1995, has observed that 'The celebration of Christian life which our Lord has left us in the Eucharist comes to us, not in one image, but in two. The Eucharist is not sacrifice alone, nor is it banquet alone. It is both sacrifice and banquet.'[18] Messiaen has highlighted these elements with his sixth and seventeenth pieces (emphasising banquet) and his eighth and ninth pieces (emphasising sacrifice).

THE TRINITARIAN CONTEXT OF THE EUCHARIST

Concerning the Trinitarian context of the Eucharist, Moloney reminds us that 'Our Lord's earthly existence was but the transposition into time of relationships between Father, Son and Holy Spirit within the Trinity.' Messiaen presents this Trinitarian context in his eleventh piece, which he describes as 'the most developed piece in the collection'. This piece is based on Jesus' post-resurrection appearance to Mary Magdalene. Here, Messiaen makes a very important musical link with one of his earlier compositions, *Méditations sur le mystére de la Sainte Trinité*. In that work, he created a type of musical language

APPENDIX – LIVRE DU SAINT SACREMENT

I: **Adoro te**
'I adore you, O hidden God!' (*Adoro te*, St Thomas Aquinas)

II: **La Source de Vie (The Source of Life)**
'May my heart always thirst after You, O Fount of Life, Source of Eternal Life.' (Prayer of St Bonaventure)

III: **Le Dieu caché (Hidden God)**
'My eyes cannot suffer the splendour of your glory. To allow for my weakness, You hide beneath the veiled Sacrament.' (Thomas à Kempis, *The Imitation of Christ*, Bk. IV, chap. ii)

IV: **Acte de Foi (Act of Faith)**
'My God, I firmly believe ...'

V: **Puer natus est nobis**
'Unto us a child is born, unto us a son is given.' (Is 9:5)

VI: **La manne et le Pain de Vie (Manna and the Bread of Life)**
'You gave them the food of angels, from heaven untiringly sending them bread already prepared, containing every delight, satisfying every taste. And the sustenance you gave demonstrated your sweetness towards your children, for, conforming to the taste of whoever ate it, it transformed itself into what each eater wished.' (Wis 16:20-21)

'The life that Christ gives us in Holy Communion is his whole life, with the special graces which he has earned for us by living for us each of his mysteries.' (Dom Columba Marmion, *Christ in His Mysteries*, chap.18)

'I am the living bread which has come down from heaven. Anyone who eats this bread will live for ever; and the bread that I shall give is my flesh, for the life of the world.' (Jn 6:51)

VII: **Les ressuscités et la lumière de Vie (The Risen and the Light of Life)**
'Anyone who follows me will not be walking in the dark, but will have the light of life.' (Jn 8:12)

VIII: **Institution de l'Eucharistie (The institution of the Eucharist)**
'This is my body. This is my blood.' (Mt 26:26,28)

IX: **Les ténèbres (The Shadows)**
'This is your hour; this is the reign of darkness.' (Lk 22:53)

'When they reached the place called The Skull, they crucified him.' (Lk 23:33)

'From the sixth hour there was darkness over all the land until the ninth hour. (Mt 27:45)

X: **La Résurrection du Christ (The resurrection of Christ)**
'Why look among the dead for someone who is alive?' (Lk 24:5)

XI: **L'apparation du Christ ressucité à Marie-Madeleine**
(The apparition of the Risen Christ to Mary Magdalene)

'Mary stayed outside near the tomb, weeping. ... She turned round and saw Jesus standing there, though she did not recognise him. ... Jesus said 'Mary!' She knew him then and said to him in Hebrew, 'Rabbuni!' – which means Master. Jesus said to her ... 'Go and find the brothers, and tell them: I am ascending to my Father and your Father, to my God and your God.' (Jn 20:11-17)

XII: **La Transsubstantiation (Transubstantiation)**
'Sight, touch and taste cannot satisfy: hearing alone assures my faith. I believe all that the Son of God said: nothing is truer than this word of Truth.' (*Adoro te*, St Thomas Aquinas)

'Under different species, which are no longer substances but only signs, hide sublime realities.' (Sequence, *Lauda Sion*)

XIII: **Les deux murailles d'eau (The two walls of water)**
'The waters parted and the sons of Israel went on dry ground right into the sea, walls of water to right and to left of them.' (Ex 14:22-23)

'If the Host is broken, do not hesitate; but remember that there is as much in each fragment as in the entire Host. Its substance cannot be divided, only the sign is broken, changing neither the state nor the grandeur of Him who is beneath the sign.' (Sequence, *Lauda Sion*)

XIV: **Prière avant la communion (Prayer before Communion)**
'Lord, I am not worthy ... but only say the word...' (Words of the centurion, Mt 8:8)

XV: **La joie de la grâce (The joy of grace)**
'I come to You, Lord, to taste the joy of the Holy Banquet which You have prepared for the poor.' (Thomas à Kempis, *The Imitation of Christ*, Bk. IV, chap. iii)

'He who loves, runs, flies! He is full of joy, he is free and nothing can stop him.' (Thomas à Kempis, *The Imitation of Christ*, Bk. III, chap. v)

XVI: **Prière aprés la communion (Prayer after Communion)**
'You are my perfume and my delight, my peace and my gentleness ... ' (Prayer of St Bonaventure)

XVII: **La Présence multipliée (The multiplied presence)**
'One receives it, a thousand receive it, one receives as much as they: all receive it without exhausting it.' (Sequence, *Lauda Sion*)

XVIII: **Offrande et Alleluia final (Final offering and Alleluia)**
'I offer you, Lord, all the transports of love and joy, ecstasies, delights, revelations, heavenly visions given to all Blessed Souls ... ' (Thomas à Kempis, *The Imitation of Christ*, Bk. IV, chap. xvii)

MUSIC AS *LOCUS THEOLOGICUS*: AN EXPRESSION OF HARMONIC GRACE

DR MAEVE LOUISE HEANEY VDMF
Santa Clara University

Our God is a God of love, of communion, and if ever there were a time in which we needed to learn how to live a unity that integrates our differences, it would appear to be now. It also seems more obvious than ever that this is a quest that is supernatural, in the best sense of the word – beyond our human capacities. The proposal of this paper is that music is a means, a symbolic form, which has the humble potential to aid in such a transformation, or as *Sacrosanctum Concilium* 112 puts it, to 'foster unity of minds'.

Alongside this more general aim, there are two specific concerns in relation to music as an art form underlying these thought:

- The first is that which, in the different countries I have worked, they refer to as 'worship wars': the deep-rooted divisions between assemblies and churches based on their tastes in music. The question needs to be asked as to why a symbolic form such as music, with the potential it has for unifying and harmonising, should be such a source of contention. I suggest it is precisely because we do not know enough about what music is and how it works, that we struggle to facilitate more mature dialogue.
- Secondly, the growing division between the worlds of the arts and the Church, which in Ireland could be identified in the phenomenon of no longer singing in church, contradictory in a musical culture such as our own in which we sing everywhere else! Creativity in music abounds, but musicians do not find their spiritual home in church. There are noteworthy exceptions, but in your average church, this is the case. Why, as music flourishes outside of church walls, and for many is becoming their first access point to God and form of expression of their faith, is it so anemic inside?

The aim of this short paper, therefore, is to offer a few foundational thoughts in relation to these issues, which could at least point in the direction of a resolution of these concerns, and lead us towards a greater understanding of music's role in liturgy and some of the tasks to be approached if we are to work towards its full potential.

In *Wuthering Heights*, Catherine speaks of her love for Heathcliff in the following terms: 'I have dreamt in my life dreams that have ... gone through and through me, like wine through water, and altered the colour of my mind.'[1] If I could paraphrase this in relation to music: 'I have sung songs that have run through me like sap through stone, and altered the shape of the world I live in.' Music is a powerful medium. PierAngelo Sequeri, Italian theologian, musician and composer, talking about music, says:

> There is a dimension of the symbolic, which human beings more typically live from, which have instead the form of action ... it does not produce objects, it transforms subjects. It establishes invisible bonds, which cannot be reduced to a meaning, to a concept, to an idea. Nor to a sign. Because they are bonds that act as strengths of interiority, not as exterior forms.[2]

As a premise to all that I will say about music, I will state that, due to the logo-centric mode of thought within which the Western world works, perhaps the easiest way to explain and comprehend music's symbolic form is, in fact, in comparison and contrast to verbal or conceptual understanding. We think 'meaning' in verbal terms, even where we know that music 'does things' differently. This does not imply that one is undervaluing or underestimating the spoken and written word. Nor am I seeking to pit one against the other. There is a place for both – indeed, in most liturgical music, the verbal word comes first, and inspires or informs the music that finally carries it. However, music is not verbal, even where it can be weaved together with words, and the effect is much more than the sum of both. However, the music that is so intrinsic to our liturgical celebrations will emerge all the more clearly in the measure that we understand it on its own terms, before, or at the same time as we integrate it with the words that clarify and complete our worship of God.

Returning to the above quotation of Sequeri, although it cannot be denied that words can be transformational (performative utterances), and can change us, they are *primarily* referential. The symbolic form that is music works differently to that of the written word. Therefore, albeit appreciating what people are attempting to say with the expression, music is *not*, in fact, a 'universal language' – first, because it is not a language (the discursive and referential nature of music is simply not how music works in semantic and semiotic terms) and second, because the way in which it is 'universal' would also need to be qualified. The 'sounds' we human beings consider to be 'music' or 'musical' are not the same. However, the dynamic of making-music as an activity may well be the place to look for the universal (and therefore unifying) capacity music has. This is a point musicologist Jean-Jacques Nattiez proposes: that 'universals' in music take place in the event and dynamic of music-making, rather than the actual 'sounds' that are considered musical in each culture. There is room and need for exploration in this area, which goes beyond the limits of this paper. But let us recognise that we need to appreciate more the specific nature of what music is, and of how it 'means', in human life.

An exercise in human apprehension: For example: I can speak 'Of the peace of our Lord', or we can listen to a piece of music by Arvo Pärt called 'Da Pacem Domine' (*Give us peace, Lord).* We listen to the music in a different way, we receive it in a different way – it affects us in a different way than words do. Hence the title of this paper: Music as *locus theologicus*; music as a theological place, space, source in the sense of embodied experience, in and through which grace can be 'heard', received and participated in, in a different way to which it is through words. I am aware that this is a challenge, as theology works in primarily verbal and conceptual forms, but it is necessary, as the 'Word', the logos, is not words, but Someone, who also 'communicates' something through music. In a similar way in which theology relies on and must be critically aware of the philosophy it draws from, so theological thought on music must draw on musicology, ethnomusicology, musical semiotics, neuroscience on music, if it is to be able to reflect intelligently on its role in relation to the different areas of theology that it touches.

Only then can we intelligently reflect upon how *Sacrosanctum Concilium* 112: invited us to consider music: 'The musical tradition of the universal Church is a treasure of inestimable value, greater even than that of any other art. The main reason for this pre-eminence is that, as *sacred song united to the words, it forms a necessary or integral part of the solemn liturgy.*'

I'd like to suggest that the phrase 'necessary or integral' should not be understood so much as an approval or exhortation to the use of music in liturgy, but rather as an epistemological form of approaching liturgical celebration. Music is not an addition, albeit a positive one, to our celebrations, but one that could colour the very way we think about them.

In order to be able to do this, we need begin to understand how music works.

The character of sign in conceptual and verbal thought works differently to how music works. Jean-Jacques Nattiez, whose approach to musical analysis could be described as a hermeneutical one (although he himself calls it Tripartitional Method, drawing from Jean Molino), explains it thus. In verbal communication, there is the 'sender' who communicates/sends a 'message' to a 'receiver'. Communication is achieved when the message is understood (whether one agrees or disagrees with it – both are forms of 'reception').

Sender **Message** **Receiver**

In musical expression, the process is different. Instead of a sender, Nattiez speaks of the 'poietic' process, the message is the 'trace',[3] and as the receiver he speaks of the 'esthesic' process. Applying and expanding his approach, in the poietic process we could include all the music-makers involved: composer, arrangers and musicians; who perform, opening a space of musical experience, in which receivers (listeners) participate and share in.

Music-makers **Musical Experience** **Listeners**

The most important element of the above 'diagram' is the direction of the arrows: the end and aim of musical experience, or performance is sharing, rather than the sending and receiving of a message. In the words of another musicologist and liturgical theologian, Willem Marie Speelman, (who draws on the semiotic school of Ferdinand de Saussure): 'The practice of musical communication is not so much a practice of a sender in opposition to a receiver, as it is *an act of sharing.*

Communication of music is not about anything else other than the sharing of the music itself.'[4]

So when is the aim of musical expression accomplished? In the very sharing. In the dynamic created between the:

- music-makers (composers, arrangers, musicians)
- Listeners/ assembly, and
- in the concrete experience of each and every musical experience.

Meaning in music works differently than in purely verbal communication. Therefore, it is not only about the 'words of the song' or even about the most appropriate the style of music, but also about the dynamic created in the musical (liturgical) experience as generated by musicians/performers, music and assembly. That assessing and discerning these performances may be complex and challenging does not mean the difficulties in doing so are insurmountable. Group and ecclesial discernment in other forums is necessary and possible. Nattiez talks about 'the trace' and indeed insists that there is no musical analysis without one. I would add that just as important, musical experience and performance, as each and every enactment of music is different, and because the very fact that it is live music means it is, in some way, performance. Rather than fighting against that fact, I suggest that in the same way as homiletics implies formation, theological aesthetics and liturgy in regard to music could enrich its thought process with some insights from performance studies. 'Performance studies does not study texts, architecture visual arts or any other item or artefact of art or culture as such ... they are studied "as" performances. That is, they are regarded as practices, events and behaviours, not as "objects" or "things".'[5]

Within the context of talking about performance, and in the context of liturgy, I suggest that the current argument over participation versus performance in liturgy, although recognising the underlying issue, is also based on a false dichotomy between silence and singing, as if silence was not participative.

Basically, music has four elements:

- Rhythm
- Melody
- Harmony
- Tone colour.

Intrinsic to rhythm (and I would suggest underlying them all) is another fifth and often not – recognised one: *silence* – the space between the notes. The shared space that opens up, not when we start to play or sing, but when we begin to count the beat; the shared space that invites us to be attentive, with all that we are, to the sounds that are about to emerge. I think this must have been what St Augustine was in touch with when he said whoever sings well, prays twice, as it does imply a level of attentiveness of mind, body and spirit which can only aid, if and when applied to prayer. What does it say about our liturgical music if it does not provoke the desire to keep quiet and listen?

We do not have the time to go further into the realms of musicology, but I will simply state that one of the common characteristics of most authors in the area is their affirmation of the embodied nature of musical meaning. Making music (singing or playing any other instrument), is embodied. It is arguably the most spiritual and yet most embodied of the art forms.

Once again, in the words of Sequeri: 'Music, in itself, puts structurally in practice the *oxymoron* that represents the background of that truth of the Christian *logos*, but also its necessary effect: *the senses are also intelligent,* not only obtuse; *the spirit is also sensitive/sensible,* not only incorporeal. The Christian *logos* is not a naked truth without style.'[6] So, even before we put words to it, music is already enacting core realities of our faith: harmonic grace – body and spirit, embodied spirits in action.

Let us venture some thought on how taking this seriously would look like in liturgy, allowing music to be an intrinsic organising form, which, among other things, can add delight to prayer, foster unity of minds, and confer greater solemnity upon the sacred rites (cf. *Sacrosanctum Concilium,* 112). Instead of looking at liturgy in a linear way, in order to identify when and where music is appropriate or necessary ...

STRUCTURE AND PARTS OF THE MASS

Introductory Rites:

- Entrance chant or hymn, penitential rites, Gloria and collect.

Liturgy of the Word:
- Readings: if sung, the words are primordial
- Psalm: should be sung, in a form that does not overshadow the other readings
- Alleluia: sung
- Gospel
- Creed
- Prayer of the Faithful.

Liturgy of the Eucharist:
- Preparation of the gifts: song/chant
- Eucharistic Prayer: centre and summit – preface dialogue through to the amen: musical unity invited. Sung as much as possible in solemnities
- Communion rite: song of Communion, after Communion, space to pray, or aid to reflection.

CONCLUDING RITES

Could we not look at it as 'musical', from beginning to end, with moments of silence, crescendo, words spoken, refrains repeated, gestures gracefully 'performed' (or danced?) and participated in by presider and assembly? Instead of words being at the centre of everything, to be enhanced by music, the whole of the liturgy could be understood as 'musical', integrating presence (first and foremost that of God), actions, words and music, orchestrated in a way in which one leads into and enhances the next. To do this would not only imply close collaboration between pastors and ministers in liturgical preparation, but also a change of mindset: music as intrinsic and necessary to liturgical preparation and praxis.

A short mention of our second concern: the separation between the worlds of the arts and the Church; that is to say: the fact that so many of our musicians, even when they still come to Church, do not find their 'creative home' in the Church, and therefore we are denied the richness their gifts would offer. It runs against the tradition of centuries in which music and religion have overlapped and interacted fruitfully.

Theologian and musician, and initiator of an initiative called Essagramma, Pierangelo Sequeri writes about the inextricable link between music and religion in the following terms: 'The prophecy of Nietzsche – "Art raises its head where the religions withdraw", has not been very listened to in music.'[7] Because the history of music has been moved by the very idea that music is able to

- initiate us into immediate contact with the divine
- attempt to represent or interpret it.

The decline or separation between the world of religion and that of music is a particularly western phenomenon. It is interesting that Sequeri does not read the current situation in purely negative terms, lamenting this separation, but identifying its potential and a possible way forward. In a book called *Musica e Mistica,* he traces these links over the centuries and suggests a 'solution', which he describes as a type of 'third way': the notion of creative thought as the 'director' of the encounter between the sacred and art, which is neither simply destined to prayer, nor necessarily estranged from religion.[8]

'Creative thought, in the form of poetic invention, of reflective seeking and hermeneutical variation has generated a new space of aesthetic culture, focused on the bond between freedom and the sacred.'[9]

There is no doubt that books and writings on the creative process are on the increase in recent years, usually coloured by the differing theological stances on human-divine collaboration underlying their theses. I would suggest that the invitation, in the current setting, is not about asking: 'why are people not composing good liturgical music', or by analysing the 'words' of a given music so as to define how 'religious' or 'sacred' it is, but rather to ask: 'where is creativity moving, and what does it have to say to the Church and to our liturgies?' In Christian terms: 'what are our artists doing?'

Sequeri talks of this third way in terms of an opening towards 'a new beginning. A purely sonorous space for invocation … in the search of a more sincere word: of religion, but even for civilisation'.[10] The balance and vision in Sequeri's analysis, both cultural and musical, is hard to overestimate. 'The idea that music is perhaps already a step ahead, beyond the crossroads of Nihilism's fatality and beauty's mediocrity in which our culture flounders, does not seem to be too astray.'[11]

It seems to me that such a position is the only way forward, as once again it suggests an integral and intrinsic way of addressing the problem, with a clear faith vision: if God is at work, if God is the author of gifts of creativity, although we may need to clarify the 'how' of human and divine interaction (nature and grace), then somehow human creativity will forge a new path from within. This implies a positive anthropology and perhaps even a theology of vocation. As a musician and composer, time and time again I come back to a short writing by Karl Rahner as my *carta magna*: In *Prayer for Creative Thinkers*, Rahner prays: 'Invoke your Holy Spirit upon them! Raise up among us people endowed with creative powers, thinkers, poets, artists (musicians). We have need of them.'

He describes such creative thinkers as '… those men and women who are engaged in constantly producing new expressions of their own nature and spirit, people who are the architects of themselves'.

If we were (are) scared of human potential, we could be fearful of the invitation to artists to realise their own beings in what they 'achieve and produce', to 'discover and express that nature which is an image and likeness of your own glory'. And who can deny that there is a fear of creative intelligence in our Church now? And yet, Rahner, grounded on his faith in grace (as a supernatural existential), poured out in every human heart, invites them, not only to express that which seems safe, but to express everything! 'And in expressing this let them express everything!' Why? Because: 'whether we realise it or not, every creative activity of the human spirit has become an element in the personal history of your Word …'

So the 'third way' which Sequeri calls for converges with the growing awareness we have of the need for true human giftedness to be placed at the service of Christian faith.

And here we come full circle: unity in diversity. Artistic creativity is highly personal and yet God-given. We live our communion in the body of Christ – in which each member has its role, at the service and in communion with the other members. Musically speaking, we will only move forward to a fuller and more beautiful expression of the faith we love, and the Triune God we seek to make present in the world if, in Sequeri's words, we allow 'convinced believers of passionate faith and real talent and formation', who are allowed to work and draw with them the interest of a culture.[12]

NOTES

1 Emily Brontë, *Wuthering Heights*, Rockville, Maryland: Arc Manor, 2008, p. 62.

2 P. Sequeri, *Estro di Dio, Saggi di Estetica*, Milan: Glossa, 2000, pp. 176–7.

3 The trace is the written musical score, without which Nattiez considers musical analysis impossible.

4 W.M. Speelman, 'Words can be understood, but music must be followed. Language and music as fundamental categories of liturgy', *The Conference: Singing God's Love Faithfully,* Notre Dame, 12th–14th April 2007, p. 3. Translated and published as 'Woorden kunnen worden verstaan, muziek moet worden gevolgd. Taal en muziek als fundamentele categorieën van de liturgie', 'Woorden kunnen worden verstaan, muziek moet worden gevolgd. Taal en muziek als fundamentele categorieën van de liturgie',Woorden kunnen worden verstaan, muziek moet worden gevolgd. Taal en muziek als fundamentale categorieën van de liturgie', M. Hoondert, ed., *Elke muziek heeft haar hemel. De religieuze betekenis van muziek,* Budel: Damon, 2009, pp. 161–83.

5 R. Schechner, *Performance Studies. An Introduction,* London: Routledge, 2002, p. 2.

6 Sequeri, *Anti-Prometeo,* p. 107.

7 P. Sequeri, *La Risonanza del Sublime,* p. 11.

8 Cf. Sequeri, *Musica e mistica,* pp. 507–8. Once again we are touching on the area of the overlap of the artistic and Christian vocations, which we will look more closely at in chapter VI.

9 Sequeri, *Musica e mistica,* p. 508.

10 Cf. P. Sequeri, *La Risonanza del Sublime,* p. 9.

11 P. Sequeri, *La Risonanza del Sublime,* p. 11.

12 Cf. P. Sequeri, 'Coscienza cristiana, ethos della fede e canone pubblico', M. Vergottini, *A misura di Vangelo,* Cinisello Balsamo: Edizioni San Paolo, 2003, p. 29.

Thursday 7th June 2012

EMERGING SCHOLARS

at the International Symposium of Theology
50TH INTERNATIONAL EUCHARISTIC CONGRESS

• • 1 • •

CHAIR: **DR CATHERINE O'LEARY**
(National University of Ireland, Maynooth)

SPEAKER: **MR AURELIO CERVIÑO**
The Alphonsian Academy, Rome
El eslabón perdido de la comunión: el mandamiento nuevo

• • 2 • •

CHAIR: **REV. DR DAVID KELLY OSA**
(Milltown Institute, Dublin)

SPEAKER: **MS NOLLAIG M. NÍ MHAOILEOIN**
St Patrick's College, Maynooth
Gairdín an Anama mar Iomhá: Samplaí as na Leabhair Urnaithe ón Naoú Aoise Déag sa Leabharlann Ruiséal, Coláiste Naoimh Phádraig, Má Nuad, le nascanna agus macallaí ón dtraidisiúin Eireannach chomh maith leis an Mhór Roinn

• • 3 • •

CHAIR: **DR TONY HANNA**
(Director of Pastoral Renewal and Family Ministry, Archdiocese of Armagh)

SPEAKER: **MS PATRICIA KELLY**
Centre for Catholic Studies, Durham University
'The Workbench is your Altar': Jozef Cardijn's Understanding of the Role of the Eucharist in the Life of the Worker

• • 4 • •

CHAIR: **SR ELEANOR CAMPION OCSO**
(Cistercian Generalate, Rome)

SPEAKER: **MR JOSÉ PEDRO LOPES ANGÉLICO**
Catholic University of Portugal
'The Eucharist as the Eager Longing of Creation': The Relational Wholeness of Reality and the Mystery of Communion

• • 5 • •

CHAIR: **REV. DR GEARÓID DULLEA**
(Secretary to the Irish Catholic Bishops' Conference)

SPEAKER: **REV. DR ALESSANDRO CLEMENZIA**
Sophia University Institute, Loppiano, Italy
The Ecclesial 'We' and the Eucharist: In Dialogue with the 'Theo-logic' of Heribert Mühlen

• • 6 • •

CHAIR: **DR DÁIRE KEOGH**
(St Patrick's College, Drumcondra)

SPEAKER: **RT REV. ANTONIO LUIZ CATELAN FERREIRA**
Catholic University of Paraná, Brazil
L'ecclesiologia di comunione di Jerome Hamer

EL ESLABÓN PERDIDO DE LA COMUNIÓN: EL MANDAMIENTO NUEVO

MR AURELIO CERVIÑO PhD Candidate
The Alphonsian Academy, Rome

INTRODUCCIÓN

'Un mandamiento nuevo os doy: que os améis unos a otros; como yo os he amado, que también vosotros os améis mutuamente' (Jn 13:34).[1]

Este mandamiento está llamado a convertirse en el espejo y el termómetro de nuestra comunión, palabra que asumimos como sinónimo de amor. Si tenemos dudas, si no sabemos por dónde comenzar a caminar, si nos parece que en nuestras relaciones no conseguimos alcanzar una genuina comunión, aquí tenemos la solución. ¿Cuál es la medida de mi amor por los demás? ¿Estoy amando y a su vez experimento el amor de los demás? ¿Puedo afirmar que en mi familia, mi trabajo, mi parroquia, mi comunidad religiosa, hacemos experiencias de reciprocidad en el amor?

En el mandamiento nuevo resaltan con fuerza dos características. La primera es la reciprocidad; resulta legítimo amar sin esperar nada a cambio y donarse con generosidad, pero se alcanza una mayor perfección en el amor cuando este es recíproco. La segunda es el 'cómo'; entendiéndolo no sólo como una medida de amor sino como un fundamento del mismo. Se trata de un 'cómo' que no describe sólo la intensidad del amor y tampoco se refiere exclusivamente a su modo o manera, sino que indica el fundamento del mismo. Retomaremos este argumento más adelante.

Por lo tanto, la relación de amor que Jesús pide a sus discípulos se fundamenta en el amor con el cual Él los ha amado. Esto nos aleja de un mero amor abstracto o metafísico para situarnos en una medida de amor histórica y concreta. El espacio y el tiempo con el cual Jesús amó es la base del amor recíproco y constituye el fundamento del amor que podemos tener entre nosotros. A su vez, en Jesús se evidencia que el amor del Padre por Él supone la base del amor de Jesús por sus discípulos. 'El Hijo ama a sus discípulos con el mismo amor divino que el Padre tiene por Él.'[2]

ANÁLISIS EXEGÉTICO-TEOLÓGICO

El mandamiento nuevo resulta una aportación eminentemente joánica. Las referencias más claras se encuentran en Jn 13,34; 15,12; 1 Jn 2:8; 3:23; 4:12 y 2 Jn 4–6. Como sabemos, el evangelio de Juan es el más tardío de los cuatro y su fecha de elaboración se remonta al periodo comprendido entre los años 90 y 100. Por lo tanto se trata de un fruto maduro que expresa un abismo de profundidad y reflexión entorno al acontecimiento Jesucristo. No podemos adentrarnos en toda la cuestión de la autenticidad del cuarto evangelio porque nos llevaría demasiado lejos.

Proponemos ahora un breve análisis exegético del pasaje bíblico, siguiendo el trabajo de Cancian:[3]

> Un nuevo mandamiento os doy:
> que os améis unos a otros;
> como yo os he amado,
> que también vosotros
> os améis mutuamente.
> En eso conocerán todos que sois discípulos míos,
> si os tuviereis amor unos a otros (Jn 13:34-35).

Llamamos enseguida la atención del lector para notar que en este pasaje existe una palabra clave: *agapaô – agapê*. La misma no aparece de forma inmediata ni antes ni después de Jn 13:34-35; lo cual resulta una primera constatación de la unidad literaria del pasaje.

Otra palabra clave es *kathôs* – como ya hicimos mención al inicio – la cual no describiría sólo el grado, la intensidad o la manera del amor, sino que hace referencia también al fundamento del mismo. ¿Qué significa esto? Concretamente nos indica que el amor – sentido último de toda la vida de Jesús en su completa expresión histórica – se transforma en la base y la fuente de la cual los suyos pueden beber para comunicar entre ellos el mismo tipo de *agapê*. Un amor de la misma naturaleza del amor que Jesús tuvo por los suyos se constituye,

Eutimio Zigabeno, después de haber retomado la sentencia de Cirilo, presenta la opinión de otros que observan que el motivo de novedad se caracteriza por la ampliación del amor incluso a los enemigos.

Entre los latinos, san **Agustín** († 430) subraya que la novedad del mandamiento se encuentra en el nuevo motivo que se le propone al amor.

San **Bernardo** († 1153) afirma que la novedad del mismo se debe establecer en la consideración del efecto que la caridad produce en quien la posee.

También san **Buenaventura** († 1274) se pregunta por los motivos de novedad y nos dice que, si bien se trata de un precepto que ya formaba parte del Antiguo Testamento, fue renovado en su modo. Antes se prescribía el amor hacia los amigos, ahora hacia los enemigos; éste sería el valor que añade 'sicut dilexi vos'. Pero el doctor Seráfico nos ofrece una interpretación moral del mandamiento cuando afirma que es nuevo porque la caridad debe permanecer siempre joven en el corazón.

En santo **Tomás de Aquino** († 1274) tendríamos que profundizar el concepto de amistad con Dios. La caridad de amistad se fundamenta en una *communicatio vitae* que permite la reciprocidad en el amor.

Durante los siglos posteriores los comentaristas se limitarán a recopilar las opiniones precedentes y raramente se detendrán para ofrecer una propia.

Por ejemplo **Cornelio a Lapide** († 1643) presenta siete motivos por los cuales el mandamiento puede considerarse como nuevo:

1) *Ratione causae efficientis*, en cuanto que posee un nuevo legislador, Cristo
2) *Ratione causae materialis*, su objeto es infinito
3) *Ratione causae formalis*, la unión que se establece entre todos los hombres en Cristo resulta un nuevo motivo de amor
4) *Ratione causae exemplaris*, como ha amado Jesús
5) *Ratione finis*, porque el amor supone transformar y renovar a los hombres
6) *Ratione praestantiae*, en relación a cualquier otro madandamiento
7) *Ratione effectus*, en cuanto otorga una fuerza nueva para cumplir heroísmos de santidad.

Por razones de espacio no desarrollo las propuestas de **Maldonado** († 1674), **Calmet** († 1757), **Simón-Prado** (ed. 1930) y **Knabenbauer** († 1914) el cual presenta cuatro opiniones que podemos considerar abarcadas en los autores ya mencionados.

Un dato significativo supone la reflexión que nace a partir de la publicación en 1943 de la encíclica *Mystici Corporis Christi*, de Pío XII. Autores como **Scheeben, Anger, Prat, Mersch, Ceriani, Jürgensmeier, Philipon, Mura**, etc. abren nuevas sendas que permiten interpretar de forma más completa y profunda el mandamiento nuevo de Jesús.

UNA ESPIRITUALIDAD DE COMUNIÓN

Habiendo atravesado el equinoccio de este trabajo conviene comenzar a sacar algunas conclusiones. Si enumeramos los puntos claves que hemos sugerido, hasta ahora, constatamos que:

- El amor manifestado en Jesucristo constituye el centro de su actuar y de su ser porque 'el amor, por su esencia, es ilimitado'[8]
- El mandamiento nuevo indica la particularidad y la característica por antonomasia del amor cristiano: la reciprocidad
- La comunión o unidad, fruto del amor mutuo, refleja la más sublime y profunda comunión que constituye la Trinidad
- Amar 'como' Jesús nos amó supone una adhesión de fe que se actualiza en una vivencia *con* y *en* Dios
- El mandamiento nuevo no se reduce a un mero precepto moral sino que indica una vivencia irrenunciable, justamente se manda debido a su valor sin igual.

Ahora bien, si la unidad o comunión constituye el legado por excelencia de Jesús, si su invitación a un amor que llegue a ser recíproco es la base y el distintivo de todo cristiano, si nuestra inhabitación en Cristo supone una comunión con cada prójimo, nos preguntamos cómo vivir y cómo actuar para que esto sea posible.

Una respuesta clara y práctica la encontramos en la Carta Apostólica *Novo Millennio Ineunte*, de Juan Pablo II. De hecho, el Papa propone 'una programación pastoral que se inspirará en el mandamiento nuevo'[9] (NMI, 42).

Una de las frases que sintetiza la intención de esta carta es la siguiente: 'Hacer de la Iglesia *la casa y la escuela de la comunión*' (43). Para

Chiara Lubich describe el mandamiento nuevo como 'resumen' o 'síntesis' de todo el evangelio. Es la 'perla' de todas las palabras de Jesús y el 'corazón' de la espiritualidad de comunión.

Un punto que merece ser aclarado es que la vida del mandamiento nuevo no supone el mero cumplimiento de un precepto o una regla, sino que conlleva una adhesión con toda la mente, con todas las fuerzas y con todo el corazón (cf. Dt 6:5).

¿Y por qué tanta insistencia en este mandamiento? Más allá de la centralidad que ocupa en el mensaje de Jesús, Chiara descubre en el amor recíproco la llave y la puerta de ingreso a la unidad. Si un grupo de cristianos se aman recíprocamente crean las condiciones necesarias para que se cumpla la promesa de Jesús: 'Pues donde quiera que estén dos o tres reunidos en mi nombre, allí estoy yo en medio de ellos' (Mt 18:20). Como podemos observar se trata de un círculo que se 'cierra' cuando habiendo realizado nuestra parte – nos hemos amado mutuamente como Él nos amó – Jesús mismo nos une con su presencia. La unidad o comunión es un don de Dios que no podemos alcanzar sólo con nuestros medios o méritos, se trata de una presencia que nos permite experimentar que somos células vivas del cuerpo místico de Cristo.

'La unidad. Pero, ¿qué es la unidad? En aquellos mismos apuntes de 1946 encontramos cierta explicación, expresada todavía con términos aprendidos en la escuela:

'No tenemos que hacer una mezcla, sino una combinación, y ésta se realizará solamente cuando uno se pierda en la unidad al calor de la llama del amor divino.

> '¿Qué queda de dos o más (personas) que se 'combinan'? Jesús-el Uno.
> '... Cuando la unidad pasa, deja una sola huella: Cristo.'
> Y he aquí, en una carta de 1947, una definición de la unidad, dada después de haberla experimentado:
> '¡Oh! ¡La unidad, la unidad! ¡Qué divina belleza!
> '¡No tenemos palabras humanas para decir lo que es! Es Jesús.'
> Después, en una carta de 1948, se lee también:
> '... ¡La unidad!
> 'Pero, ¿quién tendrá la audacia de hablar de ella?

> '¡Es inefable como Dios!
> 'Se siente, se ve, se goza ... pero, ¡es inefable!
> 'Todos gozan de su presencia, todos sufren con su ausencia.
> 'Es paz, gozo, amor, ardor, clima de heroísmo, de inmensa generosidad.
> ¡Es Jesús entre nosotros!'[11]

Antes de concluir querría presentar un último punto sin el cual resulta casi imposible comprender la experiencia de Chiara Lubich.

Se trata de Jesús crucificado y abandonado como clave de acceso a la unidad. Ya hemos descrito el recorrido que el amor recíproco genera hasta llegar a una particular presencia de Dios en medio de la comunidad. Ahora bien, esto resulta imposible sin el necesario pasaje a través de la cruz.

En el seno de la Trinidad, la dinámica de amor recíproco es una constante inhabitación de amor, pero en esta Tierra amar supone una constante elección – acto de libertad – y una permanente actuación – acto de voluntad. Por lo tanto llegar a amar siempre, enseguida y con alegría, a cada prójimo que encuentro durante el día resulta difícil. Más aún cuando nos encontramos con situaciones de sufrimiento, pecado o incomprensión. Chiara Lubich descubre precisamente en la cruz, en el abismal grito de Jesús 'Dios mío, Dios mío, ¿por qué me has abandonado?' (Mc 15:34; Mt 27:46) el secreto para construir la unidad.

La unidad y Jesús abandonado se presentan así como las dos caras de una única moneda. En una cara el dolor abrazado y ofrecido, como lo hizo Jesús, se demuestra la medida máxima del amor; en la otra el fruto, el don, de ese abandono, la unidad; cuando sea elevado sobre la tierra, atraeré a todos hacia mí (cf. Jn 8:28).

> Desde ese momento cada dolor en nosotros y fuera de nosotros tuvo un nombre, nos apareció un rostro ... todo nos recordaba a Él, pero sobre todo los dolores provocados por la desunidad, que podían verificarse en nuestra relación con Dios o con los hermanos. Cada vez que se presentaban, íbamos al fondo del corazón y los aceptábamos: eran un aspecto del dolor de Jesús abandonado. Después salíamos fuera de nosotros mismos para

vivir la voluntad de Dios del momento siguiente para reestablecer la unión con Él, si se había roto, o establecer de nuevo la unidad con los demás, y la paz y la alegría regresaban a nuestro corazón como si se tratase de una resurrección continua.[12]

De esta forma podemos apreciar cómo el amor a Jesús crucificado no supone sólo una comprensión intelectual sino que implica una clara experiencia vital, que permite actuar unas relaciones humanas que son un reflejo de las relaciones trinitarias.

CONCLUSIÓN

Partiendo de la base del amor recíproco y abrazando a Jesús crucificado y abandonado, resulta factible actuar y vivir una espiritualidad de comunión como propone *Novo Millennio Ineunte* en los cuatro puntos citados anteriormente.

El termómetro de nuestra vida cristina es el mandamiento nuevo, que significa amar y ser amado siguiendo un modelo trinitario en las relaciones. En una sublime síntesis del deber ser de las relaciones humanas, Chiara Lubich se expresa así: 'Amar significa ser Dios que ama a Dios y es a su vez amado por Dios, produciendo el Espíritu Santo en medio como Tercera Persona.'

Por lo tanto, el mandamiento nuevo constituye el espejo de la Trinidad en medio de nosotros y un eslabón indispensable en la cadena del amor. Porque el camino, que la vivencia del mandamiento nuevo nos abre, resulta la puerta de acceso al seno de Dios.

NOTES

1 'Mandatum novum do vobis, ut diligatis invicem; sicut dilexi vos ut et vos diligatis invicem' (Jn 13,34). Para todas las citas bíblicas de este trabajo sigo a: Bover María José – O'Callaghan José, *Nuevo Testamento Trilingüe* = BAC 400, Biblioteca de Autores Cristianos, Madrid 1999.

2 Brown Raymond, *The Gospel according to John XIII – XXI*, London: Geoffrey Chapman, 1971, 663.

3 Cancian Domenico, *Nuovo comandamento. Nuova alleanza. Eucaristia. Nell'interpretazione del capitolo 13 del Vangelo di Giovanni*, Edizioni L'amore Misericordioso, Collevalenza (Perugia) 1978, 168–90.

4 O'Connell Matthew J., 'The Concept of Commandment in the Old Testament', *Theological Studies* 21 (1960), 375.

5 Cancian Domenico, *Nuovo comandamento. Nuova alleanza. Eucaristia*, 223.

6 Barrett Charles Kingsley, *The Gospel According to St John. An Introduction with Commentary and Notes on The Greek Text*, London: SPCK, 1978^2, cf. 215.

7 Serrini Lanfranco M., *Un comandamento 'nuovo'. L'amore nello Spirito di Cristo*, Padova: Edizioni Messaggero Padova, 1996, 13–18.

8 Rahner Karl, *Il comandamento dell'amore*, Brescia: Paideia Editrice, 1963, 28.

9 Las citas de la Carta Apostólica han sido extraídas de la página web del Vaticano: http://www.vatican.va/holy_father/john_paul_ii/apost_letters/documents/hf_jp-ii_apl_20010106_novo-millennio-ineunte_sp.html.

10 Vandeleene Michel, *Io-Il fratello-Dio*, Roma: Città Nuova Edizione, 1999, 183–98. El aparato crítico se encuentra en ésta obra, no lo cito por razones de espacio.

11 Lubich Chiara, *La unidad y Jesús Abandonado*, Madrid: Editorial Ciudad Nueva, 1985, 35–6.

12 Vandeleene Michel, *Io-Il fratello-Dio*, 192.

GAIRDÍN AN ANAMA MAR IOMHÁ: SAMPLAÍ AS NA LEABHAIR URNAITHE ÓN NAOÚ AOISE DÉAG SA LEABHARLANN RUISÉAL, COLÁISTE NAOIMH PHÁDRAIG, MÁ NUAD, LE NASCANNA AGUS MACALLAÍ ÓN DTRAIDISIÚIN EIREANNACH CHOMH MAITH LEIS AN MHÓR ROINN

MS NOLLAIG M. NÍ MHAOILEOIN PhD Candidate
St Patrick's College, Maynooth

Osclóimid le paidir i sprid na 19ú hAois déag:

An Ainim an Athar agas an Mhic agas an Spioraid Naomh. Amen.

Osculoirsi a Thiarna mo croidh agus deanfadh mo theanga tu mholla. A Thiarna dein deifir dam cabharadh. Gloire don Athar agas don Mhac agas don Spioraid Niomh mar do bhi air tuis, mar ata anios agus math bhiaidh do shior, sioghal gan chrioch, biodh mar sin.

RÉAMHRÁ

Nuair a chuireas tús leis an dtaighde sa Leabharlann Ruiséil chuir saibhreas na mBailiúchán difriúila iontas orm. Tá sár-altanna agus leabhair scríofa ag Pádraig Ó Fiannachta, Tadhg Ó Dúshláine, Agnes Neligan agus Etain Ó Síocháin faoin áis a bhí á nochtadh os comhair mo shúile i *Lámhscríbhinní Choláiste Phádraig Má Nuad,* le Ó Fiannachta. Sna cnuasaigh feictear leabhair; dánta; scéalta; amhráin; leabhair urnaithe agus seanmóirí. Beidh na leabhair urnaithe amháin á bplé anseo. Tabharfar blaiseadh astu agus dearcadh ar:

Dia, an Trionóid agus ár dTiarna Íosa Chríost
Muire
Naomh Seosamh
Chomh maith le:
Cumhacht an Easpaig
Icóneolaíocht
Liodáin mar uirlis mhachnaimh

Scríobhadh na leabhair urnaithe sa naoú h-aois déag i rith am na bPéindlithe, dlíthe a cuireadh i bhfeidhm chun an Chreideamh Chaitlicigh, an Cultúr agus an Teanga Ghaeilge a threascairt.

Tháinig siad i bhfeidhm go dlúth i rith ama na Banríona Éilis agus ar aghaidh.[1] Seo sliocht as leabhar,*'Our Martyrs'* futhu, i rith ama na Banríona Éilis.

> VII) All Archbishops, Bishops, and every ecclesiastical minister ... shall make oath and declare her Highness ... the only supreme governor of the realm ...
>
> XII) 'Any one who by writing, printing, teaching, preaching, express words, deed, or act, advisedly, maliciously, and directly maintains the authority and jurisdiction of any foreign prince, prelate, & c., and their abettors, shall for the first offence forfeit all ... goods/or jail ... for the second offence ... the penalty of praemunire; for the third ... the penalty of death, as in cases of high treason.'[2]

Am an-dainséarach a bhí ann do gach Caitliceach, do gach sagart, nó pé duine a bhí i mbun cúrsaí scríbhneoireachta nó clódóireachta. Ceileadh ar an nGaeilge ar feadh na gcéadta bliain.[3] In ionad oibreacha nua-chumtha feictear aistriúcháin á chur i gcló sa ré seo.

Ní raibh gach rud gruama, dorcha. Saoradh an teanga scríofa ó smacht na mBard.[4] Leathnaigh comhthéacs shaothrú léann na Gaeilge amach go mór ... san ochtú, naoú cead déag.[5] Caithimid a bheith thar a bheith buíoch do na hOird, na Proinsiasaigh, na Dominicánaigh agus na hÍosánaigh, chomh maith leis na scríobhaithe Éireanneacha agus iad ag bailiú, ag scríobh agus ag cur i gcló, as Louvain na Beilge, as Salamanca na Spáinne agus ón Iodáil.[6]

Tá trí mhórchnuasach Lámhscríbhinní sa Leabharlann Ruiséil. Cnuasach Uí Mhurchú a bhronnadh in 1847. B'shin Easpag Seán O

Murchú as Chorcaí.[7] Cnuasach Uí Chomhraí a shroich an Leabharlann i 1905.[8] B'shin Eoghan Ó Chomhraí, bailitheoir clúiteach agus Ollamh in Ollscoil Chaitliceach na hÉireann; agus Cnuasach Uí Rennacháin, iar-Uachtarán Choláiste Phádraig.[9]

Bhí patrúin ag na scríobhaithe imeasc na n-easpag Caitliceach. Luaitear an tEaspag Seán Ó Murchú, an tEaspag Eoin Baiste Mac Sleighne agus an tEaspag Seán Ó Briain as Corcaigh, i ndiaidh Comhairle Thrionta.[10] Bhí foireann scríobhaithe ag an tEaspag Ó Murchú, ina measc Pól agus Micheál Ó Longáin as Charraig na bhFear. Clann scolártha ab ea na Longánaigh, ag cnuasach agus ag chóipcáil ábhar dúchais Gaeilge agus aistriúcháin ábhair cráifeacha.[11]

Na Leabhair Urnaithe

An chéad Leabhar Urnaithe ná:
Gairdín an Anma
Iar na sgríobhadh, le Pól Ó Longáin
Chum úsáide speisialta Chaitillicidhe na hEírion …
Corca: Tadhg Ó Ceallacháin, 1844.[12]

Seo íomhá amháin as na céadta díobh. Ofráileann *Gairdín an Anma*, nascaithe le Leabhar Geinisis, slite chun ár fiaile phearsanta a phiocadh, le hurnaithe, rialacha agus teagasc. Tá dhá chóip sa Leabharlann, lámhscríofa agus liotagraif, le Pól Ó Longáin, foilsithe in 1844. Míníonn Ní Úrdail gur 'aontaíodh meán na peannaireachta agus meán na priondála i saothrú an léinn sa Ghaeilge ach gurbh é cumas an scríobhaí féin … a thug an dá mheán le chéile.[13]

Luaitear Teagasc Críostaidhe do réir an 'tAthar Bonaentúradh Ó Heosa, d'Ord N. Proinsias'.[14] Osclaíonn an chéad sraith sa mhodh traidisiúnta, leis na h-urnaithe scríofa i bhfoirm dánta, B'shin módh cuimhneólaíochta, caiticeasmach na nGael. Ansin athraíonn an t-údar go haistriúcháin, ó Naomh Augustin ar aghaidh. Osclaítear le Cré an-suimiúil scríofa i bhfoirm dáin (Lch 1–8).[15] Bhí a fhios aige conas an léitheoir a mhealladh ón tús! Seo blaiseadh as.

Atáid trí dóirse air theach nDé
Ní féidir le neach fán ngréin
Gan dul tríotha so … anon don Rightheach.

Na Trí Subháilcidhe Diadha,
Creidiomh, Dothchas Gradh Cialladha.
Asiad so na dóirse adeir mé,
Do bheith air ríghtheach Neimhe.

Na heochaireacha a deirim sibh,
Airtiogal cinte an Chreidimh
A CCre na nAbstal. (Lch 1–2)

Feictear Diagacht ann.
An Tobar Diadha an tAthair ... n Athair geintear an Mac ... Uatha a son thig an Spioraid N(aomh) ... Is Dia an tAthair, Dia an Mac, Dia Fíre Fór an Spioraid N(aomh) ... Aon Dia. (Lch 2)

Íomhá traidisiúnta is ea an Tobar.
Seasann 'An Chré' don chéad doras go Neamh, an Creideamh.
Seasann 'An Phaidior' (Ár nAthair) don dara doras, an Dóthchas. (Lch 8–9)

Dóthchas an dara doiras ...
Gach itche is oircheas d'iaraidh
Atá dá hiaradh san Phaidior ...
Fágtar fút fhéin doras an 'Ghradh Cialladha' a aimsiú.
Seo blaiseadh as an 'Bheannacha Mhuire.' (Lch 9)

Dia do bheatha sa a Mhuire
A thuille lán do grásaibh.
Atá an Tighearna ad tfochair,
A ghein shochair chlann Adhaimh.
Beannuighte thusa tharnda
Deighmhná na talmhuinn uille.
'sas beannuighthean gein ríogadh
Íosa toiradh do bhruinne.
Feictear omós an údair féin ar mhná nuair a scríobhann sé 'Deighmhná na talmhuinn uille.'
Tá na Deich nAitheanta Dé agus Aitheanta na hEagluise i bhfoirm dánta. (Lch 10–11)

Tagann athrú ansin, le teagasc Naoimh Aguistín faoin Aifreann:
Má théann tú go hAifreann n tús go deiridh go mbronntar ceithre headála déag an lá sin, ina measc:

Má ofráileann tú adhradh do Dhia agus má seasann tú ag Golgotha i rith an Aifrinn osclaíonn an doras go Neamh agus dúntar an doras go hIfreann. (Lch 12)

Clúdaítear na Créanna Nicene, (Lch 14–15); Naomh Athanasius (Lch 15–20) chomh maith le Liodáin do Íosa agus Muire, na hAingil agus na Naoimh. Astriúcháin atá iontu. I 'Liottain na hAingiol agus na Naomh' luaitear na Naoimh go léir a luaitear sa Mhór Roinn ach amháin

Naomh Páttraic agus Naomh Colmcille. (Lch 101–109) Tá paidir aoibhinn do Mhuire ann, 'Umhlás Mhuire' (Lch 39–41). Luafar seo níos déanaí.

Athreoimid anois go Leabhar Urnaithe an tAth. Donchadh O'Floinn, 'Tabharthas Spioradálta nó an tSlighe go Neamh: air na thiomargadh ó Oibreachaibh Craibhtheaca, Béarla, Gaoidheilg, agus Francise durnaighthibh ... [16]

Mar a luann Ó Fiannachta i *Maigh Nuad: Saothrú na Gaeilge*, is leabhar urnaithe an-phearsanta é.[17] Feictear ag a thús sár-phrionta de sculptúr a deineadh de Naomh Pádraig leis an dealbhóir, Edward Finden.[18] Cén fáth go luaim seo? Nuair a thugas faoi ndeara go raibh an nathair nimhe greamaithe faoi smacht bhachaill Phádraig thuigeas i slí níos doimhne cumhacht gach easpaig agus iad ag stiúrú muintir Dé. Mar a deireann Íosa Críost i Lucás 10, tá cumhacht tugtha dóibh thar nathracha nimhe, thar gach neart den namhaid, ... 'ní dhéanfaidh rud ar bith dochar daoibh.'[19]

Sa chéad chuid tá eolas ginearálta, mar shampla faoi Chruthú an domhain agus Comhthionóla Gineáralta na h-Eaglaise (V–Vii). Sa dara chuid feictear paidreacha do Dhia, do Mhuire, ár nAingil Chuideachta.

Osclaíonn 'an Phaidir' leis an litir 'A' ornáideach. Seo macalla iontach ón dtraidisiún 'Icóneolaíocht' atá le feiscint i Leabhar Ceannanais. Tóg mar shampla an focal 'Alleluia'gléasta' suas sa cheol naofa.[20] Ansin féach ar an Leabhar Cheannanais. Feictear 'Focal Dé' gléasta suas go healaíonta. B'shin Icóneolaíocht na nGael. Seo teoiric Frances Hogan, atá ana-eolach faoin mBíobla. Glacaim leis an dearcadh seo. Bhí ana-shuim ag an tAth. O'Floinn sa traidisiúin céanna. An féidir linn seo a chothú arís?

Tá meascán paidreacha ann, traidisiúnta agus aistriúchán, mar Phaidreacha na Maidne; Roimh dul a chodhladh; Liodáin d'Íosa, Muire agus na Naoimh; Cré Nicene; Cré Naomh Athanasius; Ullmhú chun Faoisdine agus don Chomaoin Naofa; Teagasc faoi 'Bhrigh N-Shacrament Chuirp Chriosd' (Lch 102–106) agus paidreacha i bhFraincís don Naomh Aifrinn. Feictear leis 'Smuainte ar an mbás Naomh Prionsias de Sales,' (Lch 278–281).

Seo samplaí traidisiúnta:

A Íosa, a Spioraid Naomh, a Aithir agus Uain ... bí ár dhíon. (Lch 9)

A Thighearna do bheirim mile buidhchais díot fá mo thabhairt bhás codalta; fá mo cruthúchadh agus mo cheannach. (Lch 17)

'A Íosa Mhilis ... an Spioraid Shearc. (Lch 27–28)

Tá an 'Hail Holy Queen', 'A Bhanríoghan bheanaighthe' aistrithe. (Lch 33) Baineann an teideal 'A Bhanríoghan' go mór leis an dtraidisiún. Sna sean-lámhscríbhinní, a d'fhás as an dtraidisiún béil, feictear faoi 'Mhartairlaig Ghormain', ár dTiarna Íosa Críost mar 'Tiarna na Seacht Neimhe', i 'bhFéilire Oengusso' le Stokes.[21] I 'mBethú Phátraic' feictear Muire mar 'Bhanríoghan na Seacht Neimhe'.[22]

Clúdaíonn na Seacht Neimhe gach ní sa Cosmas agus Neamh na Tríonóide.[23]

Athreoimid anois go Leabhar *Urnaithe Foirleathan,* sínithe ag Jonathan Furlong, foilsithe i mBaile Átha Cliath, 1842.[24] Clúdaítear urnaithe, go háirithe na Liodáin, le téamaí iontu mar Pháis Chríost nó na 'Seacht nDoláis, chomh maith le dánta, teagasc, agallaimh, mar "Agalamh an Anama leis an Corp" (Lch 239–248); "Teagasg an Photaire" (Lch 340); Teagasc Críostaidhe i bhfoirm Ceist agus Freagra, gnáth fhoirm na Teagasc Críostaidhe i ndiaidh Comhairle Thrionta. Críochnáionn sé le 'Duain na Páise' (Lch 355).

Samplaí as na hOibreacha aistrithe ná:

An Sailm 'De Profundis' (Lch 133–143).

An Dies Irae as Gaeilge (Lch 155–157).

Seacht Sailm na hAithrighe – Sailm 6, 31,37,50, 101 129, 143. (Lch 190–198).

Nascaim seo le 'Umhlás Mhuire', as *Gairdín an Anma*:

> Go mbeannuightear dhuit a Mhuire, a Ríoghan an Atha(ir) Neamhda ... a Mhatha(ir) Dé asé do Mhac ... anrachas an S.pioraid N.aomh ... A Bhanríoghan Neimhe agus talamh.[26]
>
> Feictear ról Naoimh Sheosaimh sna Liodáin leis:
> In áit an Athair Sioruidhe ar talamh.
> Fear do ghairm Íosa Athair air. (Lch 87)
>
> Fear foighneach a chonaic, a chlos, a mhothaigh agus a iompraigh Íosa Críost, Mac Dé an Athair. (Lch 91–96)

Ag athrú anois go Leabhar Urnaithe tanaí C53, sínithe ag Pádraig Mac Anguinen, a osclaíonn le Liodáin do Naomh Phroinsias.[27] Tá paidreacha ann don Chroí Ró-Naofa, do Mhuire agus Naomh Sheosaimh, aistriúcháin agus ón dtraidisiúin. Mar shampla:

> A ... Mhuire ... Adhbhocóidigh mhór carthanach na bpeacach sin ná tréig ... síocháin dá nanmna ó an leanbh d'oll tú féin. (Lch 11)

Sa Phaidir 'Urnaigh cum a Naingil Chuideachta' iarrann an t-údar cabhair Mhuire mar 'An bhean a thuigeann leanaí' (Lch 6–7). Scaipthe tríd na Leabhair Urnaithe feictear 'A Thiarna na n-óg', 'a Rioghán na n-Óg'. Cinnte go n-éistíonn Dia le daoine go bhfuil meon agus croíthe naíonda acu.

Tá iomann machnamhach ann faoi ról Naoimh Sheosaimh agus an Chlann Naofa as Béarla, ina luaitear 'Crann an Beatha' ár dTiarna Íosa Críost.'

Moltar i *Mhánuel Dearbtha d'Urnuighthe Caoindúthrachtach*, le Tomás do Búrc, 'Goir mheanmha (Contemplate) ... creid a dfhulaing an Slannaighthoír ar do shon.'

'Tug thú feín go hiomlán do Dhia.'

Cabhraíonn na leabhair urnaithe linn díriú ar shaothrú ghrá Dé ionann, ionas go bhfásfaidh 'Crann an Beatha', ár dTiarna Íosa Críost, i ngairdín ár nAnama.

NOTES

1 Denis Murphy, *Our Martyrs*, Dublin: Fallon, 1896; Banríon Shasana Éilis ó 1558–1603, 9, 32–41.

2 Murphy, *Our Martyrs*, 9.

3 Pádraig Ó Fiannachta, *Léas Eile ar ár Litríocht*, Maigh Nuad, 1982, 217.

4 Agnes Neligan, ed., *Maynooth Library Treasures: From the Collection of Saint Patrick's College*, Dublin: Royal Irish Academy, 1995, 93.

5 Meidhbhín Ní Úrdail, 'Seachadadh agus Seachadóirí Téacsaí san Ochtú agus sa Naoú Céad Déag', *Studia Hibernica,* no. 32, Baile Átha Cliath: Coláiste Phádraig , 2002–3, 78.

6 Na Coláistí Cléireach Gaelacha sna tíortha seo chun na sagairt a thraenáil.

7 Easpag Seán Ó Murchú, 1772–1847.

8 Pádraig Ó Fiannachta, eag., 'Lámhscríbhinní Gailge Mhaigh Nuad', *Maigh Nuad agus an Ghaeilge: Léachtaí Cholm Cille, XXIII*, Maigh Nuad: An Sagart, 1993, 185.

9 Tomás Ó Fiaich, Má Nuad, Má Nuad: An Sagart, 1972, 31; Dr Labhrás Ó Rennacháin, 1845–57, mar Uachtarán.

10 Neligan, eag., *Maynooth Library Treasures*, 109: Easpag Eoin Baiste Mac Sleighne, 1693–1713, *Scríobhaithe Chorcaí 1700–1850* le Breandán Ó Conchúir, Baile Átha Cliath: Clócomhar, 1982, 216–18; Easpag Seán Ó Briain, 1748–69; Tadhg Ó Dúshláine, 'Seanmóirí Mhaigh Nuad', *Maigh Nuad: Saothrú na Gaeilge 1795–1995*, eag. Etaín Ó Síocháin, Maigh Nuad: An Sagart, 1995, 63–78; Easpag Seán Ó Murchú, 1772–1847.

11 Ní Úrdail, 'Seachadadh agus Seachadóirí Téacsaí san Ochtú agus sa Naoú Céad Déag', *Studia Hibernica*, 76.

12 Pól Ó Longáin, *Gairdín an Anma: Iar na sgríobhadh Chum úsáide speisialta Chaitillicidhe na hEírion*, Corca: Tadhg Ó Ceallacháin, 1844. Cláraithe mar RB226.

13 Ní Úrdail, 'Seachadadh agus Seachadóirí Téacsaí san Ochtú agus sa Naoú Céad Déag', *Studia Hibernica,* no. 32, 91.

14 Ó Longáin, *Gairdín Anma*, 1: *Teagasc Críostaidhe* an tAth. Bonaentúradh Ó Heosa, a cuireadh igcló sa Bhruiséal, 1612.

15 As *Teagasc Críostaidhe* an tAth. Bonaentúradh Ó Heosa, a cuireadh i gcló sa Bhruiséal 1612.

16 Donchadh Ó Floinn, *Tabharthas Spioradálta nó an tSlighe go Neamh: air na thiomargadh ó Oibreachaibh Craibhtheaca, Béarla,, Gaoidheilg, agus Francise durnaighthibh, bíodh duthchus is fuiniomh ad chroídhe; Is í umhlachd do stiúras chuige sin sinn, bíodh scrúdadh agus cúram aguibh chum gúidhe, is dá*

his life in and around Brussels. At seminary, he later said he had 'lived a double life: that of the student, and that of a worker's child, and these two worlds were poles apart'.[4] Returning home on holiday, he was profoundly shocked at what had happened to his former classmates: 'When fifty years ago I entered the junior seminary ... my schoolmates went out to work. They were intelligent, decent, God-fearing. When I came back for my holidays they were coarse, corrupted and lapsed from the Church – whilst I was becoming a priest. I started to make enquiries, it became the obsession of my life.'[5]

This was reinforced by his father's early death, when Jozef dedicated his priestly service to 'the salvation of the working class and young workers'.[6] Post-ordination study in sociology at Leuven, followed by overseas research in the holidays from teaching in a junior seminary, enabled Cardijn to publish a handful of articles: on working conditions in the textile industry in Germany; on single, working-class women; and on trades unionism in Britain.[7]

Arriving as curate in the parish of Laeken in 1913, Cardijn found the dichotomy between work and religious practice (limited though it often was) to be as prevalent as ever among young workers. He initially established a study circle for young needle-workers, with the aim of forming them in their faith, and offering them education – many were illiterate, innumerate, or both. At the request of young men in the parish, a study circle was soon formed for them too. By 1915, Cardijn had been appointed 'Director of social works' for the diocese, a post he held until 1925. After World War I, these parish study circles became more formalised, gradually morphing into the Young Christian Workers (male and female branches). The movement was approved by Pope Pius XI in early 1925.[8]

Key to the popularity of the Young Christian Workers, and to the support the movement received from the Pope and bishops across Western Europe during the inter-war period, was Cardijn's appropriation and development of Leo XIII's teaching in *Rerum Novarum* on 'associations of working-men'.[9] Leo was full of praise for those 'who ... have striven ... to better the condition of the working class ... They have taken up the cause of the working man, and have spared no efforts to better the condition both of families and of individuals'.[10] Cardijn's insight was to ensure that it should be, not 'men of eminence',[11] nor clergy, but the workers themselves, who '(would strive) to better the condition of the working class'. Marking a definitive move away from the paternalism which had dominated nineteenth-century social Catholicism, Cardijn transferred responsibility for improving working-class living and working conditions, and the apostolate of the working class, to members of this very group. Suddenly the Church was listening to young workers, taking their concerns seriously, and encouraging them to take their place in the Church and in society.

LAY APOSTLES

The work of the Young Christian Workers was thus two-fold: educating workers in their faith would bring them to realise their inherent dignity as children of God; and to accord themselves, their work, and their colleagues the dignity commensurate with this. It was to be 'a school' of 'lay apostolate', of 'training', 'which transforms their life of young workers into a lay priesthood and a lay apostolate'.[12] This school would also form them to bring the good news to their peers and friends; thus the workers would be the primary apostles of workers. This lay apostolate of like-to-like was to complement, not replace, the apostolic work of the priest: 'The priest cannot, must not, replace lay people in their apostolic mission.'[13]

Such apostolic work required a strong faith: the young worker 'must develop in himself the sense of faith', a faith which 'must be continually renewed in our minds by an apostolic spiritual life which is not that of a priest or religious, but working class and adapted to working-class life'.[14]

Cardijn insisted that 'ordinary daily working life cannot be separated, even in its most profane aspects, from *religious life* ... religious practices – sacraments, prayer, Mass, Communion, liturgy, religious ceremonies – are but the sources, the beginnings, the channels of the divine life which must transform and divinise all aspects and manifestations of working-class life'.[15]

Faith was to permeate daily life. 'Each morning, the young worker should be able to offer to his Creator and Redeemer, not the lives of others, but his own life ... the offering that is worth most in the sight of God.'[16] Indeed, 'the whole of life must become religious ... must, like the Host, be consecrated to God'.[17] For the young worker, work was to become the chapel and altar: 'he cannot handle his rosary or his missal while he is in the factory; he has tools in his hands and work to do. [He] must change his work into a prayer, a prolonged Mass, united to the priest at the altar.'[18]

In order to carry out the vital work of the lay apostolate, through and in their work, Young Christian Workers were to have a strong faith, which would seep into every aspect of their daily lives, particularly their work. In a very particular way, their workplace was to become the altar. This in turn required Cardijn, not only to develop foundations for a theology of work, but also to ensure that the Young Christian Workers had a profound, and correct, understanding both of the centrality of the Mass, and of the Church and their place in and contribution to it. I will therefore now turn to his concept of the Eucharist and of the mystical body, before returning to the theme of work as eucharistic.

THE EUCHARIST

For Cardijn, the Mass was 'the centre and summit of the liturgy',[19] indeed, 'the source and culmination of all Christian life' *avant la lettre*.[20] He followed the lead of Pius X[21] in encouraging more frequent attendance at Mass and reception of Communion where this was realistic: the working day at YCW headquarters always began with Mass, which all were expected to attend. At the same time, he was 'haunted by the thought of the thousands of workers who leave their homes before the church is open in the mornings, and only come home in the evening once the church is closed';[22] effectively meaning that 'daily Mass and Holy Communion [were] out of the question because of work'.[23] He nonetheless emphasised the importance for young workers of understanding the Mass. 'How must they pray, be united to Christ? Try to make them understand the Mass ... Not understanding it they get bored ... They must want to go to Mass.'[24] To this end:

> Very often, when I was in parish ministry, I would replace the meetings of the first YCWs with a live demonstration of the Mass. We would gather in the evening in the church in Laeken, and there, with the young men or young women around the altar, I

would show them the sacred vessels, explain the symbols, and carry out in front of them, and with them, the most significant actions of the eucharistic sacrifice. For most of them it was such an extraordinary revelation … that they were marked by it for life.[25]

The centrality of the Eucharist to the life of prayer was carried into the world of the lay person. *Ite, missa est.* When Mass has ended, the lay person should know it is this very sacrifice of redemption which pushes them to action in the world: 'Go now, lay people, go to your mission, to your work, which is the ongoing sacrifice of Christ! Your machine, your workbench is the altar.'[26]

The Eucharist – sacrament and sacrifice – was, for Cardijn, absolutely transformative of life, especially working life, transforming 'each worker into a lay-priest who can make his work, his workbench … an altar, united with priests at the altars of their churches …'[27] Ultimately, it was this link between Eucharist and work which enabled 'every worker to bring Christ to their friends at work'.[28]

Furthermore, as Henri de Lubac (1896–1991) pointed out, 'The Church makes the Eucharist, and the Eucharist makes the Church.'[29] The Church describes the Eucharist as a sacrament, but it is the Eucharist which builds up the Church community. 'Their life [is to become] a divine life, in constant union with Christ, so that their own life becomes the life of Christ in them, within that divine community … which is the Church.'[30] Those who receive the Body of Christ at the Eucharist make up the mystical body of Christ, the community of Christians working in the world, continuing the eucharistic sacrifice there. It is to Cardijn's understanding of the Church as mystical body of Christ that I now turn.

THE CHURCH: MYSTICAL BODY OF CHRIST

'From 1932 onwards, for the first time, [Cardijn's] ecclesiology was marked by the image of the Church as the Mystical Body of Christ, a concept which he had never before used. This position was inspired in particular by Pius XI's writings and speeches, particularly *Quadragesimo Anno* (1931).'[31] *Pace* Vos, this image was not simply due to Pius XI, but in fact formed a significant part of the theological *Zeitgeist* of the interwar period in Europe: 'during the 1920s and 1930s', Hahnenberg reminds us, 'Paul's organic image for the Church burst onto the scene'.[32] The bibliography compiled by Bluett demonstrates a dramatic growth in studies in this field between 1920 and 1937, moving from 'doctrinal expositions (and e)xegetical studies' to 'historical studies of the doctrine in the Patristic and Medieval periods'.[33] As well as Cardijn, theologians such as Romano Guardini (1885–1968), Karl Adam (1876–1966), Émile Mersch SJ (1890–1940), and Sebastiaan Tromp SJ (1889–1975), to mention but a few, studied the concept of the Church as mystical body – Tromp is widely acknowledged as the author of Pius XII's 1943 encyclical *Mystici Corporis Christi*. Perhaps most famously, de Lubac investigated the question, initially in a series of articles for *Recherches de Science Religieuse*[34] in the late 1930s, later published as *Corpus Mysticum*,[35] in which he traced the use and understanding of that expression. He would develop a deeper theology of the Church as mystical body of Christ in *Méditation sur l'Église*.[36]

The image of the Church as mystical body marks not only a retrieval of Paul's ecclesiology (Romans and 1 Corinthians describing the whole *ekklesia* as Christ's body, Ephesians/Colossians developing the motif of Christ the head of his body, the Church), but also the retrieval of patristic and medieval writings on Eucharist and Church. By taking up this important motif, Cardijn demonstrates that, despite his adamant claims that he was a man of action rather than a theologian, he clearly had his finger on the theological pulse, and intended to use it to support his beloved Young Workers.

A key aspect of mystical body ecclesiology, from Möhler's *Symbolik*[37] onwards, is the understanding of 'the Church as the continuation of the incarnation of the Son of God'.[38] For Cardijn, this fitted closely with the emphasis on work as a collaboration with God, to bring about the salvation of the world: 'the divine seal of vocation which makes every worker the immediate, personal, irreplaceable co-worker with God in his work of creation and of redemption.'[39] It also reinforced the understanding that every worker – by which he meant, every person – as a part of the mystical body, was to share in the apostolic work of evangelisation. The mystical body 'finds its foremost and full expression and realisation' in 'that apostolate, which confers on humanity all its value, and its supreme and ultimate significance'.[40] Cardijn offered Young Christian Workers the concept of the Church as mystical body, formed 'by all humanity, united to Christ',[41] as a foundation to underpin the apostolate they carried out, 'a shared apostolate to all members of the mystical body',[42] for 'the whole mystical body is to be apostolic'.[43] For, he insisted, 'only true unity will be a dynamic, transformative unity; this alone will bring about a constructive charity, the life and soul of the mystical body'.[44]

WORKBENCH AS ALTAR

Cardijn repeatedly told the Young Christian Workers that they were 'not machines, or animals, or slaves', but rather 'the sons, the collaborators, the heirs of God'; this gave them their 'unique, only, and true destiny, their *raison d'être*, reason for living, reason for working'.[45] It is because 'the Word became flesh and dwelt among us [that] every person's eternal destiny is incarnate in temporal life, where it develops and becomes concrete'.[46] For young workers, as indeed for every human person, 'there is but one eternal destiny ... either to be saved or to be damned for all eternity'.[47] All workers, as indeed, all human beings, bear the especial dignity of being created *in imago Dei*.

Cardijn was careful to demonstrate that work, far from being a 'punishment, a curse, slavery', was in fact 'a collaboration with the Creator and Redeemer. At his work, the worker is the primary minister, God's immediate and intimate collaborator'.[48] There is no doubt, for Cardijn, that work 'continues the mission of Christ the worker'; that working life 'is necessary for the redemption of the world'.[49] But crucial to this is the role of the Eucharist.

One of the difficult areas in the theology of work is the Pauline understanding of working for Christ – does it mean, doing one's work (tent-making) for the glory of Christ; or does it mean, doing Christ's work (evangelising)? Cardijn, arguing that the Eucharist 'transforms human work into the work of Christ'[50] appears to be in favour of the former interpretation. This interpretation is supported by his subsequent statements that the Eucharist 'transforms the place of work'[51] and 'consecrates the working regime'.[52]

CONCLUSION

In conclusion, Cardijn's theology of the Eucharist provides a foundational underpinning for his theology of work. A gifted orator, he was able to teach his Young Christian Workers the value of the Eucharist, the value of their work, and their own value, using his own, non-academic theological method. Underpinning his entire theology were two convictions: that 'each young worker is worth more than all the gold in the world, for they are children of God'; and that 'the Eucharist gives human work the providential place that God has granted it in his plan for the world and in the economy of salvation'.[53]

By raising work to the status of the eucharistic sacrifice, Cardijn was thus able to encourage the Young Christian Workers in their apostolate with their peers, truly enabling them to bring the Eucharist into their places of work, by ensuring that their workbenches were their altars.

NOTES

1 Joseph Cardijn, 'Sermon lors des cérémonies de la consécration de la basilique à Lisieux', KADOC archives, Cardijn microfiche #1846 (1937).

2 Joseph Cardijn, 'Avant-Propos' (1963), *Laïcs en premières lignes,* Paris: Éditions universitaires, 1963, 9–14 (10–11). Unless otherwise stated, all translations of foreign-language works are my own. Note, too, that Cardijn was baptised 'Jozef' but published (in French and English) as 'Joseph'.

3 As Cardijn pointed out, 'Pope Pius XI himself gave (Thérèse) to be the special patron of the apostles of Catholic Action in their places of work ... ' ('Lisieux', 2).

4 Jozef Cardijn, 'Ten Huize Van ... Monseigneur Cardijn', KADOC archive, Cardijn microfiche, 1964 (1962).

5 Eugene Langdale, 'Introduction', in Joseph Cardijn, *Challenge to Action,* E. Langdale trans., Chicago: Fides, 1955, 7–14 (8).

6 Cardijn, 'Point du départ d'un cheminement' (1963), *Laïcs,* 19–28 (20).

7 Joseph Cardijn, 'L'industrie à domicile en Allemagne', *Revue Sociale Catholique* 11 (1907); *Idem.* 'L'organisation ouvrière anglaise', *Revue Sociale Catholique* 15/16 (1911); *Idem.* 'L'ouvrière isolée', *Revue Sociale Catholique* 17 (1913).

8 Cardijn states that 'he had the providential grace to be received in private audience by Pius XI, who approved the YCW in its aim, method, and organisation', 'Point du départ', in *Laïcs,* 26–7. This contrasts with the rather more extraordinary accounts in some of the quasi-hagiographic literature, according to which, after a public audience, Cardijn was to have sneaked into the Apostolic Palace, past the Swiss Guards, and entered the Pope's study.

9 Leo XIII, *Rerum Novarum,* 54–6.

10 Rn, 55.

11 Rn, 55.

12 Cardijn, 'The Y.C.W.' (1938), *Challenge,* 88–96 (91).

13 'Une nécessité vitale pour l'Église' (1935), *Laïcs,* 33–41 (37).

14 'The Young Worker faces life' (1949), *Challenge,* 62–82 (79–80).

15 'L'apostolat des laics dans une de ses realisations concrètes: un laïcat ouvrier' (1935), *Laïcs,* 45–53 (47).

16 'The Hour of the Workers' Mission', *The Church and the Young Worker. Speeches and Writings of Canon Joseph Cardijn,* E. Langdale, trans., London: Young Worker Publications, 1948, 14–21 (20).

17 'The Hour of the Worker Missionaries', *The Church and the Young Worker*, 22–31 (22).

18 'The Young Worker faces life', *Challenge*, 80.

19 'La formation des laïcs à leur apostolat' (1951), *Laïcs*, 151–73 (159).

20 *Lumen Gentium* no. 11; Norman P. Tanner SJ, *Decrees of the Ecumenical Councils*, London: Sheed & Ward, 1990, ii.857.

21 Pius X, *Sacra Tridentine Synodus* (1905).

22 Cardijn, 'La formation', *Laïcs*, 158.

23 'The Young Worker faces life', *Challenge*, 80.

24 'Worker Missionaries', *The Hour of the Working Class*, 28.

25 'La formation', *Laïcs*, 160.

26 Ibid.

27 'Lisieux', 4.

28 Ibid.

29 Henri de Lubac SJ, *Méditation sur l'Église, Théologie*, Paris: Aubier, 1953, 113; also Paul McPartlan, *The Eucharist Makes the Church. Henri de Lubac and John Zizioulas in Dialogue*, Edinburgh: T&T Clark, 1993.

30 Cardijn, 'A Y.C.W. of the Masses to the Scale of the World' (1945), *Challenge*, 97–107 (98).

31 Louis Vos, 'La Jeunesse Ouvrière Chrétienne', *Histoire du Mouvement Ouvrier Chrétien en Belgique*, Emmanuel Gerard and Paul Wynants, eds, KADOC-STUDIES 16, Leuven: Leuven University Press, 1994, 424–95 (455).

32 Edward P. Hahnenberg, 'The Mystical Body of Christ and Communion Ecclesiology: Historical Parallels', *Irish Theological Quarterly* 70/3 (2005) 3–30 (3).

33 J. Bluett SJ, 'The Mystical Body: A Bibliography, 1890–1940', *Theological Studies* 3 (1942) 262–89 (262).

34 RSR, 29 (1939), RSR 30 (1940).

35 Henri de Lubac SJ, *Corpus Mysticum. The Eucharist and the Church in the Middle Ages*, Gemma Simmonds, Richard Price, and Christopher Stevens trans., Laurence Paul Hemming and Susan Frank Parsons, eds, London: SCM Press, 2006. This translation is from the second (1949) edition.

36 Paris: Seuil, 1953; ET, *The Splendor of the Church*, Michael Mason trans., San Francisco: Ignatius, 1999.

37 J. A Möhler, *Symbolism: or, the exposition of the doctrinal differences between Catholics and Protestants as evidenced by their symbolical writings*, J. B.

Robertson, trans. (3rd edn) New York: The Catholic Publication House, 1843.

38 Peter Riga, 'The Ecclesiology of Johann Adam Möhler', *Theological Studies* 22/4 (1961) 563–87 (562).

39 Cardijn, 'Lisieux', 1.

40 'Dimensions de l'apostolat des laïcs' (1951), *Laïcs*, 103–117 (108).

41 'La mission terrestre de l'homme et de l'humanité' (1951), *Laïcs*, 67–75 (70).

42 'La mission terrestre', *Laïcs*, 75.

43 'Une nécessité vitale', *Laïcs*, 38.

44 'Un laïcat ouvrier', *Laïcs*, 52.

45 JOC, ed., *Compte-Rendu de la Semaine d'Études Internationale de la Jeunesse Ouvrière Chrétienne*, Brussels: Éditions Jocistes, 1935, 71–2.

46 *Compte-Rendu*, 72.

47 Cardijn, 'Scale', *Challenge*, 98.

48 'Un laïcat ouvrier', *Laïcs*, 46.

49 Ibid., 48.

50 'Lisieux', 1.

51 Ibid., 1, 5.

52 Ibid., 7.

53 Ibid., 1.

'THE EUCHARIST AND THE EAGER LONGING OF CREATION': THE RELATIONAL WHOLENESS OF REALITY AND THE MYSTERY OF COMMUNION

MR JOSÉ PEDRO LOPES ANGÉLICO PhD Candidate
Catholic University of Portugal

> The day of the 'new creation' presupposes the ecological 'day of rest' of the original creation, if that new creation is to complete the first and not destroy it.
>
> The ecological day of rest should be a day without pollution of the environment – a day when we leave our cars at home, so that nature too can celebrate its Sabbath.[1]

Since the Second Vatican Council, sacramental theology has been defined by its return to the early sources of Christianity as well as of a new awareness of the eucharistic central place. But even before the Council, several theologians offered new insights inspired by ancient intuitions. In this way, categories such as mystery and communion have been underlined since those times in order to express the very nature of the Eucharist, and consequently of all the other sacraments. In the meantime, half a century has passed and it seems that a large part of our celebrations are gradually turning back in terms of liturgical practice.

However, emerging trends in sacramental theology seem to be exclusively stressing the category of sacrifice, we believe that the centrality of the Eucharist depends rather on the peculiar features that scripture reveals to be the nature of the Triune God: mystery and communion. Understood in terms of eschatological anticipation, the Eucharist is described by Paul as being a celebration of the life and death of Jesus, the Risen. Nevertheless, the community of his followers does not only celebrate something from the past, but also a living presence and the awaiting in hope of its consummation: the mystery of total communion. Furthermore, this sacramental experience is deep-rooted in a dialectics of absence-presence. This tension is better expressed in terms of *eager longing* (cf. Rm 8:19), which Paul assumes to be the (silent) cry of all creation. Our aim is therefore to reflect on the Eucharist as a mystery of communion, without putting aside the relational wholeness of the whole created reality, which we believe a coherent Eucharist theology should be aware of.

THE RELATIONAL LOGIC OF CHRISTIAN THEOLOGY

Salvation is undoubtedly an important and central issue for theological discourse, once categories such as promise, or promised land, forgiveness, deliverance from evil and sin, heaven, kingdom of God or eternal life are all implied in its common understanding. Nevertheless, theology needs to ask itself how should the question be brought up. I believe it should be put in the following terms: what are human beings supposed to be saved from and by whom, and what reality are they supposed to be saved for? These are three out of four questions that Adolphe Gesché raises in one of his books.[2] Anyway, I would like to begin this reflection by pointing out a renewed concept of salvation.

Twenty years have passed since Mary Midgley published her book on *Science as Salvation*.[3] When modern science came into being, it was understood as one of the means that could actually lead the human being to salvation, because 'Nature was God's creation, and to study it was simply one of the many ways to celebrate his glory. That celebration was understood to be the proper destiny of the soul, the meaning of human life'.[4] But since then, science took a path that would gradually put God aside, or push him 'into the background'.[5]

There is no need to say that science became a means of salvation to some extent. But once again the double question comes up: salvation from what and what is its purpose? In a certain way, that science has a saving power is totally acceptable if we consider its *marriage* with technology: the access to medical treatments, new ways of palliating pain when it comes to untreatable and deadly diseases, and so forth. This is indeed that renewed concept of salvation: we are being saved

EUCHARIST AND THE EAGER LONGING FOR COMMUNION

'The whole creation is waiting with eagerness for the children of God to be revealed'.[10] This assertion implies a deeper reflection. According to Jordi Sanchéz Bosch,[11] Romans 8 is part of a major doctrinal body concerning the Christian life.[12] It's all about the new law, in which live dived those whose life is breathed by the Spirit of Christ: 'Thus, condemnation will never come to those who are in Christ Jesus, because the law of the Spirit which gives life in Christ Jesus has set you free from the law of sin and death.'[13] Though, this sinfully and deadly law, from which the *Christforms* were set free, is the one into which Adam and Eve dived in the beginning.

If in the first and second chapters of Genesis everything goes towards a relational dialogue,[14] when everything was said as *tôb* and at the end of the whole creative process as *tôb me'od* (very good), in the third chapter we see the fall, the evolving degenerative process of the protological design of communion.[15] If in the first part there is a conscious voice of the universe, *quo capax Dei* (cf. Augustinus, *De Trinitate*); in the second one we find all the deadly ingredients of the relationality initially desired.

In fall's account, there is one note that must be underlined: before the fall, the first relational stage is of peace and harmony. Thus, the protological sin can be understood as paradigm of every sin,[16] for sin is essentially a free decision of rupture in the relationship between the God creator and his creatures. Therefore, matter (and consequently human body) cannot be understood as a divinity decayed[17] (Gnosticism). It is all about free will and decision (*personhood*). One of the most important elements of *personhood* is relationality, of which the immediate consequence is solidarity[18] between those who share such a structure. This solidarity, even in sin, means that the whole creation, human and not human, shares with Adam this sinful condition.[19] Thus, sin is not only personal and social but cosmic as well.[20]

What exactly do we mean by sin and death into which entered Adam and Eve?

What really happens in the fall's account is a betrayal of the created freedom by reason of a free and illusory eagerness of dissolving the ontological different peculiarity in relation to God's nature.

The snake appears as the highest possibility of denying the divine project of communion. In his eagerness of being equal to God, and thus not recognising the richness of difference, the human being refuses the enabling relational otherness. And that is the idol: a projection of the same (*id*) in the other (*alter*).[21] Idolatry is the beginning possibility of violence, in the despotic domination over the others and the cosmos, emptying the true meaning of the created reality and subjecting it to futility.

This futility is nowadays translated as destruction, but in the original Greek it is vanity,[22] for example, futility and emptiness. In that promethean eagerness of divinisation by his own will, the human being moves away not only from his created condition, but rather from the possibility of accepting it by grace. This happens for the human being remains in immanence, in pure biologic instinct. This is why he won't be able to elevate the rest of creation as he should. This is why we understand when Paul says that 'human nature has nothing to look forward to but death, while the Spirit looks forward to life and peace, because the outlook of disordered human nature is opposed to God, since it does not submit to God's law, and indeed it cannot, and those who live by their natural inclinations can never be pleasing to God'.[23]

It is thus why non-human creation is submitted to sin as well, because by virtue of human futility, creation was stripped of meaning. The meaning of this sin in the wholeness of creation is similar to a withering plant without fruits. But in Christian consciousness there is still a hope. And from the *eager longing* of creation arises a hope towards the future, desired in the present and anchored in the past. There is a hope not only for mankind, but for the whole creation as well.

Celebrating the Eucharist every Sunday,[24] we do not celebrate only the memory of what God has done for our salvation, but rather, remembering this incarnated mystery of communion in history (and in the cosmos), we also affirm our hope in the future of the full communion to come, as guaranteed and promised by the resurrection of Jesus. And it would not be full communion if the wholeness of reality was not embraced by this mystery of communion.

THE ECCLESIAL 'WE' AND THE EUCHARIST: IN DIALOGUE WITH THE 'THEO-LOGIC' OF HERIBERT MÜHLEN

REV. DR ALESSANDRO CLEMENZIA
Sophia University Institute, Loppiano, Italy

The actuality of the category of *we* in its ecclesial reference has confirmation not only in the academic field: it is enough to look at the numerous studies on the communional dimension of the Church, showing the value of relationships founded upon reciprocity, a visible expression of how the Trinity manifests itself; but also in the socio-cultural context in which the challenges rising from the process of globalisation have imposed a serious rethinking of the value of the other and of the question of unity; that is to say, what is meant by *unum*, the goal toward which we tend whether in a conscious way or not (and it is the same strategy of communication which verifies it).

In the face of these realities which initiate in the socio-cultural context and which are seen even today under the guise of 'challenges', can the Church, or rather, the 'ecclesial we' still offer a proposal that makes sense? The theologian Heribert Mühlen has tried to answer that question in all of his research, in the various theological fields he studied.

To enter into the ecclesiological dynamics of the ecclesial-*we* it is important first of all to understand what is meant by *we*. Mühlen tries to explain its significance starting with Trinitarian theology, interpreted in the light of personological categories. He starts with the personal pronoun *I*, which on the one hand indicates the identity of the person as 'incommunicable' existence, unrepeatable and unique (in saying 'I' the subject is identified as being totally distinct and distinguishable from every other). While on the other hand, the personal pronoun *I* indicates its being-in-relation: to say *I* is a declaration of one's own being before a *you* or better yet, before another *I*.

The meeting between *I* and *you* creates a twofold situation that is fundamental for a Trinitarian and ecclesiological reflection: a) a relationship of opposition: the more *I* and *you* become closer, the more the specifics which distinguish one from the other emerge, and thus the distinction between them; b) an *intentio unitiva* in which *I*, even though discovering to be 'other' than you, enters into a relationship of intentional reception of the other so much so as to generate reciprocal recognition. The twofold reality which is formed realises the *union I-you,* a unity that is composed simultaneously of a relation of opposition and a relation of reciprocal reception. This, however, is not yet the *we* (as is often said in the Italian language, 'we two' or 'us both') but rather, the *union I-you.*

So when can we talk about a *we,* since it is not the same as the result of the relationship between an *I* and a *you*? We are at the heart of the personological method of Mühlen, who after having presented and argued the fundamental structure of the meeting of the *I-you,* introduces another union, the *union-of-we* (*Wir-Vereinigung*), which is formed in the moment when the *I* and the *you* do not relate to each other in a relation of opposition but fulfil a common action, as if they were a single subject, towards a third. It is this third that transforms the *union-I-you* into the *union-of-we.*

Mühlen rereads Trinitarian theology in the light of the personological method just described, albeit in a simplified way. Basing the discussion on *Anì Jhwh,* as a formula of revelation in the Old Testament, and n *'egó eimi* in the New Testament, whereby the Father presents himself as the *I-in-person,* and the Son, as the *You-in-person,* Mühlen uses the personological method as a hermeneutical criterion for a re-examination of the Trinity-in-itself (or the Trinitarian life of God in himself).

What distinguishes the Father is his being the origin without beginning, the paternity and the active spiration. According to Mühlen, the Father uses the *I-expression,* in the Old Testament, so as not to allow for the presence of other gods next to him, and in the New Testament, to emphasise his being the origin of both the Son and the Holy Spirit. The absoluteness of the Father, his being without origin, cannot be separated from his paternity, that is from his relation to the Son. The Father thus manifests himself as the *I-intra-Trinitarian.*

The Son, on his part, presents himself as an *I* who finds the sense of his being in relation to that *You,* the Father, who constitutes him as *I*. He is the *You-in-person*, because his *I* while having all the specifics that distinguish him as *I* with respect to the Father, is nonetheless only in respect to the *You* of the Father, in truth, to the *I* of the Father. The Son is therefore the *You-intra-Trinitarian* in reference both to his response to the *I* of the Father and to the being-You-of-the-Father, in the establishment of the dialogue in which he does not lose his being without a beginning.

And where is the Trinitarian or intraTrinitarian *We* realised? On the basis of what has been affirmed through the personological method, that is that the *we* is not identified with the *union-I-you,* there needs to be a third. It is here that Mühlen introduces the discussion of the Holy Spirit, the third Person who is neither external nor extraneous but within the relationship between Father and Son. He is the same divine we-ness, the *We-in-person,* the *relationship-We-intra-Trinitarian*.

But how can a single person be the *We,* which by itself is an indication of plurality?

The Holy Spirit, within the divine life is the *nexus Patris et Filii,* and the same communication between Father and Son and, we might add, their *perichoresis in-Person,* since he personalises the intra-Trinitarian dynamics and all that can be attributed to the divine nature.

The third Person of the Trinity is the most complex because of its anonymity. It is sufficient to look at his name, 'Holy' and 'Spirit', terms which can both be said of each Person of the Trinity and of their divine nature. The anonymity of the divine Pneuma has been confirmed by the fact that in the scriptures, on the contrary to the Father or the Son, he never reveals himself as an 'I' or as a 'You'. He never speaks about himself to the people of God even though he is the condition of the possibility of the act of faith in the Father and in the Son on behalf of the individual believer and the faithful community.

I would now like to more thoroughly examine the question of the epistemological statute of *we*, starting with the suggestive intuitions of Mühlen to discover the fundamental characteristics of the ecclesial *we.*

To more completely understand Mühlen's reflections on the *We*, it is necessary to introduce a category used by him which was not given a great importance in the theological field nor was it studied deeply by the scholars who studied his ideas but which, however, seems to emphasise the specificity of his proposal: *the we-a-priori*.

This category is used here in a twofold significance – the *we-ness* intended as divine nature and the *We-in-person*, that is, the Holy Spirit. Of the few scholars who expounded on this category, most have dealt almost exclusively with the pneumatological aspect which shows a certain disregard, especially in the last decades, for a deeper speculation of the concept of divine nature. The *a priori* indicates a condition of possibility because a reality is in a certain way. It is the horizon which interprets; it is *through which* and *thanks to which* one is or has something. If the *a priori* is considered then in relation to the communion of *we*, that is, to the divine nature, then it is possible to identify the characteristics of the latter by recuperating the syntactical function of the *ablative* such as *quo* and *in quo*. Talking about the divine *we-ness* as a fundamental logic of the distinctions of the Persons, it is possible to see in Mühlen an appreciation for a classical approach, most of all in reference to St Thomas and to St Anselm. Mühlen, as he affirms repeatedly, avoids considering the divine *We* in the prospective of a tri-theism or an accidental or collective unity *a posterior* (the *we* cannot be intended as the result of the sum of an *I* and of a *you*, just because it is *a priori)*. Starting from this reference to the divine nature, the *we* appears, not so much in its personological meaning in relation to an *I* or to a *you*, but as an originating space and divine background that shows the interpersonal dynamics of the being of God. The category of the *we-a priori* is used also in reference to the *We-in-Person*, to the Holy Spirit. Through the recovery of the *neutral gender* (which does not mean *non-personal*) his action can be expressed as space and force both in the creative activity and in reference to the believer, as the force which makes the experience of faith possible. In all these meanings the Spirit is shown as the *between*-in-person.

What are the ecclesiological implications for Mühlen? We are here at the ecclesial *we*, presented by Mühlen in his ecclesiological work entitled *Una Mystica Persona*. His intention was not to write a manual of ecclesiology but to find a fundamental formula for the

Church that could express the characteristics found in scripture and in Tradition. As Trinitarian theology developed the formula 'one nature in three Persons' and Christology coined the phrase 'two natures in one Person', likewise for ecclesiology an adequate expression is to be found that remains 'open' while accounting for what is essential. In this perspective, the Church is understood as 'one Person (the Spirit) in many persons (in Christ and in us)'. Mühlen writes: 'The expression "one person" means the Holy Spirit and the expression "many persons" means Christ and us. Christ binds us to himself and binds himself to us by means of the mission of his Spirit; and thus the Spirit, while he unites himself to us and unites us to himself, achieves our union with Christ. He is, therefore, the *vinculum*, the bond of unity, he then is the numerically one person in Christ and in us'.[1]

The biblical foundation of this ecclesiological proposal moves from the biblical category of the corporative personality, included in the concept of *Great-I*, in which there is evidence of a continual oscillation from the collective to the individual, from the *I* to the *we* in mutual implication. In addition to this internal return, the corporative personality presupposes a kind of irradiation of a great personality passed on in his descendents, whereby a population seems to identify itself with the ancestor who continues to live throughout time. As far as the Church is concerned, the reference is specifically Christological since it is the *I* of Christ who shines forth in the ecclesial community.

Recuperating the Augustinian category of *Christus totus*, and the Aquinian one of *Una Mystica Persona*, Mühlen introduces the ecclesiological formula developed by him: 'One Person in many persons.' He reaches that by asking himself in what way the *I* of Christ (as the ancestor/individual) is extended in the *Great-I* of the Church (people/collective). The divine Pneuma, the *We-in-person* is the condition of possibility for the ecclesial *we*, in that he is the One in whom and by means of whom the *I* of Christ is extended and spreads in Christians through unction. The Church is the historical continuation of the unction of Christ.

As at the intra-Trinitarian level the Spirit manifests the divine *we-ness*, in his being of both the Father and the Son, so too, on the ecclesial level he achieves the *we* of the Church in his being one and the same in Christ and in Christians. The Pneuma, in the life of Jesus, has rendered public and ecclesial this event: the grace of the unction conferred on Christ was ordered *a priori* to a multitude of persons, such that what seemed to have the characteristic of singularity, that of the *I-ness* has instead a plural finality, a reference to the *we-ness*. The Church, or rather, the ecclesial *we* thus finds its origin in Christ, and its condition of possibility in the *We-in-Person,* the divine Pneuma. In fact, the ecclesial *we* is such only as the Spirit of Christ taking place in it.

The Holy Spirit is the communion and the mediation by whose power the *I* of Christ finds itself in front of the *you* of the Church in an *oppositio relationis*.

Personological categories are the interpretive horizons of the whole theological system of Heribert Mühlen. Through this, what emerges above all is the importance that the relational dimension has in a discourse about the person, expressed both in the relationship *I-You* and in the union of *We*. At the same time every personal-word expresses, together with the dynamics of reciprocity also the individuality and the particularity of every single person. Therefore, everyone *is* in his *being from-with-for-in* the other-than-himself; being and relations in the divine Persons coincide perfectly so much so that it is not possible to think of one without the other. To speak of God in personal terms has implications also in the realm of creation. Mühlen, in fact, through the personological categories that describe how every person is who he is only by entering into dialogue with those who are other-than-himself, illustrates how such a logic can have its equivalent both in the theological area and in the anthropological one. While the human person is such by engaging in dialogue with others, the divine Persons themselves are dialogue: the *I,* the *You* and the *We* are who they are in their individuality each in reference to the other-than-himself. The distinction between the relationship *I-you* and the communion of the *we* is central to the *theologic* of Mühlen: the *I* of the Spirit arises from the common gift of the mutual love of the Father and of the Son; as an initiative of the Father (as the primordial *I*) love does not enrich one's own *I* but raises a *You* in front of himself, in which he finds himself as in another self. The opening of the reciprocal relationship between the *I* and the *You* radiates beyond the two and generates a Third who makes the two 'collaborators' in a common action: from the love that is in ecstasy a new *I* is formed.

can be defined as a 'reciprocating reciprocity', to use an expression of Piero Coda in his latest book *From the Trinity*.[4] This means a form of relationship that is actuated not only in the dia-logicality but also in the opening towards others, as a fecundity of the initial gratuity and the primordial communion. This 'open gratuity' in-forms the intra-ecclesial relationships, as con-formation to divine life and, through the mediation of eucharistic logic, becomes a per-formative announcement of the ecclesial *we*.

On this overall level, the Eucharist is the hermeneutical foundation of the Church, not only because the ecclesial *we* is the given 'body' of the *I* of Christ, such that both become a corporative personality (in which, while maintaining the necessary distinction between human and divine, the profound interaction between the two is emphasised), but also because the relationships which characterise the ecclesial *res*, to make it be what it is, must enter within the same Christ-*logic* (here called eucharistic logic) which we have tried to explain here briefly.

At this point it is necessary, in ecclesiology, to recuperate and study more deeply the mystical character of the Church, founded upon the relational-Trinitarian rhythm and mediated in Christological-sacramental form.

The *we*, therefore, is not only a sign of identity and belonging to the Church but an *open space* through which the divine *We* enters in humanity to lead it to himself. In this descending and ascending dynamic, the *we* of the Church is called to realise itself, accomplishing its mission, through the eucharistic dynamic of Christification in the Spirit, the *Christus totus, a mystical Person*, who gathers all of humanity within himself, turning to the Father in the Spirit with the same invocation of the Son: Abbà-Father!

NOTES

1 H. Mühlen, *Una Mystica Persona. La Chiesa come mistero dello Spirito Santo in Cristo e nei cristiani: una Persona in molte persone*, Rome, 1968, 21.

2 S. N. Bulgakov, 'Capitoli sulla Trinitarietà', *Sergej Bulgakov*, P. Coda, Brescia 2004, pp. 67–171, p. 77.

3 S. Petrosino, 'Il Figlio ovvero Del Padre. Sul dono ricevuto', P. Gilbert – S. Petrosino, *Il dono, il Melangolo*, Genoa, 2001, pp. 49–86, p. 52.

4 Cf. P. Coda, *Dalla Trinità. L'avvento di Dio tra storia e profezia*, Rome, 2011, pp. 566–7.

L'ECCLESIOLOGIA DI COMUNIONE DI JEROME HAMER

RT REV. ANTONIO LUIZ CATELAN FERREIRA
Catholic University of Paraná, Brazil

Il tema di questa presentazione fa parte della dissertazione per il dottorato, presentata alla Pontificia Università Gregoriana l'anno scorso. L'argomento è la nozione di comunione nell'ecclesiologia di J. Hamer. Lui è nato in Bruxelles, Belgica, nel 1916. Ha studiato nello *Studium Generale* di frati Domenicani de La Sartre in Louvain. È stato professore dal 1944 al 1962 alla Università di Friburgo, Svizzera, ha ministrato corsi anche nella Pontificia Università *Angelicum* a Roma, nel *Studium Generale* de La Sartre e nel *Le Souchoir*, in Francia, del quale è stato anche Rettore. Ha svolto il lavoro di esperto del Segretariato per l'Unità dei Cristiani durante le quattro sessioni del Concilio Vaticano II. È stato Vice-Segretario e dopo Segretario di questo Segretariato, Arcivescovo Segretario della Congregazione per la Dottrina della Fede, e, per fine, Presidente della Congregazione per gli Istituti di Vita Consacrata e Società di Vita Apostolica. Morì all'età di ochenta anni, a Roma.

Fra le sue pubblicazioni il libro *L'Église est une communion*, pubblicato nel 1962 senza dubi, occupa il posto principale. Ma anche nell'ecclesiologia dell'ultimo secolo ha un posto di rilevo. S. Dianich, infatti, ha affermato che l'ecclesiologia contemporanea deve molto a questo libro.[1] Fra gli autori ai quali si riconosce alcuna influenza sulla nozione di comunione adoperata nel Concilio Vaticano II, J. Hamer è spesso citato. Un studioso di questa nozione, com'è J. Rigal, afferma che 'l'insistenza del Vaticano II sulla Chiesa-comunione è, da una parte, dovuta a lavori anteriori fra i quali di Y. Congar oppure di H. de Lubac. In loro scritti, tuttavia, l'idea è più o meno esplicita, ma non è oggetto di un trattamento privilegiato sino nell'opera di J. Hamer, dal titolo *L'Église est une communion*'.[2]

C. Möller, nello studio sulle idee che hanno avuto influsso sulla *Lumen Gentium* afferma sul libro di J. Hamer: 'questo libro marcherà tappa dentro dell'ecclesiologia, perché ha provocato la presa di coscienza dell'insieme delle ricerche precedenti che si hanno gettato in questa realtà biblica e patristica della Chiesa come comunione'.[3]

Cerchiamo di riflettere in quest'occasione sull'ambiente dentro il quale la nozione di comunione è emersa come adatta in vista di esprimere la natura della Chiesa, la sua comprensione generale nell'opera di J. Hamer e le principali caratteristiche che l'autore mete in rilievo.

L´ECCLESIOLOGIA DI J. HAMER E IL MOVIMENTO DI RINNOVAMENTO ECCLESIOLOGICO: LA NUOVA EMERGENZA DELLA NOZIONE DI COMUNIONE

La storia della ripresa della nozione di comunione nell'ambito degli studi ecclesiologici intorno agli anni cinquanta del secolo scorso, e precisamente per indicare l´essenza della Chiesa, risulta dalla collaborazione di vari fattori: il contesto culturale, l´esperienza vissuta dalla Chiesa e della riflessione teologica.

Si può dire, in modo generale, che la rivalutazione del concetto ecclesiologico di comunione come categoria privilegiata per significare la Chiesa ha maturato lentamente nel pensiero teologico durante il processo di rinnovamento dell'ecclesiologia che va dal Concilio Vaticano I al Concilio Vaticano II. Ne è precisamente uno dei suoi frutti.[4]

Lungo questo periodo, l'esperienza ecclesiale, specialmente stimolata dai grandi movimenti di rinnovamento biblico, liturgico, patristico, ecumenico, risulta in una comprensione della missione della Chiesa come fondata nella Trinità e partecipata da tutti i fedeli, compresa essenzialmente in maniera pastorale, al servizio della finalità spirituale della Chiesa. La densa e profonda esperienza della vita della Chiesa in questo periodo fornisce le condizioni per la ripresa del concetto di comunione.

Si deve tenere presente che questa nozione, come lo dimostra J. Hamer non si oppone a altre, come la di corpo di Cristo o di popolo di Dio. Al contrario, forma con loro un insieme nel quale ognuna offre contribuzioni specifiche.

L'emergenza della nozione di comunione è chiamata di ripresa oppure di riscoperte proprio perché si riscopre la sua presenza nella Scrittura, come *koinonia*, che è testimoniata in diversi modi nella Tradizione viva della Chiesa, come *communio*, e lungo la storia della Chiesa, in diverse istituzioni, fin dalla Chiesa Antica.

Proprio gli studiosi della Chiesa antica la identificano nello stilo di vita dei Cristiani e anche in precise istituzioni come le lettere di comunione fra le Chiese. Nella teologia dei Padri, la comprensione della Chiesa comunione è l'ambiente vivo del pensiero. Rimane nella teologia medievale dei grandi scolastici, nella nozione di corpo mistico e della *congregatio fidelium*. Però, proprio nel medioevo, soprattutto a partire del secolo XII, è eclissata gradualmente con la progressiva ascensione del modo predominantemente giuridico di capire la Chiesa che si è firmato a partire delle controversie tra il papato e i re, com´è classico identificare la sua figura-tipo nella relazione fra Bonifacio VIII e Filippo il Bello. Segnata dalla controversia contro la Riforma protestante, l'impostazione moderna dell'ecclesiologia si è caratterizzata in maniera apologetica, e si è fissata in termini societari, visibilisti e incentrati nella gerarchia.

All'interno di questo movimento di rinnovamento dell'ecclesiologia, alcuni autori hanno iniziato a utilizzare la categoria comunione come adatta a esprimere la natura o l'essenza della Chiesa, fra il quale, il teologo laico tedesco F. Pilgram, sembra essere stato il primo a fare uso di comunione per indicare il modo come si caratterizza la forma dell´unità della Chiesa nel importante libro *Physiologie der Kirche*, dal 1860.[5]

GLI ANNI CINQUANTA E L´EBOLLIZIONE ECCLESIOLOGICA

Circa la metà del ventesimo secolo, questa nozione può essere trovata nelle opere di teologi fra i più ripresentativi, come H. de Lubac[6] e Y. Congar.[7] È presenti anche nelle influenti ricerche storiche di L. Hertling e di Elert.[8] Circa la metà degli anni cinquanta è possibile trovare affermazione come questa, di Laberthonnièrre: 'Il vero carattere della Chiesa è il di essere una società per comunione, che non si compie che dall´interiore, per adesione intimamente acconsentita'.[9] sorta nell´ambito del movimento ecumenico, come anche, nell´anno sessanta, frutto di riflessione già abbastanza maturata, viene pubblicata la importante opera dell´ecumenista M.-J. le Guillou: *Mission et unité, les exigences de la communion.*[10] Questi sono, tuttavia, approcci su uno o altro aspetto della vita della Chiesa oppure sulle esigenze dell´ecumenismo. Non sono ancora applicazione sistematiche alla realtà ecclesiale totale.

Tener presente l'opinione del grande ecclesiologo e storico delle idee ecclesiologiche, Y. Congar su questo argomento in quello contesto può essere utile per miglior capire la contribuzione di J. Hamer. Wel 1949, Y. Congar riteneva che sarebbe importante studiare tale prospettiva. Infatti, ha fatto l´osservazione che 'tale studio non è stato mai fatto 'ex professo'.[11] Nel 1950 egli dichiarava l´intenzione di studiare questa possibilità.[12] Alcuni anni dopo, rimette in valore il tema della comunione: 'solo si conosce veramente la Chiesa quando si studia la natura della comunione, le sue condizioni, implicazioni, il modo come se la può ferire'. E ancora: 'la realtà designata dalla parola *Chiesa* nel uso Cristiano ha due aspetti ... Nella realtà finale, è comunione degli uomini con Dio e di tutti, gli uni con gli altri, in Cristo. Lei è anche l´insieme dei mezzi di codetta comunione'.[13] Nel 1960 afferma che la linea vitale dell´ecclesiologia va verso la direzione della *communio.*[14] Nel 1961, riprende il tema, presenta le sue linee generali e ritiene che uno studio approfondito sul tema richiederebbe l´investigazione di notevole documentazione.[15] Nel 1963 egli fa ancora una volta menzione a quello già antico progetto di realizzare uno studio approfondito sulla comunione, ancora non compiuto.[16]

Nel settembre 1962, un mese prima dall'inizio del Concilio Vaticano II, è pubblicata l´opera fondamentale di J. Hamer, *L´Église est une communion.*[17] In questo libro, la comunione è proposta come categoria ecclesiologica centrale. La definizione che presenta al capitolo quattro è stata proposta per essere assunta nel capitolo I della *Lumen Gentium.*[18] La sua caratteristica fondamentale è quella di essere capace di esprimere la Chiesa in modo globale: sua natura e le relazioni che in essa sono caratteristiche; a significare gli elementi interni e esterni, presentati in prospettiva unitaria. È, quanto sembra, il primo saggio di ecclesiologia sistematica a fare uso centrale della nozione di comunione. Infatti, lui afferma che 'è necessario rivalutare il termine 'comunione', così ricco e così tradizionale'.[19] Sono trattate questioni come la relazione fra le nozione di corpo di Cristo e popolo di Dio con la comunione; la relazione tra la Chiesa e il Regno di Dio; la priorità di quello che nella Chiesa è comune a tutti i cristiani; la importanza fondamentale dell´azione pastorale della Chiesa locale; le relazioni fra il primato del papa e la collegialità dei vescovi; il significato della sinassi eucaristica per la realizzazione della Chiesa, per citare soltanto i più significativi. Questi aspetti, articolati, hanno fatto emergere la percezione dell'importanza architettonica della nozione di comunione per l´avvenire dell´ecclesiologia.[20]

Il movimento ecumenico è un punto di riferimento importante per la riscoperta dell´importanza e della portata di questa nozione per l´ecclesiologia. Infatti, Laberthonnièrre, M. J. Le Guillou, Y. Congar, come anche J. Hamer sono tutti impegnati con l´ecumenismo.

Il contributo dell´opera va nella direzione del punto di convergenza dei principali obiettivi del movimento di rinnovazione dell'ecclesiologia: l´arricchimento della comprensione della Chiesa per mezzo dell´approfondimento spiritualmente e l'ingrandimento per mezzo del pieno riconoscimento della sua natura comunitaria. Proprio come voleva il movimento ecclesiologico.

LA COMPRENSIONE DELLA CHIESA IN MODO UNITARIO

Tra i diversi aspetti importanti della contribuzione di *L´Église est une communion* nel momento della sua pubblicazione, uno si distingue per la sua importanza. È anche uno degli aspetti più caratteristici dell'ecclesiologia di J. Hamer. È il carattere unitario. Infatti, J. Hamer presenta la realtà totale della Chiesa a partire della nozione di comunione.[21] Oggi, quest´osservazione può sembrare un può strana. Però, in quella situazione, le cose erano un po' diverse.

C'è la realtà storica e visibile della Chiesa. C'è anche la sua dimensione spirituale. I tentativi di definizione della Chiesa trovavano un grave inciampo in questa dualità di dimensioni. La prima metà del ventesimo secolo ha discusso molto se questa dualità non impedirebbe una definizione della Chiesa.[22] La questione della definizione faceva parte del tentativo de integrare migliore gli aspetti spirituali e comunitari nella propria definizione, come abbiamo già accennato.

Ancora una volta un paragone fra J. Hamer e Y. Congar su questo punto può essere istruttivo. Infatti, Y. Congar, l'autore contemporaneo più volte citato da J. Hamer. I due, secondo il modo come la tradizione tomista capisce la Chiesa secondo le tappe della storia della salvezza, ritengono importante per l'ecclesiologia essere sempre consapevoli delle differenze fra le fasi. Per entrambi, la realtà definitiva della Chiesa è compresa come comunione. Y. Congar afferma che nel suo fine, la Chiesa 'sarà eternamente comunione',[23] però, nel *status viae* la comunità ecclesiale ha la forma di società.[24] C'è un aspetto di comunione nella Chiesa durante il pellegrinaggio in questo mondo, ma è interiore e si riferisce ai suoi elementi istituzionali, che sono mezzi di comunione.[25] *Ex professo*, lo stilo dell´ecclesiologia di Y. Congar in questo periodo è segnato da antinomie.[26] Nel 1950, di fato, Y. Congar afferma: 'due sono le logiche attuanti simultaneamente nella Chiesa ...'[27] In altra occasione, afferma: 'il compito attuale dell'ecclesiologia ... è di non sacrificare nessun dei due poli dei quali abbiamo provato riconoscere le coordinate, anche se una certa tensione deve rimanere tra i due'.[28]

Discutendo la possibilità di definire della Chiesa, Y. Congar fa anche delle considerazioni riguardanti i due aspetti irreducibili della Chiesa, lo istituzionale e il corpo mistico. É una dualità relativa che, secondo lui, non acconsente arrivare a una definizione semplice e unificata.[29] Facendo uso di una distinzione fatta classica da Guglielmo d´Ockham,[30] considera ancora la differenza fra definizione nominale e definizione reale.[31] Reale è quella definizione che espressa l´essere di una cosa; nominale è, al contrario, la definizione che espressa il significato di un nome. La definizione nominale della Chiesa non è problema: spiega cosa significa il termine biblico *ekklesia*. Importa investigare la definizione reale. Y. Congar ha delle questioni sulla sua possibilità.[32] Per mezzo delle principali nozioni ecclesiologiche della Scrittura, dei Padri e della liturgia, lui ritiene possibile trovare un 'principio di definizione'.[33] Dopo di esaminare diversi, finisce citando Ch. Journet che la realtà chiamata da noi Chiesa 'è troppo ricca per essere contenuta in uno solo concetto e rispondere a un solo nome'.[34]

J. Hamer, a sua volta, al principio ugualmente ha fatto la differenza tra principi diversi nell´essere della Chiesa, come 'apostolicità e comunione',[35] oppure fra *communio* e *potestas* come due modi di sociabilità della Chiesa. Apostolicità e potestas, la sociabilità organizzata. La comunione, *communio*, spontanea.[36] Però, in *L'Église est une communion* ha abbandonato questa prospettiva, affermando che 'la comunione non è un vestimento temporaneo della Chiesa';[37]

la comunione è la 'forma stessa dell´unità della Chiesa', il suo 'nome strutturale', lo stesso 'vincolo della Chiesa'.[38] Non solo la condizione finale della Chiesa nel Regno, ma 'la felice e necessaria condizione di nostra peregrinazione', appartiene alla stessa 'struttura dell´essere della Chiesa'.[39] 'La comunione è um insieme',[40] 'una realtà organica allo stesso tempo interiore e esteriore ... È tutta la Chiesa nei suoi vincoli di coesione'.[41] Così, J. Hamer definisce la comunione come la 'forma della sociabilità della Chiesa'.[42]

LE ARTICOLAZIONI MAGGIORI DELL'ECCLESIOLOGIA DI J. HAMER

A partire di questa comprensione unitaria sostenuta da J. Hamer, vengono articolate i diversi elementi della ricca e complessa realtà della Chiesa, sempre però esplicitamente a partire della unità di comprensione dell´essere ecclesiale.[43] È fondato sui sacramenti e su un'esslesiologia sacramentale.[44] I sacramenti dell´iniziazione alla vita Cristiana sono la base e il permanente fondamento. Secondo questo, nella comunione l'elemento collettivo è predominante: il sacerdozio comune di tutto il popolo di Dio e la missione comune di quest´intero popolo si articolano con tutte le successive differenziazioni. È anche fondata nei sacramenti dell´ordine e del matrimonio, i quali si associano ai carismi e agli altri ministeri. In questi ultimi, la comunione trova il fondamento della diversificazione. La diversificazione, però, ha sempre caratteristiche missionarie. Per lui, la comunione fondata nei sacramenti non è soltanto una similarità nella fede oppure negli affetti. Ne è una realtà ontologica: è un essere parti uni degli altri[45] come risultato di una vera comunione con Dio.[46]

L'esistenza nella Chiesa è relazionale per sua stessa natura. In ognuno di noi c'è una dipendenza riguardante al 'tutto' proprio in quello che ci fa cristiani e membri della Chiesa. Il nostro essere e il nostro comportamento sono condizionati dal 'tutto' che ne è la Chiesa di Gesù risorto. La nostra azione è sempre quella di un membro della Chiesa, qualunque sia l'importanza del ruolo esercitano nella comunità cristiana.[47]

Così la comunione è caratterizzata per essere fondata nella partecipazione degli stessi beni salvifici ed è vissuta nella corresponsabilità missionaria. Comunione, partecipazione e corresponsabilità sono termini inseparabili nell'ecclesiologia di J. Hamer, come vedremo in seguito.

Il significato esistenziale della comunione è derivato da quel livello più profondo, ontologico, e si manifesta in comportamenti di comunione. Così si trova la prima e più fondamentale articolazione dell´ecclesiologia di J. Hamer: quella fra l´essere e l´agire. Tra il livello ontologico della comunione e i comportamenti di comunione c'è una relazione specifica: i comportamenti allo stesso tempo manifestano e producono la comunione. È percettibile, sotto intesa, la classica comprensione tomistica della relazione fra l´essere e l´agire, secondo l'assioma della tradizione aristotelica: *agere sequitur esse.*[48]

A partire di quest'articolazione fondamentale, J. Hamer fa una modificazione importante nel senso dell´assioma citato. Nella tradizione della Scolastica, viene preso su considerazione una direzione in senso unico, secondo la quale l´agire decorre dell´essere. J. Hamer la prende con doppia direzione. Le azioni che manifestano la comunione e allo stesso tempo la producono. Così, la comunione, fondata nella partecipazione sacramentale e carismatica dei beni salvifici, è vissuta nella corresponsabilità ecclesiale.[49]

Con questa articolazione: comunione fondata nella partecipazione agli stessi beni e vissuta nella corresponsabilità missionaria, gli elementi sacramentali e missionari, a partir della articolazione fondamentale istaurata fra l´essere e l´agire, la comunione è la realtà della Chiesa. Così J. Hamer ha potuto passare oltre il binomio comunione – società per espirmere la complessità della Chiesa, raggiungendo una comprensione che allo stesso tempo conserva l'unità senza sacrificare la complessità.

Così, la prima realizzazione risultante di questa comprensione unitaria della Chiesa consiste in raggiungere allo stesso tempo il doppio scopo del movimento di rinnovazione dell'ecclesiologia. L´impoverimento spirituale connesso all´uso predominante della nozione di società, che metteva in risalto lo giuridico, viene superato. Come viene anche superata la comprensione che non prendeva in sufficiente considerazione la comunità. L'elemento spirituale viene del fondamento sacramentale e della comunione con il mistero di Dio che egli comporta. Questa è la finalità ultima della Chiesa e sua natura più intima, che determina i rapporti interpersonali. La Tradizione ha messo in risalto il carattere sacro della comunione con la designazione communio sanctorum.[50] La superazione della predominanza della gerarchia e loro poteri – chiamata da Y. Congar gerarcologia[51]– in forza anche dello stesso fondamento sacramentale porta con sé importanti conseguenze.

Per miglior capire la dimensione comunitaria c'è bisogno di far risalire il suo carattere missionario. Lo studio sulla missione dei laici, fato con cura, mete in evidenza il suo fondamento sacramentale.[52] Insieme a questo si tenga presente la apertura al mondo come orizzonte della missione. 'Totalmente tensa verso il pieno compimento del Regno, la comunione non chiude la Chiesa su se stessa. È aperta al mondo ... Ella raccoglie in se la ricchezza e la varietà depositate da Dio nella sua creazione'.[53] Così la Chiesa è caratterizzata come una comunione aperta, non auto referenziata.[54] Anche il posteriore studio sulla *sacra potestas,* in chiave di comunione, fa risalire il suo carattere di servizio e la sua finalità espressamente missionaria.[55]

Con riferimento a questa doppia direzione della comprensione della comunione, J. Hamer parla di due aspetti, l´uno verticale, l´altro orizzontale,[56] il primo il caratterizza il secondo. Non possiamo lasciar di vedere in questa doppia direzione una relazione con l'approfondimento spirituale e con l'ampliazione comunitaria della comprensione della Chiesa voluta dal movimento ecclesiologico. J. Hamer parla anche di comunione interiore e esteriore, reciprocamente coinvolte.[57] Così, la nozione di comunione gli permette un approccio pienamente teologico della Chiesa.

CONSEGUENZA MAGGIORE: LA STRUTTURAZIONE DEL TRATTATO DI ECCLESIOLOGIA A PARTIRE DI UNA PERSPETTIVA DI COMUNIONE

A partire della struttura di base della comunione, essere e agire, del suo fondamento sacramentale e del suo carattere missionario, facendo uso della categoria popolo di Dio, subito dopo di considerare la Chiesa come mistero di comunione, J. Hamer espone uno schema di comprensione della vita della Chiesa in cui l'elemento collettivo, che è comune a tutti i credenti, ha la precedenza in relazione alla esposizione della missione della gerarchia e della missione dei laici.

La funzione sacerdotale, regale e profetica di Cristo, inviato dal Padre, è esercitata allo stesso tempo dal ministero generale del popolo di Dio e dal ministero speciale di quelli che il Signore ha messo da parte. Questi due ministeri sono correlativi l´uno all´altro. È l´insieme che deve essere preso in considerazione. Noi iniziamo qui dall´aspetto collettivo.[58]

Non si può dimenticare che questa comunione cosi sostituita [la comunione di tutta la Chiesa] è chiamata, anche, a un ruolo attivo, generativo della crescita della vitalità della Chiesa. Tutto il popolo sacerdotale è chiamato a 'diffondere le grandi azioni di Colui che ci ha chiamati dalle tenebre alla sua ammirabile luce' (1 Pd 2:9).[59]

Per fare questo egli si appoggia sugli studi riguardanti il fondamento sacramentale, anche nel suo aspetto strutturale, e sugli studi riguardanti la categoria popolo di Dio, che mettono in luce l'uguaglianza fondamentale di tutti i fedeli nella dignità dell'esistenza cristiana e il senso diaconale del ministero gerarchico, servizio del popolo di Dio. Questa priorità ecclesiologica della condizione cristiana fondamentale sulle ulteriori differenziazioni ministeriale non sono novità negli scritti di J. Hamer, erano già come nell´aria. Nuova è la strutturazione fatta da lui a partire dello schema *essere – agire* e della comprensione dell´unità tra gli aspetti interni ed esterni della comunione. La novità si trova nel proporre questo come cerniera della riflessione sulla Chiesa in vista dell´organizzazione di un intero trattato di ecclesiologia.

Questa procedura gli consente di configurare la trattazione in modo che il mistero della Chiesa comunione sia preso in considerazione in precedenza. Per questo un insieme d'immagini bibliche sono presi, alcune di loro sono strutturanti, come quella di corpo di Cristo, come lo è anche il riferimento al Regno di Dio. È la priorità dell´essere della comunione. Subito dopo, è preso in considerazione l´agire della comunione, nel quale la missione di tutta la Chiesa è compresa sotto gli aspetti comuni e speciali. Speciali sono i ministeri della gerarchia e dei laici.

L'importanza di questo modo di comporre la comprensione della Chiesa sarà messa in risalto nel 1963, l'anno seguente alla pubblicazione di *L'Église est une communion*. Dopo il rifiuto dello *schema* del *De Ecclesia* al finale della prima sessione del Concilio Vaticano II, la commissione di redazione si è trovata davanti a quindici proposte di schemi diversi. È stato scelto lo schema belga, conosciuto come *schema* Philips, per base della nuova redazione. Il quale prevedeva una trattazione della teologia del popolo di Dio nel capitolo dedicato ai laici, il terzo capitolo. È stata suggerita, dal Cardinale Suenens, una importante modificazione: subito dopo il capitolo primo, riguardanti il mistero della Chiesa, dovrebbe venire la considerazione dell´intero popolo di Dio, per solo dopo trattare della gerarchia e dei laici.

Questo fa che la nozione di popolo di Dio riceva una straordinaria attenzione dalla parte della teologia. Infatti, l'utilità della nozione di popolo di Dio per la comprensione della Chiesa aveva già cominciato a manifestarsi negli anni quaranta.[60] Pero, qui, più che semplicemente utilizzare la nozione, ne estrae una conseguenza strutturante per la comprensione della Chiesa. Un tale modo di impostare il discorso era nuovo all´epoca. Gli elementi sufficienti per questo erano già stati sviluppati lungo il percorso del movimento ecclesiologico, ma separatamente, e non erano ancora stati sistematizzati nei trattati ecclesiologici.

C'è, però una corrispondenza molto prossima tra questa sistematizzazione risultante della proposta del Card. Suenens e la strutturazione di *L'Église est une communion* di J. Hamer. La prima parte del libro, riguardanti il mistero della Chiesa, corrisponde al capitolo uno dello schema. In entrambi, la pluralità d'immagini bibliche sono incentrati nella nozione di corpo di Cristo. Il riferimento della Chiesa alla Santissima Trinità e al Regno di Dio sono anche comuni. La seconda parte del libro, con quattro capitoli, tratta la materia in quest'ordine: il sacerdozio comune di tutto il popolo di Dio, la missione della gerarchia presentata come funzione apostolica, i laici e il suo apostolato. C'è una corrispondenza molto stretta tra questa seconda parte del libro e i capitoli due, tre e quattro dello *schema*. La principale differenza è la questione ecumenica che compare nel secondo capitolo dello schema e non si trova nella seconda parte del libro.

Quest'organizzazione del materiale nella *Lumen Gentium* è stata accolta come 'tratto dal genio' e 'una delle rivoluzioni che hanno marcato la redazione della costituzione'.[61] Lo stesso cardinale L.J. Suenens se riferisce a questo come una 'rivoluzione copernicana'.[62]

Concediamo ora un può più di attenzione a questo punto per la sua importanza. Lo stesso cardinale racconta che la suggestione gli è stata data da Mons. Prignon Rettore del Pontificio Collegio Belga, a Roma.[63] Cl. Troisfontaines lo racconta con maggiore ricchezza di dettagli:

Il cardinale [Suenens] chiede a A. Prignon di fargli alcune suggestione riguardanti al nuovo *De Ecclesia*. Il Rettore del Collegio Belga propone che si meta il capitolo sul popolo di Dio prima del capitolo sulla gerarchia. Il cardinale accetta il suggerimento e fa passare per la commissione di coordinamento del Concilio nei giorni 3–4 luglio del 1963. Così A. Prignon sta nell'origine della così detta 'rivoluzione copernicana' del Vaticano II in materia di ecclesiologia.[64]

E aggiunge in nota:
G. Philips anche se fondamentalmente in conformità, aveva paura dai lavori che tale cambiamento provocherebbe. A. Prignon ha dovuto esortarlo molto a mettersi al lavoro. E ancora più, era necessaria l'approvazione di Papa Paolo VI. L'argomento che gli ha convinto è stato: il popolo di Dio, ultimo nell´ordine dell'esecuzione, è il primo nell´ordine dell´intenzione. A. Prignon mi ha raccontato che la formula *populus Dei, ultimus in executione, sed primus in intentione,* lui ha coniato in collaborazione con G. Philips, è stata trasmessa da Mons. Garrone a Paulo VI e guadagnò la sua adesione.[65]

Nel *Processus verbalis* della riunione della Commissione di Coordinamento di 4 di luglio di 1963 si trova il registro:

La seconda parte dello schema *De Ecclesia* viene perciò approvata e dato mandato alla Segreteria di aggiungere una nota al testo indicante la proposta della nuova divisione della materia secondo l'indicazione dell'Em.mo Suenens. Anche l'Em.mo Card. Browne, vice-Presidente della Comm. Teologica, e P. Tromp Segretario, sono consenzienti, non avanzando alcuna difficoltà alla approvazione del testo ed alla presentazione del medesimo al Concilio con la divisione della materia indicata dall'Em.mo Card. Suenens.[66]

M. Lamberigts e L. Declerck osservano, però, che l'idea, era in circolazione nel Segretariato per la promossine de l´Unità dei Cristiani, dove lavorava J. Hamer.[67] Ricordiamo ancora, che tra A. Prignon e de J. Hamer c'era conoscenza, entrambi erano belgi e che A. Prignon si riferisce a J. Hamer otto volte nel diario della quarta session del Concilio

Ostens, Berlin 1954 (trad. nord-americana: *Eucharist and Church Fellowship in the First Four Centuries*, St Louis 1966). Questi autori non hanno fato studi sistematici, ma piuttosto una ricerca sulla comprensione di comunione della Chiesa Antica.

9 L. Laberthonnièrre, *La notion chrétienne de l'autorité. Contribution au rétablissement de l' unanimité chrétienne*, Paris, 1955, 248.

10 Quest'autore approfondisce la nozione di comunione in M.J. le Guillou, *Mission et unité, les exigences de la communion*, 2 vol., Paris 1960. Egli segue e sviluppa l'approccio indicato da Y. Congar in 'Notes sur les mots "confession", "Eglise", et "communion"' (cf. *Irén*. 23 [1950] 3–36).

11 Y. Congar, 'Communion ecclésiastique', *Catholicisme*, vol. 2, Paris, 1949, col. 1375.

12 Y. Congar, *Vraie et fausse réforme dans l'Église*, Paris, 1968[2,] (la prima edizione rissale al 1950.

13 Id., *Jalons pour une théologie du laïcat*, Paris 1954[2], rispettivamente, 15 e 46.

14 Id., 'Conclusion', *Le concile et les conciles, contribution à l'historie de la vie conciliaire de l'Église*, B. Botte, ed., Paris, 1960, 319–23.

15 Id., 'De la communion des Églises a une ecclésiologie de l'Église universelle', *L'Épiscopat et l'Église universelle*, Y. Congar – B. D. Dupuy, Paris 1964[2] [la prima edizione è di 1962], 227–60, specialmente le osservazioni alla p. 231 e nota 2.

16 Y. Congar, 'Peut'on définir l'Église? Destin et valeur de quatre notions qui s'offrent a le faire', Id., *Sainte Église: Études et aprroches ecclésiologiques,* Paris, 1963, 39.

17 Questa informazione riguardo il mesme, ci è fornita allo setesso J. Hamer, 'Bulletin d'ecclésiologie', *Revue des Sciences Philosophiques et Theologiques* 46 (1962) 555, nota 19.

18 La proposta è stata fatta dai vescovi spagnoli N. Jubani Arnau e V. Enrique y Tarancón (cf. ASSCOV, vol. 2/2, Città del Vaticano, 1972, 154–6).

19 Cf. J. Hamer, *L'Église est une communion*, 99.

20 Cf. Uma breve e precisa valutazione in questo senso in C. Möhler, 'Il lievito delle idee nell'elaborazione della Costituzione', *A Igreja do Vaticano II*, G. Baraúna, ed., Petrópolis 1965, 173, nota 37.

21 Cf. J. Hamer, 'La communion, forme permanente de l'Église', Id. *L'Église est une communion*, 227–31.

22 Discutono la questione, tra altri, Adam, K., *Das Wesen des Katholizismus*, Düsseldorf 1924; Barry, D., 'A Plea for a more Comprehensive Definition of the Church', *The New York Review* 2 (1906–7), 691–7; Commer, E., *Die Kirche in ihrem Leben und Wesen dargestellt*, vol. 1, Vienne 1904; Id., 'Das Leben

der Kirche: Grundlegung', *Divus Thomas* 6 (1919) 167–88; Feckes, C., Das *Mysterium der heilige Kirche. Dogmatische Untersuchungen*, Paderborn 1934 (trad. italiana: *La santa Chiesa*, Alba 1956); Holböck, F., *Mysterium Kirche in der Sicht der theologischen Disziplinen*, vol. 1, Salzburg 1962; Koster, M.D., *Ekklesiologie im Werden*, Paderborn, 1940.

23 Y. Congar, 'Deux aspects dans l'Église', Id., *Saint Église*, 1963, 51.

24 Cf. Y. Congar, *Chrétiens désunis*, Paris, 1937, 93.

25 Cf. Y. Congar, *Jalons pour une théologie du laïcat*, Paris, 1954^2, 46 (la prima edizione è di 1953).

26 Cf. Famerée, 'Schèmes ecclésiologiques fondamentaux des écrits congariens de 1937 a 1959', Id., *L'Ecclésiologie d'Yves Congar avant Vatican II*, Leuven 1992, 401–436; Id., 'Évolution progressive du P. Congar sur certains points d'ecclésiologie après 1959', in Ibid., 437–57.

27 Y. Congar, *Vraie et fausse réforme dans l'Église*, Paris, 1968^2, 271, (la prima edizione è di 1950).

28 Id., 'Le Saint-Esprit et le corps apostolique, réalisateurs de l'oeuvre Du Christ', Id., *Esquises du Mystère de l'Église*, Paris, 1953^2, 178, la prima edizione è di 1941.

29 Y. Congar 'Le Saint-Esprit et le Corps apostolique,', 129–79 (cf. Id., 'Position de l'Église, dualité et unité', 45–67, dove fa uso sistematico dell´espressione *entre-deux*. Lo stesso approccio se mantiene fin più tardi, per esempio in Y. Congar 'Peut-on définir l'Église? Destin et valeur de quatre notions que s'offrent a le faire', in AA.VV., *Jacques Leclercq. L'homme, l'oeuvre et ses amis*, Tornai – Paris 1961, 233–54 (in *Saint Église*, Paris, 1963, 21–44). In questa riedizione Y. Congar fa alcune aggiunte, come la menzione alla pubblicazione di *L'Église est une communion*, de J. Hamer (cf. p. 39, nota 3). Dopo di considerare che sia possibile utilizzare il termine comunione in vista della definizione della Chiesa e di una sistematizzazione dell'ecclesiologia (cf. Ibid., 22), non ostante prognosticare un buon futuro per la nozione (cf. Ibid., 39), considera anche alcune difficoltà ('molto lavoro sarà ancora necesario' [Ibid.]).

30 'Definizione si capisce in due modi. A volte definizione espressa il *quid* di uma cosa; a volte espressa cosa è um nome' (*Summa totius logicae*, Pars I, c. XXVI; apud R. Robinson *Definition*, Oxford, 1972, 12–148. Anche F. Pilgram ha utilizato questa distinzione (cf. *Physiologie de l'Église*, 11, 19).

31 Y. Congar 'Peut-on définir l'Église?', Id., *Saint Église*, Paris 1963, 21–44.

32 Cf. Y. Congar 'Peut-on définir l'Église?', 42.

33 Ibid., 22.

34 Cf. Ch. Journet *L'Église du Verbe incarné*, vol. 2, Paris 1951, 50. E, in favore di questa opinione, cita E. Commer, 'Von Wesen der Kirche', 10.

Vatikanischen Konzil, München 2004]; Treffler, ed., *Julius Kardinal Döpfner. Briefe und Notizen* [no. 9], 352), (M. Lamberigts – L. Declerck, 'The Role of Cardinal L.J. Suenens at Vatican II', 103, nota 210).

68 J. Hamer, 'Iglesia y comunión, introducción al tema eclesiológico', CELAM *La Iglesia del Señor, algunos aspectos hoy*, Bogotá, 1983, 18.

69 J. Hamer, *L'Église est une communion*, 237.

70 Ibid., 99.

• • 4 • •

CHAIR: **SR CONSILIO ROCK RSM**

(Member of the Theology Forum of the Irish Inter-Church Meeting)

SPEAKER: **MS ANASTASIA WOODEN**

Catholic University of America, Washington DC

The Eucharistic Ecclesiology of Nicholas Afanasiev and Catholic Ecclesiology: History of Interaction and Future Perspectives

• • 5 • •

CHAIR: **REV. PAUL PRIOR**

(St Patrick's College, Maynooth)

SPEAKER: **REV. DR BILLY SWAN**

Gregorian University, Rome

The Eucharist, Communion and Formation

• • 6 • •

CHAIR: **MR BRENDAN O'REILLY**

(National Director for Catechetics, Irish Bishops' Conference)

SPEAKER: **MS SIOBHAN LEAHY**

All Hallows College, Dublin

Nurturing Children's Spirituality in the Presence of the Eucharist

• • 7 • •

CHAIR: **REV. DR MICHAEL SHORTALL**

(St Patrick's College, Maynooth)

SPEAKER: **REV. DR ANTONIO JOSÉ DE ALMEIDA**

Pontifical Catholic University of Paraná, Brazil

Comunità e Eucaristia nella V Conferenza Generale dell' Episcopato dell' America Latina

COMMUNION, CHURCH AND CRISIS: COMMUNION ECCLESIOLOGY IN AN ANGLICAN CONTEXT

MR EIMHIN WALSH PhD Candidate
Trinity College, Dublin

At the Lambeth Conference of Anglican Bishops in 2008, Cardinal Walter Kasper asked 'what else can our dialogue be but an expression of our intent and desire to be fully one in him in order to be fully joint witnesses to his gospel?'[1] Kasper's theory of receptive ecumenism asks firstly what can be learnt from Christians of other denominations rather than insisting upon conformity. It strives to move ecumenism in ways that would deepen respective ecclesial identities and draw them together in communion. However, when pushed to specify what Roman Catholics could learn from the Anglican communion Kasper stated 'In its current situation, the Anglican communion has nothing to teach the Catholic Church about communion.'[2] The purpose of this paper then, is to consider two questions: firstly what is Anglican communion ecclesiology, and secondly, is there anything which the Anglican experience can teach the Catholic Church about communion?

ECCLESIOLOGY IN ANGLICANISM

The limitations of this investigation need to be admitted. Any discussion of 'Anglicanism' is necessarily limited because of the degree of theological independence afforded to individual Anglican provinces. The dispersed nature of authority with its correlative acceptance of the integrity of national Churches and provinces to make theological decisions based on their own processes of discernment renders a definition of a pan-Anglican solution to any theological problem almost impossible. Indeed, Archbishop Michael Ramsey even commented that 'the use of the word Anglicanism can be very misleading' as 'the Anglican will not suppose that he has a system or a confession that can be defined ... side by side with those of others'.[3]

Most Anglican scholars agree that Anglicanism is not a confession or a system of belief but rather exists as a distinctively theological ethos, a method. Anglican theologians specify the method but not the outcome of theological investigation and can respectably disagree on the grounds of fidelity to method. This gives rise to a rather dynamic approach to tradition, an issue which shall be returned to.

Nevertheless, Anglicanism is not a theology in which anything goes. While it has been argued that Anglican comprehensiveness is merely an excuse for muddled theological thinking, the history of Anglicanism reveals that the proper use of this comprehensive model of doing theology and of being Church is rooted in a desire to maintain communion by specifying only the essential elements of Christian faith.[4] This essentialist approach was defined by Archbishop Robert Runcie in 1988 as the 'minimum structuring of our mutual interdependence – that which is actually required for the maintenance of communion and no more'.[5]

The very existence of the Anglican Communion as a family of Churches that share a common or related origins, albeit with divergent theological perspectives, gives rise to a challenge to the notion that Anglicanism possesses no special doctrines of its own.[6] In fact, the special doctrine of Anglicanism is its ecclesiology, and as it shall be argued, this in *esse* is an ecclesiology of communion.

Foundational to each of the local Churches that comprise the Anglican Communion is the diocese, overseen by a bishop. Each local worshipping community gathers to celebrate the Eucharist, which is an anticipation of the universal Church.[7] As Newman explained: 'each diocese is a perfect independent Church, sufficient for itself; and the communion of Christians one with another, and the unity of them all together lie ... in what they are and what they have in common.'[8] While the mystical oneness of multiple local eucharistic communities is essentially complete, it is not independent of other like communities.[9] Although higher instruments of a synodical nature have proved undesirable for the Anglican Communion, local bonds of culture, language, economy and of relationship with secular government have facilitated associations between local eucharistic communities, gathered together into provinces.[10] Thus, relationships between local communities, national Churches and global communion is one of mutual interdependence. The local is always bound to the universal as both are supremely complementary; both are mutually dependent manifestations of the body of Christ.[11]

The Anglican Communion, however, does not regard itself as the universal Church, but always as a provisional manifestation. A hallmark of Anglican ecclesiology is that it does not make exclusive claims for itself.[12] It recognises that union with Christ is the true sign of ecclesiality and that, consequently, all faithful constitute the Church empirically.[13] Anglican ecclesiology sees itself, and all churches, as provisional in light of the one, holy, Catholic and apostolic Church. This self-understanding gives Anglican ecclesiology its distinctive character, and it is for this reason that Anglicanism does not need much specific doctrine, since it is comfortable drawing upon the common inheritance of Christian tradition, supplemented with contemporary experience.[14]

It is this provisionality, amongst other things, that provides Anglicans with the impetus for ecumenical engagement. Its emphasis on common inheritance expresses a desire to be Catholic, that is to be part of the whole. Anglicans would generally accept Cardinal Willebrands description of Catholicity as 'a fellowship of local Churches, each with its own style and personality bound together by a single faith expressed in sacramental communion, but not necessarily organisation and control'.[15] Stephen Bayne appropriated this perspective when he said that 'the vocation of Anglicanism is to disappear because Anglicanism does not believe in itself but believes only in the Catholic Church of Christ; therefore it is forever restless until it finds its place in that one body'.[16] Robert Runcie, again, emphasised that the provisional nature of Anglicanism mandates us to look outside of individual Churches towards greater ecclesial communion amongst fellow-believers:

> We must never make the survival of the Anglican Communion an end in itself. The Churches of the Anglican Communion have never claimed to be more than a part of the one holy Catholic and apostolic Church. Anglicanism has a radically provisional character which we must never allow to be obscured.[17]

As a consequence of provisionality, Michael Ramsey observed that Anglicanism's credentials become 'its incompleteness ... [therefore] it is clumsy and untidy, it baffles neatness and logic ... by its very brokenness [it is] to point to the universal Church wherein all have died.'[18] Classical Anglican ecclesiology, then, is rooted in an idea of communion, that is mutual interdependence. Through its provisional character Anglicanism is profoundly uncomfortable with ecclesiological disunity, and so it holds within it divergent opinions in creative tension as an attempt to maintain unity and communion.

But is this comprehensive, provisional vision purely aspirational? Pragmatically, Anglicans have sought to enact communion, albeit with those other Churches with whom there is a more organic relationship, that is other Anglican Churches. In 1886, a movement began to define what is essential for enacting communion between these Churches. The 1888 Chicago-Lambeth Quadrilateral affirmed that the Holy Scriptures as the Word of God, the historic creeds, the two dominical sacraments and the historic episcopate were the four fundamental non-negotiables for communion. It specified what bishops thought was a helpful account of the unity that Anglicans sought with one another and also with other non-Anglican Christians.[19] Although more recently additional qualifications have been articulated, the Quadrilateral constitutes the basis of the common witness of Anglicanism as a communion of local churches, aspiring to unity with the Church universal.

Bishop Peter Elliott has claimed that Anglicans have never fully resolved the issue of how the particular Church relates to the universal, and that this is the fuel that fires all Anglican disputes.[20] The ostensibly muddled appearance of Anglicanism prompts the question ecclesiologically speaking, what is the Anglican Communion? Is it a Church? Is it a federation of Churches with shared theological convictions? Is it a particular expression of the mystical Church bound together in grace? Although the Anglican Communion possess certain ecclesial qualities such as professing the creeds and the interchangeability of ministry, it is not a Church. It lacks a central authority, and common canon law, liturgy and uniformity of doctrine. The Church of Ireland is legitimately a 'Church' inasmuch as it possess enforceable canons, but the Anglican Communion possesses no such structures so cannot really be termed 'Church'. Neither is the Anglican Communion simply a federation of like-minded Churches, its

amongst Anglicans by articulating a common fundamental theology, and second it articulated the ecumenical orientation of Anglicanism by expressing what Anglicans believed to be essential for ecclesial communion with other Christians.[31] The turn towards an institutional form of ecclesial communion has caused Anglicans to become more introspective, emphasising unity within rather than balancing it with unity outside the Anglican Communion. A sense of self-preservation has emerged which contrasts that earlier self-understanding that the vocation of Anglicanism is to disappear.

The Anglican Communion has sailed through its recent storms with this newer infrastructure *in situ*. The greater ecclesiality has created the expectation of closer doctrinal uniformity.[32] The *Windsor Report*, which addressed the structural considerations of communion, has recommended the establishment of an Anglican Covenant to affirm the essentials of the Quadrilateral yet specify the 'relational consequences' of doctrinal disagreements across the communion.[33] The establishment of a structure, enforceable through a new instrument called the 'Standing Committee', could limit the participation by national Churches in the common life of the communion, wherever such Churches had taken decisions that it deemed 'incompatible with the Covenant'.[34] The recommendation was welcomed by the Roman Catholic Church which, understandably saw in it a more united Anglicanism with which it could continue its conversations. However, the covenant has been seen by many Anglicans as adopting a new normative form of Anglicanism which establishes a more unified Church rather than a communion. At this stage it appears that the covenant will not gain the required level of global support. The covenant experiment has attempted to link the Churches together by shared convictions, that is an increased measure of enforced orthodoxy and orthopraxis, in contrast to the essentialist position of the past. The alternative for Anglicans is to continue along the difficult path of dialogue and disagreement while bound together in a *koinonia,* which permits diversity. It seems that the only way forward is, actually, backwards, towards a communion ecclesiology that is rooted in the local Church, seen in relation to a mystical Church. Thankfully, this return to an early framework of communion provides a space to counteract introspection and revitalise the external/internal balance implicit in the Quadrilateral.

An introspective mentality can be ecumenically dangerous. Kasper has said that the 'only obstacles to ecumenical dialogue ... come from the internal tensions within the Anglican world'.[35] This seems, however, unfair in light of the publication of *Dominus Iesus* in 2000. While the Churches of the Anglican Communion are recognised as 'ecclesial communities' its structures are not constituted in a way that enables communion between 'true particular Churches', which subsists within the twenty-three particular Churches of the Catholic Church. By implication, any Anglican local particular Churches are not Churches in the proper sense.[36] This appears to run contrary to the definitions of ecclesiality in the ARCIC dialogues. Furthermore, *Anglicanorum Coetibus* in 2009 has revealed additional complications. Roman Catholic responses to *Anglicanorum Coetibus* have tended towards exclusivism. The permission of Anglicans entering the personal ordinariate to maintain their Anglican 'patrimony' yet surrender their ecclesiological heritage reveals a misunderstanding about Anglican fundamentals, since Anglican patrimony is effectively ecclesiological. Indeed, a recent series of essays reduced Anglican 'patrimony', to Church music and married clergy![37] These authors compare an idealised Roman Catholicism with Anglicanism as it is, in all its acknowledged brokenness. *Anglicanorum Coetibus* is a sure sign of the urgency of renewing ecumenical dialogue. Both communions, then, are in dire need of dialogue to counterbalance recent trends towards introspection.

HAVE ANGLICANS ANYTHING TO OFFER TO COMMUNION ECCLESIOLOGY?

When Anglicanism appears in media reports, it usually partnered with the world 'crisis'. The anticipation of 'schism' seems an ever-present spectre. Yet this is nothing new. The formative period of post-Reformation Anglican identity was one of successive political crises, while both the Lambeth Conferences and the Quadrilateral emerged in the aftermath of conflict. Inter-Anglican 'crisis' or debate is part of Anglican DNA, yet it is important to note that Anglicans do not see this as a problem, rather it is a consequence of Anglican ecclesiology. Conflict and disagreement are not unhealthy, nor are they a sign that the Anglican Communion is dysfunctional. Conflict is a reality of being Church, and Anglicans are comfortable in acknowledging its existence.[38] Despite frequent disagreement, Anglicanism has an impressive track record at staying united through major controversies.[39] Although there are certain circumstances where communion is 'impaired', Anglican Churches maintain their communion with the See of Canterbury as a symbol of mutual interdependence, despite disagreements. While the 'certain yet imperfect' cliché is usually applied to Anglican-Roman Catholic relations, it can be said of the Anglican Communion itself. It is certain through its struggle to hold together, yet imperfect through its human frailty, disagreement and in light of the universal Church. Although it is untidy, incomplete and eclectic Anglicanism is willing to admit and embrace its provisionality.[40] As such, Anglican ecclesiology has been described by Paul Avis as modest.

It is also modest in its general avoidance of making exclusive claims for itself. Anglican provisionality prohibits such claims. Expressions of exclusivist ideas, such as those of *Dominus Iesus* are anathema to Anglican ecumenical encounters.[41] If there is one thing that the Anglican experiment can teach it is that in a divided Christian Church there cannot be any Church that is not provisional; all Churches are provisional in light of the one, holy, Catholic and apostolic Church that Christians aspire to be, yet constantly fall short of being.

In conclusion, it is imperative to renew both communions' fellowship, and that these conversations be conducted in a spirit of receptive ecumenism, with a radical openness to whatever this might require, rather than the introspection that both communions have tended towards in recent years. Both communions need to reaffirm that 'grave obstacles from the past and of recent origins must not lead us into thinking that there is no further room for growth towards fuller communion'.[42] Whatever difficulties and disagreements emerge, an ecclesiology of communion requires mutual striving towards the highest possible degree of communion with God and with one another. Cardinal Willebrands offered some words of advice which the current round of ARCIC ought to hear: 'dialogue is not enough. To renew oneself, to reform oneself means to sacrifice oneself.'[43] Perhaps it is through the rhetoric of sacrifice that tension between local and universal can be resolved definitively?

NOTES

1 Walter Kasper, 'Address to the Lambeth Conference', presented at Lambeth, United Kingdom, 31st July 2008.

2 Mark Woodruff, 'Anglican Orders – Recognised or Received?' *The Messenger of the Catholic League,* 292 (2010): 80.

3 Michael Ramsey, 'What is Anglican theology?', *Theology* 48 (1945), 6.

4 Andrew Pierce, 'Anglican Incomprehensiveness', *Search* 33 (2010), 127.

5 *The Truth Shall Make You Free: The Lambeth Conference 1988,* London: Church House, 1988, 16.

6 Colin Podmore, *Aspects of Anglican Identity,* London: Church House, 2005, 40.

7 G.R. Evans, *Authority in the Church: a challenge for Anglicans,* Norwich: Canterbury Press, 1990, 39.

8 John Henry Newman, 'The Catholicity of the Anglican Church', *Essays Critical and Historical,* London: Basil Montagu Pickering, 1890, II. 20.

9 Evans, *Authority in the Church,* 40.

10 Ibid., 56–7.

11 Martin Foord, 'Recent directions in Anglican Ecclesiology', *Churchman* 115 (2004), 326.

12 Paul Avis, *The Identity of Anglicanism,* London: T&T Clark, 2007, 157.

13 A perspective particularly advanced by Irish brothers A.T. Hanson and R.P.C. Hanson., *The Identity of the Church,* London: SCM Press, 1987, cf. Foord, 'Recent directions in Anglican Ecclesiology', 318.

14 Avis, *The Identity of Anglicanism,* 156–7.

15 Gerard Noel, 'Rome, Canterbury and World-Wide Christianity: Hopes for the Future', *Anglicanism and the Western Christian Tradition: Continuity, Change and the Search for Communion,* Stephen Platten, ed., Norwich: Canterbury Press, 2003, 211.

16 S.F. Bayne, 'Anglicanism – the contemporary situation: this nettle, Anglicanism', *Pan-Anglican: A Review of the World-wide Episcopal Church* 5 (1954), 43–4.

17 *The Truth Shall Make You Free,* 13. Cf. Podmore, *Aspects of Anglican Identity,* 40–1.

18 Michael Ramsey, *The Gospel and the Catholic Church,* London: Longmans, Green & Co., 1936, 220. Cf. Podmore, *Aspects of Anglican Identity,* 40–1.

19 Pierce, 'Anglican Incomprehensiveness', 128.

20 Peter Elliott, 'Understanding Pope Benedict XVI's offer to Traditional Anglicans', *The Messenger of the Catholic League* 292 (2010), 34.

21 Paul Avis, 'Catholicity outweighs Autonomy', *Our Unity in Christ,* 1st April 2011.

22 The Final Report of the 1985 Extraordinary Synod.

23 ARCIC, Final Report, 9.

24 ARCIC, Church as Communion, 43.

25 Ibid., 45.

26 Walter Kasper, *Harvesting the Fruits,* London: Continuum, 2009, 75.

27 ARCIC, Gift of Authority, 37.

28 Kasper, *Harvesting the Fruits,* 76. Cf. ARCIC, Church as Communion, 4.

29 Archbishop Rowan Williams at a meeting with Pope Benedict XVI in March 2012. Cf. *Church of Ireland Gazette,* 23rd March 2012.

30 The Instruments of Communion are identified as the personal ministry of the Archbishop of Canterbury, the Lambeth Conference, the meeting of Anglican Primates and the Anglican Consultative Council.

31 Pierce, 'Anglican Incomprehensiveness', 129.

32 Jonathan Clatworthy, 'Decision time for the Anglican Covenant', *Search* 33 (2010): 166

33 Anglican Covenant, Final Draft, section 4.2.7.

34 Ibid., section 4.2.6.

35 *Osservatore Romano,* 14th November 2009.

36 Woodruff, 'Anglican Orders – Recognised or Received?', 85.

37 Stephen Cavanaugh, ed., *Anglicans and the Roman Catholic Church: Reflections on recent developments,* San Francisco: Ignatius Press, 2011.

38 Avis, *The Identity of Anglicanism,* 153.

39 Jonathan Clatworthy, 'Decision time for the Anglican Covenant', 165.

40 Avis, *The Identity of Anglicanism,* 155.

41 Ibid., 156–7.

42 ARCIC, *Church as Communion,* 56.

43 Jan Willebrands, 'To what extent can or should there be diversity in a United Church? – Freedom and Authority', *Anglican/Roman Catholic Dialogue: the work of the Preparatory Commission,* Alan Clark and Colin Davey, eds, Oxford: Oxford University Press, 1974, 73.

THE SECOND VATICAN COUNCIL AND THE ECCLESIOLOGY OF COMMUNION WITH SPECIAL REFERENCE TO MATTHEW 18:20

REV. DR TOMÁS SURLIS DD
Gregorian University, Rome

In this paper, I would like to indicate how Matthew 18:20 – which is referred to thirty-eight times in the *Acta et Documenta* of Vatican II and four times in the conciliar documents – provides an important perspective to aid our interpretation of the intent and purpose of Vatican II.[1] The references to Matthew 18:20 in the Council documents indicate the importance of this dominical saying for a deeper and fuller appreciation of the purpose of an ecumenical council of the Church. These same references also act as an aid to theological discussion on how best to interpret the insights of the documents of Vatican II in fidelity to the living Tradition of the Church and the authority of the Magisterium. It is the same Jesus, who promised to be with his Church until the end of time (cf. Mt 28:20), who guided and directed the deliberations and teachings of the bishops of Vatican II and who continues to lead the community of his disciples towards the fulfilment of God's plan for the Church and the world.

Before reviewing the references to Mt 18:20 in the Council, I want to note that in underlining Mt 18:20 I am mindful of Pope Benedict XVI's words that 'it is clear that this commitment to expressing a specific truth in a new way demands new reflection on this truth and a new vital relationship with it; it is also clear that new words can only develop if they come from an informed understanding of the truth expressed, and on the other hand, that a reflection on faith also requires that this faith be lived.'[2] It is only with a balanced sense of continuity, of renewal within tradition, and of the attempt to find new and attractive ways of communicating the message of the gospel that we can seek to engage in the ongoing attempt to better understand an emerging theological development in ecclesiological reflection, namely, the ecclesiology of communion.[3] It is in that context I offer this short reflection on Mt 18:20 in Vatican II.

THE DOCUMENTS OF THE COUNCIL ON MATTHEW 18:20

Matthew 18:20 in the Constitution on the Sacred Liturgy, *Sacrosanctum Concilium*, 7

The first mention of Matthew 18:20 in the *Acta et Documenta* (*Antepraeparatoria*) of Vatican II, with reference to the presence of Christ in the Liturgy, is in a letter written by Antonio Jannucci, Bishop of Penne Pescara, to the preparatory commission, in which he raises the question of the manifold presence of Christ in the Church.[4] From the beginning, this was an important question, both for those who drafted the schema and for the Council Fathers who debated it, as shall be seen when the way the presence of Christ in the community is described by the other three conciliar documents which quote Matthew 18:20 is examined.[5]

Since it was the first conciliar document to be approved, the first instance in which the final text of the documents of the Council made reference to Matthew 18:20 is in the Constitution on the Sacred Liturgy, *Sacrosanctum Concilium* (SC, 7). In this section of the Constitution, the Council Fathers present the gathering of the community of disciples for prayer in Jesus' name as one of the principles for understanding the presence of Christ in the Church's liturgy.[6] The manner in which *Sacrosanctum Concilium* lists the various ways in which Christ is present in the liturgy is based on Pius XII's encyclical *Mediator Dei* (*On the Sacred Liturgy*), which was written in 1947.[7] By comparing and contrasting the two passages, it becomes clear that the drafters of *Sacrosanctum Concilium* did not simply repeat verbatim what Pope Pius XII wrote. Rather, they adapted it and indeed added to it. Jean Galot observes that the conciliar document augments *Mediator Dei*'s list of the modes of Christ's presence 'by noting his presence in the word'.[8] Judith M. Kubicki agrees and adds that 'the conciliar articulation of the manifold presence of Christ, *Sacrosanctum Concilium*, article seven, is the usual point of reference today for discussions of the various modes of Christ's presence'.[9]

Galot goes on to explain the meaning of the conciliar language used to signify presence: *praesens adest*. He comments that '[*a*]*dest* means an existence oriented toward someone. This intentionality of the presence shows that it is not simply an action of the Lord in the liturgy. Christ wants to be present to those who take part in the liturgical action, and such a presence highlights the relationship of one person to another. Thus, Christ is more clearly seen as the centre of interpersonal relations between human beings.'[10] This theological observation is important because it draws attention to interpersonal relations and draws out the meaning of gathering in the name of Jesus. According to Kubicki, the intention of the Council in using Mt 18:20 in this context *and* by placing it where it does is to emphasise the fact that it is Christ's presence in the midst of those who are assembled in his name 'that forms the basis for the possibility for all the other modes of presence'.[11]

While emphasising Christ's presence in the eucharistic liturgy, *Sacrosanctum Concilium* in no way denies his presence in other liturgical activities. The Constitution draws heavily on *Mediator Dei* and while it reorders the modes of Christ's presence it does not take away from anything Pius XII said. In fact, it adds to it the presence of Christ in the proclaimed word of scripture. Kubicki stresses that 'a significant point that can easily be overlooked is that in *Mediator Dei* the introduction to the listing of the modes clearly asserts that in *every* liturgical action Christ is present. This includes such non-sacramental celebrations as the Liturgy of the Hours, even when it is celebrated in a space without the reserved sacrament.'[12] The purpose of Christ's presence in the midst of the disciples gathered in his name is to build up unity among believers who, in their turn, are called to bring all people into the unity the Church shares in the unity of the Father, the Son and the Holy Spirit. This is in keeping with what the Second Vatican Council would later say in its *Pastoral Constitution on the Church in the Modern World* (*Gaudium et Spes*, 32).

The emphasis on unity – evident in *Gaudium et Spes,* 32 – is implicit in *Sacrosanctum Concilium,* 7. Christ is present whenever his Church gathers to pray and he is present precisely because he wishes to draw men and women into more intimate communion with him and through him with the Father in the bond of love which is the Holy Spirit. To help his followers to imitate him in prayer as a means of entering into deeper communion with God, Jesus gave an example. Peter E. Fink notes that 'Jesus never did anything of significance without first withdrawing to pray.'[13] Jean Galot adds that '[w]e must remember that through his prayer, Christ inaugurated Christian prayer, and it is through him that his Church continues to pray'.[14] While Christ is present in the most sublime manner when the Church gathers to celebrate the Eucharist and he is also present when the Church gathers to celebrate the Liturgy of the Hours, it may also be said that when small groups gather to pray and deliberate over a problem, Christ is present there too.

Matthew 18:20 in the Decree on Ecumenism, *Unitatis Redintegratio*, 8

As Pope Paul VI indicated in his discourse for the opening of the second period of the Council, the bringing together of Christians in unity was to be one of the major foci of Vatican II.[15] Therefore, the work put in to the decree on Ecumenism by the Council Fathers was very important, especially because there were two often competing theologies of ecumenism at work among the bishops.[16]

The decree shows that an imperfect unity already exists which makes it possible for Christians to pray together for reconciliation and for the unity of the Church, but that degree of unity has not yet been achieved which would allow for us to legitimately share in the Eucharist together. UR, 8 does not speak of the *sacramental* presence of Christ in the context of ecumenical gatherings to pray for Christian unity. But it does speak of a real presence nonetheless. Though separated Christians cannot celebrate the Eucharist together, the Decree on Ecumenism strongly suggests that they can and should share together in the presence of Christ, through the power of the Holy Spirit, by uniting in prayer in Jesus' name. For this reason, it seems to be the case that the first two conciliar references to Matthew 18:20 in SC, 7 and UR, 8 are speaking about the presence of Christ from two different, yet complementary, angles. Christ unites the Church to himself most profoundly through the sacred action of the Eucharist, yet he does not deny a mode of his presence to separated

Christians who gather in prayer for the precise purpose of asking God to grant their petition for his will to be done and for full, visible unity to be achieved. In that sense, the Decree on Ecumenism calls upon all Christians to first focus on what we *can* do together rather than on what we *cannot* do because, as the second of the two principles upon which common worship is based says, gathering together in prayer for unity allows for 'sharing in the means of grace' to achieve the unity we pray for.[17]

Matthew 18:20 in the Decree on the Sensitive Renewal of Religious Life, *Perfectae Caritatis*, 15[18]

In the much-revised Conciliar *Schema Decreti De Accomodata Renovatione Vitae Religiosae*, the reality of the members of a religious community being gathered in the name of Jesus is described in terms of the love of God which is diffused into their hearts by the Holy Spirit, making of them a community and a real family, gathered in the name of the Lord and rejoicing (*gaudet*) in his presence among them.[19] An earlier draft had made no mention of the presence of Christ, rather it had restricted itself to referring to religious being gathered in the name of Christ. The *Acta et Documenta* do not explain the reasons for the change but it appears that the Commission for Religious wanted to emphasise that the renewal of religious life should focus on religious communities being a fellowship of faith, hope and love which rejoices in the presence of Christ in its midst, rather than emphasising separation from the world, which the first draft had implied. The revised text was to remain in the document, which was approved by Paul VI and the Council Fathers during the Seventh Public Session of the Council on 28th October 1965.[20]

In the *Decree on the Sensitive Renewal of Religious Life,* the Council wishes to show that '[f]raternal community of life is one of the ultimate motifs of Catholic religious life'.[21] This is because communities of religious men and women have, as part of their *raison d'être,* the task of making visible the beauty of a common life, lived in unity and charity, thereby heralding the fulfilment of the divine plan. The decree implies that this was not always easy to achieve in the past.

It is because religious are members of one another in Christ that they make it one of their basic aims to give witness to the powerful presence of Christ in the midst of the community which works, prays and lives a common life together. This requires effort and a shared vision, which is why each community operates out of a rule, but it is not as simple as having a rule and leaving it at that. Community life is built up and strengthened by a keen awareness of the presence in the midst of the community of the One who has gathered them together in his name. This keen awareness deepens each individual's appreciation of having been called to devote his/her entire self to God and the building of his kingdom on earth. It also deepens each person's knowledge of the love God has for him/her, a love which he invites them to share with all those among whom they live, work and pray.

The Fathers of the Council were aware that some of what had come to characterise traditional religious life at the time of Vatican II stood in the way of true community. Therefore, the Decree called for appropriate and sensitive renewal of religious life. Some of the things which obstructed the building up of genuine fraternal community included: 'the anonymity of the individual, the assumed distance from one another, the customary largeness of communities, overwork, and, not least, the constitution of modern man who on the one hand desires community, on the other withdraws from it, who needs contact and yet is bad at making it, who would like to love, and yet finds it hard to rise above himself.'[22] All or a combination of some of these factors were wholly unconducive to a way of life which, at its best, was intended to gradually yet steadily form each member of the community into being a person-for-others, and in this way achieving their greatest potential as disciples of Christ. The Decree does not specify precisely how this reform and renewal was to come about, except to call for a return to the original vision of the founder in each order, congregation and institute of apostolic life.

In his post-synodal exhortation, *Vita consecrata* (1996), Pope John Paul II refers to Matthew 18:20 in chapter II of his post-synodal exhortation, which bears the title, 'Consecrated Life as a Sign of Communion in the Church.' In it he notes that 'in community life ... it should in some way be evident that, more than an instrument for carrying out a specific mission, fraternal communion is a *God-enlightened space* in which to experience the hidden presence of the Risen Lord (cf. Mt 18:20).'[23] Thus, Pope John Paul teaches that religious community life is not simply about the apostolate but, more fundamentally, such a common life seeks to generate and rejoice in the presence of Christ in the midst of those who gather in his name. The phrase 'God-enlightened space' points to the effect of living with Jesus in the midst of the community: the minds and hearts of those who live such a life are enriched by the power and wisdom of God. They live in the space of the *Shekinah*, overshadowed by the divine presence, and, as such, they are a powerful witness to the world of what it means to call God *Emmanuel* (cf. Mt 1:23; 18:20; 28:20).[24]

Thus, *Perfectae Caritatis*, which forms the background to *Vita Consecrata*, helps the Church to better appreciate the effective sign value of the religious life. The task which the Council puts before religious men and women is to teach humanity how to live in communion, a communion which has as its vital life-force the presence of the Risen Jesus in the midst of those striving to live a common life in faith, hope and love (cf. Mt 18:20).

Matthew 18:20 in the Decree on the Apostolate of Lay People, *Apostolicam Actuositatem*, 18

The Commission on the Apostolate of the Laity was a late addition to the Preparatory Commission at the express wish of Pope John XXIII who referred to it as 'the "newest mark" of the Council and entrusted [it] with the study of "the apostolate of the laity, religious and social Catholic action"'.[25] In the final preparatory document on the laity, as a result of revisions worked on by the commission, explicit mention of the key biblical text with which this present paper is concerned appears in the final draft.[26]

Article 18, especially by making direct reference to the presence of Christ in the midst of those who work together in an apostolate, shows that Christ associates himself with all aspects of the lives of his disciples and does not confine his presence to the moments when they gather together in formal prayer. He is with them in their work, particularly when that work is directed towards promoting the values of the kingdom and the mission of the Church. When the members of the apostolate are united, Jesus can achieve great things with and through them – far greater than that which would be achieved were an individual working alone. As William Henn observes in his book, *Church: The People of* God, '[t]he Church, therefore, is the community of Jesus' disciples who, by witness, worship and service, in their words and actions, are sent by their Lord to invite others to become disciples too. This mission is a genuine service to people.'[27] The Spirit of the Risen One binds believers together, inspires them to draw on the wealth of resources which he has placed in their hearts, minds and souls and teaches them to rely on each other and on Christ and thereby discover the peace and joy which genuine communion brings.

This is why the decree says that 'common activity must reveal itself in the apostolate within the family, the parish, the diocese, and also within freely chosen groups – *coetus* was chosen on purpose to indicate the widest possible term for such associations. In all these forms of common endeavour the Church should appear as the community that she really is.'[28] The fruits of collaboration are made plain by the decree in the light of the ecclesiology of communion. These are the fruits of 'the greater effectiveness of the common apostolate in the ecclesiastical communities proper, as well as in the various milieus: it gives the individual support, facilitates the formation for the apostolate as well as its planning and direction.'[29] This provides the theological rationale for any number of apostolic activities at family, group, parish and diocesan levels. By working together, with Jesus in the midst, the work of the apostolate bears fruit in plenty (cf. Jn 15:4-5). There is strength in the unity which comes from sharing in the bond of love which unites the Father, the Son and the Holy Spirit. It is in this light that the decree *Apostolicam Actuositatem* cites Matthew 18:20 as a scriptural clarion call to the disciples of Jesus to underpin their activity with prayer offered in unity so that all that is done is his name will bear fruit for the building up of the kingdom of God on earth.[30]

CONCLUSION

From these considerations of the way in which the Second Vatican Council understands the Lord's promise to be present in the midst of the community of disciples that gathers to pray in his name, the ecclesiological significance of Matthew 18:20 has begun to emerge. To be conscious of Jesus' presence when the Church celebrates the liturgy, when Christians pray together for unity, when religious men and women bear witness to the fulfilment of God's promises and when the laity work together for the upbuilding of God's kingdom of justice and peace means being ever more deeply aware that God is with us and God is for us. Jesus founded his Church to be a sign for the entire world to see, a leaven in the midst of society which works to raise the expectations and hopes of men and women for a world of justice and peace and brotherhood among people. The more consciously aware the members of the Church are of the constant presence of Christ in the midst of those who gather in his name, the more perfectly they are able to act as a leaven for society – each according to his/her own proper gifts bestowed upon all the baptised by the Christ through the power of the Holy Spirit (cf. Mt 18:20; Eph 4:10-13). Of course, from the perspective of Catholic ecclesiology, the two or three who gather in the name of Jesus should do so conscious of their communion with the local bishop, who acts as its representative at a council of the universal Church and is 'the principal dispenser of the mysteries of God' for the Church entrusted to his care.[31] Yet *all* the members of the Church have a responsibility in this regard and this responsibility is perfectly in keeping with the understanding of the Church as communion in light of the gospel promise: 'where two or three are gathered together in my name, there I am in the midst of them' (Mt 18:20).[32]

ABBREVIATIONS[33]

AAS	Acta Apostolicae Sedis
ADCOV	*Acta et documenta Concilio Oecumenico Vaticano II apparando*
ASCOV	*Acta synodalia sacrosancti Concilii Oecumenici Vaticani II*
DH	Denzinger, H., *The Sources of Catholic Dogma*, Fitzwilliam, [NH]: Loreto Publications, 2004.
ND	Neuner, J. Dupuis, J., *The Christian Faith in the Doctrinal Documents of the Catholic Church*, New York: Alba House, 2001.
SCDSOCVS	*Schemata Constitutionum et Decretorum Sacrosanctum Oecumenicum Concilium Vaticanum Secundum*

NOTES

1 Mt 18:20 Is quoted directly in *Sacrosanctum Concilium,* 7, *Unitatis Redintegratio,* 8, and *Apostolicam Actuositatem,* 18, and is cited in the body of the text in *Perfectae Caritatis,* 15. For a list of the references to Mt 18:20 In The *Acta Et Documenta* Of Vatican II, See Footnote 4 Below And T. Surlis, *The Presence Of The Risen Christ In The Community Of Disciples: An Examination Of The Ecclesiological Significance Of Matthew 18:20,* Roma, Editrice Pontificia Università Gregoriana, 2011, 197–8.

2 Pope Benedict XVI, 'Address Of His Holiness Benedict XVI To The Roman Curia Offering Them His Christmas Greetings', 22nd December 2005, *Vatican II: Renewal Within Tradition,* M.I. Lamb and M. Levering, eds., Oxford, 2008, xi.

3 For an examination of the meaning and significance of the emerging Ecclesiology of Communion for the post-conciliar church, see T. Surlis, *The Presence Of The Risen Christ In The Community of Disciples,* Rome: Gregorian & Biblical Press, 2011, pp. 179–94.

4 Cf. *Adcov,* i:ii/3, 523. This reference was discovered while researching each volume of the *acta et documenta.* In the absence of a biblical index to accompany the *acta et documenta synodalia* of Vatican II, the researcher must read through each volume to discover the references to a specific biblical text. A complete list of the 38 references made to Mt 18:20 Runs as follows: **1.** *Scdsocvs,* iv, 385; **2.** *Adcov,* i:ii/3, 523; **3.** *Adcov,* ii:i, 275–83, at 279; **4.** *Adcov,* ii:ii/3, 29; **5.** *Adcov,* ii:ii/3, 77; **6.** *Adcov,* ii:ii/4, 537; **7.** *Adcov,* ii:ii/4, 787; **8.** *Adcov,* ii:iii/2, 12; **9.** *Ascov,* i/1, 265; **10.** *Ascov,* i/1, 421; **11.** *Ascov,* i/1, 479; **12.** *Ascov,* i/3, 696–7; **13.** *Ascov,* vi/2, 415; **14.** *Ascov,* ii/2, 893; **15.** *Ascov,* ii/3, 609; **16.** *Ascov,* ii/3, 614; **17.** *Ascov,* ii/5, 421–2; **18.** *Ascov,* ii/5, 499; **19.** *Ascov,* ii/5, 871; **20.** *Ascov,* ii/5, 873; **21.** *Ascov,* ii/6, 143; **22.** *Ascov,* ii/6, 259; **23.** *Ascov,* ii/6, 411; **24.** *Ascov,* iii/4, 340; **25.** *Ascov,* iii/7, 19; **26.** *Ascov,* iii/7, 764–5; **27.** *Ascov,* iii/8, 766; **28.** *Ascov,* iv/1, 127; **29.** *Ascov,* iv/2, 339; **30.** *Ascov,* iv/2, 630; **31.** *Ascov,* iv/3, 524; **32.** *Ascov,* iv/4, 932; **33.** *Ascov,* iv/5, 590; **34.** *Ascov,* iv/6, 85; **35.** *Ascov,* iv/6, 622; **36.** *Ascov,* v/1, 415; **37.** *Ascov,* v/1, 468; **38.** *Ascov,* v/2, 266.

5 For a detailed analysis of the interventions and debates that surrounded the question of the modes of Christ's presence, see T. Surlis, *The Presence Of The Risen Christ In The Community of Disciples,* Rome, 2011, 197–205.

6 *Sacrosanctum Concilium,* 7. Cf. A. Flannery, *Vatican II,* Vol. I, Dublin, 1975, 4–5. Cf. Council Of Trent, Session 22: Doctrine On The Holy Sacrifice of the Mass, Ch. 2. Cf. St Augustine, *Tractatus In Ioannem* Vi, ch. 1, no. 7.

7 Pope Pius XII, *Mediator Dei* (*On The Sacred Liturgy,* 24. Cf. *Aas* 39 (1947): 528; dh 2297; nd 1331.

8 J. Galot, 'Christ: Revealer, Founder Of The Church, And Source Of Ecclesial Life', *Vatican II: Assessments And Perspectives, Twenty-Five Years After,* R. Latourelle, I-Iii, Mahwah, 1988, 1989, 397.

9 J.M. Kubicki, *The Presence Of Christ In The Gathered Assembly*, New York, 2006, 47.

10 J. Galot, 'Christ: Revealer, Founder of the Church, and Source of Ecclesial Life', 397.

11 J.M. Kubicki, *The Presence of Christ in the Gathered Assembly*, 47.

12 Ibid., 49.

13 P.E. Fink, 'Public And Private Moments In Christian Prayer', *Worship* 58/6, November 1984, 487.

14 J. Galot, 'Christ: Revealer, Founder of the Church, and Source of Ecclesial Life', 398.

15 Pope Paul VI, 'Discorso di Apertura del 2º Periodo del Concilio,' 29 Settembre 1963, 'Salvete Fratres', *Enchiridion Vaticanum II*, 99. Cf. G. Alberigo and J. Komonchak, eds, *History Of Vatican II,* Vol. IV, Maryknoll, 2003, 413–4.

16 Cf. C. Soetens, 'The Ecumenical Commitment of the Catholic Church', *History of Vatican II,* Vol. III: *The Mature Council. Second Period And Intersession September 1963–September 1964*, G. Alberigo and J. Komonchak, eds, Maryknoll, 1997, 263.

17 Cf. *Unitatis Redintegratio*, 8, N.P. Tanner, *Decrees of the Ecumenical Councils*, Vol. II, Washington, 1990, 914.

18 'Sensitive' is tanner's translation. Some commentators say 'appropriate' while others, including flannery, say 'up-to-date'.

19 Cf. *Ascov*, iv/3, 524. The Text Reads: 'Caritate Enim Dei in Cordibus per Spritum Sanctum Diffusa (cf. Rm 5:5, Communitas ut vera Familia, in nomine Domini Congregata, Eius Praesentia Gaudet, [Cf. Mt 18:20]).'

20 Cf. *Ascov*, iv/5, 590.

21 F. Wulf, 'Decree On The Appropriate Renewal of the Religious Life', H. Vorgrimler, *Commentary on the Documents of Vatican* II, Vol. II, New York, 1967, 365.

22 Ibid., 366.

23 Pope John Paul II, post-synodal apostolic exhortation, *vita consecrata*, 42 in: www.Vatican.Va/roman_curia/congregations/ccscrlife/documents/hf_jp-ii_exh_ 25031996_vita-consecrata_en.Html (accessed on 14th January 2010). (Emphases original.)

24 Cf. T. Surlis, *The Presence of the Risen Christ in the Community of Disciples*, 85–91, especially p. 87, for an exposition of the meaning of '*shekinah*'.

25 J. A. Komonchak, 'The Struggle for the Council during the Preparation of Vatican II', *History of Vatican II,* Vol. I: *Announcing and Preparing Vatican Council II, Toward a New Era in Catholicism*, G. Alberigo and J. Komonchak,

eds, Maryknoll, 1995, 196. Cf. Footnote 123: 'See The Pope's Autograph Notes, 1st June 1960, quoted in V. Carbone, "Il Cardinale Domenico Tardini E La Preparazione Del Concilio Vaticano II", *RschIt* 45 (1991) 78n.'

26 The work of the commission is elaborated upon more fully in T. Surlis, *The Presence of the Risen Christ in the Community Of Disciples*, Rome, 2011, 223–6.

27 W. Henn, *Church: The People Of God*, London/New York, 2004, 94–5.

28 F. Klostermann, 'Decree On The Apostolate Of The Laity', Vorgrimler III, 349.

29 Ibid., 349.

30 See E. Lanne, 'L'église Locale: Sa Catholicité Et Son Apostolicité', *Istina* 14, 1969, 64.

31 Cf. Vatican Council II, Decree On The Pastoral Office of Bishops in The Church, *Christus Dominus*, 4 and 15 and Dogmatic Constitution on The Church, *Lumen Gentium*, 22, A. Flannery, *Vatican Council II*, Vol. I, 566, 572 and 375.

32 Two of the contributions of Pope John Paul II are especially important for the Church on the threshold of the Third Millennium as she seeks to more fully understand her nature and mission as a Communion of Jesus' Disciples called to bring the whole world into that intimate union she enjoys with the Holy Trinity. They are: Pope John Paul II, encyclical on commitment to ecumenism, *Ut Unum Sint*, 21 in: www.vatican.va/holy_father/john_paul_ii/encyclicals/documents/hf_jp-ii_enc_25051995_ut-unum-sint_en.html [Accessed on 11 February 2010]. And apostolic letter to mark the close of the jubilee year 2000, *novo millennio ineunte*, esp. 43 In: *aas* 93 (2001) 266–309, at 296–7: 'to make the church the home and the school of communion: that is the great challenge facing us in the millennium which is now beginning ... communion must be cultivated and extended day by day and at every level in the structures of each church's life. There, relations between bishops, priests and deacons, between pastors and the entire people of god, between clergy and religious, between associations and ecclesial movements must all be clearly characterised by communion.'

33 In as far as possible, the use of abbreviations follows the system proposed by S.M. Schwertner, *International Glossary of Abbreviations for Theology and Related Subjects*, New York/Berlin, 1992.

THE EUCHARIST AS COMMUNITY BUILDER: EUCHARISTIC COMMUNION AND SOCIAL TRANSFORMATION

DR IZUNNA OKONKWO
Archdiocese of Glasgow, Scotland

The Eucharist is the source and summit of the Church's life and mission (LG, 11). It occupies a central locus in the Catholic Church's doctrinal and pastoral teaching to such an extent that some of its essential elements, namely communal and ecclesial aspects, seem to be taken for granted. This is partly in an effort to protect the classical scholastic sacramental (onto) theology which highlights Christ's true, real and substantial presence in the Eucharist, under the species of bread and wine, as it relates to devotion, adoration[1] and salvation of the recipient of the Eucharist from misconceptions, heresies and abuses. In a world that is pervaded by the likes of humanism, relativism and individualism, it is both necessary and urgent for the vertical[2] and horizontal communal dimensions of the Eucharist to be given the attention it deserves both in theory and practice.

This paper, against the background of orthodoxy and ortho-praxis, explores whether/how the communion and sharing experienced in the Eucharist could be employed in the fight against hunger in a world of plenty and abundant resources. At the same time, one witnesses a scandalous gap between the rich and the poor, the well-fed and the hungry. Can eucharistic Communion form a veritable basis for alleviation and eradication of hunger?

TOWARDS AN UNDERSTANDING OF SACRAMENTS

The traditional (scholastic) understanding of the sacrament as the outward sign of the inward grace instituted by Christ to confer grace to the soul of the recipient so much prevailed in the Church that the sacraments were more or less seen as mechanical and automatic transmitters of grace.[3] As the view was maintained, the involvement of the recipient and that of the celebrant seems to be regarded as passive. The scholastic theology of the sacraments, borrowing from Aristotelian hylemorphic dualism of matter and form, substance and accident, and *causa* explained the efficacy of the sacraments within the context of a mystery one cannot but receive in wonder and amazement.[4] The Council of Trent appears to have promoted this way of understanding sacramental efficacy, and gave it a significant place in Catholic theology.[5] William J. Bausch observes that the first Christians 'were interested in the whole community celebrating the wonderful works of God in Jesus, not in individuals privately manipulating objects to tease out grace'.[6] The approach has significantly 'changed' such that a 'new model' – a paradigm shift, has become both necessary, and urgent. Such a 'new way' of perceiving Sacraments, however, is not and should not be viewed as a deviation from or contradictory to traditional sacramentology. But what does it entail? This takes us to exploration of sacraments from the perspectives of onto-theology (orthodoxy) and ortho-praxis.

Sacramental Onto-Theology

The apostles and the Fathers of the Church had a way of handling doctrine. Partly this was by appealing to the scriptures, without, of course ignoring the Tradition. However, 'the desire to be faithful to the scriptures was primordial'.[7] Invariably 'the tendency to associate doctrine, as distinct from theology, with magisterial teaching is not found until after the Council of Trent'.[8]

One of the preoccupations of the Council was to protect the Catholic Church's teachings from the aftermath of Protestant Reformation.[9] In the light of this, Thomas D. McGonigle and James F. Quigley have this to say: 'on the institutional level, the Roman Catholic Church addressed the issues raised by the Protestant Reformation when Pope Paul III (1543–9) summoned the Council of Trent. Meeting in three different sessions between 1545 and 1563, the council reaffirmed the fundamental doctrinal teachings of the Church.'[10] The opening question which received a unanimous 'yes' gives a clear picture of why the Council was summoned.

> ... for the increase and advance in esteem of the faith and Christian religion, for the uprooting of heresies, for the peace and unity of the church, for the reform of the clergy and the Christian people, for the crushing and complete removal of the enemies of the Christian name, is it your wish to declare that the holy and general Council of Trent is beginning and has begun? [They replied: Yes].[11]

Further discussions involved debate on the original sin, the dogma of justification and gave doctrines of the Church on the sacraments a central place in Trinitarian theology. At their seventh Session on 3rd March 1547, the Fathers established the link between the decree on the sacraments and other doctrines already promulgated and even referred to it as 'the completion of the doctrine of salvation concerning justification'.[12] The council underlined the number and author of the sacraments in these words:

> If anyone says that the sacraments of the new law were not all instituted by our Lord Jesus Christ; or that there are more or fewer than seven: namely, baptism, confirmation, eucharist, penance, last anointing, order, matrimony; or that one or other of these seven is not truly and in the full sense a sacrament: let him be anathema.[13]

At its third canon on the sacraments in general, the council fathers made it explicit that all the sacraments are not at the same par: 'If anyone says that these seven sacraments are so equal to each other that on no ground is one of greater dignity than another; let him be anathema.'[14] Surprisingly, no further elaboration was given by the council with regard to the sequence or fact of their quality. Moreover, the Council seems not to have categorised the sacraments in their order of importance. All the same, no one may be in doubt of the status given to the Eucharist. On 11th October 1551, during its thirteenth session, a decree on the Most Holy Sacrament of the Eucharist was promulgated. By calling it the most holy, venerable and divine sacrament, the Eucharist was dealt with in a way that no other sacrament was treated. The Council of Trent, with its decrees and doctrinal formulations gave the Eucharist a significant locus in the Church's life and mission.[15] We will now look at the Eucharist to see (among others) if the Council's teachings were able to link it to concrete situations of humanity, with particular reference to the problem of hunger.

Trent: Focus on the Sacrament of the Eucharist
Conspicuous in the Council of Trent is the concern to address prevalent heresies in an attempt to offer the faithful a better sense of direction with regard to articles of faith. It [the council] was, therefore, resolved to:

> ... tear up root and branch the tares of those detestable errors and schisms which the enemy in these calamitous times has sown in the teaching of faith in the most holy Eucharist and its use and liturgy, the very sacrament which the saviour left in his Church as a symbol of its unity as love, whereby he wished all Christians to be mutually linked and united (with Christ and one another).[16]

The Council paid special attention to the Eucharist. Partly because 'in the Eucharist the author of holiness himself is present before their use'.[17] This involves a change – transubstantiation, which brings about Christ's true, holistic, substantial and realistic presence: 'for Christ exists whole and entire under the form of bread and under any part of that form, and likewise whole under the form of wine and under its parts.'[18] Consequently, if anybody denies that in the 'Eucharist there are contained truly, really and substantially, the body and blood of our lord Jesus Christ together with the soul and divinity, and therefore the whole Christ, but says that he is present in it only as in a sign or figure or by his power: let him [or her] be anathema.'[19] The Eucharist stands out as a sacrament, and has the 'power' of transforming the recipient. By being transformed to become like Christ (who is present in the sacrament), he/she is expected to become 'a new person' in his/her approach to daily realities of life.

For our concern here, it is a transformation for the possibility of being Christ to the vulnerable in the society; among who are the hungry. If we approach the Eucharist only from a material point of view, we will miss the essential ingredient which makes it a transformative force. Unlike ordinary food and drink, St Augustine, against the background of transubstantiation, says of those who receive 'eucharistic Christ': 'you will not change me into you like the food your flesh eats, but you will be changed into me.'[20] The Council rejected some theologians' opinion that the Church came to her faith in the real presence of Christ through her teaching on transubstantiation. It rather insisted that 'the Church comes to her statement of true change (called transubstantiation) through her biblical faith in the truth of Christ's words: "This is my body", "This is my blood"'.[21] This was a doctrine, which the council expounded in her three different sessions, namely: Session XIII, Session XXI (July 1562) and Session XII (September 1562). In all these one sees, among others, effort to strengthen the Church's teaching on the Eucharist, without clearly highlighting if/how this sacrament can be connected to people's concrete life situation.

The Council of Trent witnessed great opposition to its work, from the Church and the political power of the time. However, David N. Power observes that 'any examination of the teachings of Trent on Mass, or any consideration of its dogmas, has to keep in mind that doctrine and practice belong essentially together'.[22] Perhaps, it was the elaborate way in which it dealt with the sacrament of the Eucharist that other subsequent councils did not delve much into doctrinal definition of sacraments.[23] For instance, Vatican II appears to be more interested in fashioning out how celebration of sacraments could reflect in day-to-day life of Christians. This is our major concern in the next section.

VATICAN II: FROM ONTO-THEOLOGY TO ORTHOPRAXIS?

The Second Vatican Council brought renewal in the Church.[24] This is evident in the sphere of liturgy. Liam G. Walsh observes that the Council dwells on the 'mystery of the Eucharist rather than telling Catholics how to defend their faith against heresy on particular points'.[25] Besides, the Council did not concentrate on the dogmatic issues settled by Trent at the time of the Reformers.[26] A brief look at some of the Council's documents has become necessary.

Constitution on the Sacred Liturgy: *Sacrosanctum Concilium*

The Constitution on the Sacred Liturgy's concerns involves putting in place, in the light of sound tradition, new vigour to meet contemporary circumstances and needs.[27] One sees this in the way the Council Fathers dealt with the sacrament of the Eucharist. The Council not only made the celebration of the Eucharist more meaningful to the faithful, but also highlighted its nature as a sacrament of love, a sign of unity and a bond of love.[28] Such understanding of the Eucharist can go a long way in solving the problem of detaching liturgy from the experience of the Christian community which clamours for liberation.[29]

nature.[40] An encounter with Jesus in the Eucharist should therefore spur Christians into action full of concern for the other and the environment. Paul apostle gives a clue on how this could be done.

THE EUCHARIST: MEMORIAL AND COMMUNION

Paul's treatise on the Eucharist is phenomenal.[41] He was the first to write in the world of the New Testament. Like other evangelists, he never used the word Eucharist, but his narrative is very close to what is obtainable in most Christian Churches today. His condemnation of the disparity between the rich and the poor who gather for the celebration of the Lord's Supper makes more evident the necessity of linking *diakonia* (service) and *koinonia* (communion). Such link abhors discrimination and makes all one in Christ and enhances commensality.[42] Paul, reproaches the Corinthians for acting otherwise: 'When you meet together, it is not the Lord's Supper that you eat. For in eating, each one goes ahead with his own meal, and one is hungry and another is drunk' (cf. 1 Cor 11:20-21).

For Paul, the Lord's Supper has a direct link with social concerns, among which is hunger. The coming together of people with varied social status brought to the fore the necessity of protecting the less privileged.[43] Paul teaches that 'there can be no real celebration of the Lord's Supper as long as their [Christians'] liturgical assemblies are marred by unworthy conduct that is divisive and factious and not marked by the same concern "for others" that Jesus manifested at the Last Supper'.[44] His outright condemnation of the attitude of those who over feed themselves when others are hungry is a clear testimony. Social problems in the Christian community at the time was even more: 'They had to do with the use and appreciation of charismatic gifts, the meal that accompanied the ritual, the place of the poor in the assembly, and the public use of their gifts by women members.'[45] In the face of these problems, some Christians rested their hope on eschatology[46] which is always proclaimed at every eucharistic celebration.

In Paul's day, it was not a question of insufficient resources. Rather it was the scandal of inequitable distribution of abundant resources. Thus, some people were living in abundance while others were languishing in poverty and hunger. What was happening in Paul's day has not disappeared in our own era, it has increased. However, nature has a lot to offer humanity. Its productive capacity is far from being explored. In the words of Grassi: 'we are faced by the scandal of enormous surpluses of foodstuffs that certain countries periodically destroy, because of the lack of a wise economy which would have guaranteed the useful employment of these surpluses.'[47] This could be considered as it concerns a community in connection with global communities on the one hand,[48] and as it pertains to a local community on the other hand. As such, celebration of the Eucharist (normally done by a particular community) fits well into the schema as it has universal character. Consequently:

> When we receive 'Holy Communion' we are receiving into ourselves that way of being together – *without favouritism*. By standing and approaching Holy Communion, I publicly commit myself to step into a *holy community*. But I am not stepping only into this community around me here, not just the local community assembled around me: it is a commitment to consider *all people* as holy, *all people* as noble and *all reality* as impregnated with the presence of God.[49]

Pauline theology on the Eucharist is nothing short of this call for community orientedness and commitment to the pursuit of social justice. Against this background, Benedict XVI presents the Eucharist as a mystery to be believed, celebrated and lived.[50] This spirit seems to be lacking in the Corinthian community, hence Paul rebuked them for being unworthy of the Lord's Supper and showing contempt for God's Church.[51]

The community presented by Luke in the Acts of the Apostles seems to be different. For Craig L. Nessan, 'The apostolic Church of Acts is remembered for its generosity, flowing out from its table fellowship.'[52] To some extent, the apostolic table fellowship has been pictured as one of the foremost approaches to the problem of hunger. This, however, can not be taken as a perfect situation. Especially when one recalls that: 'A man named Ananias with his wife Saphira sold a piece of property, and kept back some part of the proceeds, and brought only a part and laid it at the apostles' feet' (Acts 5:1-2). This account has a very important message for both Christians and non-Christians. For the former, selfishness is inimical to the practice of life of sacrifice, love, and generosity Christ propagated.[53] For the non-Christian it serves as a caveat to those who wish to belong. The Eucharist is remembrance of what Christ did for his followers and serves as an invitation to those who take part in it to do the same for their fellow human beings.[54] To be overfed or drunk while one's neighbour is hungry, therefore, is counter-eucharistic celebration and action. Benedict XVI calls for a eucharistic spirituality which does not terminate at participation and devotion, but rather involves the entire life.[55] By extending the liturgical celebration of Christ's memorial sacrifice into real life, one can talk of the link the Eucharist has with social transformation.

EVALUATION AND CONCLUSION

For several years, the Catholic sacramentology concerned itself more with orthodoxy. Then, more attention seems to have been paid to the vertical dimension of the Eucharist. In the Middle Ages for example, heated debates focused more on the doctrine of Christ's real presence in the Eucharist.[56] These debates lingered until the twentieth century.[57] Consequently, little attention was paid to the horizontal impact of the Eucharist in the world. In another dimension, preoccupation was on the nature of the Eucharist as a meal vis-à-vis the traditional teaching of the Catholic Church on the Eucharist as a sacrifice.[58] Common to these approaches are vertical and transcendental proclivity. Understanding the Eucharist against the backdrop of its horizontal dimension refers to 'the connection between the Eucharist and charity, neighbour and life'.[59] This can be possible if vertical impulse (orthodoxy) of the Eucharist is properly applied to practical situation (ortho-praxis).

The effect of the Eucharist will be felt more in the society if it is understood and projected – in theory and practice – as communion with Christ and with one another.

NOTES

1 John Paul II, *Ecclesia de Eucharistia: On the Eucharist and the Church*, London: Catholic Truth Society, 2003, no. 25.

2 John Paul II, *Ecclesia de Eucharistia*, no. 15 and 16.

3 Lambert J. Leijssen, *With the Silent Glimmer of God's Spirit: A Postmodern Look at the Sacraments,* Mahwah, NJ: Paulist Press, 2006, 9.

4 Leijssen, *With the Silent Glimmer of God's Spirit,* 9.

5 Karl Rahner, *Theological Investigations vol. XIV: Ecclesiology, Questions in the Church, the Church in the World,* David Bourke, trans., London: Longman and Todd, 1976, 136.

6 William J. Bausch, *A New Look at the Sacraments*, Mystic, CT: Twenty-Third Publications, 1984, 1. They celebrated (in adoration praise and thanksgiving) ritual and sign as people favoured by God and through Christ even without calling their activities sacraments.

7 David N. Power, *The Eucharistic Mystery: Revitalizing the Tradition,* Dublin: Gill and Macmillan, 1992, 242. See also Omutah, *From Vatican II to African Synod: Catholic Social Teaching in African Context*, Onitsha, Nigeria: Tansi Publications, 2003, 12–13.

8 Power, *The Eucharistic Mystery*, 242.

9 Joseph Martos, *The Sacraments: An Interdisciplinary and Interactive Study*, Collegeville, MN: Liturgical Press, 2009, 116–8.

10 Thomas D. McGonigle and James F. Quigley, *A History of the Christian Tradition: From Its Jewish Origins to the Reformation*, New York, NY, Mahwah, NJ: Paulist Press, 1988, 203.

11 Council of Trent (1545–63) Session 1, 13th December 1545, *Decrees of the Ecumenical Councils, Vol 2, Trent to Vatican II*, Norman P. Tanner, ed., Washington, DC: Georgetown University Press, 1990: 657–800, 660. Though the Council of Trent officially opened on 13th December 1545, discussion on the sacraments was kept until when the fathers gathered for their seventh Session, on 3rd March 1547

12 Council of Trent (1545–63) Session 7, 3rd March 1547.

13 Ibid., This is the first of thirteen canons with which the Council of Trent defined the sacraments in general. There are other definitions on other particular sacraments.

14 Council of Trent (1545–63) Session 7, 3rd March 1547.

15 Izunna Okonkwo, *The Eucharist and World Hunger: Socio-Theological Exploration*, Bloomington, IN: Xlibris, 2011, 202–3.

16 Council of Trent (1545–63) Session 13, 11th October 1551, The Council of

Trent's Decree on the Holy Eucharist was composed during its thirteenth session in eight chapters. This quote is taken from its introductory statement.

17 Council of Trent (1545–63) Session 13, Chap. 3.

18 Ibid.

19 Council of Trent (1545–63) Session 13, 11th October 1551. This is contained in the first chapter which treats of 'The Real Presence of Our Lord Jesus Christ in the Most Holy Sacrament of the Eucharist.' And it is the first of the eleven canons on the most holy sacrament of the Eucharist as articulated by the fathers of the Council of Trent. Other ten canons may be seen as derivations from and explications of this very canon.

20 St Augustine, *The Confessions*, Henry Chardwick, trans., Oxford, New York: Oxford University Press, 1991, Bk. 7, 10.

21 Joseph M. Powers, *Eucharistic Theology*, New York, NY: The Seabury Press, 1967, 39.

22 David N. Power, *The Sacrifice We Offer: The Tridentine Dogma and its Reinterpretation*, Edinburgh: T&T Clark, 1987, 29.

23 Powers, *The Sacrifice We Offer*, 31–3.

24 Joseph Martos, *Doors to the Sacred: A Historical Introduction to Sacraments in the Catholic Church,* revised and updated edition, Missouri: Liguori/Triumph, 2001, 260.

25 Liam G. Walsh, *The Sacraments of Initiation: Baptism, Confirmation, Eucharist*, London: Geoffery Champman, 1988, 260.

26 Walsh, *The Sacrament of Initiation,* 260. By making such an observation Walsh was referring to the Christological reality of the Eucharist that led to some definitions by the Council of Trent. Apparently Vatican II was more concerned with ecclesiological reality inherent in the Eucharist.

27 Second Vatican Council, The Constitution on the Sacred Liturgy *Sacrosanctum Concilium*, 4th December 1963, *Decrees of the Ecumenical Council*, Vol. II, Nornam P. Tanner, ed., Washington: Washington University Press, 1990, no. 4. This document is hereafter to be referred to as SC.

28 SC, 47.

29 Ralph A. Keifer, *Blessed and Broken*, Wilmington: Michael Glazier, 1984, 84.

30 Bernard Cooke, *Sacraments and Sacramentality*, Mystic, CT: Twenty-Third Publications, 1994, 155.

31 SC, 10.

32 LG, 1.

33 LG, 3.

34 LG, 11.

35 Second Vatican Council, Pastoral Constitution on the Church in the Modern World: *Gaudium et Spes*, 7th December, 1965, no.1. This is hereafter to be referred to as GS.

36 GS, 42.

37 GS, 43.

38 GS, 63.

39 GS, 69.

40 Benny Koottanal, 'Eucharist: Love in Action', *Indian Journal of Spirituality* 18 (2005), 372–390, 380.

41 Okonkwo, *The Eucharist and World Hunger*, 169–72.

42 John Paul II, *Ecclesia de Eucharistia*, no. 24.

43 Elisabeth Schüssler Fiorenza, 'Table Sharing and the Celebration of the Eucharist', Concilium 152 (1982), 3–12.

44 Joseph A. Fitzmyer, *First Corinthians: A New Translation with Introduction and Commentary*, London: Yale University Press, 2008, 426.

45 Power, *The Eucharistic Mystery*, 59.

46 John Paul II, *Ecclesia de Eucharistia*, 20.

47 Joseh A. Grassi, *Broken Bread and Broken Bodies: The Lord's Supper and World Hunger*, second ed., Maryknoll, NY: Orbis, 2004, 104.

48 Benedict XVI, *Caritas in Veritate – Charity in Truth*, London: Catholic Truth Society, 2009, no. 34–8.

49 Frank Andersen, *Making the Eucharist Matter*, Notre Dame, ID: Ave Maria Press, 1999, 116.

50 Benedict XVI, *Post Synodal Exhortation on the Eucharist: Sacramentum Caritatis*, Vatican: Liberia Editrice, 2007, see especially numbers 6, 34 and 70.

51 Fitzmyer, *First Corinthians: A New Translation with Introduction and Commentary*, 426.

52 Craig L. Nessan, *Give Us This Day: A Lutheran Proposal for Ending World Hunger*, Minneapolis, MN: Augsburg Fortress, 2003, 26.

53 John Paul II, *Ecclesia de Eucharistia: On the Eucharist and the Church*, London: Catholic Truth Society, 2003, nos. 3 and 13. See also Izunna Okonkwo, 'The Sacrament of the Eucharist (as Koinonia) and African Sense of Communalism: Towards a Synthesis', *The Journal of Theology for Southern Africa* (2010), 88–103, 101–3.

54 Though there are some subtle variations in Paul and Luke's theology of the Eucharist there is still a point of convergence: both included 'do this in memory of me'. This aspect is missing in the account of other evangelists.

55 Benedict XVI, *Sacramentum Caritatis*, no. 77.

56 Dermot A. Lane, *Foundations for a Social Theology: Praxis, Process and Salvation*, Dublin: Gill and Macmillan, 1984, 142.

57 See Augustine U. Nebechukwu, 'The Eucharist and Praxis of Love' *Bigard Theological Studies* 12 (1993): 43–8, 43. One of the theories involved in the debate is transfinilisation; a theory on consecration proposed by F.J. Leenhardt, a Protestant theologian. He presented it with an ecumenical mind, full of hopes that both Protestants and Catholics could be in agreement. Many Protestants saw the theory as explaining too much, believing that it pointed to a metaphysical change in the element which they could not accept. On the other hand, for most Catholic theologians the theory explained too little because it admitted that the elements were changed but it did not explain fully how it happens. Though some Catholic theologians uphold transignification, transubstantiation to many, appears to be the most favoured in the Catholic belief in the real presence of Christ in the Eucharist. Martin Luther, in the period of Reformation denied transubstantiation, considering it to be a private opinion. In its place, he proposed consubstantiation; which suggests a continuation of the substances of bread and wine as well as the Body and Blood of Jesus Christ even after the words of consecration. For him, Christ is present from the time of the proclamation of the words till the time of consumption of the species. Therefore, he rejected the eucharistic devotion and adoration.

58 Lane, *Foundations for a Social Theology*, 43.

59 Edward J. Kilmartin, *Church, Eucharist and Priesthood: A Theological Commentary on 'The Mystery and Worship of the Most Holy Eucharist'*, Ramsey: Paulist Press, 1981, 18.

THE EUCHARISTIC ECCLESIOLOGY OF NICHOLAS AFANASIEV AND CATHOLIC ECCLESIOLOGY: HISTORY OF INTERACTION AND FUTURE PERSPECTIVES

MS ANASTACIA WOODEN PhD Candidate
Catholic University of America, Washington DC

The goal of this paper is to show that an encounter of the eucharistic ecclesiology of the Russian Orthodox theologian Nicholas Afanasiev and Catholic theology in the 1950s was a truly fruitful instance of reciprocal learning between Orthodox and Catholic theologies. I also hope to show that this example has not only historical significance but it continues to be a source of insight for Catholic ecclesiology.

Father Nicholas Afanasiev (1893–1966) is known for coining the phrase 'eucharistic ecclesiology'. The claim that his thought exerted certain influence on Catholic ecclesiology prior to Vatican II is confirmed by the fact that he was mentioned three times in the preparatory documents for the Council's Constitution on the Church.[1] In this paper I will explore two questions arising from this fact: a historical question of *how* Afanasiev became known to the Fathers of the Council and a theological question of *why* his work was considered significant enough to warrant mention. This paper will conclude with a discussion about what Afanasiev's teaching can offer today to the study of the Council's ecclesiology.

CATHOLIC THEOLOGY'S ENCOUNTER WITH AFANASIEV'S EUCHARISTIC ECCLESIOLOGY

In the beginning of the twentieth century the Catholic Church saw an influx of interest in the liturgical and spiritual life of the Eastern Churches. This interest led to the creation in 1917 (during the pontificate of Benedict XV) of the Congregation for Eastern Churches and the opening of the Pontifical Oriental Institute in Rome. In 1924, Pope Pius XI commissioned the Benedictines to work toward unity with the Orthodox Churches, especially with the Russian Orthodox Church. For this reason, a dual rite Benedictine monastery was founded by Dom Beaduin in 1926 in Amay-sur-Meuse, Belgium (the monastery moved to Chevetogne in 1939).

The Catholic interest in Orthodoxy went beyond the sphere of ecclesial politics. Orthodox Churches were viewed – perhaps, romantically – as living communities that preserved their genuine identity with Christian origins and for that reason were considered as kind of a model for renewal of the Catholic Church.[2]

Providentially, as a result of the tragic demise and exile of the Russian Orthodox Church following the revolution of 1917 in Russia, a number of very prominent Russian Orthodox theologians gathered in Paris around the St Sergius' Orthodox Theological Institute (1925), where these theologians engaged in an ecumenical dialogue with the best Western scholars of their time. One of the most important but less-known venues of this dialogue was the *Liturgical Weeks* – the scholarly ecumenical gatherings centred on liturgical issues which have been held by the St Sergius' Institute annually since 1953. The organisers, headed by Fr Cyprian Kern and Nicholas Afanasiev, were able to gather many leading French and Belgian liturgical scholars of their time, almost all of whom eventually played an important part in the work of Vatican II, especially in preparation of the Council's *Constitution on the Sacred Liturgy* (see Appendix 1 at the end of this paper).

One needs to remember that ecumenical gatherings like *Liturgical Weeks* were rare in the 1950s and they did not receive eager approval of ecclesial authorities. For example, Fr Danielou did not obtain his superior's authorisation in 1953, even though he promised to give a talk. (Fortunately, he was able to come back since then more than once, the last time when he was cardinal.)[3]

Afanasiev was one of the leading voices in ecclesiology from St Sergius at that time. He also spoke at the first *Liturgical Weeks* in 1953 on the topic of 'Sacrament of Assembly'. I believe that it is from this talk that Catholic theologians first encountered Afanasiev's term 'eucharistic ecclesiology' and became familiar with its principles. After 1953, Afanasiev continued to present his ecclesiology to the Catholic colleagues in a number of important essays published in French in such Catholic theological journals as *Irenikon* and *Istina*.

I still continue my research of the *Liturgical Weeks* in St Sergius Institute's archives. However, it is already clear that these gatherings played a crucial role in introducing Catholic scholars to Orthodox theology in general and Afanasiev's work in particular. Later, these scholars, as members of preparatory committees of the Vatican II and *periti* to the bishops, in their turn, brought his work to the attention of the Council.

Having established how Afanasiev's name and work became known to the Fathers of the Council, I now turn to the question of what in Afanasiev's work might have attracted the attention of the Catholic theologians.

AFANASIEV'S EUCHARISTIC ECCLESIOLOGY AND LITURGICAL PARTICIPATION

In 1944, de Lubac formulated what became a main principle of eucharistic ecclesiology: 'The Eucharist makes the Church.' A similar statement is found in a footnote to the second draft of what became Vatican's II Constitution on the Church, *Lumen Gentium*: 'If the Church alone makes the Eucharist, it is also true that the Eucharist makes the Church.'[4]

From this statement one may infer that those *who* make the Eucharist *are* the Church. So I want to approach my presentation of Afanasiev's thought as an answer to the question closely related with a question of liturgical participation: *Who makes the Eucharist*? Afanasiev had his own one-line definition of the main principle of eucharistic ecclesiology: 'Where there is the eucharistic assembly, there is Christ, and there is the Church of God in Christ.'[5] In this formulation we already see the answer to our question, which became the hallmark of Afanasiev's ecclesiology – the eucharistic assembly makes the Eucharist. It is important to note that Afanasiev's ecclesiological reflections are guided not by the Eucharist as an abstract 'one of the sacraments', but primarily as a eucharistic gathering, the Eucharist as an act of the people of God gathered in one place. For him, to interpret the meaning of the eucharistic assembly, beginning with the very act of gathering and ending with dismissal, is to interpret the meaning and the structure of the Church. Therefore, no matter which topic he discusses – the ministry of bishops, Church unity, or Roman primacy, the *celebrating community becomes not just the start of reflection, but it remains at the core of his thinking* and gives Afanasiev's ecclesiology 'a sensation of concreteness and cohesion'.[6]

Since Afanasiev's eucharistic ecclesiology rests on his notion of the eucharistic assembly, I want to mention four building blocks, or key elements of the latter, on which the rest of Afanasiev's ecclesiology is built upon: *the Holy Spirit, the royal priesthood, epi to auto, and concelebration.*[7]

1) The Holy Spirit. Afanasiev begins with the belief that the Church is born out of and exists through the Spirit. The grace of the Spirit was not only given to some group in the Church long ago, but everybody in the Church is endowed with charisms, while the Church itself is 'the place of Spirit's activity'.[8] Describing the pneumatological foundations of the Church, Afanasiev often quotes the prophesy mentioned in Acts 2:17: 'In the last days it shall be, God declares, that I will pour out my spirit upon all flesh.' The Church that flowed from Christ's pierced side and which was actualised at Pentecost is the fulfilment of this prophecy. Therefore, says Afanasiev, 'the beginning of the Church lies in the Spirit. Through the Spirit and in the Spirit [the] Church lives'.[9]

2) The royal priesthood. The charismatic character of the Church is reflected in ecclesial ministries.[10] The charisma of the royal priesthood is bestowed on all members of the Church in the sacraments of initiation, consequently, installing *every* member of the Church for ecclesial ministry. Afanasiev often repeats that 'in the Church there are no gifts of the Spirit without ministry and there is no ministry without gifts'.[11] Since the Holy Spirit is the principle of all activity in the Church, then, says Afanasiev, in the Church *life and ministry are one and the same*, and the whole of the life in the Church can be seen as 'a permanent ministry, in which the Christian serves God through the Church, and serves the Church itself'.[12]

Although the ministry is given to all members of the Church, these ministries differentiate in accordance with the gifts of the Spirit, as shown by St Paul in 1 Cor 12:4-6. Accordingly, the differentiation between laity and the ecclesiastical hierarchy reflects the diversity of the forms of ministry and it would be erroneous to say that some members of the Church have ministries and others do not.[13]

3) Epi to auto. These words, frequently found in the writings of St Paul and of St Ignatius of Antioch, are hard to translate into English in a precise and definitive way without some context. Afanasiev insisted that they describe the fundamental principle of Church life according to which all Church members always act *epi to auto*, meaning always together 'for one and the same thing'. Therefore, there can be no separate acts in the Church which are not linked with the action of all. The priestly ministry of all members of the Church finds its expression in the eucharistic assembly in which all celebrate, led by one presider. In the eucharistic celebration, the faithful are gathered by the Holy Spirit into the body of Christ to offer sacred service to God. Since Christ is one, then his body is one and it always acts as one – *epi to auto*. According to Afanasiev, such was the basic understanding of the eucharistic assembly in the early Church and this phrase, *epi to auto*, came to designate the eucharistic assembly itself, as seen in the Acts of the Apostles: 'The Lord was adding to the ones being saved day by day in the same place *epi to auto*.' (Acts 2:47)[14]

Since no single group in the Church constitutes the Church in separation from the other – like the hierarchy and laity, for example – then no group in the Church can act independently. In other words, *epi to auto means that the acting subject in the Church is always the Church itself and the Church is always united in its actions*.

Afanasiev applies the principle of *epi to auto* also to the relationship of local Churches, stating that the unity of the eucharistic assembly constitutes the foundation for the internal universalism of one Church.[15] Most of the secondary literature on Afanasiev is focused on this point of his ecclesiology. For Afanasiev, the oneness and completeness of the body of Christ in the Eucharist defines the oneness and completeness of the local Church in the eucharistic assembly. However, a locally celebrated Eucharist is never only local, because only the Church in all her fullness can celebrate the Eucharist.[16]

Therefore, empirical unity of the local celebrating assembly preserves and manifests the oneness of the Church of God in Christ so that 'each local Church contained in itself all remaining local Churches'.[17] Afanasiev concludes that with time the principle of internal universality grew weaker in the Church as the unity of the eucharistic assembly was dissolving. Eventually, the whole ecclesial organisation reoriented 'from internal toward external universalism'.[18]

4) Liturgical concelebration. Afanasiev notes that misconceptions of the royal priesthood range from 'its minimisation to a meaningless formula to entitling any member of the Church to accomplish any of the acts of the liturgy'.[19] Contrary to both of these extremes, Afanasiev affirms that 'concelebration by the laity is effective and real, not ceremonial'.[20] However, the priesthood belongs to God's people as a whole, and nobody can fulfil this ministry for him or herself, but only when the liturgical acts are fulfilled by the Church as a whole: meaning when God's people gather together with their presider in the Church assembly. The difference between the members of the eucharistic assembly is expressed not in the degree of their liturgical participation but in the places they occupy during the eucharistic celebration.[21] The place that Jesus had at the Last Supper is now occupied by the bishop who is a presider of the eucharistic assembly.

Afanasiev considers the exclusion of laity from priestly ministry as 'one of the paradoxes of our contemporary life' since this is in fact a distinct function of the people of God as described in different New Testament texts, most notably in 1 Peter 2: 9: 'People of God, chosen race, royal priesthood, a holy nation, God's own people.'[22] He insists that the very essence of participation in the Eucharist contains in it the common priestly service to God by all baptised, the service that is completed by the common 'partaking' of the eucharistic bread and wine.

To summarise, Afanasiev says that the Eucharist is celebrated by the eucharistic assembly – an assembly of all baptised gathered by the Holy Spirit in the Body of Christ for service to God. In this assembly, *everybody concelebrates, but only one presides at the Eucharist, and nobody celebrates separately from the whole assembly*. Afanasiev also adds that *the very hierarchical structure of the Church emerged in the consciousness of Christian communities in a Spirit-guided process of living out their main Christian vocation – worship of God in Christ.*

I believe that a very similar understanding of eucharistic ecclesiology can be found already in the first constitution of Vatican II – *Constitution on Sacred Liturgy*, especially in its notion of 'active participation' to which I now turn.

NOTION OF 'ACTIVE PARTICIPATION' IN THE CONSTITUTION ON SACRED LITURGY

I propose the notion of the people of God actively and responsively constituting the Church by participating in the liturgical celebration. For example, Council's notion of active participation contains the ecclesiology of the *Constitution on the Sacred Liturgy (Sacrosanctum Concilium)*.

As Frederick McManus noticed, at least one-third of the *Constitution's* 131 articles are concerned directly with the active participation of the worshipping assembly.[23] The text mentions 'active participation' fifteen times, rightfully making it, in the words of Josef Jungmann, 'the refrain of the Constitution'.[24]

By expounding Christ's continuous presence in his Church, especially in her liturgical celebrations, SC, 7 shows that the work of Christ and the work of the Church most fully coincide in the eucharistic celebration. The liturgy is an exercise of Christ's priestly office which is aimed at glorification of God and sanctification of man. These are not two parallel goals of the liturgy. As Godfrey Diekmann comments on this paragraph, 'The glorification of God is without doubt the ultimate aim of the liturgy, it is primary in order of intention: but God is glorified in sacramental action precisely by the transformation of man, by man's conscious turning to God in faith and love which the sacramental action accomplishes.'[25] Since the sanctification of man 'is not merely an objective of the liturgy, but is constitutive of it', then 'the willing engagement of free persons is the obvious aim' of the Constitution[26] and of its notion of active liturgical participation.

This desired 'willing engagement' is fully described in SC, 14 which also states that the entire Church is the subject of liturgy and that the entire Church is called to participate in it as the priestly people of God by reason of their baptism. The liturgical role of the assembly is further reinforced in SC, 26, 28–29, noting that this participation of the whole body is accomplished not only by delegation to the ordained minister, but by direct participation in the performance of liturgy. Finally, the most precise description of the active participation is given in SC, 48:

> The Church, therefore, earnestly desires that Christ's faithful, when present at this mystery of faith, should not be there as strangers or silent spectators; on the contrary, through a good understanding of the rites and prayers they should take part in the sacred action conscious of what they are doing, with devotion and full collaboration. They should be instructed by God's word and be nourished at the table of the Lord's body; they should give thanks to God; by offering the Immaculate Victim, *not only through the hands of the priest, but also with him*, they should learn also to offer themselves; through Christ the Mediator, they should be drawn day by day into ever more perfect union with God and with each other, so that finally God may be all in all.[27] (SC, 48)

After describing the desired 'active participation', article 41 of the constitution places it in the most fitting ecclesiological setting of a communal celebration of the Eucharist presided by a bishop, who is the High Priest of the Church. Here the Christian community locally gathered around the bishop is depicted as an active subject of the manifestation of the Church.[28]

There are fundamental similarities in how both Afanasiev and the *Constitution on the Sacred Liturgy* connect liturgical participation with ecclesiology. Reflecting on the most vital activity of the Church, the Eucharist, in which its nature is most visible and most perfectly manifested, both Afanasiev and the constitution show that the visible hierarchical structures of the Church should follow the pattern of the eucharistic celebration. By affirming that the Church is most perfectly manifested as a Spirit-filled assembly of baptised Christians gathered around their bishop for the service of God in Christ, the *Constitution on the Sacred Liturgy* demonstrated an emergence of a new self-awareness of the Church and laid the foundations for *the 'liturgical' reorientation of Catholic ecclesiology*.

The meaning of the liturgical orientation of ecclesiology

If the Eucharist is understood as an exercise of ministry aimed at glorification of God through sanctification of human beings, then the ministerial structure of the Church reflects the very goal of the Church's existence and becomes the foundation of ecclesiology. It is through the call to ministry that the Holy Spirit gathers the Church into the body of Christ. In this paper I attempted to show that this ecclesiology already manifested itself in the Council's first constitution – *Constitution on the Sacred Liturgy*, especially in its notion of active participation. Therefore, this constitution holds a hermeneutical key to the *study and teaching* of the council's ecclesiology as a whole. It means that other documents of the Council, including the *Constitution on the Church,* can be interpreted and evaluated in light of the ecclesiological principles reflected in the *Constitution on the Sacred Liturgy.* This approach to study of the council's ecclesiology should contribute to the healing of the chronic disconnect of liturgy from ecclesiology and pastoral theology and to the concrete task of formulating a ministry-based understanding of the Church. Perhaps Afanasiev's thoughts again can be helpful for the latter task. Ultimately, all these efforts should find their final fulfilment in preaching and catechetical instruction through which all the baptised – laity and clergy alike – may become 'convinced that the principle manifestation of the Church consists in the full, active participation of all God's holy people in the same liturgical celebrations' (SC, 41) and thus they will be enabled 'to express in their lives and to manifest to others the mystery of Christ and the real nature of the true Church' (SC, 2).

NOTES

1 *Acta Synodalia Sacrosancti Concilii Oecumenici Vaticani Secundi,* Vatican City, 1970–3. 1. *Congregatio generalis* 31, see 1, 4, 87; 2. *Congregatio generalis* 37, see 2, 1, 252; 3. *Congregatio generalis* 80, see 3, 1, 254.

2 For example, according to Aidan Nichols, Yves Congar held a similar opinion. See A. Nichols, *Yves Congar,* Wilton, CT: Morehouse-Barlow, 1989, p. 138.

3 Ibid.

4 Paul McPartlan, '*Ressourcement,* Vatican II, and Eucharistic Ecclesiology', *Ressourcement: A Movement for Renewal in Twentieth-Century Catholic Theology,* Gabriel Flynn and Paul D. Murray, eds, Oxford: Oxford University Press, 2012, 392.

5 Nicolas Afanasiev, 'Una Sancta', *Tradition Alive: On the Church and the Christian Life in Our Time,* Michael Plekon, ed., Lanham: Rowman & Littlefield, 2003, 14.

6 Mattijs Ploeger, *Celebrating Church. Ecumenical Contributions to a Liturgical Ecclesiology,* Netherlands Studies in Ritual and Liturgy, Tilburg: Liturgisch Instituut van de Universiteit Tilburg, 2008, 54.

7 For more on Afanasiev's ecclesiological vision see Anastacia Wooden, 'eucharistic Ecclesiology of Nicholas Afanasiev and its Ecumenical Significance: A New Perspective', *Journal of Ecumenical Studies* 45, no. 4, 2010, pp. 543–60.

8 Ibid., 1.

9 Nicholas Afanasiev, *The Church of the Holy Spirit,* Notre Dame: University of Notre Dame Press, 2007, p. 5.

10 Afanasiev developed his own original theology of the ministry. It is most fully expounded in his book *Sluzhenie mirian v cerkvi* [*Ministry of Laity in the Church*] which was published only in Russian in 1955. A summary of this book can be found in his essay under the same title in *Called to Serve: Readings on Ministry from the Orthodox Church,* William C. Mills, ed., New Hampshire: Orthodox Research Institute, 2010, 4–14.

11 *The Church of the Holy Spirit,* 3.

12 Nicholas Afanasiev, 'The Ministry of Laity in the Church', *Called to Serve: Readings on Ministry from the Orthodox Church,* William C. Mills, ed., New Hampshire: Orthodox Research Institute, 2010, 6.

13 Ibid.

14 The Russian [and RSV] translation gives a different reading: 'The Lord added to their number [the Church] day by day those who were being saved.' Actually this was one and the same for the apostolic time since *epi to auto*

was the complete expression for the Church. However, undoubtedly, the rendering *epi to auto* is more ancient than the rendering 'to the Church'.

15 *The Church of the Holy Spirit*, 4–5.

16 Nicholas Afanasiev, *Trapeza Gospodnia* [Lord's Supper], chap. 1, I–3; available in Russian at http://www.golubinski.ru/ecclesia/trapeza_poln.htm.

17 *The Church of the Holy Spirit*, 4.

18 Ibid., 5.

19 'The Ministry of Laity in the Church', 7–8.

20 Ibid., 8.

21 *Trapeza Gospodnia*, chap. 2, II–5.

22 'The Ministry of Laity in the Church', 7. Interestingly, Diekmann notes that the citation from 1 Peter 2:9 is one of the most frequently quoted scripture texts in the conciliar documents: 'and all of them, in treating on the laity's role, invariably call attention to its baptismal, liturgical foundation.' [Diekmann, 412] It is also the passage very frequently quoted by Afanasiev.

23 Frederick McManus, *Liturgical Participation: An Ongoing Assessment*, Washington DC: The Pastoral Press, 1988, 10.

24 Josef Jungmann, 'Constitution on the Sacred Liturgy', *Commentary on the Documents of Vatican II*, H. Vorgrimler, ed., New York: Herder and Herder, 1967, volume I, 17.

25 Diekmann, 418.

26 Ibid., 417.

27 Austin Flannery OP, *Vatican Council II: The Conciliar and Post-Conciliar Documents*. New York: Costello Publishing Company, 1975. Here and later italics are added unless noted otherwise.

28 This evaluation by Prof. Herve-Marie Legrand is mentioned by J. F. Puglisi in 'International Colloquium on the Ecclesiology of Vatican II', *Journal of Ecumenical Studies* 17, no. 3, 1980, 580.

APPENDIX 1
Catholic Participants of the first Liturgical Weeks in 1953[29]:

Dom Lambert Beauduin OSB – founder of the Benedictine monastery in Amay-sur-Meuse, Belgium; d. 1960;

Dom Bernard Botte OSB – Liturgical Institute, Paris; consultor of the Preparatory Conciliar Commission on the Liturgy, consultor for the Consilium;

Dom Bernard Capelle OSB – member of the Preparatory Conciliar Commission on the Liturgy, d. 19th October–1961;

Canon Aime-Georges Martimort – Catholic Institute, Toulouse; consultor of the Preparatory Conciliar Commission on the Liturgy, *periti* to the member of the Conciliar Commission on the Liturgy, consultor for the Consilium;

Pierre-Marie Gy OP – director of the Liturgical Institute, Paris; consultor of the Preparatory Conciliar Commission on the Liturgy, consultor for the Consilium;

Dom Olivier Rousseau OSB – *Irenikon*, (submitted almost annual accounts of the *Liturgical Weeks* to *Irenikon*);

Christophe-Jean Dumont OP – founder and director of the Dominican Center *Istina*; *periti* to the member of the Conciliar Commission on the Church;

Irenee Henry Dalmais OP – Catholic Institute, Paris; consultor for the Consilium;

Alphonse Raes SJ – prefect of the Vatican Library; consultor for the Consilium.

THE EUCHARIST, COMMUNION AND FORMATION

REV. DR BILLY SWAN
Gregorian University, Rome

The theme of the 50th International Eucharistic Congress: 'The Eucharist: Communion with Christ and with One Another', draws attention to the relationship between the Eucharist and ecclesial communion. While it is conventional to associate the Eucharist as the place where communion is celebrated and received, the importance of the Eucharist as the *locus* where communion is formed has arguably received insufficient attention. This paper highlights the importance of communion with Christ and with one another being continually formed by the action of the Spirit when Eucharist is celebrated: a time and space when we are *formed* into the people of God the Father, *conformed* to the image and likeness of Christ and *transformed* by the Spirit into the body of Christ. I argue that this reality of being transformed by the Eucharist calls for constant awareness, if Christianity is to retain its effectiveness as the means through which God unites and transforms all things in Christ (cf. Eph 1:10).

The Second Vatican Council saw the retrieval by the Church of Tertullian's insistence that Christians are 'made not born':[1] that Christian life is not static, but a living and dynamic existence. For the Christian, the permanency of Jesus Christ and God's constant offer of salvation in him, lead to change, growth and formation of those who accept that gift. Recovered here is the power of the Spirit of Christ who transforms all things, especially the existence of man, 'for whatever the Holy Spirit touches is surely sanctified and changed'.[2] This is especially true in the liturgy, where the lives of participants are constantly immersed, purified and transformed by the Paschal mystery.[3] Prior to the Council, two movements contributed enormously to the rediscovery of faith as a formative virtue in the believer, opening new horizons of understanding of how God's creative action transforms man as 'a living being capable of becoming divine'.[4]

The revival in Biblical studies, which was given particular impetus by *Divino Afflante Spiritu* in 1943, paved the way for a new appreciation not only of God but of the human person. When scholars considered man's relationship with God in the history of salvation, a new anthropology of transcendence leading to growth emerged as a constant theme. In the Old Testament, Israel is described as a child begotten of Yahweh in love whom he nourishes and invites to adulthood (cf. Is 49:1-6, 15-16; Hos 11:1-4). Israel is loved (cf. Deut 7:8, 23:5; Jer 31:3; Hos 11:1), fed (cf. Ex 16:32; Deut 8:16; Ps 78:72) and grows to 'blossom like the lily' to 'become beautiful as the olive' and 'flourish as a garden' (cf. Hos 14:5-7). In the New Testament, the parables of the sower and the vine communicate the effects evident in a people faithful to Jesus. They bear grain and fruit in abundance (cf. Mt 13:1-9; Mk 4:2-9; Lk 8:9-15; Jn 15:1-6). On several occasions, Paul uses the image of a parent and child for his relationship to his converts (cf. 1 Cor 4:14, 17; 2 Cor 6:13; 7:14; Phil 2:22; 1 Th 2:11). Of particular interest to our theme of formation is Galatians 4:19, where Paul calls the nascent Christian community his 'little children with whom I am again in travail until Christ be *formed* in you!' The verb *morphoun* used here by Paul is found elsewhere in his letters, and is used in the present tense signifying an ongoing process of formation.[5] Paul's uses the language of image and glory to describe progressive conformity to Christ (cf. Rm 8:29; 2 Cor 3:18).[6] This is a dynamic process of 'putting off the old' and 'putting on the new' (cf. Gal 3:27), of sharing Christ's death and risen life (cf. Gal 2:19; 6:14).[7] What is also worthy of note is the use by Paul of the plural in this Galatians text: formation of Christ is *en hymin* ... in you, referring to the community. Formation does not belong to individual believers alone. In sum, key aspects of Biblical anthropology include the fulfilment of the gift of grace in humanity that is accomplished in an ongoing and nurturing relationship with God, leading to a process of transformation into the image of Christ. This transformation in Christ takes place both in the individual and in the community, where humanity's growth is actualised in relationship with others.

The second pre-Conciliar development that led to a renewed appreciation of the concept of formation was a retrieval of the Jewish origins of the Eucharist. This development took place as part of a greater understanding of the Jewish identity of Jesus and Christianity's relationship to Judaism.[8] For Justin Martyr, the celebration of the Eucharist took place on Sunday not only because of the resurrection but because of creation, when God 'brought forth the world from darkness and matter'.[9] This testifies to an early understanding of the Eucharist that developed against the backdrop of intertwining themes of creation by God and re-creation by Christ.[10] Of particular relevance to our argument is the fact that for the early Christians, most of whom were Jews, the Eucharist of Jesus Christ was inseparable from the Jewish celebration of Passover.[11] For it was in the context of the Passover meal, the *seder*, that Jesus uttered the command to 'do this in memory of me' and proclaimed the coming reign of God that would be accomplished by his death and resurrection (cf. Mk 14:25; Mt 26:29; Lk 22:18). In our own age, this transforming power given by Christ at the Last Supper to make all things new (cf. Is 43:19; Rv 21:1), continues in the Eucharist, for it is the same Christ who works through the sacrament by his Spirit and actualises his saving presence in all times and places.[12] Here emerges the full significance of the Eucharist as a formative experience where it makes present the grace it signifies.[13] Like all the sacraments that 'make the Church',[14] the Eucharist celebrates and creates the communion of believers with the Trinity while at the same time strengthening the bonds of communion between believers as fellow members of one body. Hence the Eucharist is both 'a sign and sublime cause of that communion in the divine life and that unity of the people of God'.[15] In this sense it is a celebration of Passover from what already is to a prophetic anticipation of future glory when this communion with Christ and one another will be definitively consummated and when Christ will be all in all (cf. 1 Cor 15:28). Therefore, with a renewed anthropology which sees humanity as existentially open to transformation and an understanding of the Eucharist's inherent power to transform, we are now in a position to appreciate the Eucharist as a celebration when the bonds of communion are formed and deepened.

First, the Eucharist *forms* Christians into the new people of God, into an organic community with a singular identity. Just as by celebrating the *seder*, the Jewish people remembered their election by God and gathering by him to be *qahal* or a nation (cf. Deut 4:10; 10:4; 18:16), so the Eucharist gathers into one a people of all ages, cultures and nations, where all differences are subordinate to a shared ontological identity as children of the Father and brothers and sisters in Christ.[16] For Paul, the Eucharist constitutes the Church as one, for 'we who are many are one body, for we all partake in the one bread' (1 Cor 10:17). It makes visible the 'one body of faith, one baptism' where we are united in worship of 'one God and Father of us all' (Eph 4:4-5).[17] As the Church is a sign of unity, so she is called to be an instrument of unity 'to gather the whole human race into one'. In a world torn by strife, this visible unity seen at the Eucharist is called to 'shine forth as a sign of prophetic unity and concord'.[18] Finally, for many of the Fathers, this unity of all peoples through the Eucharist had both vertical and horizontal aspects. The Mass effected unity among God's people on earth, but also joined God's people on earth to those in heaven at the wedding feast of the lamb.[19] Hence the Eucharist remains a powerful formative experience when participants in heaven and earth are united in communion with the Trinity that embraces Christians of every age, in time and eternity.

At the Eucharist and by the Eucharist, participants are united in communion as one people of God, united in Christ to whom they are *conformed*. This profound communion with Christ was first sealed at baptism when Christians were irreversibly bonded us to the person of Christ, to his life, death and glorification.[20] This unique intimacy with Christ and fundamental orientation of one's life towards him, is confirmed at the Eucharist in a way that conforms us ever closer to him. This active conformation is made possible by the inherent power of God's word, *dabar*, that transforms those who hear and accept it.[21] This is possible because 'the word of God addressed to us always presupposes the word of God within us, insofar as we have been created in the word'.[22] At the Eucharist, God's word is explicated: first by the spoken word and then by the visible word made flesh in the Body and Blood of Christ. In both cases, Christ continues to reveal who the Father is and communicates himself to us. And so the Eucharist is the 'externalisation' of the Father's love in Christ made visible to the faithful.[23] This externalisation on the part of God and beholding of man absorbs the participant into the act of contemplation where the believer becomes more like the One he or she contemplates.[24] At the Eucharist we 'see him as he really is' and so 'become like him' (cf. 1 Jn 3:2). Here the object of contemplation is 'the unsearchable riches of Christ' (Eph 3:8): his beauty, truth, self-giving and obedience to the Father. So too is revealed the new world in him: 'a glorious ray of the heavenly Jerusalem which lights up our journey.'[25] In this act of contemplation the subject sees himself with greater clarity: his own creatureliness, sinfulness, but above all his divine identity and calling.[26] Following the initiative of God's love that evokes responses of love, blessing and thanksgiving, the subject is drawn into the mystery of transformation. At the Eucharist, this conformation of the participants to Christ is consummated with the reception of communion when 'the outward action of eating becomes the expression of that intimate penetration of two subjects ... the fusion of existences'.[27] In the Eucharist, the mutual indwelling of Christ in the believer and the believer in Christ is given full expression and leads to a deeper assimilation of the believer to Christ and a fuller immersion into Trinitarian life.[28] This process of assimilation is accomplished by the Eucharist and is described by the Fathers as providing nourishment that leads to growth while conferring the gift of immortality.[29]

Finally, the Eucharist not only conforms us to Christ individually but *transforms* us collectively into his body by the power of the Holy Spirit. 'In him all become one',[30] for 'Christ is the centre where all lines converge'.[31] Paul testifies to the power of the Eucharist to transform the early Christians into the body of Christ and to heal divisions that threatened the importance of that unity.[32] All become one in Christ, for he is the Word through whom all were created and in whom all are recreated.[33] An indispensable part of forming this communion is forgiveness, which is why sins are acknowledged at the beginning of Eucharist and forgiveness sought. The Eucharist continues to effect the power of Christ's sacrifice, reconciling God to humanity and humanity to itself, for 'as often as his blood is poured out, it is poured out for the forgiveness of sins'.[34] Reconciliation is always cruciform: vertical and horizontal. The community are reconciled to the Father, for they offer their lives to him in union with Christ. Thus, the one who offers the sacrifice is the *Totus Christus in capite et in corpore*, Christ the head together with his members. Since *ubi divisium ibi peccatum*, the Eucharist is 'the sacrifice of perfect reconciliation ... the saving banquet that takes away everything that estranges us from one another'.[35] Seeds of disunity among Christians are countered by the unifying power of the Mass, the bond of love,[36] where communion is restored by the gift of Christ's forgiveness received and shared. This occurs through the healing power of the Holy Spirit invoked in the eucharistic Prayer that moulds the community into 'one body, one Spirit in Christ'.[37] Just as the Spirit transforms bread and wine into the Body and Blood of Christ, so does she transform the Church into the visible image of Christ, becoming 'one Spirit with him' (1 Cor 6:17). In this way, the Church becomes the body of Christ filled with the same Spirit as Christ himself.[38] As his body was given *pro nobis* so the Church offers herself in service to the world, united by the Spirit to the life and mission of Christ himself.[39]

The drama of Christian existence is most intense and active where believers and the mystery of Christ are brought into intimate contact at the Eucharist. For this reason, 'all the activities of the Christian life are bound up with the Eucharist, flow from it and are ordered to it'.[40] If we are 'God's work of art' (Eph 2:10) then the Eucharist is God's studio where his innovation is seen at its best, where communion is formed and the Church is made. It is the place where formation, conformation and transformation of Christians occur in a single Trinitarian act 'that transfigures every aspect of life'.[41] This paper has highlighted the transformative power of the Eucharist to form communion with Christ and with one another. May awareness of this power, transform and rekindle 'eucharistic amazement'[42] and lead to a greater conviction of the Eucharist's 'supreme effectiveness for the transformation of the world in justice, holiness and peace'.[43]

NOTES

1 Tertullian, *Apologeticus adversus gentes pro Christianis*, 18, 4; *Patrologiae latina* (PL) 1, 378.

2 Cyril of Jerusalem, *Catechesis*, 5, 7; *Patrologiae graeca,* PG, 33, 514.

3 Cf. *Presbyterorum Ordinis*, 5.

4 Gregory of Nazianzus, *Orations*, 45, 7; PG, 36, 631. For Origen, the image of God in the human is but an incipient deification: the final goal is to become as like God as possible. Origen, *De principiis*, 3, 6, 1; *Die griechischen christlichen Schriftsteller* (GCS), 5, 256–7. For a study on the transcendent nature of man as an essential requisite to the possibility of faith, see F. Scanziani, 'The Parameter of Otherness and its Importance for Dogmatic Theology', *Formation and the Person*, A. Manenti, S. Guarinelli and H. Zollner, eds, Peeters 2007, 125–39. On Post-Conciliar interpretations of the human person, see L.M. Rulla, F. Imoda, J. Ridick, 'Anthropology of the Christian Vocation', *Vatican II: Assessment and Perspectives*, R. Latourelle, ed., New York: Paulist Press, 1988, 402–459.

5 Cf. Rm 12:12 where Paul urges Christians in Rome to be transformed *metamorphizomai* by the renewal of their minds; 2 Cor 3:18 speaks of believers being changed ... *metamorphizomai* into the likeness of the Lord; Phil 3:10 refers to the hope of being conformed ... *summorphizomai* to the death of Christ. See J.D.G. Dunn, *The Theology of Paul the Apostle*, London: T&T Clark, 1998, 466–72.

6 Commenting on Gal 4:19, Cyril of Alexandria wrote: 'Christ is formed in you by nothing else but irreproachable faith and the way of the gospel', *Festal Letter*, 10, 1; *Sources Chrétiennes* (SCh) 392, 194–6. For Augustine: 'Paul speaks here in person of the Church as mother. This forming has to do with strengthening and perfecting faith'; PL, 35, 2131–2.

7 According to B.R. Gaventa, individual and community transformation takes place against the backdrop of transformation of the whole cosmos and the birth of a new age. In Gal 4:19, the verb dinein, to be in travail, is also used in Mark 13:8 and is associated with the coming of the new created order inaugurated by the death and resurrection of Christ. B.R. Gaventa, 'The Maternity of Paul: an Exegetical Study of Galatians 4:19', *The Conversation Continues: Studies in Paul and John*, R. T. Fortna and B. R. Gaventa, eds., Nashville: Abingdon Press, 1990, 189–201.

8 Cf. J. P. Meier, *A Marginal Jew: Rethinking the Historical Jesus*, vols. 1–3, New York: Doubleday, 1991–2001.

9 Justin Martyr, *First Apology*, 67; *The Ante-Nicene Fathers* (ANFa), 1, 186.

10 There are numerous allusions to the creation story in the resurrection appearance narratives. Cf. Jn 20:15; 20:19; 21:4.

11 For Bouyer, the first Christian liturgies were, quite simply, Jewish texts

with added Christological and Trinitarian language. L. Bouyer, *Eucharist: Theology and Spirituality of the Eucharistic Prayer*, University of Notre Dame Press: Notre Dame, 1968. See also E.J. Fisher, ed., *The Jewish Roots of the Christian Liturgy*, New York: Paulist Press, 1990.

12 Leo the Great, 'What was visible in our Saviour has passed over into his mysteries'; *Sermon* 74, 2; PL, 54, 398; cf. Council of Trent, H. Denzinger, P. Hünermann, *Enchiridion Symbolorum: definitionum et declarationum de rebus fidei et morum*, DS, 1740.

13 Cf. Council of Trent (1547); DS, 1605.

14 Augustine, 'The Sacraments make the Church'; *De civ. Dei* 22, 17; PL, 41, 779.

15 Congregation of Rites, *Instr. Eucharisticum mysterium* 6. *Lumen Gentium* described ecclesial unity as being both 'expressed and brought about' when the Eucharist is celebrated; LG, 3. Cf. *Unitatis Redintegratio* 2.

16 Cf. 1 Pet 2:9. As *Lumen Gentium* clarifies, God wills to save people 'not merely as individuals without any mutual bonds but by making them into single people'; LG, 9. As we pray in the preface of a Mass for the Church on the path to unity: 'by the word of your Son's Gospel you have brought together one Church from every people, tongue and nation', *Roman Missal*, Preface of Mass for Church on the Path of Unity, Dublin: Veritas, 2011, 659.

17 Similarly in the *Didache*: 'even as this broken bread was scattered over the hills and was gathered together and became one, so let your Church be gathered together from the ends of the earth into your kingdom', *Didache* 9. Ignatius of Antioch: 'Take care then to have only one Eucharist. For there is one flesh of our Lord Jesus Christ, and one cup to show forth the unity of his blood'; *Letter to the Philadelphians* 4, SCh, 10, 143. On the early Church conviction of the unifying power of the Eucharist, see H. de Lubac, *Catholicism: a study of dogma in relation to the corporate destiny of mankind*, New York: Mentor Omega Books, 1950.

18 *Roman Missal*, eucharistic Prayer for Church on the Path of Unity, 662. For Aquinas, the true *res* of the Eucharist is the unity of the Church. T. Aquinas, *Summa Theologica*, III, 73.6.

19 Cf. Heb 12:22ff; Rv 19:9. For Irenaeus, the earthly altar was united with the altar of heaven. Irenaeus, *Against the heresies*, 4, 18, 6; PG, 7, 1029. Cf. J. Danielou, *The Bible and the Liturgy*, Notre Dame: University of Notre Dame Press, 1956, 128ff. 'The Eucharist unites heaven and earth. It embraces and permeates all creation'; John Paul II, *Ecclesia de Eucharistia*, 8.

20 Cf. Rm 8:15; Gal 4:6-7. Cf. *Catechism of the Catholic Church*, 1272.

21 Cf. Is 55:10-11; 1 Pt 1:23. *Verbum Domini* refers to the 'performative character of the word' and 'sacramentality of the word', 53, 56. For John Chrysostom, the transforming power of God's word proclaimed at the

Eucharist was no less powerful than his word at the dawn of creation: 'The priest, in the role of Christ, pronounces these words, but their power and grace are God's. This is my body he says. This word transforms the things offered'. John Chrysostom, *De prod. Jud.* 1, 6; PG, 49, 380C.

22 H. Urs Von Balthasar, *Prayer*, San Francisco: Ignatius Press, 1986, 26.

23 For Augustine, the Eucharist is a *verbum visibile*, a word that is visible. Augustine, *In Ioannem*, 80, 3; PL, 35, 1040.

24 'Contemplation transforms and man becomes more and more like that which he contemplates', H. Crouzel, *Théologie de l'image de Dieu chez Origène*, Paris: Aubier-Montaigne, 1956, 232ff. Origen, commenting on 2 Cor 3:18, gave an active meaning to the word *katoptizomenoi*, looking as in a mirror in an act that transforms. Origen, *Fragmenta in Lamentations Jeremiae*, 116, GCS, 3, 276.

25 John Paul II, *Ecclesia de Eucharistia*, 18.

26 'Looking at myself in you, I have seen that I am your image', Catherine of Siena, *Dialogue on Divine Revelation*, 167. For Catherine, 'we see neither our own dignity nor the defects which spoil the beauty of our soul unless we look at ourselves in the peaceful sea of God's being in which we are imaged'. Catherine of Siena, *Letter* 226, in M. O'Driscoll, ed., *Catherine of Siena: Passion for Truth, Compassion for Humanity*, New York: New City Press, 2008, 26. See also Benedict XVI, *Verbum Domini*, 10: 'The word of God makes us change our concept of realism'.

27 J. Ratzinger, *Called to Communion*, San Francisco: Ignatius Press, 1996, 37.

28 Cf. Jn 6:56. Augustine, 'I am the bread of the strong, eat me! But you will not transform me and make me part of you: rather, I will transform you and make you part of me'; *Confessions*, 7, 10, 16; PL, 32, 742. Also, 'it is your own mystery that is placed on the Lord's table! It is your own mystery that you are receiving! You are saying 'Amen' to what you are ... Be what you see; receive what you are'; Augustine, *Sermon* 272; PL, 38, 1246. Leo the Great, 'Our sharing in the body and blood of Christ has no other purpose than to transform us into that which we receive'; *Sermon* 63, 7; PL, 54, 357C; cf. LG, 26.

29 Metaphors of food and drink leading to growth in Christ are found in 1 Cor 3:3; 1 Pt 2:2 and Heb 5:12-14. For Clement of Alexandria, 'I am he who feeds you, giving myself as bread. I am he who gives daily the drink of immortality'; *Who is the rich man that shall be saved*, 23; PG, 9, 627. In the West with Tertullian 'the flesh feeds on the body of Christ so that the soul might grow fat on God'; *The Resurrection of the Body*, 8. Cf. Jerome, *Epistle to the Galatians*, 2, 4, 19; PL, 26, 385BC. Ignatius of Antioch called the Eucharist 'the medicine of immortality, the antidote for death and the food that makes us live forever in Jesus Christ'; *Ad. Eph* 20, 2; SCh 10, 91. See also Irenaeus, *Against the Heresies*, 4, 18, 5; PG, 7, 1028.

30 Irenaeus, *Oratio* 2, 23; PG, 35, 433A.

31 Maximus the Confessor, *Mystagogia* 1; PG, 91, 668.

32 Cf. Acts 2:46.

33 Cf. Eph 1:10 and Augustine, *In Iohannis evangelium tractatus*, 1, 12; PL, 35, 1385.

34 Ambrose, *De sacr.* 4, 6, 28; PL, 16, 464.

35 *The Roman Missal*, Eucharist Prayer for Reconciliation II, 654.

36 'The Eucharist is the sacrament of unity and the bond of love', Augustine, *In Iohannis evangelium tractatus* 26, 6, 13; PL, 35, 1613.

37 *The Roman Missal*, eucharistic Prayer III, 520.

38 'We are joined to him in the same body and share his life and are his members', N. Cabasilas, *Life in Christ* 1; PG, 150, 501C.

39 Cf. *Catechism of the Catholic Church*, 1091–2.

40 Cf. *Sacrosanctum Concilium*, 10; *Presbyterorum ordinis*, 5; *General Instruction of Roman Missal*, 16.

41 Benedict XVI, *Sacramentum Caritatis*, 71.

42 John Paul II, *Ecclesia de Eucharistia*, 6.

43 Paul VI, *Insegnamenti*, 16, 1978, 476.

NURTURING CHILDREN'S SPIRITUALITY IN THE PRESENCE OF THE EUCHARIST

MS SIOBHAN LEAHY PhD Candidate
All Hallows College, Dublin

This paper aims to present my recent and current research in the area of children's spirituality. It is appropriate to mention that this research is conducted through a Christian lens. I have chosen to research within my own faith tradition, the Catholic tradition. I did this in order to be able to dialogue with what other traditions have to say about children's spirituality. Spirituality has been described in contemporary literature as a level of connectedness that a person may feel towards themselves, their communities, the world around them, and to a 'Transcendent Other'.[1] My working definition of children's spirituality is: the Divine's relentless search for contact with the child and the child knowing that within and beyond herself something seems to seek contact with her, leading the child to realise that she is indeed connected and in relationship with all around her. If I was to define spirituality in two words I would do so by using the words: *connected relationship*.

Recent Surge of Interest in Children's Spirituality

Many agree there appears to be a recent surge of interest in the area of children's spirituality. Donald Ratcliff and Scottie May, two children's spirituality scholars pinpoint the 1990s as a time when interest in children's spirituality began to flourish.[2] They state this new interest is the result of previous interest in children's religious development declining. Many scholars contend this gradual surge of interest is due to a greater awareness of the sufferings and marginalisation of children. Also the UN Convention on the Rights of the Child (1991) accepted spiritual development as a category of human development and health worthy of rights protection. Article 27 recognises the right of every child to a standard of living adequate for the child's physical, mental, spiritual, moral and social development.[3] The recent revival of interest in children's spirituality has attempted to express itself in terms other than religious. For example, the 1996 UK Education Act, section 351, proclaims that education is also about promoting the spiritual development of the child.[4] The Dalai Lama had the same message when he visited Ireland in 2011. Even though there seems to be a recent revival of interest in children's spirituality, many of the Catholic Christian mystics showed a deep level of interest in children's spirituality. Julian of Norwich wrote how she imagined that Jesus wants us to become just like children in our want for him. She spoke about Jesus wanting us to run to him like a child runs hastily to its mother for help.[5] Catholic theologian Karl Rahner stated 'A child is a human being, it is not that he grows into a person but is a person right from the start'. Rahner believed each child is endowed with grace.[6] Rahner understood that children can indeed experience the depths of love and blessedness.

Recent research in the area of children's spirituality

My recent research in the area of children's spirituality asked, 'What can be learned about children's spirituality by observing them engaging in contemplative practice?' The contemplative practice used was the John Main style of Christian meditation. This contemplative practice involves silence, stillness and the repetition of the mantra, *Maranatha,* meaning, 'Come Lord Jesus'. The idea was to observe how children engaged with contemplative practice and observe if a silent practice could be used to understand more about children's spirituality.

Children's spirituality through silence

This research looked at observing children's spirituality through silence. Rebecca Nye speaks of important periods of silence in children's prayer and therefore the importance of making room for silence in children's prayer. Many contend that there seems to be a 'pathological busyness' in today's culture, making silence 'counter cultural'.[7] Karen Marie Yust contends that we need to help children develop an aptitude and appetite for silence because today's young people are prisoners of noise.[8] Tobin Hart encourages silence for children. He believes in the silence children can leave the chattering mind of the ego behind and enter into the larger stream of conciousness.[9]

Children's spirituality through stillness

This research looked at observing children's spirituality through stillness. Many scholars believe encouraging physical stillness for children encourages inward stillness.[10] Many agree today's children need some time for stillness in their hectic lifestyle which often leaves no time for stillness. John Main explained stillness is not a state of passivity but a state of full openness.[11] Many agree 'Children are victims of a hyperactive and fast-speed world'[12] and that we must encourage children to practice stillness.

Children's spirituality through the repetition of a mantra

John Main recommended repeating the ancient aramaic word, *Maranatha*, from beginning to end of the meditation session. In the *Cloud of Unknowing*, it encouraged Christian meditators to fix the word close to their hearts to avoid being carried away with thoughts.[13] Some literature states children are capable and even enjoy repeating words as they are fascinated by beat and repetition. This is evident in the way young children enjoy the repetition in nursery rhymes.[14] Lawerence Freeman believes encouraging children to repeat a mantra helps them to deal with distractions.

The principal objectives of this study:

- To investigate how a specific group of eleven children from a Catholic school that caters for mildly to severely intellectually challenged children behaved when engaging with the contemplative practice over a six-week period of one session per week
- To record the observations as a participant observer
- To reflect on the recordings of the observations and see what important themes may have emerged.

Research Design

The historical origin of the current ethical principles for conducting research with children arises from the amended *Declaration of Helsinki*, which now includes an examination of the issues of children as research participants. This declaration suggests that the study method used should be appropriate to children. The declaration mentions it is vital from the onset of research with children to be mindful of the fact that they are potentially vulnerable to unequal power relationships between adult researcher and child participant.[15] Also, current research on best practices when researching with children states, 'Reflexivity should be a central part of the research process with children where researchers critically reflect not only on their role and their assumptions but also on the choice of methods and their applications'.[16] Mary Frohlich names 'interiority' as a 'methodological principle' fundamental to the study of spirituality.[17] Frohlich states 'our starting point must be critical reflection on what we are actually doing when we live, teach and study spirituality'.[18] Self appropriation and self presence were the goals of interiority in this research project. At the start of this research I had to be mindful of the fact that, 'If I scan "the world" from where I stand, there is a limit to what I can see'.[19]

Mystagogic method

Kees Waaijman explains how the mystagogic method is similar to spiritual accompaniment.[20] This method allows for a recognition of entering into the level of mystery, therefore this method was chosen as it was seen as the most appropriate for observing children engaging in this ancient prayer practice. The mystagogic method facilitated the creation of an unobtrusive, sacred space for them to tell their own unique sacred stories of how the prayer practice was for them. It created an openness and surrender to the children's words so that what they were saying could be fully heard. The mystagogic method allowed for a silent presence as a participant observer of what was going on. This method did not place the children in an uncomfortable, unfamiliar interview setting.

Participant Observation

Samantha Punch states, 'Participant observation with children in their own spaces can enable them to feel more comfortable'.[21] This research needed to enter into the inner territory of eleven children with the awareness that it was a foreign land with a new landscape and a new sacred story that needed to be heard. An aim in this research was to avoid what Elizabeth Grave and Daniel Walsh state about how often research with children is inaccurate, when too often, 'What was intended to be a study of children becomes an evaluation of adults' interactions with children'.[22]

SELECTION OF PARTICIPANTS

This research was carried out in a mixed class that consisted of eleven children aged between eleven and thirteen years of age. The group of children were already practising meditation. They weren't using a mantra, it was more a mindful style of meditation. Written consent was obtained from the teacher who acted as gatekeeper, the principal, the children's parents and also the children. It was made clear both verbally and in writing that any child was free to pull out at any stage and there was no reason for that decision necessary, there were provisions set in place for children to colour or draw if they didn't want to take part. The children were reminded of this at the beginning of each session. The data was recorded by observing the children at the practice for approximately ten minutes and listening to what the children had to say afterwards if they choose to comment.

Ethical Issues

Bernard Lonergan speaks of, 'a judgement not what appears to me, not what I imagine, not what I wish, not what I would be inclined to say, not what seems to me, but what is so'.[23] In order to try to arrive at this judgement it was vital to take ethical concerns serious in this research. Ethical guidelines call on researchers to avoid undue intrusion. The participant observer method was unobtrusive and non-confrontational. The teacher was present at all times. No names were recorded even in my notes and no pseudonyms allocated. The name of the school and teacher had to remain confidential. All handwritten data was shredded as soon as it was entered.

Presentation of Data

I choose to present the data exactly as it was recorded so that each child's authentic voice could be heard. In the data analysis the children's comments were never altered, they were analysed as they were recorded. I reflected on all words spoken by the children, no text was removed. Recorded observations and reflections were read many times and I looked for what kind of responses kept recurring. What were the deviations from these? What themes began to emerge? The teacher was provided with the data and analysis to check for accuracy. The resulting data analysis involved a combination of emerging themes and observations. To recap, in the data analysis the mystagogic method of analysis involved striving hard with the aid of every facial expression to penetrate every word to the inner core of the speaker.

RESPONSES OF THE CHILDREN

I would like to take this opportunity to share with you some of the responses of the children. Because of time limitations it is not possible to share all the comments but I have tried to select at least one comment from each child.

- It was great, like a happy place.
- I tried to close my eyes but the word (referring to the mantra *Maranatha*) sounded like a scary Church bell sound.
- It felt good like James Bond in Goldfinger.
- Was I still?
- Very relaxing, it feels like a big room. It felt like there was space in the room.
- Good, because it was quiet, it's just like myself.
- I like it, it's like when I am with my mam, safe and happy.
- No, it's confusing. I can't think of anything. I find it hard not to think of anything.
- I don't like the quiet, it's scarlet when I close my eyes.
- I couldn't say the word. It's like a horror movie.
- I like it, inside my soul. I guess it's just myself.

ANALYSIS, FINDINGS AND CONCLUSIONS

No God Talk

Over the six-week period an unexpected finding was that none of the children used any predictable 'God talk' when describing the prayer practice. They used metaphor and simile that was available and familiar to them in their normal everyday life. They described the prayer practice being similar to a 'big room', indicating Christian meditation involves locating space within. Another child, 'Like James Bond', indicating Christian meditation involves action, something mysterious and exciting. Other children used words like 'no nothing' indicating that there was no sense of anything occurring or happening or anything of relevance as they engaged with the practice. The children seemed to be authentic in the way they chose to describe the experience of meditation. The prevalence of religious language recorded in some children's spirituality studies seems to be in contrast to the findings in this particular study. Tobin Hart states that children's spirituality branches into every aspect of the child's life. Some of the current literature contends that children know the words of faith without really understanding the dept of meaning that is involved. In this study this problem did not seem to present itself as the children used no predictable words of faith and yet they appeared to demonstrate a deep understanding of the prayer practice and expressed this understanding in a very real and unique way.

Stillness, Silence and Repetition of a Mantra

The eleven children in this research demonstrated, that, overall the silence of this practice was not a problem. As the sessions progressed, most children seemed to become better able to stay still, indicting that the practice of stillness was not immediately available but rather seemed to develop over time. This research found that the majority of the children were not at ease with the repetition of *Maranatha*. The unfamiliarity of this word seemed to not suit this particular group of children. Some current literature suggests that using this mantra can help lead the children into real relationship with Christ. Whereas in this research, many expressed that repeating *Maranatha* felt scary. The children were put first and the teacher decided she would leave out encouraging the children to repeat it. The research seemed to continue well without the use of the mantra *Maranatha*. It seemed it was better to make room for the children's individuality than conform them all to using the same word. Rebecca Nye states that a signal that can alert us to times when children are genuinely speaking from the heart, in their spiritual voice, is when they show signs of individuality.[24] The children's spiritual voice in this research seemed to say let us pick our own sacred word as it is a personal word that cannot be forced.

Contemplative Practice, A Key to Feelings

Some current literature contends that Christian meditation allows children the chance to 'come home' to themselves and connect inward. This research seems to agree that children are afforded the possibility of interiority by engaging in Christian meditation. Some children went from not offering any comments in the first weeks to, in later sessions, articulating their feelings in comments like: 'Good, I like it. It's peaceful. Inside it's comfortable.' This also seems to agree with some current literature that states Christian meditation is proven to make children calmer and more relaxed.[25] It seems the more these children became familiar with the practice the deeper they journeyed within. What is interesting is that two children who seemed less able to do the practice were also involved in this increased ability to express their feelings. One child went from 'No I couldn't do it' on week one, to 'I don't like the quiet, it's scarlet when I close my eyes'. Over the weeks the children seemed to journey to a deeper place within where they could find words for their feelings. They seemed to almost increase in confidence in their ability to express their inner feelings. This research seems to agree with some current literature that states Christian meditation is good for children's overall health and well-being.

A Born Contemplative

One of the most interesting findings in this study came from the child who appeared to be the most intellectually challenged of the eleven children. On my initial meeting with this child he refrained to talk and covered his head; he didn't join in with the others to share his name. However, this child appeared the most able to engage with the practice of silence and stillness. This child appeared to almost yearn for the silence in so far as expressing his annoyance at the ones who made noise during the practice. He said he wanted to be 'alone, away from the others'. The child seemed to want the solitude of meditation. The child went from not saying his name to being able and willing to articulate how the prayer practice 'brought his mood back'. The child presented the most intriguing statement of all with sophisticated soul talk: 'I like it inside my soul, I guess it's just myself.' This was the most succinct description of Christian meditation, of the practice that involves getting a person in touch with the real self or the soul – with the sacred that lies within. His use of the words 'just myself' were poignant. It was not a changed, transformed or holier self but the real authentic self, no more, no less. This child had a lesson to teach, that Christian meditation involves encountering the reality of oneself. The child, who appeared to be the most intellectually challenged, seemed to demonstrate a great aptitude and insight into the ancient prayer practice of the desert mothers and fathers. This seems to contradict some writings such as Piaget and Golding who seem to link the ability of a child to have a spiritual experience with cognitive ability.[26] Rebecca Nye suggests that spiritual perception has nothing to do with what a child of a particular age can do or know.[27] Many childhood spirituality scholars contend that, over the past thirty years, the dominance of cognitive development theory in the field of religious education has lead to a severe neglect of the study of the spirituality of the child and to a distortion of what really goes on.

Strengths and Limitations

This was a small-scale study of eleven children. All the children stemmed from the same class and geographical area. Because of time constraints I only had six weeks with the children. However, the small scale of this study meant that all the participating children's voices could be considered. There was no screening out of a child's voice because it was deemed irrelevant to this study. The small scale of the study was intimate and familiar to the children. No fake settings or rigid interviews were put in place. The children had a choice to answer or not as they so chose. The general question 'how was that?' was asked and some children chose not to answer on some weeks, which was respected. The collected data was given to the teacher for examination, which meant that the data collected was less likely to be biased by my possible and unintentional agenda.

CONCLUSIONS

This research shows that a rich insight into children's spirituality was gained by observing children engage in the contemplative practice of Christian meditation. These conclusions are what led to my current research in the area of children's spirituality in the Catholic tradition.

Nurturing Children's Spirituality in the Presence of the Eucharist

My current research asks the question, 'Can children's spirituality be nurtured by allowing them time to sit in silence and stillness in the presence of the Eucharist?' Again this research is being carried out in a Catholic school that caters for mildly to severely intellectually challenged children. All the participating children have made their First Holy Communion. This research is not a theology of the Eucharist; I see my role as facilitating the children to 'come and see'. The conviction that Father, Son and Holy Spirit are blazingly radiating from the monstrance in the presence of the children is indeed a powerful means within the Catholic tradition to nurture children's spirituality. This current research is in its infancy, however I will share that the participating class consists of twelve children who come to the prayer room with their teacher to engage in the contemplative practice in the presence of the Eucharist. The bare Eucharist in a silvery monstrance is placed on the altar facing the children who sit before it. The ten-minute sessions begin with a joint recital of the Lord's Prayer. As I have said this current research is in the very early stages and so I will leave you with a spontaneous comment that a child made in the first week of this research when she sat down and looked at the Eucharist. She spontaneously exclaimed out loud, 'Wow! That's beautiful!' Pope John Paul II made many requests such as, 'I urge priests, religious and lay people to continue and redouble their efforts to teach the younger generations the meaning and value of the Eucharistic adoration and devotion.' (The Vatican, 28th May 1996).

NOTES

1 Marian De Souza, 'Contemporary Influences on Spirituality', *International Journal of Children's Spirituality* 8, 2003, 271.

2 Donald Ratcliff, *Children's Spirituality: Christian Perspectives, Research, and Applications*, Eugene, OR: Cascade Books, 2004, 10.

3 Daniel G. Scott, 'Spirituality in Child and Youth Care: Considering Spiritual Development and "Relational Consciousness"', *Child and Youth Forum 32*, 2003, 117–31 at 117.

4 Mark Charter, 'Child and Youth Spirituality: Current research and practice issues, and some strategic pointers', *Studies in Spirituality* 15, 2005, 254–6.

5 Don S. Browning and Marcia J. Bunge, eds., *Children and Childhood in World Religions*, London: Rutgers, 2009, 117–18.

6 Ibid., 142.

7 See, Shirley Lancaster, 'Children need more meditation and less stimulation.' http://www.guardian.co.uk/commentisfree/belief/2011?Jan/11/children-meditation-australia (accessed 10th March 2011).

8 Karen Marie Yust, *Nurturing Child and Adolescent Spirituality*, Maryland: Rowman & Littlefield Publishers, 2006, 217.

9 Tobin Hart, *The Secret Spiritual World of Children*, California: New World Library, 2003, 42.

10 Ernie Christie, *Coming Home: A Guide to Teaching Christian Meditataion To Children*, London: Medio Media John Garratt Publishing, 2008, 119.

11 John Main, *Word Into Silence*, New York: Continuum, 1998, 20.

12 Christie, *Coming Home: A Guide To Teaching Christian Meditation to Children*, 18.

13 See, 'World Community For Christian Meditation', http://www.meditation withchildren.com/recommendlength.html (accessed 1st March 2010).

14 C. Carlson and others, *Perspectives on Children's Spiritual Formation*, Tennessee: Broadman & Holman Publishers, 2006, 70.

15 Anne Greig and Jane Taylor, *Doing Research With Children,* London: Sage Publications, 1999, 148.

16 Pia Christenson and Allison James, eds., *Research With Children: Perspectives and Practices*, New York: Routledge, 2008, 126.

17 Mary Frohlich, 'Spiritual Discipline, Discipline of Spirituality: Revisiting Questions of Definition and Method', *Minding the Spirit: The Study of Christian Spirituality: Contours and Dynamics of a Discipline*, Elizabeth A. Dreyer and Mark S. Burrows, eds, Baltimore: Johns Hopkins University Press, 2005, 66.

18 Ibid.,70.

19 Bruce Lescher, 'The Truth That Makes You Free', *The Way* 4, 2004, 135–45 at 141.

20 Kees Waaijman, *Spirituality: Forms, Foundations, Methods*, Leuven: Peeters Press, 2002, 869–945.

21 Samantha Punch, 'Research With Children: The Same or Different from Research with Adults', *Childhood 9* (2002): 321–41 at 330.

22 Elizabeth Grave and Daniel Walsh, eds., *Studying Children In Context: Theories, Methods and Ethics*, xvii.

23 Bernard Lonergan, *Method In Theology*, London: Darton, Longman & Todd, 1972, 104.

24 Rebecca Nye, *Children's Spirituality: What it is and Why it Matters*, London: Church House Publishing, 2009, 32.

25 See Shirley Lancaster, 'Children Need More Meditation And Less Stimulation'.

26 Ronald Goldman, *Religious Thinking From Childhood to Adolescence*, London: Routledge & Kegan Paul, 1964, 226.

27 Rebecca Nye, *Children's Spirituality: What is it and Why it Matters*, 16–17.

COMUNITÀ E EUCARISTIA NELLA V CONFERENZA GENERALE DELL' EPISCOPATO DELL' AMERICA LATINA

REV. DR ANTONIO JOSÉ DE ALMEIDA
Pontifical Catholic University of Paraná, Brazil

IGREJA E COMUNHÃO TRINITÁRIA

O tema é 'Comunhão eclesial, eucaristia e ministério de comunhão à luz da Conferência de Aparecida', celebrada no Brasil em 2007; trata-se da V Conferência Geral do Episcopado da América Latina e do Caribe; as anteriores foram celebradas no Rio de Janeiro (1955), Medellín (Colômbia) (1968), Puebla (México) (1979) e Santo Domingo (República Dominicana) (1992); o tema da V Conferência foi: 'Discípulos e missionários de Jesus Cristo, para que nossos povos nele tenham vida - Eu sou o Caminho, a Verdade e a Vida' (Jo 14, 6).

O vocabulário da 'comunhão' é abundante, mais que isto, onipresente, no documento final: 144 ocorrências (enquanto 'povo de Deus', por exemplo, aparece 34 vezes); as menções propriamente eclesiológicas estão concentradas no capítulo V, que aborda o tema 'a comunhão dos discípulos missionários na Igreja. A fundação trinitária da Igreja enquanto 'mistério de comunhão' (DAp, 547) é afirmada em mais de uma passagem: 'O mistério da Trindade é a fonte, o modelo e a meta do mistério da Igreja: "um povo reunido pela unidade do Pai, do Filho e do Espírito", chamado em Cristo "como sacramento ou sinal e instrumento da íntima união com Deus e da unidade de todo o gênero humano" (DAp, 155); "a comunhão dos fiéis e das Igrejas locais do Povo de Deus se sustenta na comunhão com a Trindade" (DAp, 155); 'o mistério e a realidade da Igreja [que] devem refletir a Santíssima Trindade'" (DAp, 304).

As dioceses, as paróquias e diversos outros tipos de comunidades são apresentados sob o signo do 'povo de Deus', da 'comunhão' e da 'missão':

a) *Dioceses* – 'No povo de Deus, "a comunhão e a missão estão profundamente unidas entre si ... A comunhão é missionária e a missão é para a comunhão" (DAp, 176). 'Nas Igrejas particulares, todos os membros do povo de Deus, segundo suas vocações específicas, somos convocados à santidade na comunhão e na missão (DAp, 163); 'Reunida e alimentada pela Palavra e pela Eucaristia, a Igreja Católica existe e se manifesta em cada Igreja particular, em comunhão com o Bispo de Roma. Esta é, como afirma o Concílio, 'uma porção do povo de Deus confiada a um bispo para que a apascente com seu presbitério' (DAp, 165); 'A diocese, em todas as suas comunidades e estruturas, é chamada a ser 'comunidade missionária' (DAp, 168);

b) *Paróquias* – 'Entre as comunidades eclesiais, nas quais vivem e se formam os discípulos e missionários de Jesus Cristo, sobressaem as Paróquias. São células vivas da Igreja e o lugar privilegiado no qual a maioria dos fiéis tem uma experiência concreta de Cristo e a comunhão eclesial. São chamadas a ser casas e escolas de comunhão (DAp, 170);

c) *Comunidades eclesiais de base* – 'As comunidades eclesiais de base, no seguimento missionário de Jesus, têm a Palavra de Deus como fonte de sua espiritualidade e a orientação de seus pastores como guia que assegura a comunhão eclesial. Demonstram seu compromisso evangelizador e missionário entre os mais simples e afastados, e são expressão visível da opção preferencial pelos pobres. São fonte e semente de variados serviços e ministérios a favor da vida na sociedade e na Igreja. Mantendo-se em comunhão com seu bispo e inserindo-se no projeto de pastoral diocesana, as CEBs se convertem em sinal de vitalidade na Igreja particular (DAp, 179);

d) *Pequenas comunidades* – 'Como resposta às exigências da evangelização, junto com as comunidades eclesiais de base, existem outras formas válidas de pequenas comunidades, inclusive redes de comunidades, de movimentos, grupos de vida, de oração e de reflexão da palavra de Deus. Todas as comunidades e grupos eclesiais darão fruto na medida em que a Eucaristia for o centro de sua vida e a Palavra de Deus for o farol de seu caminho e de sua atuação na única Igreja de Cristo (DAp, 180).

'A vocação ao discipulado missionário [tema central da V Conferência] é con-vocação à comunhão em sua Igreja. Não há discipulado sem comunhão (DAp, 156). Com efeito, ao abordar teologicamente os 'discípulos missionários - em sua dupla dimensão de filhos e irmãos - Aparecida recorre insistentemente também à categoria de 'comunhão':

a) *A filiação divina* – Por obra do Espírito Santo, mediante o os sacramentos da iniciação cristã (o batismo, a confirmação e a eucaristia), 'somos chamados a ser discípulos missionários de Jesus Cristo e entramos na comunhão trinitária da Igreja' (DAp 153); os discípulos de Jesus, na verdade, 'são chamados a viver em comunhão com o Pai (1 Jo 1,3) e com seu Filho morto e ressuscitado, na 'comunhão no Espírito Santo' (1 Cor 13:13) (DAp, 155);

b) *A comunhão fraterna* - O fato de 'sermos filhos e filhas do Pai' nos torna 'irmãos e irmãs em Cristo' (DAp, 158). 'NEle, somos todos filhos do mesmo Pai e irmãos entre nós. (DAp, 193) 'O 'irmão' de Jesus (cf. Jo 20,17) participa da vida do Ressuscitado, Filho do Pai celestial, porque Jesus e seu discípulo compartilham a mesma vida que procede do Pai: o próprio Jesus, por natureza (cf. Jo 5:26; 10:30) e o discípulo por participação (cf. Jo 10:10). A conseqüência imediata desse tipo de vínculo é a condição de irmãos que os membros de sua comunidade adquirem (DAp, 132; cf. 336; 392: Hb 2:11-12).

Em breve: 'Essa realidade [da comunhão] se faz presente em nossa vida por obra do Espírito Santo, o qual também nos ilumina e vivifica através dos sacramentos. Em virtude do batismo e da confirmação, somos chamados a ser discípulos missionários de Jesus Cristo e entramos na comunhão trinitária na Igreja. Esta tem seu ponto alto na Eucaristia, que é princípio e projeto da missão do cristão. 'Assim, pois, a Santíssima Eucaristia conduz a iniciação cristã à sua plenitude e é como o centro e fim de toda a vida sacramental' (DAp, 153).

COMUNHÃO ECLESIAL E EUCARISTIA

Na verdade, nenhuma Conferência anterior do episcopado da América Latina e do Caribe insistiu tanto quanto Aparecida no tema da Eucaristia, seja para a constituição da Igreja, seja para a constituição do cristão, seja para a comunhão eclesial, seja para a vida cristã em suas distintas dimensões. Um dos mais belos, densos e fortes textos sobre a Eucaristia encontra-se na primeira seção ('chamados a viver em comunhão') do capítulo quinto que versa sobre 'a comunhão dos discípulos missionários na Igreja': 'Igual às primeiras comunidades de cristãos, hoje nos reunimos assiduamente para 'escutar o ensinamento dos apóstolos, viver unidos e tomar parte no partir do pão e nas orações' (At 2:42). A comunhão da Igreja se nutre com o Pão da Palavra de Deus e com o Pão do Corpo de Cristo. A Eucaristia, participação de todos no mesmo Pão de Vida e no mesmo Cálice de Salvação, nos faz membros do mesmo Corpo (cf. 1 Cor 10:17). Ela é a fonte e o ponto mais alto da vida cristã, sua expressão mais perfeita e o alimento da vida em comunhão. Na Eucaristia, nutrem-se as novas relações evangélicas que surgem do fato de sermos filhos e filhas do Pai e irmãos e irmãs em Cristo. A Igreja que a celebra é 'casa e escola de comunhão', onde os discípulos compartilham a mesma fé, esperança e amor a serviço da missão evangelizadora (DAp, 158).

Encontro do discípulo com o Senhor, a Eucaristia nos põe ao mesmo tempo em relação com o Pai e com os irmãos e irmãs, o que implica a vivência das dimensões teologal (crer), litúrgica (celebrar) e ética (viver) da vocação cristã, dando 'forma eucarística' e 'pascal' à vida do discípulo missionário:

> A Eucaristia é o lugar privilegiado do encontro do discípulo com Jesus Cristo. Com este Sacramento, Jesus nos atrai para si e nos faz entrar em seu dinamismo em relação a Deus e ao próximo. Existe estreito vínculo entre as três dimensões da vocação cristã: crer, celebrar e viver o mistério de Jesus Cristo, de tal modo que a existência cristã adquira verdadeiramente forma eucarística. Em cada Eucaristia, os cristãos celebram e assumem o mistério pascal, participando nEle. Os fiéis devem, portanto, viver sua fé na centralidade do mistério Pascal de Cristo através da Eucaristia, de maneira que toda a sua vida seja cada vez mais vida eucarística. A Eucaristia, fonte inesgotável da vocação cristã é, ao mesmo tempo, fonte inextinguível do impulso missionário. Aí, o Espírito Santo fortalece a identidade do discípulo e desperta nele a decidida vontade de anunciar com audácia aos demais o que tem escutado e vivido. (DAp, 251)

Ao mesmo tempo, os bispos chamam a atenção para a 'coerência eucarística' (cf. DAp, 436), ou seja, para as exigências eclesiais e éticas da Eucaristia: 'A Eucaristia, sinal da unidade com todos, que prolonga e faz presente o mistério do Filho de Deus feito homem (cf. Fl 2:6-8), nos propõe a exigência de uma evangelização integral. A imensa maioria dos católicos de nosso continente vive sob o flagelo da pobreza. Esta tem diversas expressões: econômica, física, espiritual, moral, etc. Se Jesus veio para que todos tenhamos vida e vida em abundância, a paróquia tem a maravilhosa ocasião de responder às grandes necessidades de nossos povos. Para isso, tem que seguir o caminho de Jesus e chegar a ser uma Igreja samaritana como ele. Cada paróquia deve chegar a concretizar em sinais solidários seu compromisso social nos diversos meios em que se move, com toda 'a imaginação da caridade'. Não pode ser alheia aos grandes sofrimentos que a maioria de nossa gente vive e que com muita frequência são pobrezas escondidas. Toda autêntica missão unifica a preocupação pela dimensão transcendente do ser humano e por todas as suas necessidades concretas, para que todos alcancem a plenitude que Jesus Cristo oferece (DAp, 176).

Diante do fato desafiador de que muitos cristãos não participam da Eucaristia dominical, nem recebem com regularidade os sacramentos, nem se inserem ativamente na comunidade eclesial (Cf. DAp, 301), os bispos afirmam insistentemente a importância da Eucaristia: 'A Santíssima Eucaristia conduz a iniciação cristã à sua plenitude e é como o centro e fim de toda a vida sacramental (DAp, 153; cf. SC, 17). Afirmam reiteradamente a relação entre Eucaristia e vida paroquial: 'Seguindo o exemplo da primeira comunidade cristã (cf. At 2:46-47), a comunidade paroquial se reúne para partir o pão da Palavra e da Eucaristia e perseverar na catequese, na vida sacramental e na prática da caridade (DAp, 175). Apresentam a Eucaristia como fonte de renovação da paróquia, de fortalecimento da comunidade dos discípulos e escola de vida cristã:

> Na celebração eucarística ela [a paróquia] renova sua vida em Cristo. A Eucaristia, na qual se fortalece a comunidade dos discípulos, é para a Paróquia uma escola de vida cristã ... A Eucaristia, fonte e ponto alto da vida cristã, faz com que nossas paróquias sejam sempre comunidades eucarísticas que vivem sacramentalmente o encontro com o Cristo Salvador.

(DApAS) Com efeito, a Eucaristia é momento privilegiado do encontro das comunidades com o Senhor ressuscitado: 'Com diversas celebrações e iniciativas, especialmente com a Eucaristia dominical, que é "momento privilegiado do encontro das comunidades com o Senhor ressuscitado", os fiéis devem experimentar a paróquia como uma família na fé e na caridade, onde mutuamente se acompanhem e se ajudem no seguimento de Cristo (DI, 4).' (DAp, 305)

A Igreja una, santa, católica e apostólica existe e se manifesta – como ensinou o Concílio (cf., sobretudo LG, 26) – na Igreja local, sobretudo, quando esta se reúne em assembleia para se deixar edificar por aqueles dois elementos essenciais de sua constituição, que são, justamente, a Palavra e a Eucaristia: 'Reunida e alimentada pela Palavra e pela Eucaristia, a Igreja Católica existe e se manifesta em cada Igreja local em comunidade com o Bispo de Roma (ChL, 85) (DAp, 165).

A Eucaristia, além disso, é vista, em Aparecida, não só em relação à edificação da Igreja, mas também em relação à construção da civilização do amor: 'Só da Eucaristia brotará a civilização do amor que transformará a América latina e o Caribe para que, além de ser o Continente da esperança, seja também o Continente do amor!' (DI, 4; cf. DAp, 543) A V Conferência, aliás, vai mais longe, uma vez que afirma que 'a Eucaristia é o centro vital do universo, capaz de saciar a fome de vida e felicidade: 'Aquele que se alimenta de mim, viverá por mim' (Jo 6:57) (DAp, 354).

CELEBRAÇÃO DA EUCARISTIA E ESCASSEZ DE PRESBÍTEROS

Constata-se, entretanto, a falta regular e assídua da celebração da Eucaristia em milhares de comunidades: 'O número insuficiente de sacerdotes e sua não equitativa distribuição impossibilitam que muitíssimas comunidades possam participar na celebração da Eucaristia (DAp, 100).

Esta situação gera preocupação: 'Recordando que é a Eucaristia que faz a Igreja, preocupa-nos a situação de milhares de comunidades cristãs privadas da Eucaristia dominical por longos períodos de tempo. Tem crescido a consciência da importância do preceito de 'viver segundo o domingo' (DAp, 253), 'como uma necessidade interior do cristão, da família cristã, da comunidade paroquial (DAp, 253). Donde o pedido de especial atenção para que os fiéis possam ter acesso à Eucaristia: 'A experiência positiva destas comunidades *torna necessário que recebam uma especial atenção para que tenham a Eucaristia* [o itálico é meu] como centro de sua vida e cresçam em solidariedade e integração eclesial e social.[1] Em nossa modesta opinião, trata-se do texto ao mesmo tempo mais sábio e ousado da Conferência, em relação a essa questão da falta habitual da Eucaristia em milhares de comunidades latino-americanas: a experiência positiva das comunidades torna necessário que elas recebam uma especial atenção para que tenham a Eucaristia! As comunidades – que já são julgadas positivas – só serão plenas quando puderem ter a Eucaristia, justamente porque a Eucaristia é 'centro de sua vida' e fonte de seu crescimento em 'solidariedade e integração eclesial e social'. A 'especial atenção' só pode ter um sentido: não bastam medidas provisórias e paliativas; é preciso encontrar uma solução permanente e cabal para que essas comunidades 'tenham a Eucaristia'!

A V Conferência, porém, só viu saída imediata, para a falta crônica de Eucaristia, na intensificação da celebração da palavra:

> Com profundo afeto pastoral às milhares de comunidades com seus milhões de membros, que não têm a oportunidade de participar da Eucaristia dominical, que também elas podem e devem viver 'segundo o domingo'. Podem alimentar seu já admirável espírito missionário participando da 'celebração dominical da Palavra', que faz presente o Mistério Pascal no amor que congrega (cf. 1 Jo 3:14), na Palavra acolhida (cf. Jo 5:24-25) e na oração comunitária (cf. Mt 18:20). (DAp, 253)

Fora isso, a solução está nas mãos dos fiéis – que 'devem desejar a participação plena na Eucaristia dominical' e 'orar pelas vocações' – ... e, portanto, nas mãos de Deus! Aparecida teria, segundo muitos, perdido a chance de ser mais corajosa e criativa, simplesmente resgatando a prática da Igreja Antiga em matéria de ministério eucarístico.[2] Diz jocosamente um teólogo espanhol que 'orar pelas vocações', dentro da atual estrutura ministerial da Igreja católica, é tentar a Deus, pois, em princípio, mais da metade dos membros da Igreja (as mulheres) estão excluídos, e também cerca de noventa por cento dos homens (que *grosso modo* são os que se casam)... Onde então encontrar vocações, nos pouco mais de dez por cento restantes, levando-se em conta ainda as demais exigências da Igreja católica para a seleção dos candidatos?

Estamos convencidos de que a resposta possa estar na própria dinâmica das centenas de milhares de comunidades eclesiais que contam com serviços e ministérios vários, exercidos por leigos e leigas, e se reúnem todas as semanas para a Celebração da Palavra de Deus, pois só esporadicamente podem contar com a presença de algum presbítero para a celebração da Eucaristia.

Há questões que não são de 'instituição divina', mas de 'instituição eclesiástica' e que a Igreja, sem maior tardar, mas com serena, aprofundada e espiritual ponderação, deveria enfrentar, antes que prejuízos de várias ordens afetem ainda mais a vida e a missão da Igreja. Sabe-se que, não obstante poucos aumentos pontuais das vocações para o ministério presbiteral, o número de presbíteros é cada vez menos suficiente para atender às necessidades da pastoral e da evangelização. Ao mesmo tempo, não se vislumbra uma mudança para melhor neste quadro, a menos que entrem em cena fatores imponderáveis no momento.

Alguns propõem a ordenação de alguns líderes dessas comunidades – que permaneceriam em seu estado de vida e dividiriam o serviço à comunidade com o trabalho profissional – para presidi-las e presidir a celebração da Eucaristia nessas comunidades.[3]

Argumenta Zulehner: 'A unidade profunda existente nas e entre as comunidades da Igreja, bem como entre as Igrejas locais (e certamente também entre as diversas Igrejas cristãs) se exprime na celebração da Eucaristia e é por ela fundada e reforçada. Por isso, toda comunidade de crentes tem o direito de celebrar a Eucaristia (cf. *Ecclesia de Eucharistia*, de João Paulo II). A Igreja se preocupa que para estas celebrações haja presbíteros suficientes e 'acessíveis' e, mais ainda, que eles vivam possivelmente na comunidade. Para atingir este objetivo, em caso de necessidade, a Igreja flexibilizará os critérios com base nos quais uma pessoa é admitida para a ordenação presbiteral. Na hierarquia dos valores da Igreja, o bem da celebração da Eucaristia nas comunidades dos fiéis deverá preceder a 'salvaguarda' do bem da forma de vida célibe dos presbíteros.[4] 'Entre as tantas pessoas profundamente inseridas na vida comunitária, não se pode pensar em escolher formar e ordenar três para um "*team of elders*" local?' (Fritz Lobinger)[5]

PROPOSTA NOVA PARA PROBLEMA ANTIGO

A proposta de Lobinger, bispo emérito de Aliwal, África do Sul, na verdade, é original. Não se trata da 'simples proposta de ordenar homens casados para suprir a carência de padres. Lobinger conhece 'os inconvenientes desse caminho e as razões sensatas de Roma o rejeitar, como medida universal para toda a Igreja. Em seu lugar, insiste na formação do espírito comunitário, de maneira que os fieis se entendam como uma comunidade que se sente responsável de prover para si os diversos ministérios. Muitas já dispõem de vários deles. Agora consistiria em ampliar a diversidade de ministérios e carismas, escolhendo alguns dos fieis para serem ministros ordenados. O bispo

> insiste que não se trata de ordenar indivíduos, mas de ordenar uma equipe que assuma o ministério ordenado. As pessoas permanecem como membros da comunidade, sem nenhuma separação e distinção externa. Elas presidem as eucaristias, nunca isoladamente, mas em equipe, por turno, quando as comunidades o requerem. A intuição fundamental e original consiste em que se pense tal ministério como serviço à comunidade e não como ordenação de indivíduos, constituídos sagrados pelo fato de serem ordenados. E o sacerdote celibatário, de tempo integral, assumiria a função principal de ser formador desses ministros. Os ministros ordenados pertenceriam normalmente à comunidade, continuando a vida de família e profissional, tal como acontece com tantos outros ministérios já existentes: das exéquias, da Eucaristia, da crisma, da catequese, de curso de noivos. Entre eles haveria os ministros ordenados que não se distinguiriam externamente dos outros, mas simplesmente pela diferença do ministério exercido. Aliás, é o que acontece com todos os outros.[6]

Não se é contra o celibato, carisma que vem do Alto; não se advoga o fim do modelo atual de presbíteros, que, com sua formação e experiência, podem colaborar na formação e no acompanhamento dos presbíteros que seriam ordenados para presidirem a comunidade, e, assim, como na Igreja antiga, presidirem a Eucaristia. Válidas vocações para o presbiterado não faltam; faltam antenas para captá-las e valorizá-las onde elas se manifestam, dando-lhes nova configuração, uma configuração que seja, ao mesmo tempo, fiel ao Novo Testamento, à Igreja antiga e aos tempos atuais, com seus desafios, necessidades e possibilidades.

NOTES

1 Este texto estava no texto aprovado pela Assembleia, mas não consta mais no texto 'reconhecido' pelo Vaticano. O original espanhol dizia: 'La experiencia positiva de estas comunidades hace necesaria una especial atención para que tengan a la Eucaristía como centro de su vida y crezcan en solidaridad e integración eclesial y social. (TA 196). ('TA' significa *Texto da Assembleia*). Em seu lugar, consta o seguinte: 'Todas as comunidades e grupos eclesiais darão fruto na medida em que a Eucaristia for o centro de sua vida e a Palavra de Deus for o farol de seu caminho e de sua atuação na única Igreja de Cristo' (A, 180).

2 Na linha sugerida, por exemplo, por F. Lobinger – P.M. Zulehner, *Padres para amanhã. Uma proposta para comunidades sem Eucaristia,* Paulus, São Paulo, 2007; F. Lobinger, *Equipes de ministros ordenados. Uma solução para a Eucaristia nas comunidades,* Paulus, São Paulo, 2009; IDEM, *Altar vazio. Podem as comunidades pedir a ordenação de ministros próprios?* Editora Santuário, Aparecida, 2010. Sabe-se, aliás, que um grupo de bispos, em certa altura da Conferência de Aparecida, foi conversar, com um alto dignitário do Vaticano, sobre a questão da ordenação de ministros próprios para as comunidades que não têm acesso dominical regular à celebração da Eucaristia. Ouviram duas respostas. Primeira: 'I tempi non sono ancora maturi'. Segunda: 'Questo non è lo spazio adeguato per una simile discussione'! Quando é que os tempos estarão maduros? Qual seria o fórum adequado? Um concílio? Um sínodo universal? Mas por que não se poderia, ao menos, ventilar a questão numa conferência intercontinental?

3 Cf. F. Lobinger, *Padres para amanhã,* op. cit.; *Idem, Equipes de ministros ordenados. Uma solução para a Eucaristia nas comunidades: Altar vazio. Podem as comunidades pedir a ordenação de ministros próprios?*

4 P. Zulehner, *Cambi di prospettiva. Dieci linee guida per il rinnovamento della Chiesa;* em: Il Regno (Attualità) LVII, 2012, p. 307.

5 Ibid.

6 *Altar vazio. As comunidades podem pedir ordenação de ministros próprios?,* por Fritz Lobinger. Editora Santuário, Aparecida 2010, 1 vol. br., Recensão de João Batista Libânio SJ, em: REB LXXII, fascículo 285/janeiro de 2012, pp. 252–3.